Ordnance Survey

STREET ATLAS
Nottinghamshire

Contents

PHILIP'S

First edition published 1994
First colour edition published 1999 by

Ordnance Survey®   and George Philip Ltd., a division of
Romsey Road   Octopus Publishing Group Ltd
Maybush   Michelin House
Southampton   81 Fulham Road
SO16 4GU   London SW3 6RB

ISBN 0-540-07541 8 (hardback)
ISBN 0-540-07542 6 (spiral)

To the best of the Publishers' knowledge, the information in this
atlas was correct at the time of going to press. No responsibility
can be accepted for any errors or their consequences.

The representation in this atlas of a road, track or path is no
evidence of the existence of a right of way.

**The mapping between pages 1 and 223 (inclusive) in this atlas
is derived from Ordnance Survey® Large Scale and Landranger®
mapping, and revised using OSCAR® and Land-Line® data.**

Ordnance Survey, OSCAR, Land-line and Landranger are registered
trade marks of Ordnance Survey, the national mapping agency of
Great Britain.

Printed and bound in Spain by Cayfosa

Digital Data

The exceptionally high-quality mapping
found in this book is available as digital
data in TIFF format, which is easily
convertible to other bit-mapped (raster)
image formats.

The index is also available in digital form
as a standard database table. It contains
all the details found in the printed index
together with the National Grid reference
for the map square in which each entry
is named and feature codes for places
of interest in eight categories such as
education and health.

For further information and to discuss
your requirements, please contact the
Ordnance Survey Solutions Centre on
01703 792929.

Motorway (with junction number)		**Railway station**	Walsall
Primary route (dual carriageway and single)		**Midland Metro**	
A road (dual carriageway and single)		**Metrolink station**	
B road (dual carriageway and single)		**Underground station**	
Minor road (dual carriageway and single)		**Docklands Light Railway station**	
Other minor road (dual carriageway and single)		**Tyne and Wear Metro**	
Road under construction		**Private railway station**	
Pedestrianised area		**Bus, coach station**	
Post code boundaries DY7		**Ambulance station**	
County and Unitary Authority boundaries		**Coastguard station**	
Railway		**Fire station**	
Tramway, miniature railway		**Police station**	
Rural track, private road or narrow road in urban area		**Accident and Emergency entrance to hospital**	
Gate or obstruction to traffic (restrictions may not apply at all times or to all vehicles)		**Hospital**	
Path, bridleway, byway open to all traffic, road used as a public path		**Church, place of worship**	
The representation in this atlas of a road, track or path is no evidence of the existence of a right of way		**Information centre** (open all year)	

Adjoining page indicators

126

94

164

The map area within the pink band is shown at a larger scale on the page indicated by the red block and arrow

Acad	**Academy**		Meml	**Memorial**	
Crem	**Crematorium**		Mon	**Monument**	
Cemy	**Cemetery**		Mus	**Museum**	
C Ctr	**Civic Centre**		Obsy	**Observatory**	
CH	**Club House**		Pal	**Royal Palace**	
Coll	**College**		PH	**Public House**	
Ent	**Enterprise**		Recn Gd	**Recreation Ground**	
Ex H	**Exhibition Hall**		Resr	**Reservoir**	
Ind Est	**Industrial Estate**		Ret Pk	**Retail Park**	
Inst	**Institute**		Sch	**School**	
Ct	**Law Court**		Sh Ctr	**Shopping Centre**	
L Ctr	**Leisure Centre**		TH	**Town Hall/House**	
LC	**Level Crossing**		Trad Est	**Trading Estate**	
Liby	**Library**		Univ	**University**	
Mkt	**Market**		YH	**Youth Hostel**	

Right column symbols:

P P&R **Parking, Park and Ride**

PO PO **Post Office**

Important buildings, schools, colleges, universities and hospitals — Prim Sch

Water name — River Medway

Stream

River or canal (minor and major)

Water

Tidal water

Woods

Houses

Non-Roman antiquity — House

Roman antiquity — VILLA

■ The dark grey border on the inside edge of some pages indicates that the mapping does not continue onto the adjacent page ■ The small numbers around the edges of the maps identify the 1 kilometre National Grid lines

The scale of the maps is 5.52 cm to 1 km (3½ inches to 1 mile)

0	¼	½	¾	1 mile
0 250m 500m 750m 1 kilometre				

The scale of the maps on pages numbered in red is 11.04 cm to 1 km (7 inches to 1 mile)

0	220 yards	440 yards	660 yards	½ mile
0 125m 250m 375m ½ kilometre				

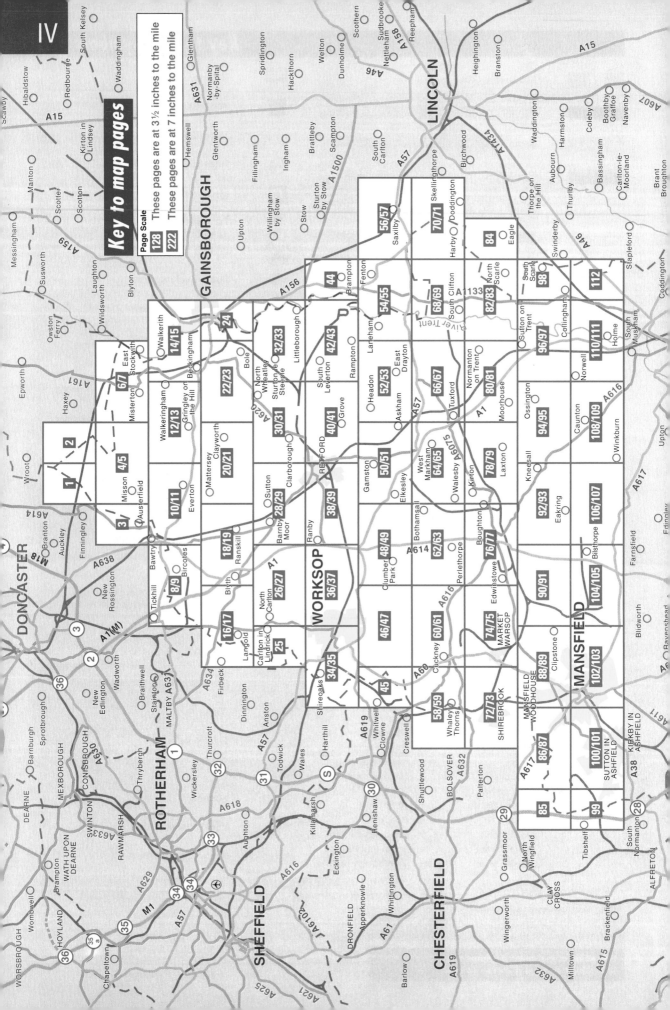

Key to map pages

Page Scale

128 These pages are at 3½ inches to the mile

222 These pages are at 7 inches to the mile

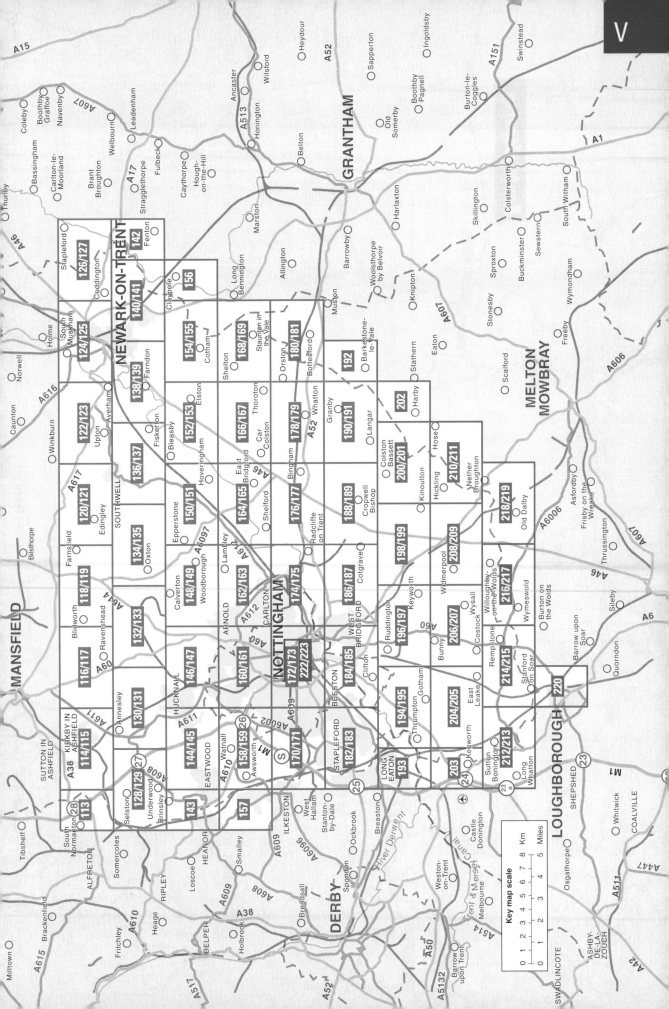

Route planning

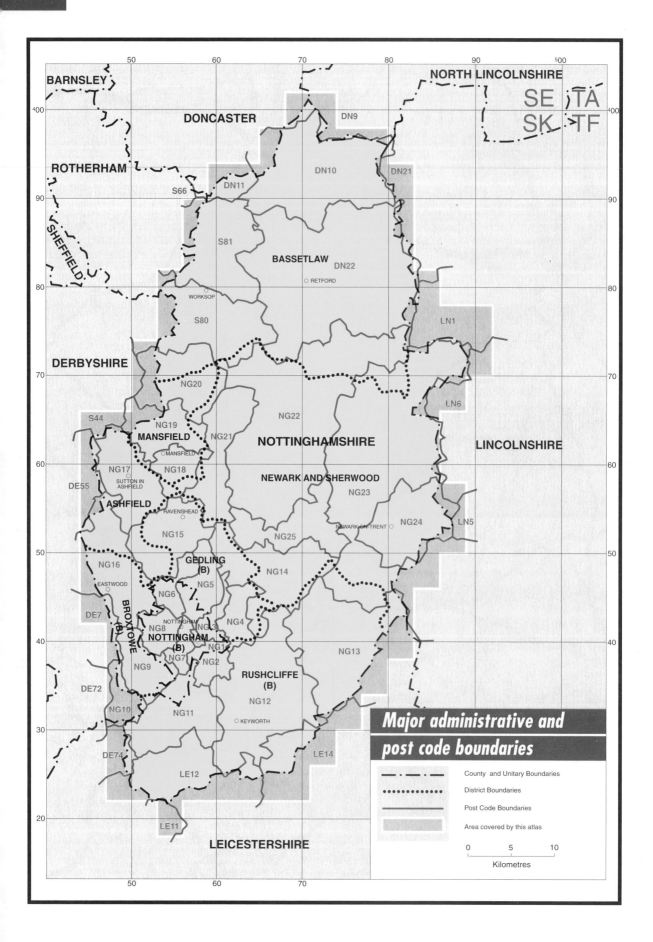

BARNSLEY

ROTHERHAM

SHEFFIELD

DERBYSHIRE

DONCASTER

NORTH LINCOLNSHIRE

SE TA
SK TF

DN9

DN10

DN11

DN21

S66

S81

BASSETLAW

DN22

○ RETFORD

○ WORKSOP

S80

LN1

NG20

NG22

LN6

NG19

NG21

MANSFIELD

NOTTINGHAMSHIRE

LINCOLNSHIRE

S44

○ MANSFIELD

NG17

NG18

NEWARK AND SHERWOOD

DE55

SUTTON IN
ASHFIELD

NG23

ASHFIELD

RAVENSHEAD
○

NG24

LN5

NEWARK-ON-TRENT

NG15

NG16

GEDLING
(B)

NG25

NG5

NG14

EASTWOOD
○

NG6

DE7

NG4

BROXTOWE
(B)

NG8

NG3

NOTTINGHAM
NOTTINGHAM
(B)

NG1

NG13

NG7

NG2

DE72

NG9

RUSHCLIFFE
(B)

DE74

NG10

NG11

NG12

○ KEYWORTH

LE14

LE12

LE11

LEICESTERSHIRE

Major administrative and post code boundaries

–··–··–··–	County and Unitary Boundaries
··············	District Boundaries
─────	Post Code Boundaries
▨	Area covered by this atlas

0   5   10
Kilometres

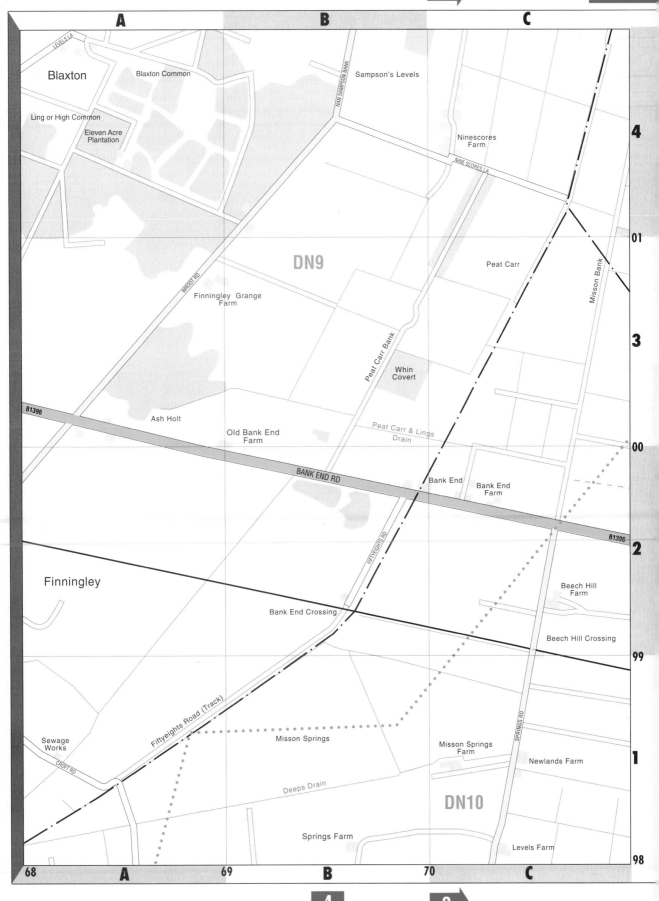

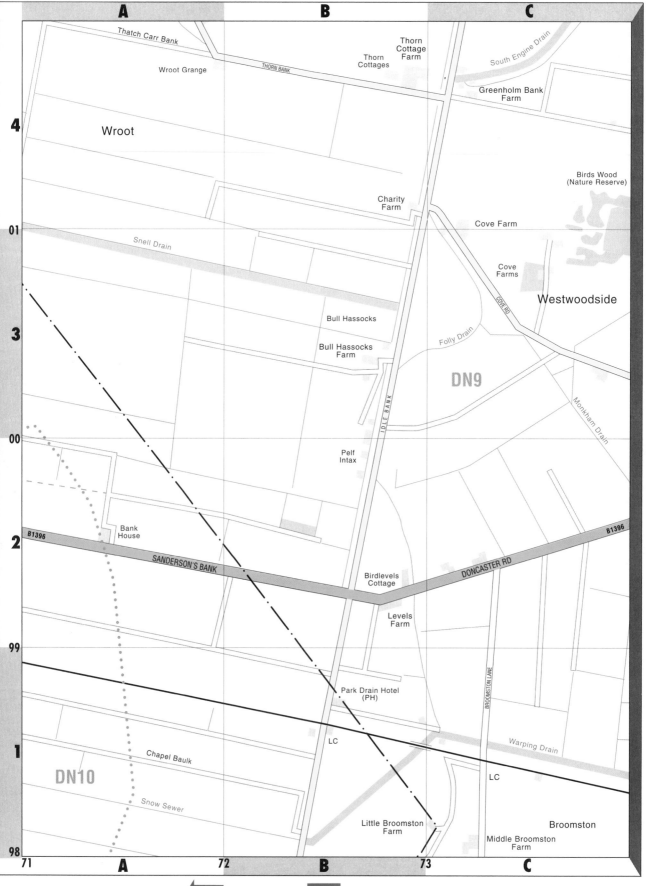

A · B · C

Thatch Carr Bank

THORN BANK

Wroot Grange

Thorn Cottages

Thorn Cottage Farm

Thorn Cottages

South Engine Drain

Greenholm Bank Farm

4

Wroot

Birds Wood (Nature Reserve)

Charity Farm

Cove Farm

01

Snell Drain

Cove Farms

Westwoodside

3

Bull Hassocks

Bull Hassocks Farm

Folly Drain

IDLE BANK

DN9

Monkham Drain

00

Pelf Intax

2

B1396

Bank House

B1396

SANDERSON'S BANK

DONCASTER RD

Birdlevels Cottage

Levels Farm

99

BROOMSTON LANE

Warping Drain

Park Drain Hotel (PH)

1

Chapel Baulk

LC

LC

DN10

Snow Sewer

Broomston

Little Broomston Farm

Middle Broomston Farm

98

71 · A · 72 · B · 73 · C

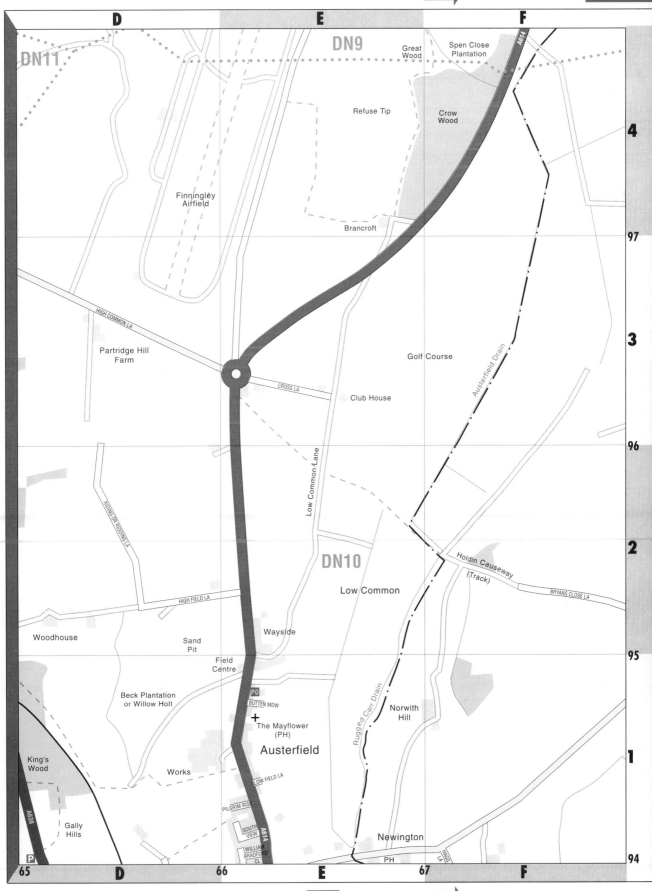

DN11

DN9

DN10

D   **E**   **F**

Great
Wood

Spen Close
Plantation

Refuse Tip

Crow
Wood

Finningley
Airfield

Brancroft

HIGH COMMON LA

Golf Course

Austerfield Drain

Partridge Hill
Farm

CROSS LA

Club House

Low Common Lane

RIDING OR RIDING LA

Holdin Causeway

(Track)

BRYANS CLOSE LA

Low Common

HIGH FIELD LA

Woodhouse

Sand
Pit

Wayside

Field
Centre

Rugged Carr Drain

Beck Plantation
or Willow Holt

PO

BUTTEN MDW

Norwith
Hill

The Mayflower
(PH)

Austerfield

King's
Wood

Works

LOW FIELD LA

A638

Gally
Hills

PILGRIM RISE

SOUTH
VIEW

A614

WILLIAM
BRADFORD
CL

Newington

PH

HAGG LA

P

D   **E**   **F**

65   66   67

94 95 96 97

1 2 3 4

A614

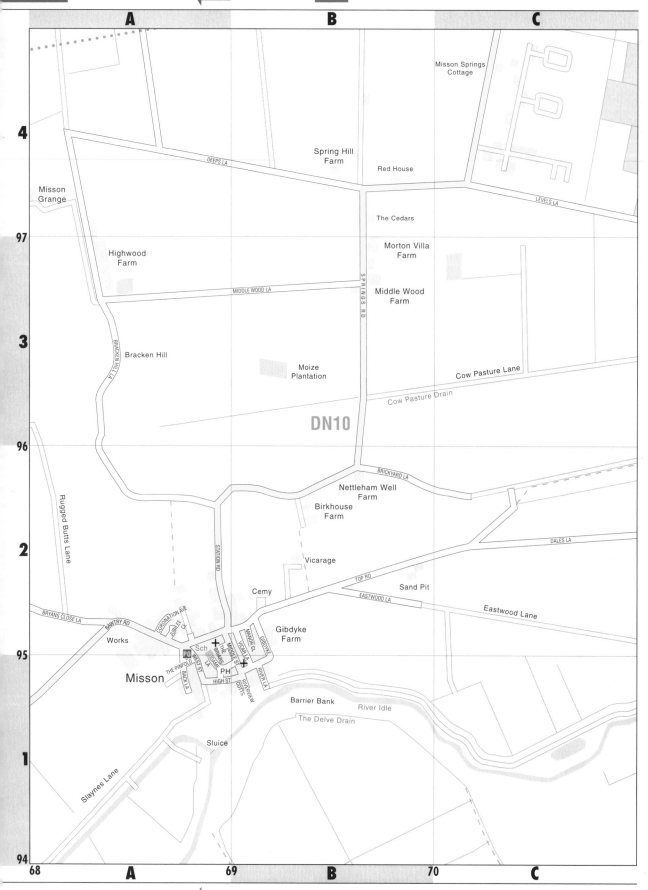

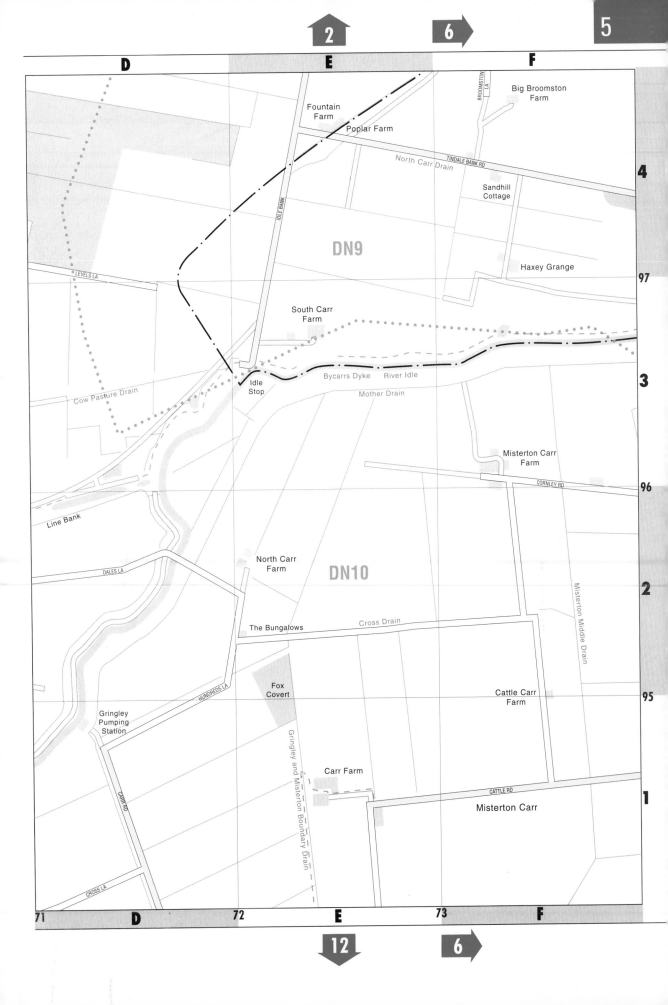

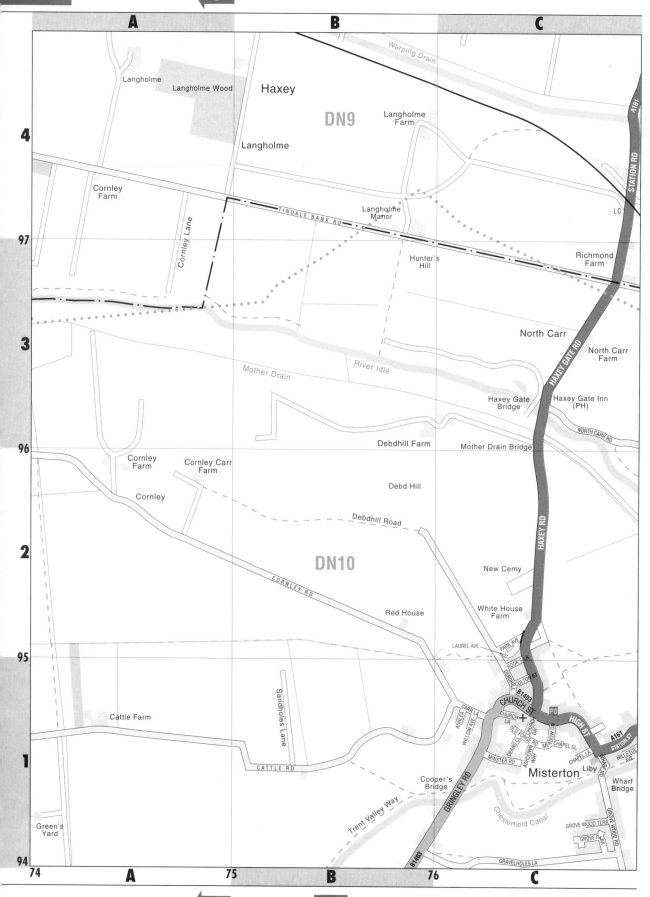

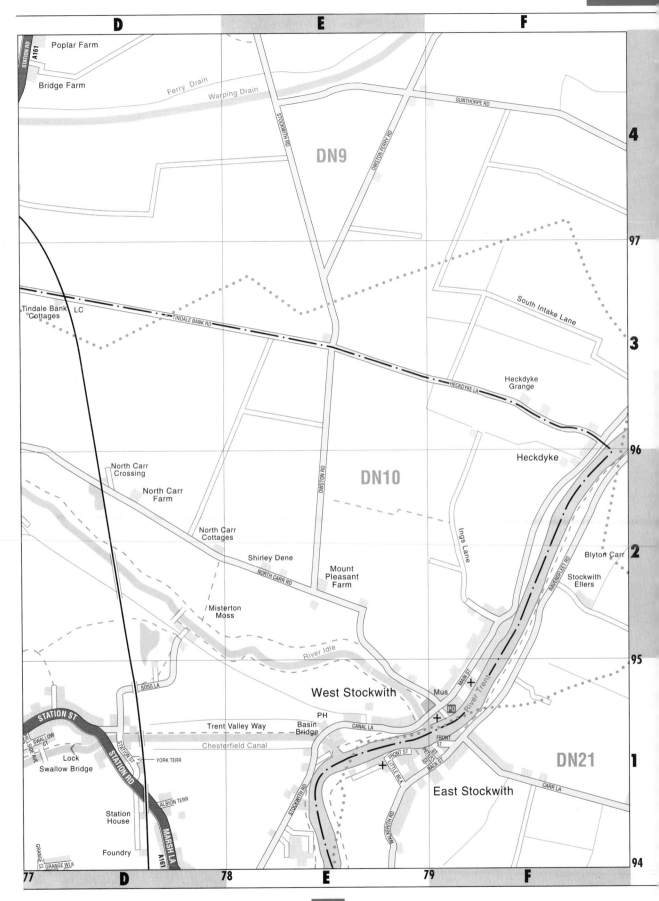

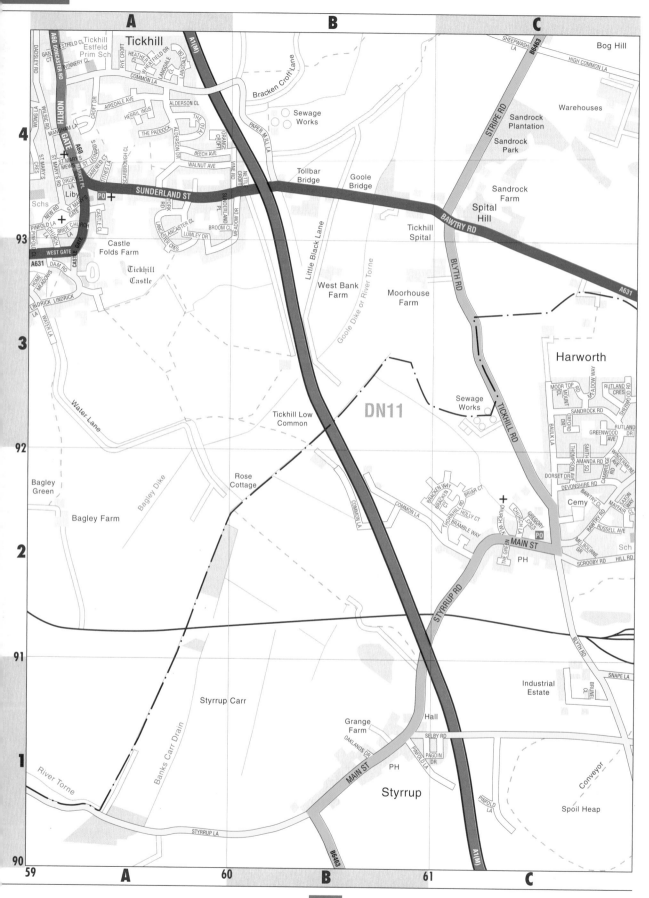

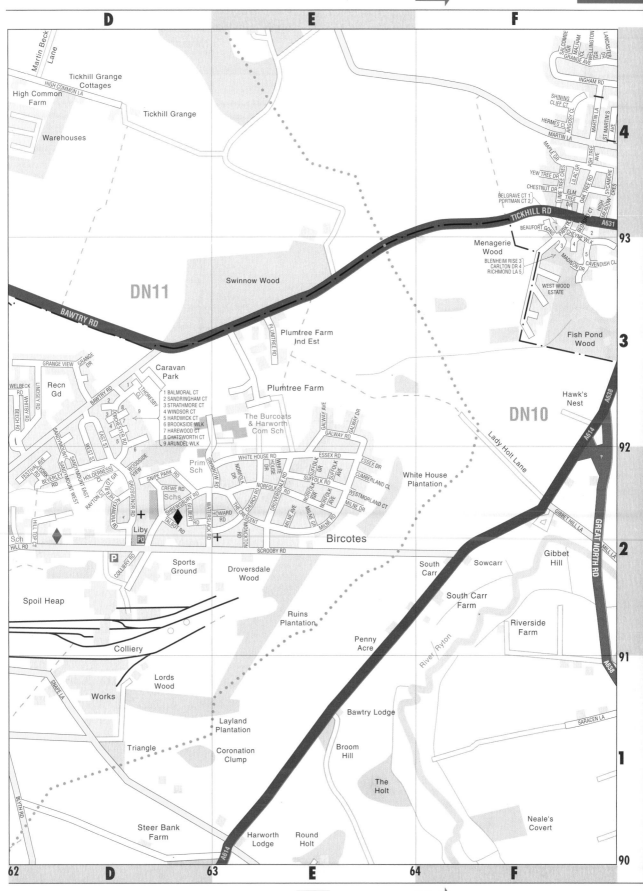

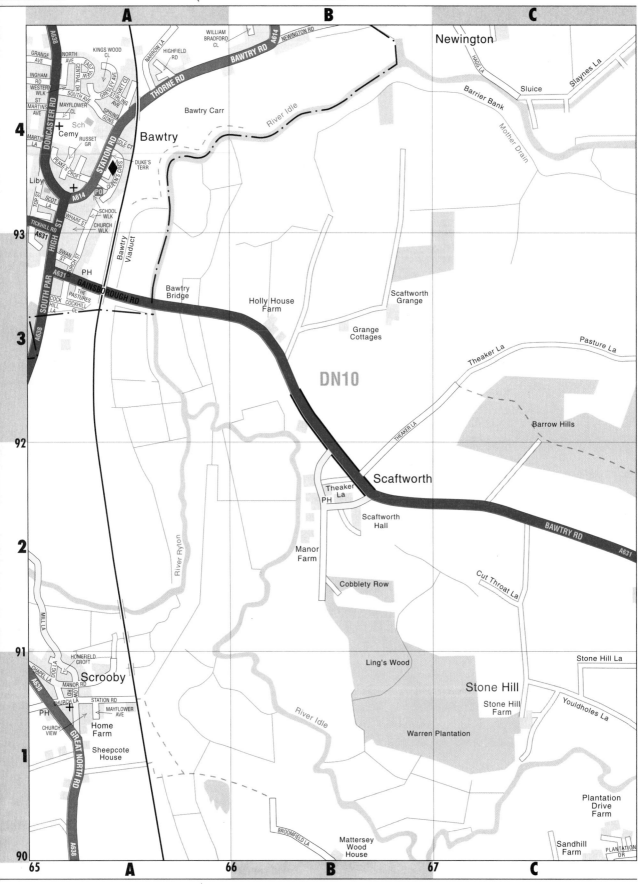

A   B   C

10

9

3

Newington

William Bradford Cl

Bawtry Rd A614

Newington Rd

Thorne Rd

Bawtry Rd

Narrow La

Highfield Rd

Kings Wood Cl

Grange Ave

North Ave

Easy Rd

Central Dr

Greley Ave

Stirling Cl

Ingham Rd

Western Wlk

South Ave

Mayflower Cl

Spring Gdns

St Martins Ave

Sch

Cemy

Russet Gr

Bawtry Carr

Bawtry

Martin La

Doncaster Rd A638

Station Rd

Idle Ct

Duke's Terr

Liby

Peakes Croft

Queen's Cres

A614

PO

Top St

Scot La

Wharf St

School Wlk

Church Wlk

Tickhill Rd

A631

Swan St

Church St

South Par

A631

Gainsborough Rd

PH

The Pastures

Cockhill La

Cock Hill Gr

Cockhill

Bawtry Viaduct

Bawtry Bridge

River Idle

Barrier Bank

Sluice

Slaynes La

Haggs La

Mother Drain

Scaftworth Grange

Holly House Farm

Grange Cottages

DN10

Theaker La

Pasture La

Barrow Hills

Theaker La

River Ryton

Scaftworth

Theaker La PH

Scaftworth Hall

Bawtry Rd A631

A638

Manor Farm

Cut Throat La

Cobblety Row

Milll La

Homefield Croft

Stone Hill La

Scrooby

Dog La

Manor Rd

Ling's Wood

Stone Hill

Stone Hill Farm

Youldholes La

Chapel La

A638

Low Rd

Church La

Station Rd

Mayflower Ave

PH

Church View

Home Farm

Sheepcote House

Great North Rd

River Idle

Warren Plantation

Plantation Drive Farm

Broomfield La

Mattersey Wood House

Sandhill Farm

Plantation Dr

A638

4

93

3

92

2

91

1

90

65   66   67

A   B   C

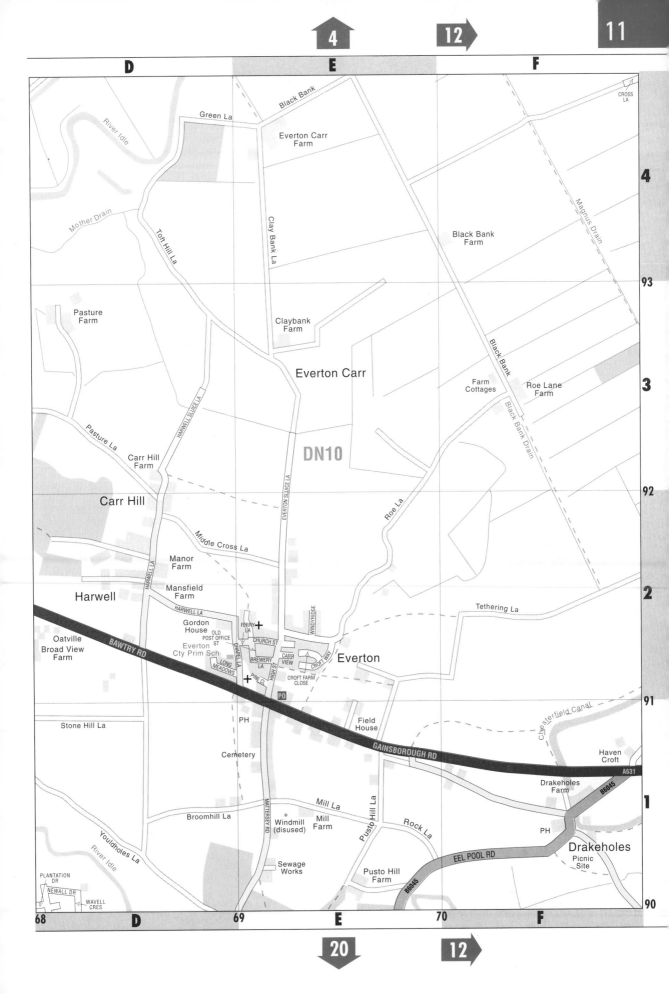

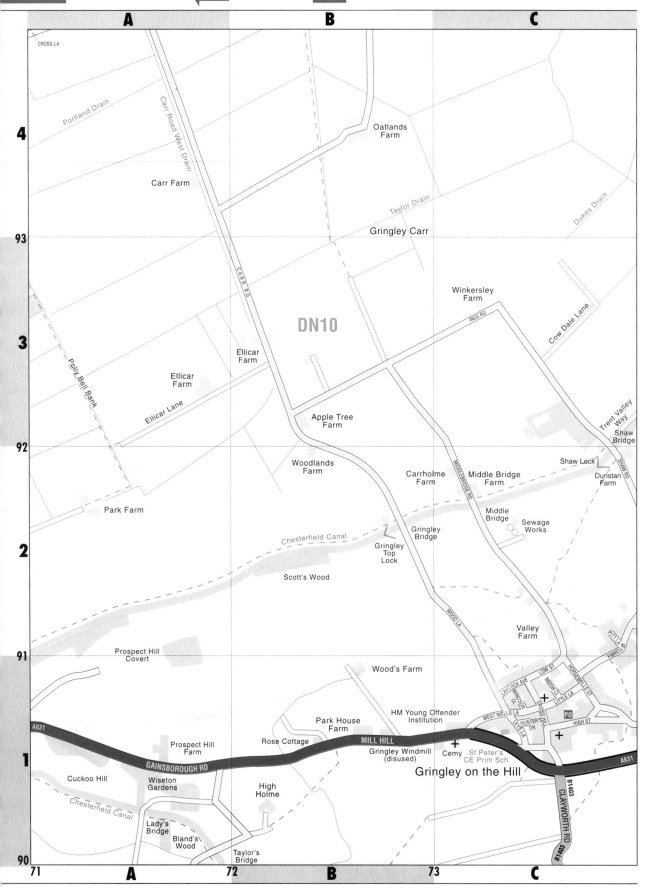

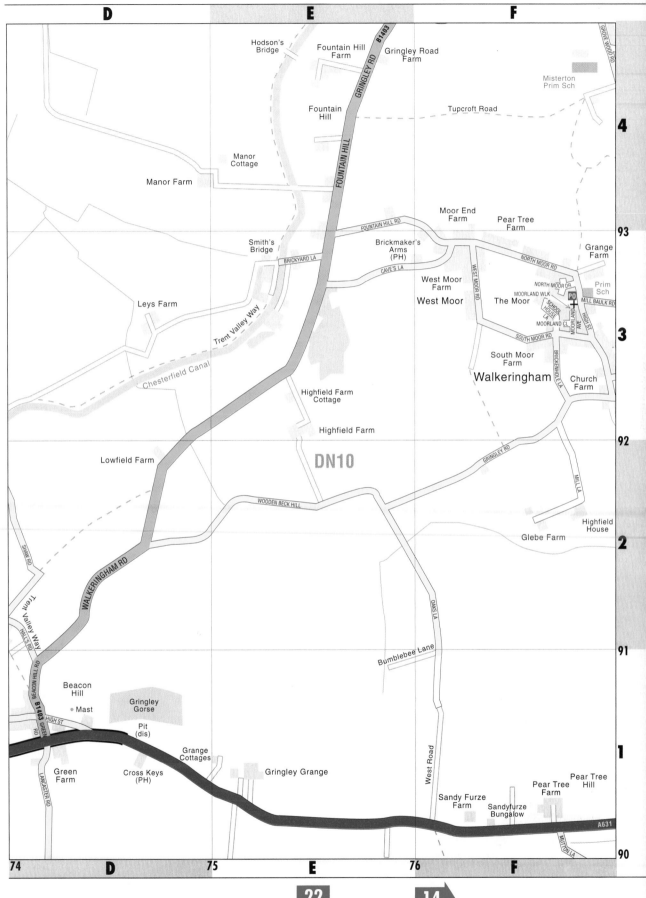

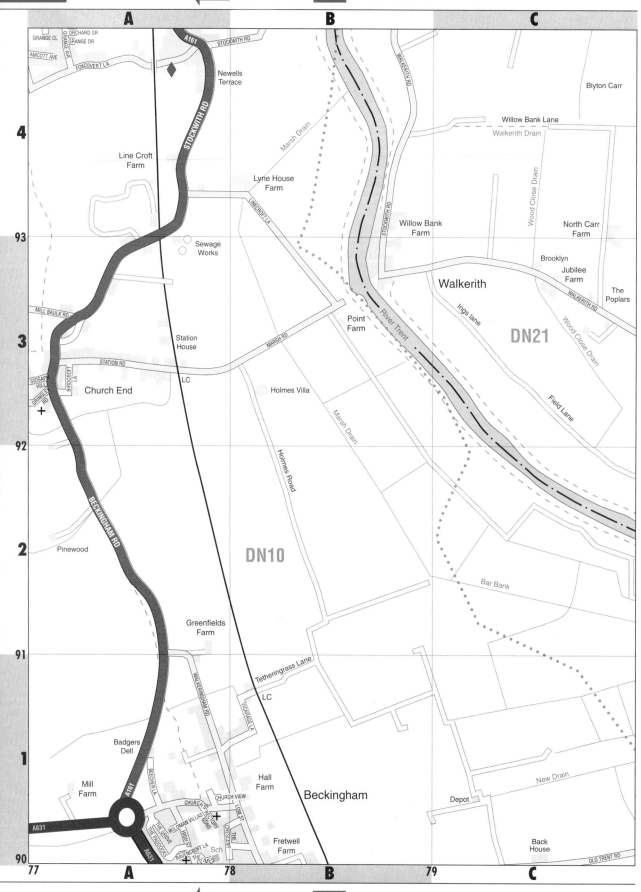

A   B   C

GRANGE CL
ORCHARD GR
GRANGE AVE
GRANGE DR
AMCOTT AVE
FOXCOVERT LA

A161
STOCKWITH RD
Newells
Terrace

Blyton Carr

Line Croft
Farm

Lyne House
Farm

Willow Bank Lane
Walkerith Drain

Marsh Drain

LINECROFT LA

WALKERITH RD

Wood Close Drain

4

93

Sewage
Works

Willow Bank
Farm

STOCKWITH RD

North Carr
Farm

Walkerith

Brooklyn
Jubilee
Farm

DN21

The
Poplars

WALKERITH RD

Wood Close Drain

MILL BAULK RD

Point
Farm

River Trent

Ings lane

3

Station
House

MARSH RD

STATION RD

LC

Holmes Villa

Field Lane

SIDSAPLE HILL
BIRDCROFT LA
GRINGLEY RD

Church End

+

92

Marsh Drain

Holmes Road

BECKINGHAM RD

Pinewood

DN10

Bar Bank

2

91

Greenfields
Farm

New Drain

WALKERINGHAM RD

Tetheringrass Lane

LC

VICARAGE LA

Badgers
Dell

1

Mill
Farm

A161

BEECHER LA

Hall
Farm

CHURCH VIEW

Beckingham

Depot

Back
House

A631

CHURCH ST
RECTORY GDNS
WILDSMAN VILLAS
HIGH ST
THE LESONE
THE PADDOCKS
RAVENCROFT LA
THE HOLMES
LOW ST
THE CRESCENT
Sch
+
+

Fretwell
Farm

OLD TRENT RD

90

77   A   78   B   79   C

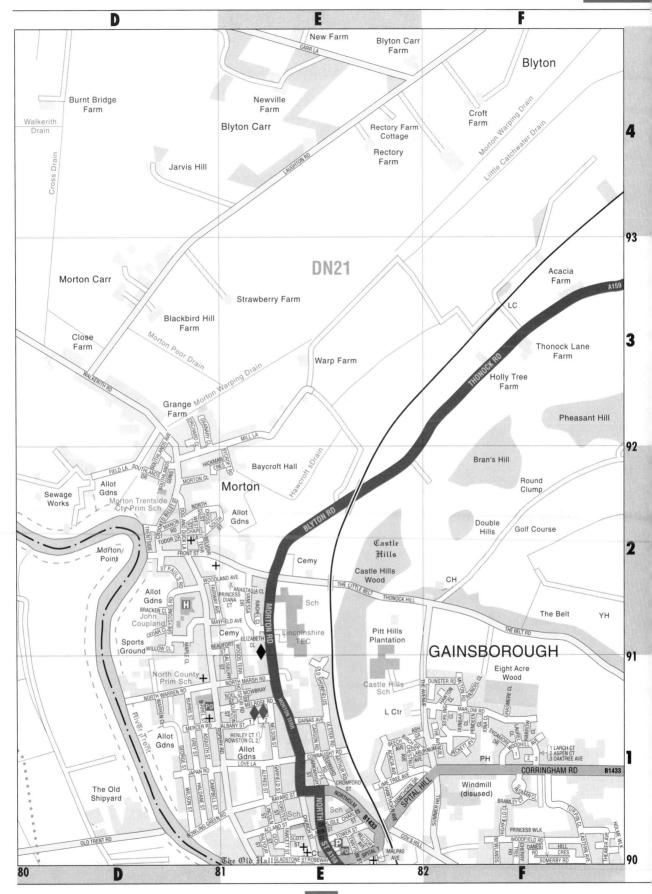

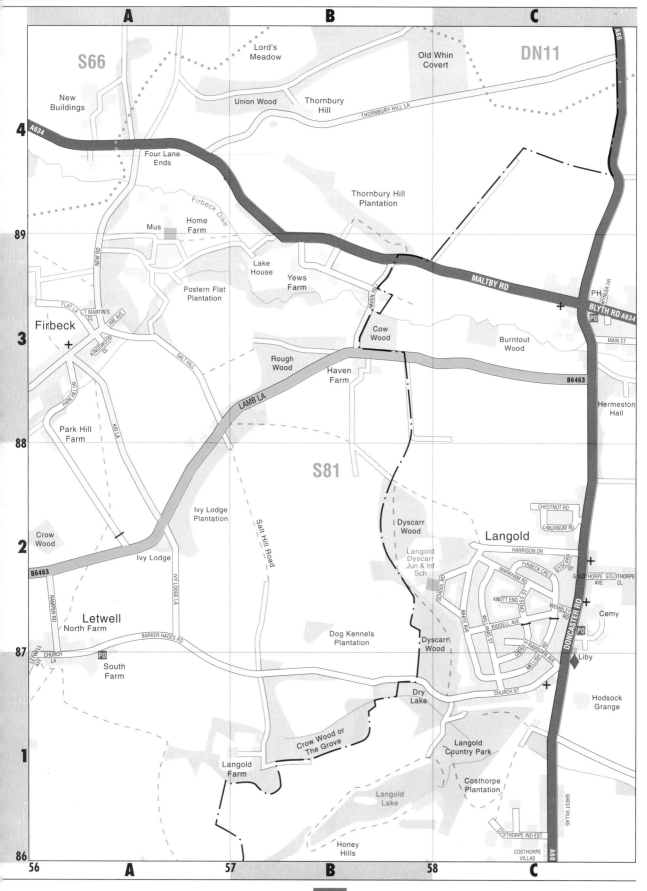

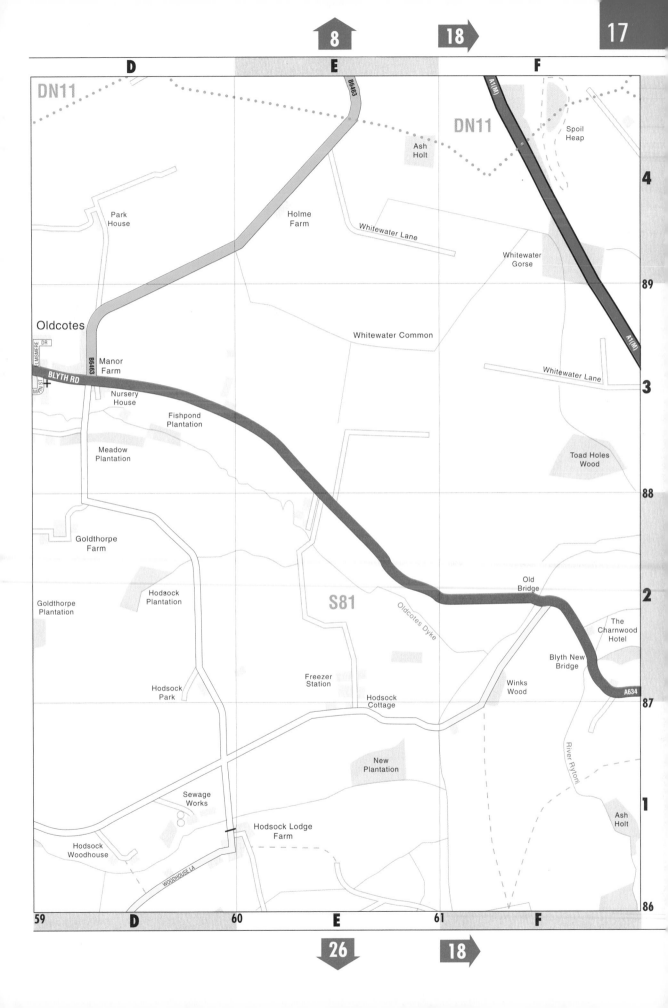

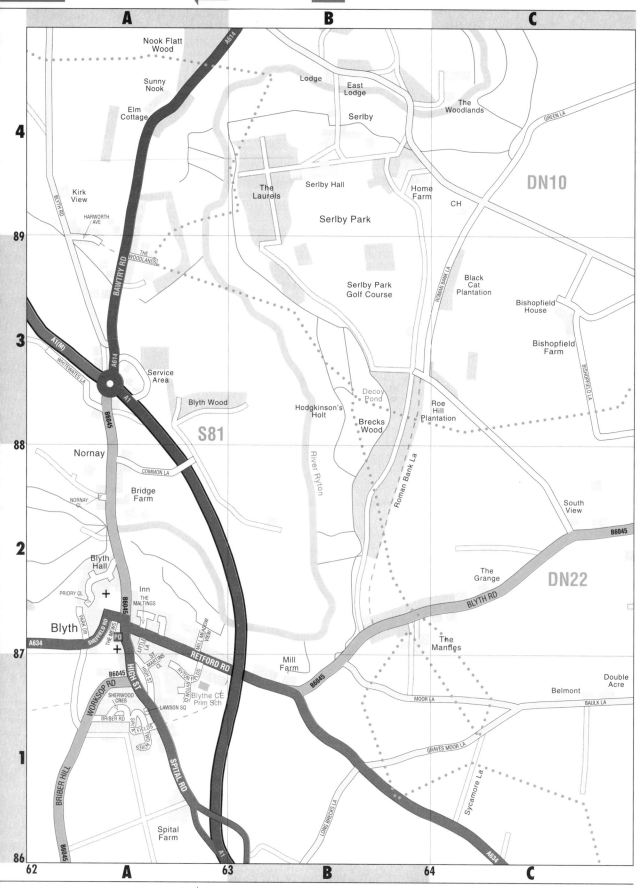

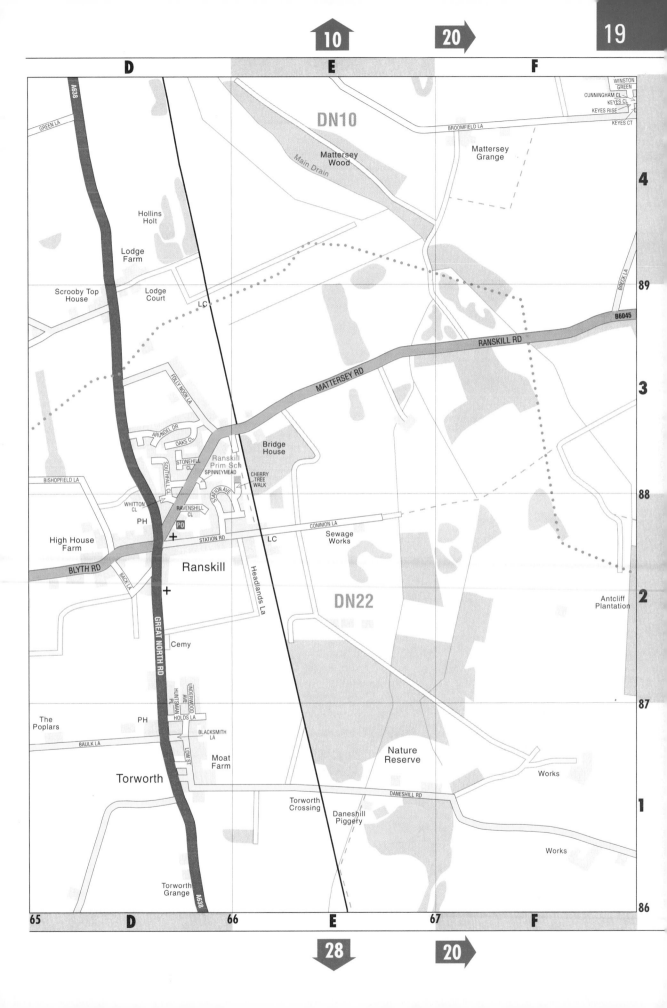

D   E   F

GREEN LA

A638

DN10

Mattersey Wood

Main Drain

WINSTON GREEN

CUNNINGHAM CL

KEYES CL

KEYES RISE

KEYES CT

BROOMFIELD LA

Mattersey Grange

BRECK LA

4

Hollins Holt

Lodge Farm

Scrooby Top House

Lodge Court

LC

B6045

89

RANSKILL RD

MATTERSEY RD

3

FOLLY NOOK LA

ARUNDEL DR

OAKS CL

Bridge House

STONEHILL CL

Ranskill Prim Sch

SPINNEYMEAD

CHERRY TREE WALK

SOUTHFIELD CL

BISHOPFIELD LA

WHITTON CL

PH

RAVENSHILL CL

STATION AVE

88

PO

COMMON LA

Sewage Works

LC

High House Farm

BLYTH RD

BACK LA

STATION RD

+

Ranskill

Headlands La

DN22

2

+

GREAT NORTH RD

Cemy

Antcliff Plantation

The Poplars

PH

UNDERWOOD AVE

HUNTSMAN PL

HOLDS LA

BLACKSMITH LA

87

BAULK LA

Torworth

LOW ST

Moat Farm

Nature Reserve

Works

1

Torworth Crossing

DANESHILL RD

Daneshill Piggery

Works

Torworth Grange

A638

86

65   D   66   E   67   F

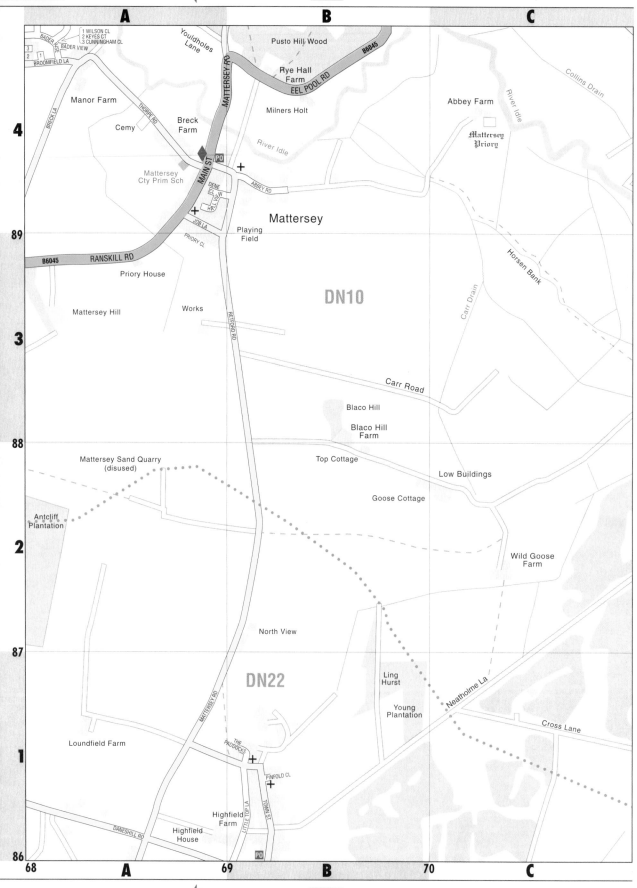

A   B   C

1 WILSON CL
2 KEYES CT
3 CUNNINGHAM CL

BADER VSE
BADER VIEW
BROOMFIELD LA

Youldholes Lane

Pusto Hill Wood

B6045

Rye Hall Farm

EEL POOL RD

Collins Drain

Manor Farm

BRECK LA

THORPE RD

Cemy

Breck Farm

Milners Holt

River Idle

Abbey Farm

River Idle

Mattersey Priory

4

MAIN ST

MATTERSEY RD

PO

Mattersey Cty Prim Sch

DENE
PL
VW
HALL
CL

ABBEY RD

Mattersey

89

JOB LA

PRIORY CL

Playing Field

B6045   RANSKILL RD

Horsen Bank

Priory House

Carr Drain

DN10

Mattersey Hill

Works

RETFORD RD

Carr Road

3

Blaco Hill

Blaco Hill Farm

88

Mattersey Sand Quarry (disused)

Top Cottage

Low Buildings

Goose Cottage

Antcliff Plantation

2

Wild Goose Farm

North View

87

Ling Hurst

DN22

Young Plantation

Neatholme La

Cross Lane

MATTERSEY RD

Loundfield Farm

THE PADDOCKS

1

PINFOLD CL

LITTLE TOP LA

TOWN ST

DANESHILL RD

Highfield Farm

Highfield House

PO

86

68   A   69   B   70   C

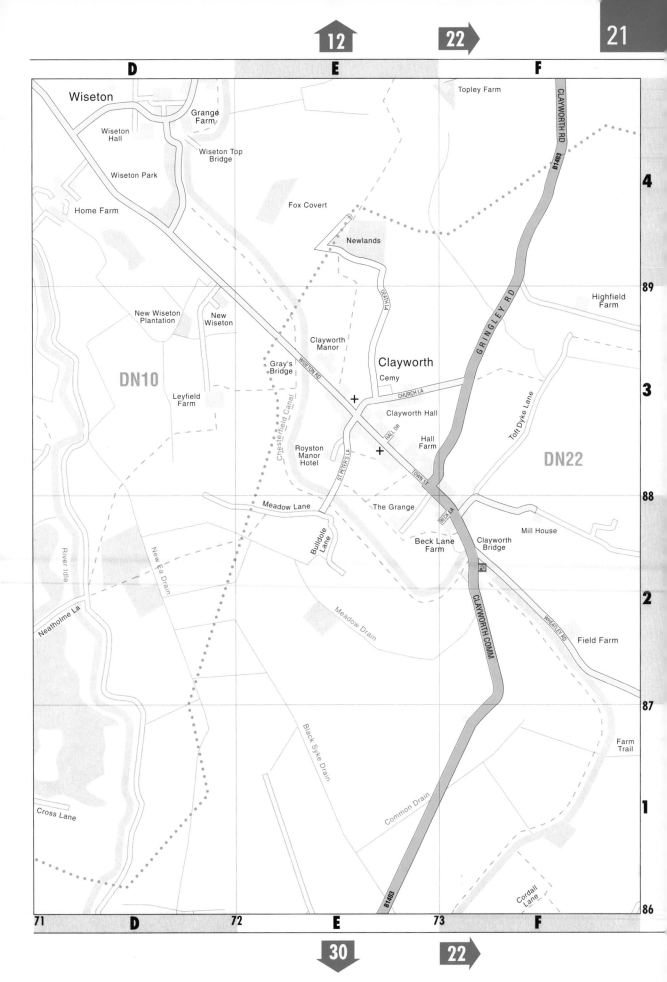

A **B** **C**

DN10

South Sandy-Furze Farm

MUTTON LA

WOOD LA

Ash Lea

LANCASTER RD

4

Wood Farm

Beckingham Wood

Tong's Wood

89

Clayworth Woodhouse

Dogholes Wood

Saundby Park Farm

3

Lovers' Lane

Wheatley Wood

Hangman Lane

Trent Valley Way

Freeman's Gorse

88

Wheatley Wood Farm

Wheatley Grange

Walk Lane

2

DN22

87

WHEATLEY RD

Northfield Leys Road

Trough Baulk Lane

WOOD LA

A620

GAINSBOROUGH RD

1

North Point

Eastfield

Hayton Castle Farm

Long Plantation

Allot Gdns

HAUGHGATE HILL

Greenacres

A620

86

74 **A** 75 **B** 76 **C**

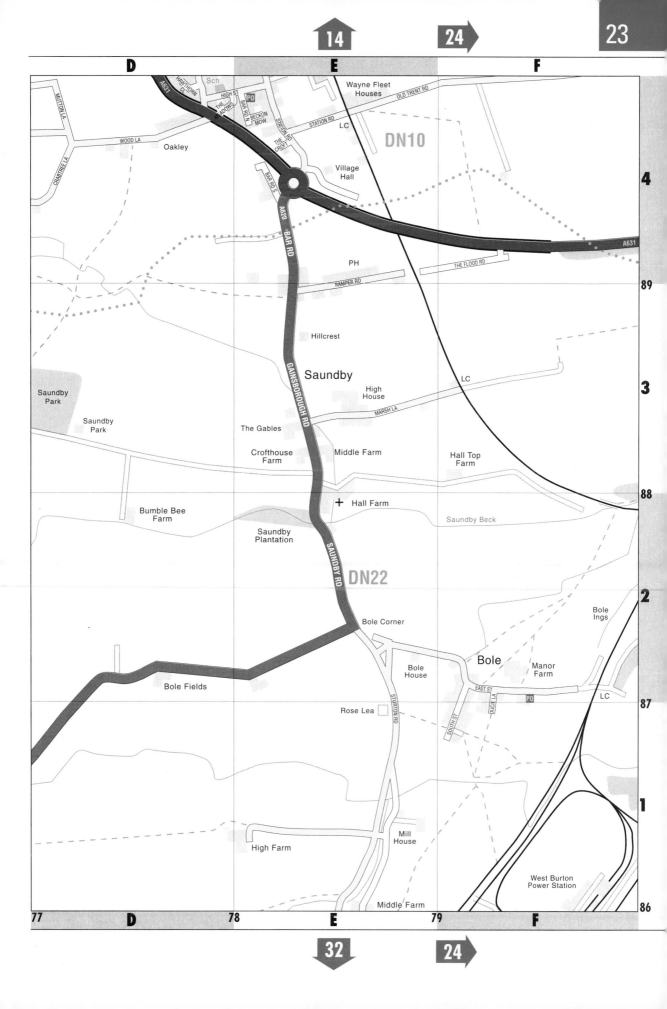

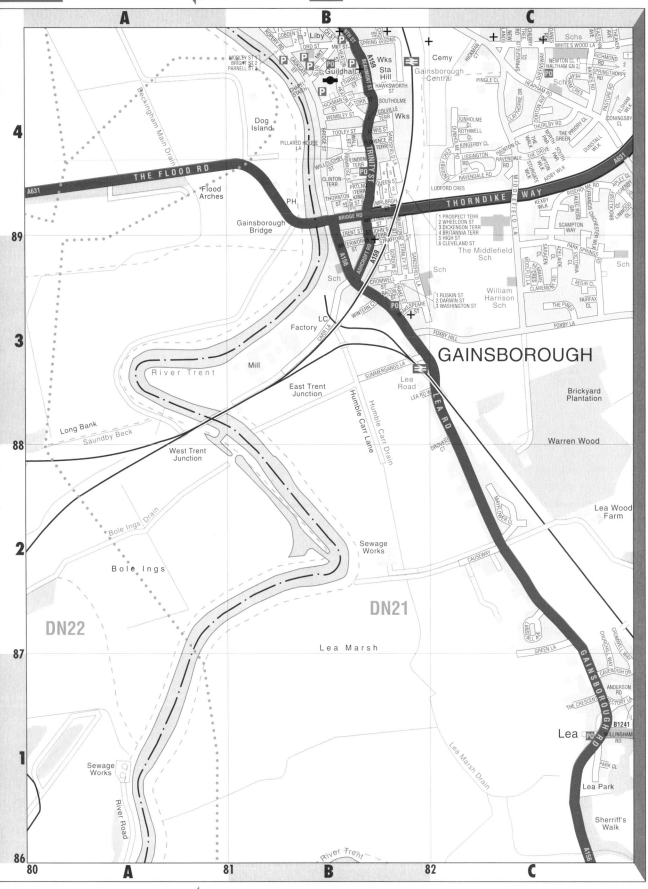

GAINSBOROUGH

DN21

DN22

Lea

Miller Lands

Acorn Piece

Langold Holt

Woodland Farm

Buckwood Farm

ROTHERHAM BAULK

WALLINGWELLS LA

Castle Garden

Wallingwells

Wallingwells Hall

S81

Wallingwells Park

Owlands Wood

Corn Mill Farm

The Ashes

Hollin Hills

The Bottoms

Wks

Owlands Wood Dike

Holme House Farm

OWDAY LA

Woodsetts

Owday Wood

The Homestead

Rough Piece

WORKSOP RD

WOODSETTS LA

WORKSOP RD

A57 GATEFORD RD

Fox Covert

Ashes Wood

Dog Kennel Plantation

Owday Plantation

Nab's Ashes Wood

Whipman Wood

Cocked Hat Wood

Sand Hill Plantation

WEST VIEW

Costhorpe

Ingham Bungalows

Trading Estate

DONCASTER RD

A60

PINFOLD DR 1
COPPICE WAY 2
HARVEST CL 3
PLOUGH DR 4

PH

CHILTERN WAY 1
PENTLAND DR 2
HAMBLETON CT 3
LOWTHER SQ 4
CLEVELAND CL 5
BEVERLEY WLK 6
CHICHESTER WLK 7
CHEVIOT CT 8
MENDIP CT 9
CANTERBURY WLK 10
LICHFIELD WLK 11
COTSWOLD CT 12

LAWN RD

NORTHUMBERLAND AVE

SUTHERLAND CL

HIGHFIELD VILLAS

CUMBERLAND CL

WEST WAY

WORK WAY

DAXLEY RD

A60

LINDRICK CL

LILAC GR

OAK TREE RISE

WILLOW AVE

LIME TREE AVE

BEECH GR

SYCAMORE RD

LE BRUN SQ

BECKETT AVE

PO

RAMSDEN CRES

MULBERRY CRES

HAWTHORN WAY

KNATON RD

STEWART CL

STEWART RD

KINGSTON RD

AMANDA AVE

LONG LA

QUEENS RD

OXFORD RD

Liby

CARISBROOK RD

CRATHIE RD

CRAIGSTON RD

WINDSOR GDNS

STIRLING CL

GLAMIS RD

PEMBROKE DR

RICHMOND RD

BALMORAL

CONWAY DR

STRATHAVEN DR

STRATHMORE DR

KENILWORTH DR

WARWICK AVE

Schs

WINDSOR RD

ARUNDEL DR

Green Lane

Wallingwells Wood

Carlton Wood

Carlton in Lindrick

CARLTON HALL LA

The Lawns

Mus

CHURCH LA

Carlton Lake

South Carlton

Field House Farm

Hardwick Ashes

Broom Farm

Little Broom Wood

CARLTON RD

A60

Holme Wood

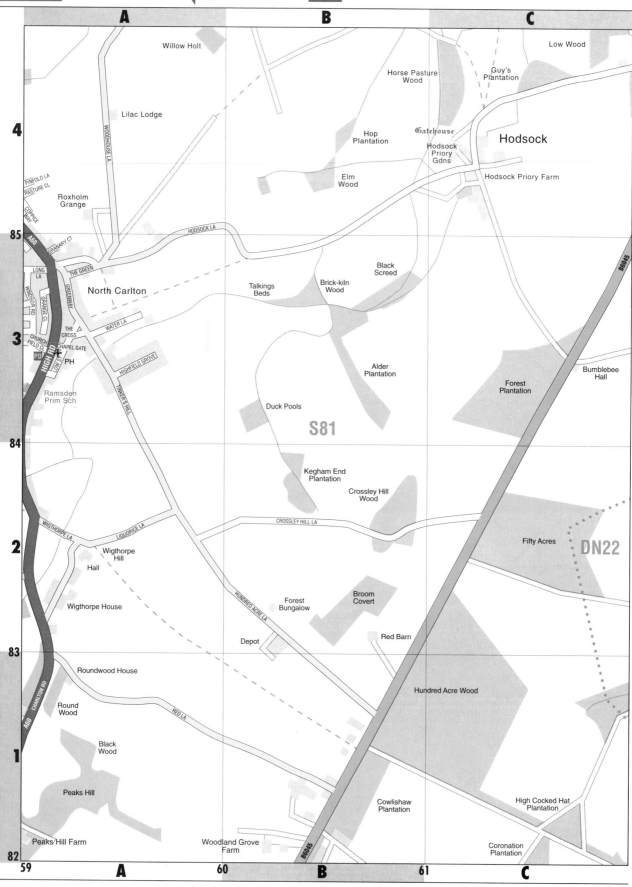

A   B   C

Willow Holt

Horse Pasture Wood

Guy's Plantation

Low Wood

Lilac Lodge

Hop Plantation

Gatehouse

Hodsock

Elm Wood

Hodsock Priory Gdns

Hodsock Priory Farm

PINFOLD LA

PASTURE CL

Roxholm Grange

COPPICE WAY

A60

GRANARY CT

HODSOCK LA

85

LONG LA

THE GREEN

Black Screed

WINDSOR RD

GRANGE CL

GREENWAY

North Carlton

Talkings Beds

Brick-kiln Wood

WATER LA

THE CROSS

CHURCH

CHAPEL GATE

3

FIELD CL

HIGH RD

LOW ST

PH

Alder Plantation

Forest Plantation

Bumblebee Hall

B6045

PO

HIGHFIELD GROVE

Ramsden Prim Sch

Duck Pools

S81

TINKER'S HILL

84

Kegham End Plantation

Crossley Hill Wood

WIGTHORPE LA

LIQUORICE LA

CROSSLEY HILL LA

Fifty Acres

DN22

2

Wigthorpe Hill

Hall

HUNDRED ACRE LA

Forest Bungalow

Broom Covert

Wigthorpe House

Red Barn

83

Depot

Roundwood House

Hundred Acre Wood

CHARLTON RD

A60

Round Wood

RED LA

1

Black Wood

Peaks Hill

High Cocked Hat Plantation

Peaks Hill Farm

Woodland Grove Farm

B6045

Cowlishaw Plantation

Coronation Plantation

82

59   A   60   B   61   C

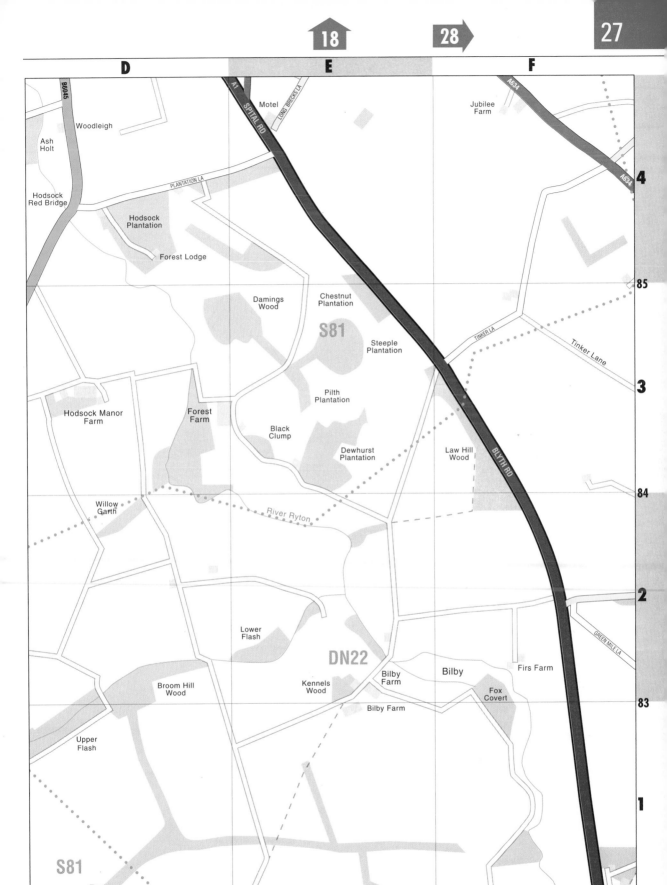

18
28

D   E   F

B6045

A1

SPITAL RD

LONG BRECKS LA

Motel

A63A

A634

Jubilee
Farm

Woodleigh

Ash
Holt

PLANTATION LA

Hodsock
Red Bridge

4

Hodsock
Plantation

Forest Lodge

85

Damings
Wood

Chestnut
Plantation

S81

TINKER LA

Tinker Lane

Steeple
Plantation

3

Pilth
Plantation

Hodsock Manor
Farm

Forest
Farm

Black
Clump

Dewhurst
Plantation

Law Hill
Wood

BLYTH RD

84

Willow
Garth

River Ryton

2

Lower
Flash

DN22

GREEN MILE LA

Bilby

Firs Farm

Broom Hill
Wood

Kennels
Wood

Bilby
Farm

Fox
Covert

83

Bilby Farm

Upper
Flash

1

S81

Church
Clump

Whin
Hill

The Barracks

A1

82

62   D   63   E   64   F

28

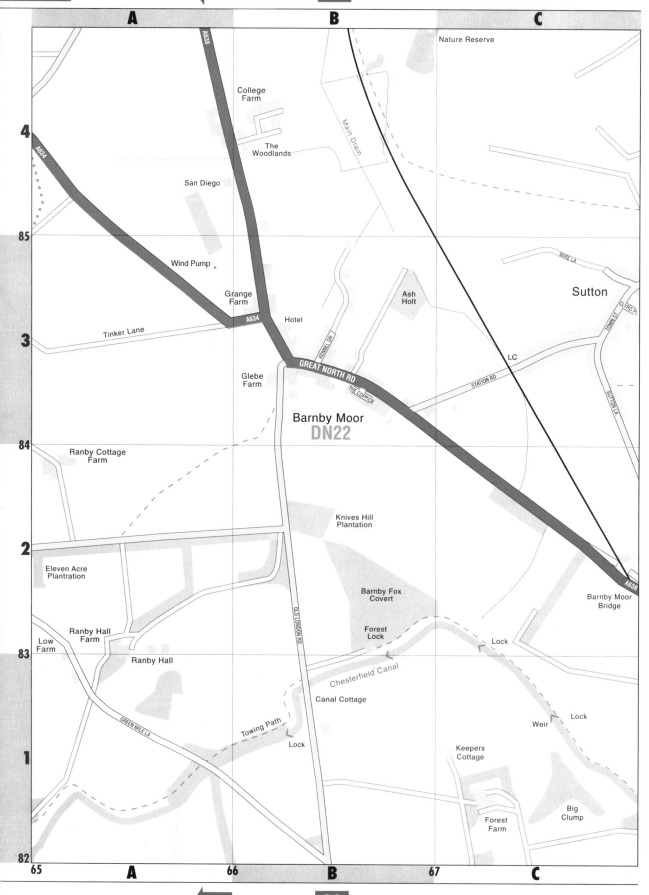

A   **B**   **C**

4

85

Nature Reserve

College Farm

A638

The Woodlands

Main Drain

San Diego

Sutton

MIRE LA

Wind Pump

Grange Farm

A634

Ash Holt

TOWN ST

CLYRO PL.

Hotel

KENNEL DR

3

Tinker Lane

GREAT NORTH RD

LC

STATION RD

SUTTON LA

Glebe Farm

THE COPPICE

Barnby Moor
DN22

84

Ranby Cottage Farm

Knives Hill Plantation

2

Eleven Acre Plantration

Barnby Fox Covert

A638

Barnby Moor Bridge

Ranby Hall Farm

Forest Lock

Lock

Low Farm

83

Ranby Hall

Chesterfield Canal

OLD LONDON RD

Canal Cottage

Weir

Lock

GREEN MILE LA

Towing Path

Keepers Cottage

1

Lock

Forest Farm

Big Clump

82

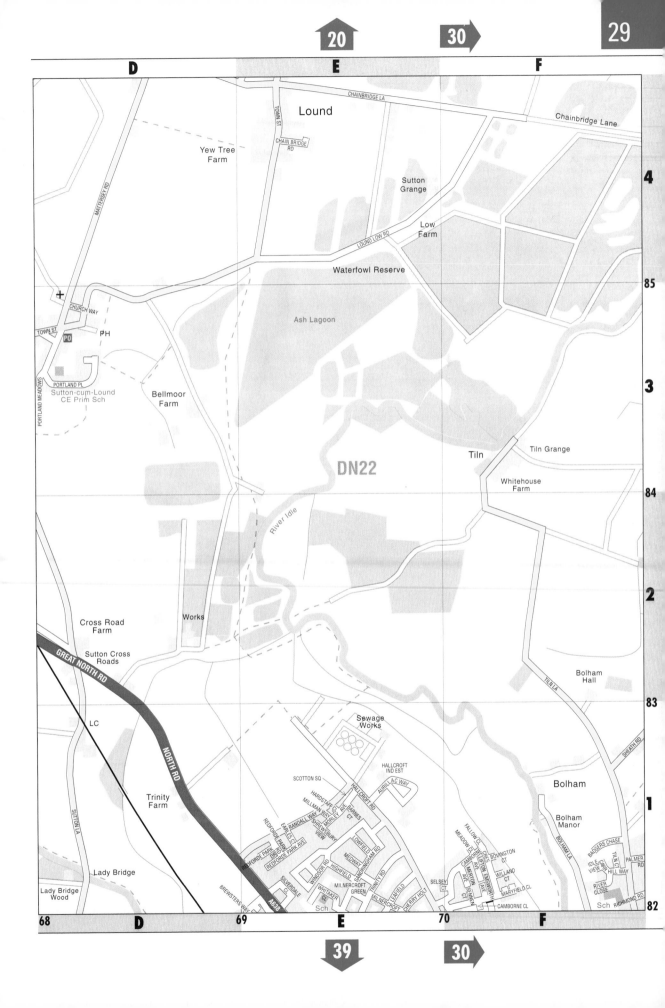

D   E   F

CHAINBRIDGE LA

Lound

Chainbridge Lane

Yew Tree
Farm

CHAIN BRIDGE RD

TOWN ST

MATTERSEY RD

Sutton
Grange

Low
Farm

LOUND LOW RD

Waterfowl Reserve

4

85

+

CHURCH WAY

TOWN ST

PH

PO

Ash Lagoon

PORTLAND PL

Sutton-cum-Lound
CE Prim Sch

PORTLAND MEADOWS

Bellmoor
Farm

DN22

Tiln

Tiln Grange

Whitehouse
Farm

3

84

River Idle

Works

Cross Road
Farm

Sutton Cross
Roads

GREAT NORTH RD

Bolham
Hall

TILN LA

2

83

LC

NORTH RD

SUTTON LA

Trinity
Farm

Sewage
Works

Scotton Sq

HALLCROFT
IND EST

HARDSTAFF CL

AURIL AC WAY

Bolham

SHEATH RD

Bolham
Manor

1

Lady Bridge

Lady Bridge
Wood

BREWSTERS WAY

A638

HALLCROFT RD

BARNES CT

MILLMAN WAY

MORLEY CT

RANDALL WAY

SHREWSBURY

REDFORDE PARK

REDFORDE PARK DR

REDFORDE PARK AVE

EARL CL

MEDWAY

LOWFIELD

HIGHFIELD

WINDSOR RD

SILVERDALE

WHITAKER RD

Sch

MILNERCROFT
GREEN

SANDRINGHAM RD

TRINITY RD

LEAFIELD

CHERRY HOLT

MILNERCROFT RD

MEADOW CL

FALLOW CL

CAMBORNE CL

CROFT RD

LITTON EADWARD

MERTON CL

AVE BENNENT

SELSEY
CT

CAMBORNE CL

BOVINGTON
CT

WILLAND
CT

MARYFIELD CL

BOLHAM LA

BADGERS CHASE

IDLE
VIEW

HILL WAY

TILN CT

RIVER
CLOSE

PALMER
RD

Sch

RICHMOND RD

82

68   D   69   E   70   F

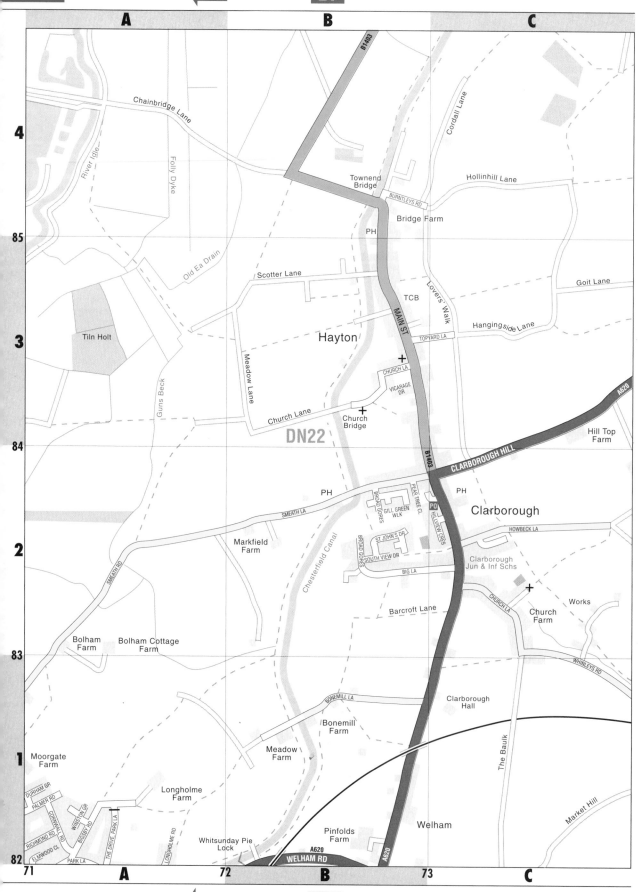

A   B   C

4

85

3

84

2

83

1

82

Chainbridge Lane

River Idle

Folly Dyke

Old Ea Drain

Tiln Holt

Scotter Lane

Meadow Lane

Guns Beck

Church Lane

Hayton

Church Lane

Church Bridge

DN22

B1403

Townend Bridge

BURNTLEYS RD

PH

Bridge Farm

MAIN ST

TCB

CHURCH LA

VICARAGE DR

TOPYARD LA

Cordall Lane

Hollinhill Lane

Lovers' Walk

Goit Lane

Hangingside Lane

Hill Top Farm

A620

B1403

CLARBOROUGH HILL

PH

SMEATH LA

Markfield Farm

SMEATH RD

Chesterfield Canal

BROAD GORES

BROAD GORES

GILL GREEN WLK

PEAR TREE CL

St JOHN'S DR

SOUTH VIEW DR

BIG LA

Barcroft Lane

PO

PH

HILLVIEW CRES

Clarborough

HOWBECK LA

Clarborough Jun & Inf Schs

CHURCH LA

Church Farm

Works

WHINLEYS RD

Bolham Farm

Bolham Cottage Farm

Moorgate Farm

DURHAM GR

PALMER RD

CORNWALL RD

BIGSBY RD

RICHMOND RD

ELMWOOD CL

PARK LA

WINSTON GR

THE DRIVE

PARK LA

LONGHOLME RD

Longholme Farm

Whitsunday Pie Lock

BONEMILL LA

Bonemill Farm

Meadow Farm

Pinfolds Farm

Clarborough Hall

The Baulk

Market Hill

Welham

A620

A620

WELHAM RD

71   A   72   B   73   C

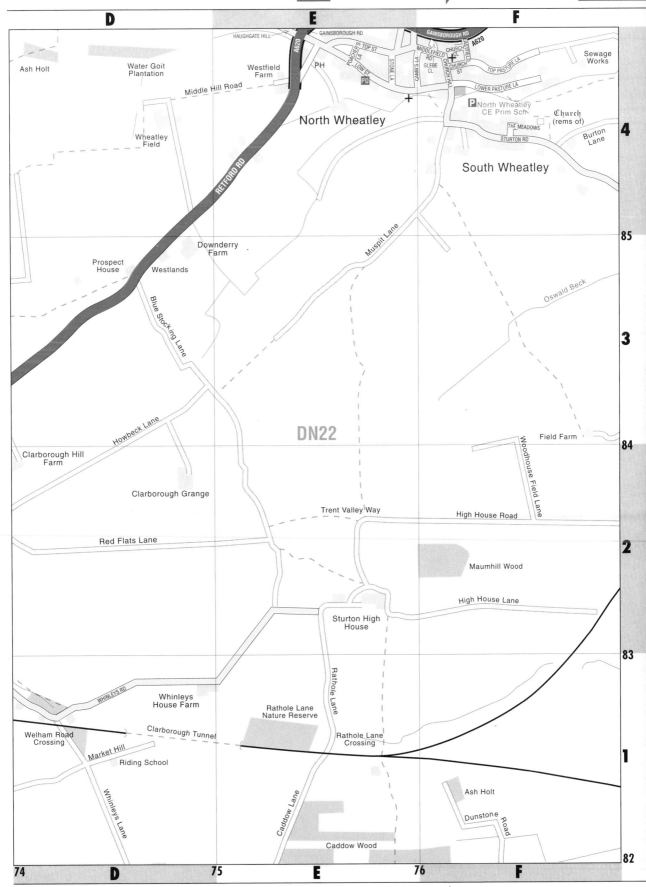

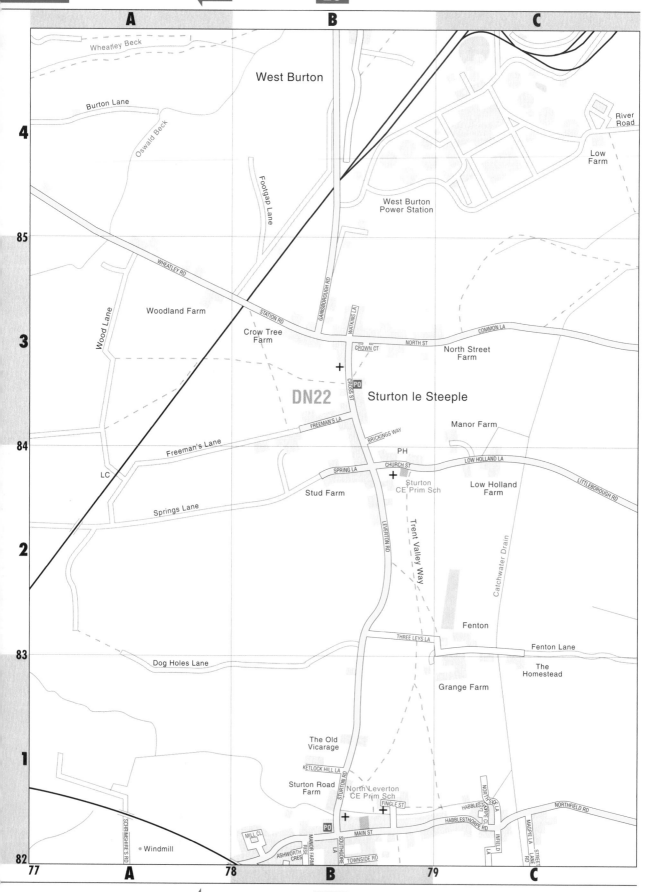

A B C

4

85

WHEATLEY RD

Wheatley Beck

Burton Lane

Oswald Beck

West Burton

Footgap Lane

GAINSBOROUGH RD

STATION RD

West Burton
Power Station

River
Road

Low
Farm

Wood Lane

Woodland Farm

Crow Tree
Farm

WATKINS LA

CROWN CT

PO

CROSS ST

DN22

Sturton le Steeple

NORTH ST

COMMON LA

North Street
Farm

3

Freeman's Lane

LC

Freeman's Lane

FREEMAN'S LA

BRICKINGS WAY

Manor Farm

84

Spring Lane

Stud Farm

SPRING LA

CHURCH ST

PH

Sturton
CE Prim Sch

LOW HOLLAND LA

Low Holland
Farm

LITTLEBOROUGH RD

Springs Lane

LEVERTON RD

Trent Valley Way

Catchwater Drain

2

Fenton

Dog Holes Lane

THREE LEYS LA

Fenton Lane

83

The
Homestead

Grange Farm

The Old
Vicarage

KETLOCK HILL LA

Sturton Road
Farm

STURTON RD

North Leverton
CE Prim Sch

FINGLE ST

NORTH SIDE LA

HABBLESTHORPE CT

NORTHFIELD RD

1

HABBLESTHORPE RD

INFIELD

MAGPIE LA

STREET LANE RD

MILL CL

Windmill

SCRIMSHIRE'S RD

ASHWORTH
RISE

CRES

MANOR FARM
LA

SOUTHGORE
LA

PO

MAIN ST

TOWNSIDE RD

82

77 A 78 B 79 C

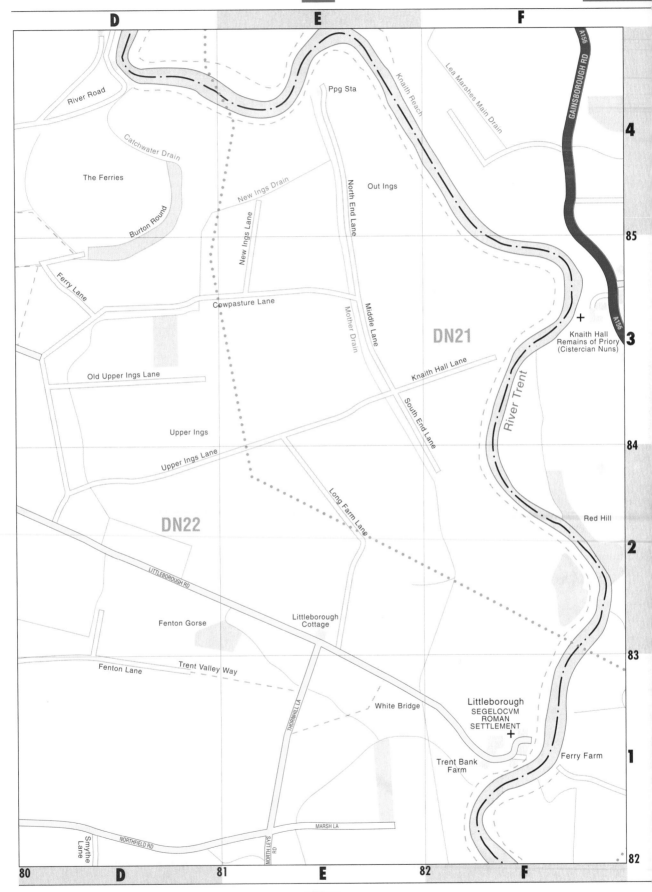

River Road

Catchwater Drain

The Ferries

Burton Round

Ferry Lane

New Ings Drain

New Ings Lane

Cowpasture Lane

Old Upper Ings Lane

Upper Ings

Upper Ings Lane

DN22

LITTLEBOROUGH RD

Fenton Gorse

Fenton Lane

Trent Valley Way

THORNHILL LA

White Bridge

Smythe Lane

NORTHFIELD RD

NORTH LEYS RD

MARSH LA

Ppg Sta

North End Lane

Out Ings

Mother Drain

Middle Lane

Knaith Hall Lane

South End Lane

Long Farm Lane

DN21

Littleborough Cottage

Littleborough
SEGELOCVM
ROMAN
SETTLEMENT

Trent Bank Farm

A156

GAINSBOROUGH RD

Lea Marshes Main Drain

Knaith Reach

River Trent

A156

Knaith Hall
Remains of Priory
(Cistercian Nuns)

Red Hill

Ferry Farm

4

85

3

84

2

83

1

82

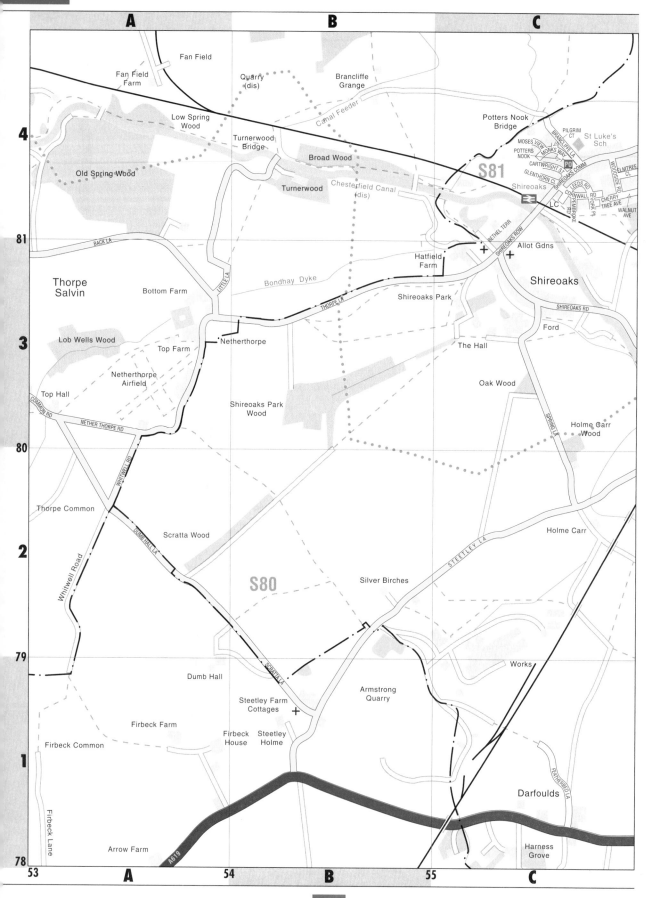

Fan Field

Fan Field
Farm

Quarry
(dis)

Brancliffe
Grange

Canal Feeder

Potters Nook
Bridge

PILGRIM
CT

St Luke's
Sch

Low Spring
Wood

MOSES VIEW

MONKS WAY

BRANCLIFFE LA

4

Turnerwood
Bridge

POTTERS
NOOK

SHEDOAKS COMM

CARTWRIGHT ST

GLENTHORN CL

PO

WOODSIDE RD

ELMTREE
CL

Broad Wood

S81

LEEDS RD

CORNWALL RD

YORK RD

PEARROBE RD

CHERRY
TREE AVE

WALNUT
AVE

Old Spring Wood

Turnerwood

Chesterfield Canal
(dis)

Shireoaks

LC

BETHEL TERR

81

BACK LA

Bondhay Dyke

Hatfield
Farm

Allot Gdns

SHIREOAKS ROW

Shireoaks

Thorpe
Salvin

Bottom Farm

THORPE LA

Shireoaks Park

SHIREOAKS RD

LITTLE LA

3

Lob Wells Wood

Top Farm

Netherthorpe

The Hall

Ford

Netherthorpe
Airfield

Shireoaks Park
Wood

Oak Wood

SPRING LA

Holme Carr
Wood

Top Hall

COMMON RD

NETHER THORPE RD

80

WHITWELL RD

Thorpe Common

Scratta Wood

Holme Carr

DUMB HALL LA

STEETLEY LA

2

Whitwell Road

S80

Silver Birches

Works

79

Dumb Hall

SCRATTA LA

Armstrong
Quarry

Steetley Farm
Cottages

Firbeck Farm

Firbeck
House

Steetley
Holme

FEATHERBED LA

1

Firbeck Common

Darfoulds

Firbeck Lane

Arrow Farm

A619

Harness
Grove

78

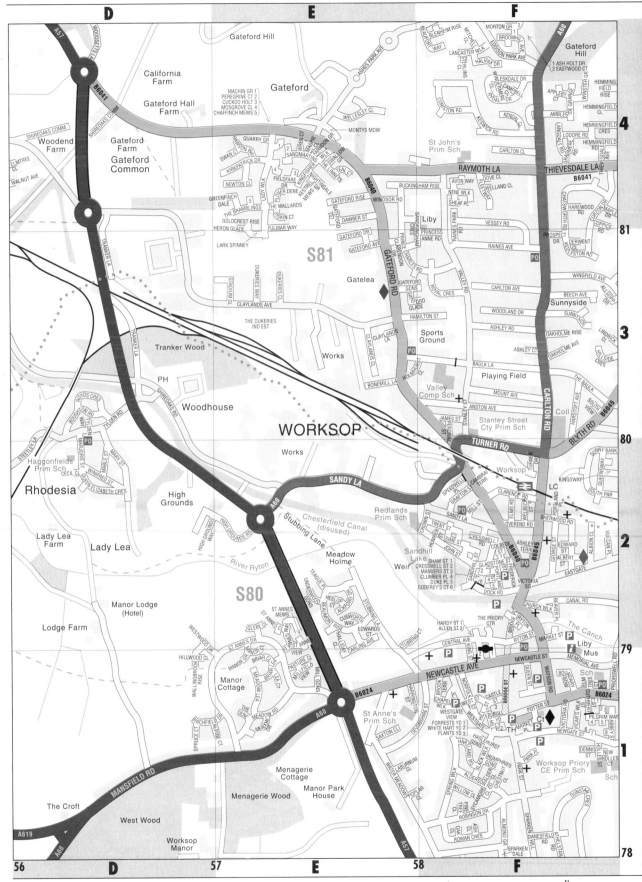

F1
1 LANGLEY ST
2 MELROSE WLK
3 LANERCOST MEWS
4 BUSHMEAD MEWS
5 NEWBURY MEWS
6 NOSTELL MEWS
7 EVESHAM MEWS
8 LAVENHAM MEWS

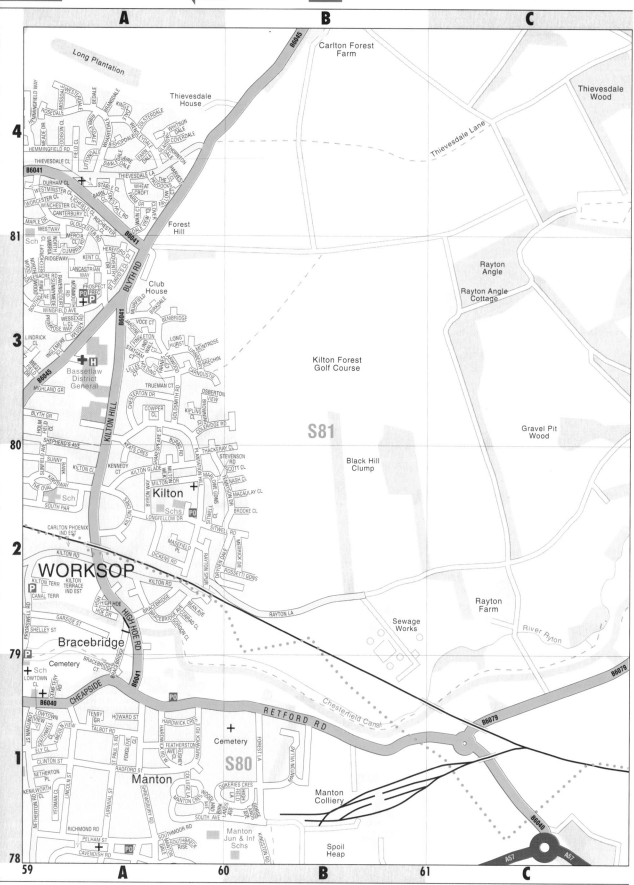

Long Plantation

Carlton Forest Farm

Thievesdale Wood

Thievesdale House

4

Thievesdale Lane

B6041

Forest Hill

81

Rayton Angle

Rayton Angle Cottage

Club House

Kilton Forest Golf Course

3

Bassetlaw District General

S81

80

Gravel Pit Wood

Black Hill Clump

Kilton

2

WORKSOP

Rayton La

Sewage Works

Rayton Farm

River Ryton

Bracebridge

79

Cemetery

B6079

CHEAPSIDE

B6079

Chesterfield Canal

B6040

RETFORD RD

Cemetery

1

S80

Manton

Manton Colliery

B6040

Manton Jun & Inf Schs

Spoil Heap

78

A57

A57

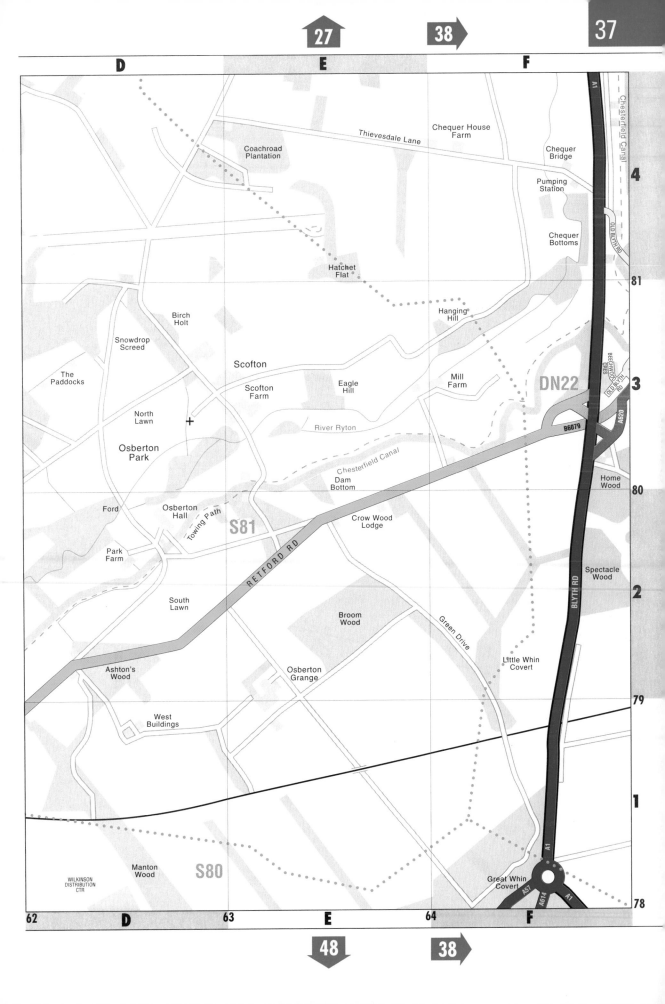

D
E
F

Chesterfield Canal

A1

Thievesdale Lane

Chequer House Farm

Coachroad Plantation

Chequer Bridge

Pumping Station

Old Blyth Rd

4

Chequer Bottoms

81

Hatchet Flat

Birch Holt

Hanging Hill

Snowdrop Screed

Scofton

Mill Farm

DN22

BEECHWOOD CRES

OLD BLYTH RD

3

The Paddocks

Scofton Farm

Eagle Hill

A620

North Lawn

River Ryton

B6079

Osberton Park

Chesterfield Canal

Home Wood

Ford

Dam Bottom

80

Osberton Hall

Towing Path

S81

Crow Wood Lodge

Spectacle Wood

Park Farm

RETFORD RD

BLYTH RD

2

South Lawn

Broom Wood

Green Drive

Little Whin Covert

Ashton's Wood

Osberton Grange

79

West Buildings

1

Manton Wood

S80

Great Whin Covert

A57

A614

A1

A1

WILKINSON DISTRIBUTION CTR

78

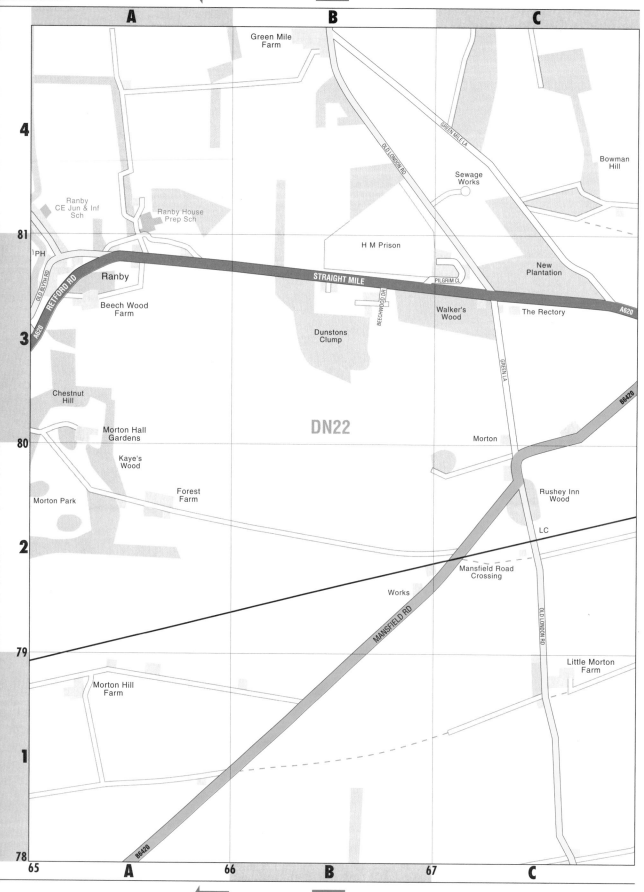

A
B
C

4

Green Mile Farm

GREEN MILE LA

OLD LONDON RD

Sewage Works

Bowman Hill

81

Ranby CE Jun & Inf Sch

Ranby House Prep Sch

H M Prison

New Plantation

PH

OLD BLYTH RD

RETFORD RD

Ranby

STRAIGHT MILE

PILGRIM CL

Walker's Wood

The Rectory

A620

Beech Wood Farm

BEECHWOOD DR

3

A620

Dunstons Clump

DN22

GREEN LA

B6420

Chestnut Hill

Morton Hall Gardens

Morton

80

Kaye's Wood

Rushey Inn Wood

Morton Park

Forest Farm

LC

2

Mansfield Road Crossing

OLD LONDON RD

Works

MANSFIELD RD

79

Little Morton Farm

Morton Hill Farm

1

B6420

78

65
A
66
B
67
C

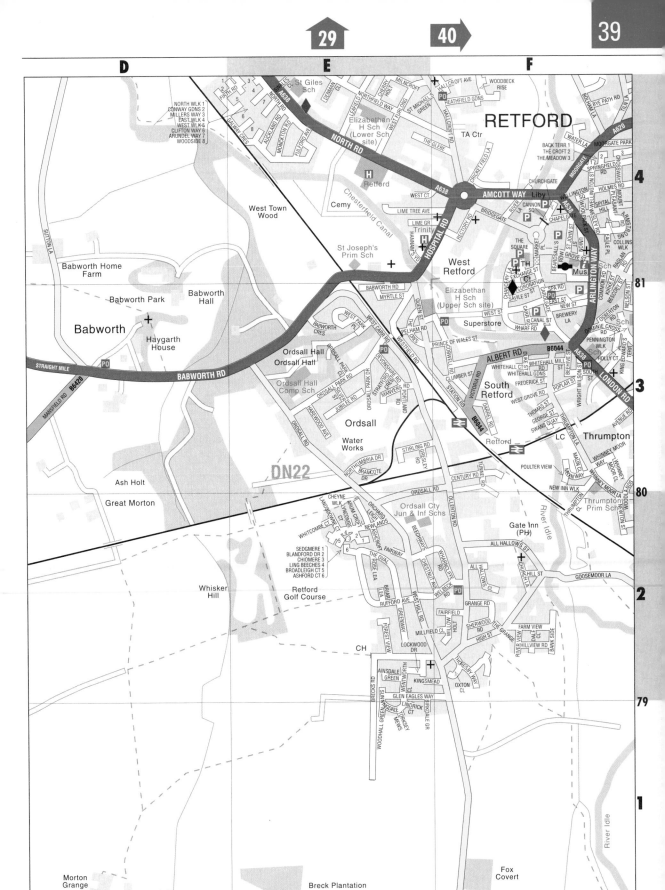

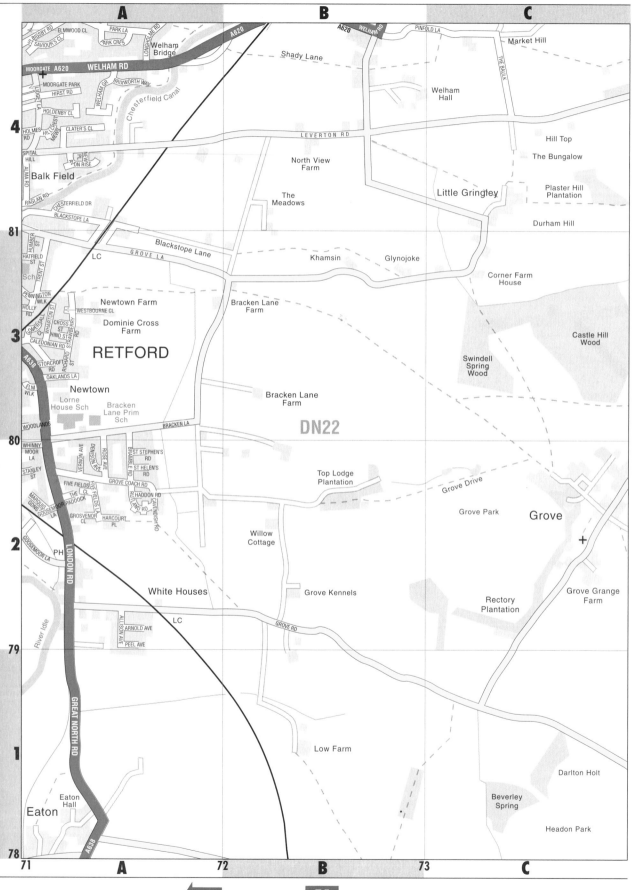

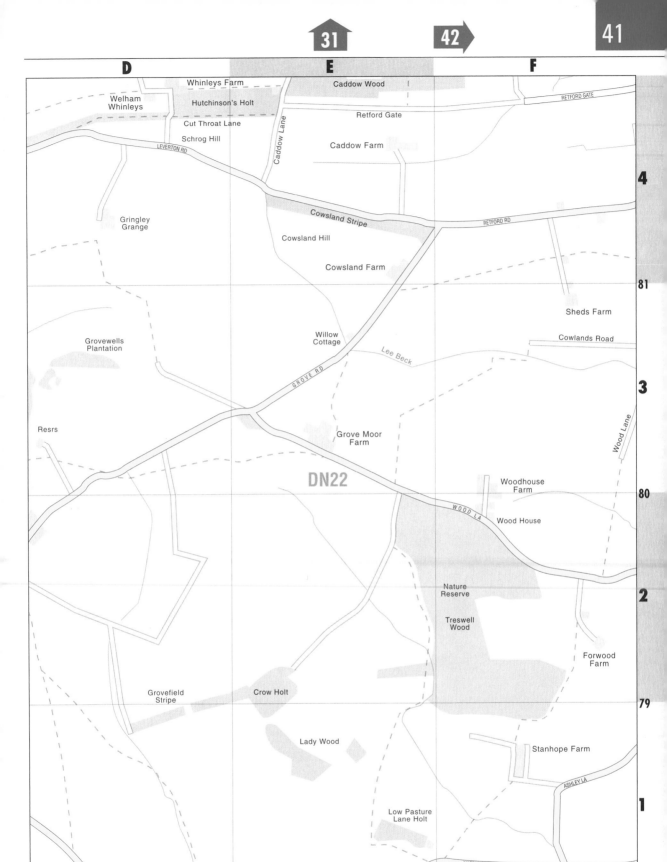

D

Whinleys Farm

Caddow Wood

Welham
Whinleys

Hutchinson's Holt

Retford Gate

RETFORD GATE

Cut Throat Lane

Caddow Lane

Retford Gate

Schrog Hill

LEVERTON RD

Caddow Farm

4

Cowsland Stripe

RETFORD RD

Gringley
Grange

Cowsland Hill

Cowsland Farm

81

Sheds Farm

Grovewells
Plantation

Willow
Cottage

Lee Beck

Cowlands Road

GROVE RD

3

Resrs

Grove Moor
Farm

Wood Lane

DN22

Woodhouse
Farm

80

WOOD LA

Wood House

Nature
Reserve

2

Treswell
Wood

Forwood
Farm

Grovefield
Stripe

Crow Holt

79

Lady Wood

Stanhope Farm

ASHLEY LA

1

Low Pasture
Lane Holt

HAZELWOOD LA

Ladywell Rise

Bottom Woodbeck
Farm

78

74

D

75

E

76

F

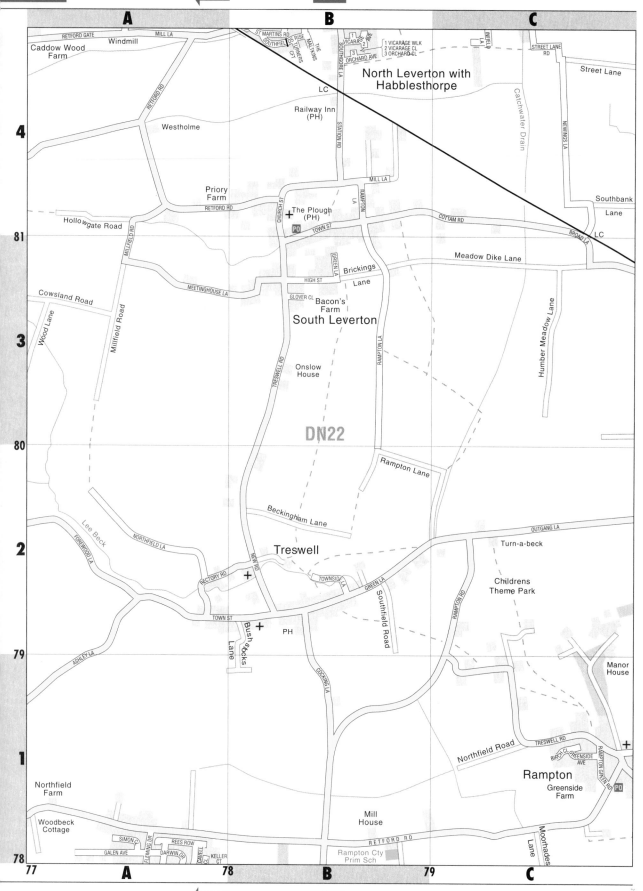

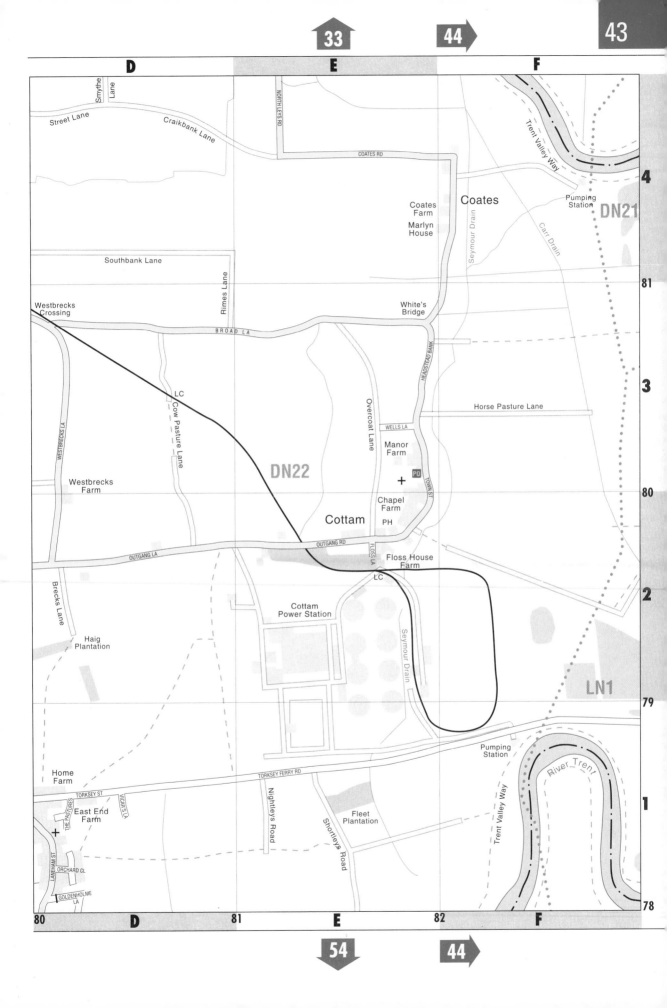

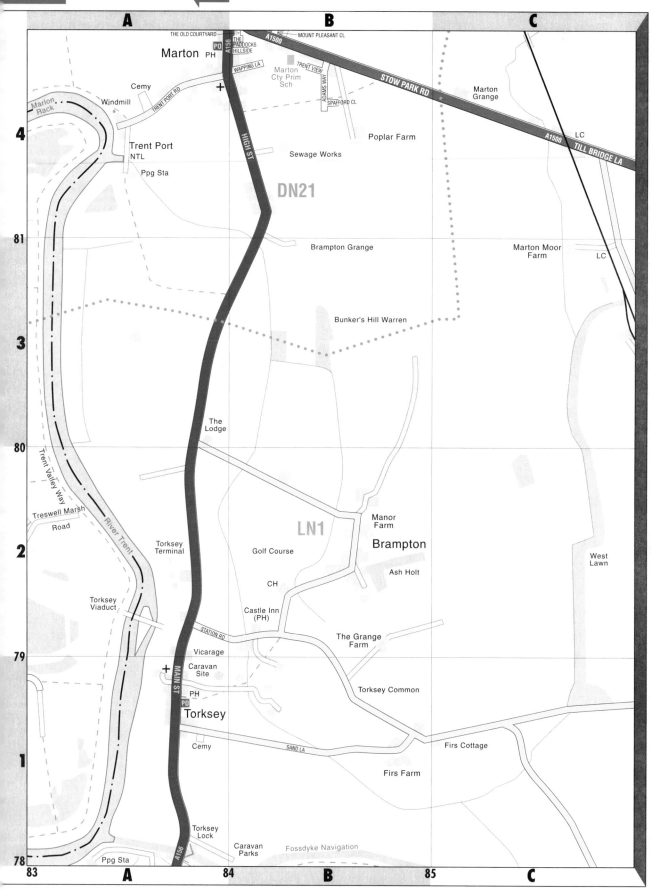

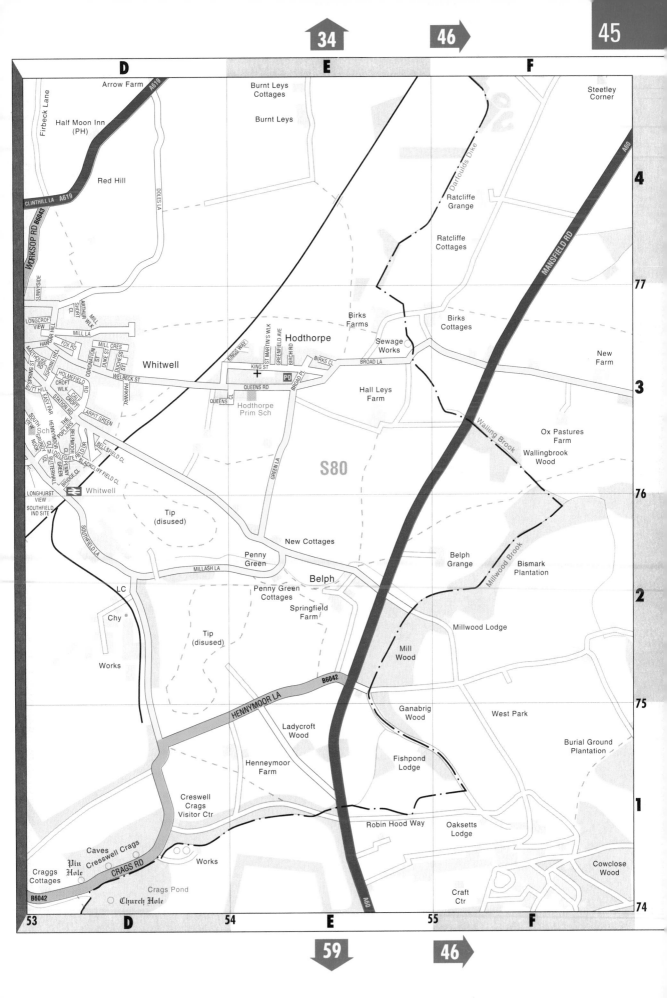

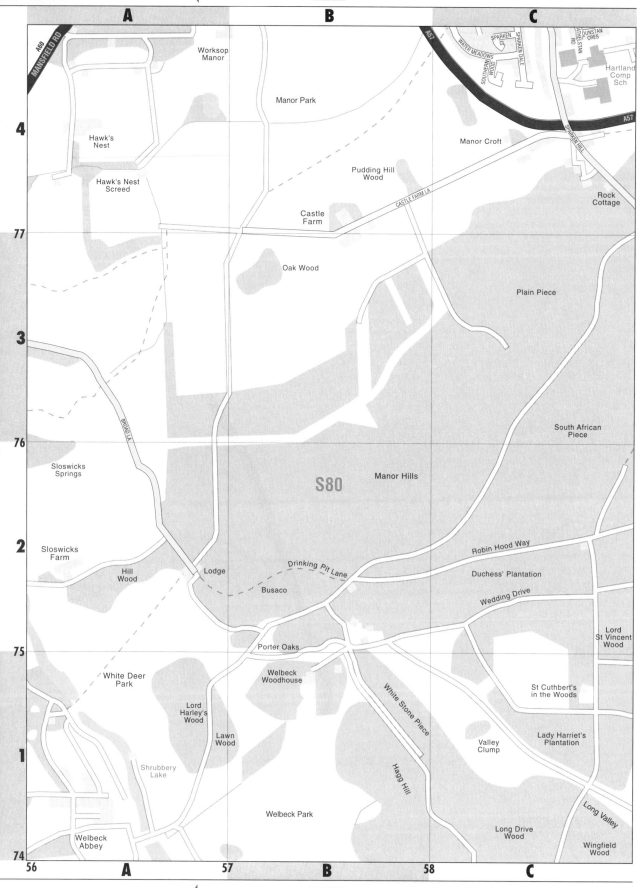

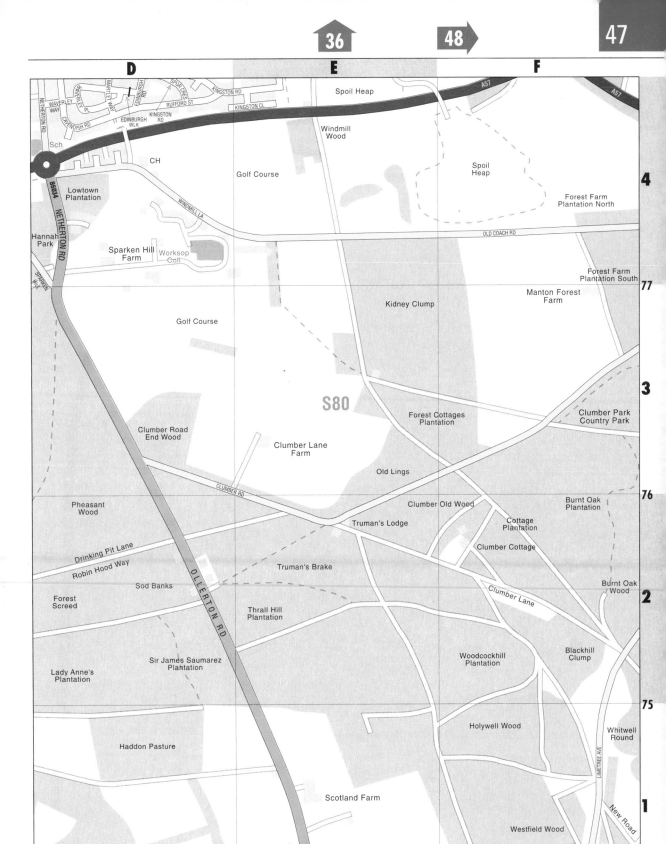

D
E
F

Spoil Heap

A57

A57

Kingston Rd

Spur Cres

Rufford St

Kingston Cl

Kingston Rd

Waverley Way

Waverley Pl

Martley Way

Edinburgh Pl

Cavendish Rd

Edinburgh Wlk

Windmill Wood

Sch

CH

Spoil Heap

Golf Course

4

Netherton Rd

B6034

Lowtown Plantation

Forest Farm Plantation North

Windmill La

Hannah Park

Old Coach Rd

Sparken Hill Farm

Worksop Golf

Forest Farm Plantation South

Sparken Hill

77

Manton Forest Farm

Kidney Clump

Golf Course

S80

3

Forest Cottages Plantation

Clumber Park Country Park

Clumber Road End Wood

Clumber Lane Farm

Old Lings

Clumber Rd

Clumber Old Wood

Burnt Oak Plantation

76

Pheasant Wood

Truman's Lodge

Cottage Plantation

Drinking Pit Lane

Clumber Cottage

Robin Hood Way

Truman's Brake

Burnt Oak Wood

Ollerton Rd

Sod Banks

Clumber Lane

2

Forest Screed

Thrall Hill Plantation

Lady Anne's Plantation

Sir James Saumarez Plantation

Woodcockhill Plantation

Blackhill Clump

75

Haddon Pasture

Holywell Wood

Whitwell Round

Limetree Ave

Scotland Farm

1

New Road

Westfield Wood

Lord Howe's Plantation

Long Valley Screed

Long Valley Lodge

B6034

74

59
D
60
E
61
F

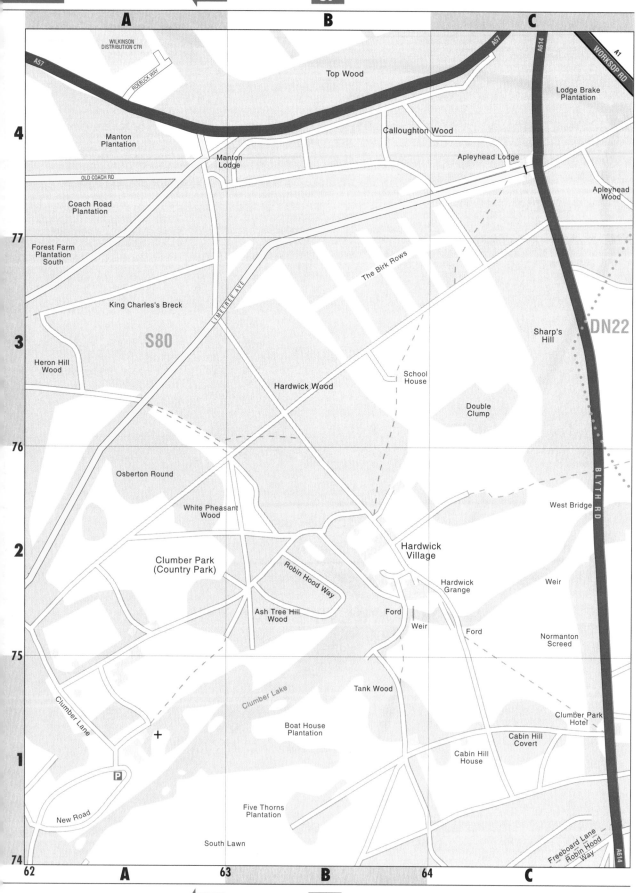

A   B   C

WILKINSON
DISTRIBUTION CTR

A57

ROEBUCK WAY

Top Wood

A57

A614

WORKSOP RD

A1

Lodge Brake
Plantation

Manton
Plantation

Calloughton Wood

Manton
Lodge

Apleyhead Lodge

Apleyhead
Wood

OLD COACH RD

Coach Road
Plantation

Forest Farm
Plantation
South

The Birk Rows

King Charles's Breck

LIMETREE AVE

S80

Sharp's
Hill

SDN22

Heron Hill
Wood

Hardwick Wood

School
House

Double
Clump

Osberton Round

White Pheasant
Wood

West Bridge

BLYTH RD

Clumber Park
(Country Park)

Robin Hood Way

Hardwick
Village

Ash Tree Hill
Wood

Ford

Hardwick
Grange

Weir

Weir

Ford

Normanton
Screed

Clumber Lane

Clumber Lake

Tank Wood

Clumber Park
Hotel

Boat House
Plantation

Cabin Hill
Covert

Cabin Hill
House

P

New Road

Five Thorns
Plantation

South Lawn

Freeboard Lane
Robin Hood
Way

A614

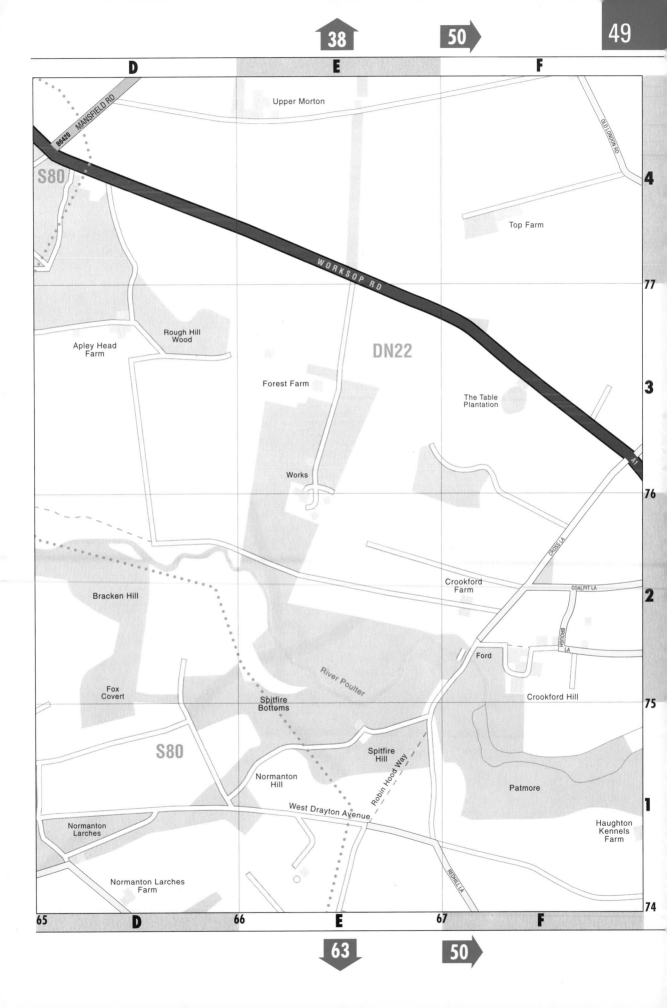

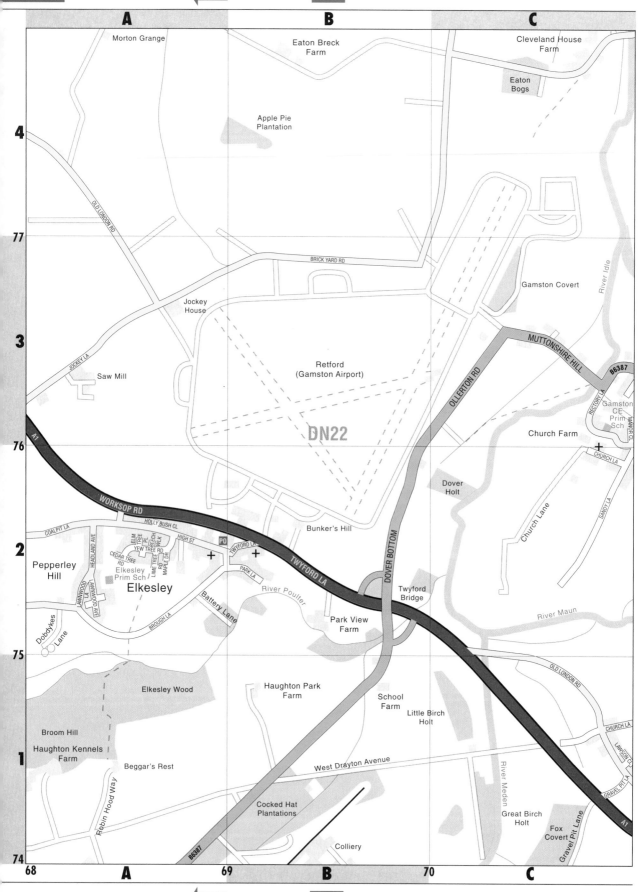

A
B
C

Morton Grange

Eaton Breck
Farm

Cleveland House
Farm

Eaton
Bogs

Apple Pie
Plantation

4

OLD LONDON RD

77

BRICK YARD RD

Gamston Covert

River Idle

Jockey
House

MUTTONSHIRE HILL

3

JOCKEY LA

Saw Mill

Retford
(Gamston Airport)

OLLERTON RD

B6387

Gamston
CE
Prim
Sch

RECTORY LA

MANOR CL

DN22

Church Farm

Church Lane

SANDY LA

CHURCH LA

76

A1

Dover
Holt

WORKSOP RD

HOLLY BUSH CL

Bunker's Hill

Church Lane

COALPIT LA

HEADLAND AVE

ELM TREE PL

YEW TREE RD

HIGH ST

PO

TWYFORD LA

DOVER BOTTOM

2

Pepperley
Hill

CEDAR TREE RD

Elkesley
Prim Sch

LIME TREE RD

BEECH WALK

MAPLE DR

PARK LA

TWYFORD LA

Twyford
Bridge

River Maun

Elkesley

LAWNWOOD LA

LAWNWOOD AVE

BROUGH LA

Battery Lane

River Poulter

Park View
Farm

Dobdykes
Lane

75

Elkesley Wood

Haughton Park
Farm

School
Farm

Little Birch
Holt

OLD LONDON RD

CHURCH LA

LAWSON CL

Broom Hill

Haughton Kennels
Farm

Beggar's Rest

West Drayton Avenue

River Meden

Great Birch
Holt

Fox
Covert
Holt

GRAVEL PIT LA

CHURCH LA

1

Robin Hood Way

B6387

Cocked Hat
Plantations

Colliery

Gravel Pit Lane

A1

74

68
A
69
B
70
C

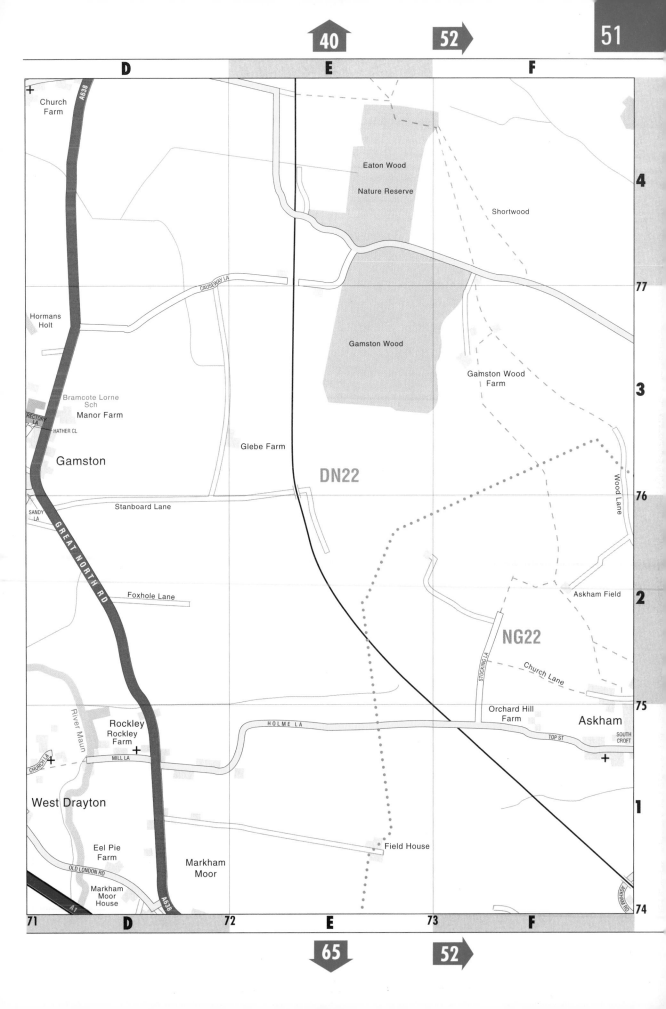

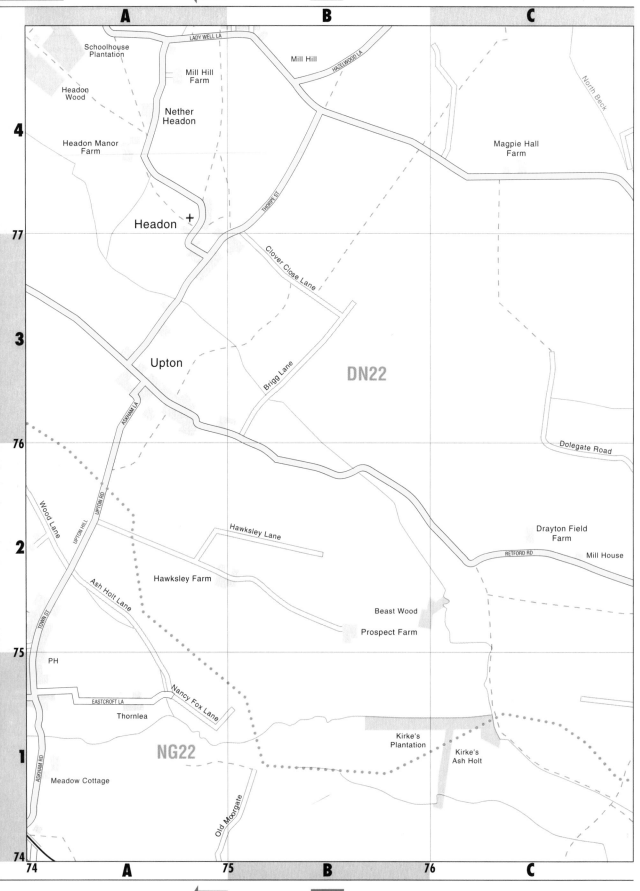

LADY WELL LA

Schoolhouse
Plantation

Mill Hill

Mill Hill
Farm

HAZELWOOD LA

Headon
Wood

Nether
Headon

Magpie Hall
Farm

North Beck

4

Headon Manor
Farm

THORPE ST

Headon +

77

Clover Close Lane

DN22

3

Upton

Brigg Lane

ASKHAM LA

76

Dolegate Road

Wood Lane

UPTON HILL

UPTON RD

Hawksley Lane

Drayton Field
Farm

RETFORD RD

Mill House

2

Hawksley Farm

Ash Holt Lane

TOWN ST

Beast Wood

Prospect Farm

75

PH

EASTCROFT LA

Nancy Fox Lane

Thornlea

Kirke's
Plantation

Kirke's
Ash Holt

ASKHAM RD

NG22

1

Meadow Cottage

Old Moorgate

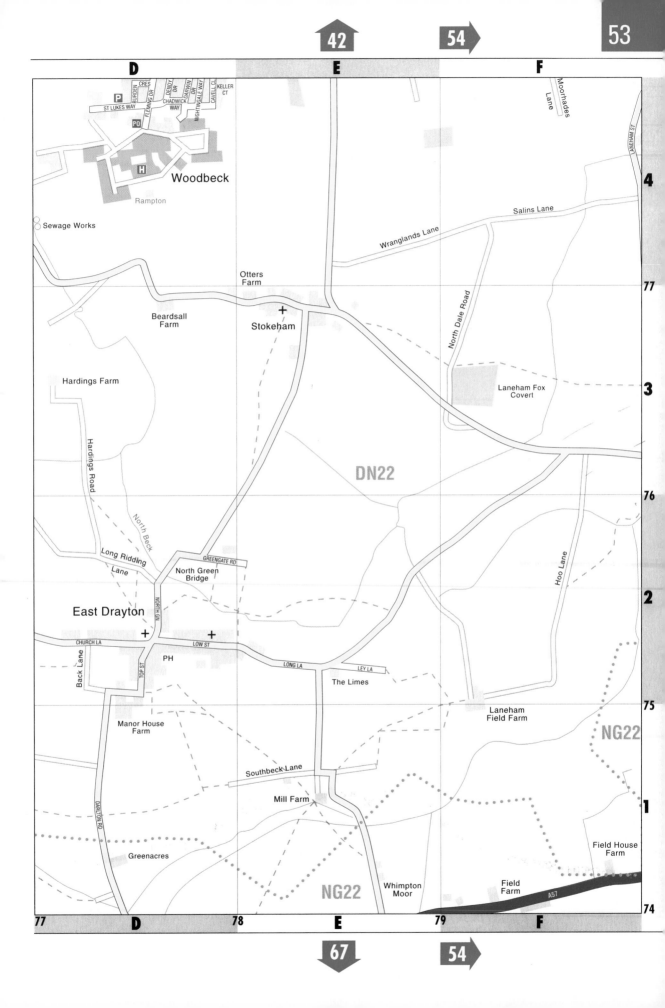

D E F

4

St Lukes Way

P

PO

H

Woodbeck

Rampton

Sewage Works

BURDEN CRES
FLEMING DR
DENDY DR
DARWIN DR
CHADWICK WAY
NIGHTINGALE WAY
CAVELL CL
KELLER CT

Otters Farm

Beardsall Farm

Stokeham

Hardings Farm

Hardings Road

North Beck

Long Ridding Lane

North Green Bridge

GREENGATE RD

East Drayton

NORTH GN

CHURCH LA

Back Lane

TOP ST

PH

LOW ST

LONG LA

LEY LA

The Limes

Manor House Farm

DARLTON RD

Southbeck Lane

Mill Farm

Greenacres

NG22

Whimpton Moor

Wranglands Lane

Salins Lane

North Dale Road

Laneham Fox Covert

DN22

Hoo Lane

Laneham Field Farm

NG22

Field Farm

Field House Farm

A57

Moorhades Lane

LANEHAM ST

77

76

75

74

3

2

1

77 78 79

D E F

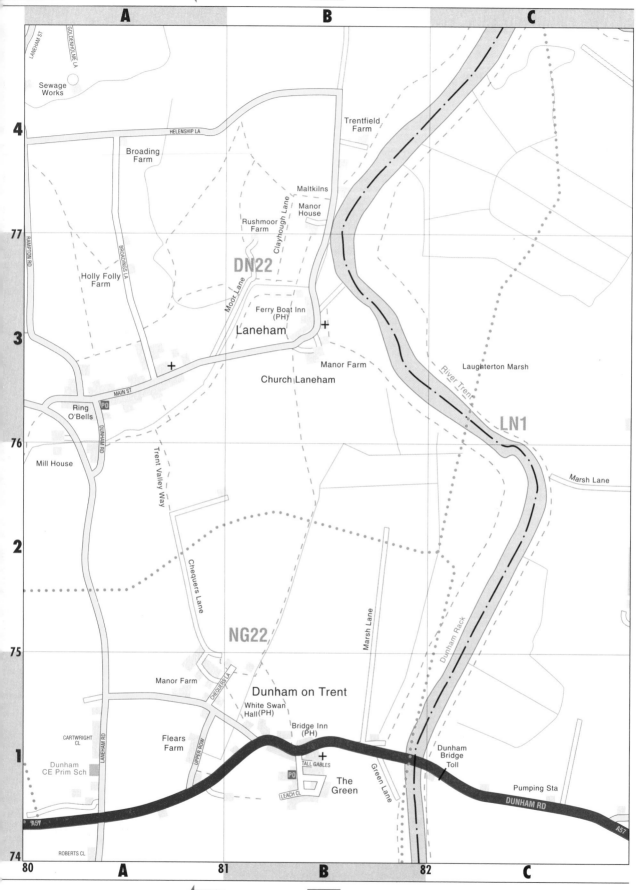

LANEHAM ST

GOLDENHOLME LA

Sewage
Works

HELENSHIP LA

4

Broading
Farm

Trentfield
Farm

Maltkilns

Manor
House

RAMPTON RD

77

Rushmoor
Farm

Clayhough Lane

DN22

BROADINGS LA

Holly Folly
Farm

Moor Lane

Ferry Boat Inn
(PH)

Laneham

3

Manor Farm

Laughterton Marsh

Church Laneham

River Trent

MAIN ST

Ring
O'Bells

PO

DUNHAM RD

LN1

76

Mill House

Trent Valley Way

Marsh Lane

Chequers Lane

2

NG22

Marsh Lane

Dunham Rack

75

Manor Farm

CHEQUERS LA

Dunham on Trent

White Swan
Hall(PH)

CARTWRIGHT
CL

LANEHAM RD

Flears
Farm

UPPER ROW

Bridge Inn
(PH)

TALL GABLES

Green Lane

Dunham
Bridge
Toll

1

Dunham
CE Prim Sch

PO

LEACH CL

The
Green

Pumping Sta

DUNHAM RD

A57

A57

74

ROBERTS CL

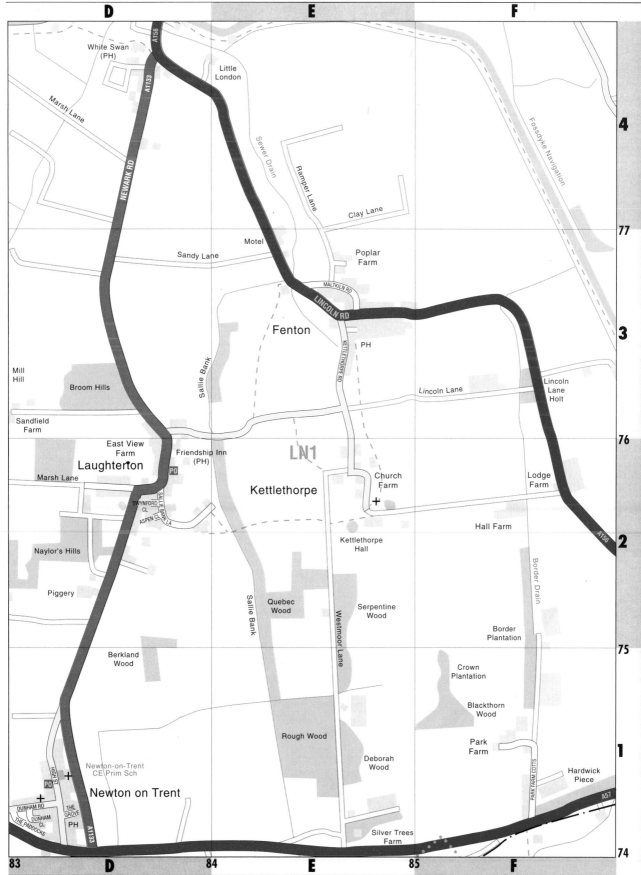

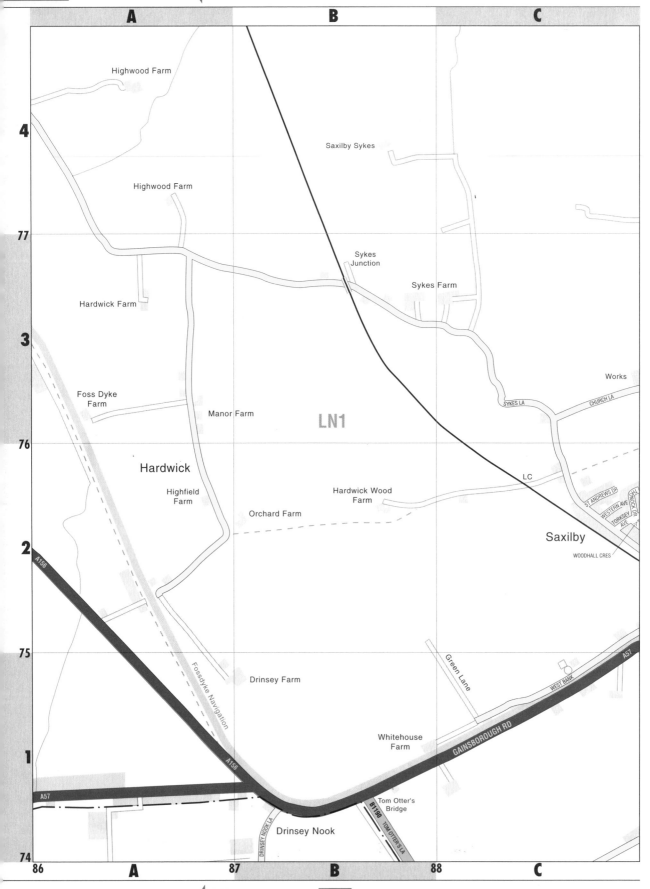

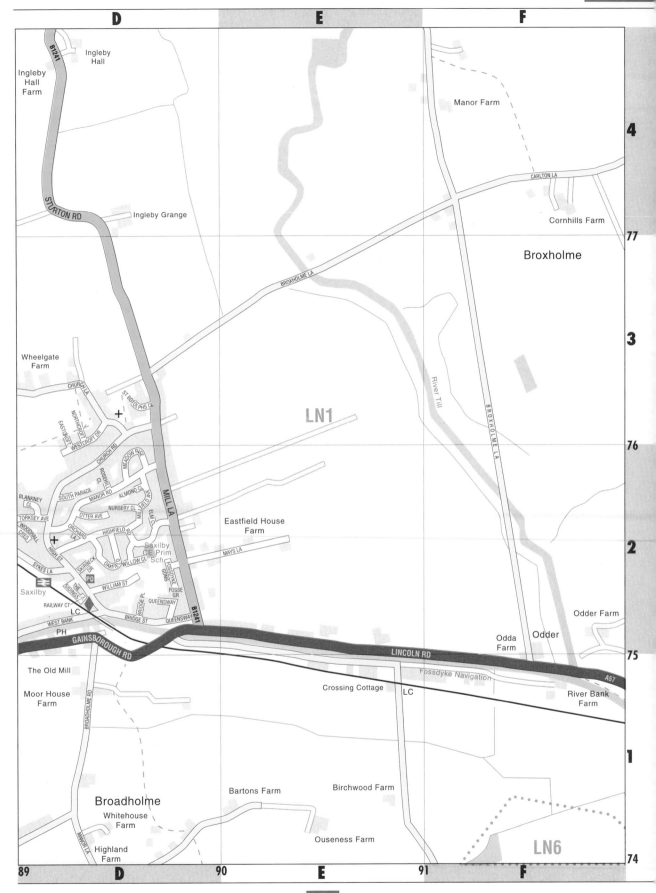

Ingleby Hall

Ingleby Hall Farm

B1241

Manor Farm

4

CARLTON LA

STURTON RD

Ingleby Grange

Cornhills Farm

77

Broxholme

BROXHOLME LA

Wheelgate Farm

3

River Till

CHURCH LA

ST BOTOLPHS CL

BROXHOLME LA

LN1

NORTHCROFT
EASTCROFT
WESTCROFT DR

CHURCH RD

MEADOW RI/GR

76

BLANKNEY CL

SOUTH PARADE

ROSEHILL CL

MANOR RD

ALMOND CL

MILLFIELD AVE

MILL LA

TORKSEY AVE

NURSERY CL

ELM CL

Eastfield House Farm

2

WOODHALL CRES

HIGH ST

ORCHARD LA

OTTER AVE

HIGHFIELD RD

OAK CL

WILLOW CL

Saxilby CE Prim Sch

MAYS LA

Odder Farm

SKIRBECK DR

THE SIDINGS

PO

WILLIAM ST

FOSSDYKE

BONIS

FOSSE GR

QUEENSWAY

B1241

SYKES LA

RAILWAY CT

BRIDGE PL

BRIDGE ST

QUEENSWAY

Odda Farm

Odder

Saxilby

LC

WEST BANK

PH

GAINSBOROUGH RD

LINCOLN RD

A57

River Bank Farm

75

The Old Mill

Moor House Farm

BROADHOLME RD

Fossdyke Navigation

Crossing Cottage

LC

1

Broadholme

Whitehouse Farm

MANOR LA

Bartons Farm

Birchwood Farm

Ouseness Farm

LN6

Highland Farm

74

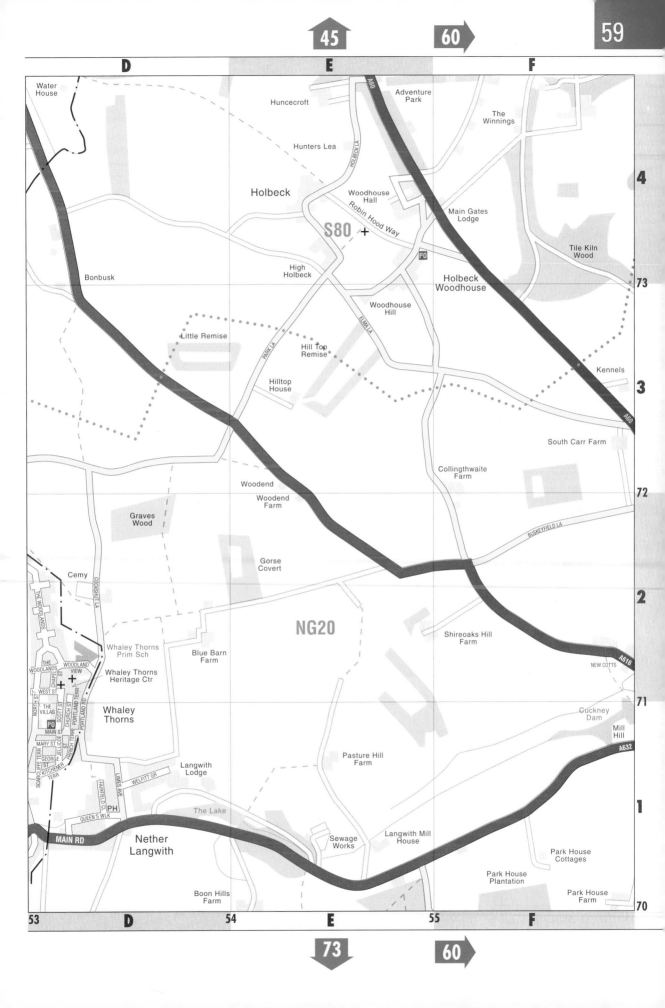

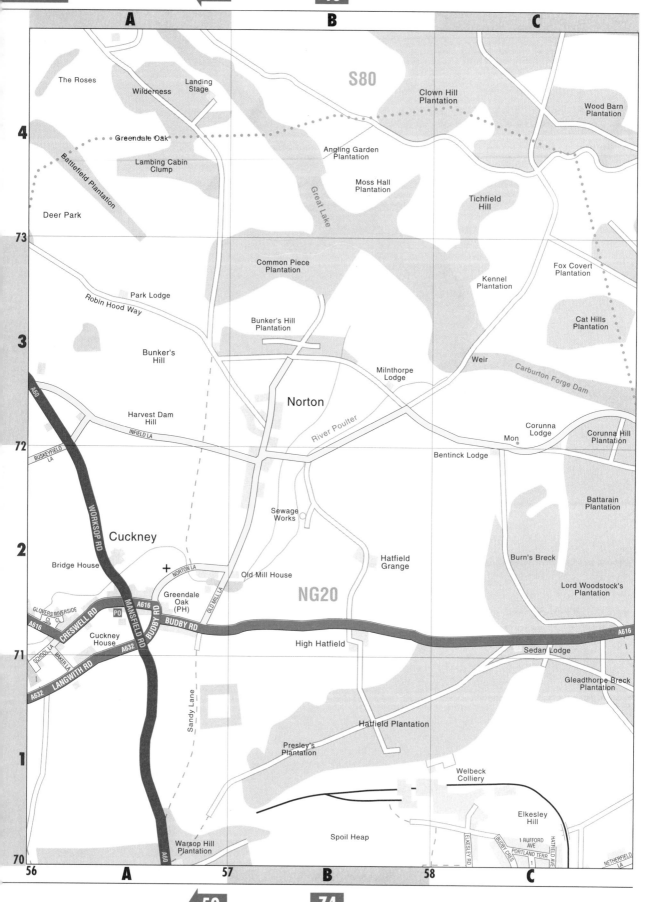

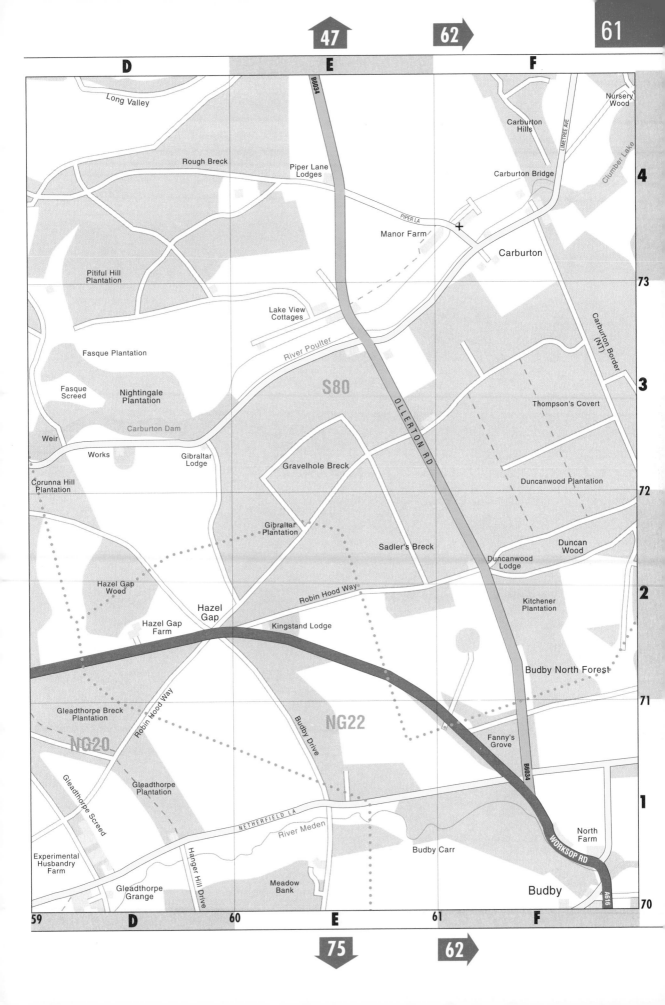

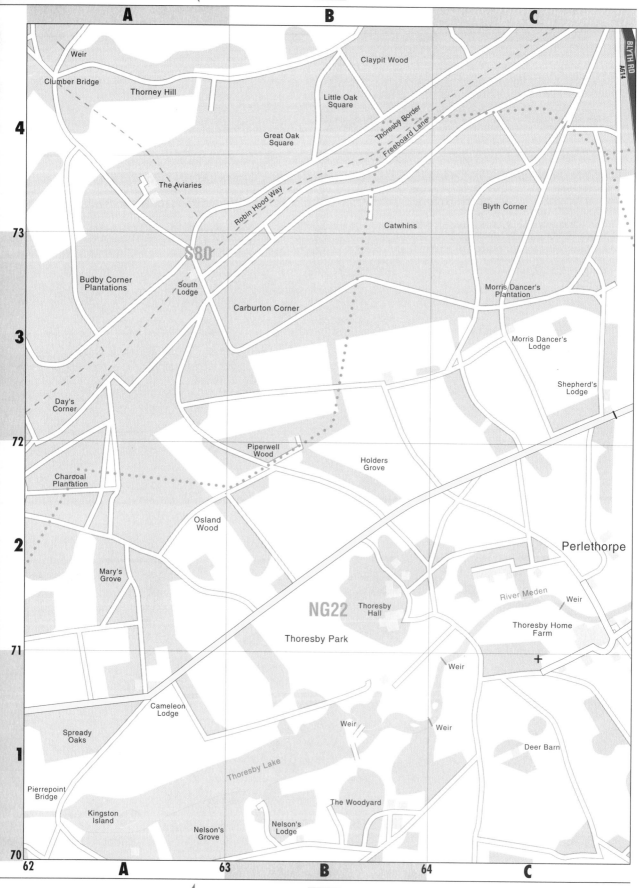

Weir

Clumber Bridge

Thorney Hill

Claypit Wood

Little Oak Square

Great Oak Square

Thoresby Border

Freeboard Lane

4

The Aviaries

Robin Hood Way

Blyth Corner

73

Catwhins

S80

Budby Corner Plantations

South Lodge

Carburton Corner

Morris Dancer's Plantation

3

Morris Dancer's Lodge

Shepherd's Lodge

Day's Corner

72

Piperwell Wood

Holders Grove

Charcoal Plantation

Osland Wood

Perlethorpe

2

Mary's Grove

River Meden

Weir

NG22

Thoresby Hall

Thoresby Home Farm

71

Thoresby Park

Weir

Cameleon Lodge

Weir

Weir

Spready Oaks

Deer Barn

1

Thoresby Lake

Pierrepoint Bridge

Kingston Island

The Woodyard

Nelson's Grove

Nelson's Lodge

70

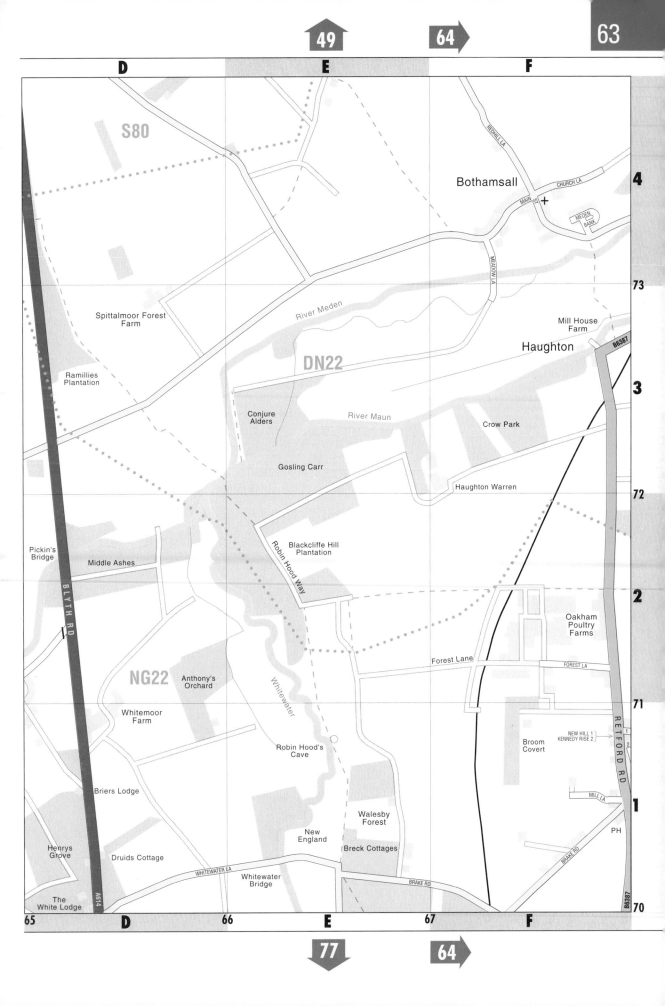

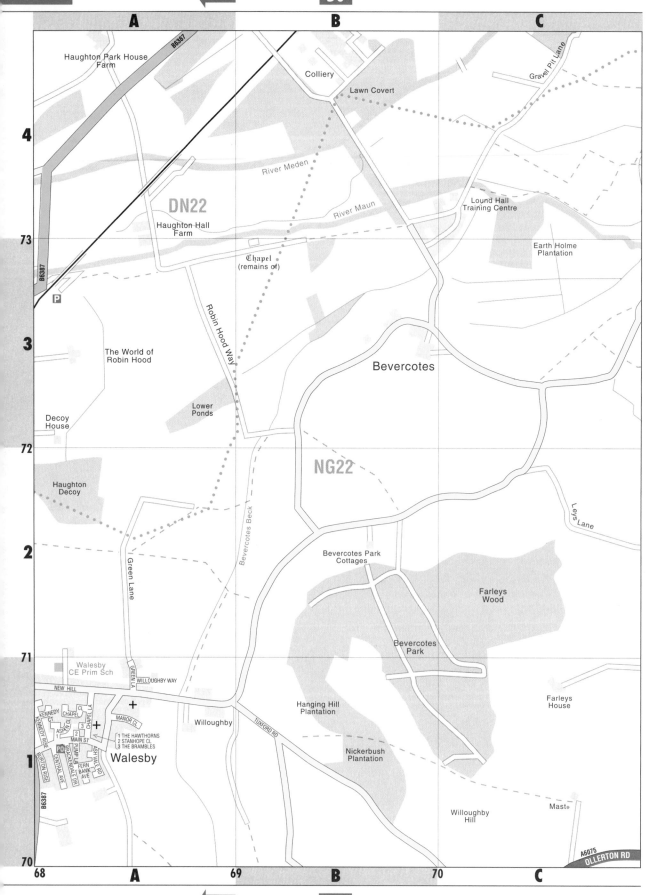

A   **B**   **C**

4

Haughton Park House Farm

B6367

Colliery

Lawn Covert

Gravel Pit Lane

River Meden

River Maun

Lound Hall Training Centre

DN22

73

Haughton Hall Farm

Chapel (remains of)

Earth Holme Plantation

B6367

P

3

The World of Robin Hood

Robin Hood Way

Bevercotes

Decoy House

Lower Ponds

72

NG22

Haughton Decoy

Bevercotes Beck

Leys Lane

2

Bevercotes Park Cottages

Farleys Wood

Green Lane

71

Walesby CE Prim Sch

GREEN LA

WILLOUGHBY WAY

Bevercotes Park

Farleys House

NEW HILL

KENNEDY CT

CHAPEL CL

ASPEN CL

CHAPEL LA

MANOR CL

Willoughby

TUXFORD RD

Hanging Hill Plantation

KENNEDY RISE

MAIN ST

1 THE HAWTHORNS
2 STANHOPE CL
3 THE BRAMBLES

BURTON RISE

PUMP LA

BRACKENDALE DR

FERN BANK AVE

ASH VALE RD

CENTRAL AVE

PO

1

Walesby

Nickerbush Plantation

Farleys House

B6367

Willoughby Hill

Mast

A6075

OLLERTON RD

70

68   **A**   69   **B**   70   **C**

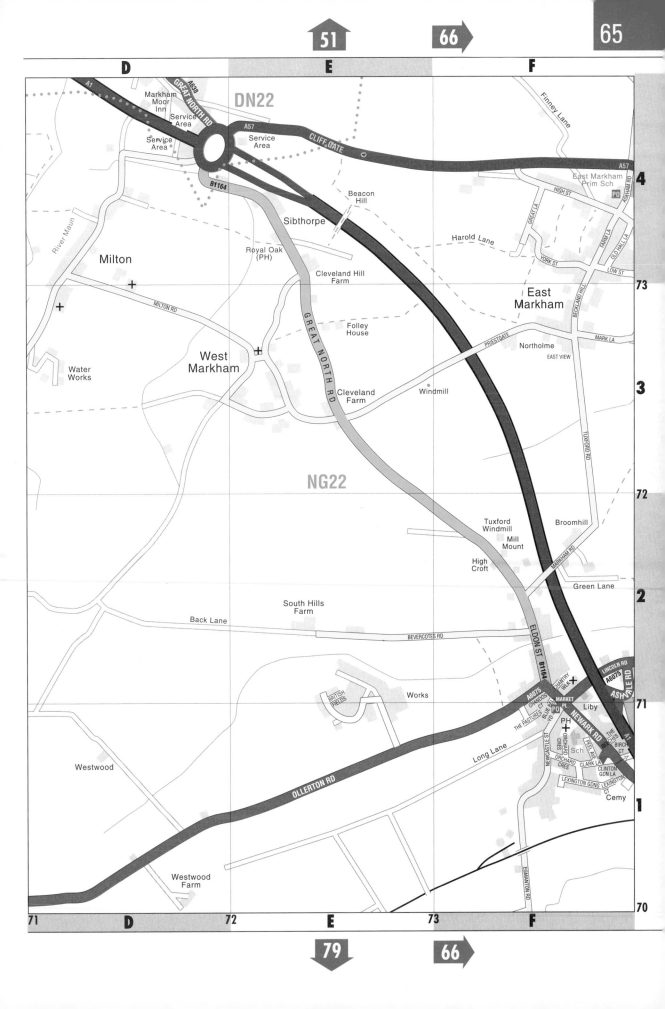

A1
Markham Moor Inn
GREAT NORTH RD
A638
Service Area
Service Area
DN22
A57
Service Area
CLIFF GATE
Finney Lane
A57
B1164
East Markham Prim Sch
PO
ASKHAM RD
HIGH ST
GREAT LA
PARK LN
OLD HALL LA
4
Beacon Hill
Sibthorpe
Harold Lane
YORK ST
LOW ST
River Maun
Royal Oak (PH)
Cleveland Hill Farm
BECKLAND HILL
East Markham
73
Milton
+
+
Folley House
PRIESTGATE
Northolme
EAST VIEW
MARK LA
MILTON RD
GREAT NORTH RD
TUXFORD RD
Water Works
West Markham
+
Cleveland Farm
Windmill
3
NG22
72
Tuxford Windmill
Broomhill
Mill Mount
High Croft
MARKHAM RD
Green Lane
South Hills Farm
2
Back Lane
BEVERCOTES RD
ELDON ST
B1164
A6075
LINCOLN RD
ASHVALE RD
BRITISH FIELDS
Works
CHANTRY WLK
MARKET PL
Liby
A1
71
A6075
CHANDOS
PO
NEWARK RD
THE PASTURES
BLUE BELL YD
Long Lane
LEXINGTON GDNS
ORCHARD CRES
CLARK LA
CLINTON GDN LA
LEXINGTON CT
Sch
THE BEECHES
BIRCH CT
PH
+
Cemy
1
Westwood
OLLERTON RD
Westwood Farm
EGMANTON RD
70

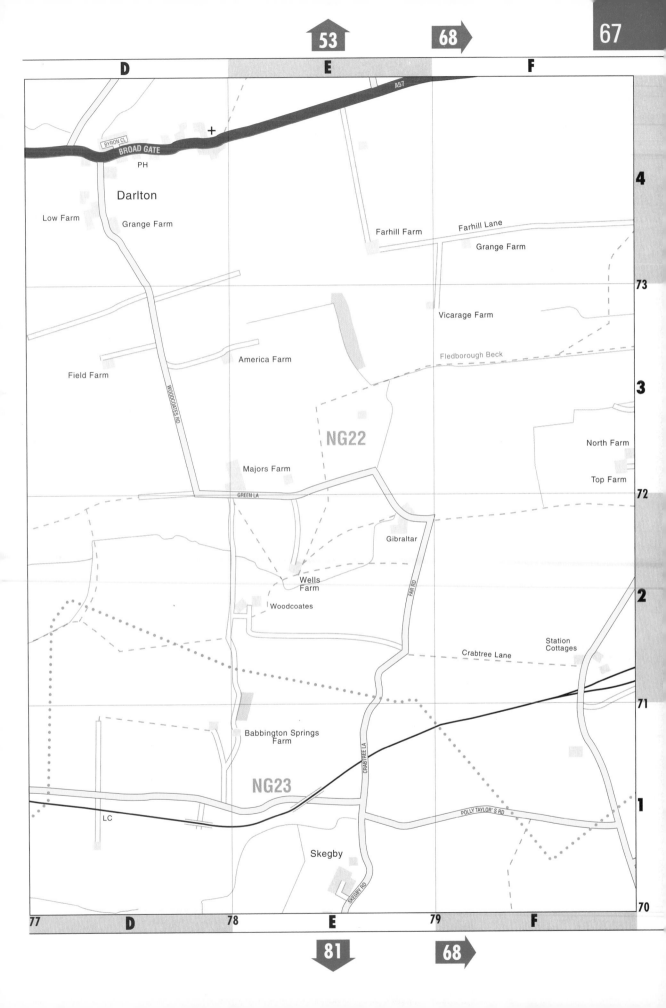

D · E · F

A57

BYRON CL
BROAD GATE
PH

Darlton

Low Farm

Grange Farm

Farhill Farm · Farhill Lane

Grange Farm

4

73

Vicarage Farm

WOODCOATES RD

Field Farm

America Farm

Fledborough Beck

3

NG22

North Farm

Majors Farm

Top Farm

GREEN LA

72

Gibraltar

FAR RD

Wells Farm

Woodcoates

2

Station Cottages

Crabtree Lane

71

Babbington Springs Farm

CRABTREE LA

NG23

1

POLLY TAYLOR'S RD

LC

Skegby

SKEGBY RD

70

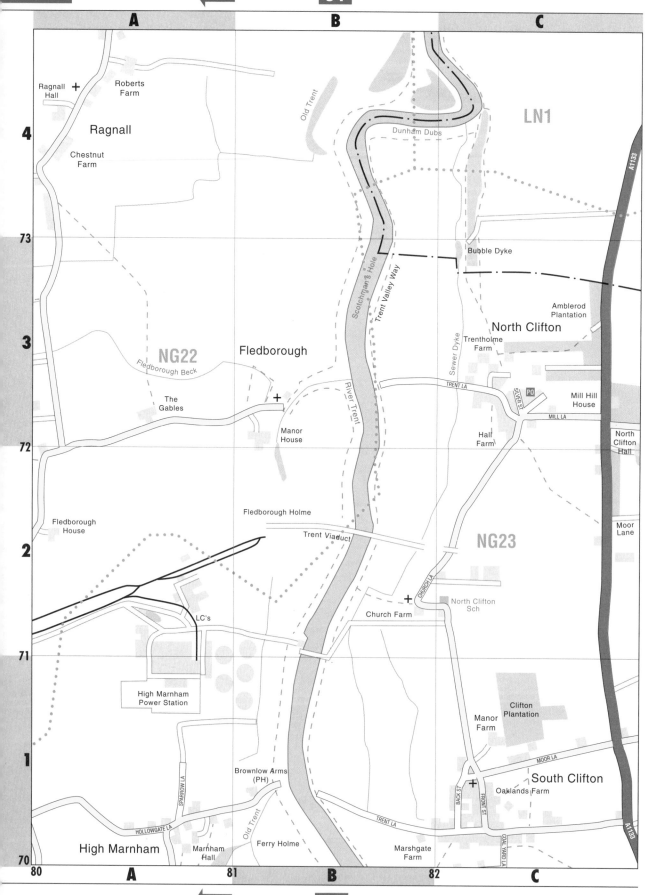

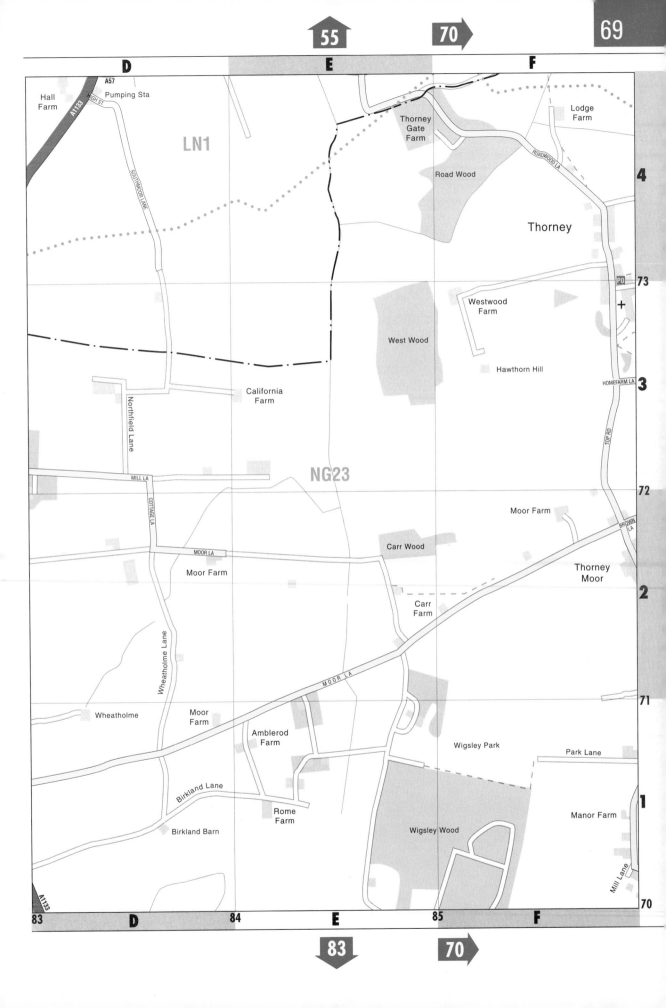

D **E** **F**

Hall Farm

A57

HIGH ST

Pumping Sta

A1133

LN1

SOUTHMOOR LANE

Thorney Gate Farm

Road Wood

Lodge Farm

ROADWOOD LA

Thorney

4

PO

73

Westwood Farm

West Wood

Hawthorn Hill

HOMEFARM LA

3

Northfield Lane

California Farm

NG23

MILL LA

TOP RD

72

COTTAGE LA

Moor Farm

BROWN LA

Moor Farm

MOOR LA

Carr Wood

Thorney Moor

Moor Farm

Carr Farm

2

Wheatholme Lane

MOOR LA

71

Wheatholme

Moor Farm

Amblerod Farm

Wigsley Park

Park Lane

1

Birkland Lane

Rome Farm

Manor Farm

Birkland Barn

Wigsley Wood

Mill Lane

A1133

70

83 **D** **84** **E** **85** **F**

A **B** **C**

LN1

B1190

Spring Wood

Gibbet Wood

SAND LA

4

Saxilby Moor

TOM OTTER'S LA

Springwood Farm

The Ring

Gibbetwood Farm

Gibbet Lane Cottages

DRINSEY NOOK LA

Glover's Wood

73

Five Lane Ends

Crow Wood

Castle Farm

Ox Pasture Drain

Saxilby Moor Farm

CARR LA

Lee Nook Farm

HOMEFARM LA

3

Plot Farm

North Harby

B1190

Grange Farm

Half Moon Plantation

Fir Tree Farm

Wallrudding Farm

BROWN LA

Manor Farm

NG23

72

Thorney Brown

Lodge's Farm

Station Farm

2

LN6

71

Plot Wood

Wigsley Drain

Manterfield Farm

Queen Eleanor Cty Prim Sch

Clay Lane

STATION RD

Ox Pasture Drain

Bottle and Glass (PH)

MILL FIELD CL

LOW ST

PO

HIGH ST

Harby

WIGSLEY RD

CROSS LA

1

Wigsley

CHURCH RD

Grange Farm

70

86 **A** 87 **B** 88 **C**

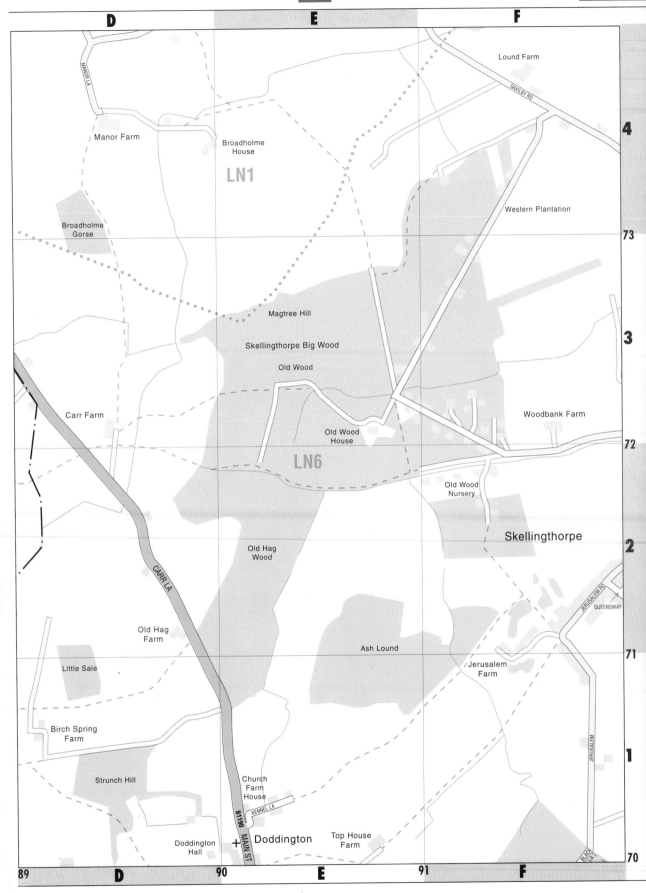

D E F

Lound Farm

SAXILBY RD

Manor Farm

Broadholme
House

LN1

4

Western Plantation

Broadholme
Gorse

73

Magtree Hill

Skellingthorpe Big Wood

3

Old Wood

Carr Farm

Woodbank Farm

Old Wood
House

72

LN6

Old Wood
Nursery

Skellingthorpe

Old Hag
Wood

2

CARR LA

JERUSALEM RD

QUEENSWAY

Old Hag
Farm

Little Sale

Ash Lound

71

Jerusalem
Farm

Birch Spring
Farm

JERUSALEM

1

Strunch Hill

Church
Farm
House

B1190

KENNEL LA

MAIN ST

Doddington

Top House
Farm

BLACK LA

70

Doddington
Hall

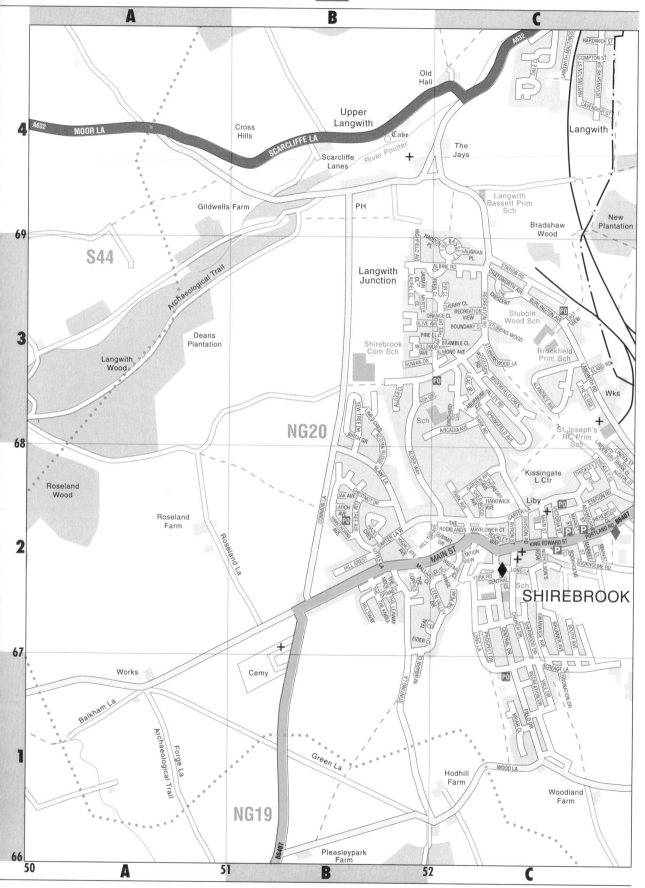

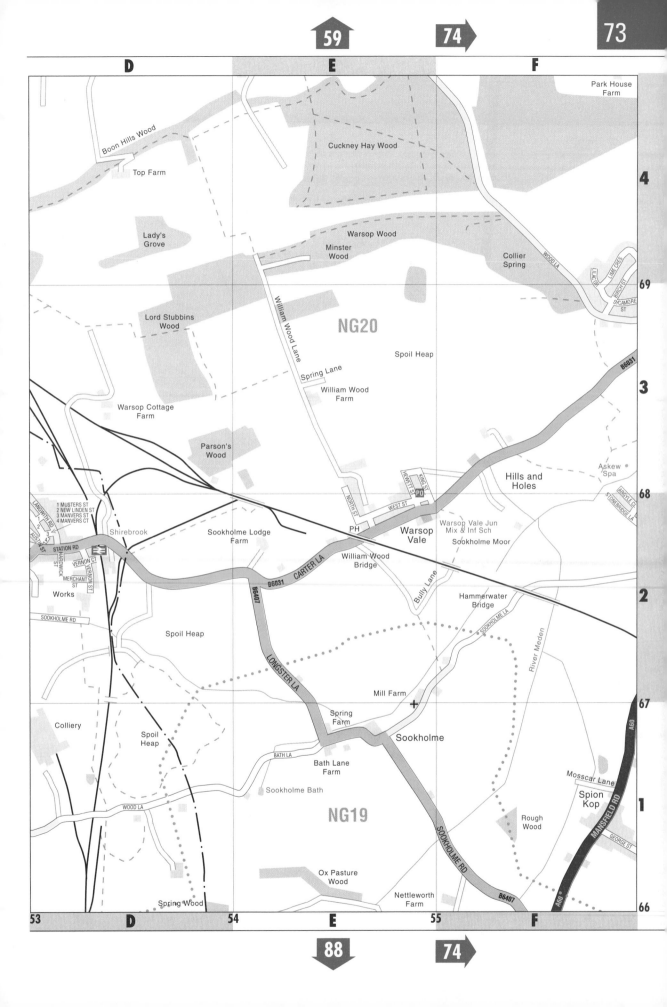

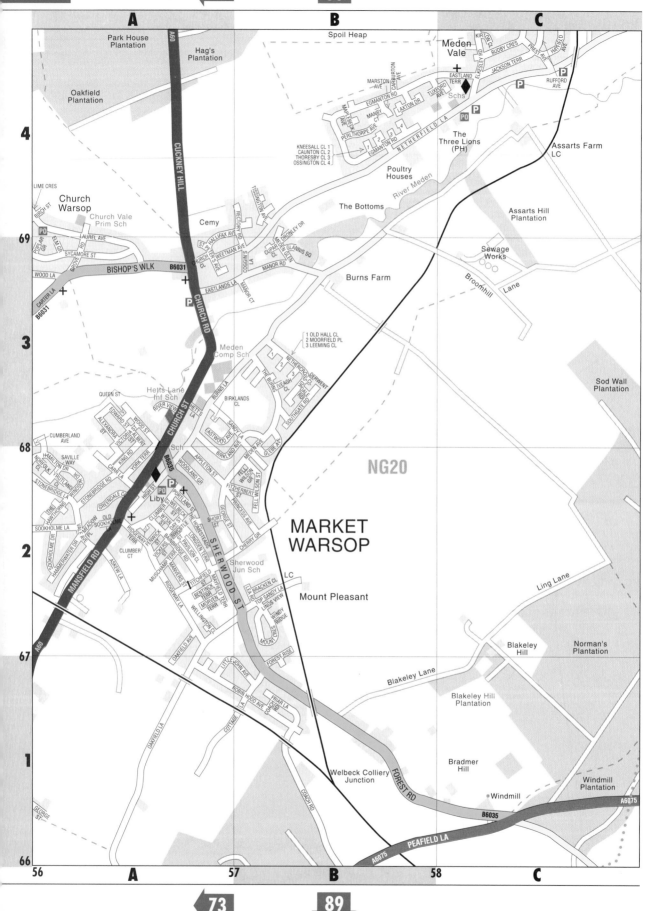

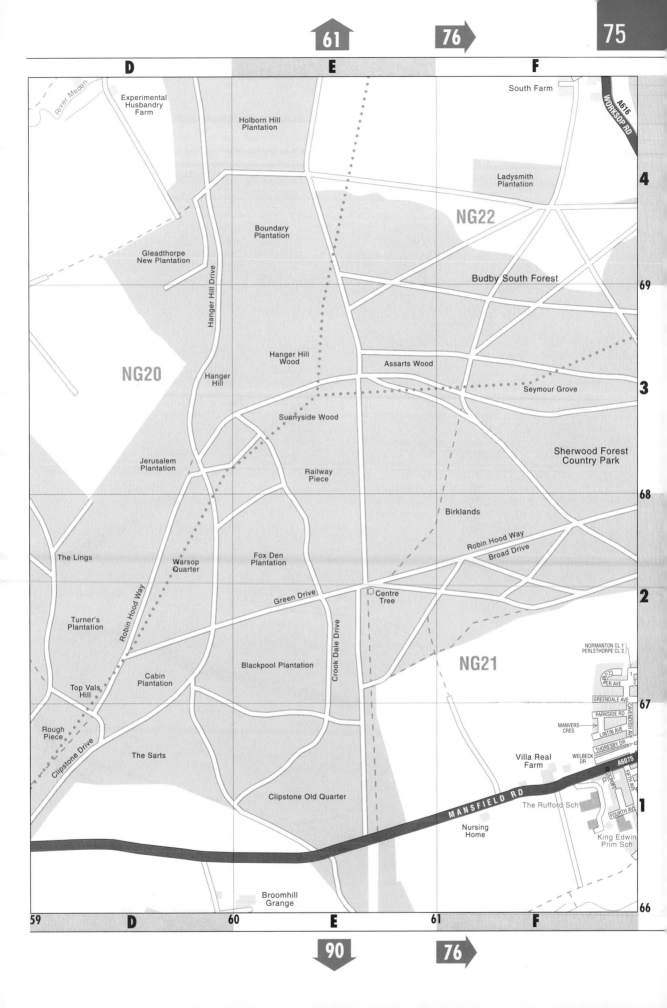

D
E
F

River Meden

South Farm

WORKSOP RD
A616

Experimental
Husbandry
Farm

Holborn Hill
Plantation

Ladysmith
Plantation

4

NG22

Boundary
Plantation

Budby South Forest

69

Gleadthorpe
New Plantation

Hanger Hill Drive

Hanger Hill
Wood

Assarts Wood

NG20

Hanger
Hill

Seymour Grove

3

Jerusalem
Plantation

Sunnyside Wood

Sherwood Forest
Country Park

Railway
Piece

68

Birklands

Robin Hood Way

Robin Hood Way

Broad Drive

The Lings

Warsop
Quarter

Fox Den
Plantation

Green Drive

Centre
Tree

2

NORMANTON CL 1
PERLETHORPE CL 2

Turner's
Plantation

Crook Dale Drive

NG21

GREENDALE AVE

67

Blackpool Plantation

PARKSIDE RD

MANVERS
CRES

LINTIN AVE

Cabin
Plantation

Top Vals
Hill

WELBECK
DR

THORESBY DR

A6075

Villa Real
Farm

Rough
Piece

Clipstone Drive

The Sarts

FIFTH AVE

BRIDGNETT

MANSFIELD RD

1

Clipstone Old Quarter

The Rufford Sch

Nursing
Home

FOURTH AVE

King Edwin
Prim Sch

66

Broomhill
Grange

59
D
60
E
61
F

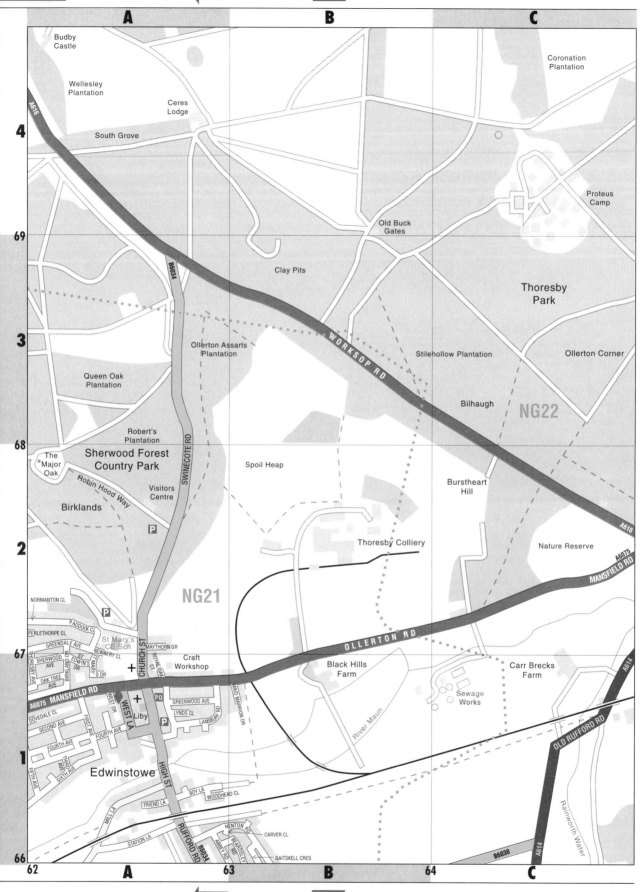

A   B   C

Budby Castle

Coronation Plantation

Wellesley Plantation

Ceres Lodge

4

South Grove

A616

Proteus Camp

69

Old Buck Gates

B6034

Clay Pits

Thoresby Park

WORKSOP RD

3

Ollerton Assarts Plantation

Stilehollow Plantation

Ollerton Corner

Queen Oak Plantation

Bilhaugh

NG22

Robert's Plantation

SWINECOTE RD

68

The Major Oak

Sherwood Forest Country Park

Spoil Heap

Burstheart Hill

Robin Hood Way

Visitors Centre

A616

Birklands

P

Nature Reserve

A6075

MANSFIELD RD

Thoresby Colliery

2

NORMANTON CL

NG21

P

PADDOCK CL

PERLETHORPE CL

GREENDALE AVE

SHERWOOD AVE

OAK TREE AVE

THORESBY AVE

BIRCHEND DR

ST EDWIN'S DR

ST MARY'S DR

St Mary's CE Sch

NEWBERY CL

CHURCH ST

MAYTHORN GR

ROYAL OAK CT

Craft Workshop

OLLERTON RD

Black Hills Farm

Carr Brecks Farm

A614

67

A6075 MANSFIELD RD

WEST DR

WEST LA

PO

Liby

P

GREENWOOD AVE

LYNDS CL

LANSBURY RD

MAID MARRION DR

Sewage Works

River Maun

OLD RUFFORD RD

DOVEDALE CL

SECOND AVE

FIRST AVE

FOURTH AVE

FOURTH AVE

THIRD AVE

FIFTH AVE

SIXTH AVE

1

Edwinstowe

HIGH ST

BOY LA

WOODHEAD CL

A614

MILL LA

FRIEND LA

Rainworth Water

STATION LA

RUFFORD RD

B6034

HENTON RD

CARVER CL

ABBEY RD

BEARDSLEY RD

GAITSKELL CRES

B6030

66

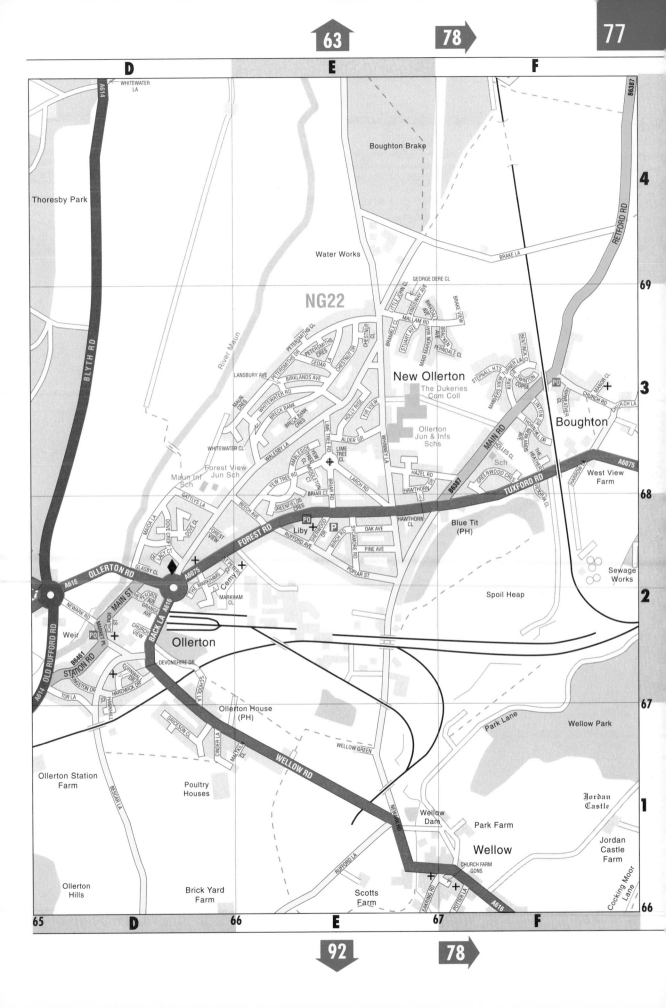

A **B** **C**

4

Collinridge Wood

TUXFORD RD

A6075 OLLERTON RD

Priors Park Farm

Manor Farm

PH

Pasture Farm
Carriage Mus

Hall Farm

PO

Goosemoor Dyke

69

RECTORY GDNS

SANDFIELD LA

KIRTON PARK

Kirton

Winson Hill

Doncaster Farm

CHURCH LA

CHARLOTTE CL

KIRTON CT

THE FURZE

Kirton Wood

3

Manor Farm

MAIN ST

PRIMROSE LA

NG22

BROUGHTON IND EST

A6075

Brick Works

68

Cocking Hill Farm

MEDEN RD

TRENT RD

GLEN CL

BROUGHTON WAY

MAUN WAY

Marl Pit

Norton Wood

Golden Hill

West Field

2

Birkhill Wood

COCKING HILL

Wellow Park

Laxton Common

67

Cocking Moor

Westwood Farm

ACRE EDGE RD

1

Jordan Castle Farm

Cocking Moor La

Ompton Lodge

SHORTWOOD LA

66

68 **A** **69** **B** **70** **C**

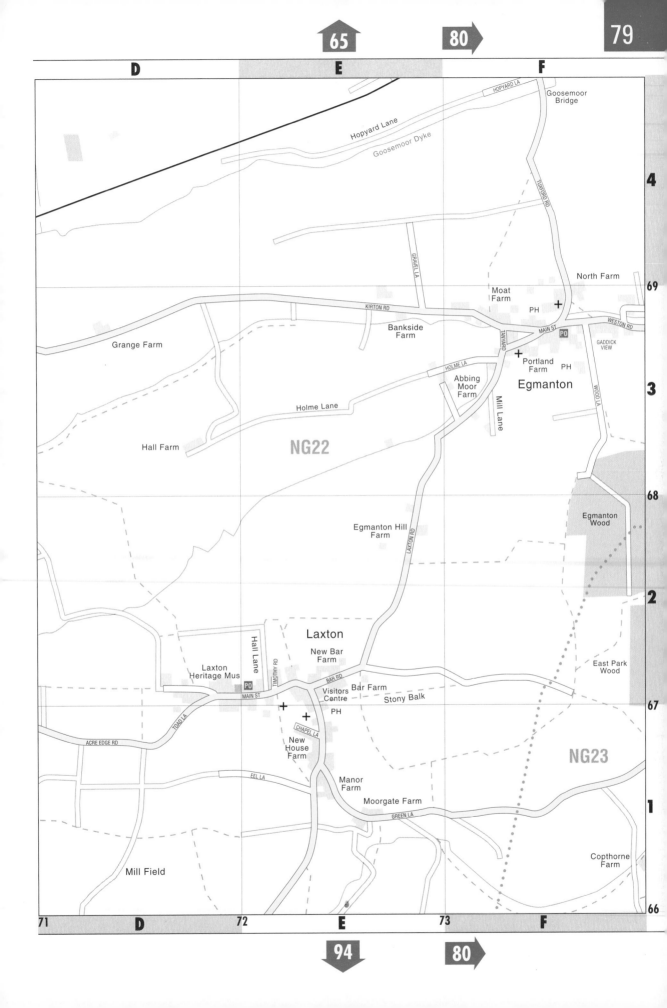

D   E   F

Hopyard La

Goosemoor
Bridge

Hopyard Lane

Goosemoor Dyke

TUXFORD RD

4

North Farm

69

Moat
Farm

PH

KIRTON RD

Bankside
Farm

GRAVEL LA

Main St

PO

WESTON RD

Grange Farm

TANYARD

GADDICK
VIEW

HOLME LA

Portland
Farm

PH

Egmanton

Abbing
Moor
Farm

3

Holme Lane

Holme Lane

Mill Lane

WOOD LA

Hall Farm

NG22

68

Egmanton Hill
Farm

Egmanton
Wood

LAXTON RD

2

Laxton

East Park
Wood

Hall Lane

New Bar
Farm

TIMOTHY RD

Laxton
Heritage Mus

PO

BAR RD

Bar Farm

Visitors
Centre

Stony Balk

MAIN ST

PH

67

TOAD LA

ACRE EDGE RD

CHAPEL LA

New
House
Farm

NG23

EEL LA

Manor
Farm

Moorgate Farm

1

GREEN LA

Mill Field

Copthorne
Farm

66

71   D   72   E   73   F

79
66

A   B   C

A1

B1164

4

Egmanton Crossing

Ruddings Cottage

Stone Road End Farm

Windmill (dis)

Goosemoor Dyke

69

WESTON RD

Scarthingmoor Mill

GREAT NORTH RD

Scarthingmoor House Farm

NG22

BURNMOOR LA

Scarthingmoor Farm

3

Gipsy Lodge Farm

Scarthingmoor Cottage Farm

HAGG LA

Lady Wood

Bell Farm

B1164

Egmanton Common Farm

LADYWOOD LA

68

Ladywood Farm

Egmanton Wood

MOORHOUSE RD

2

East Park Wood

Breck's Farm

NG23

Moorhouse Beck

WAMNAIL LA

A1

67

Breck Cottage

GREEN LA

Aggrie House Farm

+

Church Farm

1

Moorhouse

Thorpe Farm

Wadnal Plantation

Cocked Hat Plantation

Copthorne Farm

Brookdale Farm

Commonside Plantation

66

North Park Farm

74   A   75   B   76   C

79
95

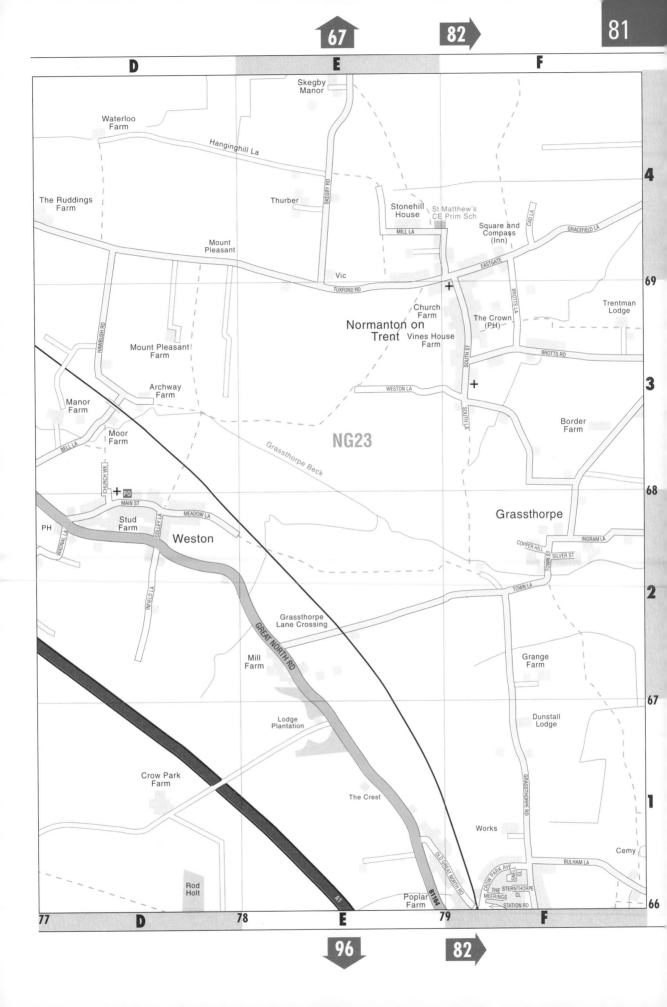

D   E   F

Skegby Manor

Waterloo Farm

Hanginghill La

4

The Ruddings Farm

Thurber

Stonehill House

St Matthew's CE Prim Sch

Square and Compass (Inn)

Gracefield La

OLD LA

MILL LA

Mount Pleasant

Vic

EASTGATE

69

TUXFORD RD

Church Farm

The Crown (PH)

Trentman Lodge

Normanton on Trent

Vines House Farm

BROTTS LA

HAWBUSH RD

Mount Pleasant Farm

SOUTH ST

BROTTS RD

Manor Farm

Archway Farm

WESTON LA

3

BELL LA

Moor Farm

SOUTH LA

Border Farm

NG23

Grassthorpe Beck

PH

CHURCH WK

PO

MAIN ST

68

Stud Farm

MEADOW LA

COLLEY LA

WADNAL LA

Weston

Grassthorpe

INGRAM LA

COPPER HILL

SILVER ST

TOWN ST

INFIELD LA

TOWN LA

2

Grasthorpe Lane Crossing

GREAT NORTH RD

Mill Farm

Grange Farm

67

Lodge Plantation

Dunstall Lodge

GRASSTHORPE RD

Crow Park Farm

1

The Crest

Works

Cemy

BULHAM LA

A1

B1164

OLD GREAT NORTH RD

CROW PARK AVE

SNELL

THE MEERINGS

STERNTHORPE CL

STATION RD

Rod Holt

Poplar Farm

66

77   D   78   E   79   F

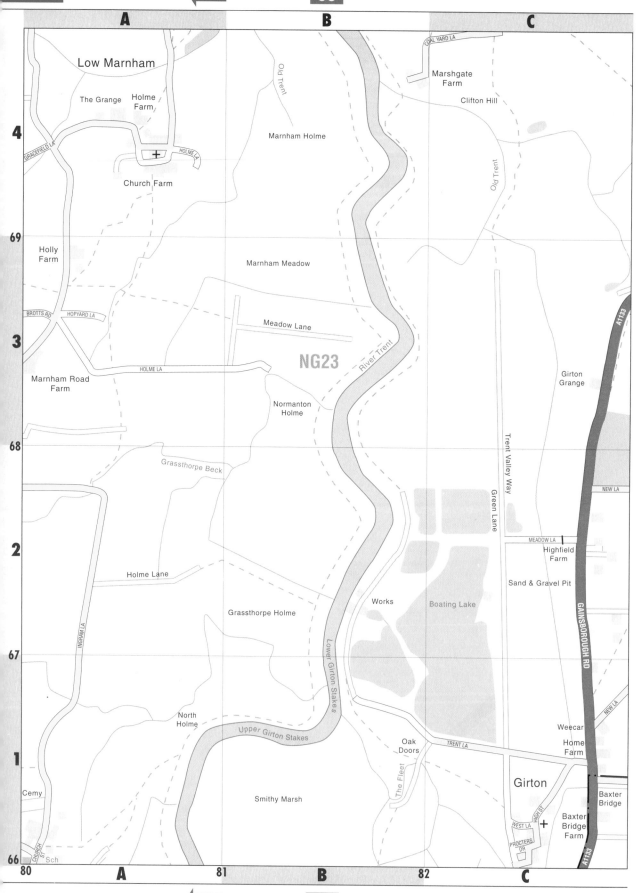

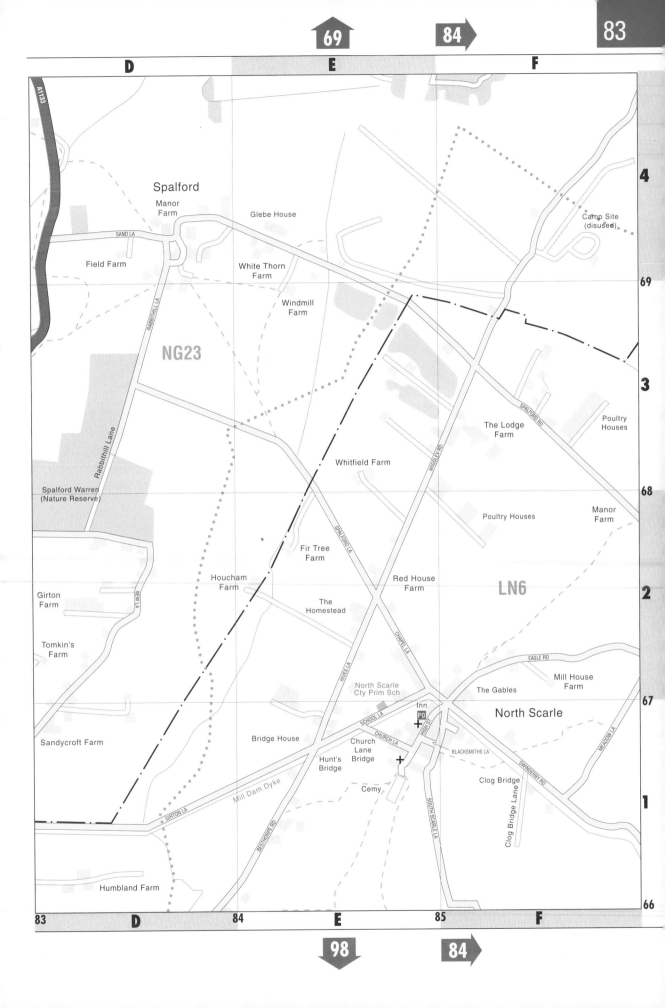

Spalford

Manor
Farm

Glebe House

Camp Site
(disused)

SAND LA

Field Farm

White Thorn
Farm

RABBITHILL LA

Windmill
Farm

NG23

Rabbithill Lane

SPALFORD RD

The Lodge
Farm

Poultry
Houses

Whitfield Farm

WESLEY RD

Spalford Warren
(Nature Reserve)

Manor
Farm

Poultry Houses

SPALFORD LA

Fir Tree
Farm

LN6

NEW LA

Houcham
Farm

Red House
Farm

Girton
Farm

The Homestead

CHAPEL LA

Tomkin's
Farm

EAGLE RD

Mill House
Farm

HIVES LA

North Scarle
Cty Prim Sch

The Gables

North Scarle

SCHOOL LA

Inn
PO

HIGH ST

Sandycroft Farm

Bridge House

Church
Lane
Bridge

CHURCH LA

BLACKSMITHS LA

SWINDERBY RD

MEADOW LA

Hunt's
Bridge

Clog Bridge

Mill Dam Dyke

Cemy

SOUTH SCARLE LA

Clog Bridge Lane

GIRTON LA

RESTHORPE RD

Humbland Farm

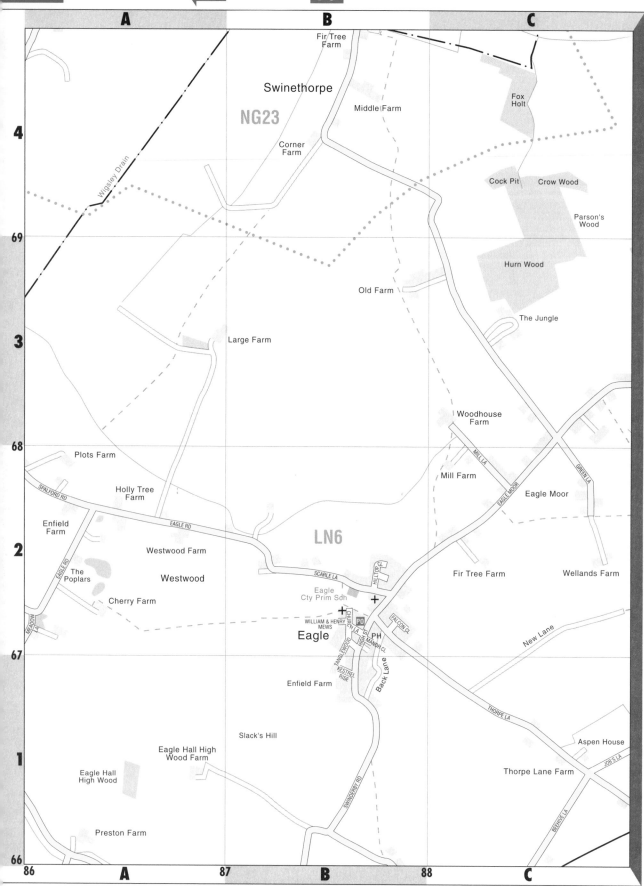

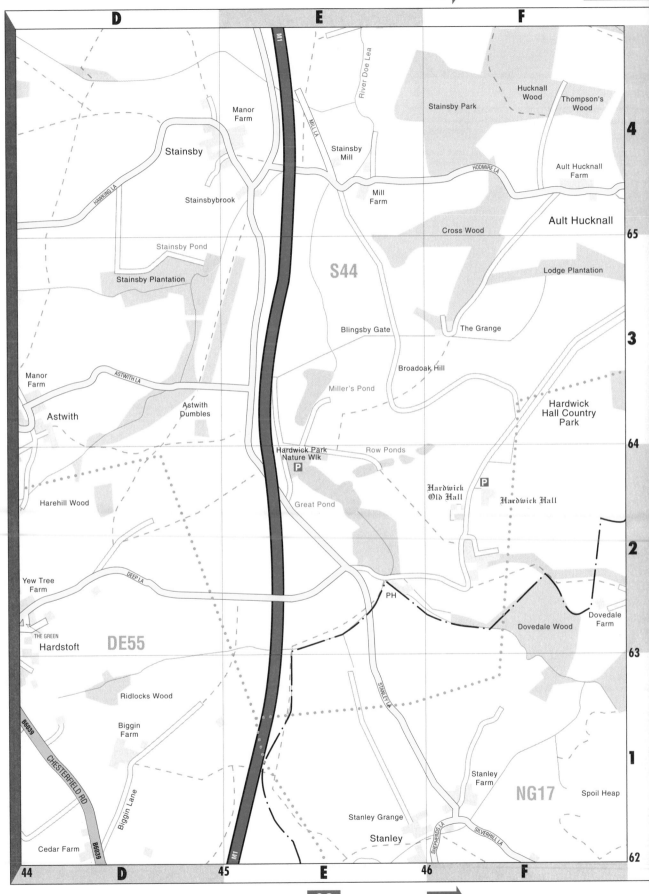

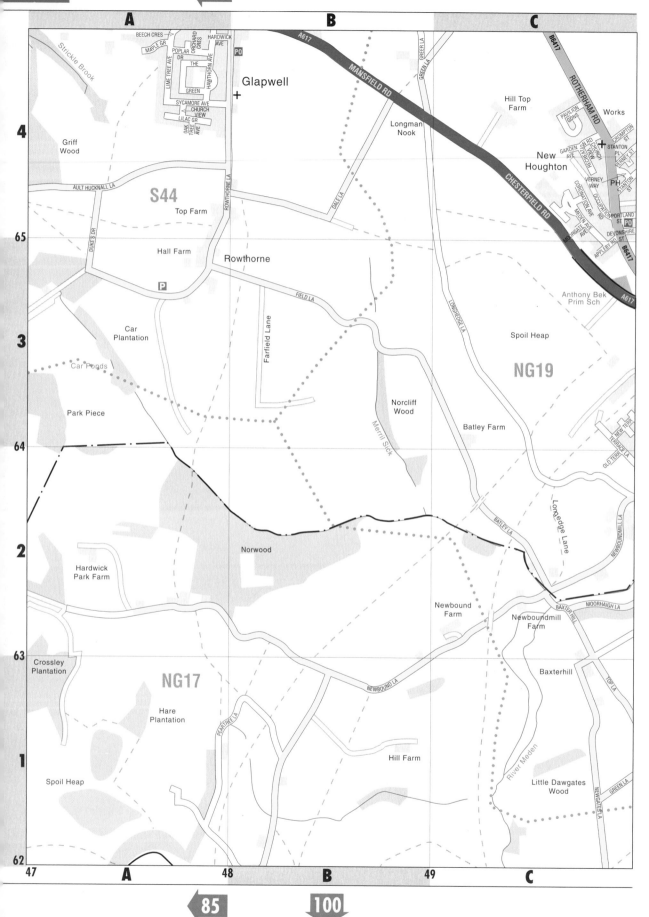

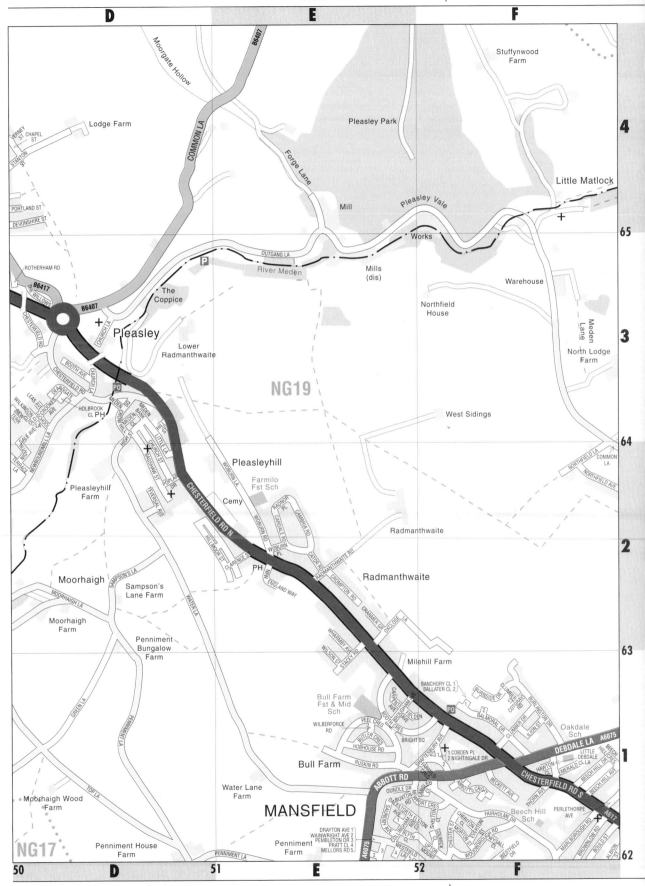

D   E   F

4

Stuffynwood
Farm

Moorgate Hollow

Lodge Farm

VERNEY ST
CHAPEL ST
STANTON ST

PORTLAND ST

DEVONSHIRE ST

COMMON LA

B6407

Pleasley Park

Little Matlock

Forge Lane

Mill

Pleasley Vale

65

ROTHERHAM RD

B6417

THE WILLOWS

B6407

Works

Mills
(dis)

River Meden

OUTGANG LA

Warehouse

The Coppice

Northfield
House

Meden Lane

3

Pleasley

Lower
Radmanthwaite

North Lodge
Farm

CHESTERFIELD RD

CHURCH LA

BOOTH AVE

PO

HOLBROOK CL PH

LEAS AVE

WILKINSON CL

GALE AVE

NEWBOUND LA

NG19

West Sidings

Pleasleyhill

NORTHFIELD LA

COMMON LA

NORTHFIELD AVE

64

CHURCH ST

BAGSHAW ST

HIGH ST

LITTLE LA

POPLAR DR

WOBURN RD

Farmilo
Fst Sch

Cemy

RADNOR PL

CARDALE RD

CAMBRIA RD

Pleasleyhill
Farm

FEVERSAL AVE

CHESTERFIELD RD N

HILLMOOR ST

CLARENCE ST

WOBURN PL

CATOR RD

RADMANTHWAITE RD

Radmanthwaite

2

Moorhaigh

SAMPSON'S LA

Sampson's
Lane Farm

WATER LA

PH

ENGLAND WAY

CROMPTON RD

CRAMMER GR

ORCLOSE LA

MOORHAIGH LA

Moorhaigh
Farm

Penniment
Bungalow
Farm

WHARMBY AVE

WILSON ST

STACEY AVE

Milehill Farm

BANCHORY CL 1
BALLATER CL 2

BURNSIDE DR

LUMLEY DR

CLUMBER DR

BIRLINGTON DR

Oakdale
Sch

DEBDALE LA

A6075

63

GREEN LA

PENNIMENT LA

TOP LA

Bull Farm
Fst & Mid
Sch

WILBERFORCE RD

PEEL CRES

BUTLER CRES

HOBHOUSE RD

RUSKIN RD

CARPENTER AVE

BRONTE AVE

FIELDEN AVE

BOOTH CRES

Bright Sq

BALMORAL DR

PO

LION ST

CLUMBER DR

Little
Debdale

HAWTON CL

BEECH HILL DR

1

Moorhaigh Wood
Farm

Penniment House
Farm

Water Lane
Farm

MANSFIELD

Penniment
Farm

DRAYTON AVE 1
WAINWRIGHT AVE 2
PEMBLETON DR 3
PRATT CL 4
MELLORS RD 5

ABBOTT RD

OUNDLE DR

OXBUXTON DR

CHATSWORTH AVE

1 COBDEN PL
2 NIGHTINGALE DR

SHAFTESBURY AVE

FARNELD

BECKETT AVE

THORN AVE

Beech Hill
Sch

PERLETHORPE AVE

CHESTERFIELD RD S

A617

NG17

PENNIMENT LA

A6075

ASHGROVE RD

BEST AVE

OAKSWORTH

SHELTON CL

CARRINGTON CL

WESTFIELD MOUNT

CHESTER ST

CHINNOCK

FAIRHOLME DR

WOODBOROUGH RD

WESTFIELD DR

MARLBOROUGH RD

BROWNLOW RD

BOLD ST

ALBION ST

62

50   D   51   E   52   F

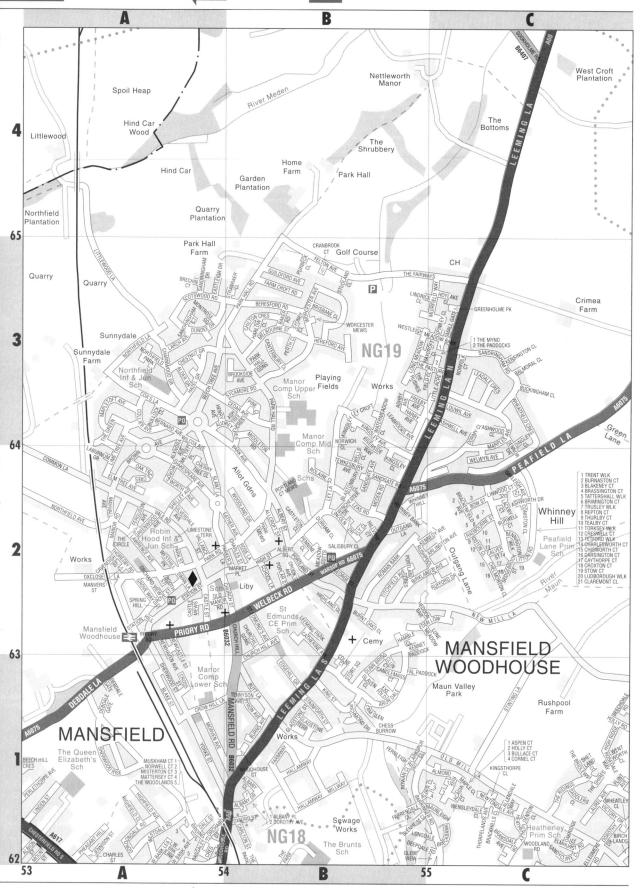

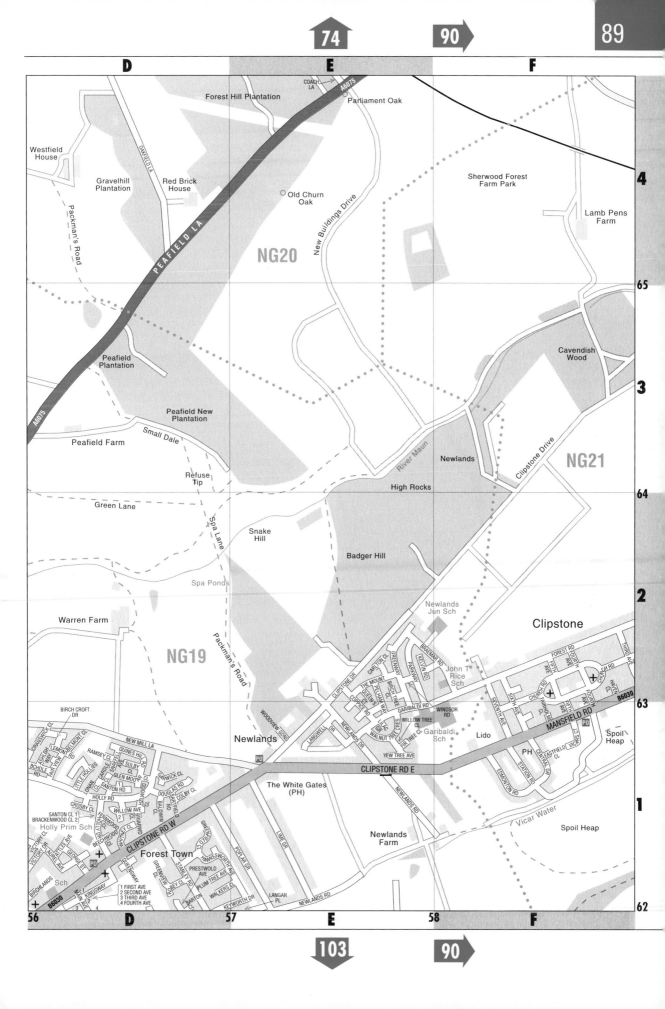

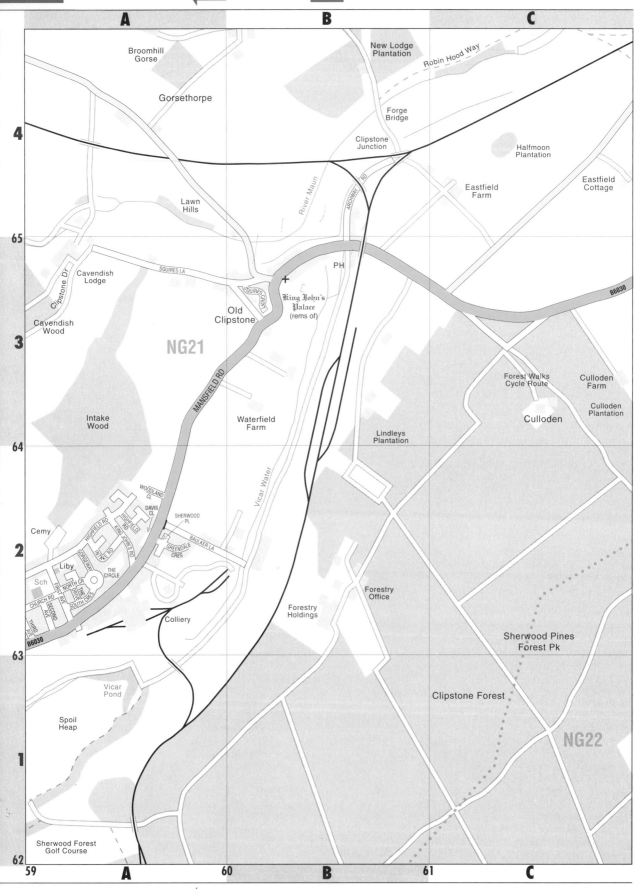

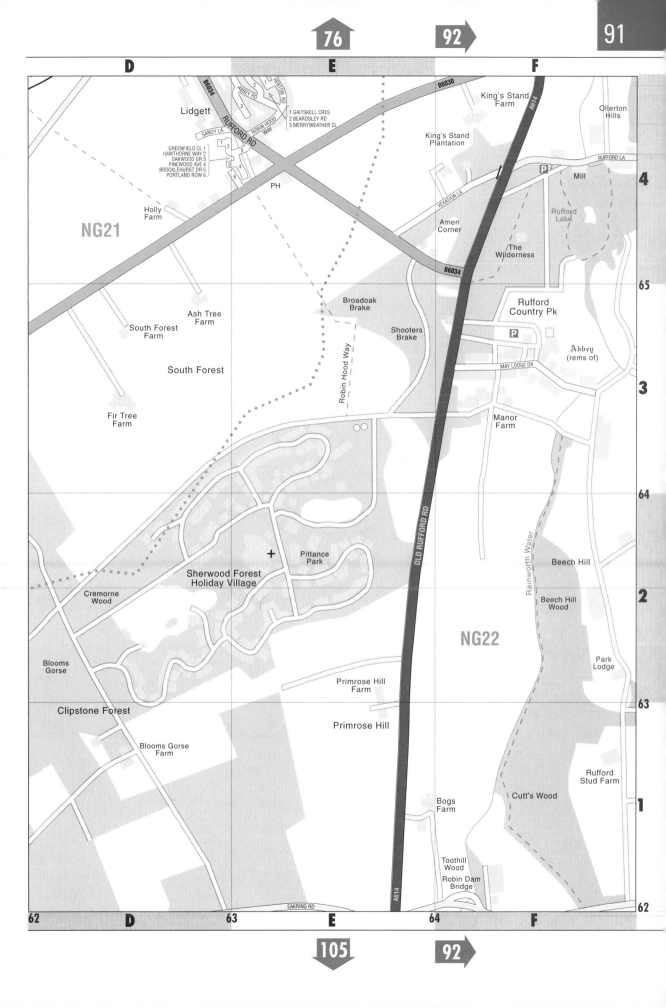

D
E
F

B6034
ABBEY RD
HENTON RD
RUFFORD RD
ROBIN HOOD WAY
Lidgett

B6030
King's Stand Farm
Ollerton Hills

1 GAITSKELL CRES
2 BEARDSLEY RD
3 MERRYWEATHER CL

SANDY LA

King's Stand Plantation

GREENFIELD CL 1
HAWTHORNE WAY 2
OAKWOOD GR 3
PINEWOOD AVE 4
BROCKLEHURST DR 5
PORTLAND ROW 6

RUFFORD LA

P
Mill
4

VEXATION LA

Amen Corner

A614

PH

Rufford Lake

Holly Farm

NG21

The Wilderness

B6034

65

Broadoak Brake

Rufford Country Pk

Ash Tree Farm

Shooters Brake

P

Abbey (rems of)

South Forest Farm

Robin Hood Way

MAY LODGE DR

3

South Forest

Manor Farm

Fir Tree Farm

OLD RUFFORD RD

64

Pittance Park

Rainworth Water

Beech Hill

Sherwood Forest Holiday Village

Beech Hill Wood

Cremorne Wood

2

Blooms Gorse

NG22

Park Lodge

Clipstone Forest

Primrose Hill Farm

63

Blooms Gorse Farm

Primrose Hill

Rufford Stud Farm

Cutt's Wood

1

Bogs Farm

Toothill Wood

Robin Dam Bridge

A614

EAKRING RD

62

62
D
63
E
64
F

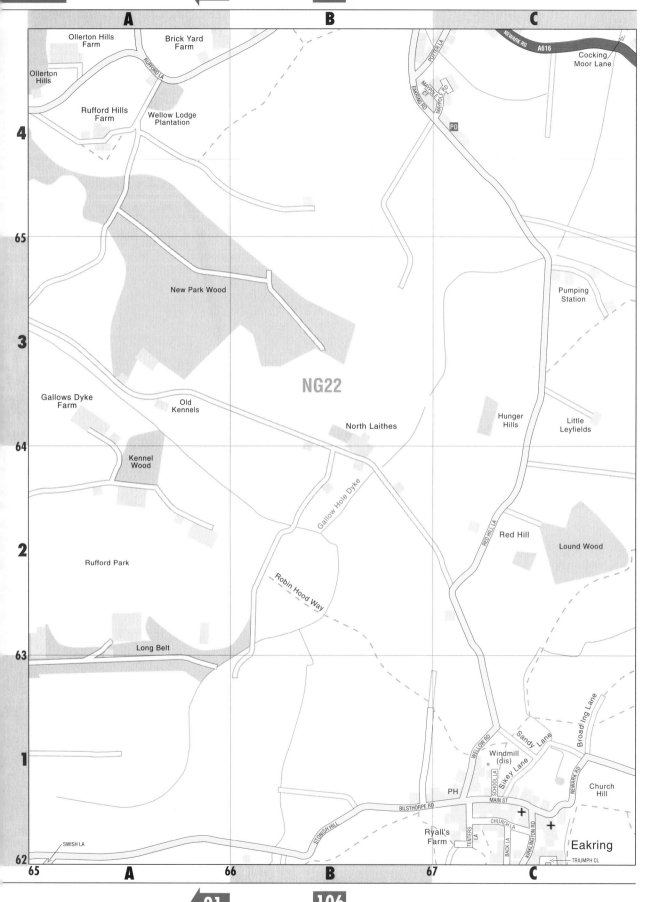

A   B   C

NEWARK RD   A616

Cocking
Moor Lane

POTTER LA

Ollerton Hills
Farm

Brick Yard
Farm

RUFFORD LA

MAYPOLE
CT

MAYPOLE RD

EAKRING RD

Ollerton
Hills

Rufford Hills
Farm

Wellow Lodge
Plantation

PO

4

65

New Park Wood

Pumping
Station

3

NG22

Gallows Dyke
Farm

Old
Kennels

North Laithes

Hunger
Hills

Little
Leyfields

64

Kennel
Wood

Gallow Hole Dyke

Red Hill

Red Hill

Lound Wood

2

Rufford Park

Robin Hood Way

Long Belt

63

WELLOW RD

Sandy
Lane

Broading Lane

1

SCHOOL LA

Windmill
(dis)

Sikey Lane

NEWARK RD

Church
Hill

PH

Main St

BILSTHORPE RD

STONISH HILL

Ryall's
Farm

CHURCH LA

TENTERS LA

BACK LA

KIRKLINGTON RD

Eakring

SWISH LA

TRIUMPH CL

62

65   A   66   B   67   C

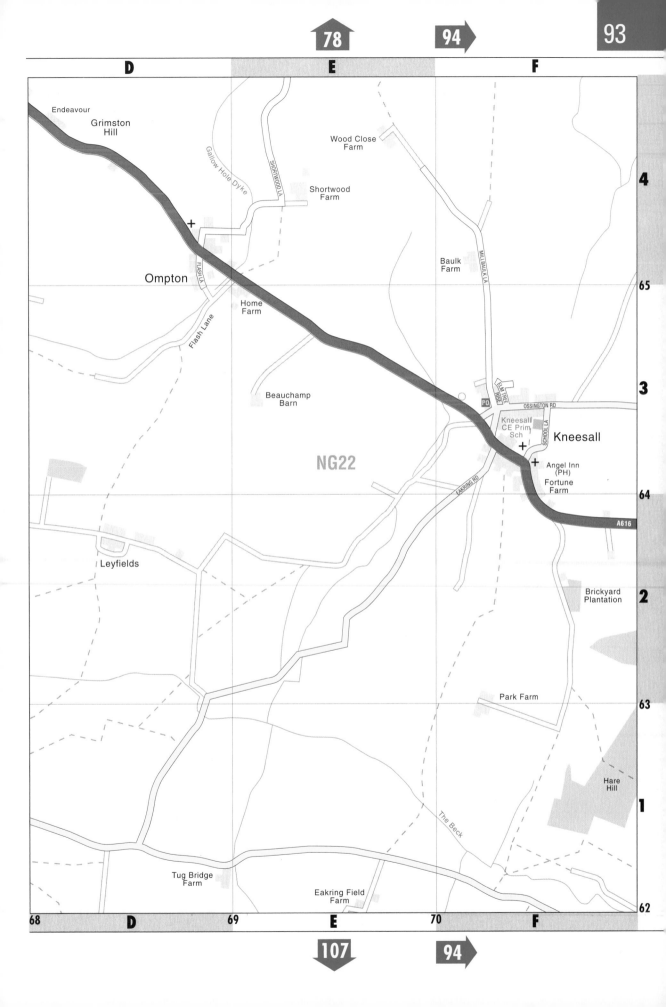

D
E
F

Endeavour
Grimston
Hill

Wood Close
Farm

Gallow Hole Dyke

SHORTWOOD LA

Shortwood
Farm

4

Baulk
Farm

MILL BAULK LA

Ompton

FLASH LA

65

Home
Farm

Flash Lane

ELM TREE RISE

PO

OSSINGTON RD

3

Beauchamp
Barn

Kneesall
CE Prim
Sch

SCHOOL LA

Kneesall

NG22

+
+

Angel Inn
(PH)
Fortune
Farm

FAKRING RD

64

A616

Leyfields

Brickyard
Plantation

2

Park Farm

63

Hare
Hill

1

The Beck

Tug Bridge
Farm

Eakring Field
Farm

62

68
D
69
E
70
F

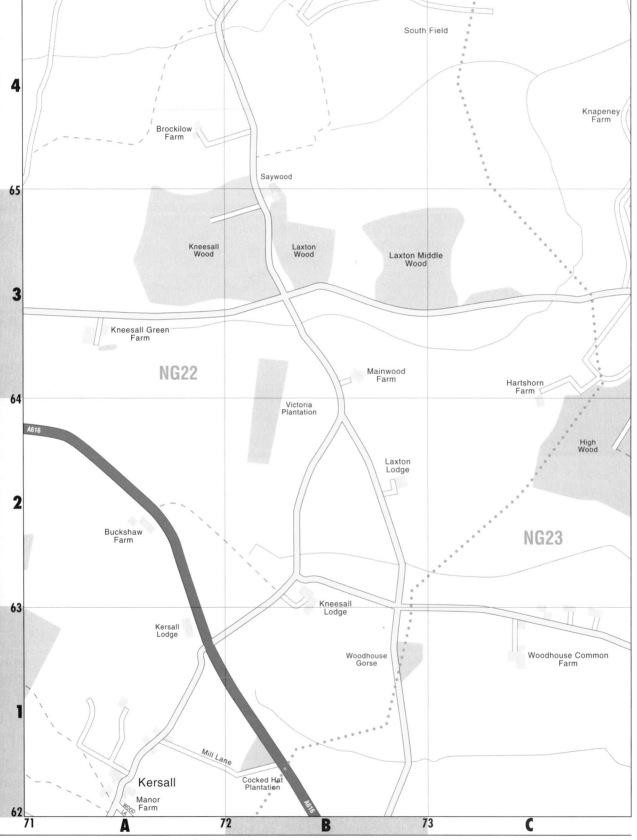

4

South Field

Knapeney
Farm

Brockilow
Farm

65

Saywood

Kneesall
Wood

Laxton
Wood

Laxton Middle
Wood

3

Kneesall Green
Farm

NG22

Mainwood
Farm

Hartshorn
Farm

64

Victoria
Plantation

High
Wood

A616

Laxton
Lodge

2

Buckshaw
Farm

NG23

63

Kneesall
Lodge

Kersall
Lodge

Woodhouse
Gorse

Woodhouse Common
Farm

1

Mill Lane

Kersall

Cocked Hat
Plantation

A616

62

Manor
Farm

WOOD LA

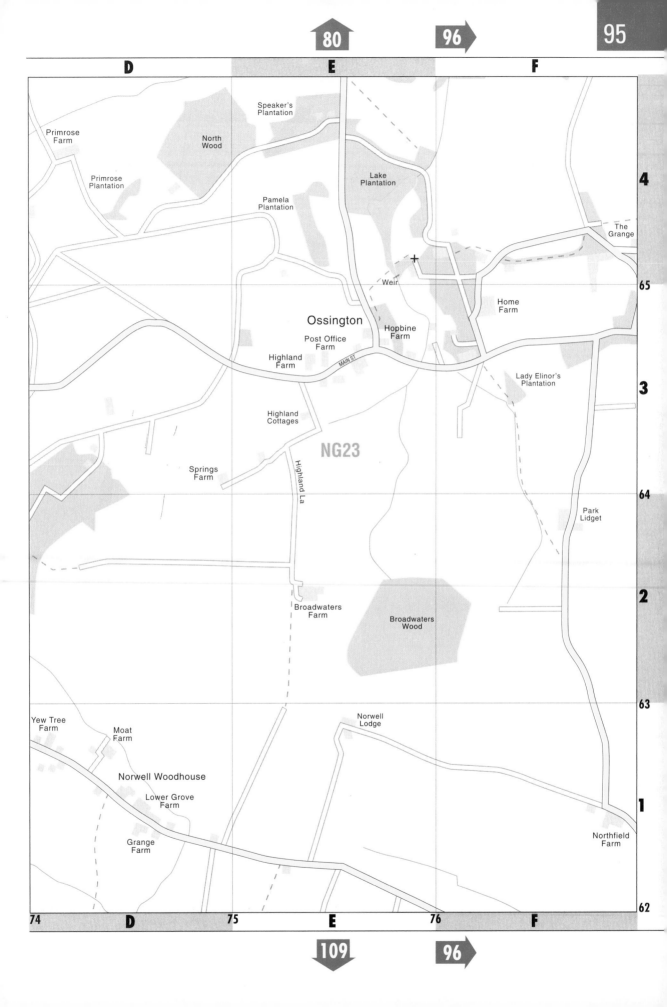

D E F

4

Primrose
Farm

Primrose
Plantation

North
Wood

Speaker's
Plantation

Lake
Plantation

Pamela
Plantation

The
Grange

65

Weir

Ossington

Home
Farm

Post Office
Farm

Hopbine
Farm

Highland
Farm

MAIN ST

Lady Elinor's
Plantation

3

Highland
Cottages

NG23

Springs
Farm

Highland La

64

Park
Lidget

2

Broadwaters
Farm

Broadwaters
Wood

63

Yew Tree
Farm

Norwell
Lodge

Moat
Farm

Norwell Woodhouse

Lower Grove
Farm

1

Grange
Farm

Northfield
Farm

62

A B C

4

65

3

64

2

63

1

62

The Grange

Common Farm

Brimblebeck Lane

Lady Charlotte's Plantation

Barrel Hill

Crow Park Bridge

B1164

OLD GREAT NORTH RD

STATION RD

PH

PO

FORGE JCU

HIGH ST

HEMPLANDS LA

NURSERY LA

HOUNSFIELD WAY

POPLAR CL

TWITCH LA

PALMER RD

ROSE FARM DR

RD

BARREL HILL RD

MILL CL

MAIN ST

Sutton on Trent

FLORAL VILLAS

Carlton Wood

Stud Farm

Castlehill

NG23

Great Northern Inn (PH)

GREAT NORTH RD

LC

B1164

Whiteley Plantation

Hill Farm

Carlton-on-Trent

B1164

OLD BELL LA

Willoughby Farm

Willoughby Farm

The Beck

The Poplars

Vicarage

GREAT NORTH RD

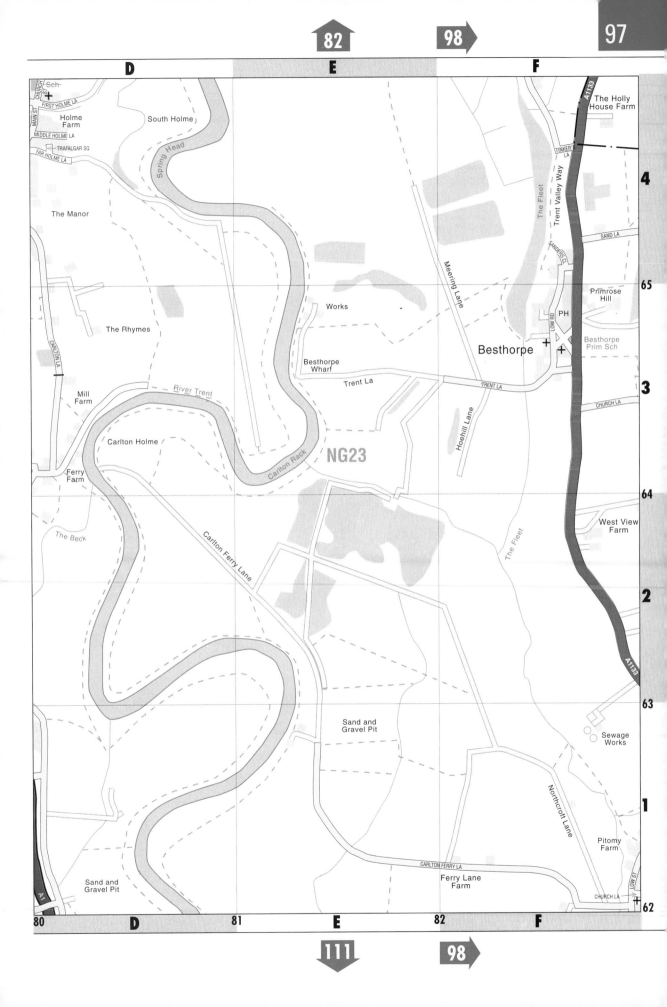

Sch
CHURCH ST
FIRST HOLME LA
Holme Farm
MAIN ST
MIDDLE HOLME LA
TRAFALGAR SQ
FAR HOLME LA

South Holme

Spring Head

The Holly House Farm

TINKER'S LA

The Fleet

Trent Valley Way

A1133

SAND LA

4

The Manor

Primrose Hill

65

The Rhymes

Meering Lane

Works

SANDERS CL

LOW RD

PH

Besthorpe Prim Sch

CARLTON LA

Besthorpe

Ferry Farm

Mill Farm

River Trent

Besthorpe Wharf

Trent La

Trent La

TRENT LA

CHURCH LA

3

Carlton Holme

NG23

Hoehill Lane

Carlton Rack

64

The Beck

Carlton Ferry Lane

The Fleet

West View Farm

2

Sand and Gravel Pit

A1133

63

Sewage Works

Sand and Gravel Pit

Northcroft Lane

1

A1

Pitomy Farm

CARLTON FERRY LA

Ferry Lane Farm

LOW ST

CHURCH LA

62

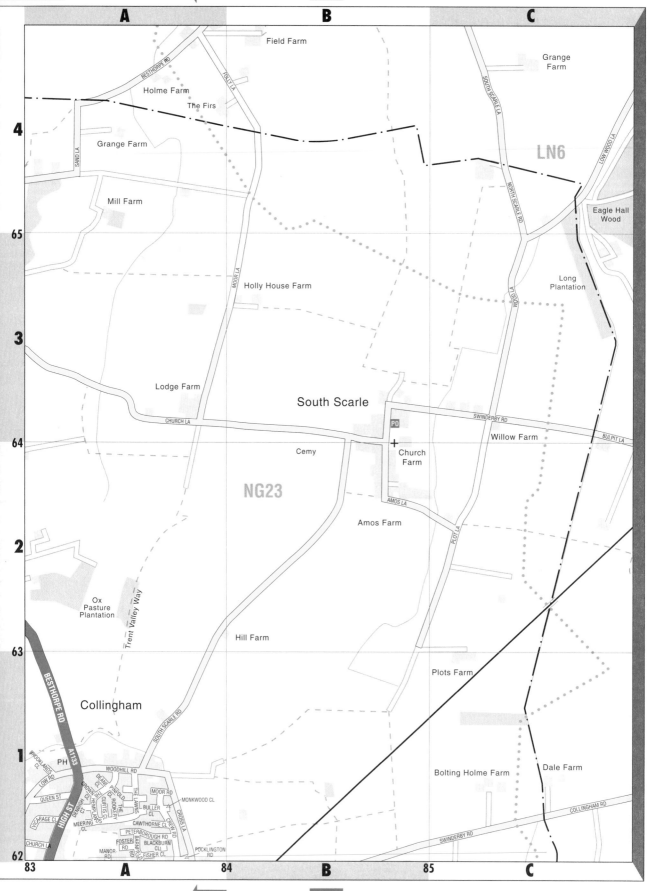

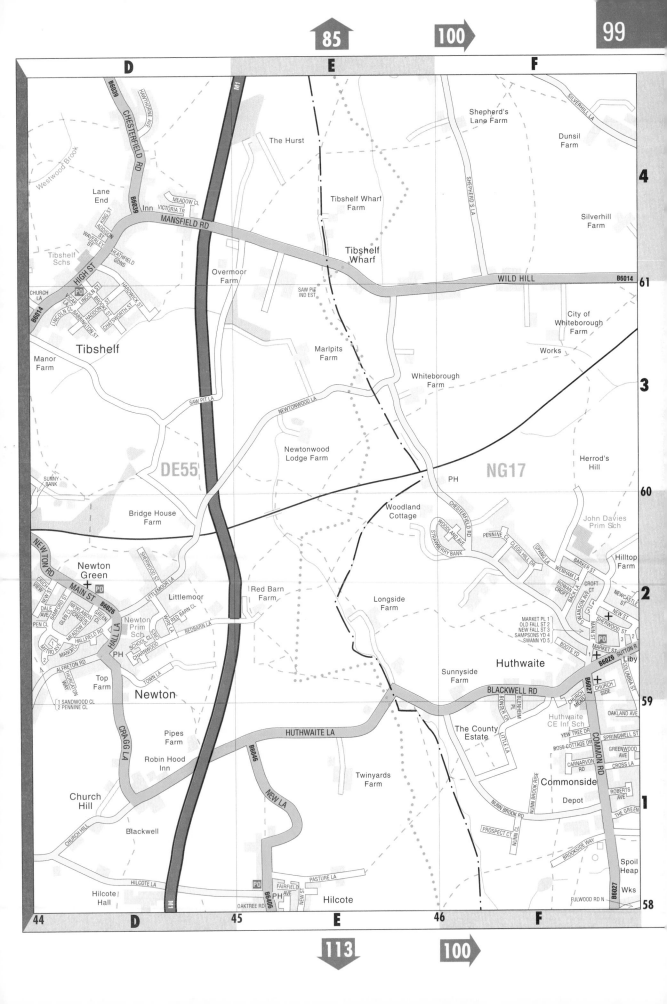

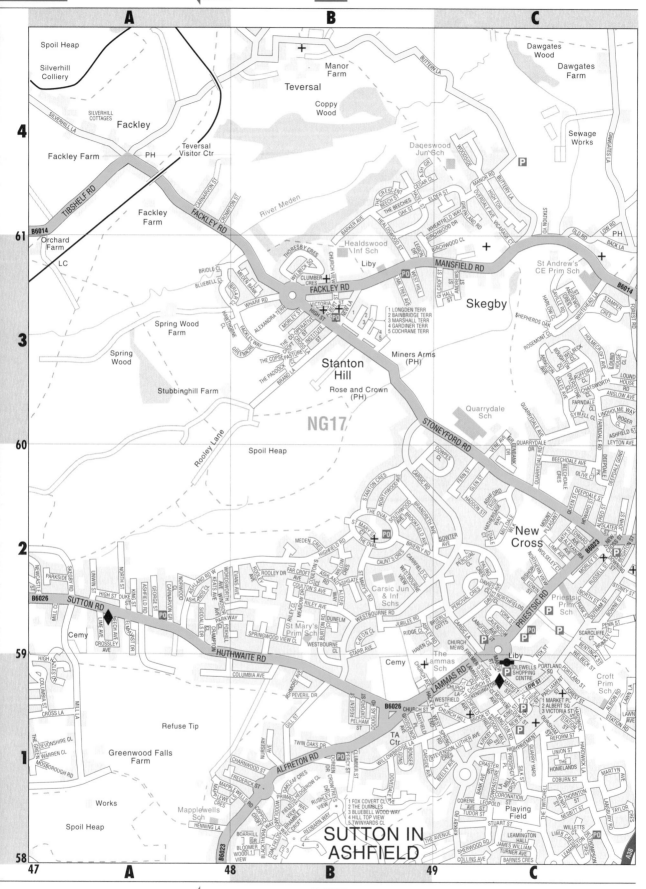

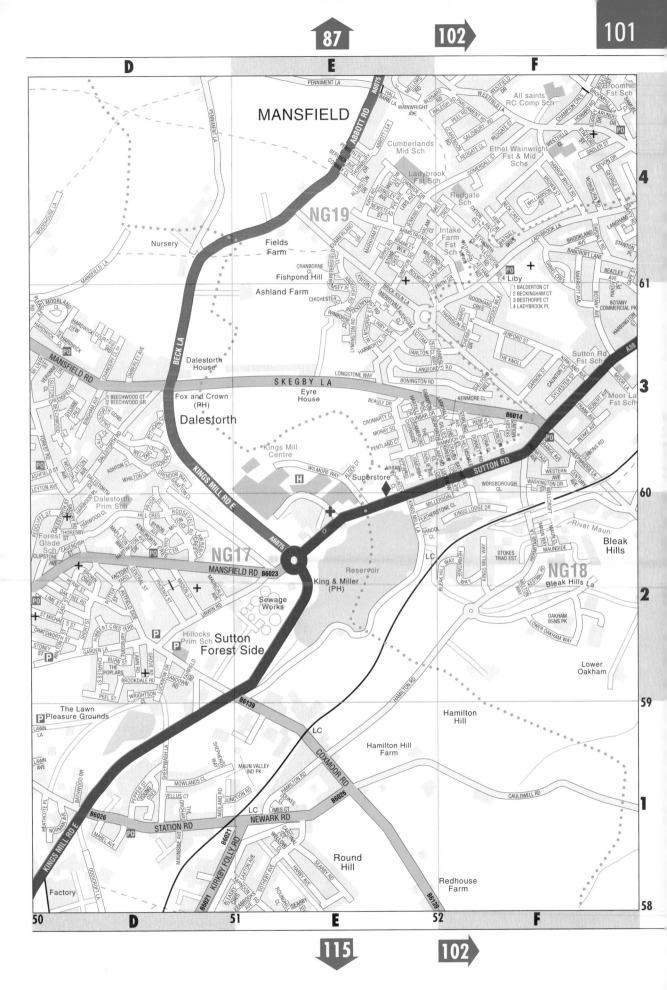

A3
1 RADFORD ST
2 PEACOCK ST
3 GARDEN RD
4 CLERKSON ST
5 COMMERCIAL ST
6 GROVE ST

7 HIGH ST
8 HIGHFIELD TERR
9 WHARF RD
10 SHERWOOD ST
11 ACORN BSNS PK
12 BEECH AVE

A4
1 THE ROOKERY
2 MOUNT PLEASANT
3 THORESBY ST
4 NEWCASTLE ST
5 BROWNING ST
6 KIPLING ST

A4
7 BEARDALL ST
8 CORPORATION ST
9 ST JOHN'S PL
10 TENNYSON ST
11 LAYTON BURROUGHS
12 CASTLE ST

13 WEST GATE
14 CLIFTON PL
15 ECLIPSE YD
16 ALFRED CT
17 HANDLEY ARC
18 CLERKSON'S ALLEY
19 TOOTHILL RD

20 STOCKWELL GATE
21 MARKET PL
22 QUEEN ST
23 QUAKER LA
24 MARKET HOUSE PL
25 EXCHANGE ROW
26 QUEENS WLK

27 MARKET ST

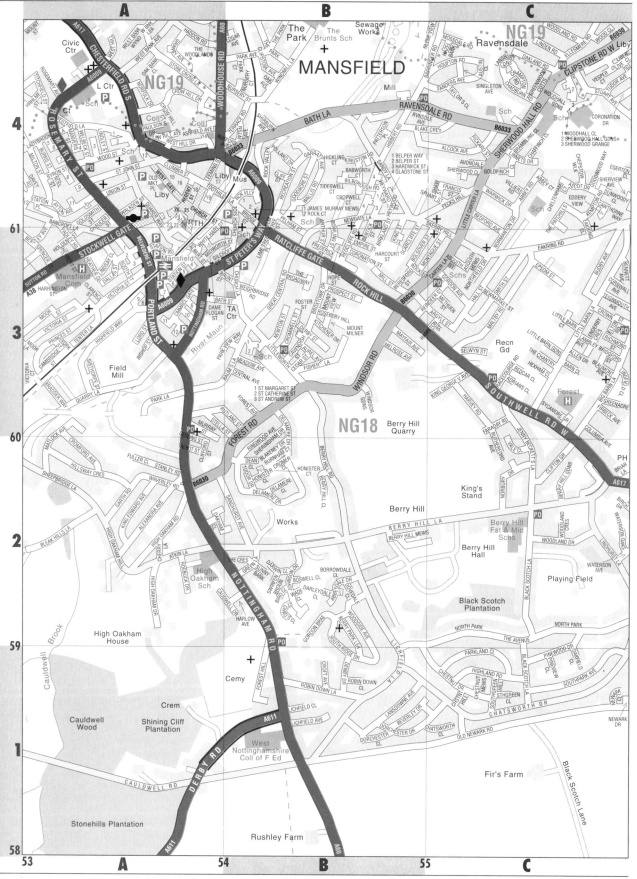

101 88 101 116

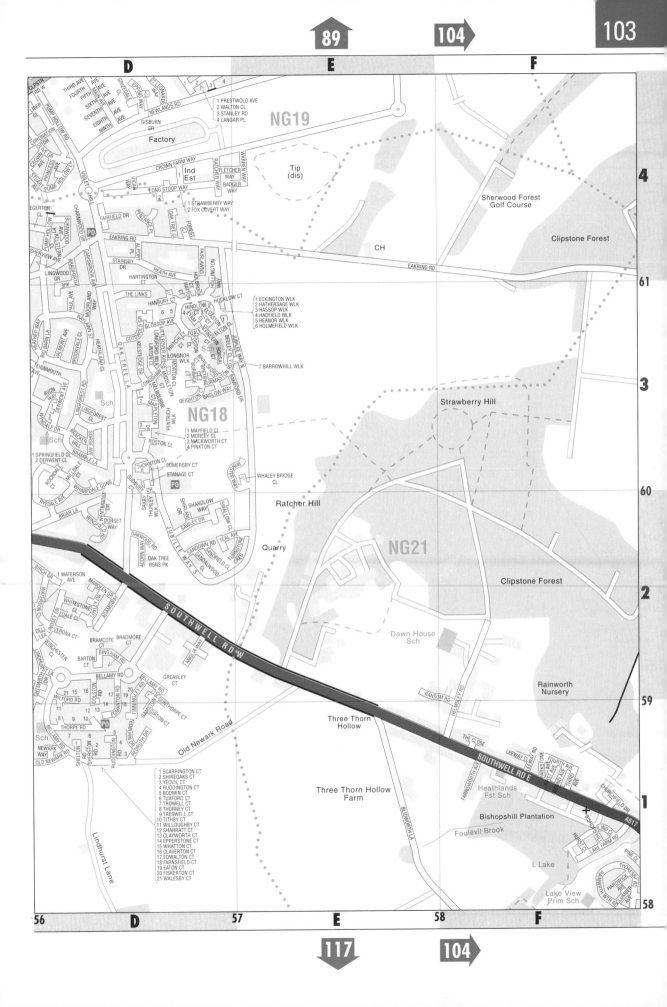

Sherwood Forest
Golf Course

Clipstone Forest

Brown's
Covert

Birch Row

4

EAKRING RD

61

Near Round
Plantation

3

LC

LC

Far Round
Plantation

Black Hill

NG22

Rufford
Colliery

NG21

60

Inkersall Grange
Farm

Rainworth Water

The Hundred
Acres

2

Spring
Hill

Watch Hill

Sewage
Works

59

1

Python Hill
Jun & Inf
Sch

KIRKLINGTON RD

A617

PO

Rufford Forest
Farm

A617

PH

GARDEN AVE

TOP ST

BRIAR CL

BIRCH AVE

LIME TREE PL

BRECON CL

1 FOREST CL
2 CHEDDAR CL

DENBIGH

HOLLYWOOD

NORTH AVE

RUFFORD CT

SHERWOOD CL

RUFFORD AVE

EGHAM CL

WEBSTER

CROSS DR

AMBER

DALE AVE

WARSOP LA

B6020

PINE

ST PETERS

STATION RD

SOUTH AVE

JUBS

CURZON

LITTLE JOHN DR

PYTHON HILL RD

THE HOLLIES

SYCAMORE CL

HATFIELD CL

DIAMOND AVE

OPAL CL

AMETHYST CL

COOPERS
RISE

WAY

THE
SQUARE

DARRICOTT
CL

HOLBECK
WAY

BEVERLEY CL

PERL CT

SAPPHIRE CL

58

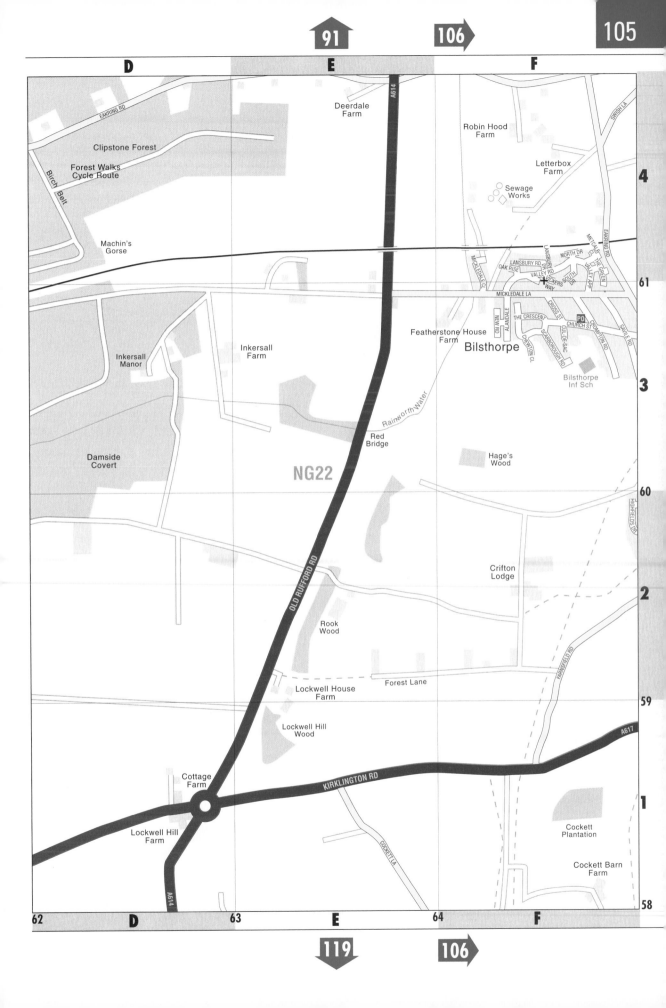

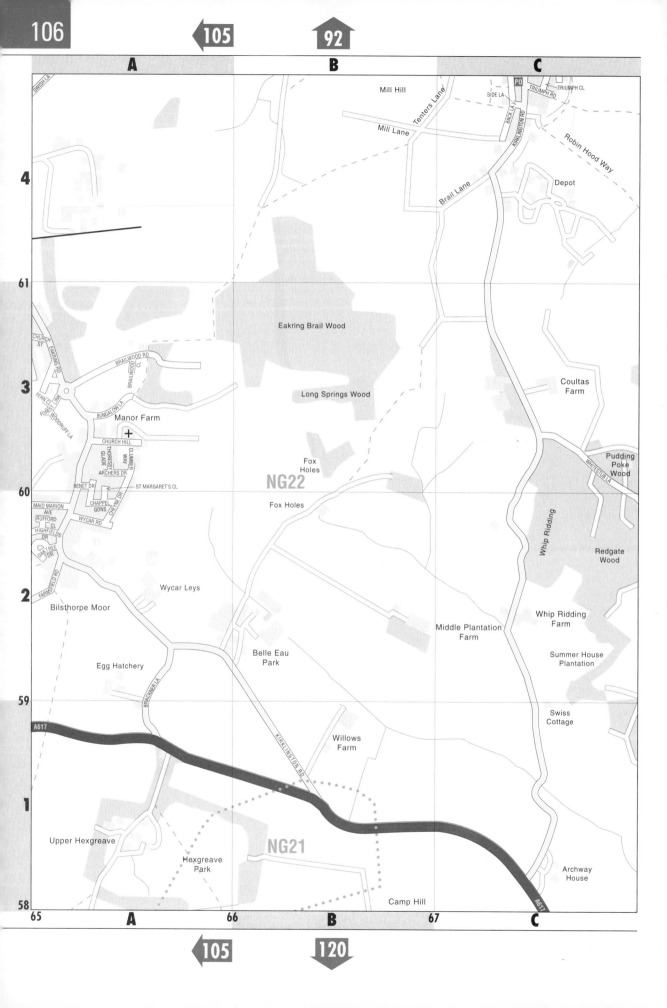

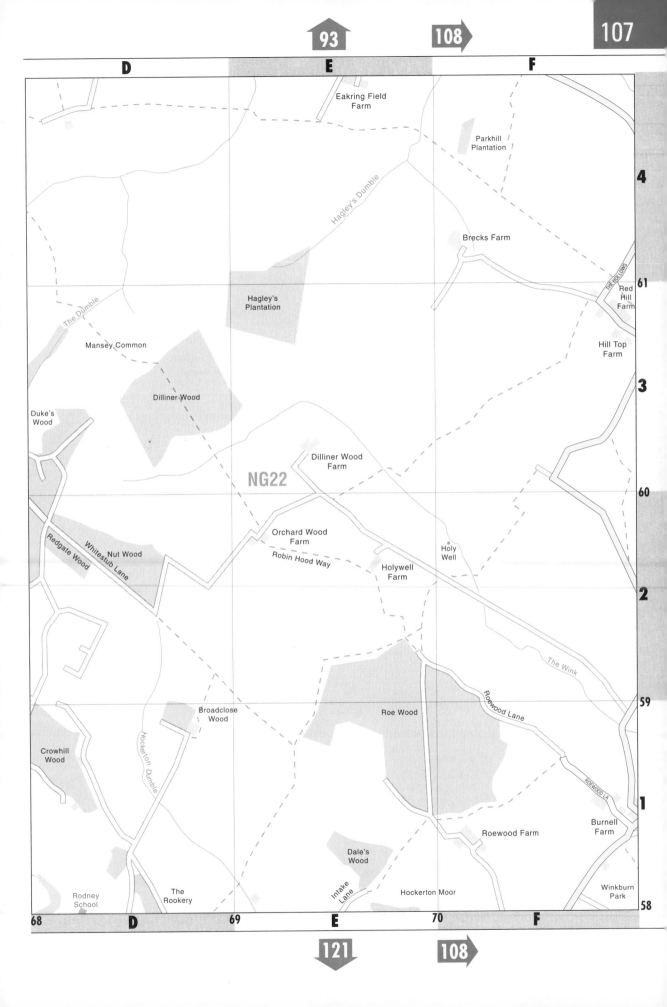

Eakring Field
Farm

Parkhill
Plantation

4

Hagley's Dumble

Brecks Farm

THE HOLLOWS

61 Red
Hill
Farm

The Dumble

Hagley's
Plantation

Mansey Common

Hill Top
Farm

Dilliner Wood

3

Duke's
Wood

Dilliner Wood
Farm

NG22

60

Orchard Wood
Farm

Redgate Wood

Whitestub Lane

Nut Wood

Robin Hood Way

Holy
Well

Holywell
Farm

2

The Wink

59

Broadclose
Wood

Roe Wood

Roewood Lane

Hockerton Dumble

Crowhill
Wood

1

ROEWOOD LA

Burnell
Farm

Roewood Farm

Dale's
Wood

Rodney
School

The
Rookery

Intake
Lane

Hockerton Moor

Winkburn
Park

58

A B C

Kersall

WOOD LA

The Elms
Farm

Caunton
Lodge Farm

Caunton Common
Farm

A616

4

THE HOLLOWS

Lodge
Cottages

Lodge Farm

61

Maplebeck

Maplebeck
Farm
Low
Farm

CHURCH LA

Beesthorpe
Farm

Beesthorpe
Lodge

MILL LA

3

Holme
Farm

The Beck

Beesthorpe
Hall Farm

Beesthorpe
Hall

NG23

The Farmstead

A616

NG22

MAPLEBECK RD

60

Readyfield
Farm

Duke's
Wood

Readyfield
Wood

2

North Lodge
Farm

Earlshaw
Farm

Mather
Wood

Lady
Wood

59

Coppice
Wood

Lady
Wood

1

Home
Farm

Hall
Farm

THE WINK

Winkburn

Winkburn
Hall

NG25

Park Spring
Wood

Park Spring
Farm

58

71 A 72 B 73 C

D
E
F

4

School
House
Farm
PH

Highfield
House

Brunk
Wood

Southfield
Farm

Mount
Pleasant

Park
Wood

Glebe
Farm

61

Moor La

Watermill
Farm

Mill
Bridge

Flags
Farm

Hill House
Farm

3

Windmill

PH

MILL LA

The
Woovers

NG23

Bathleyhill
Farm

CHAPEL
LA

Bathleyford
Bridge

Bathleyhill
Cottages

Dean Hole
CE Sch

FIELD LA

MAIN ST

DEAN'S CL

AMEN CNR

NORWELL RD

60

MANOR RD

PH

SCHOOL LA

Winterset La

CAUNTON RD

Home
Farm

The Beck

Holme
Farm

NEWARK RD

Caunton

Hunger
Barn

Newbottles
Plantation

2

Red
Lodge

Worner
Wood

59

Knapthorpe

Middlethorpe
Grange

Dean Hall
Farm

Knapthorpe
Manor

Doncaster's
Plantation

1

Cold Harbour
Plantation

OLLERTON RD

A616

58

74
D
75
E
76
F

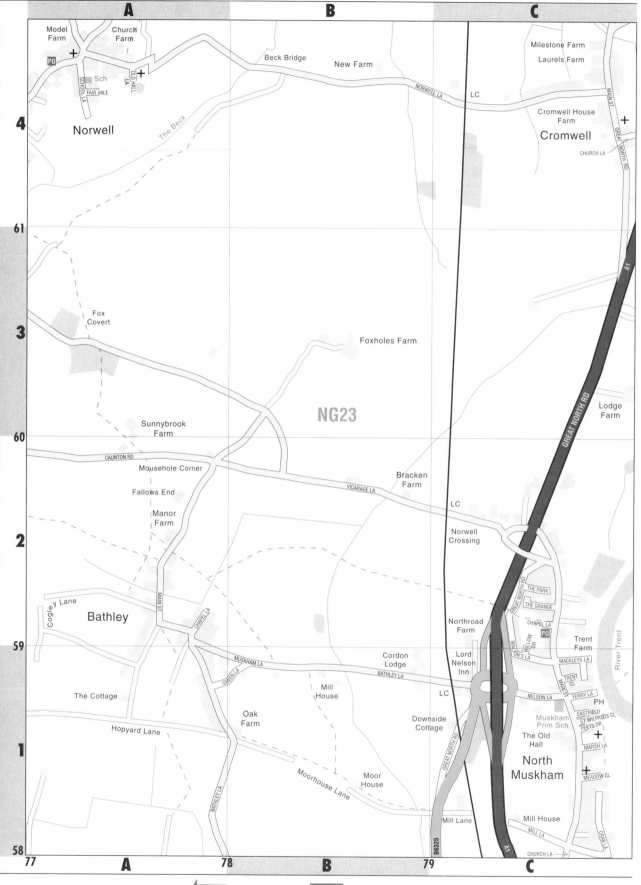

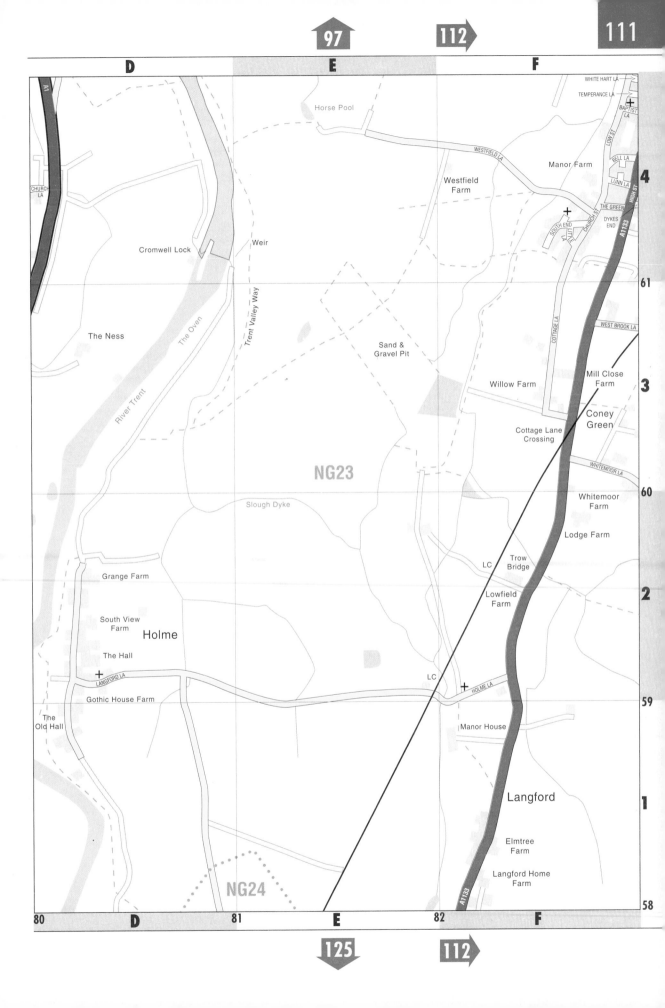

D · E · F

4

WHITE HART LA
TEMPERANCE LA
BAPTIST LA

Horse Pool

WESTFIELD LA

Manor Farm

LOW ST

BELL LA

LUNN LA

Westfield
Farm

CHURCH
LA

THE GREEN

HIGH ST

SOUTH END

LITTLE
CHURCH ST
DYKES
END

A1133

Cromwell Lock

Weir

61

Trent Valley Way

The Ness

The Oven

COTTAGE LA

WEST BROOK LA

Sand &
Gravel Pit

Willow Farm

Mill Close
Farm

3

Coney
Green

River Trent

Cottage Lane
Crossing

WHITEMOOR LA

NG23

60

Whitemoor
Farm

Slough Dyke

Lodge Farm

Grange Farm

LC

Trow
Bridge

2

Lowfield
Farm

South View
Farm

Holme

The Hall

LC

Gothic House Farm

LANGFORD LA

Holme LA

59

The
Old Hall

Manor House

1

Langford

NG24

Elmtree
Farm

Langford Home
Farm

A1133

58

80 · D · 81 · E · 82 · F

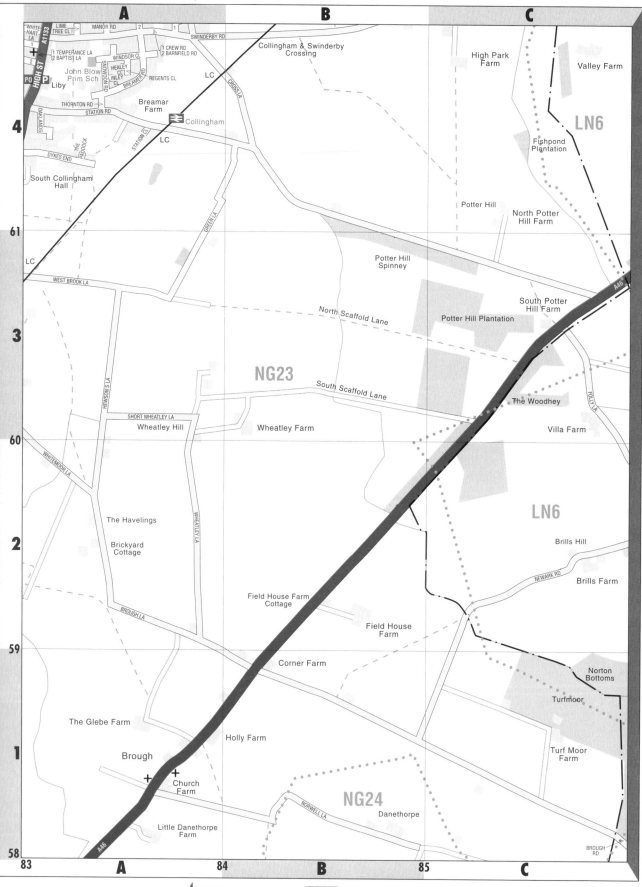

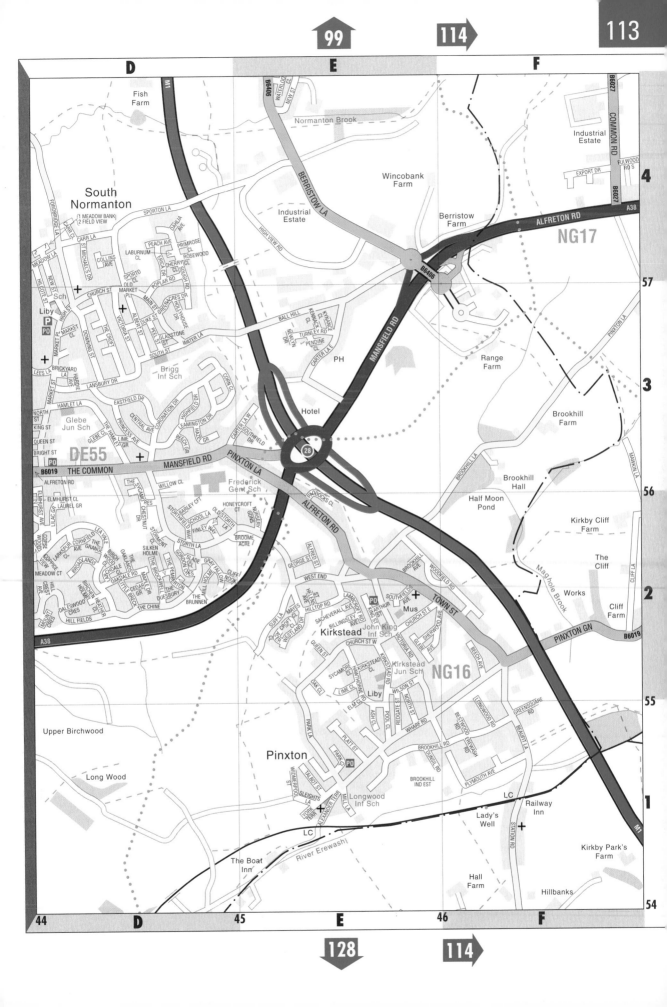

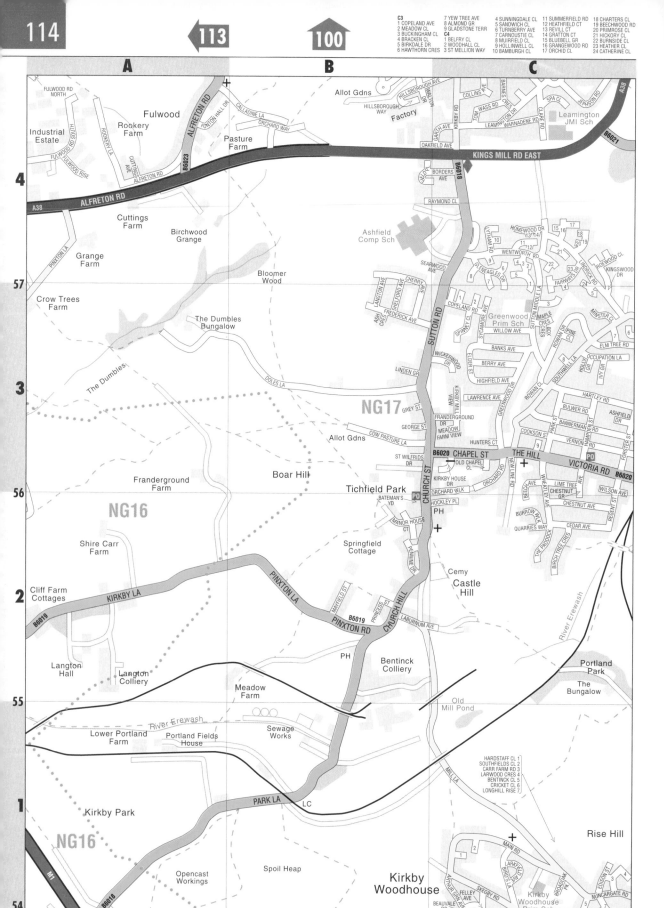

C3
1 COPELAND AVE
2 MEADOW CL
3 BUCKINGHAM CL
4 BRACKEN CL
5 BIRKDALE DR
6 HAWTHORN CRES

7 YEW TREE AVE
8 ALMOND GR
9 GLADSTONE TERR
C4
1 BELFRY CL
2 WOODHALL CL
3 ST MELLION WAY

4 SUNNINGDALE CL
5 SANDWICH CL
6 TURNBERRY AVE
7 CARNOUSTIE CL
8 MUIRFIELD CL
9 HOLLINWELL CL
10 BAMBURGH CL

11 SUMMERFIELD CL
12 HEATHFIELD CT
13 REVILL CT
14 GRATTON CT
15 BLUEBELL GR
16 GRANGEWOOD RD
17 ORCHID CL

18 CHARTERS CL
19 BEECHWOOD RD
20 PRIMROSE CL
21 HICKORY CL
22 BURNSIDE CL
23 HEATHER CL
24 CATHERINE CL

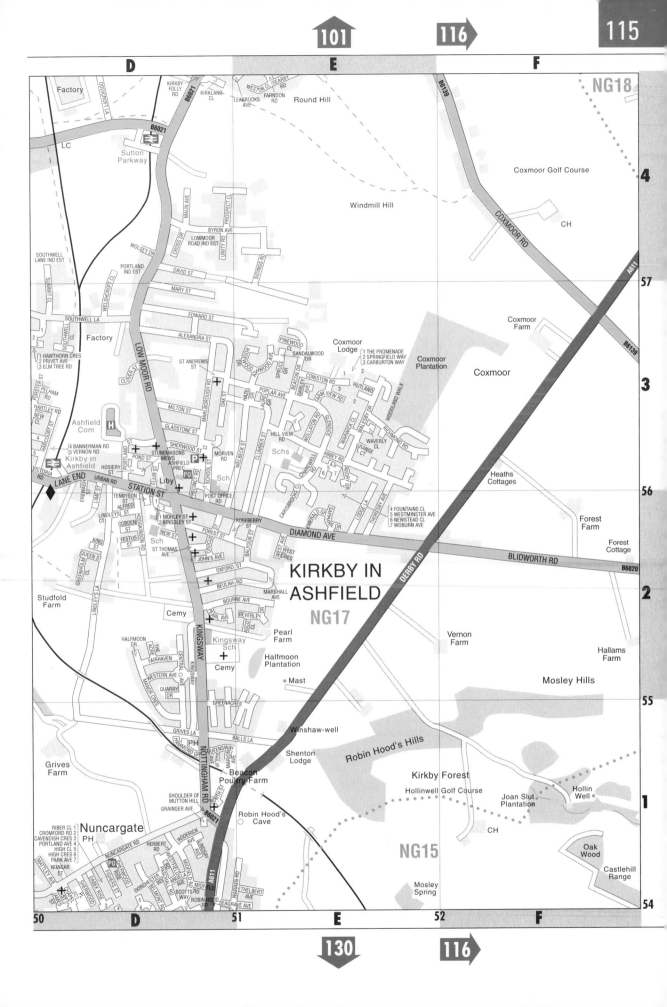

115 102

A   B   C

4

Stonehills Farm

DERBY RD

A611

A611

A60

Works

NOTTINGHAM RD

NG18

Two Oaks Farm

Thieves' Wood

Harlow Wood

57

B6139

Portland College for People with Disabilities

Forest Walks

Fountaindale Sch

Robin Hood Way

NG21

3

COXMOOR RD

Sheppard's Stone

Woodlands Farm

Nomanshill Wood

56

P

P

Forest Walks

RICKET LA

Holly Lodge

NG17

Little Nomanshill Wood

Campfield Farm

Twin Hill

B6020

BLIDWORTH RD

B6139

KIRKBY RD

LITTLE RICKET LA

MANSFIELD RD

The Larch Farm

BEECH AVE

PO

B6020

MAIN RD

2

High Leys Dr

Fairfield Copse Dr

Haggnook Wood

BYRON CRES

WOODSIDE RD 1
HASLEMERE GDNS 2

ROSEDALE LA
WESTBROOK

SUMMERCOURT DR

LINWOOD CRES

Gosford Plantation

NG15

Gunthorpe Hagg Wood

NOTTINGHAM RD

CAMBOURNE GDNS
DOVER BECK CL

55

2

SWINTON DR

PO

SHEPWALK LA
THE HOLLIES

CHURCH DR

Knightcross Dale

+

MILTON DR

VERNON CRES

Monksbarn Farm

Newstead Park

Pilgrim Oak

PILGRIM CL

MANSFIELD RD

Hotel

LONGDALE LA

VERNON AVE

1

Reedwater

Swinecotte Dale

+

Knightcross

Lady Wildman's Wood

MISTERTON CRES

Castle Wood

Upper Lake

REGINA CRES
CRES

54

53   A   54   B   55   C

A60

D
E
F

Lindhurst La
Lindhurst Farm

NG18

Rainworth
The Joseph Whitaker Sch

Rainworth Lodge

The Archer (PH)

B6020

WARSOP LA

4

+

BLIDWORTH LA

Cottage Farm

New Farm

57

Providence Farm

High Park

Norwood Hill Close

Fountain Dale

Greenfields

CROSS LA

Robin Hood Way

Brick Kiln Hill

B6020

3

Copt Hill Farm

NEW LA

MANSFIELD RD

Ling Farm

RICKET LA

NG21

Redgate Farm

Norwood Hill Farm

56

MARRIOTS LA

COTTAGE CL

BUTLER DR

B6020

+ PH

Rock Farm

MAIN ST

PH

+

2

Silverland Farm

ROBIN HOOD TERR

SANDY LA

Fishpool Farm

Tel Ex

FISHPOOL RD

+

FIELD LA

PH

MAIN RD

PH

Cottage Farm

WOODSIDE RD
DOVERIDGE CL
THE BIRCHS
CROMFORD CT
BRETTON RD
ASHOVER RD
CHATSWORTH CL
HATHERSAGE RISE
BRACKENFIELD RISE
HADDON RD
CAROLINE CL
LITTON CL
HEREFORD RD
ASHFORD DR
WINSTER AVE

1 CHERNSIDE
2 STANLEY CL
3 CASTLETON

TASWELL CL

3
1
2

Schs

SWINTON RISE

WALTHAM RD

BOURNE DR

DENBURY RD

CHERITON DR

DOWNHAM GDNS

55

SOUTHVIEW GDNS

NG15

CHURCH DR

Bottom Farm

CHAPEL LA

PH

WOODLAND RISE 1
RIDGEWOOD GR 2
MILTON CRES

HIGHFIELD CL

1
2

WOOD END DR

LEA RD

LEA CL

Jackson's Hill

MILTON DR

MAVIS AVE

BIRCH CL

DUNCAN DR

1

Sch

ROBIN GR

Ravenshead

HEAVYTREES AVE

VERNON CRES

CHERNSIDE CL

Robin Hood Way

RIGG LA

THE KEYES
GORSE HILL
LONGDALE AVE
BARBERS WOOD CL
ROWAN DR
OAKWOOD DR
SILVERWOOD AVE
PRIORY AVE
BIRCHWOOD DR

BIRCHWOOD CL

CHESTNUT AVE

LONGDALE LA

REGINA CRES

QUARRY RD

FERN CL

Blidworth Dale

54

56

D

57

E

58

F

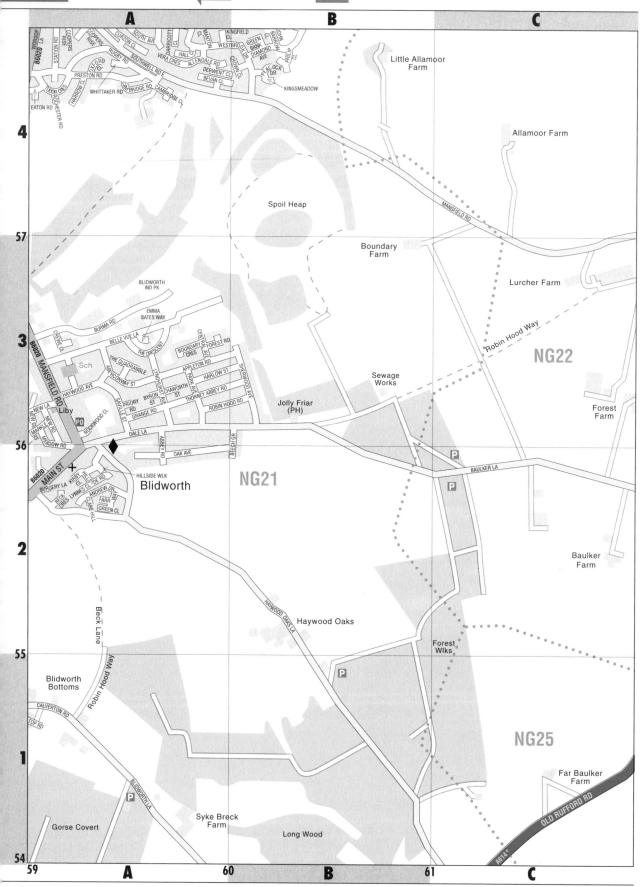

WORKSOP
B6020
STATION RD
COOPERS RISE
COOPERS CL
CURZON CL
SOUTH AVE
DARRICOTT CL
MARLTON
HALL CL
KINGFIELD CL
WESTBROOK CL
GREEN BANK
JOHN BADROW
DIAMOND AVE
PHILIP CL
PEACOCK DR

Little Allamoor Farm

Allamoor Farm

MANSFIELD RD

4

Spoil Heap

57

Boundary Farm

Lurcher Farm

BLIDWORTH IND PK

EMMA BATES WAY

Robin Hood Way

NG22

BURMA RD
BELLE VUE LA
THE CRESCENT
CENTRAL FOREST RD
BOUNDARY CRES
CREWE CL

3

B6020 MANSFIELD RD

Sch

THE QUADRANGLE
ARCONWAY ST
HAYWOOD AVE
PRIORY RD
BYRON ST
CHAWORTH ST
APPLETON RD
PARK AVE
HARLOW ST
THORNEY ABBEY RD
LYNDHURST AVE
SAVILLE ST
GRANGE RD
ROBIN HOOD RD
SHERWOOD AVE

Sewage Works

Forest Farm

NEW LA
NEW RD
MARPLE
ROCKWOOD CL
Liby
PO
DALE LA
ABBEY RD
BEECH GR
OAK AVE

Jolly Friar (PH)

56

MARPLE
MEADOW RD

B6020 MAIN ST
SURGERY LA
KIRBY CL
HILL
ANDREW DR
FARR
CLARE HILL
BECK CRES
LYNNES CL
HILLSIDE WLK
GREEN CL

Blidworth

P

BAULKER LA

P

NG21

Baulker Farm

2

Beck Lane

Robin Hood Way

HAYWOOD OAKS LA

Haywood Oaks

Forest Wlks

P

55

Blidworth Bottoms

CALVERTON RD
TOP RD

P

NG25

Far Baulker Farm

1

BLIDWORTH LA

OLD RUFFORD RD

Gorse Covert

Syke Breck Farm

Long Wood

A614

54

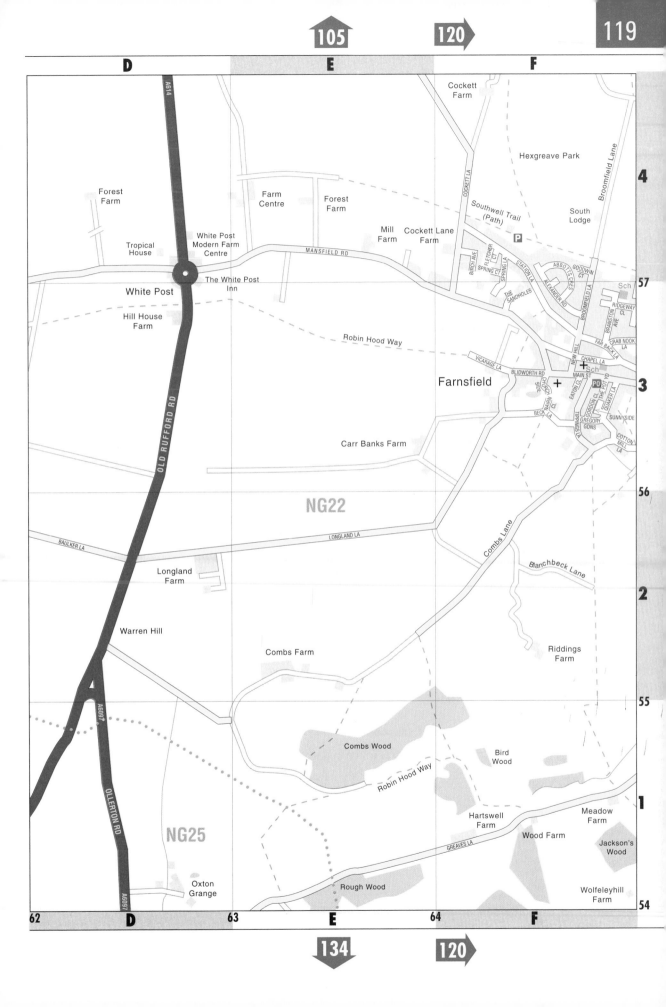

A B C

4

Lower Hexgreave Farm

Hexgreave Park

Kirklington

Home Farm

NEWARK RD

KIRKLINGTON RD

A617

Kirklington Cty Prim Sch

Mill Farm

Park Plantation

Moor Farm

River Greet

Robin Hood Way

THE GREEN

SOUTHWELL RD

SCHOOL

57

RIDGEWAY CL
D'AYNCOURT WLK

MEADOW CL

THE RIDGEWAY

LONG MEADOW

WOODLAND CL

GREENVALE

MILLDALE RD

WOODSIDE

GREENWOOD CL

Pumping Station

Southwell Trail

Spring's Farm

Osmanthorpe Manor

BRICKYARD LA

Collyeat House

NETHER CT

Cotton Mill Dyke

Edingley Beck

STATION RD

3

1 CRAB NOOK LANE
2 CHAPEL LA
3 MAIN ST

NG22

COTTON MILL LA

Sewage Works

Edingley Mill

Valley Farm

SOUTHWELL RD

PH

Edgehill Prep Sch

STATION RD

Harlow Fields

56

MANSFIELD RD

Cotton Mill Farm

ALLESFORD LA

Manor House Farm

Edingley

MAIN ST

Diamond Cottage Farm

EDINGLEY HILL

HOLME LA

2

New Manor Farm

GREAVES LA

LITTLE LA

Woodendale

Grange Farm

Halam Mill

Old Hall Farm

Littledale

55

New Hall Farm

NEWHALL LA

St HELEN'S LA

Halam Beck

Halam CE Sch

SCHOOL LA

1

CARVER'S HOLLOW

Little Turn Croft Farm

Brockley Farm

Middlebeck Farm

GRAY LA

Halam

St MICHAEL'S CL

PH

HALAM HILL

RADLEY RD

Wolfeleyhill La

Turncroft Farm

Machin's Farm

Manor Farm

CHURCH LA

Halam House Farm

RADLEY RD

54

Cutlersforth

65 A 66 B 67 C

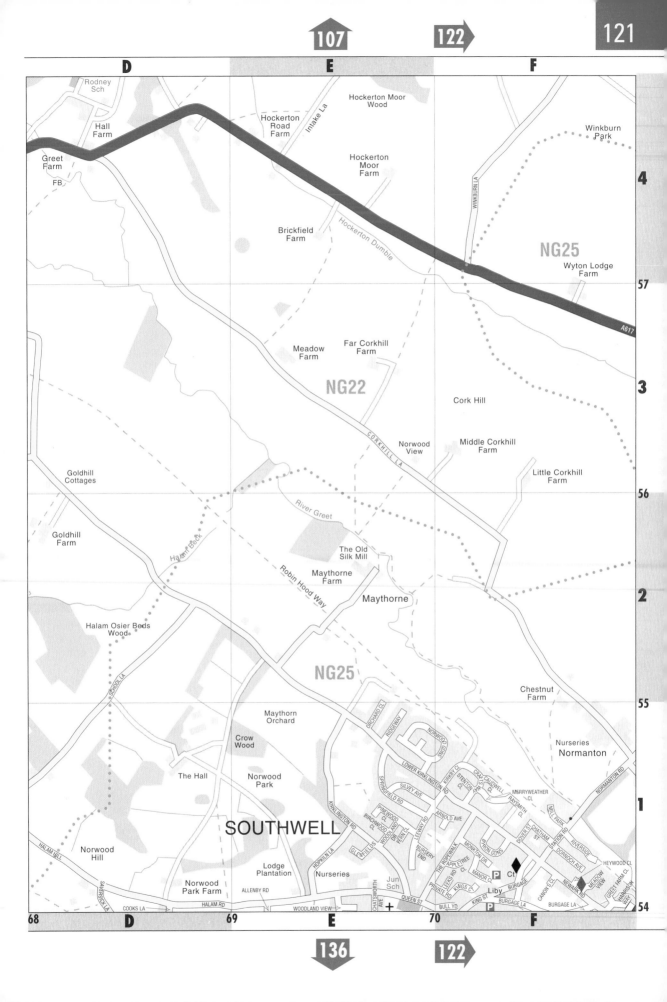

Rodney Sch

Hall Farm

Greet Farm

FB

Hockerton Road Farm

Intake La

Hockerton Moor Wood

Hockerton Moor Farm

Winkburn Park

WINKBURN LA

NG25

Wyton Lodge Farm

Brickfield Farm

Hockerton Dumble

A617

57

4

Meadow Farm

Far Corkhill Farm

NG22

CORKHILL LA

Cork Hill

Norwood View

Middle Corkhill Farm

Little Corkhill Farm

3

56

Goldhill Cottages

River Greet

Goldhill Farm

Halam Beck

The Old Silk Mill

Robin Hood Way

Maythorne Farm

Maythorne

2

Halam Osier Beds Wood

SCHOOL LA

NG25

Chestnut Farm

55

Maythorn Orchard

Crow Wood

ORCHARD CL

RIDGEWAY

NORWOOD GDNS

Nurseries Normanton

NORMANTON RD

The Hall

Norwood Park

Lower Kirklington Rd

SPRINGFIELD RD

SILVEY AVE

KIRKBY CL

STENTON CL

CL

CL

CROFT

MERRYWEATHER CL

DOVER ST

CHATHAM ST

MILL PARK

RIVERSIDE

1

Norwood Hill

HALAM HILL

KIRKLINGTON ROAD

PINEWOOD CL

BIRCHWOOD CL

FERN CL

WOODLAND DR

LEEWAY RD

ARNOLD AVE

NURSERY END

THE ROPEWALK

THE APPLETREE

MONKTON DR

PRIVATE RD

IRON GDNS

CANON ST CL

NEWARK RD

DORNOCH AVE

HEYWOOD CL

MEADOW VIEW

GREET FARM CL

HADDISON VIEW

SOUTHWELL

HOPKIN LA

GLEBE FIELDS

Lodge Plantation

Nurseries

Norwood Park Farm

SAVERSICK LA

ALLENBY RD

Jun Sch

CHATSWORTH AVE

Queen St

KINGS CL

MANOR RD

LEEKS RD

BULL YD

Libv

Ct

P

BURGAGE

KING ST

BURGAGE LA

P

BURGAGE LA

54

COOKS LA

HALAM RD

WOODLAND VIEW

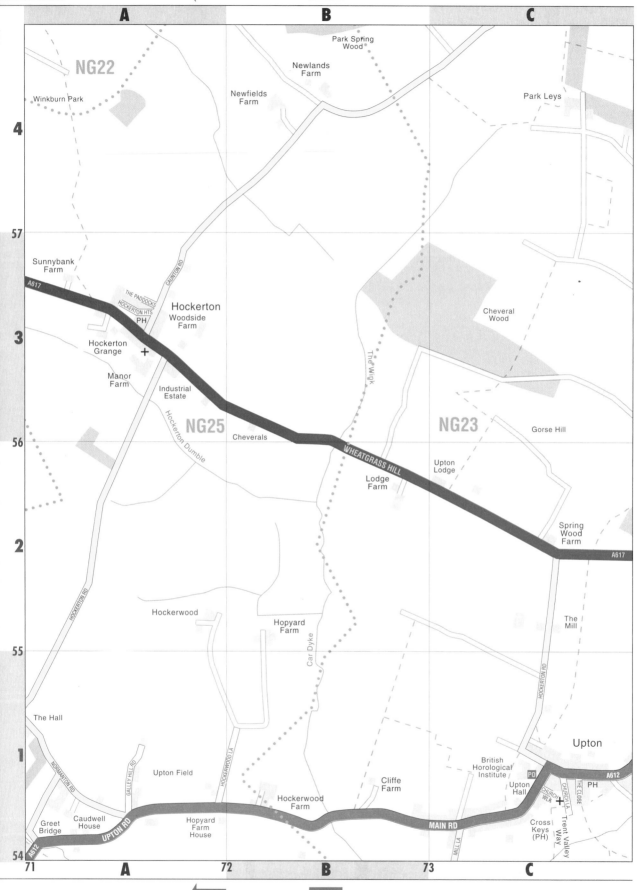

NG22

Winkburn Park

Park Spring Wood

Newlands Farm

Newfields Farm

Park Leys

4

57

Sunnybank Farm

A617

THE PADDOCKS
HOCKERTON HTS
PH

CAUNTON RD

Hockerton
Woodside Farm

Cheveral Wood

The Wigk

3

Hockerton Grange

Manor Farm

Industrial Estate

Hockerton Dumble

NG25

Cheverals

NG23

Gorse Hill

56

WHEATGRASS HILL

Upton Lodge

Lodge Farm

Spring Wood Farm

A617

2

Hockerwood

Hopyard Farm

Car Dyke

HOCKERTON RD

The Mill

55

The Hall

Upton

1

NORMANTON RD

GALLEY HILL RD

Upton Field

HOCKERWOOD LA

Hockerwood Farm

Cliffe Farm

British Horological Institute

Upton Hall

PO
HOCKERTON RD
CHURCH WLK
CHURCH LA
THE CLOSE
PH

A612

Greet Bridge

Caudwell House

UPTON RD

Hopyard Farm House

MAIN RD

MILL LA

Cross Keys (PH)

Trent Valley Way

54

A612

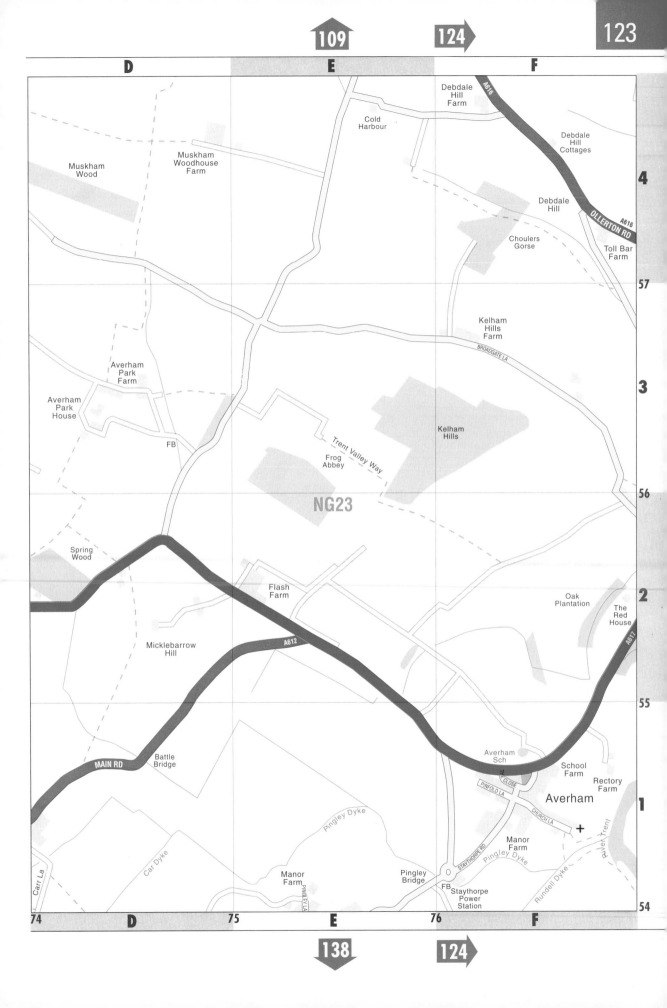

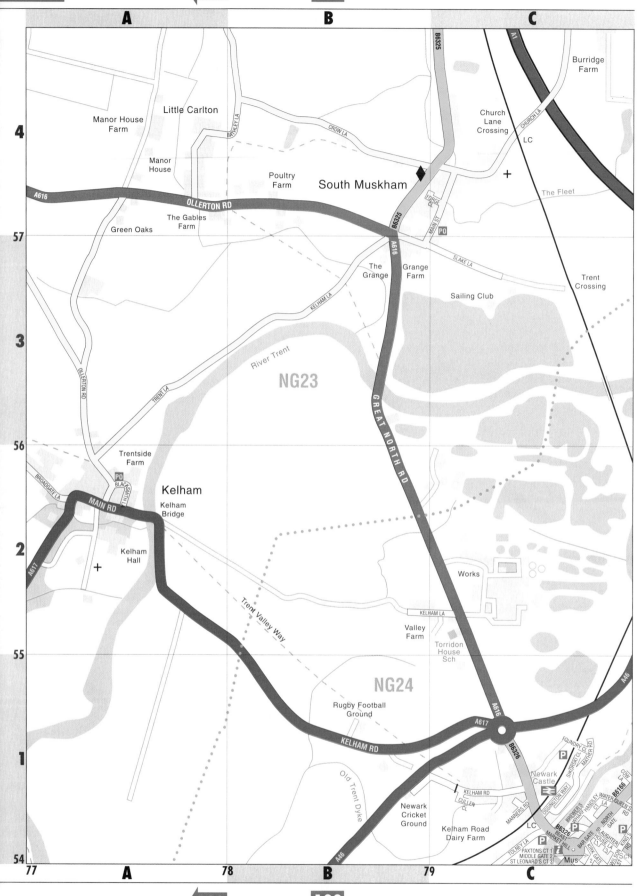

Burridge Farm

Little Carlton

Manor House Farm

Church Lane Crossing

LC

Manor House

Poultry Farm

South Muskham

The Fleet

A616 OLLERTON RD

The Gables Farm

Green Oaks

PO

The Grange

Grange Farm

SLAKE LA

Trent Crossing

Sailing Club

KELHAM LA

River Trent

NG23

GREAT NORTH RD

Trentside Farm

PO

Kelham

Kelham Bridge

Kelham Hall

Works

Trent Valley Way

KELHAM LA

Valley Farm

Torridon House Sch

NG24

Rugby Football Ground

A617

Newark Castle

A616

B6326

FOUNDRY LA

MATHER RD

P

SHORESKI CL

COW LA

NORTH GATE

B6166

QUEEN'S

KELHAM RD

BROMLEY'S

WHARF

HANDLEY

WATER LA

P

Newark Cricket Ground

Kelham Road Dairy Farm

CULLEN CL

MANNERS RD

OSSINGTON WAY

LC

B6326

MARKET HILL

BAR GATE

HOUSE LA

SLAUGHTER

P

P

KIRK GATE

KING'S RD

TOLNEY LA

PAXTONS CT 1
MIDDLE GATE 2
ST LEONARD'S CT 3

WILSON ST

i

Mus

A46

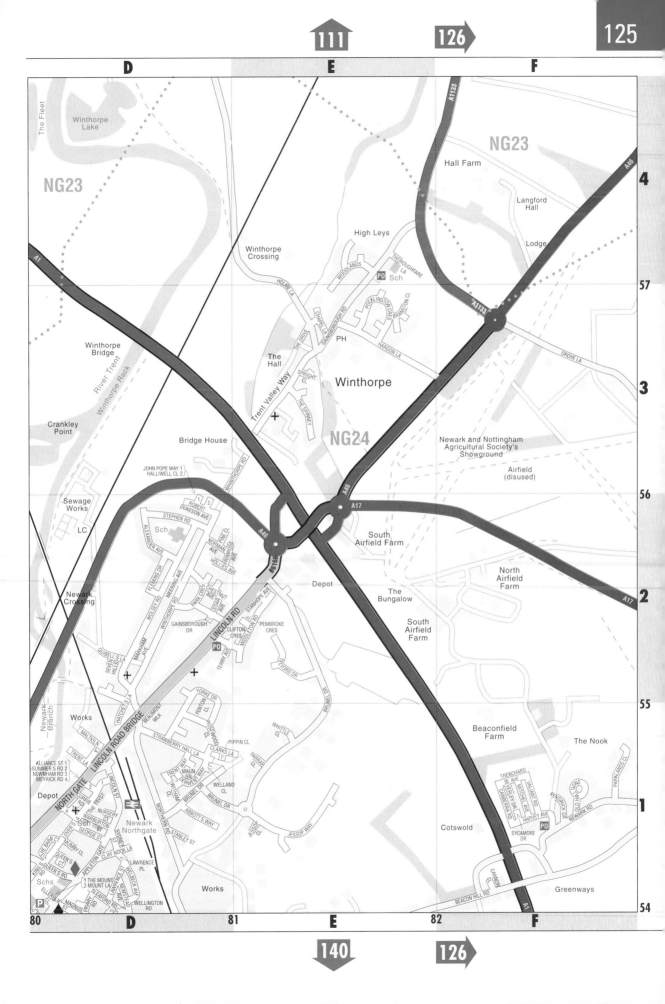

A

B

C

NG23

Thorpe Field
Farm

NG23

Danesthorpe Hill

4

Danethorpe Hill
Farm

Little Danethorpe
Farm

High
Wood

LN6

57

Langford Moor
Farm

3

Lingspot
Farm

Langford Moor

NG24

Stapleford Wood

CODDINGTON LA

Newark Air
Museum

HIGHFIELD DR

56

Northlea

DROVE LA

Drove Cottage
Farm

2

A17

The Bungalow

Moor
Brats

The
Cottage

STAPLEFORD LA

Moor
Plantation

55

Flawford
Farm

THE
GREEN

Coddington

The
Tinderbox

Coddington
Moor

MORGANS CL

THORPE CL

Hall
Farm

PH

PARKES CL

ROSS CL

SLEAFORD RD

A17

NEWARK
RD

VALLEY VIEW

CHAPEL LA

MAIN ST

1

Kelwick
Wood

BROWNLOW'S HILL

Manor
Farm

Coddington
CE Prim
Sch

BALDERTON LA

Newark Golf Course

LONG LA

Vale Farm

Club
House

54

83

A

84

B

85

C

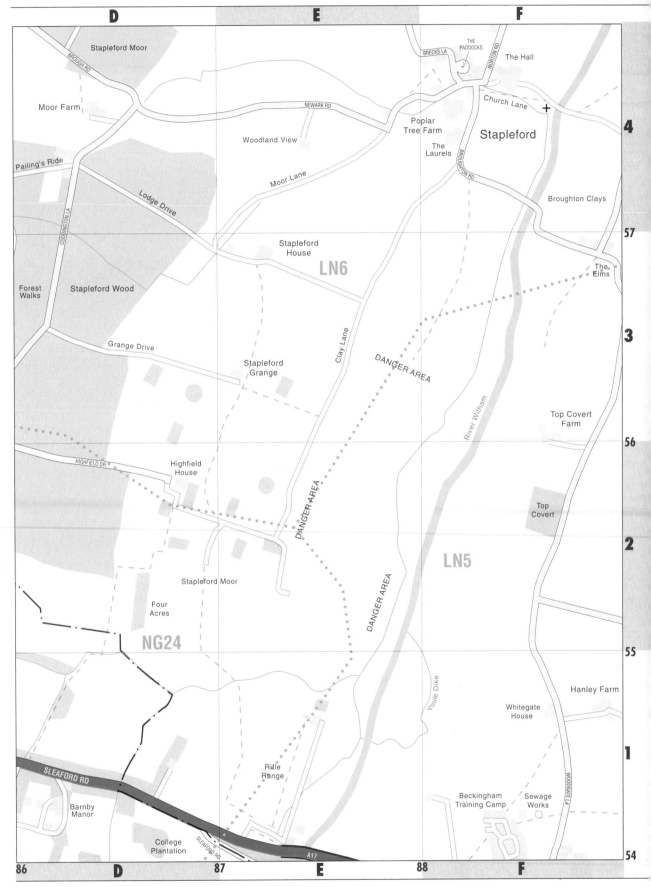

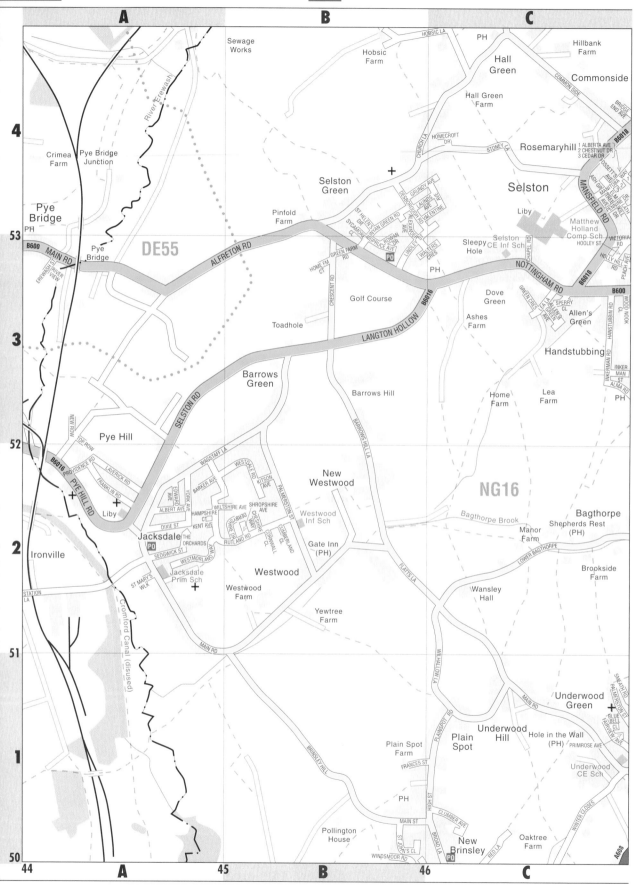

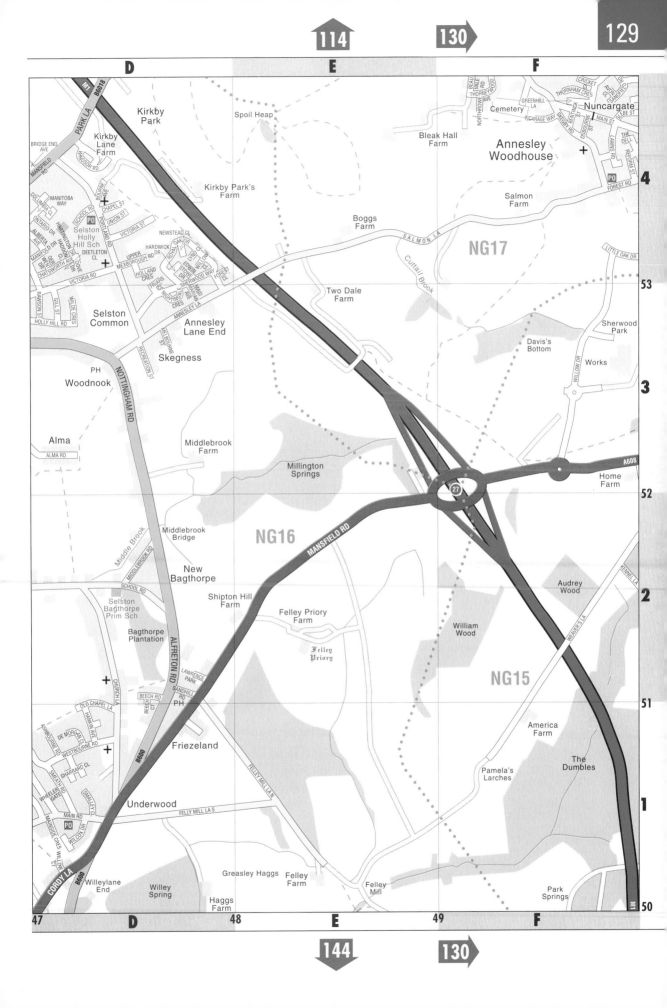

D   E   F

Park La
M1
B6018

Kirkby
Park

Bridge End
Ave
Mansfield Rd
Kirkby Lane
Farm
Windsor Rd

Columbia Dr
Manitoba
Way
School Rd
Portland Rd
Chapel St
Union St
Ontario Dr
Harrington St
Hadon St
Victoria St
Newstead Cl
Alberta Ave
Mansfield Rd
Stove
Chatsworth Dr
Hadon Dr
Deetleton Cl
Selston Holly
Hill Sch
PO

Spoil Heap

Kirkby Park's
Farm

Boggs
Farm

Salmon La

Salmon
Farm

NG17

Cemetery
Annesley
Woodhouse
Beau
Vale
Thorney
Ave
Northrowe
Greenhill
La
Vicarage Way
Thornham Cres
Bentinck
Osbourne St
Skegby Rd
Avon
Cl
Sandpit
Cricket Cl
Main St
Glebe St
The
Dell
Lawns Rd
Reform St
Forest Rd
PO

4

Little Oak Dr

53

Hardwick
Royal Oak Dr
Victoria Rd
Rawson St
Gill St
Wilde Cres
Holly Hill Rd

Upper
Mexborough Rd
Holland
Cres
Friars
Nightingale
Cres
Sherwood Main
Annesley La
Forest Cl
Edwin
Melbourne St
Recreation St
Willow Cl

Selston
Common

Annesley
Lane End
Skegness

PH
Woodnook
Nottingham Rd

Alma
Alma Rd

Middlebrook
Farm

Millington
Springs

Two Dale
Farm

Cuttall Brook

Davis's
Bottom

Sherwood
Park

Works

Willow Dr

3

52

NG16

Mansfield Rd

27

Home
Farm

A608

Middlebrook
Bridge

Middle Brook
Middlebrook Rd
School Rd

New
Bagthorpe

Shipton Hill
Farm

Felley Priory
Farm

Felley
Priory

William
Wood

Audrey
Wood

Kennel La

Weaver's La

2

Selston
Bagthorpe
Prim Sch

Bagthorpe
Plantation

Alfreton Rd

Lawrence
Park

NG15

Old Chapel La
Church La
Beech Rd
Beech Ct
Sandhill Rd
PH

America
Farm

51

De Morgan La
Hankin Ave
Westbourne Rd
Ashbourne Rd

Friezeland
B600

The
Dumbles

Pamela's
Larches

Sharrard Cl
Smalley Cl
Wheeler Gate
Sneath Rd
Main Rd
Wilcox Dr
PO
Mansie Cres
Willow Ct

Underwood
Felly Mill La
Felly Mill La S

Greasley Haggs
Felley
Farm

1

Cordy La
B600

Willeylane
End
Willey
Spring

Haggs
Farm

Felley
Mill

Park
Springs

M1

50

47   D   48   E   49   F

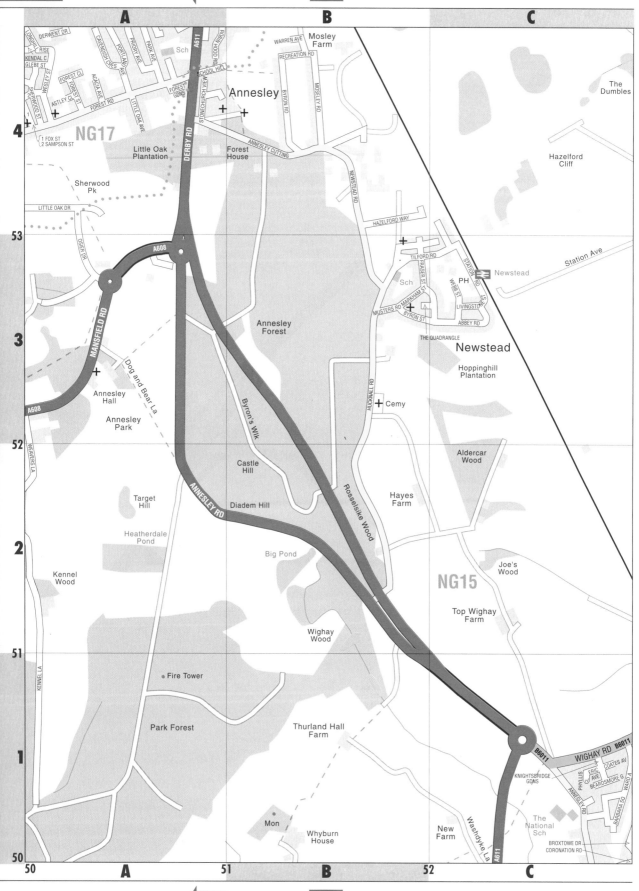

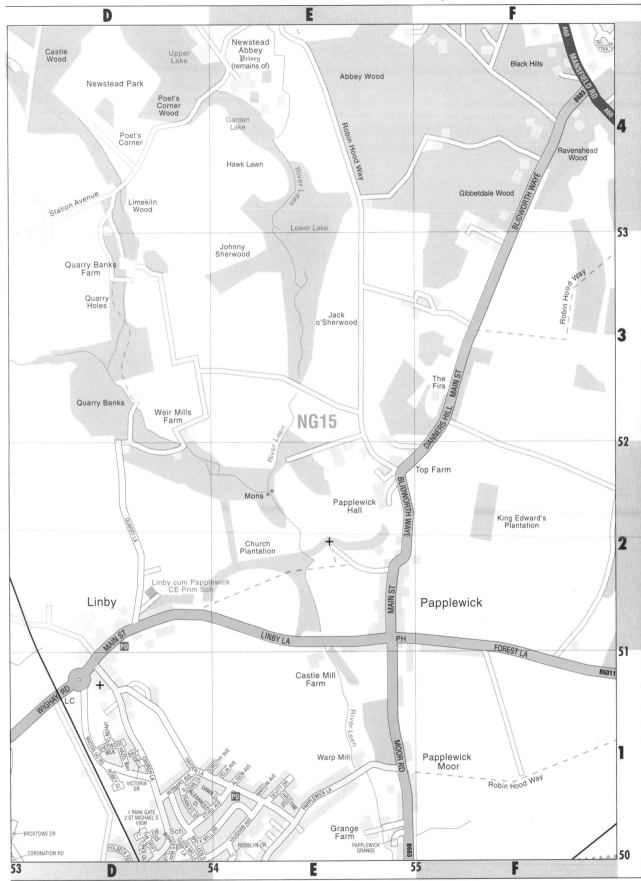

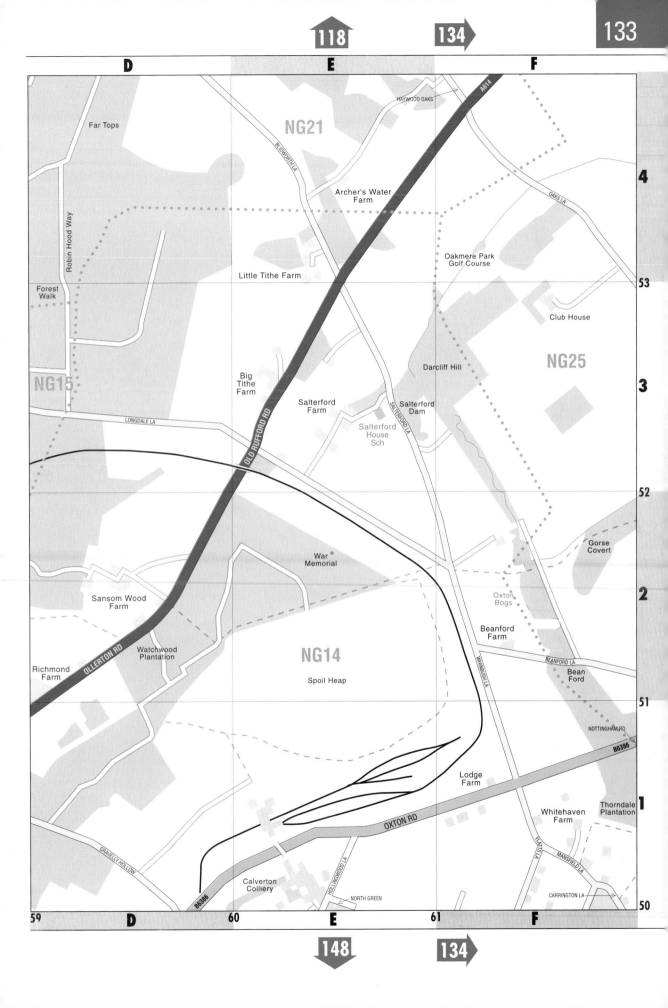

D   E   F

NG21

Far Tops

HAYWOOD OAKS

A614

Robin Hood Way

Archer's Water
Farm

4

OAKS LA

Oakmere Park
Golf Course

Forest
Walk

Little Tithe Farm

53

Club House

NG15

Big
Tithe
Farm

Darcliff Hill

NG25

LONGDALE LA

OLD RUFFORD RD

Salterford
Farm

Salterford
Dam

SALTERFORD LA

3

Salterford
House
Sch

52

War
Memorial

Gorse
Covert

Sansom Wood
Farm

Oxton
Bogs

2

Beanford
Farm

OLLERTON RD

Watchwood
Plantation

NG14

BEANFORD LA

WHINBUSH LA

Bean
Ford

Richmond
Farm

Spoil Heap

51

NOTTINGHAM RD

B6386

Lodge
Farm

Thorndale
Plantation

1

GRAVELLY HOLLOW

OXTON RD

Whitehaven
Farm

HOLLINGWOOD LA

TEATS LA

MANSFIELD LA

B6386

Calverton
Colliery

NORTH GREEN

CARRINGTON LA

50

59   D   60   E   61   F

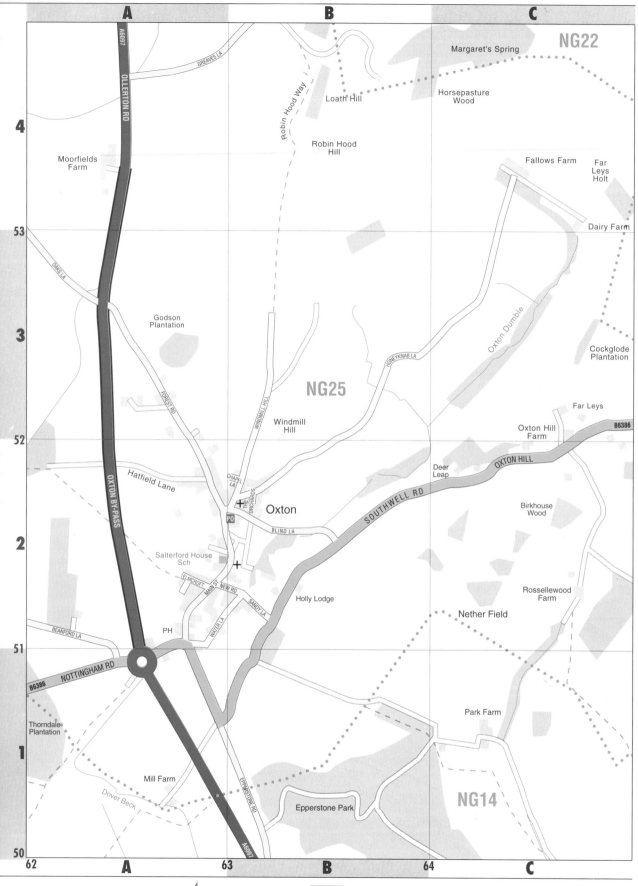

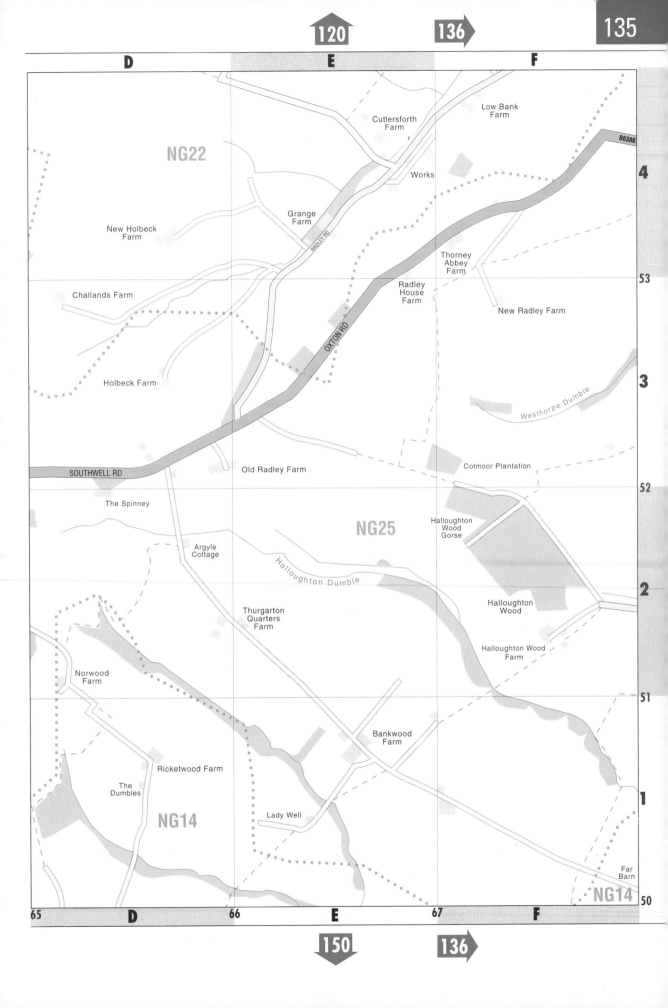

D   E   F

NG22

Cutlersforth Farm

Low Bank Farm

B6386

Works

4

Grange Farm

RADLEY RD

New Holbeck Farm

Thorney Abbey Farm

Radley House Farm

53

Challands Farm

OXTON RD

New Radley Farm

3

Holbeck Farm

Westhorpe Dumble

SOUTHWELL RD

Old Radley Farm

Cotmoor Plantation

52

The Spinney

NG25

Halloughton Wood Gorse

Argyle Cottage

Halloughton Dumble

2

Halloughton Wood

Thurgarton Quarters Farm

Halloughton Wood Farm

Norwood Farm

51

Ricketwood Farm

Bankwood Farm

The Dumbles

NG14

Lady Well

1

Far Barn

NG14

50

65   D   66   E   67   F

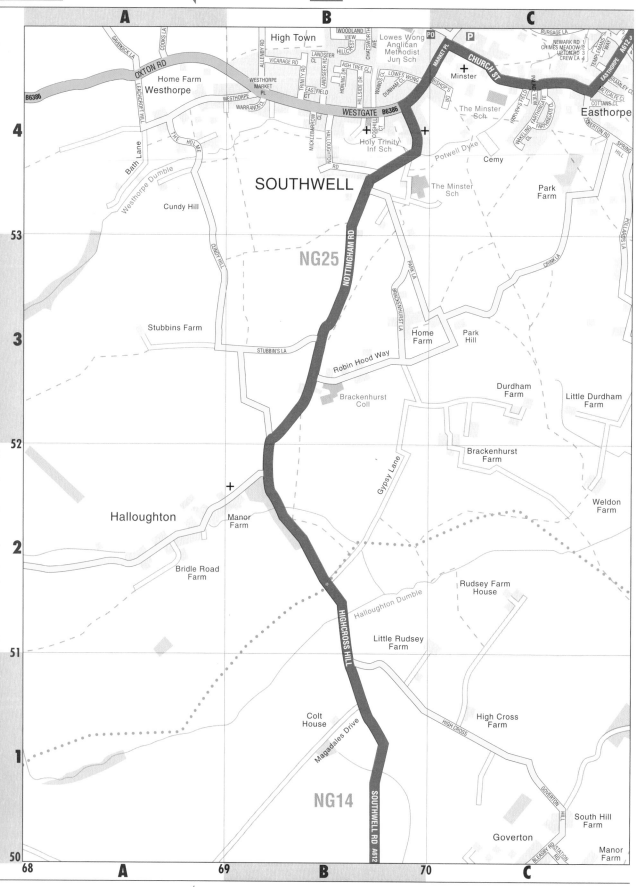

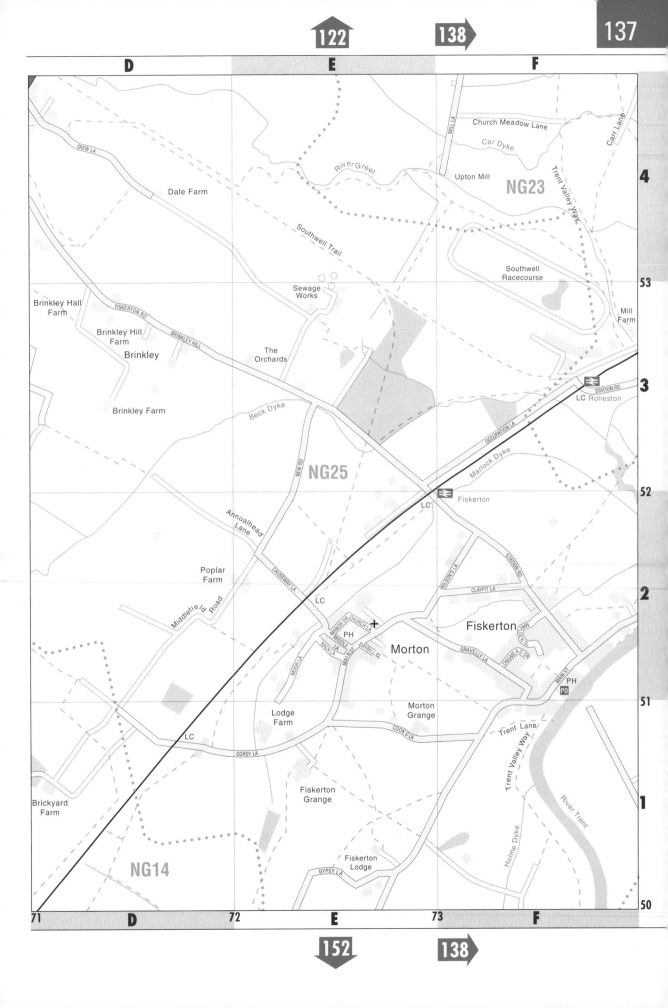

D   E   F

Church Meadow Lane

MILL LA

Car Dyke

River Greet

Upton Mill

NG23

Trent Valley Way

Car Lane

CREW LA

Dale Farm

4

Southwell Trail

Southwell Racecourse

53

Sewage Works

Brinkley Hall Farm

FISKERTON RD

Brinkley Hill Farm

BRINKLEY HILL

Brinkley

The Orchards

Mill Farm

Brinkley Farm

Beck Dyke

STATION RD

LC Rolleston

3

OCCUPATION LA

Marlock Dyke

NEW RD

NG25

LC   Fiskerton

52

Annualhead Lane

STATION RD

Poplar Farm

CAUSEWAY LA

WILSON'S LA

CLAYPIT LA

2

Middlefield Road

LC

MANOR DR   CHURCH LA

PH

Fiskerton

CRNW

LOCK CL

MOOR LA

MIDDLE LA

DAYBILL CL

Morton

GRAVELLY LA

LONGMEAD DR

MAIN ST

PH

BACK LA

MAIN ST

PO

51

Lodge Farm

Morton Grange

Trent Lane

Trent Valley Way

LC

GORSY LA

COOK'S LA

River Trent

1

Brickyard Farm

Fiskerton Grange

NG14

Fiskerton Lodge

Holme Dyke

GYPSY LA

71   72   73   50

D   E   F

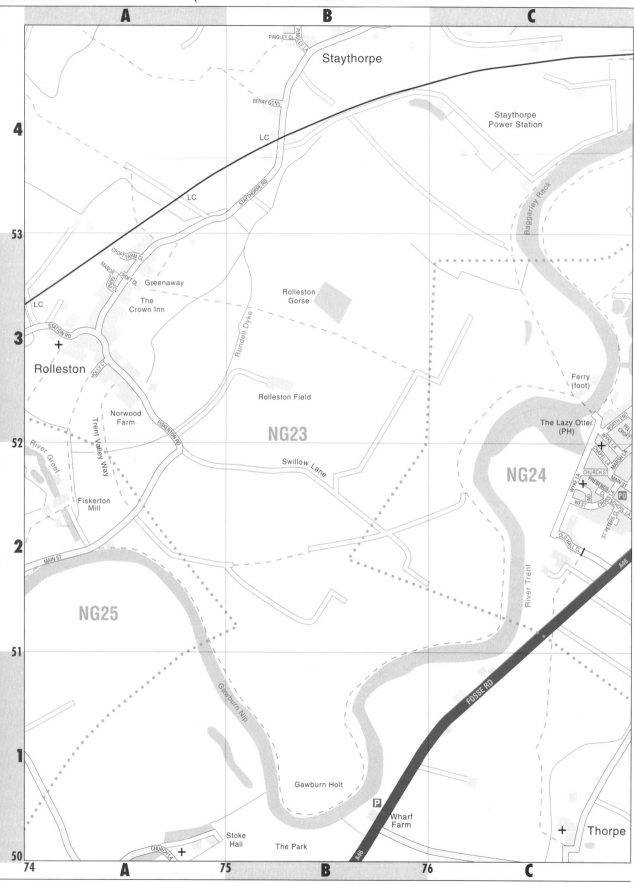

Staythorpe

PINGLEY CL
PINGLEY LA

BERAY GDNS

Staythorpe
Power Station

LC

STAYTHORPE RD

LC

53

CROFT FARM CL

Baggarley Rack

LC

MANOR CL
CROFT CL

Greenaway

Rolleston
Gorse

The
Crown Inn

Rundell Dyke

STATION RD

Ferry
(foot)

3

+

HOLLY CL

Rolleston

Rolleston Field

The Lazy Otter
(PH)

NORTH END
FELL
CROFT

Norwood
Farm

FISKERTON RD

NG23

WYKE LA

MARSH LA

CHAPEL LA

MAIN ST

52

River Greet

Trent Valley Way

CHURCH ST

WYKE LA

PREBENDS
CL

PO

Swillow Lane

NG24

WEST
END

CROSS
SCHOOL LA

Fiskerton
Mill

ST PETERS CL

OLD HALL CL

2

MAIN ST

River Trent

A46

NG25

51

FOSSE RD

Gawburn Nip

1

Gawburn Holt

P

A46

Wharf
Farm

+

Thorpe

50

Stoke
Hall

CHURCH LA

+

The Park

74

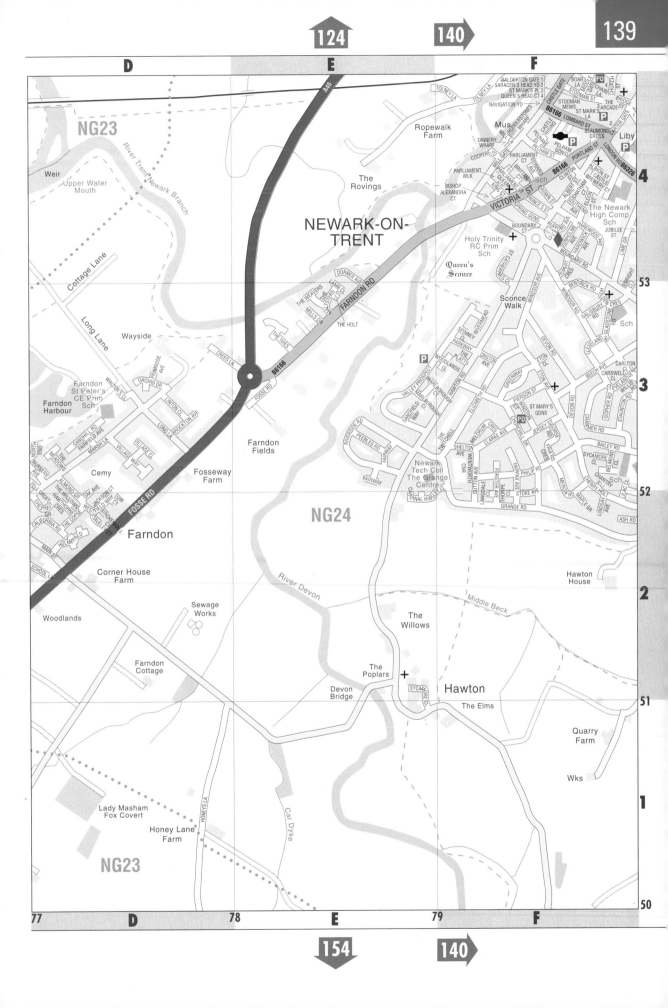

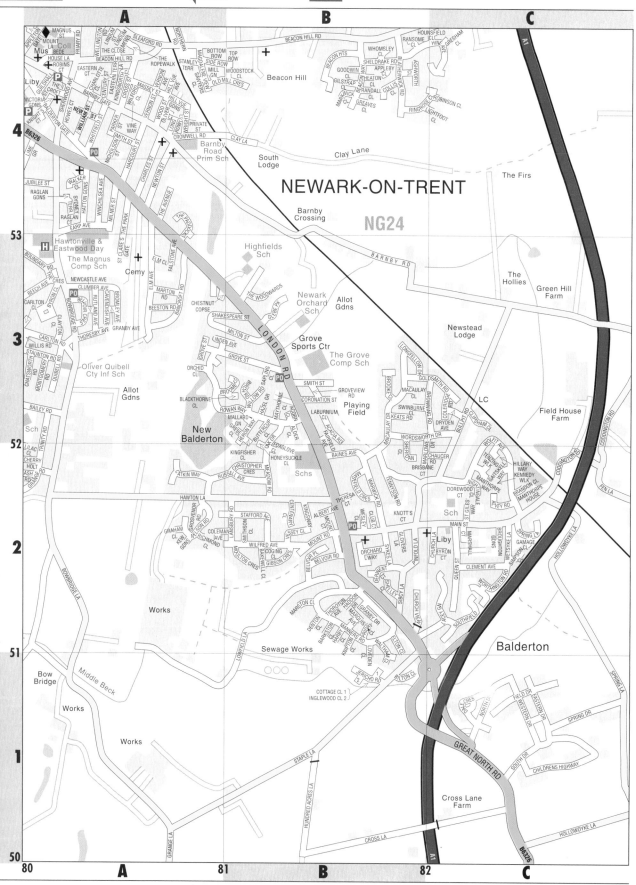

NEWARK-ON-TRENT

NG24

Balderton

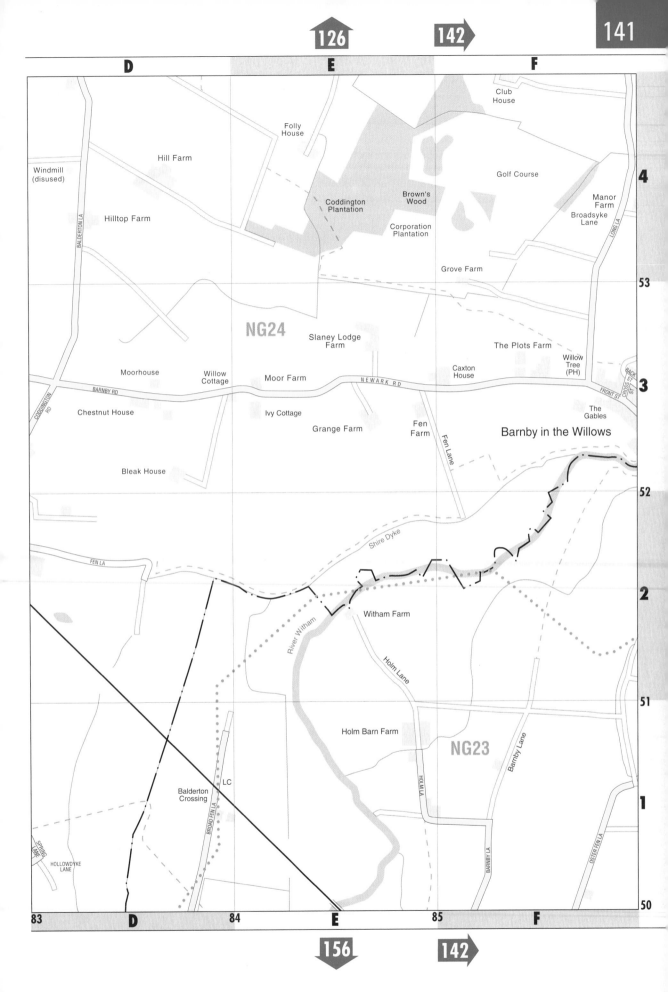

141
127

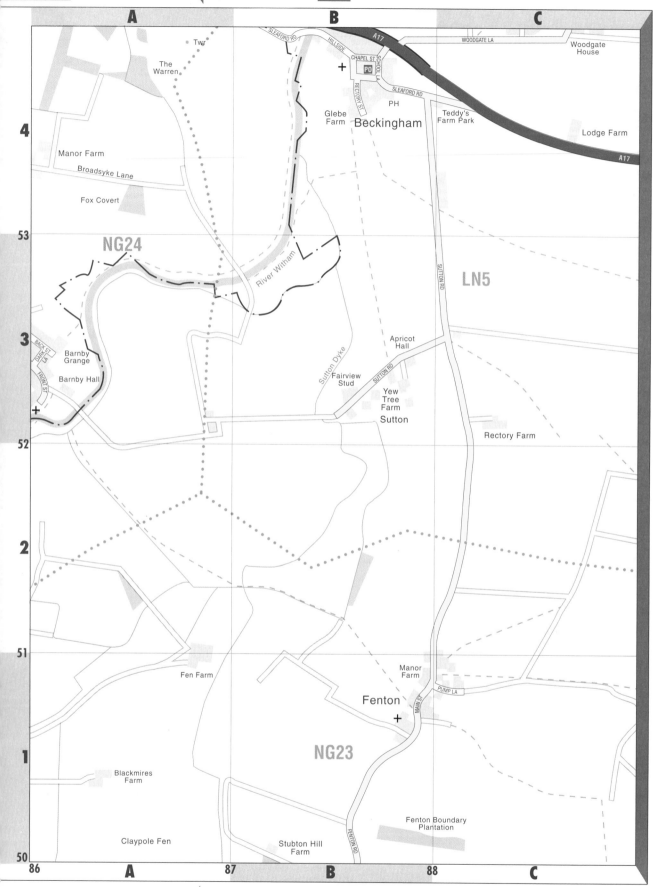

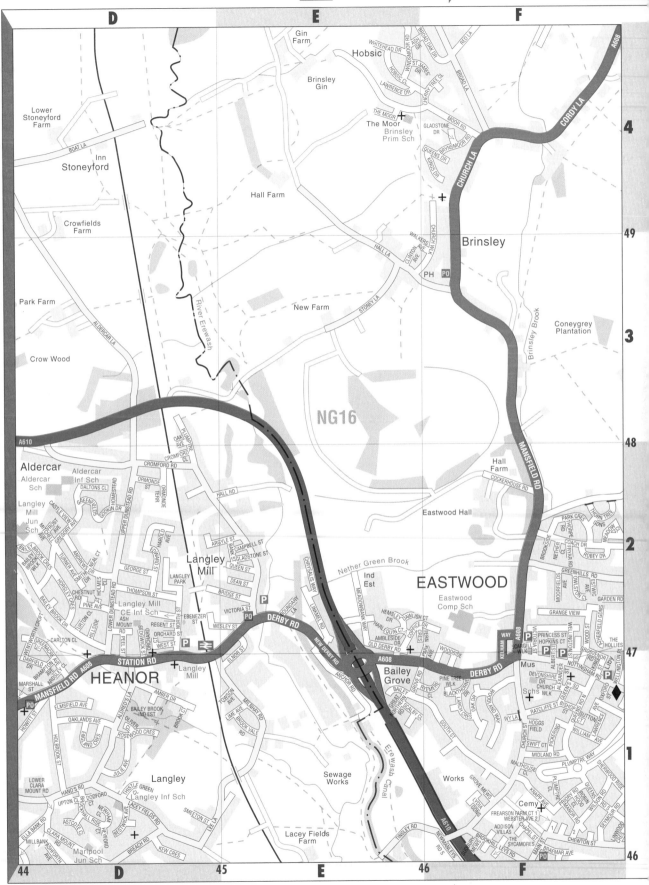

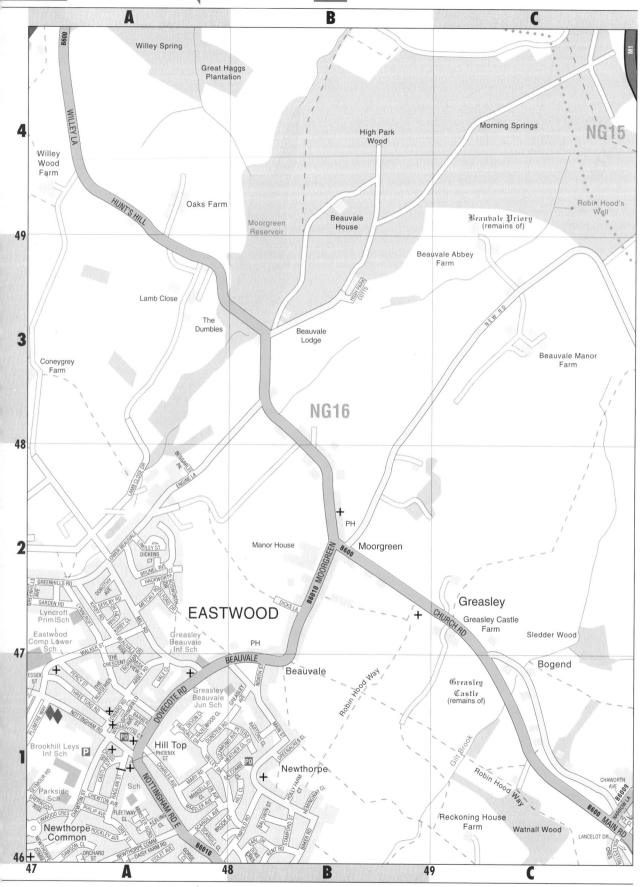

D | E | F

Park Springs

Whyburn Farm

Dobpark

Misk Hollows
Recn Gd
QUEEN ST
ST MARY'S WAY

Silo Farm

Misk Hill

Whyburn Prim Sch

Misk Farm

WHYBURN LA

Long Hill

Beacon Hill

Beauvale

BEAUVALE RD

NG15

HUCKNALL

The Annie Holgate Cty Jun & Inf Schs

Coppice Farm

Wathall Coppice

The Holgate Comp Sch

Ruffs

FOX MEADOW
LACEY AVE

Brooksbreasting Farm

Chys

Edgewood Prim Sch

Eelhole Wood

Westville
HUCKNALL IND PK

Crowhill Farm

NG16

Watson's Wood

Starthwood Farm

Starth Wood

Stubbing Wood Farm

Works

Hollybush Farm

Eel Hole Farm

Airfield

Littlefields Farm

Bulwell Woodhall Farm

Robin Hood Way

NG6

Long La

Bulwell Wood

Blenheim

1 CHAWORTH AVE
2 MAIN RD
3 LANCELOT DR

Blenheim

50 | D | 51 | E | 52 | F | 46

4

49

3

48

2

47

1

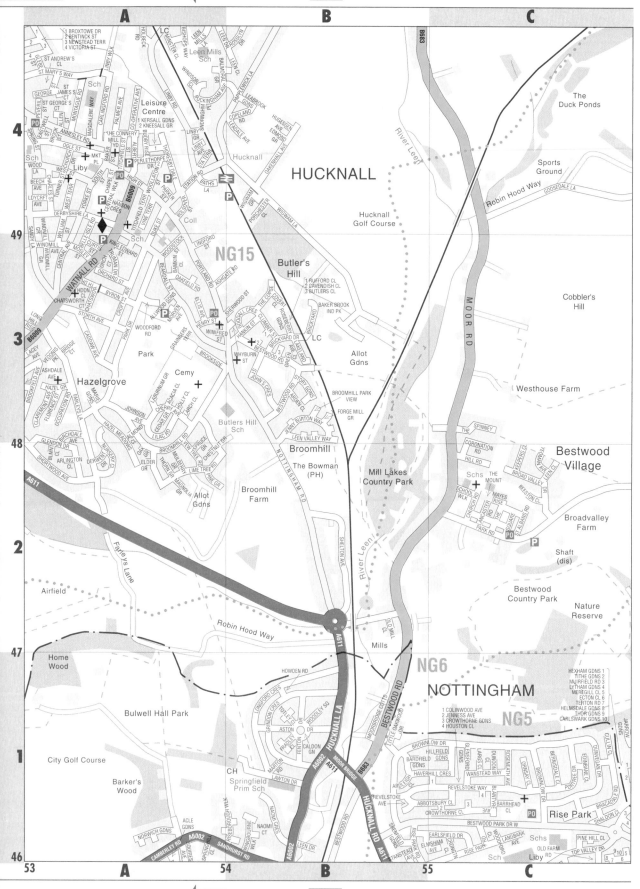

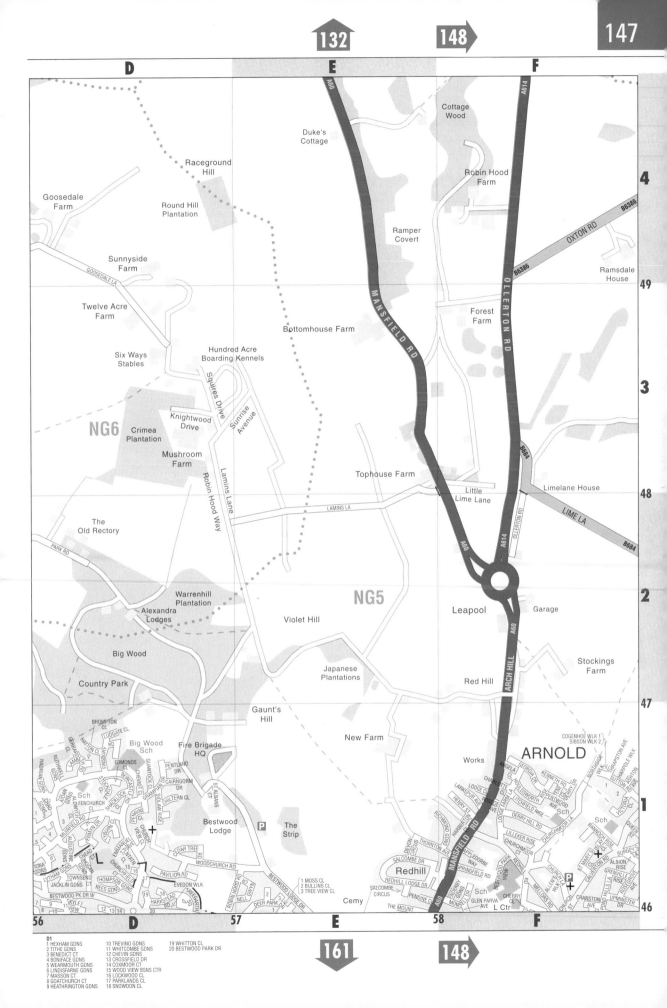

D **E** **F**

Raceground Hill

Round Hill Plantation

Goosedale Farm

Duke's Cottage

Cottage Wood

Robin Hood Farm

4

Sunnyside Farm

GOOSEDALE LA

Ramper Covert

OXTON RD

B6386

B6386

Ramsdale House

49

Twelve Acre Farm

Bottomhouse Farm

MANSFIELD RD

Forest Farm

Six Ways Stables

Hundred Acre Boarding Kennels

Squires Drive

NG6

Knightwood Drive

Crimea Plantation

Sunrise Avenue

Tophouse Farm

Little Lime Lane

B684

Limelane House

48

Mushroom Farm

Lamins Lane

Robin Hood Way

LAMINS LA

OLLERTON RD

OLLERTON RD

LIME LA

B684

The Old Rectory

PARK RD

A60

A614

Warrenhill Plantation

NG5

Leapool

Garage

2

Alexandra Lodges

Violet Hill

Big Wood

Japanese Plantations

Red Hill

ARCH HILL

A60

Stockings Farm

Country Park

Gaunt's Hill

New Farm

47

Brompton CL

Big Wood

Fire Brigade Sch

Fire Brigade HQ

Works

ARNOLD

COGENHOE WLK 1
SIBSON WLK 2

Sch

1

St ALBANS CT

CHILTERN CL

Bestwood Lodge

P

The Strip

MANSFIELD RD

Sch

Sch

Redhill

REDHILL LODGE DR

SALCOMBE CIRCUS

1 MOSS CL
2 BULLINS CL
3 TREE VIEW CL

P

Cemy

THE MOUNT

A60

Glen Parva L Ctr

46

56 **57** **58**

D **E** **F**

D1
1 HEXHAM GDNS
2 TITHE GDNS
3 BENEDICT CT
4 BONIFACE GDNS
5 WEARMOUTH GDNS
6 LINDISFARNE GDNS
7 MASSON CT
8 GOATCHURCH CT
9 HEATHRINGTON GDNS
10 TREVINO GDNS
11 WHITCOMBE GDNS
12 CHEVIN GDNS
13 CROSSFIELD DR
14 COXMOOR CT
15 WOOD VIEW BSNS CTR
16 LOCKWOOD CL
17 PARKLANDS CL
18 SNOWDON CL
19 WHITTON CL
20 BESTWOOD PARK DR

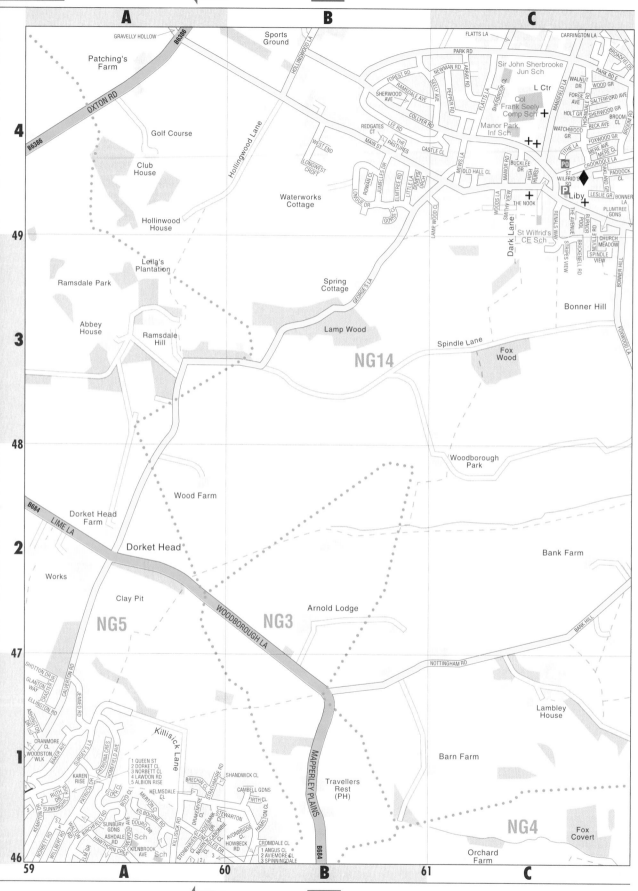

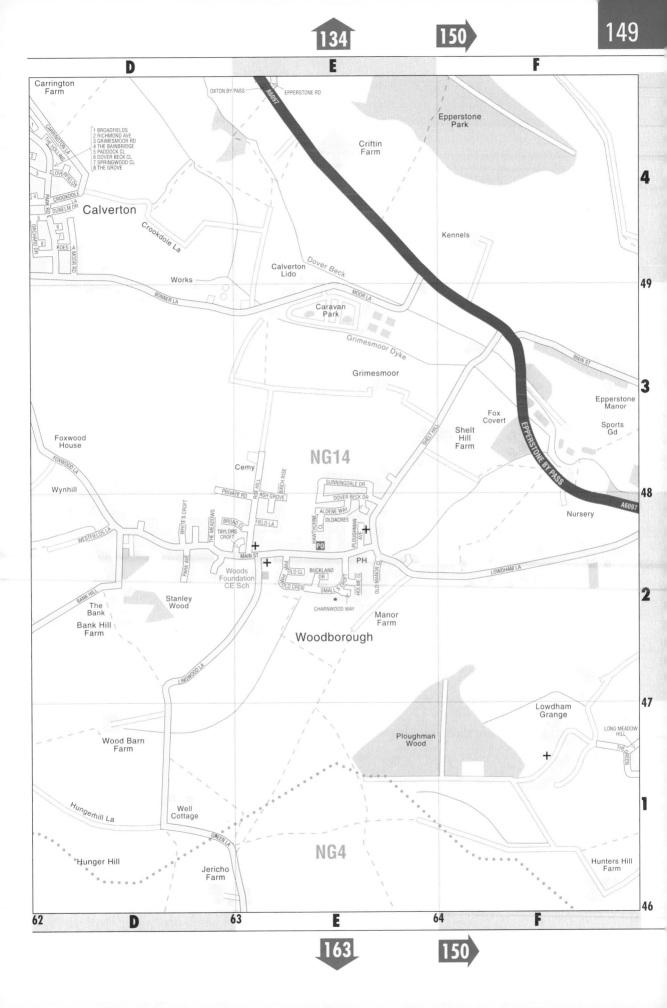

149
135

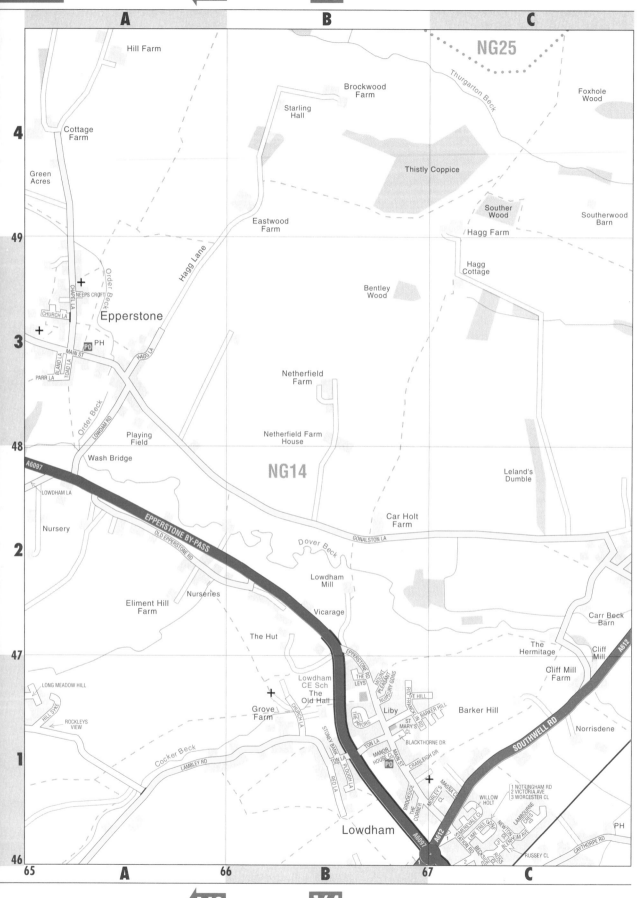

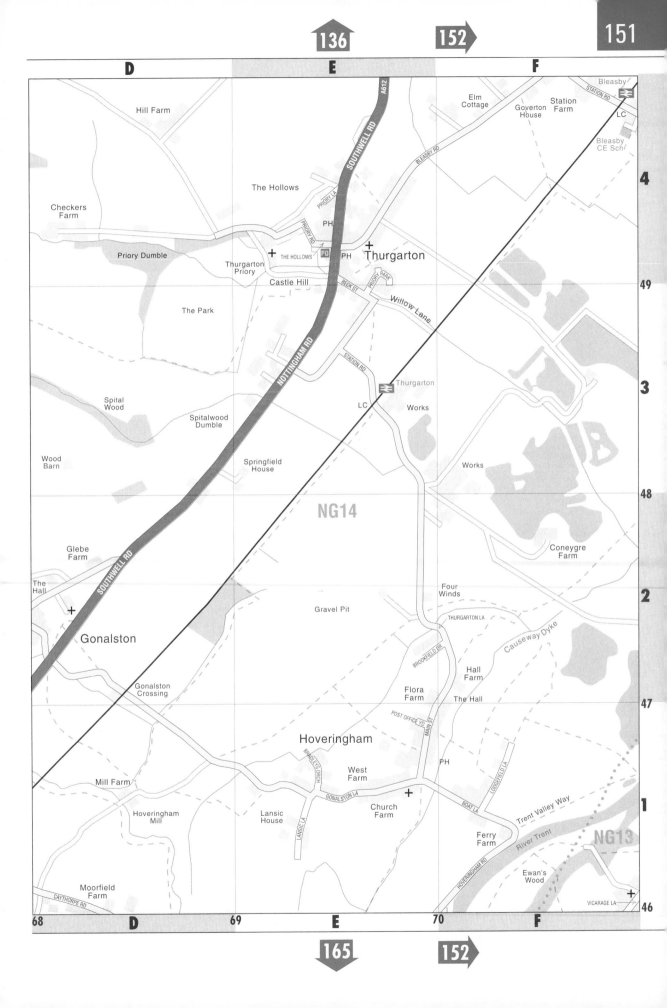

D **E** **F**

A612

SOUTHWELL RD

Hill Farm

Elm
Cottage

Goverton
House

Station
Farm

Bleasby

STATION RD

LC

Bleasby
CE Sch

The Hollows

BLEASBY RD

4

Checkers
Farm

PRIORY LA

PH

Priory Dumble

PRIORY RD

THE HOLLOWS

PO

PH

PH

Thurgarton

49

Thurgarton
Priory

Castle Hill

BECK ST

PRIORY PARK

Willow Lane

The Park

NOTTINGHAM RD

STATION RD

Thurgarton

Spital
Wood

LC

Works

3

Spitalwood
Dumble

Wood
Barn

Springfield
House

Works

NG14

Coneygre
Farm

48

Glebe
Farm

SOUTHWELL RD

The
Hall

Four
Winds

2

Gonalston

Gravel Pit

THURGARTON LA

Causeway Dyke

Hall
Farm

BROOKFIELD DR

The Hall

Gonalston
Crossing

Flora
Farm

POST OFFICE YD

MAIN ST

47

Hoveringham

PH

West
Farm

BRADLEYS ORCH

LODGEFIELD LA

Mill Farm

GONALSTON LA

Church
Farm

BOAT LA

Trent Valley Way

1

Hoveringham
Mill

Lansic
House

LANSIC LA

Ferry
Farm

HOVERINGHAM RD

River Trent

NG13

Ewan's
Wood

Moorfield
Farm

CAYTHORPE RD

VICARAGE LA

46

68 **D** **69** **E** **70** **F**

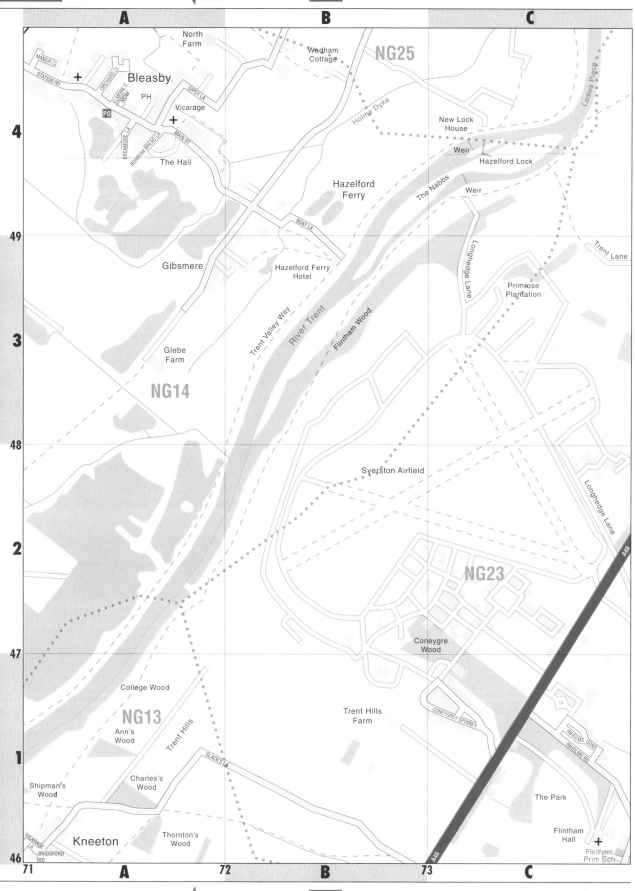

A   B   C

North Farm

Wadham Cottage

NG25

MANOR CL

STATION RD

ORCHARD CL

Bleasby

GIPSY LA

Holme Dyke

New Lock House

ELMORE'S MDW

PH

Vicarage

Ladies Piece

4

PO

SYCAMORE LA

The Hall

BORROW BREAD LA

MAIN ST

Hazelford Ferry

The Nabbs

Weir

Hazelford Lock

Weir

BOAT LA

49

Gibsmere

Hazelford Ferry Hotel

Longhedge Lane

Trent Lane

Primrose Plantation

Trent Valley Way

River Trent

Flintham Wood

3

Glebe Farm

NG14

48

Syerston Airfield

2

NG23

Longhedge Lane

A46

47

Coneygre Wood

College Wood

NG13

Trent Hills Farm

CONEYGREY SPINNEY

Ann's Wood

Trent Hills

INHOLMS GDNS

INHOLMS RD

1

SLACK'S LA

Shipman's Wood

Charles's Wood

The Park

Flintham Hall

VICARAGE LA

Kneeton

Thornton's Wood

Flintham Prim Sch

BRIDGFORD RD

A46

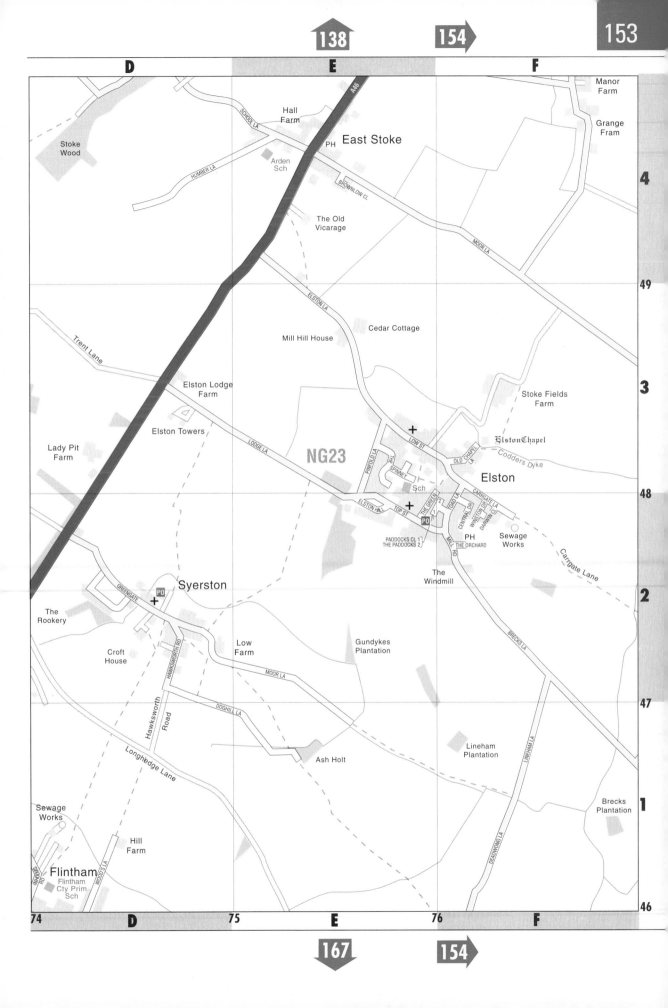

D   E   F

A46

Hall Farm

East Stoke

SCHOOL LA

PH

Stoke Wood

Arden Sch

HUMBER LA

BROWNLOW CL

The Old Vicarage

4

MOOR LA

Manor Farm

Grange Fram

49

ELSTON LA

Trent Lane

Cedar Cottage

Mill Hill House

Elston Lodge Farm

3

Stoke Fields Farm

Elston Towers

Elston Chapel

Codders Dyke

Lady Pit Farm

LODGE LA

NG23

Elston

SPINNEY

PINFOLD LA

LOW ST

OLD CHAPEL LA

48

Sch

CARRGATE LA

ELSTON HALL

TOP ST

THE GREEN

TOAD LA

CENTRAL DR

WINSTON CL

DARWIN CL

PO

Sewage Works

Syerston

PO

PADDOCKS CL 1
THE PADDOCKS 2

PH
THE ORCHARD

MILL RD

Cargate Lane

The Rookery

GREENGATE

Croft House

The Windmill

2

HAWKSWORTH RD

Low Farm

Gundykes Plantation

BRECKS LA

MOOR LA

Hawksworth Road

DOGHILL LA

47

Longhedge Lane

Ash Holt

Lineham Plantation

LINEHAM LA

Brecks Plantation

1

Sewage Works

SPINNEY RD

Hill Farm

Flintham
Flintham Cty Prim Sch

WOODS LA

DEADWONG LA

46

74   D   75   E   76   F

153
139

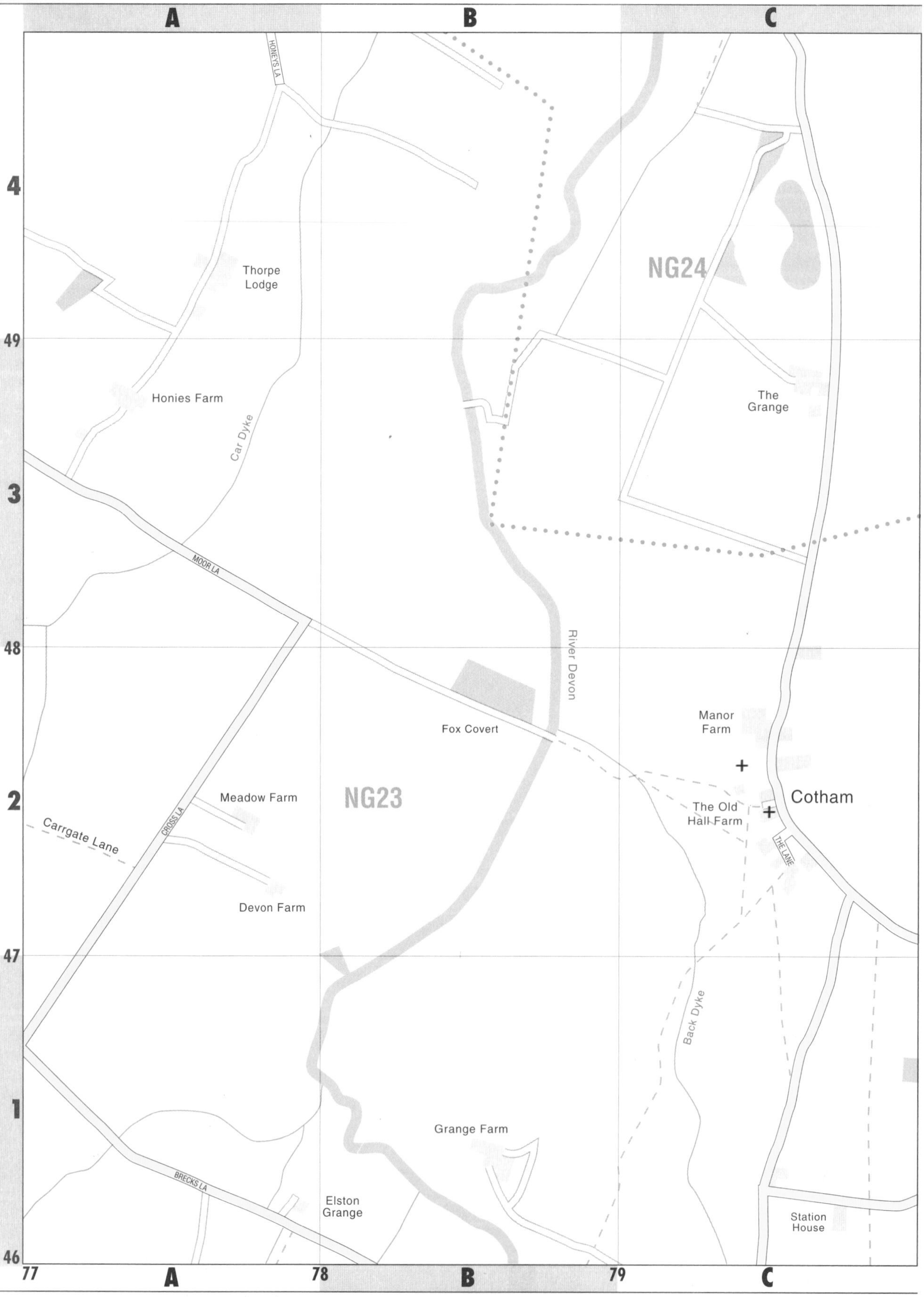
A
B
C
4
49
3
48
2
47
1
46
77
78
79
HONEY'S LA
Thorpe
Lodge
NG24
Honies Farm
The
Grange
Car Dyke
MOOR LA
River Devon
Manor
Farm
Fox Covert
Meadow Farm
NG23
Cotham
The Old
Hall Farm
Carrgate Lane
CROSS LA
THE LANE
Devon Farm
Back Dyke
Grange Farm
BRECKS LA
Elston
Grange
Station
House

153
168

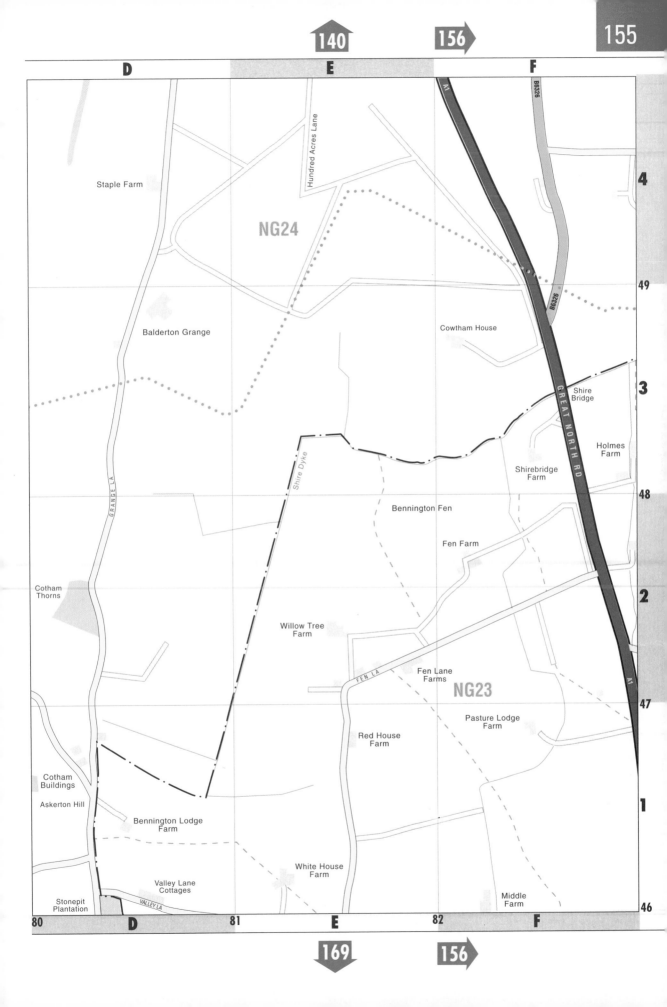

D
E
F

B6326

A1

4

Staple Farm

NG24

49

Hundred Acres Lane

Balderton Grange

Cowtham House

Shire Bridge

3

Holmes Farm

Shirebridge Farm

48

GREAT NORTH RD

Shire Dyke

Bennington Fen

Fen Farm

GRANGE LA

Cotham Thorns

2

Willow Tree Farm

Fen Lane Farms

NG23

FEN LA

Pasture Lodge Farm

47

Cotham Buildings

Red House Farm

A1

Askerton Hill

1

Bennington Lodge Farm

White House Farm

Valley Lane Cottages

Middle Farm

Stonepit Plantation

VALLEY LA

46

80
D
81
E
82
F

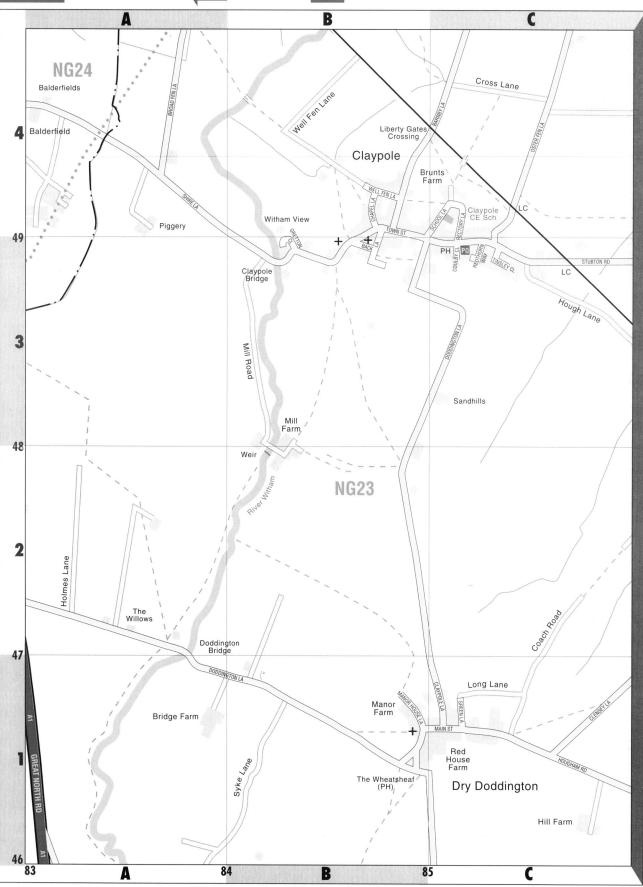

NG24

Balderfields

Balderfield

Piggery

Shire La

Broad Fen La

Well Fen Lane

Liberty Gates
Crossing

Claypole

Brunts
Farm

Cross Lane

Barnaby La

Oster Fen La

Witham View

Gretton Cl

Well Fen La

Chapel La

Town St

Back La

School La

Rectory La

Claypole
CE Sch

LC

Claypole
Bridge

PH   PO

Coulby Cl

Redthorn
Way

Tinsley Cl

Stubton Rd

LC

Hough Lane

Mill Road

Doddington La

Sandhills

Mill
Farm

Weir

River Witham

NG23

Holmes Lane

The
Willows

Doddington
Bridge

Doddington La

Bridge Farm

Coach Road

Long Lane

Manor
Farm

Manor House La

Claypole La

Green La

Clensey La

Main St

Red
House
Farm

Hougham Rd

A1

Great North Rd

Syke Lane

The Wheatsheaf
(PH)

Dry Doddington

Hill Farm

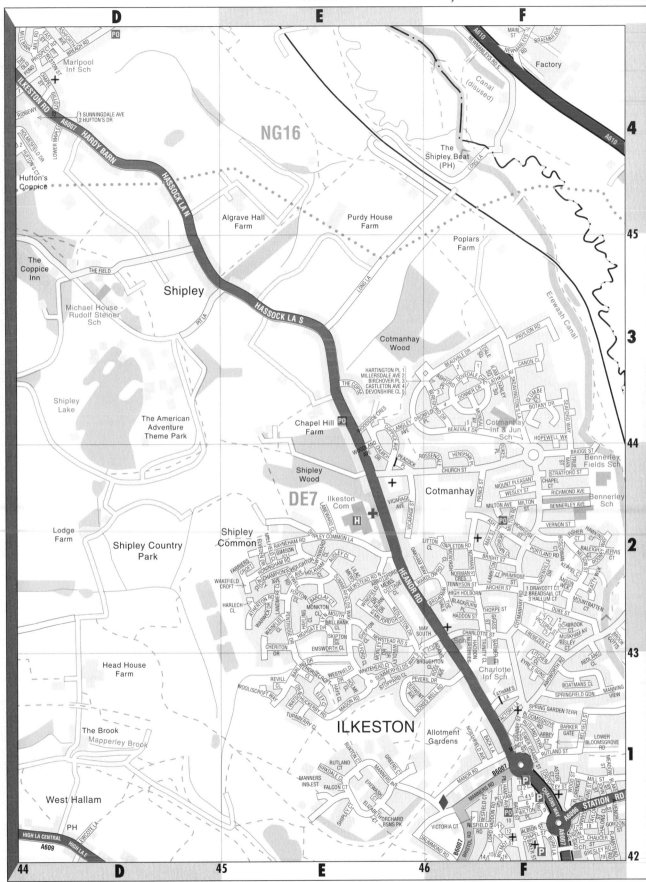

4

45

3

44

2

43

1

42

158 →

F1
1 BRUSSELS TERR
2 BURLEIGH ST
3 STAMFORD ST
4 ESSEX ST
5 DURHAM ST
6 NORTHGATE ST
7 WILTON ST
8 WEST TERR
9 NORTH ST
10 STATION CT
11 FULLWOOD AVE
12 PROVIDENCE PL
13 FULLWOOD ST
14 WHARNCLIFFE RD
15 JACKSON AVE
16 GREGORY ST
17 CHAPEL ST
18 LOWER CHAPEL ST
19 RIGLEY AVE

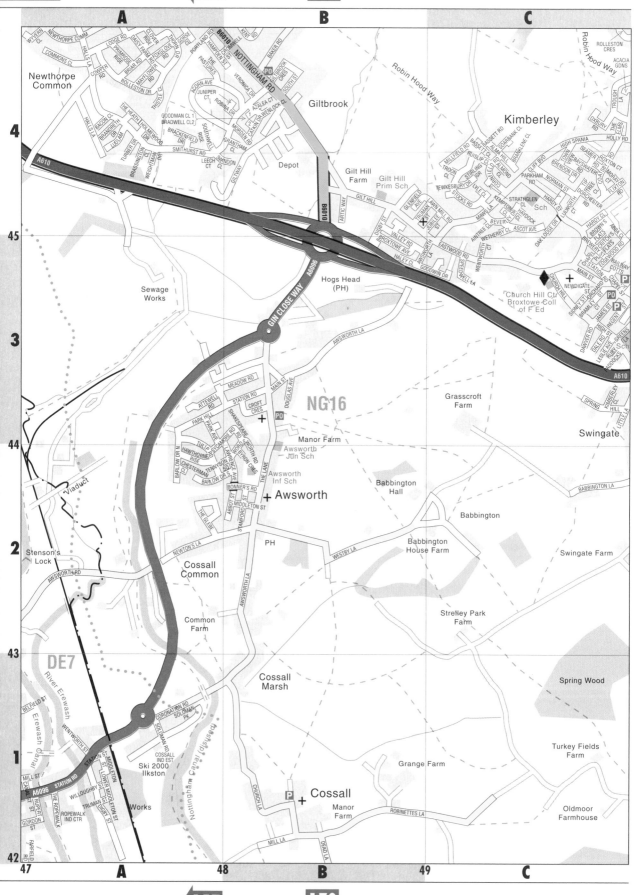

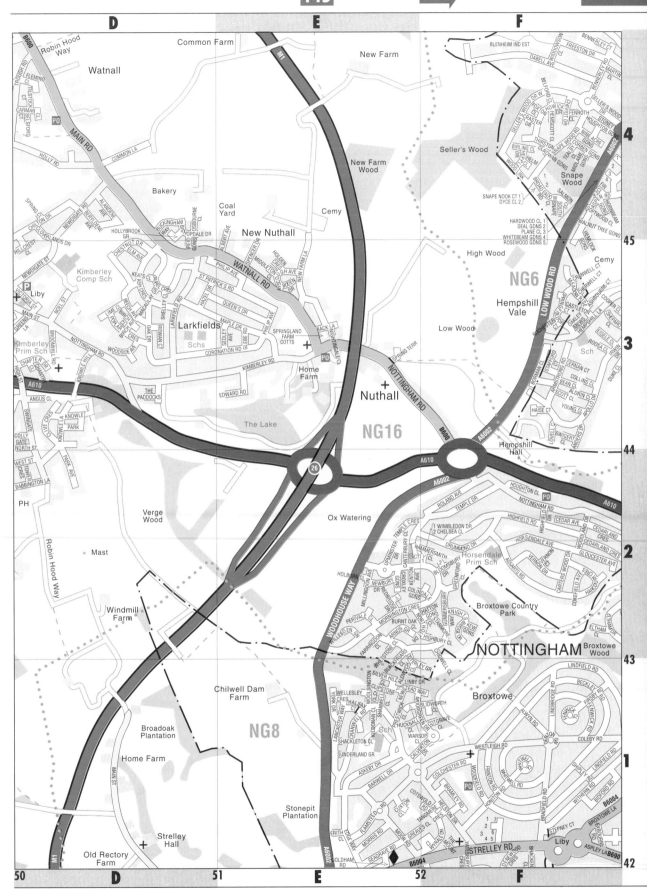

F1
1 ROSEMARY CL
2 LAVENDER CL
3 MAGNOLIA CL
4 HONEYSUCKLE CL
5 JASMINE CL
6 BRIDGE GREEN WALK
7 LILAC CL

160

A4	
1 MULBERRY GDNS	7 WAYFORD WLK
2 BACTON GDNS	8 DOWNING GDNS
3 ACLE GDNS	9 DUCHESS GDNS
4 CAWSTON GDNS	10 HARDWOOD CL
5 HETHERSETT GDNS	11 SKETCHLEY CT
6 HEMSBY GDNS	12 UTILE GDNS
	13 MUSTERS WLK

159

A4	
14 RUFFORD WLK	
15 BETHNAL WLK	
16 HAZELHURST GDNS	
17 STOCKTON ST	
18 DUKE ST	
19 COMMERCIAL RD	

146

A4	
20 TISHBITE ST	
21 PILKINGTON ST	
22 MARKET SIDE	
23 CALDER WLK	
24 BANK YD	

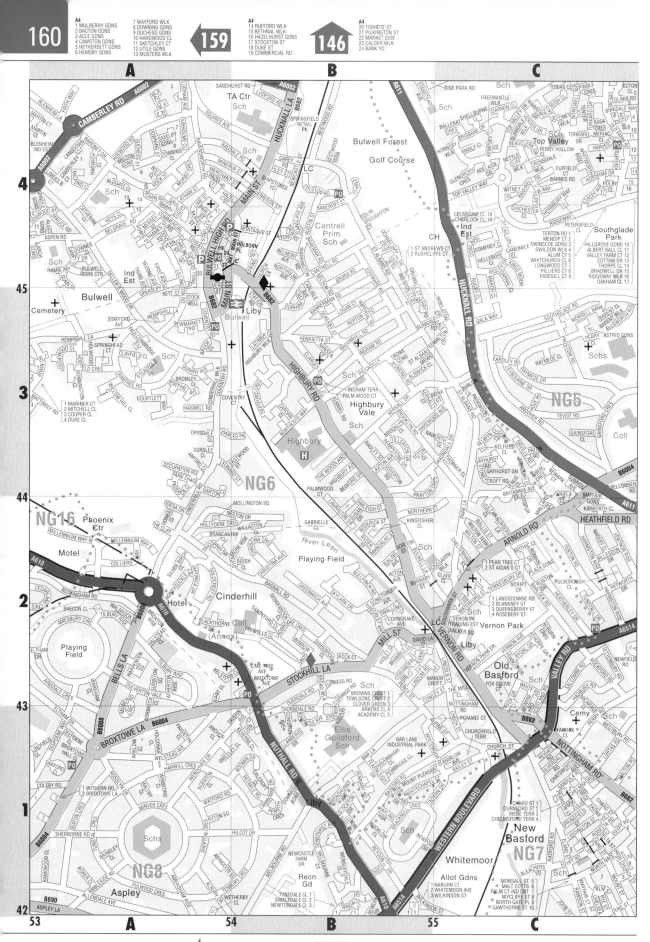

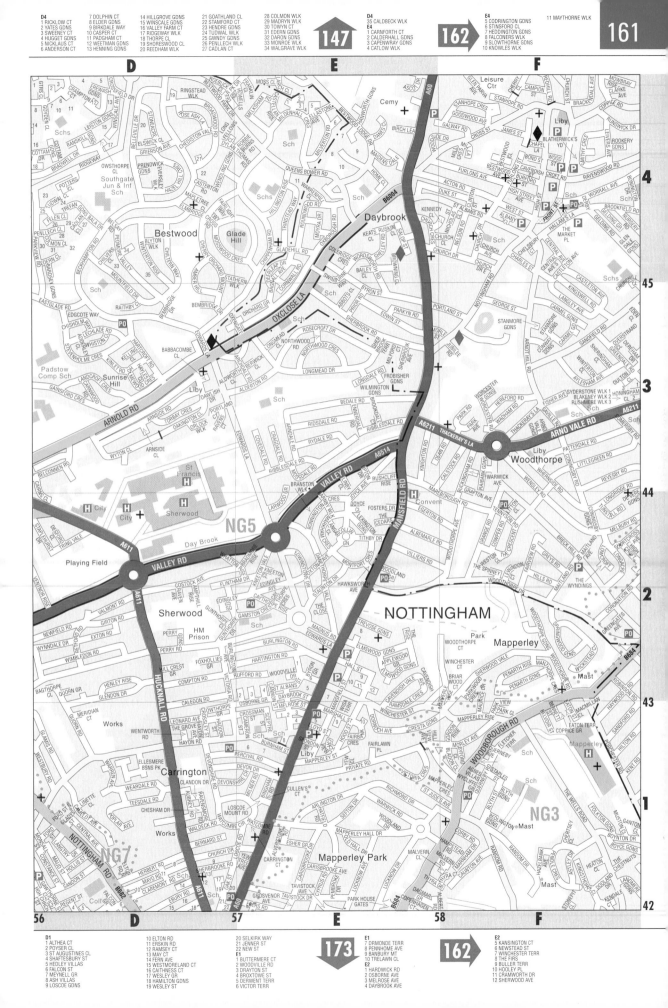

161 148

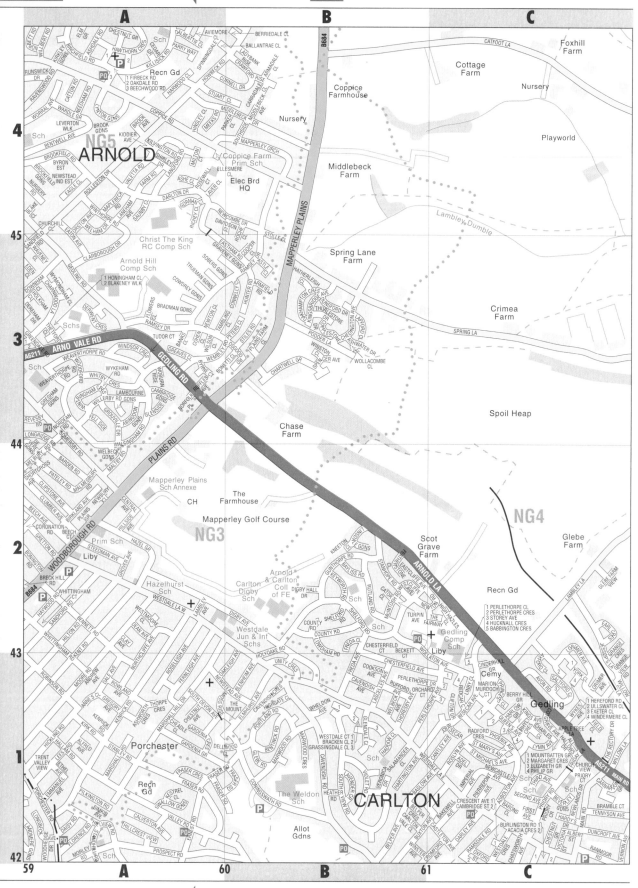

161 174

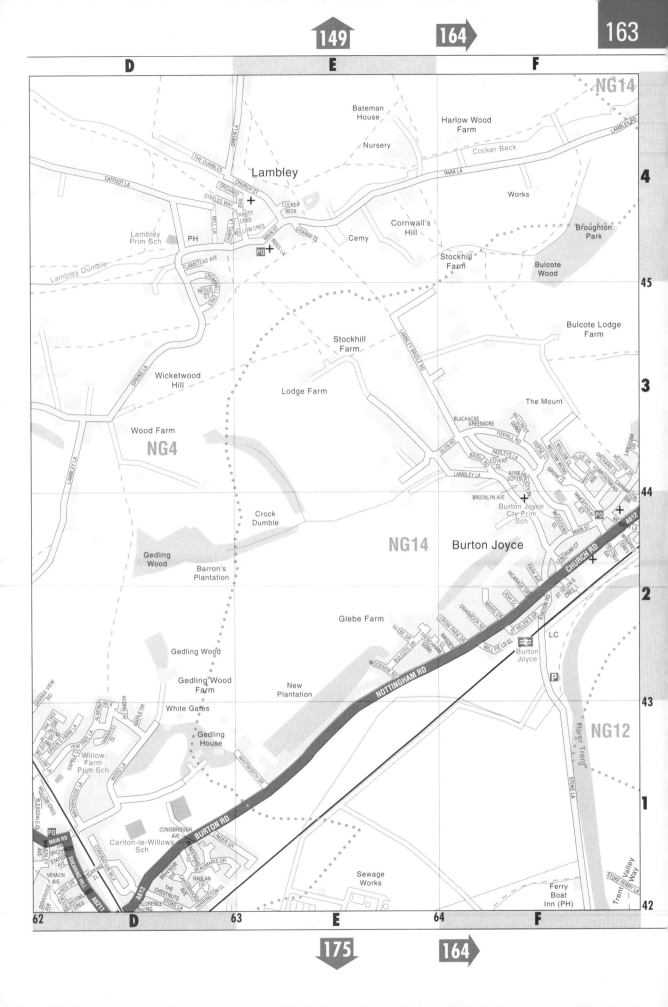

D   E   F

NG14

Bateman House

Harlow Wood Farm

Nursery

Cocker Beck

THE DUMBLES

CHURCH ST

GREEN LA

Lambley

PARK LA

Works

4

CATFOOT LA

ORCHARD

STEELES WAY

MILL CA

CHAPEL LA

TRINITY CRES

WILLOW CRES

RISE

Cocker Beck

Cornwall's Hill

Lambley Prim Sch

PH

FLAMSTEAD AVE

MAIN ST

ROSS LA

GRANGE CL

Cemy

Stockhill Farm

Broughton Park

PO

Bulcote Wood

Lambley Dumble

CROMWELL CRES

NEGUS CT

45

Bulcote Lodge Farm

SPRING LA

Wicketwood Hill

Stockhill Farm

LAMBLEY BRIDLE RD

The Mount

3

LAMBLEY LA

Lodge Farm

BLACKACRE GREENACRE

HILLCREST GDNS

FOXHILL RD

GLEN RD

BRIDLE RD

PADLEYS LA

COVERT CL

CORSE CL

WILLOW CL

OLIVE GR

ORCHARD CL

CARNARVON

LANGHAM DR

HILLSIDE DR

BROADMEAD

GROVE CL

Wood Farm

NG4

LAMBLEY LA

ROSE COTTS

BUSBY PL

MATLEY

AVE

44

Crock Dumble

BROOKLYN AVE

Burton Joyce Cty Prim Sch

WOODSEND

MAIN ST

PO

GLIM LA

A612

Gedling Wood

Barron's Plantation

NG14

Burton Joyce

LENDRUM CT

CHURCH RD

CHESTNUT

WHARF CRES

2

Gedling Wood

Glebe Farm

VICARAGE DR

PARK AVE

CRAGMOOR RD

MARIS DR

ASH CL

GT HELEN'S CR

STANTON RD

ST HELEN'S CRES

LC

Gedling Wood Farm

WOODSIDE RD

BULCOTE DR

GLEBE DR

TRENCHAM

MASSEY

CROW PARK DR

MILL FIELD CL

Burton Joyce

P

43

White Gates

New Plantation

NOTTINGHAM RD

River Trent

NG12

GRANGE VIEW RD

OAK TREE DR

JAYNE CL

ALM CL

SAPELE CL

ALMOND

WLK

YEW TREE LA

GREEN'S FARM LA

ACORN DR

TAMARLT CL

MAPLE DR

WOOD LA

WHITWORTH DR

Gedling House

STOKE LA

1

WILLOW LA

WATERHOUSE LA

WILLOW CRES

BLEASDALE CL

Willow Farm Prim Sch

CONISBROUGH AVE

BURTON RD

LINDEN GR

PO

MAIN RD

THE ORCHARDS

STATION AVE

WAVERLEY AVE

SHEARING HILL

HDS DR

CORONATION WLK

Carlton-le-Willows Sch

BRAEMAR DR

CARISBROOK

RAGLAN DR

THE CHESTNUTS

HARRINGTON CL

Sewage Works

STOKE FERRY LA

Trent Valley Way

Ferry Boat Inn (PH)

VERNON AVE

DOVERIDGE AVE

A612

A6211

BEAUMARIS DR

STOKE LA

FLORENCE RD

STOKE VALLEY WAY

42

62   D   63   E   64   F

163

150

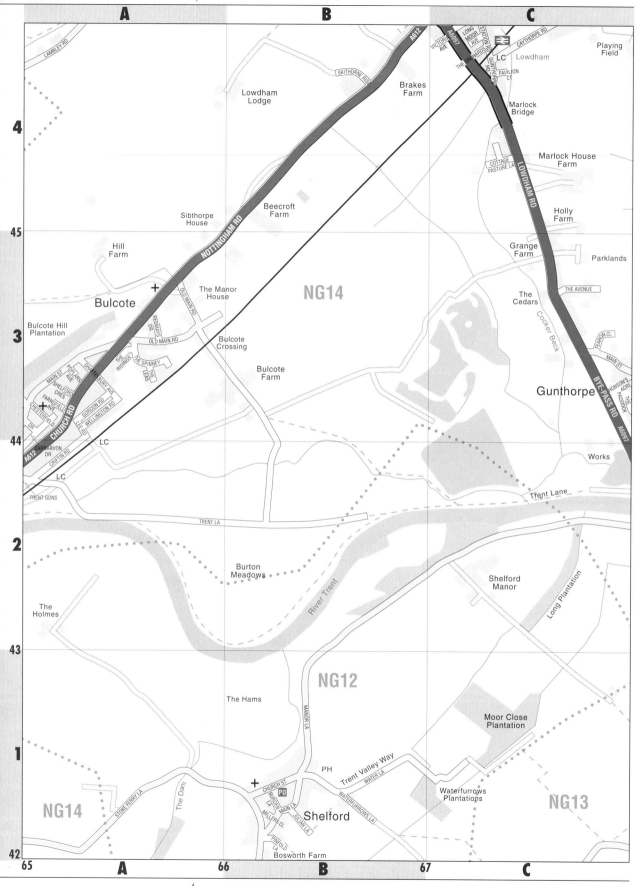

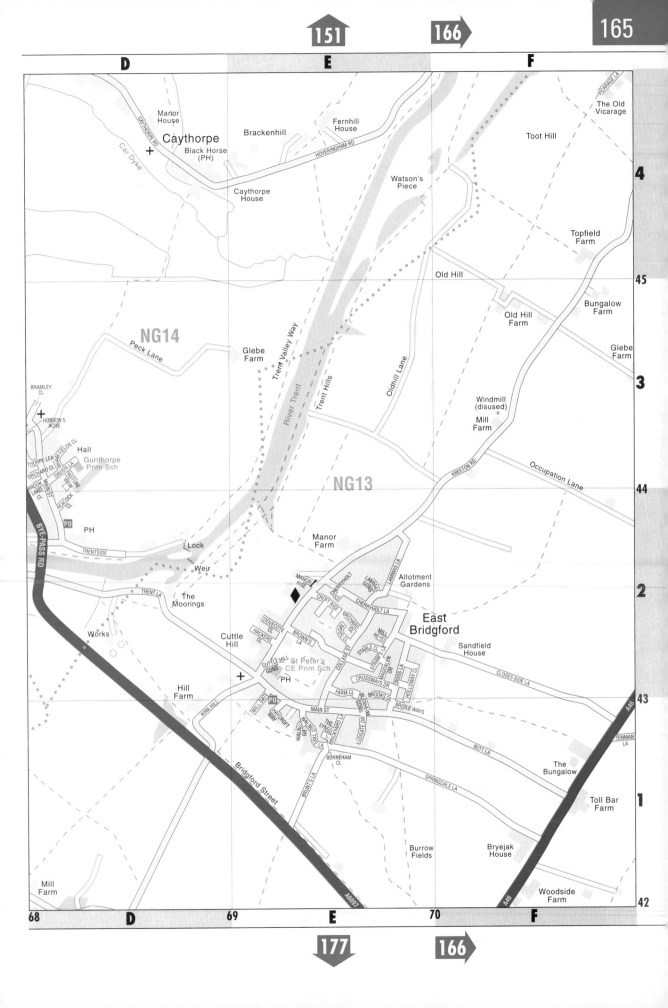

165
152

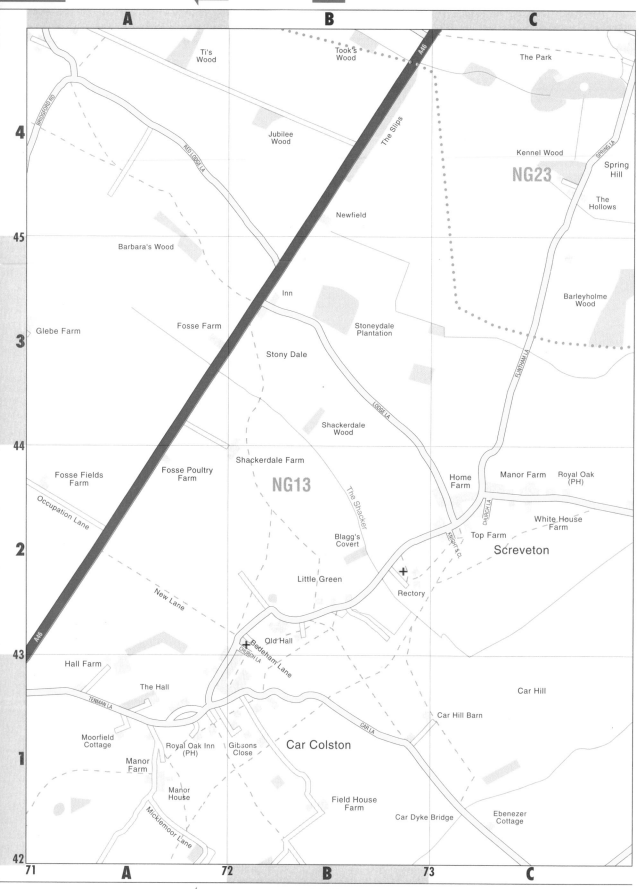

165
178

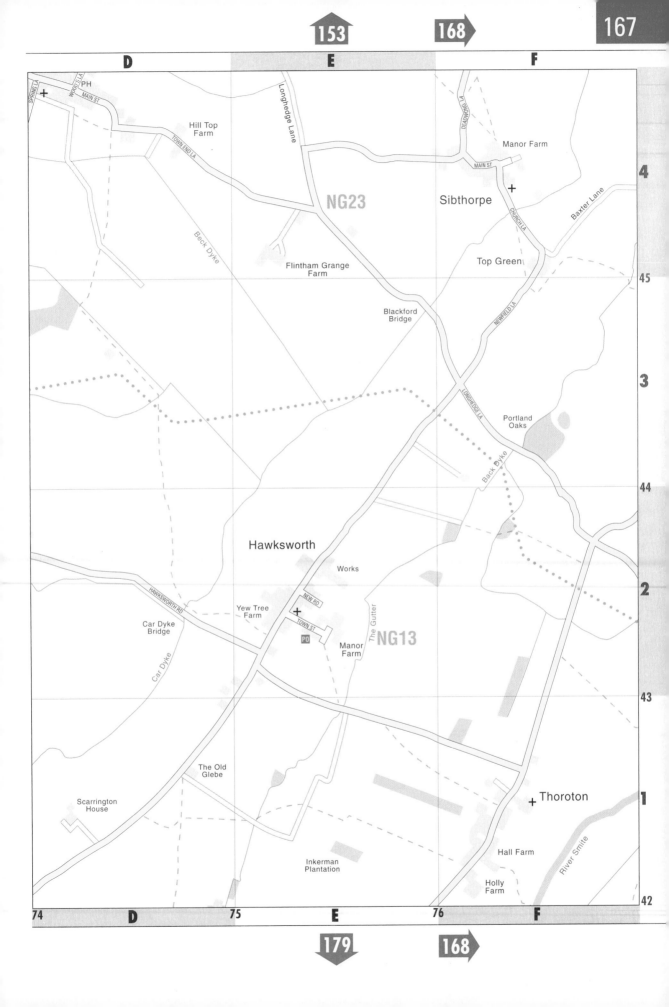

D
E
F

NG23

Hill Top Farm

SPRING LA

WOOD'S LA

PH

MAIN ST

TOWN END LA

Longhedge Lane

DEADWONG LA

Manor Farm

MAIN ST

Sibthorpe

4

CHURCH LA

Baxter Lane

Beck Dyke

Flintham Grange Farm

Top Green

45

Blackford Bridge

NEWFIELD LA

3

LONGHEDGE LA

Portland Oaks

Back Dyke

44

Hawksworth

Works

HAWKSWORTH RD

2

Yew Tree Farm

NEW RD

The Gutter

NG13

Car Dyke Bridge

TOWN ST

PO

Manor Farm

Car Dyke

43

The Old Glebe

Scarrington House

Thoroton

1

Inkerman Plantation

Hall Farm

River Smite

Holly Farm

42

74

D

75

E

76

F

167
154

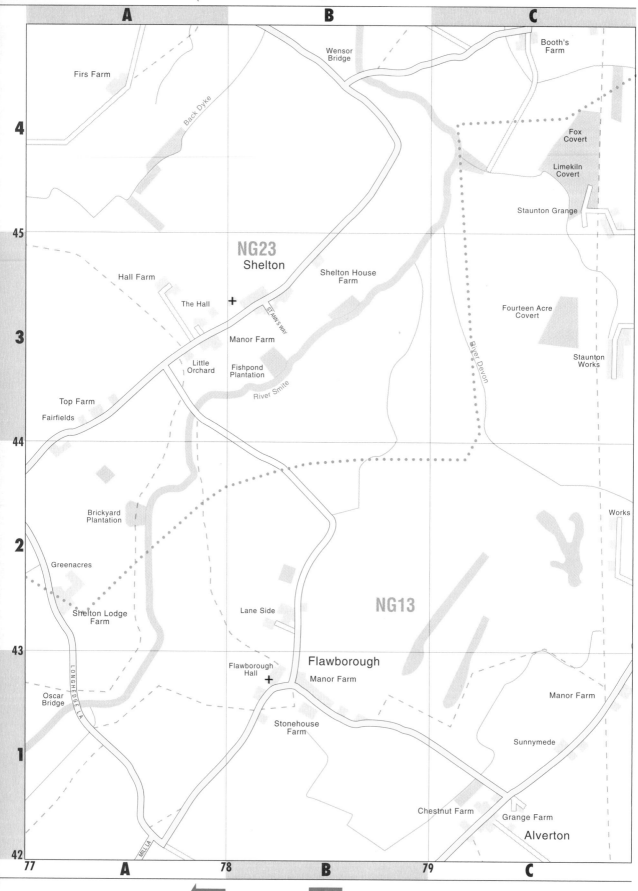

A B C

Firs Farm

Wensor Bridge

Booth's Farm

Back Dyke

4

Fox Covert

Limekiln Covert

45

Staunton Grange

NG23

Shelton

Hall Farm

Shelton House Farm

The Hall +

ST ANN'S WAY

Fourteen Acre Covert

3

Manor Farm

River Devon

Staunton Works

Little Orchard

Fishpond Plantation

Top Farm

River Smite

Fairfields

44

Works

Brickyard Plantation

2

Greenacres

NG13

Shelton Lodge Farm

Lane Side

43

Flawborough

LONGHEDGE LA

Flawborough Hall +

Manor Farm

Oscar Bridge

Manor Farm

Stonehouse Farm

Sunnymede

1

Chestnut Farm

Grange Farm

MILL LA

Alverton

42

77 A 78 B 79 C

167
180

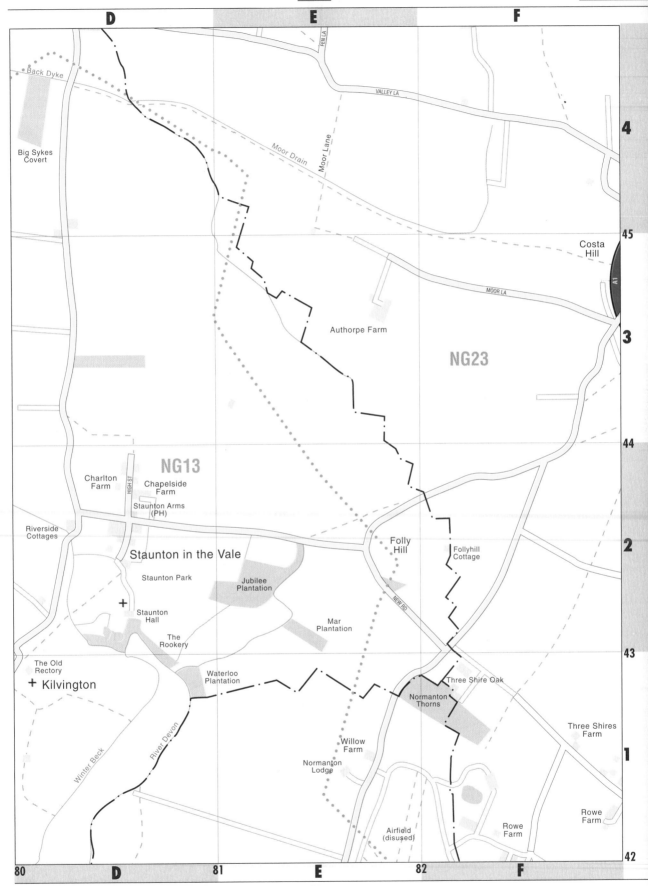

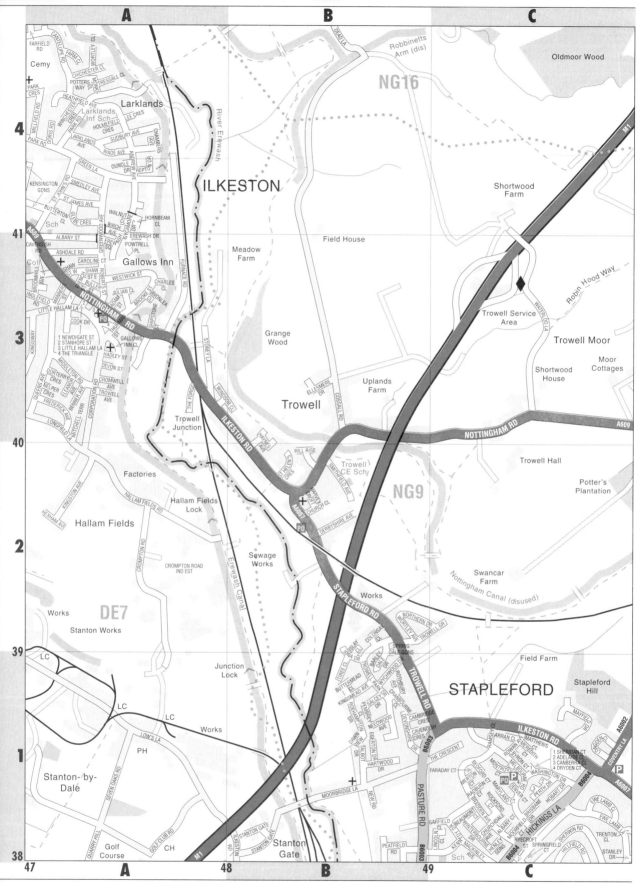

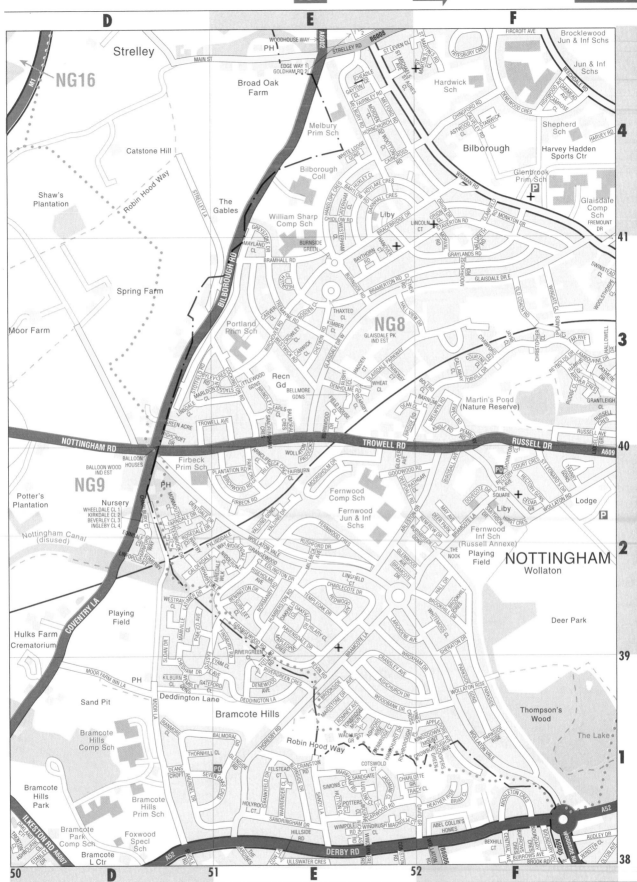

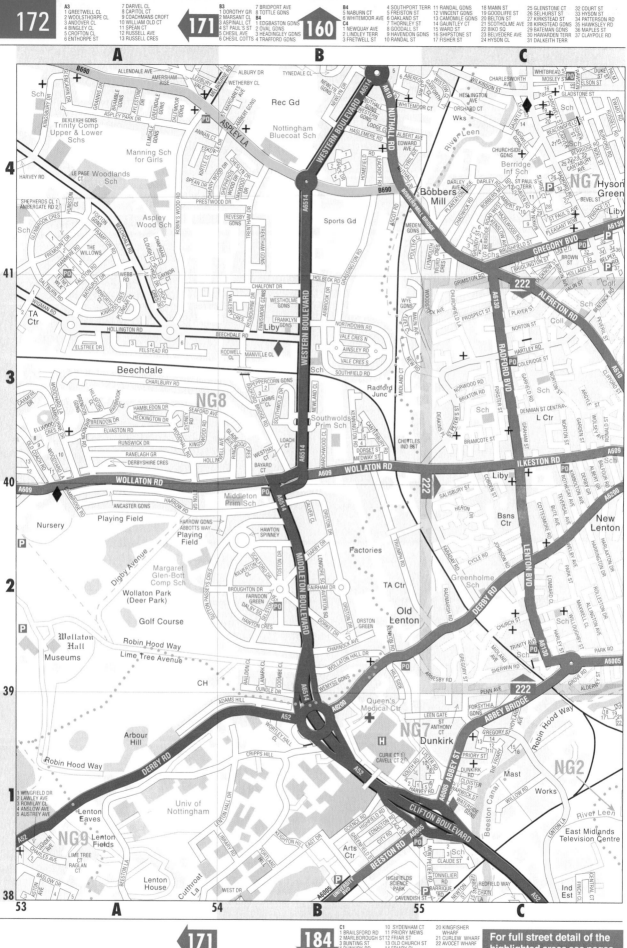

171 160

171 184

For full street detail of the highlighted areas see pages 222 and 223.

D4		
1 HIGH CHURCH ST	7 MYRTLE AVE	14 COLVILLE VILLAS
2 BRADGATE RD	8 ARNO AVE	15 COLVILLE TERR
3 TISSINGTON CL	9 NEWBURY CT	
4 LAURIE CL	10 PELHAM CT	**E4**
5 STANLEY AVE	11 CLARENDON CT	1 DENMARK GR
6 LESLIE AVE	12 AENEAS CT	2 RAVENSDENE CT
	13 MANSFIELD ST	3 MAPPERLEY PARK DR

4 SYCAMORE PL	11 LORNE WLK	18 PLOWRIGHT CT
5 MELVILLE CT	12 CHEVERTON CT	19 BOWERS AVE
6 FOTHERGILL ST	13 CRANMER GR	**F3**
7 EGERTON WLK	14 LITTLE JOHN WLK	1 SARGENT GDNS
8 BANGOR WLK	15 FOUNTAIN DALE CT	2 JOHN CARROLL CT
9 CONWAY WLK	16 VERBENA CL	3 MASSEY GDNS
10 LORNE CL	17 PLOWRIGHT CT	4 NORTHAMPTON ST

161

F3	
5 CENTRAL ST	
6 NUGENT GDNS	
7 HAWK RIDGE GDNS	
8 ROBIN HOOD IND EST	
9 ABERDEEN ST	
10 AVE E	

174

F3		17 ST CUTHBERT'S RD
11 LONGDEN ST		18 CHEDWORTH CL
12 ST LUKE'S ST		19 CARDIFF ST
13 ASHLEY ST		20 BILBY GDNS
14 KINGSTON ST		21 GRANVILLE GR
15 STONEBRIDGE CT IND EST		22 SWINBURNE ST
16 HAWKSWORTH ST		23 GRANVILLE CT

173

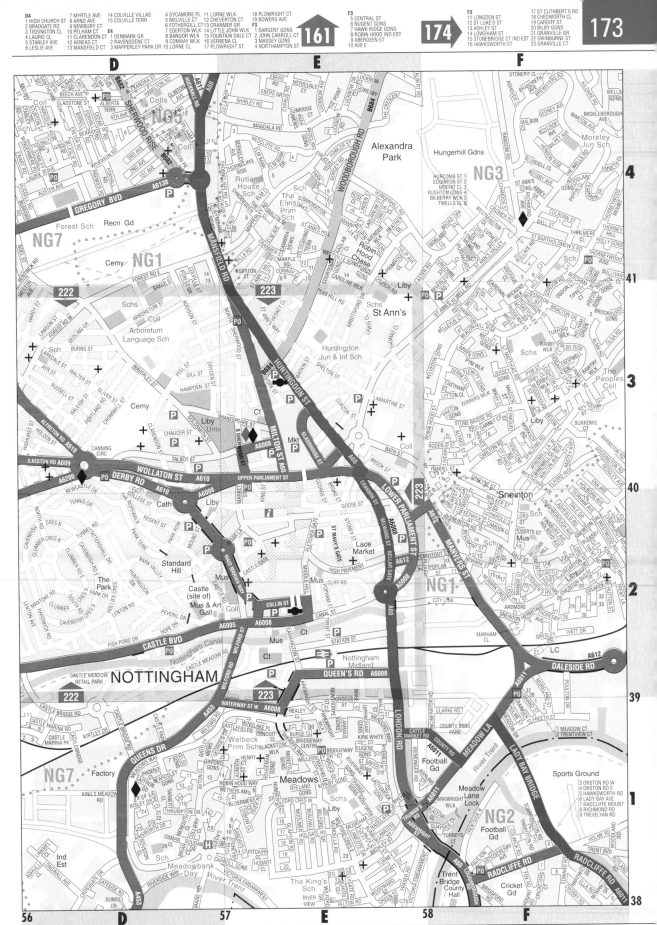

D1				
1 KINGFISHER WHARF	10 MIDDLE FURLONG MEWS	20 BARRA MEWS		
2 DUNLIN WHARF	11 MIDDLE FURLONG GDNS	21 HAWTHORN CL		
3 PLOVER WHARF	12 LYBSTER MEWS	22 HAWTHORN CL		
4 TEAL WHARF	13 BALFRON GDNS	23 HATLEY CL		
5 FLAMINGO CT	14 STROME CL	24 CASTLETON CL		
6 LAWRENCE WAY	15 MICKLEDEN CL	25 AMMER CL		
7 LOTHMORE CT	16 GLARAMARA CL	26 BOSWORTH WLK		
8 CRAMMOND CL	17 FERNGILL CL	**E1**		
9 CROMARTY CT	18 LOUGHRIGG CL	1 STROME CT		
	19 CAUSEWAY MEWS	2 LEVICK CT		

3 BRANKSOME CT	13 WILLOWBROOK CT	
4 BURTON MANDERFIELD CT	14 SWEET LEYS RD	
5 HETHBETH CT	15 BARNSLEY TERR	
6 HOOPERS WLK	16 BARNSLEY TERR	
7 HELVELLYN CL	17 CONGSBROUGH TERR	
8 REMON CT	18 DONCASTER TERR	
9 DOYNE CT	19 ECKINGTON TERR	
10 CAVAN CT	20 FERRIBY TERR	
11 BLAIR CT	21 CHURCH MEWS	
12 ARNE CT	22 PAVILION CL	

185

E1	
23 DISEWORTH GR	
24 WHICKHAM CT	
25 PRUDHOE CT	
26 KESWICK CT	
27 NORTH ST	
F2	
1 WEST WLK	
2 HAYWOOD CT	
3 KESWICK CT	
4 NORTH ST	
5 MORLEY CT	
6 HENRY ST	
7 BYRON CT	
8 HARTFORD CL	
9 MANVERS CT	

10 THORESBY ST	20 SANDRINGHAM RD	30 THURGARTON AVE
11 EVELYN ST	21 JUBILEE ST	31 ST CHRISTOPHER ST
12 LOWER ELDON ST	22 PULLMAN RD	32 DAVIDSON ST
13 MILLVERY CT	23 VICTORIA AVE	33 CARLTON FOLD
14 AINSLEY CT	24 MILLVIEW CL	34 HOTEN RD
15 LOWREY AVE	25 ST STEPHEN'S AVE	35 BECKFORD RD
16 NEWARK AVE	26 HERMITAGE SQ	36 RADBOURNE RD
17 MANOR AVE	27 MEADOW LA	37 MORELAND ST
18 PERLETHORPE AVE	28 LINDUM GR	38 MORELAND PL
19 DURHAM CT	29 COSBY RD	

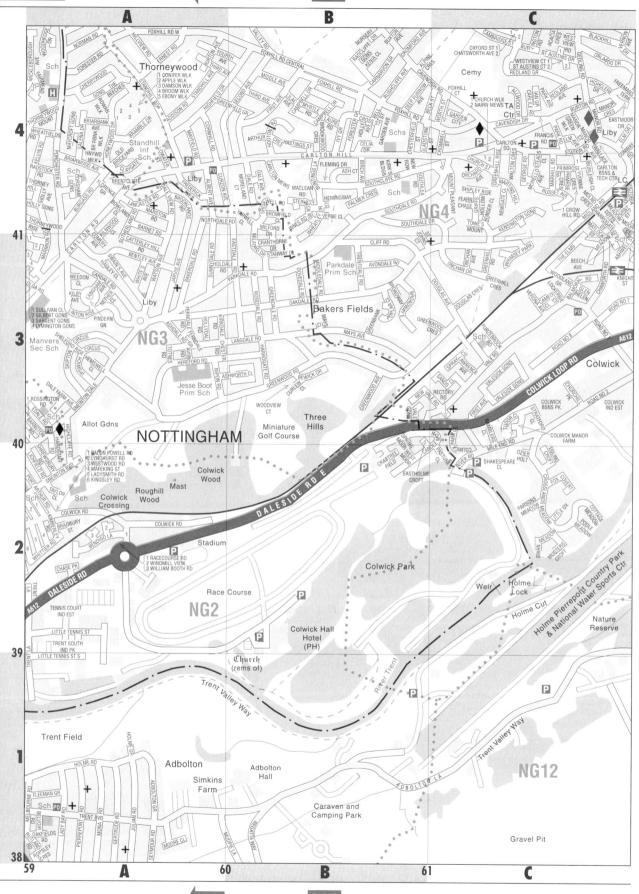

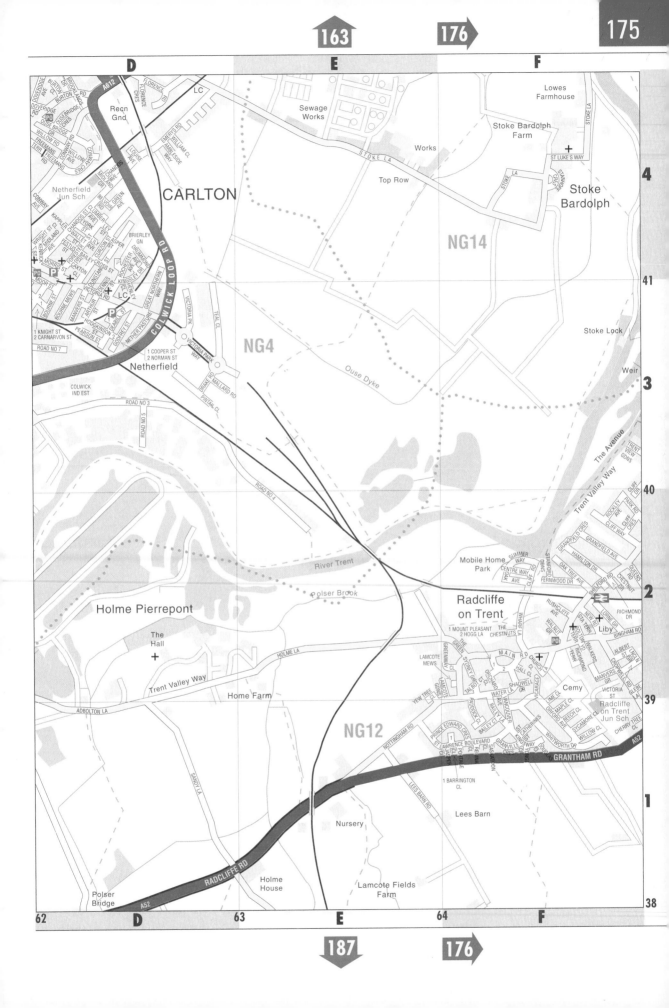

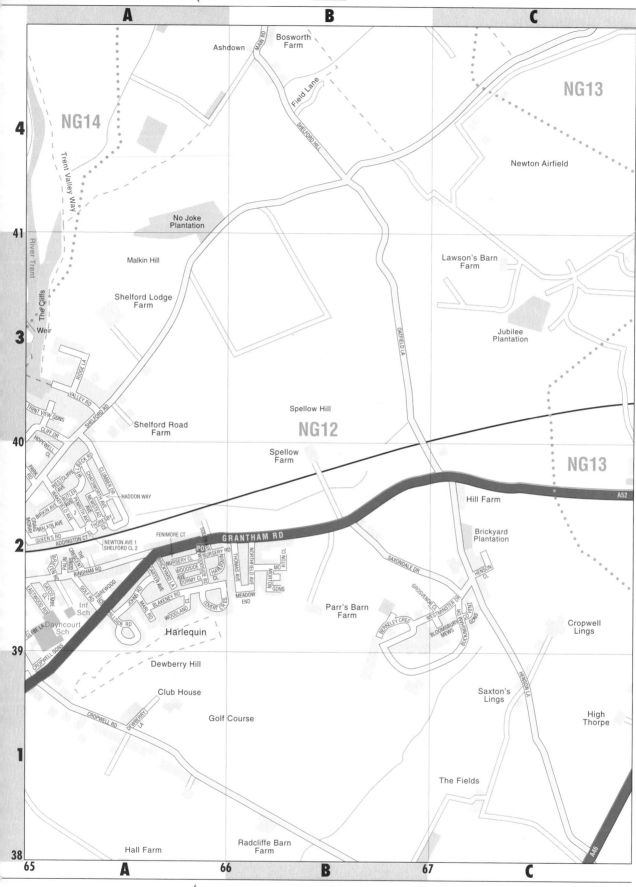

A   B   C

NG14

NG13

Trent Valley Way

River Trent

Ashdown

Bosworth Farm

MAIN RD

Field Lane

SHELFORD HILL

Newton Airfield

No Joke Plantation

Malkin Hill

Shelford Lodge Farm

The Cliffs

Weir

Lawson's Barn Farm

OATFIELD LA

Jubilee Plantation

RIDGE LA

VALLEY RD

SHELFORD RD

Shelford Road Farm

Spellow Hill

NG12

TRENT VIEW GDNS

CLIFF DR

HOPEWELL CL

Spellow Farm

NG13

A52

PARK RD

BECK RD

WEST CLIFFE RD

WINKFIELD AVE

BUTLER

CLUMBER DR

CHESWORTH AVE

HADDON WAY

NEWSTEAD

MERRITT AVE

THORESBY

Hill Farm

Brickyard Plantation

CRAIG MORAY

BIRKIN AVE

MALKIN AVE

QUEEN'S RD

ADDINGTON CT

FENIMORE CT

NEWTON AVE 1
SHELFORD CL 2

GRANTHAM RD

PO

NURSERY CL

NURSERY RD

SOUTH

WOODSIDE AVE

DORMY CL

HARLE

THOMAS AVE

NORTHFIELD AVE

RTN CL

MO

MORTON

GDNS

SAXONDALE DR

HENSON CL

HENSON LA

BINGHAM RD

THE CRESCENT

PATH

BARLOW RD

GOLF RD

HAREWOOD CL

JOHNS RD

CARTER AVE

BRICKYARD LA

BLAKENEY RD

MARL RD

WOODLAND CL

COVERT CRES

MEADOW END

Parr's Barn Farm

BERKELEY CRES

GROSVENOR CL

BLOOMSBURY MEWS

WESTMINSTER DR

BUCKINGHAM

BUCKINGHAM GDNS

Cropwell Lings

EASTWOOD CL

GATCOMBE CL

GLEBE LA

Inf Sch

Dayncourt Sch

HILLSIDE RD

Harlequin

CROPWELL GDNS

Dewberry Hill

Club House

CROPWELL RD

DEWBERRY LA

Golf Course

Saxton's Lings

HENSON LA

High Thorpe

The Fields

A46

Hall Farm

Radcliffe Barn Farm

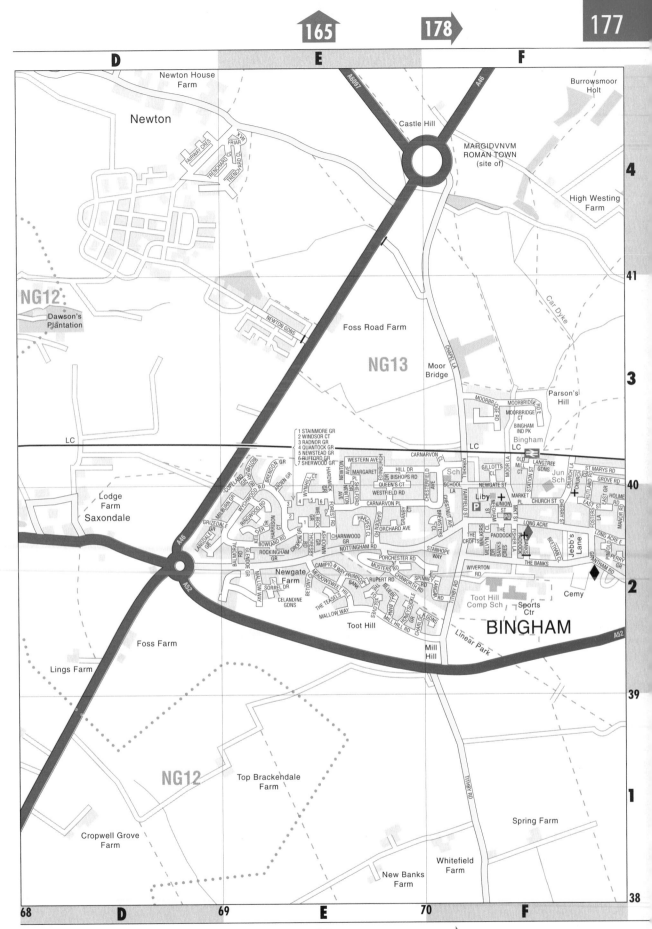

A B C

4

Thoroughfare
Holt

Bottom
Plantation

Longmoor La

The Old
Vicarage

Hall

Hawksworth Rd

Scarrington

Manor
Farm

Main St

The Saucers

41

Holme
Farm

New La

Mill La

3

Sewage
Works

Moor La

NG13

Abbey La

Sch

Abbey
Farm

Walnut

Fields Dr

The Capes

Abbey Cl

LC

Grove Rd

Priors Cl

Browns Rd

St Marys
Rd

Abbey Rd

Victoria R

Carr R

Douglas Rd

40

Butt Rd

Cogley La

Nursery Rd

Carr Banes Rd

LC

Aslockton
Hall

Holme
Rd

Crow Ct

Carnarvon
Prim Sch

Brocker
Farm

Green Wlk

Beverleys
Ave

Long
Acre E

Rowan Cl

Larch Cl

Poplar Cl

Aspen Cl

Oak Ave

Holly

Nursery

Smite Cl

Cottage Ave

Dark La

Raymond Dr

Ash Cl

Cedar
Cl

Willow Rd

Maple
Cl

Juniper

Beech
Ave

Blackthorn Cl

HM Young Offender
Institution

Sewage
Works

2

Elm A

Hazel Cl

Derry La

Grantham Rd

Belvoir
Cl

Cromwell Rd

Cranmer A

Sycamore Cl

A52

Grantham Rd

A52

Aslockton
Grange

39

River Smite

Granby La

Conery La

1

Starnhill
Farm

Thorough
Bridge

Starnhill
Plantation

Vicars
Croft

38

71 A 72 B 73 C

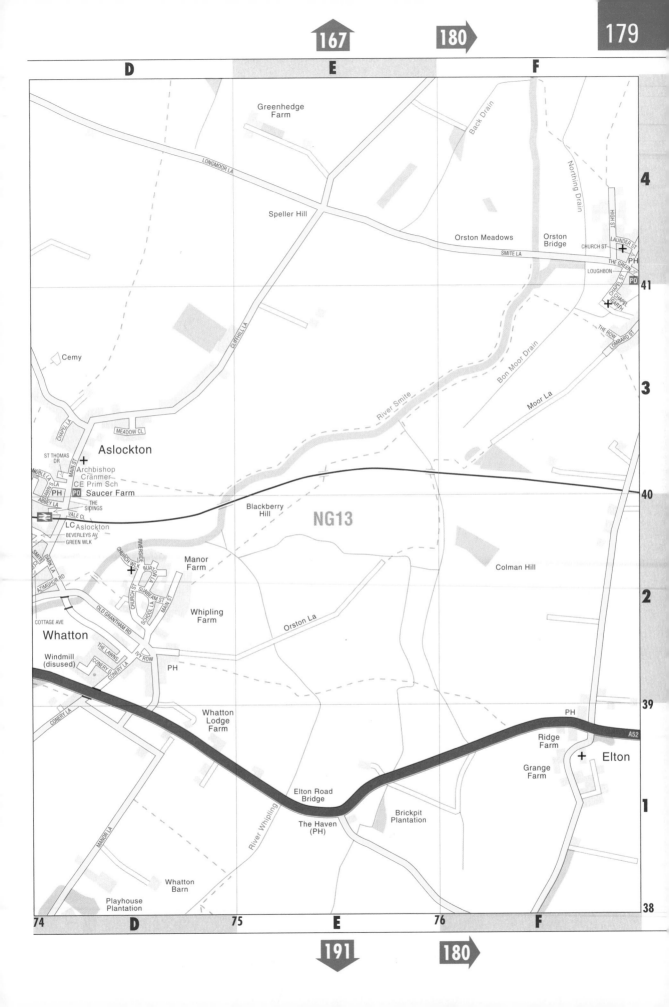

← 179
↑ 168

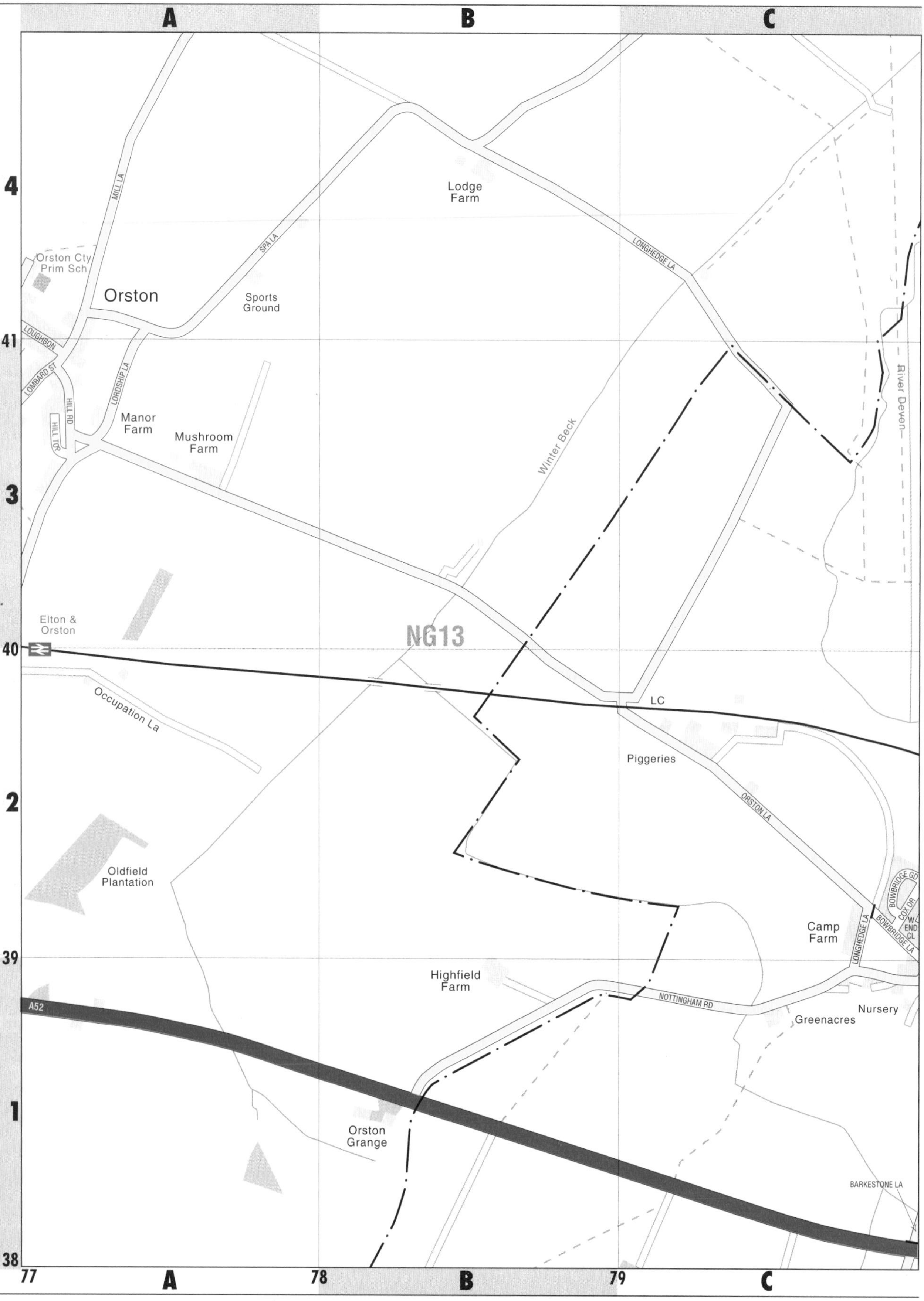

A   **B**   **C**

4

Lodge Farm

LONGHEDGE LA

MILL LA

SPA LA

Orston Cty Prim Sch

Orston

Sports Ground

41

LOUGHBOM

LOMBARD ST

LORDSHIP LA

HILL RD

HILL TOP

Manor Farm

Mushroom Farm

Winter Beck

River Devon

3

Elton & Orston

NG13

40

⊞

Occupation La

LC

Piggeries

ORSTON LA

2

Oldfield Plantation

Camp Farm

LONGHEDGE LA

BOWBRIDGE GD

COW LA

W. END

BOWBRIDGE LA

39

Highfield Farm

NOTTINGHAM RD

Nursery

Greenacres

A52

1

Orston Grange

BARKESTONE LA

38

77   **A**   **78**   **B**   **79**   **C**

← 179
↓ 192

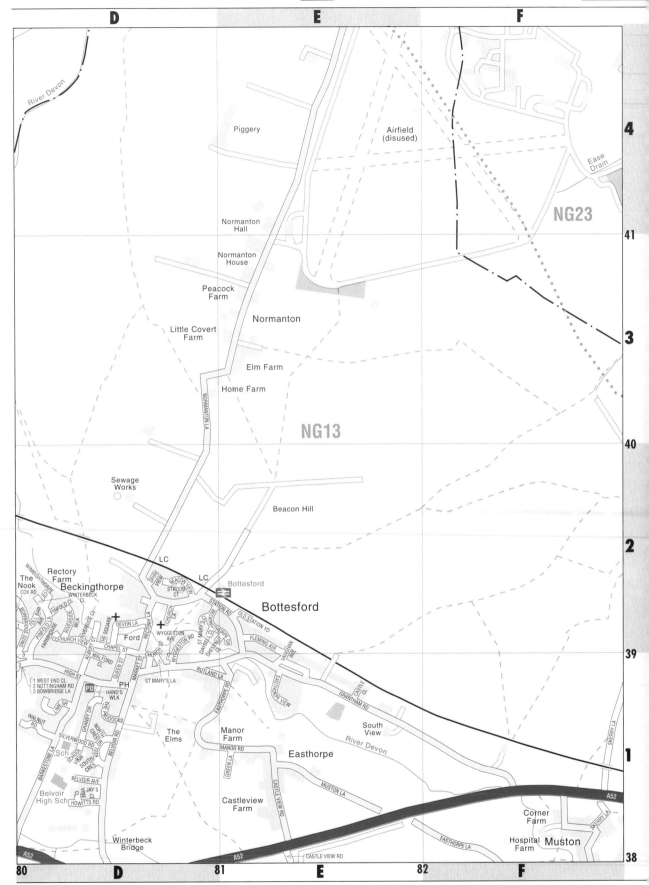

4

NG23

41

River Devon

Piggery

Airfield
(disused)

Ease
Drain

Normanton
Hall

Normanton
House

Peacock
Farm

Little Covert
Farm

Normanton

NG13

3

Elm Farm

NORMANTON LA

Home Farm

40

Sewage
Works

Beacon Hill

2

Rectory
Farm

LC

The
Nook
COX RD

Beckingthorpe

SPIRE VIEW

LC

BEACON VIEW

STROUD CT

Bottesford

WIMBRIGHTHORPE

WINTERBECK

PINFOLD CL

TOLL BAR

PINFOLD LA

RIVERSIDE CL

Bottesford

DEVON LA

THE SQUARE

CHURCH LA

Ford

CHURCH ST

RECTORY LA

ST MARY'S CH

WYGGESTON
AVE

STATION RD

DARBELL CH

OLD STATION YD

FLEMING AVE

VAUGHAN AVE

BOWBRIDGE LA

FARMHOUSE

CHURCH VIEW

ALBERT ST

WALFORD CL

CHAPEL ST

QUEEN ST

MARKET ST

CHURCH ST

RUTLAND LA

CHESTNUT DR

EASTHORPE RD

CASTLE CL

39

HIGH ST

1 WEST END CL
2 NOTTINGHAM RD
3 BOWBRIDGE LA

PD

PH

HAND'S WLK

ST MARY'S LA

EASTHORPE VIEW

GRANTHAM RD

WALNUT
RD

LANE GR

GRANBY DR

THE PADDOCKS

NORTH CRES

BELVOIR RD

The
Elms

Manor
Farm

South
View

River Devon

Easthorpe

SILVERWOOD CL

BARKESTONE LA

Sch

SCHOOL

SOUTH VIEW

KEEP

BELVOIR AVE

MANOR RD

GREEN LA

MUSTON LA

SKERRY LA

A52

Belvoir
High Sch

JAY'S CL

VINE CL

HOWITTS RD

Castleview
Farm

CASTLE VIEW RD

Corner
Farm

SKERRY LA

A52

Winterbeck
Bridge

A52

CASTLE VIEW RD

EASTHORPE LA

Hospital
Farm

Muston

1

38

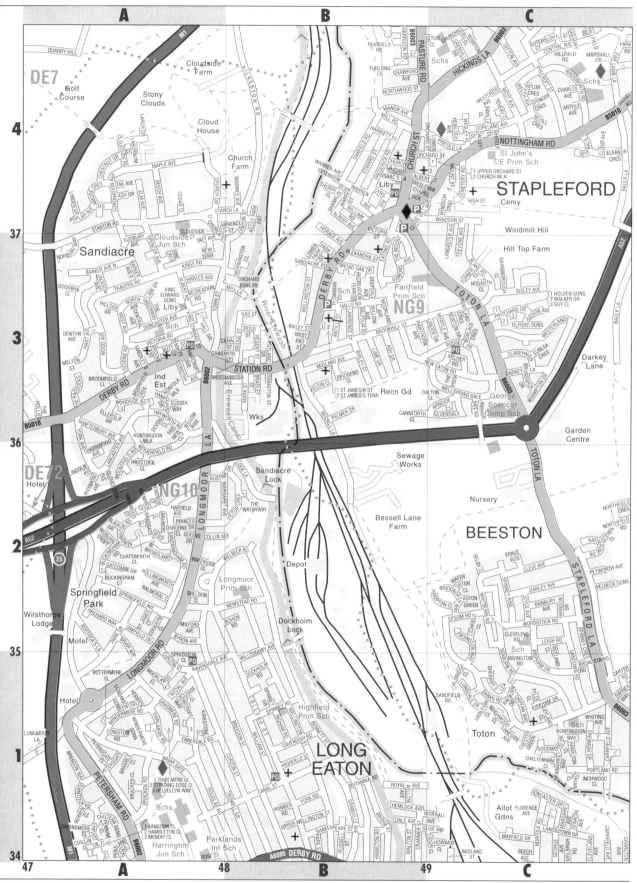

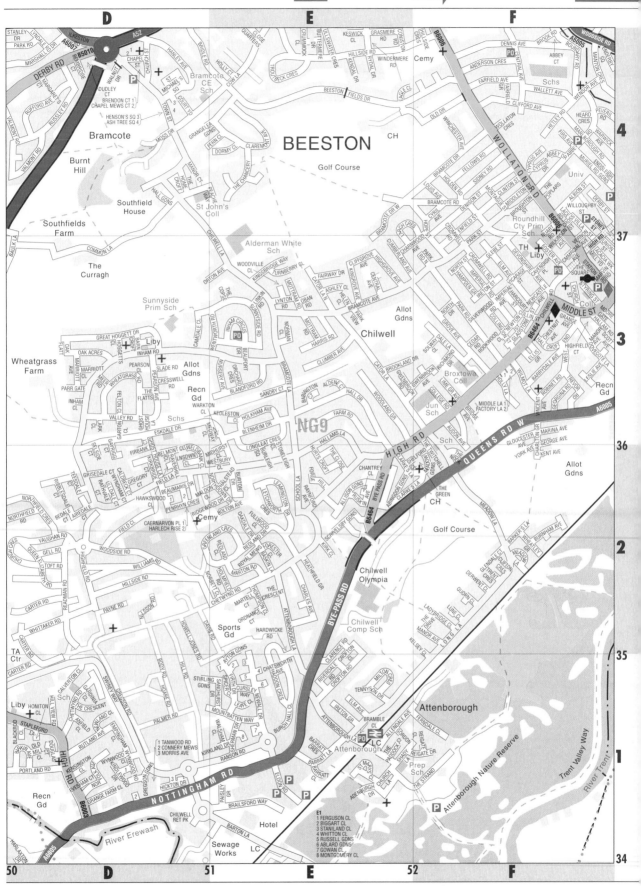

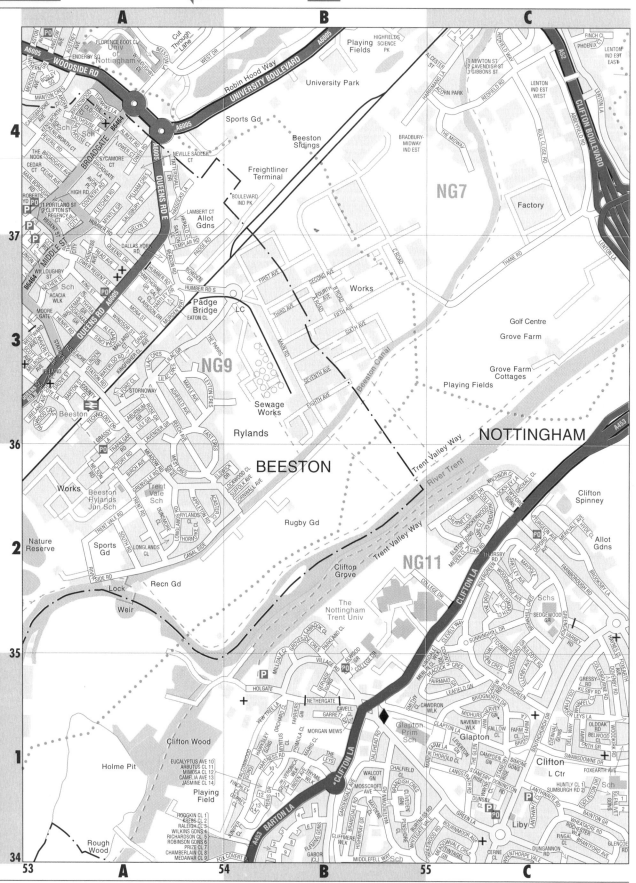

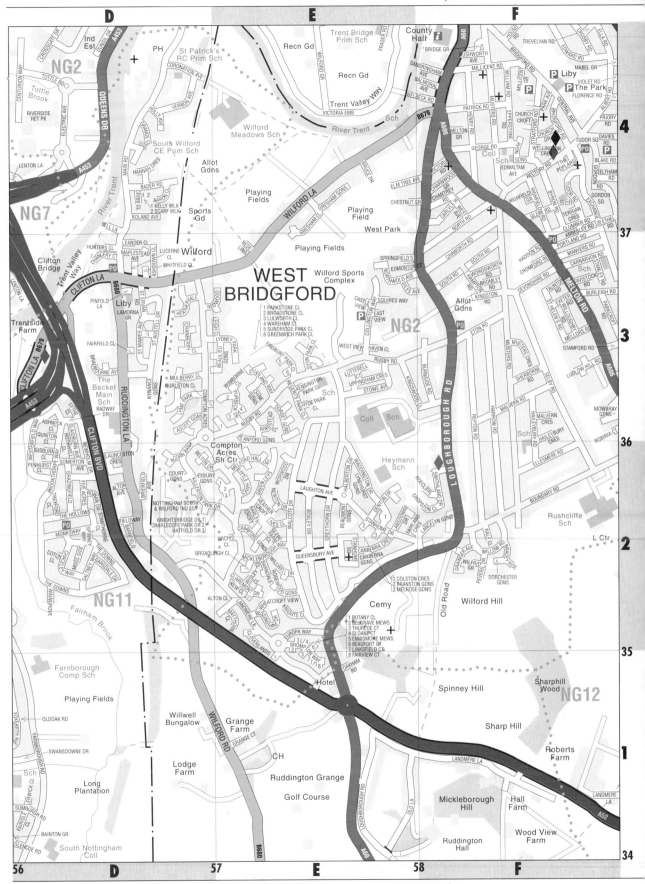

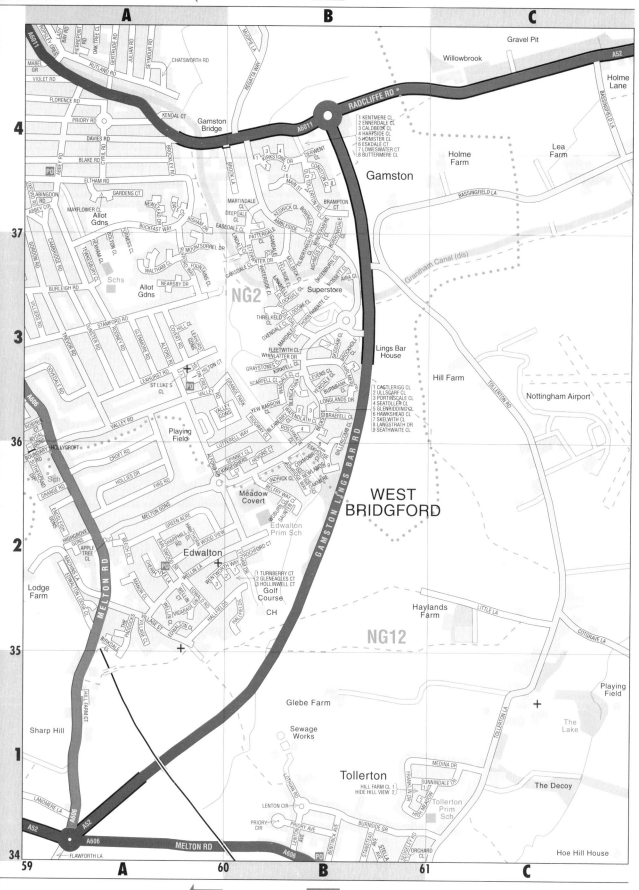

A   B   C

4

37

3

36

2

35

1

34

59   A   60   B   61   C

A52

RADCLIFFE RD

A6011

Gamston Bridge

Gamston

1 KENTMERE CL
2 ENNERDALE CL
3 CALDBECK CL
4 HARPSIDE CL
5 HONISTER CL
6 ESKDALE CT
7 LOWESWATER CT
8 BUTTERMERE CL

Willowbrook

Gravel Pit

Holme Lane

Holme Farm

Lea Farm

BASSINGFIELD LA

Grantham Canal (dis)

Superstore

Lings Bar House

Hill Farm

TOLLERTON RD

Nottingham Airport

NG2

1 CASTLERIGG CL
2 ULLSCARF CL
3 PORTINSCALE CL
4 SEATOLLER CL
5 GLENRIDDING CL
6 HAWKSHEAD CL
7 SKELWITH CL
8 LANGSTRATH DR
9 SEATHWAITE CL

Playing Field

WEST BRIDGFORD

GAMSTON LINGS BAR RD

Meadow Covert

Edwalton Prim Sch

Edwalton

1 TURNBERRY CT
2 GLENEAGLES CT
3 HOLLINWELL CT

Golf Course

CH

NG12

Haylands Farm

LITTLE LA

COTGRAVE LA

Lodge Farm

MELTON RD

A606

Playing Field

The Lake

Sharp Hill

Glebe Farm

Sewage Works

Tollerton

The Decoy

HILL FARM CL 1
HIDE HILL VIEW 2

Tollerton Prim Sch

A52

A606

MELTON RD

A606

FLAWFORTH LA

LANDMERE LA

Hoe Hill House

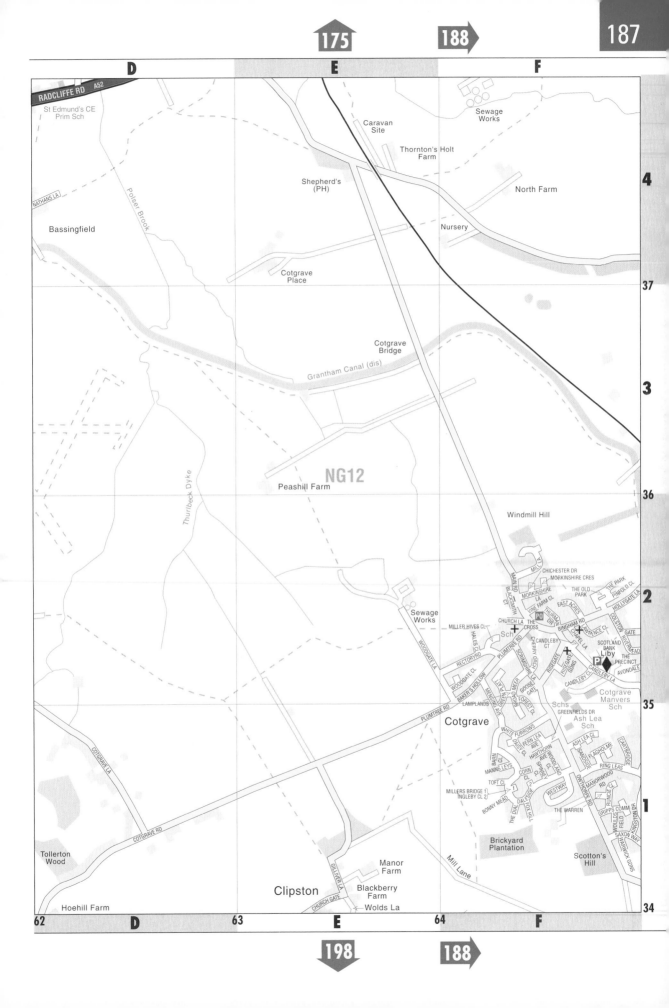

175
188

D
E
F

RADCLIFFE RD A52

St Edmund's CE Prim Sch

Caravan Site

Sewage Works

Thornton's Holt Farm

Shepherd's (PH)

North Farm

Bassingfield

Polser Brook

Nursery

4

Cotgrave Place

37

Cotgrave Bridge

Grantham Canal (dis)

3

Thurlbeck Dyke

NG12

Peashill Farm

36

Windmill Hill

Chichester Dr
Morkinshire Cres

THE PARK
PINFOLD CL
THE OLD PARK
HOLLYGATE CL

Sewage Works

Miller Hives Cl

MAIN RD
MILL LA
BLACKSMITH CT
MORKINSHIRE LA
VINE FARM CL
EAST ACRES
RUBINAL DR
BINGHAM RD
COLSTON GATE
BUCKFAST WAY

2

CHURCH LA
THE CROSS
SPENCE CL
CHAPEL LA
CANDLEBY CT
CHERRY ORCH
RISEGATE GDNS
RISEGATE
CANDLEBY LA
SCOTLAND BANK
Liby
THE PRECINCT
AVONDALE

HALES CL
WOODGATE LA
RECTORY RD
WOODGATE CL
BAKER'S HOLLOW
LAMPLANDS
MENSING AVE
GREAT FLATT
BROAD MEER
PLUMTREE RD
SCRIMSHIRE LA
CHERRY ORCH
GOOSE GATE
FOREST CL

Sch

Cotgrave Manvers Sch

35

GREENFIELDS DR
Ash Lea Sch
Schs

Cotgrave

Plumtree Rd

WHITE FURROWS
DAISY CL
FERN LEA AVE
HAWTHORN AVE
WOODLAND SPINNEY
BARN CL
MANNS LEYS
CORN CL
TOFT CL
THE DALE
DALE CL
FOX HILL
BONNY MEAD
WESTWAY
ASH LEA CL
SANDS DR
FLAGHOLME
OWTHORPE RD
MANORWOOD RD
PRINCE CL
RING LEAS
CARTBRIDGE CL

MILLERS BRIDGE 1
INGLEBY CL 2

THE WARREN

GRIPPS COMM FIELD 1
WOLDS DR
SAXON WAY
KINGSTON DR
WARWICK GDNS

1

Cotgrave La

Cotgrave Rd

Tollerton Wood

Brickyard Plantation

Scotton's Hill

GILLIVER LA
CHURCH GATE

Manor Farm

Blackberry Farm

Mill Lane

Clipston

Wolds La

Hoehill Farm

34

62
D
63
E
64
F

198
188

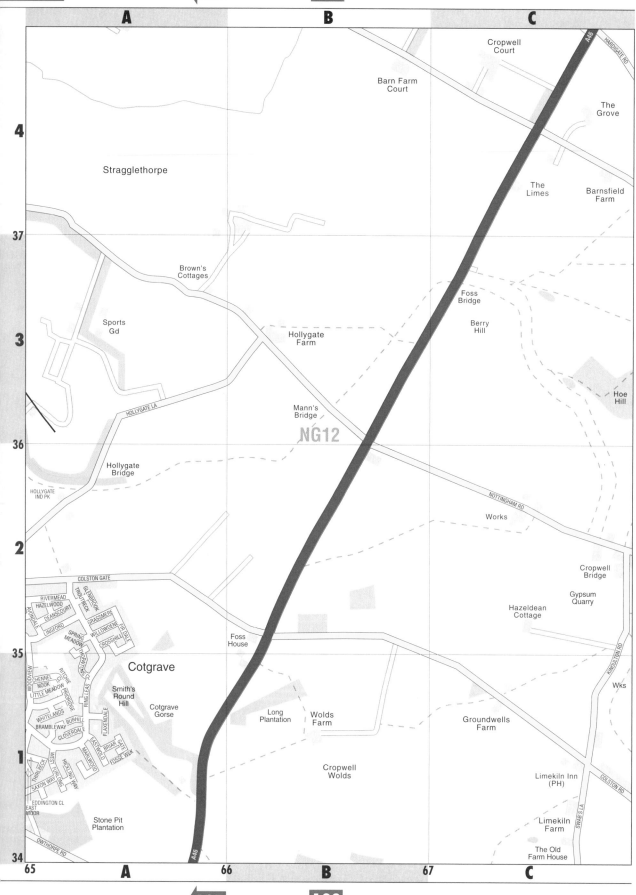

A   **B**   **C**

4

Stragglethorpe

37

Brown's
Cottages

Sports
Gd

3

Hollygate
Farm

Mann's
Bridge

HOLLYGATE LA

NG12

36

Hollygate
Bridge

HOLLYGATE
IND PK

NOTTINGHAM RD

Works

2

COLSTON GATE

RIVERMEAD
HAZELWOOD
AVONDALE   DEANSCOURT
LINGFORD   GLENBROOK
TROUT BECK
GRASSMERE
SPRING   WILLOWDENE
MEADOW   PIR DALE
CROSSHILL

Cropwell
Bridge

Gypsum
Quarry

Hazeldean
Cottage

35

WOODVIEW   CHENNEL
NOOK
LITTLE MEADOW
RITCHIE
PRIORBRIDGE
RING LEAS
SMITHY

Cotgrave

Smith's
Round
Hill

Cotgrave
Gorse

Foss
House

Long
Plantation

Wolds
Farm

Groundwells
Farm

Wks

KINDLTON RD

WHITELANDS
BRAMBLEWAY
BURHILL
CLOVERDALE
FLAXENDALE
EASTMOOR

1

THIRLBECK
SAXON WAY
HICKLING WAY
WEST FURLONG
MANYARD
OTOWN
BRIAR GATE
FOSSE WLK

Cropwell
Wolds

Limekiln Inn
(PH)

COLSTON RD

SWAB S LA

EDDINGTON CL
EAST
MOOR

Stone Pit
Plantation

Limekiln
Farm

34

OWTHORPE RD

A46

The Old
Farm House

65   **A**   66   **B**   67   **C**

Barn Farm
Court

Cropwell
Court

The Grove

The Limes

Barnsfield
Farm

A46

HARDIGATE RD

Foss
Bridge

Berry
Hill

Hoe
Hill

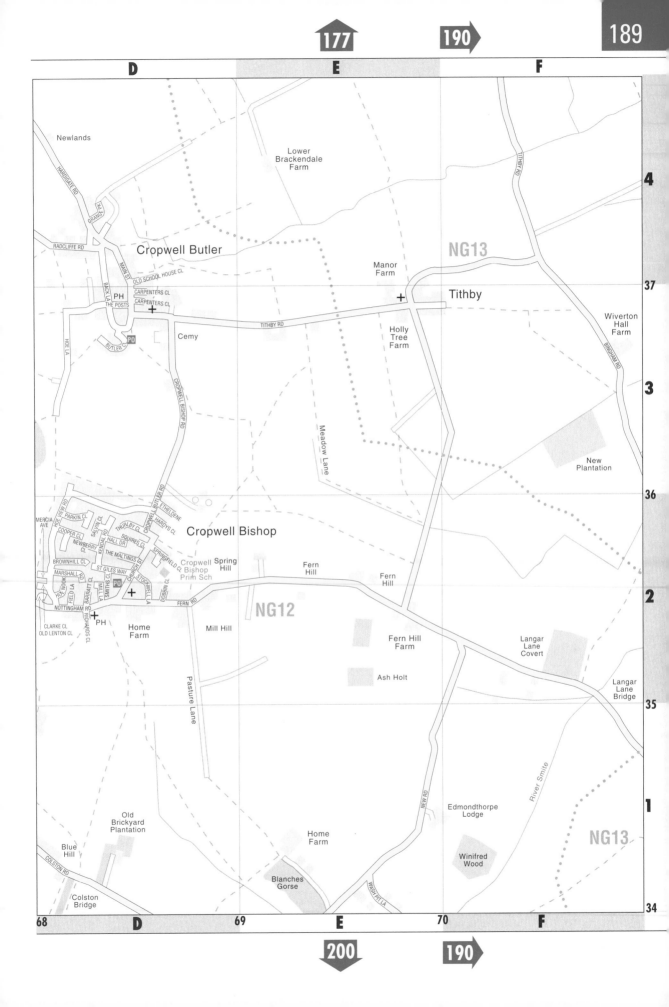

Tythby Grange

Whatton Fields

Manor Lodge

GRANBY LA

MANOR LA

4

Crane's Covert

37

Smite Hill Covert

Moat Covert

River Smite

3

Wiverton Hall

Smite Hill Farm

NG13

36

Northfield Farm

Wiverton Smite Bridge

BINGHAM RD

Walnuts Farm

MAIN RD

Church Farm

ORCHARD CL

2

Roadside Farm

PARK RD

Barnstone

NG12

Stroom Dyke

Works

Works

35

Langar CE Sch

BARNSTONE RD

NUSTERS RD

Langar

Hall

RECTOR CRES

EAST HYKE CRES

MAIN ST

WILLOW LA

PO

P

PH

Works

Works Farm

1

Stroom Dyke

CROPWELL RD

Wild Flower Farm

HARBY RD

Stroomfields

LANGAR LA

Ragnal Farm

COACH GAP LA

Works

34

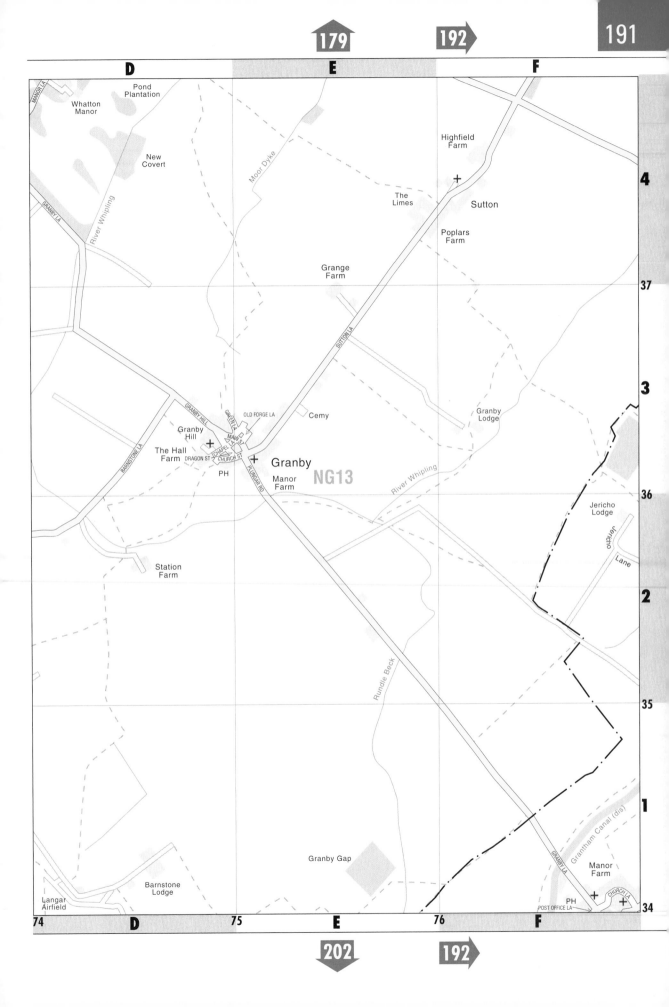

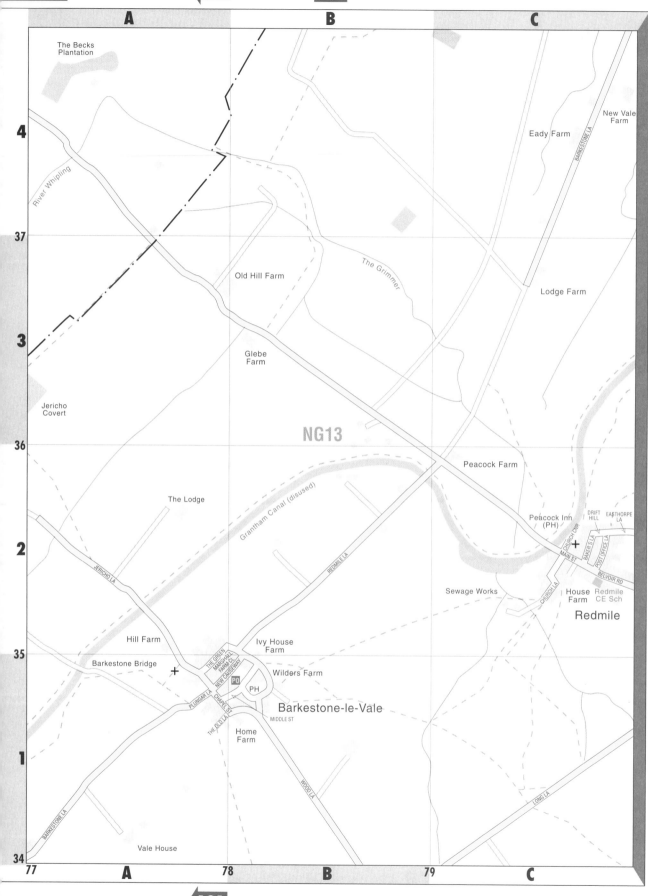

The Becks
Plantation

A   B   C

4

River Whipling

Eady Farm

New Vale
Farm

BARKESTONE LA

37

Old Hill Farm

The Grimmer

Lodge Farm

3

Glebe
Farm

Jericho
Covert

NG13

36

Peacock Farm

The Lodge

Grantham Canal (disused)

Peacock Inn
(PH)

DRIFT
HILL

EASTHORPE
LA

2

Jericho La

REDMILE LA

CHURCH CNR

MAIN ST

BAKER S LA

POST OFFICE LA

BELVOIR RD

Sewage Works

CHURCH LA

House
Farm

Redmile
CE Sch

Redmile

Hill Farm

Ivy House
Farm

35

Barkestone Bridge

THE GREEN

MARSHALL
FARM CL

NEW CAUSEWAY

Wilders Farm

PO

PH

Barkestone-le-Vale

PLUNGAR LA

CHAPEL LA

THE OLD LA ST

MIDDLE ST

1

Home
Farm

WOOD LA

Long La

34

Vale House

77   A   78   B   79   C

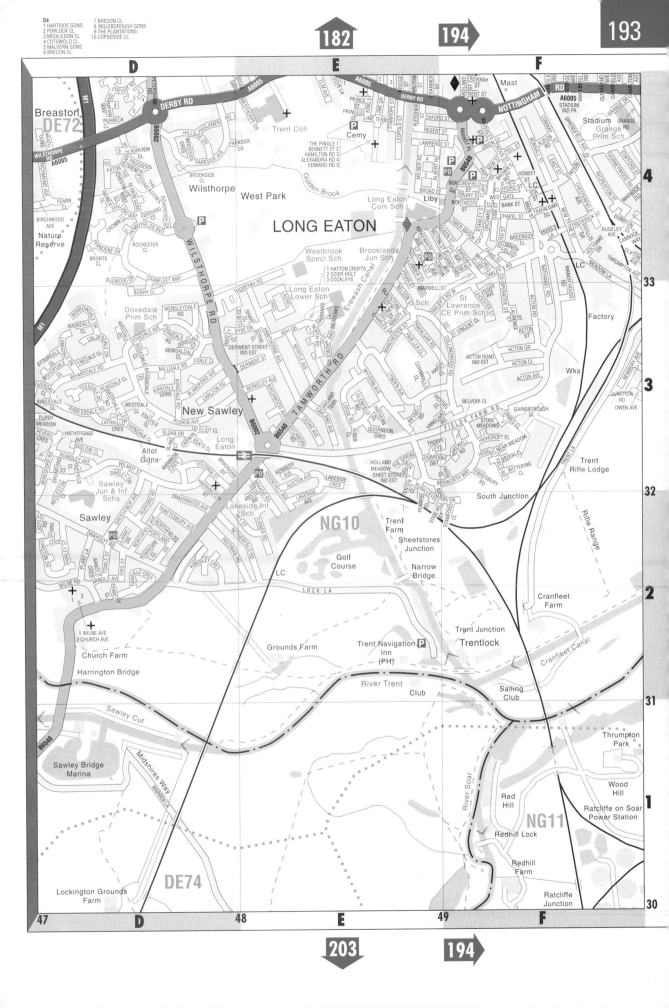

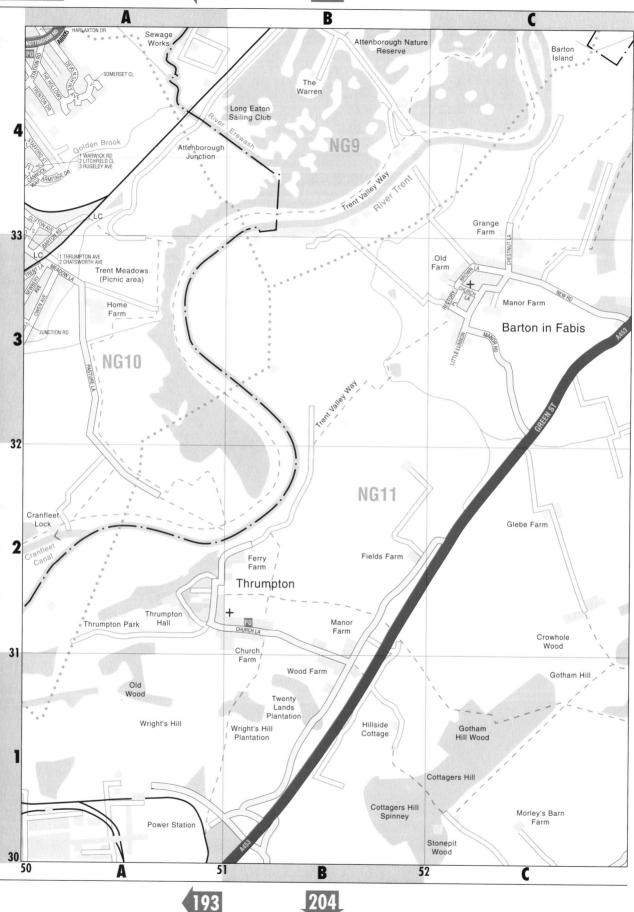

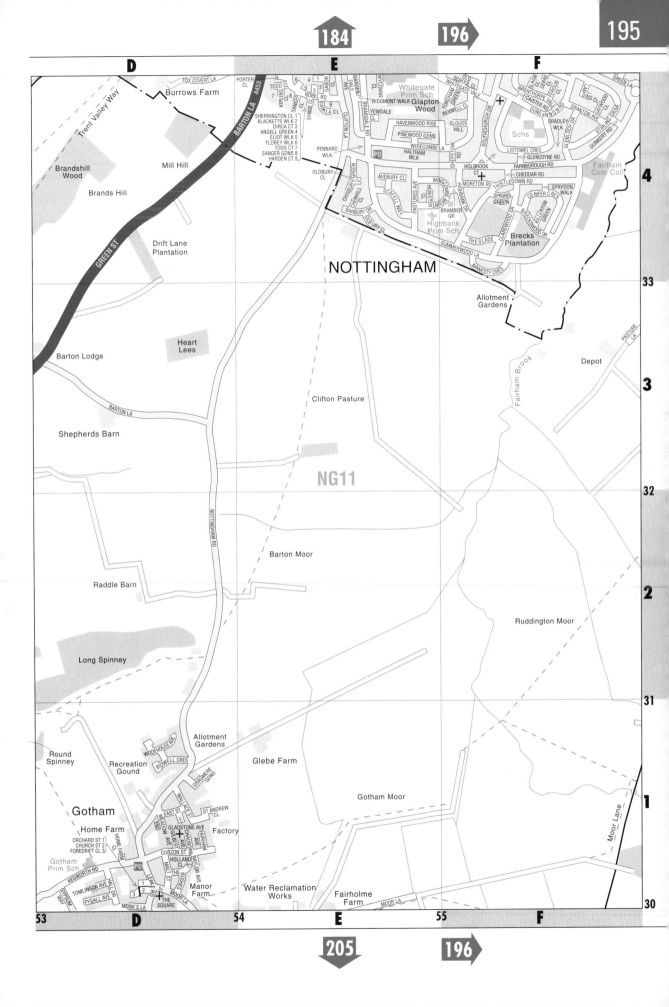

D   E   F

Burrows Farm

Trent Valley Way

Fox Covert La

PORTER CL

BARTON LA A453

TODD CL
KIPLING CL
SYNGE CL
NOBEL RD
SANGER CL
GABOR
BARALA CL

SHERRINGTON CL 1
BLACKETTS WLK 2
DIRCA CT 3
ANGELL GREEN 4
ELIOT WLK 5
FLOREY WLK 6
TODD CT 7
SANGER GDNS 8
HARDEN CT 9

GARDEN DALE AVE
WYCOMBE CL
BRANSDALE RD
YEWDALE

Whitegate Prim Sch

RIDGMONT WALK

Glapton Wood

OLD SCHOOL CL
WHITEGATE VALE
GREEN WAY
FORDHAM GREEN
BLAISE CL
CERNE CL
FERJUS CL
GREEN LA

WRENTHORPE VALE
CAISTER RD
LANSING CL
GRANTON AVE
CLAYWOOD CL
STIRLING GROVE

Brandshill Wood

Mill Hill

Brands Hill

Drift Lane Plantation

PENNARD WLK

HAVENWOOD RISE
PINEWOOD GDNS
WIDECOMBE LA
HALTHAM WLK

BEXWELL CL
CLOUDS HILL

SOUTHCHURCH DR

Schs

DUNGANNON RD

BRADLEY WLK

GLENLOCH CL
DUNKERY RD

Fairham Com Coll

4

OLDBURY CL

CHISBURY GREEN
CHERHILL CL

AVEBURY CL

SCAFELL WAY

PO

PASTURES AVE

HALTHAM WLK

HOLBROOK CT

MORETON RD

FARNBOROUGH RD

CHEDDAR RD

LISTOWEL CRES
GLENCOYNE RD

SPRYDON WALK

NOTTINGHAM

BARBURY DR
SILBURY CL

HONISTER

WINSCOMBE

HIGHBANK DR

SPRING GREEN

CO NIFER CRES

KILLERTON GREEN

Brecks Plantation

33

Heart Lees

Barton Lodge

BARTON LA

Clifton Pasture

Fairham Brook

PASTURE LA

Depot

3

Shepherds Barn

NG11

32

NOTTINGHAM RD

Barton Moor

Ruddington Moor

2

Raddle Barn

31

Long Spinney

Round Spinney

WODEHOUSE AVE

BIDWELL CRES

Allotment Gardens

Recreation Gound

GRASMERE GDNS

WALL ACE ST

EAST ST
ST ANDREW CL

Glebe Farm

Gotham Moor

Moor Lane

1

Gotham

Home Farm

ORCHARD ST 1
CHURCH ST 2
FOREDRIFT CL 3

Gotham Prim Sch

PO

KEGWORTH RD

TOMLINSON AVE
HALL DR

GYPSUM WAY

PYGALL AVE

MONK'S LA

MEADOW END
GLADSTONE AVE
GILBERT AVE

CHARNWOOD AVE
FAIRHAM AVE

CURZON ST
HOLLAND CL

NAYLOR AVE

RUSHES

MALL ST

LEAKE RD
MOOR LA
THE SQUARE

Factory

Manor Farm

Water Reclamation Works

Fairholme Farm

MOOR LA

30

53   D   54   E   55   F

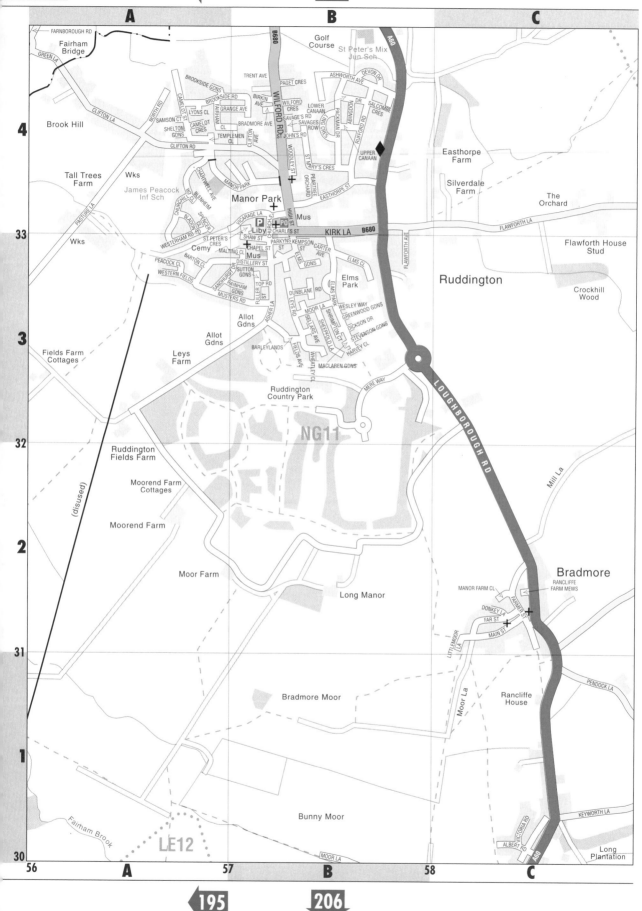

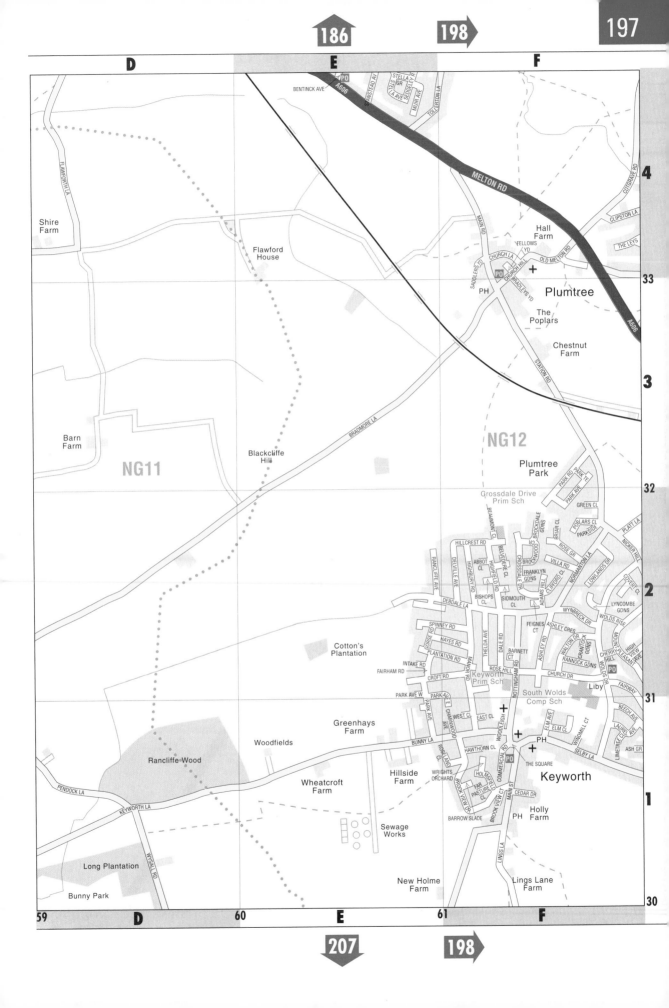

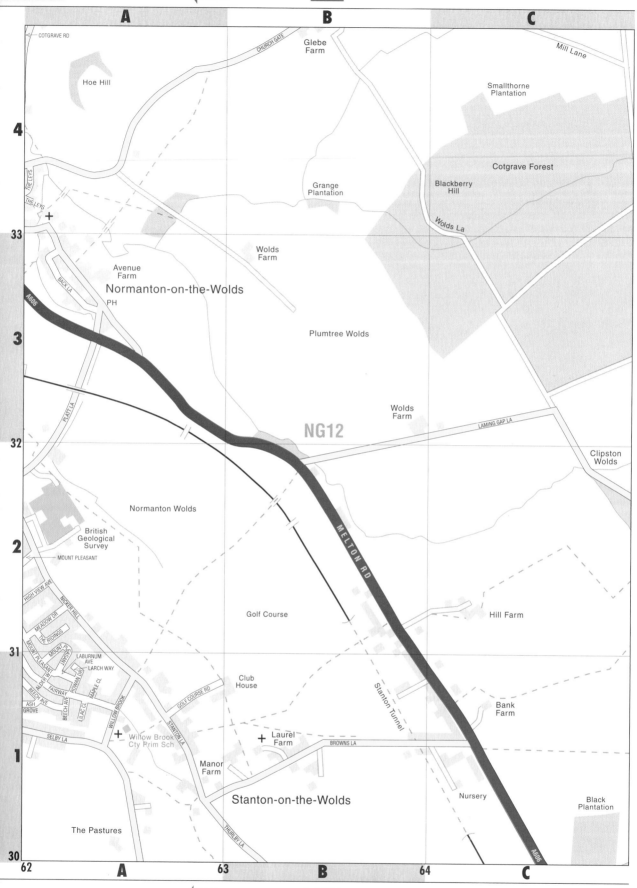

199
189

A **B** **C**

Old Gorse

NEW RD

HALL GROUNDS DR

China Bridge

WASH PIT LA

Home Farm

LANGAR LA

NG13

The Lodge

Sandpit Hollow

HALL GROUNDS

Colston Hall

4

HALL LA

Smite Bridge

CHURCH GATE

Church Farm

Colston Bassett

PO

+

BAKER'S LA

Manor House Farm

Martin's Arms (PH)

SCHOOL LA

Colston Basset Prim Sch

BUNNISON LA

33

Oddhouse Farm

Bunnison Lane Farm

Spencer's Bridge

HARBY LA

Grantham Canal (disused)

3

Kaye Wood

Kaye Wood Farm

Hills Farm

32

NG12

Barges Spinney

River Smite

2

Hall Farm

Dalby Brook

Manor Farm

HALL LA

Home Farm

GARDNER DR

HALL LA

PO

Water Reclamation Works

31

PH

MAIN ST

BOSWELL CL

NEVILE DR

Kinoulton

Sausethorpe Farm

LE14

1

HICKLING RD

Grove Farm

Kinoulton Grange

30

68 **A** 69 **B** 70 **C**

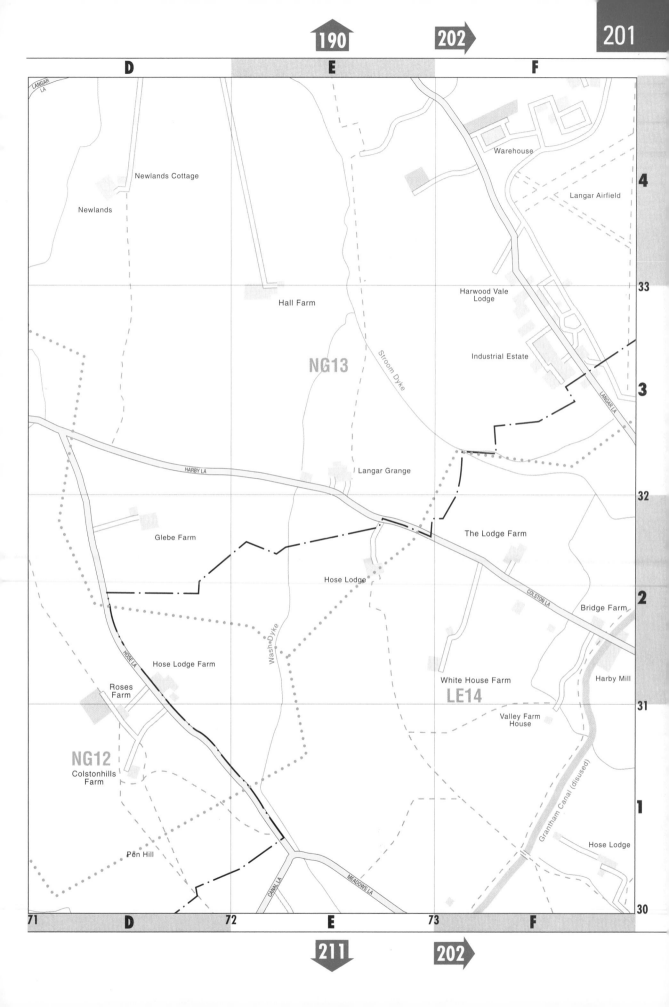

D   E   F

4

Newlands Cottage

Newlands

Warehouse

Langar Airfield

33

Hall Farm

NG13

Stroom Dyke

Harwood Vale Lodge

Industrial Estate

LANGAR LA

3

HARBY LA

Langar Grange

Glebe Farm

The Lodge Farm

COLSTON LA

32

Hose Lodge

Bridge Farm

2

Wash Dyke

HOSE LA

Hose Lodge Farm

White House Farm

LE14

Harby Mill

Roses Farm

31

Valley Farm House

NG12

Colstonhills Farm

Grantham Canal (disused)

1

Pēn Hill

Hose Lodge

CANAL LA

MEADOWS LA

30

71   D   72   E   73   F

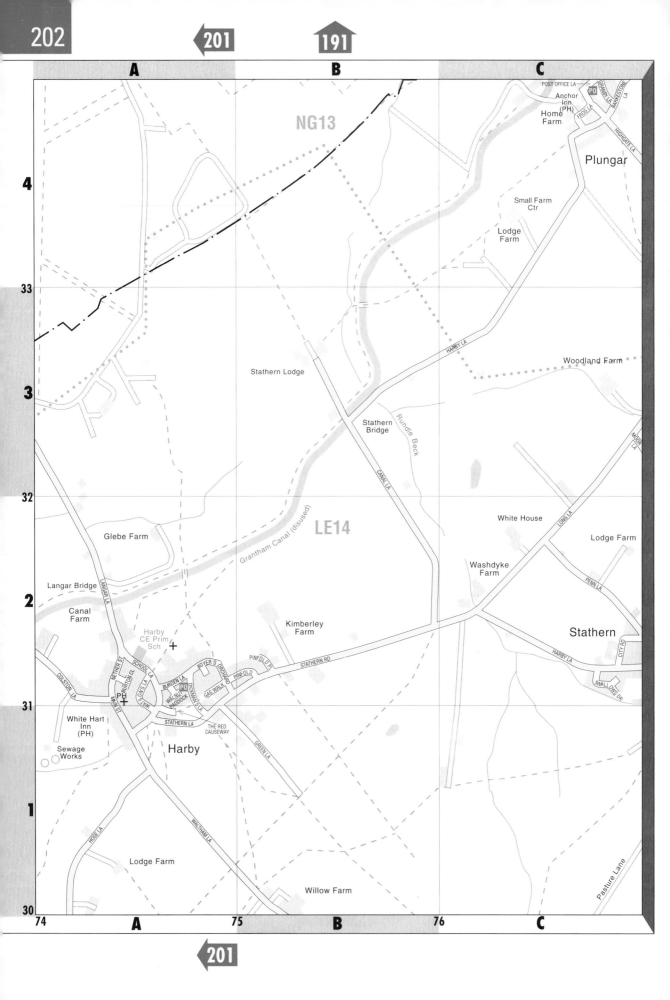

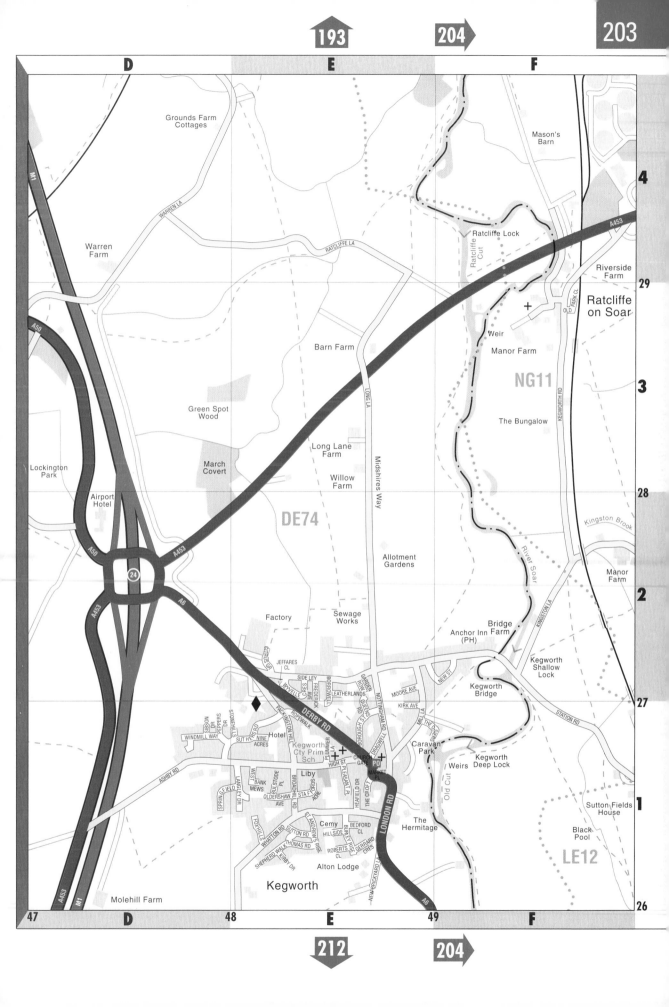

A **B** **C**

Power Station

A453

Winking Hill Farm

Fox Covert

Winking Hill

Stonepit Farm

KEGWORTH RD

Woodlands

4

A453

Gotham Wood

Hillside Farm

WOOD LA

Kingston Spinney

The Odells

Cuckoo Bush Farm

29

Hillside

New Kingston

Kingston Works

Moor Wood

GOTHAM RD

NG11

Crownend Wood

Whitehills Farm

3

W LEAKE LA

The Cottage

Kingston Park

Kingston Fields Farm

Lodge

KINGSTON CT

28

Kingston Hall

Lumbry Wood

Lodge

Church Farm

KEGWORTH RD

THE GREEN

LONG ROW

The Pool

WOSSOCK LA

2

Kingston on Soar

Station Plantation

STATION RD

Woodside

Scotland Farm

27

Scotland Wood

DE74

Cattle Breeding Centre

LE12

Moulter Hill

DARK LA

STATION RD

VILLAGE FARM GL

1

MELTON LA

Midshires Way

Kingston Brook

MAIN ST

COLLEGE RD

Sewage Works

Froghole Farm

Domleo's Spinney

PITHOUSE LA

PH

BRICKYARD LA

Univ of Nottingham Sutton Bonington Campus

LANDCROFT LA

TROWELL LA

26

50 **A** 51 **B** 52 **C**

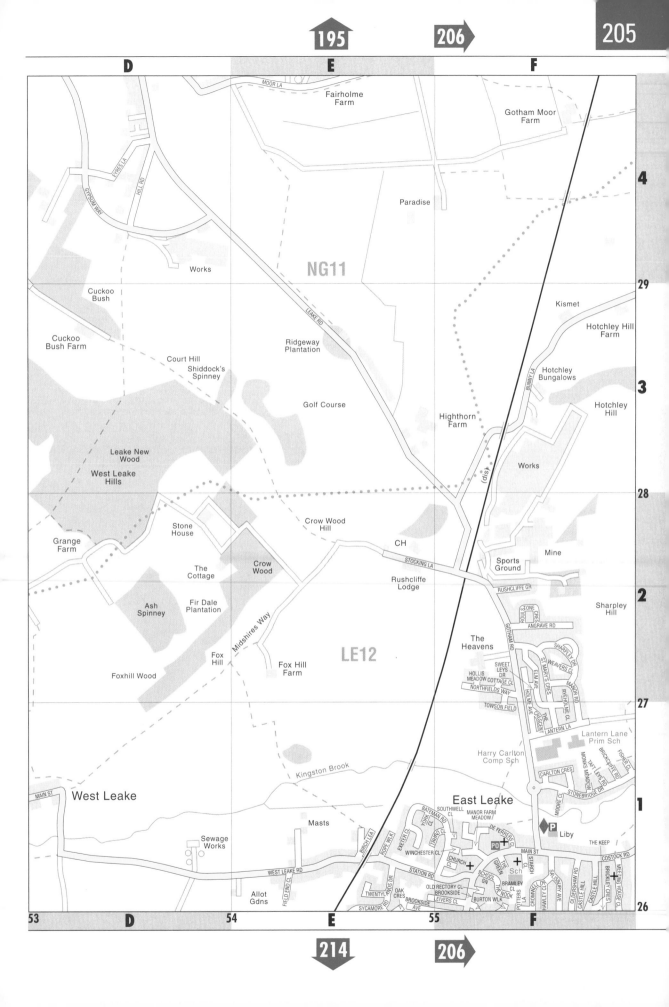

D

E

F

4

Fairholme Farm

Gotham Moor Farm

MOOR LA

EYRES LA

GYPSUM WAY

HILL RD

Paradise

Works

NG11

29

Cuckoo Bush

Kismet

Cuckoo Bush Farm

Court Hill

Shiddock's Spinney

Hotchley Hill Farm

Ridgeway Plantation

LEAKE RD

Hotchley Bungalows

Highthorn Farm

3

Hotchley Hill

Golf Course

BUNNY LA

Leake New Wood

West Leake Hills

Works

(dis)

28

Stone House

Crow Wood Hill

CH

Grange Farm

The Cottage

Crow Wood

STOCKING LA

Mine

Sports Ground

Ash Spinney

Fir Dale Plantation

Rushcliffe Lodge

RUSHCLIFFE GR

Sharpley Hill

2

Fox Hill

Midshires Way

The Heavens

LONE CRES

ANGRAVE RD

Foxhill Wood

Fox Hill Farm

LE12

Sweet Leys Dr

SHARPLEY DR

ST MARY'S CRES

WEAVERS CL

ELM AVE

RYEHOLME CL

MANOR RD

Hollis Meadow Cottage CL

NORTHFIELDS WAY

THE CRESCENT

HOLME AVE

TOWSON FIELD

LANTERN LA

Lantern Lane Prim Sch

27

Harry Carlton Comp Sch

CARLTON CRES

MOONS MEADOW

BRICKCLIFFE RD

FISHER CL

Kingston Brook

STONEBRIDGE DR

MOORE CL

East Leake

1

West Leake

MAIN ST

P

Liby

Masts

BIRCH LEA

Sewage Works

SOUTHWELL CL

Manor Farm Meadow

DE FERRERS CL

THE KEEP

BATEMAN RD

YORK CL

TRURO CL

PO

MAIN ST

STARCH

COSTOCK RD

ROPE WLK

EXETER CL

WINCHESTER CL

CHURCH CL

THE GREEN

SALISBURY AVE

OLDERSHAW RD

CASTLE HILL

MEETING HOUSE CL

BRICKLEY CRES

WEST LEAKE RD

STATION RD

Sch

GN

BRAMLEY CL

THE NOOK

DERWENT DR

CASTLE HILL

Allot Gdns

OAK CRES

FIELD END CL

TWENTYLANDS DR

Old Rectory Cl

BROOKSIDE

LEIVERS CL

BURTON WLK

POPLAR

SYCAMORE AVE

BROOKSIDE AVE

53

D

54

E

55

F

26

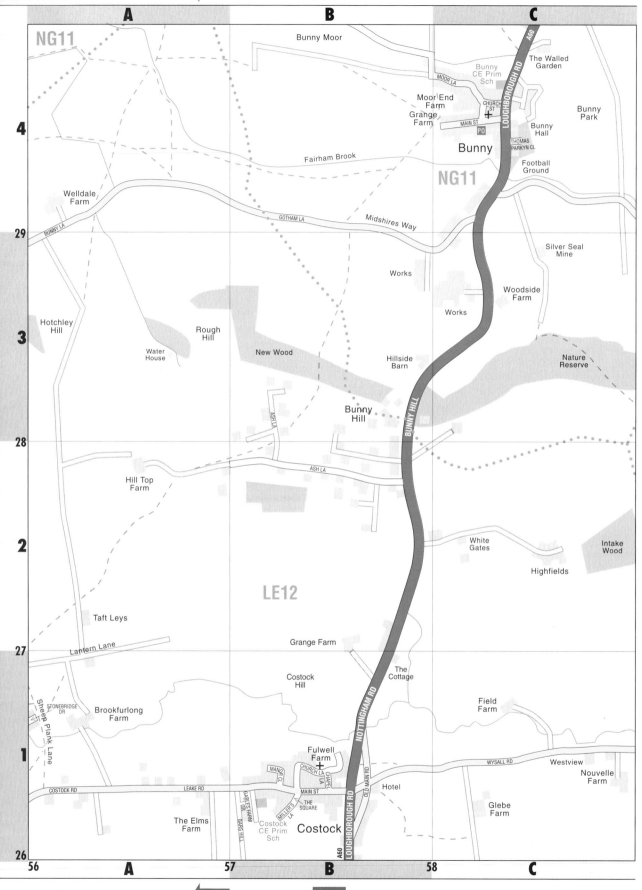

NG11

Bunny Moor

The Walled
Garden

Bunny
CE Prim
Sch

Moor End
Farm
Grange
Farm

CHURCH
ST

MAIN ST

PO

Bunny
Hall

Bunny
Park

THOMAS
PARKYN CL

Bunny

NG11

Football
Ground

Fairham Brook

Welldale
Farm

GOTHAM LA

Midshires Way

Silver Seal
Mine

BUNNY LA

Works

Woodside
Farm

Hotchley
Hill

Rough
Hill

Works

Water
House

New Wood

Hillside
Barn

Nature
Reserve

ASH LA

Bunny Hill

BUNNY HILL

Hill Top
Farm

ASH LA

White
Gates

Intake
Wood

Highfields

LE12

Taft Leys

Grange Farm

Lantern Lane

The
Cottage

Costock
Hill

Field
Farm

Stonebridge
DR

Brookfurlong
Farm

Sheep Plank Lane

NOTTINGHAM RD

WYSALL RD

Westview

Fulwell
Farm

CHURCH LA

CHAPEL

OLD MAIN RD

Hotel

Nouvelle
Farm

MAN CL

COSTOCK RD

LEAKE RD

MAIN ST

Glebe
Farm

THE
SQUARE

The Elms
Farm

GABLES FARM
DR

MILLER'S
LA

BARS HILL

Costock
CE Prim
Sch

Costock

A60
LOUGHBOROUGH RD

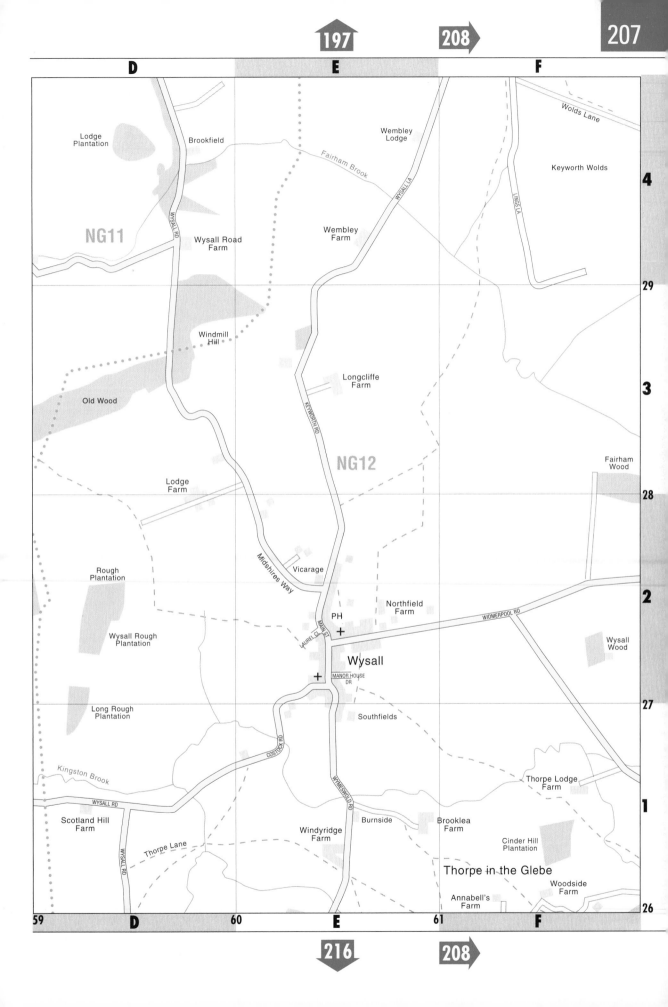

197
208

D E F

4

Wolds Lane

Lodge Plantation

Brookfield

Wembley Lodge

Keyworth Wolds

Fairham Brook

WYSALL LA

LINGS LA

NG11

WYSALL RD

Wysall Road Farm

Wembley Farm

29

Windmill Hill

Longcliffe Farm

Old Wood

KEYWORTH RD

3

NG12

Fairham Wood

Lodge Farm

28

Rough Plantation

Midshires Way

Vicarage

Wysall Rough Plantation

Northfield Farm

WIDMERPOOL RD

2

PH

Wysall Wood

MAIN ST

LAUREL CL

Wysall

MANOR HOUSE DR

27

Long Rough Plantation

Southfields

COSTOCK RD

Kingston Brook

WYSMESWOLD RD

Thorpe Lodge Farm

1

WYSALL RD

Scotland Hill Farm

WYSALL RD

Thorpe Lane

Windyridge Farm

Burnside

Brooklea Farm

Cinder Hill Plantation

Thorpe in the Glebe

Woodside Farm

Annabell's Farm

26

59 D 60 E 61 F

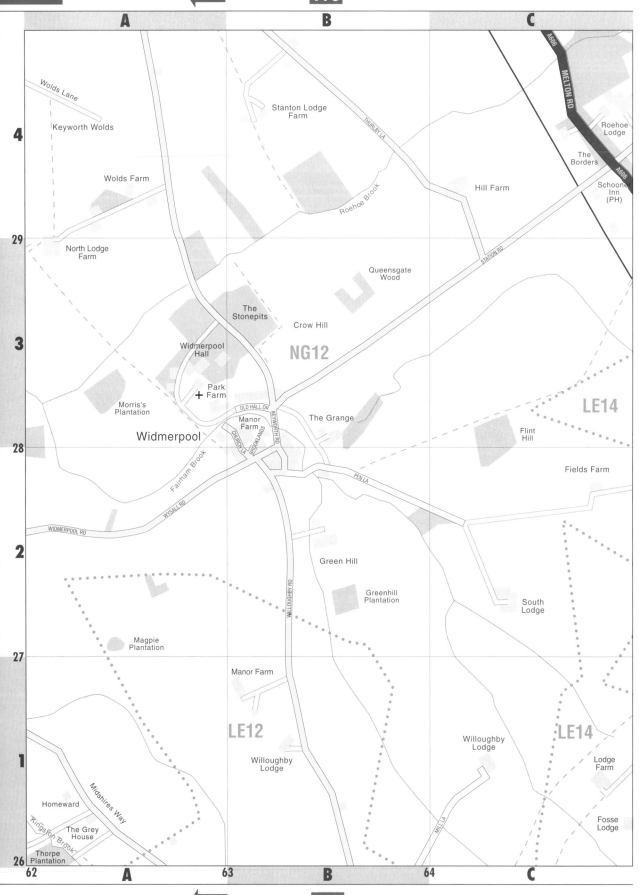

Wolds Lane

Keyworth Wolds

4

Wolds Farm

29

North Lodge
Farm

Stanton Lodge
Farm

THURLBY LA

Roehoe Brook

Hill Farm

A606

MELTON RD

A606

Roehoe
Lodge

The
Borders

Schooner
Inn
(PH)

STATION RD

Queensgate
Wood

The
Stonepits

Crow Hill

NG12

3

Widmerpool
Hall

LE14

Morris's
Plantation

Park
Farm

OLD HALL DR

The Grange

Flint
Hill

Manor
Farm

KEYWORTH RD

BROXLANDS

Widmerpool

CHURCH LA

Fairham Brook

28

Fields Farm

WYSALL RD

PEN LA

Green Hill

WIDMERPOOL RD

2

Greenhill
Plantation

South
Lodge

WILLOUGHBY RD

Magpie
Plantation

27

Manor Farm

LE12

LE14

1

Willoughby
Lodge

Willoughby
Lodge

Lodge
Farm

Midshires Way

MILL LA

Homeward

Kingston Brook

The Grey
House

Fosse
Lodge

26

Thorpe
Plantation

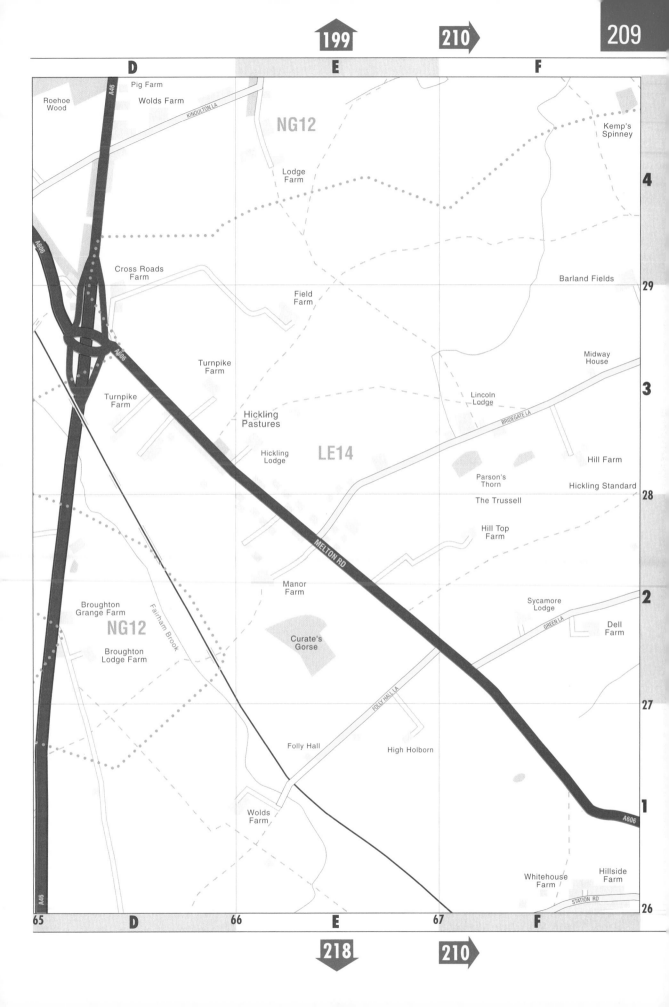

D E F

Pig Farm
Roehoe Wood
Wolds Farm
KINOULTON LA
A46

NG12

Kemp's Spinney

Lodge Farm

4

Cross Roads Farm
A606

Field Farm

Barland Fields

29

Turnpike Farm
A606

Midway House

Lincoln Lodge

BRIDEGATE LA

3

Turnpike Farm

Hickling Pastures

Hill Farm

Hickling Lodge

LE14

Parson's Thorn

Hickling Standard

The Trussell

28

Hill Top Farm

Manor Farm

MELTON RD

2

Broughton Grange Farm

NG12

Fairham Brook

Curate's Gorse

Sycamore Lodge

GREEN LA

Dell Farm

Broughton Lodge Farm

FOLLY HALL LA

27

Folly Hall

High Holborn

A606

1

Wolds Farm

Whitehouse Farm

Hillside Farm

STATION RD

26

65 D 66 E 67 F

209
200

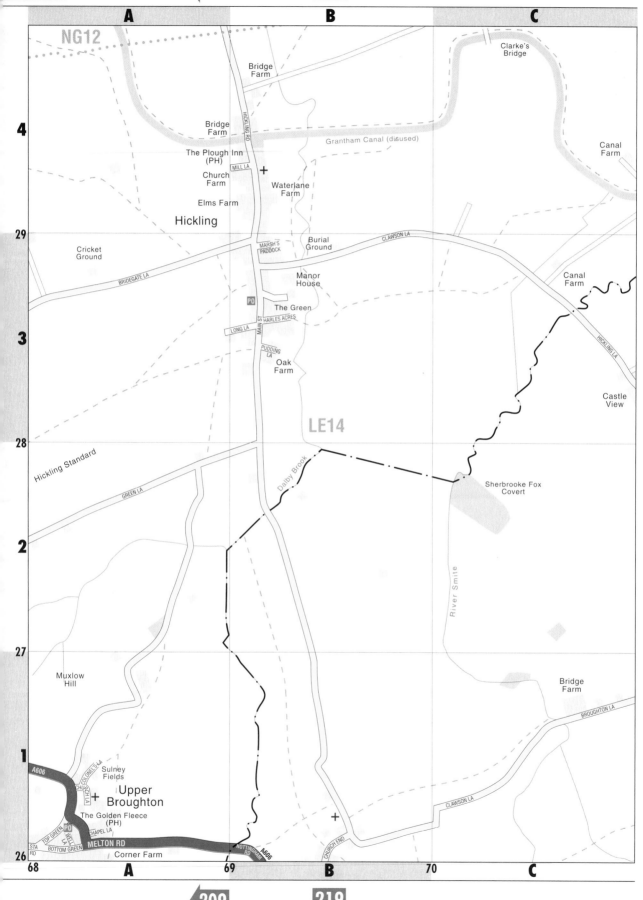

A   B   C

209
219

NG12

Bridge
Farm

Clarke's
Bridge

Bridge
Farm

Grantham Canal (disused)

Canal
Farm

The Plough Inn
(PH)

MILL LA

Church
Farm

Waterlane
Farm

Elms Farm

Hickling

29

Cricket
Ground

MARSH'S
PADDOCK

Burial
Ground

CLAWSON LA

Canal
Farm

BRIDEGATE LA

Manor
House

PO

The Green

Canal
Farm

LONG LA

HARLES ACRES

MAIN ST

HICKLING LA

3

PUDDING
LA

Oak
Farm

Castle
View

LE14

28

Hickling Standard

Dalby Brook

Sherbrooke Fox
Covert

GREEN LA

2

River Smite

27

Muxlow
Hill

Bridge
Farm

BROUGHTON LA

1

A606

COLONEL'S LA

Sulney
Fields

CHURCH LA

Upper
Broughton

The Golden Fleece
(PH)

CLAWSON LA

TOP GREEN

PO

WELL LA

CHAPEL LA

STA
RD

BOTTOM GREEN

MELTON RD

A606

NOTTINGHAM RD

A606

CHURCH END

26

Corner Farm

68   A   69   B   70   C

HICKLING RD

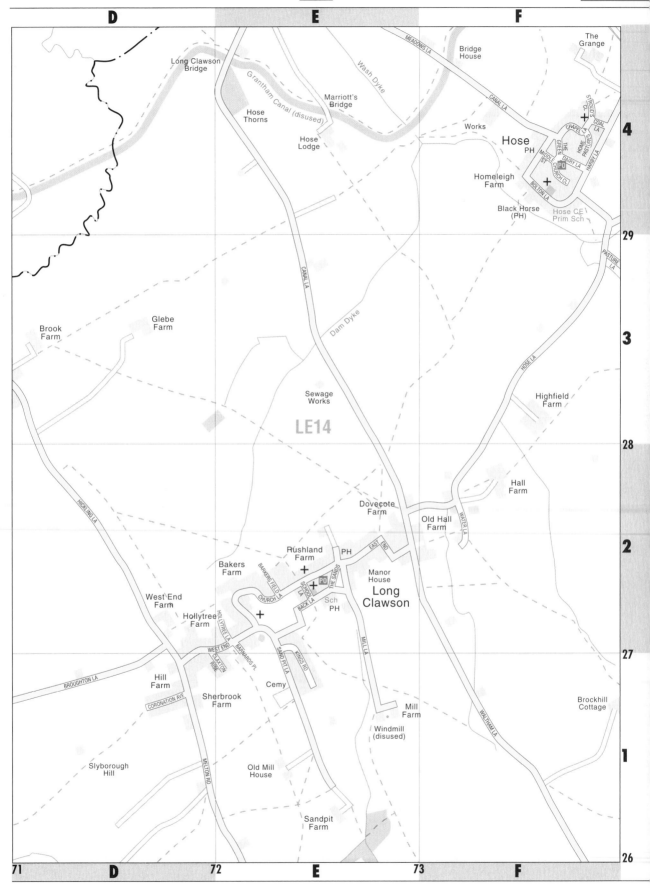

D E F

The Grange

MEADOWS LA

Bridge
House

Long Clawson
Bridge

Wash Dyke

CANAL LA

STROUDS CL

Grantham Canal (disused)

Marriott's
Bridge

Works

COAL LA

Hose Thorns

CHAPEL LA

Hose
4

Hose
Lodge

HOME PASTURES LA

PH

HARBY LA

THE GREEN

DAIRY LA

Homeleigh
Farm

MIDDLE ST

CHURCH CL

PO

CANAL LA

Black Horse
(PH)

BOLTON LA

Hose CE
Prim Sch

29

PASTURE LA

Brook
Farm

Glebe
Farm

Dam Dyke

HOSE LA

Highfield
Farm

3

Sewage
Works

LE14

28

Hall
Farm

HICKLING LA

Dovecote
Farm

Old Hall
Farm

WATER LA

2

Rushland
Farm

PH

EAST END

Bakers
Farm

BARKERS FIELD

Manor
House

West End
Farm

SCHOOL LA

PO

THE SANDS

Long
Clawson

CHURCH LA

Sch
PH

BACK LA

Hollytree
Farm

HOLLYTREE LA

MILL LA

27

Hill
Farm

WEST END

CLAXTON RISE

BARNARDS PL

SAND PIT LA

KINGS RD

BROUGHTON LA

Cemy

Brockhill
Cottage

CORONATION AVE

Sherbrook
Farm

Mill
Farm

1

WALTHAM LA

Slyborough
Hill

MELTON RD

Old Mill
House

Windmill
(disused)

Sandpit
Farm

26

71 D 72 E 73 F

203

ASHBY RD
A453
M1
A453
A42
A42
M1

Springhouse Farm

DE74

4

WHATTON RD

Slade Farm

25

PH

Slade Spinney

LONDON RD

Devil's Elbow

Windmill Farm

River Soar

His Lordships

Intensive Dairy Unit

3

Lodge

Home Farm

Woodyard Plantation

Whatton House

Five Acre

KEGWORTH LA

Ash Spinney

24

Gallow's Wood

Gorse Covert

Manor House Farm

Marylea Farm

Lodge

WEST END

Long Whatton

MILL LA

Whatton Fields Farm

2

Long Whatton Brook

Long Whatton Mill

BARNFIELD CL

MAIN ST

MANOR CL

PH

PO

Manor Farm

CRANSHAW CL

LE12

Sewage Works

THE GREEN

PH

23

PIPER CL

PIPER DR

HATHERN RD

Hathern Turn

A6006

ZOUCH RD

DERBY RD

Rose Hill

SMITHY LA

SPRING LA

TURREY LA

OAKLEY DR

WHATTON RD

B5324

DRY POT LA

PH

1

Works

WIDE LA

Piper Farm

ASHBY RD

22

B5324

M1

Mitchell's Spring Farm

Oakley Wood

Oakley Grange Farm

SHEPSHED RD

47   A   48   B   49   C

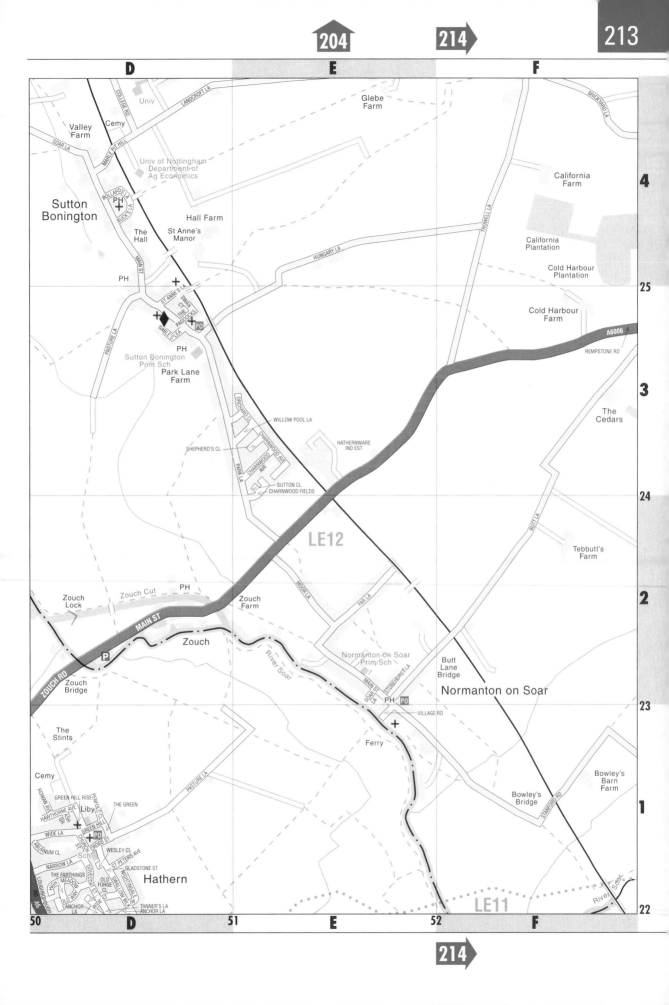

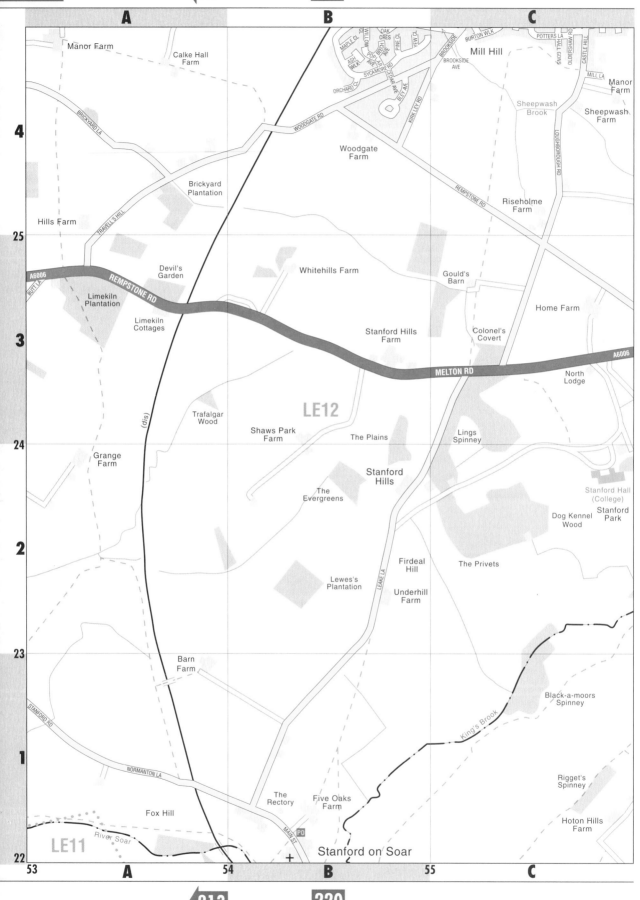

A   B   C

Manor Farm

Calke Hall
Farm

MAPLE CL
WILLOW
OAK
PINE CL
YEW CL
ASH
BECH
WLK
POP LAR
AVE
BLET AVE
ORCHARD CL
SYCAMORE RD
KIRK LEY RD
BROOKSIDE
AVE
BROOKSIDE

BURTON WLK
POTTERS LA
HALL GDNS
OLD ASHBY RD
CASTLE HILL
MILL LA

Mill Hill

Manor
Farm

Sheepwash
Brook

Sheepwash
Farm

BRICKYARD LA

WOODGATE RD

Woodgate
Farm

REMPSTONE RD

Riseholme
Farm

LOUGHBOROUGH RD

4

Brickyard
Plantation

TRAVELL'S HILL

Hills Farm

25

A6006

REMPSTONE RD

Devil's
Garden

Whitehills Farm

Gould's
Barn

Home Farm

BUTT LA

Limekiln
Plantation

Limekiln
Cottages

Stanford Hills
Farm

Colonel's
Covert

A6006

3

MELTON RD

North
Lodge

(dis)

Trafalgar
Wood

Shaws Park
Farm

LE12

The Plains

Lings
Spinney

Stanford Hall
(College)

24

Grange
Farm

Stanford
Hills

Stanford
Park

The
Evergreens

Dog Kennel
Wood

2

LEAKE LA

Firdeal
Hill

The Privets

Lewes's
Plantation

Underhill
Farm

23

Barn
Farm

Black-a-moors
Spinney

STANFORD RD

King's Brook

1

NORMANTON LA

Rigget's
Spinney

The
Rectory

Five Oaks
Farm

Hoton Hills
Farm

Fox Hill

MAIN ST

PO

LE11

River Soar

22

Stanford on Soar

53   A   54   B   55   C

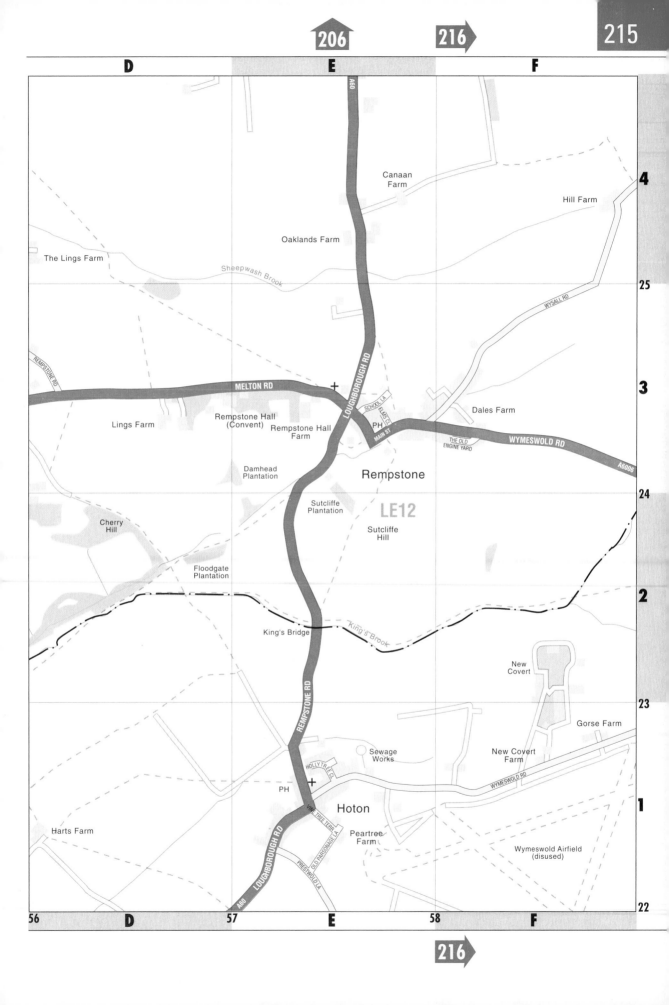

4

Canaan
Farm

Hill Farm

Oaklands Farm

The Lings Farm

Sheepwash Brook

25

WYSALL RD

REMPSTONE RD

MELTON RD

3

LOUGHBOROUGH RD

SCHOOL LA

ELMS CL

Dales Farm

Lings Farm

Rempstone Hall
(Convent)

Rempstone Hall
Farm

PH

MAIN ST

THE OLD
ENGINE YARD

WYMESWOLD RD

A6006

Damhead
Plantation

Rempstone

Sutcliffe
Plantation

LE12

24

Cherry
Hill

Sutcliffe
Hill

Floodgate
Plantation

2

King's Bridge

King's Brook

New
Covert

23

REMPSTONE RD

Gorse Farm

Sewage
Works

New Covert
Farm

HOLLY TREE CL

WYMESWOLD RD

PH

PINE TREE TERR

Hoton

1

Harts Farm

LOUGHBOROUGH RD

OLD PARSONAGE LA

PRESTWOLD LA

Peartree
Farm

Wymeswold Airfield
(disused)

A60

22

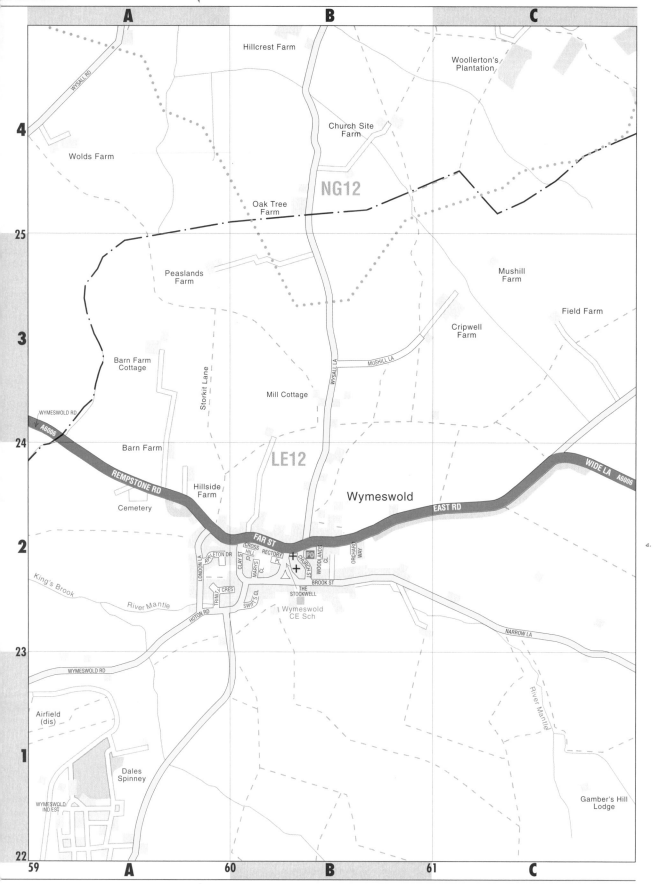

A B C

4

Wysall Rd

Hillcrest Farm

Woollerton's Plantation

Church Site Farm

Wolds Farm

NG12

Oak Tree Farm

25

Peaslands Farm

Mushill Farm

Field Farm

Cripwell Farm

3

Barn Farm Cottage

Storkit Lane

Wysall La

Mushill La

Mill Cottage

Wymeswold Rd

A6006

Barn Farm

24

LE12

Wymeswold

Wide La A6006

Rempstone Rd

Hillside Farm

East Rd

Cemetery

Far St

2

London La

Appleton Dr

Clay St

Cross Hill Pl

Rectory Pl

PO

Orchard Way

Mary's Cl

Church St

Woodlands Cl

Brook St

Trinity Cres

Hoton Rd

Swift's Cl

The Stockwell

Wymeswold CE Sch

King's Brook

River Mantle

23

Wymeswold Rd

Narrow La

River Mantle

Airfield (dis)

1

Dales Spinney

Gamber's Hill Lodge

Wymeswold Ind Est

22

59 A 60 B 61 C

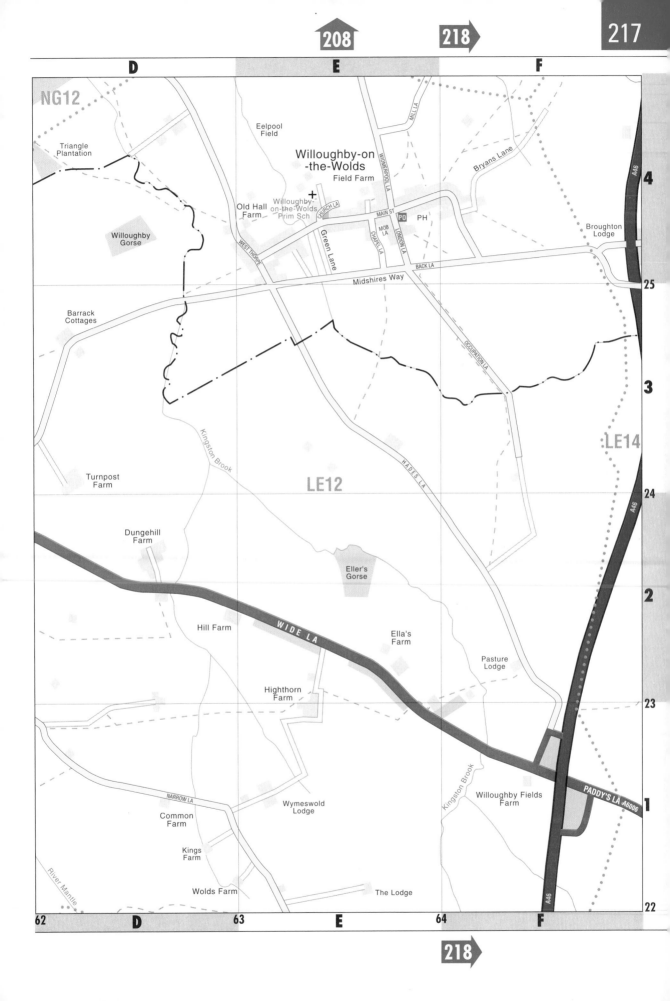

NG12

Triangle
Plantation

Eelpool
Field

**Willoughby-on
-the-Wolds**

Field Farm

MILL LA

Bryans Lane

WOMERPOOL LA

Old Hall
Farm

Willoughby-
on-the-Wolds
Prim Sch

CHURCH LA

MAIN ST

PO

PH

Broughton
Lodge

Willoughby
Gorse

Green Lane

MOB
LA

CHAPEL LA

LONDON LA

BACK LA

WEST THORPE

Midshires Way

A46

4

Barrack
Cottages

OCCUPATION LA

25

Kingston Brook

LE12

HADES LA

LE14

Turnpost
Farm

3

A46

24

Dungehill
Farm

Eller's
Gorse

2

Hill Farm

WIDE LA

Ella's
Farm

Pasture
Lodge

Highthorn
Farm

23

NARROW LA

Kingston Brook

Willoughby Fields
Farm

PADDY'S LA A6006

Common
Farm

Wymeswold
Lodge

1

Kings
Farm

River Mantle

Wolds Farm

The Lodge

A46

22

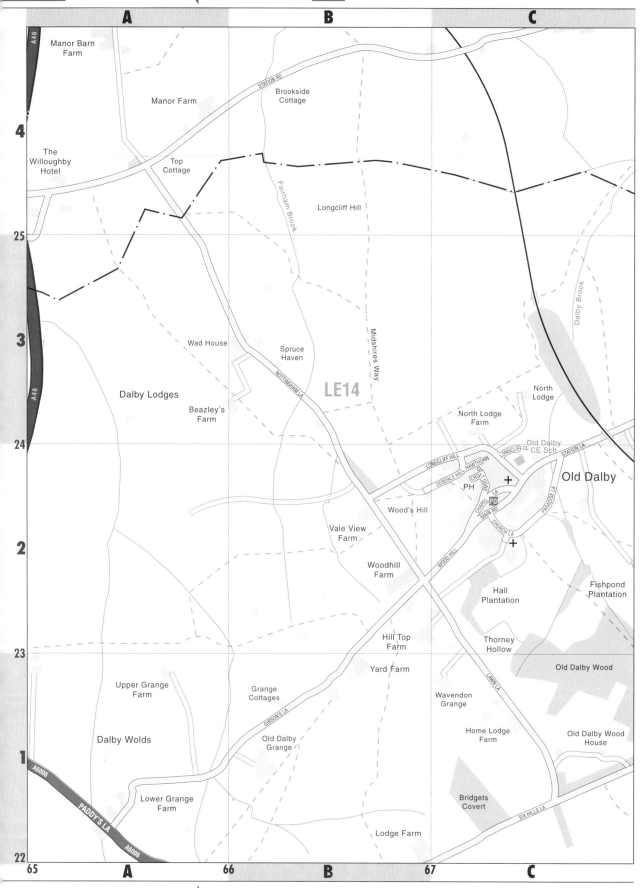

A46

Manor Barn Farm

Manor Farm

STATION RD

Brookside Cottage

4

The Willoughby Hotel

Top Cottage

Fairham Brook

Longcliff Hill

25

A46

Wad House

Spruce Haven

Midshires Way

LE14

Dalby Lodges

Beazley's Farm

3

North Lodge

North Lodge Farm

Old Dalby CE Sch

STATION LA

LONGCLIFF HILL

DEBDALE HILL

HAWTHORN CL

CROC-KLDS LA

LONGCLIFF CL

PARADISE LA

Old Dalby

24

PH

Wood's Hill

CHAPEL LA

PO

MAIN RD

Dalby Brook

Vale View Farm

WOOD HILL

CHURCH LA

✝

2

Woodhill Farm

Hall Plantation

Fishpond Plantation

Hill Top Farm

Thorney Hollow

Old Dalby Wood

23

Yard Farm

LAWN LA

Upper Grange Farm

Grange Cottages

Wavendon Grange

Dalby Wolds

GIBSON'S LA

Old Dalby Grange

Home Lodge Farm

Old Dalby Wood House

1

A6006

PADDY'S LA

Lower Grange Farm

Bridgets Covert

SIX HILLS LA

A6006

Lodge Farm

22

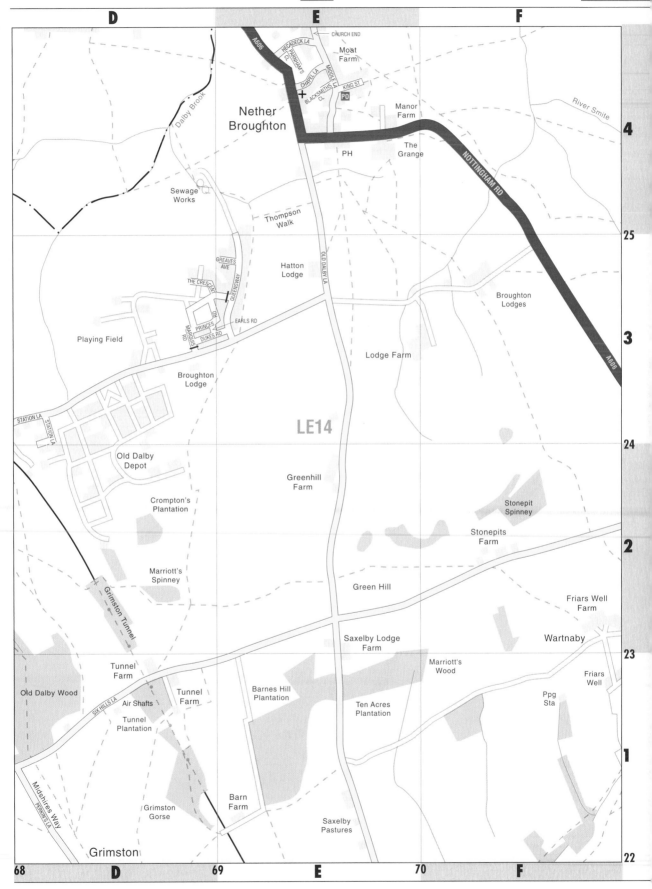

D
E
F

CHURCH END

A606

HECADECK LA
PARNHAM'S CL
CHAPEL LA
BLACKSMITHS CL
MIDDLE LA
KING ST
PO

Moat Farm

Nether Broughton

Manor Farm

River Smite

4

PH

The Grange

NOTTINGHAM RD

Dalby Brook

Sewage Works

Thompson Walk

25

GREAVES AVE

Hatton Lodge

OLD DALBY LA

Broughton Lodges

THE CRESCENT
QUEENSWAY

Playing Field

PRINCES RD
EARLS RD
MARQUIS RD
DUKES RD

Lodge Farm

3

A606

STATION LA
STATION LA

Broughton Lodge

LE14

24

Old Dalby Depot

Greenhill Farm

Crompton's Plantation

Stonepit Spinney

Stonepits Farm

2

Marriott's Spinney

Green Hill

Friars Well Farm

Grimston Tunnel

Saxelby Lodge Farm

Wartnaby

23

Tunnel Farm

Marriott's Wood

Old Dalby Wood

SIX HILLS LA

Air Shafts

Tunnel Farm

Barnes Hill Plantation

Ten Acres Plantation

Friars Well

Ppg Sta

Tunnel Plantation

1

Midshires Way

PERKIN'S LA

Barn Farm

Grimston Gorse

Saxelby Pastures

Grimston

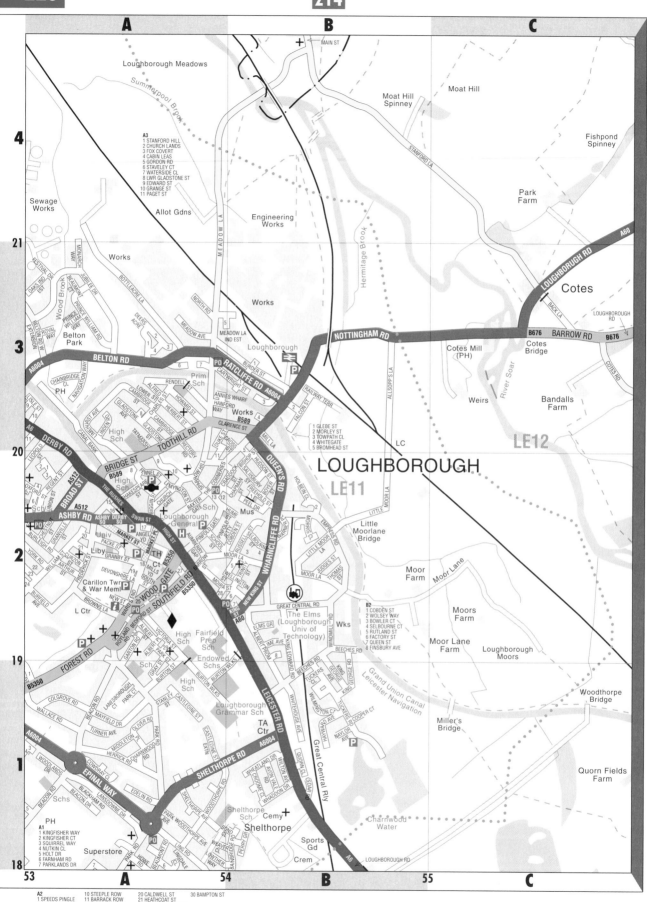

LOUGHBOROUGH

LE11

LE12

Cotes

A3
1 STANFORD HILL
2 CHURCH LANDS
3 FOX COVERT
4 CABIN LEAS
5 GORDON RD
6 STAVELEY CT
7 WATERSIDE CL
8 LWR GLADSTONE ST
9 EDWARD ST
10 GRANGE ST
11 PAGET ST

1 GLEBE ST
2 MORLEY ST
3 TOWPATH CL
4 WHITEGATE
5 BROMHEAD ST

B2
1 COBDEN ST
2 WOLSEY WAY
3 BOWLER ST
4 SELBOURNE CT
5 RUTLAND ST
6 FACTORY ST
7 QUEEN ST
8 FINSBURY AVE

A1
1 KINGFISHER WAY
2 KINGFISHER CT
3 SQUIRREL WAY
4 NUTKIN CL
5 HOLT DR
6 FARNHAM RD
7 PARKLANDS DR

A2
1 SPEEDS PINGLE
2 PLEASANT CL
3 ARMITAGE CL
4 GRANGER CT
5 ST MARY'S CL
6 HASTINGS ST
7 RADMOOR RD
8 DEAD LA
9 RECTORY PL
10 STEEPLE ROW
11 BARRACK ROW
12 PINFOLD GDNS
13 SPARROW HILL
14 BROOK SIDE
15 GREENCLOSE LA
16 ORCHARD ST
17 GEORGE YD
18 CATTLE MARKET
19 DEVONSHIRE SQ
20 CALDWELL ST
21 HEATHCOAT ST
22 TRUE LOVERS WLK
23 SEWARD ST
24 CHESTER CL
25 BEDFORD SQ
26 BEE HIVE LA
27 PACK HORSE LA
28 GREGORY ST
29 PRINCESS ST
30 BAMPTON ST

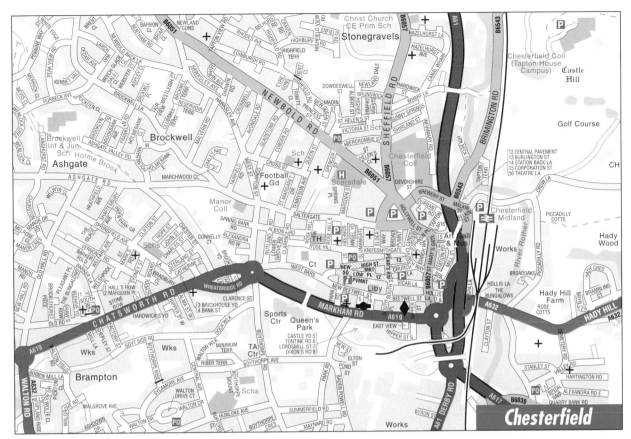

Chesterfield

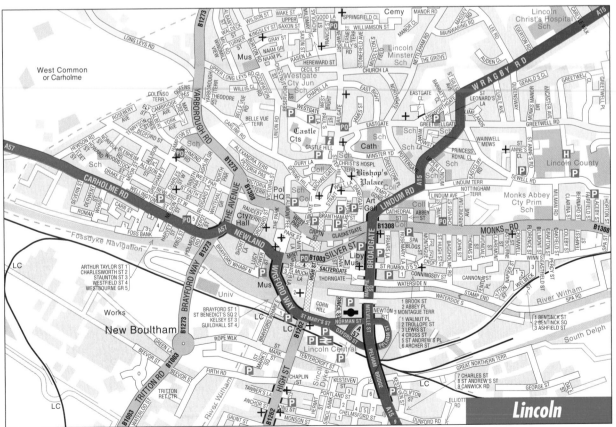

Lincoln

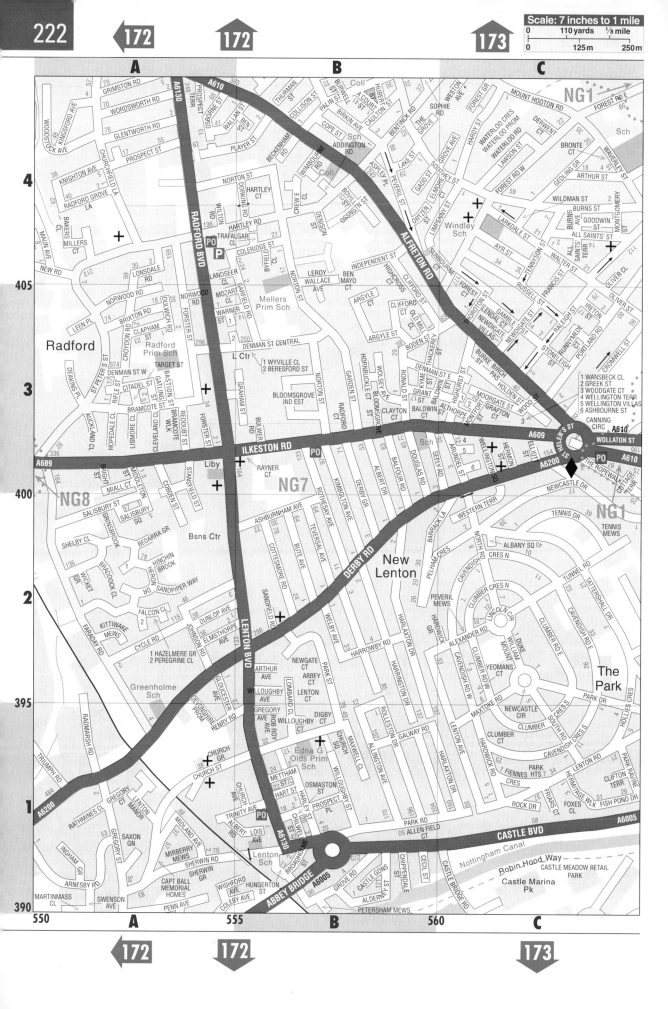

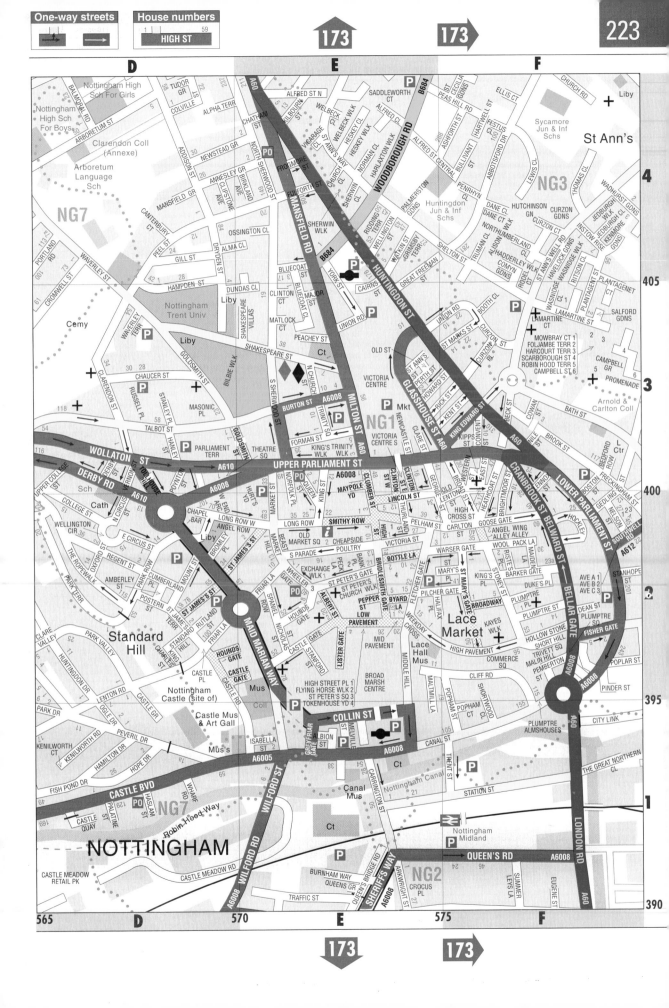

Index

Street names are listed alphabetically and show the locality, the Postcode District, the page number and a reference to the square in which the name falls on the map page

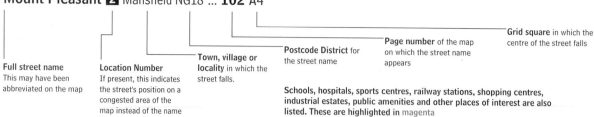

Full street name
This may have been abbreviated on the map

Location Number
If present, this indicates the street's position on a congested area of the map instead of the name

Town, village or locality in which the street falls.

Postcode District for the street name

Page number of the map on which the street name appears

Grid square in which the centre of the street falls

Schools, hospitals, sports centres, railway stations, shopping centres, industrial estates, public amenities and other places of interest are also listed. These are highlighted in magenta

Abbreviations used in the index

App	Approach	Comm	Common	Est	Estate	N	North	Sq	Square
Arc	Arcade	Cnr	Corner	Gdns	Gardens	Orch	Orchard	Strs	Stairs
Ave	Avenue	Cotts	Cottages	Gn	Green	Par	Parade	Stps	Steps
Bvd	Boulevard	Ct	Court	Gr	Grove	Pk	Park	St	Street, Saint
Bldgs	Buildings	Ctyd	Courtyard	Hts	Heights	Pas	Passage	Terr	Terrace
Bsns Pk	Business Park	Cres	Crescent	Ho	House	Pl	Place	Trad Est	Trading Estate
Bsns Ctr	Business Centre	Dr	Drive	Ind Est	Industrial Estate	Prec	Precinct	Wlk	Walk
Bglws	Bungalows	Dro	Drove	Intc	Interchange	Prom	Promenade	W	West
Cswy	Causeway	E	East	Junc	Junction	Ret Pk	Retail Park	Yd	Yard
Ctr	Centre	Emb	Embankment	La	Lane	Rd	Road		
Cir	Circus	Ent	Enterprise	Mans	Mansions	Rdbt	Roundabout		
Cl	Close	Espl	Esplanade	Mdw	Meadows	S	South		

Town and village index

Bayswater Rd NG16 158 C4
Baythorn Rd NG8 171 E3
Beacon Dr
Kirkby in A NG17 115 E3
Loughborough LE11 220 A1
Beacon Hill Dr NG15 145 E3
Beacon Hill Rd
Gringley on t H DN10 13 D1
Newark-on-T NG24 140 B4
Beacon Hill Rise NG3 173 F3
Beacon Hts NG24 140 B4
Beacon Rd Beeston NG9 184 A3
Loughborough LE11 220 A1
Beacon View NG13 181 D2
Beacon Way NG24 140 B4
Beaconsfield St
Long Eaton NG10 193 F4
Nottingham NG7 172 C4
Bean Ave S80 36 A2
Bean Cl NG6 159 F3
Beanford La
Calverton NG14 133 F2
Oxton NG25 134 A2
Beardall St
Hucknall NG15 146 A3
7 Mansfield NG18 102 A4
Beardall Street Prim Sch
NG15 146 A3
Beardsall's Row DN22 39 F4
Beardsley Gdns NG2 173 D1
Beardsley Rd NG21 76 B1
Beardsmore Gr NG15 130 C1
Beast Market Hill
Newark-on-T NG24 124 C1
Nottingham NG1 223 E2
Beatty Wlk DE7 157 F2
Beauclerk Dr NG5 160 C4
Beaufit La NG16 113 F1
Beaufort Ct NG2 185 E2
Beaufort Dr NG9 183 E3
Beaufort Gdns DN10 9 F4
Beaufort St DN21 15 E2
Beaufort Way S81 35 F4
Beaulieu Gdns NG2 185 E3
Beauly Dr NG19 101 E3
Beaumaris Dr
Beeston NG9 183 D2
Carlton NG4 163 D1
Beaumond Cross NG24 139 F4
Beaumont Ave NG18 102 C3
Beaumont Cl
Keyworth NG12 197 F2
Stapleford NG9 170 C1
Beaumont Ct LE11 220 A3
Beaumont Gdns NG2 185 E2
Beaumont Rd LE11 220 A1
Beaumont Rise S80 35 E2
Beaumont St
Gainsborough DN21 24 B4
Nottingham NG2 173 F2
Beaumont Wlk NG24 125 D1
Beauvale NG16 144 B1
Beauvale Cres NG15 145 F3
Beauvale Dr DE7 157 F3
Beauvale Rd
Annesley Woodhouse NG17 114 C1
Hucknall NG15 145 F3
Nottingham NG2 173 E1
Beauvale Rise NG16 144 A2
Beaver Pl S80 35 F2
Beazley Ave NG18 101 F4
Beck Ave NG14 148 C4
Beck Cres
Blidworth NG21 118 A2
Mansfield NG19 101 F4
Beck La Clayworth DN22 21 F2
Farnsfield NG22 119 F3
Sutton in A NG17, NG19 101 D3
Beck St Carlton NG4 174 C4
Nottingham NG1 223 F3
Thurgarton NG14 151 E4
Beckenham Rd NG7 222 B4
Becket Main Sch The
NG11 185 D3
Becket Sch The NG2 185 E4
Beckett Ave
Carlton in L S81 25 F4
Gainsborough DN21 15 F1
Mansfield NG19 87 F1
Beckett Ct NG4 162 B2
Beckford Rd 35 NG2 173 F2
Beckhampton Rd NG5 161 D4
Beckingham Ct NG19 101 F4
Beckingham Prim Sch
DN10 23 D4
Beckingham Rd DN10 14 A2
Beckingthorpe Dr NG13 181 D2
Beckland Hill NG22 65 F3
Beckley Rd NG8 159 F1
Beckon Mdw DN10 23 E4
Beckside Lowdham NG14 150 C1
West Bridgford NG2 186 B3
Bedale S81 36 A4
Bedale Ct NG9 183 D2
Bedale Rd NG5 161 E3
Bedarra Gr NG7 222 A2
Bede House La NG24 140 A4
Bede Ling NG2 185 E3
Bedford Ave NG18 102 C4
Bedford Cl DE74 203 E1
Bedford Ct Bawtry DN10 9 F4
Stapleford NG9 170 C1
Bedford Gr NG6 160 B3
Bedford Row NG1 223 F3
Bedford Sq 25 LE11 220 A2
Bedford St LE11 220 A2
Bedlington Gdns NG3 161 F1
Bee Hive La 26 LE11 220 A2
Beech Ave Beeston NG9 184 A3
Bingham NG13 178 A2
Carlton NG4 174 C3
East Leake LE12 214 B4
Gainsborough DN21 15 F1
Hucknall NG15 146 A4
Huthwaite NG17 100 A2
Keyworth NG12 198 A1
Kirkby in A NG17 114 C3
Long Eaton NG10 182 C1
12 Mansfield NG18 102 A3
New Ollerton NG22 77 E2
Nottingham, Hyson Green
NG7 173 D4
Nottingham, Mapperley
NG3 162 A2
Nuthall NG16 159 D3
Pinxton NG16 113 F2
Ravenshead NG15 116 C2
Sandiacre NG10 182 A4
Tickhill DN11 8 A4
Worksop S81 35 F3
Beech Cl
Gringley on t H DN10 12 C1
Nottingham NG6 160 B2
Radcliffe on T NG12 175 F1
West Bridgford NG12 186 A2
Beech Cres S44 86 A4
Beech Ct Nottingham NG3 162 A2
Selston NG16 129 D2
Beech Gr Blidworth NG21 118 B3
Carlton in L S81 25 F4
South Normanton DE55 113 D3
Beech Hill Ave NG19 87 F1
Beech Hill Cres NG19 87 F1
Beech Hill Dr NG19 87 F1
Beech Hill Sch NG19 87 F1
Beech Rd Harworth DN11 9 D3
Selston NG16 129 D2
Beech St NG17 100 B4
Beech Tree Ave NG19 88 A3
Beech Wlk DN22 50 A2
Beecham Ave NG3 173 F4
Beechcroft S81 36 A3
Beechdale Ave NG17 100 C2
Beechdale Cres NG17 100 C2
Beechdale Rd
Mansfield Woodhouse NG19 89 D1
Nottingham NG8 172 A4
Beecher La DN10 14 A1
Beeches Rd LE11 220 B1
Beeches The Carlton NG3 174 A4
Sutton in A NG17 100 B4
Tuxford NG22 65 F1
Beechways DN22 39 E2
Beechwood Cl
Mansfield Woodhouse NG19 89 D1
Sutton in A NG17 101 D3
Beechwood Cres DN22 37 F3
Beechwood Ct NG17 101 D3
Beechwood Dr DN22 38 B3
Beechwood Gr NG17 101 D3
Beechwood Rd
Arnold NG5 162 A4
19 Kirkby in A NG17 114 C4
Beehive La LN6 84 C1
Beehive St DN22 39 F3
Beeley Ave NG17 100 C1
Beeley Cl NG18 103 D3
Beeston Cl NG6 146 C2
Beeston Ct NG6 160 B3
Beeston Fields Dr NG9 183 E4
Beeston Fields
Jun & Inf Schs NG9 183 E3
Beeston La NG9 184 A4
Beeston Rd
Newark-on-T NG24 140 A3
Nottingham NG7 172 B1
Beeston Rylands Jun Sch
NG9 184 A2
Beeston Sta NG9 184 A3
Beethan Cl NG13 177 F2
Beggarlee Pk NG16 144 A2
Behay Gdns NG23 138 B4
Beighton Ct NG18 103 D3
Beighton St NG17 100 C2
Belconnen Rd NG5 161 D3
Belfmoor Cl S80 45 D3
Belford Cl NG6 159 F4
Belfry Cl 1 NG17 114 C4
Belfry Way NG2 186 B2
Belgrave Ct DN10 9 F4
Belgrave Rd NG6 160 A4
Bell Foundry Mus LE11 220 B2
Bell La Collingham NG23 111 F4
Nottingham NG11 185 D4
Weston NG23 81 D3
Bell St NG4 174 B4
Bellamy Rd NG18 103 D1
Bellar Gate NG1 223 F2
Belle Vue La NG21 118 A3
Belle-isle Rd NG15 146 A4
Belleville Dr NG5 161 D4
Bellevue Ct NG3 173 F3
Bellmore Gdns NG8 171 E3
Bells La NG8 160 A2
Bellsfield Cl S80 45 D3
Belmond Cl NG24 139 F3
Belmont Ave NG6 160 B4
Belmont Cl Beeston NG9 183 D2
Hucknall NG15 146 A2
Mansfield Woodhouse NG19 89 D1
Belmont Rd NG17 115 D1
Belper Ave NG4 162 B1
Belper Cres NG4 162 B1
Belper Rd NG7 172 C4
Belper St NG18 102 B4
Belper Way NG18 102 B4
Belsay Rd NG5 161 D4
Belsford Ct NG16 159 D4
Belt Rd The DN21 15 F2
Belton Cl NG10 182 A2
Belton Dr NG2 185 D2
Belton Rd LE11 220 A3
Belton Rd West Extension
LE11 220 A3
Belton St 20 NG7 172 C4
Belvedere Ave 23 NG7 172 C4
Belvedere St NG18 102 A3
Belvoir Ave NG13 181 D1
Belvoir Cl Aslockton NG13 178 C2
Long Eaton NG10 193 F3
Belvoir Cres Langar NG13 190 B1
Newark-on-T NG24 140 A3
Belvoir High Sch NG13 181 D1
Belvoir Hill NG2 173 F2
Belvoir Pl NG24 140 B2
Belvoir Rd Balderton NG24 140 B2
Bottesford NG13 181 D1
Carlton NG4 175 D4
Redmile NG13 192 C2
West Bridgford NG2 174 A1
Belvoir St Hucknall NG15 145 F4
Nottingham NG3 161 F1
Belvoir Terr DN21 15 D2
Belward St NG1 223 F2
Belwood Cl NG7 184 C1
Bembridge S81 36 A3
Bembridge Ct NG9 183 D4
Bembridge Dr NG5 161 D3
Ben Mayo Ct NG7 222 B4
Ben St NG7 222 B4
Bendigo La NG2 174 A2
Benedict Ct 3 NG5 147 D1
Benet Dr NG22 106 A3
Benington Dr NG8 171 E2
Benner Ave DE7 170 A3
Bennerley Ave DE7 157 F2
Bennerley Ct NG6 159 F4
Bennerley Fields Sch
DE7 157 F2
Bennerley Rd NG6 159 F4
Bennerley Sch DE7 157 F2
Bennett Ave NG18 102 C3
Bennett Rd NG3 162 A2
Bennett St
Long Eaton NG10 182 B1
Nottingham NG3 161 F1
Sandiacre NG10 182 A3
Benneworth Cl NG15 145 F3
Bennington Wlk NG19 88 C2
Bentick St NG18 102 B4
Bentinck Ave NG12 186 B1
Bentinck Cl
Annesley Woodhouse NG17 114 C1
Boughton NG22 77 F3
Bentinck Ct 8 NG2 173 F2
Bentinck Prim Sch NG7 222 B4
Bentinck Rd Carlton NG4 162 B1
Newark-on-T NG24 139 F3
Nottingham NG7 222 B4
Bentinck St
Annesley Woodhouse NG17 129 F4
Hucknall NG15 145 F4
Sutton in A NG17 100 C2
Bentinck Terr NG20 74 A2
Bentley Ave NG3 174 A3
Bentwell Ave NG5 162 A4
Beresford Dr DE7 157 F3
Beresford Rd
Long Eaton NG10 193 D3
Mansfield Woodhouse NG19 88 B3
Beresford St
Mansfield NG18 102 B3
Nottingham NG7 222 A3
Berkeley Ave
Long Eaton NG10 193 E3
Nottingham NG3 173 E4
Berkeley Cres NG12 176 B2
Bernard Ave
Hucknall NG15 131 D1
Mansfield Woodhouse NG19 88 A3
Bernard Rd NG19 101 F4
Bernard St NG5 161 D1
Bernisdale Cl NG5 146 C1
Berridge Inf Sch NG7 172 C4
Berridge Jun Sch NG7 172 C4
Berridge Rd NG7 173 D4
Berridge Rd W NG7 172 C4
Berriedale Cl NG5 162 B4
Berristow La DE55 113 E4
Berry Ave NG17 114 C3
Berry Hill Cl NG18 102 B2
Berry Hill Fst Sch NG18 102 C2
Berry Hill Gdns NG18 102 C2
Berry Hill Gr NG4 162 C1
Berry Hill La NG18 102 B2
Berry Hill Mews NG18 102 B2
Berry Hill Mid Sch NG18 102 C2
Berry Hill Rd NG18 102 B2
Berry Park Lea NG18 102 B2
Berwick Ave NG19 101 E4
Berwick Cl NG5 161 E3
Berwin Cl NG10 182 A1
Beryldene Ave NG16 159 D4
Bescar La NG22 77 D1
Bescoby St DN22 39 F4
Besecar Ave NG4 162 C1
Besecar Cl NG4 162 C1
Bessell La NG9 182 B3
Bessingham Dr NG2 185 E2
Besthorpe Ct NG19 101 F4
Besthorpe Prim Sch NG23 97 F3
Besthorpe Rd
Collingham NG23 98 A1
North Scarle LN6 83 E1
Bestwick Ave DE75 143 D1
Bestwood Ave NG5 161 F4
Bestwood Cl NG5 161 F4
Bestwood Ctry Pk NG6 146 C2
Bestwood Lodge Dr NG5 161 E4
Bestwood Park Dr NG5 161 D4
Bestwood Park Dr W
NG5 146 C1
Bestwood Park View NG5 147 F1
Bestwood Rd
Hucknall NG15 146 B3
Nottingham NG6 146 B1
Pinxton NG16 113 F1
Bestwood Terr NG6 160 B4
Bethel Gdns NG15 145 E3
Bethel Terr S80 34 C3
Bethnal Wlk 15 NG6 160 A4
Betony Cl NG13 177 E2
Betula Cl NG11 184 B1
Beulah Rd NG17 115 D2
Bevan Cl NG21 118 A4
Bevel St NG7 172 C4
Bevercotes Rd NG22 65 E2
Beverley Cl
Nottingham NG8 171 D2
Rainworth NG21 104 B1
Beverley Dr
Coddington NG24 125 F1
Kimberley NG16 158 C4
Kirkby in A NG17 115 E2
Mansfield NG18 102 B1
Beverley Gdns NG4 162 C1
Beverley Rd DN11 9 D2
Beverley Sq NG3 173 F3
Beverley Wlk S81 25 F4
Beverleys Ave NG13 178 C2
Bewcastle Rd NG5 147 D1
Bewick Dr NG3 174 B3
Bexhill Ct NG8 171 F1
Bexwell Cl NG11 195 F4
Biant Cl NG8 160 A2
Bidford Rd NG8 159 F1
Bidwell Cres NG11 195 D1
Big Barn La NG18 102 C3
Big La DN22 30 B2
Big Wood Sch NG5 147 D1
Biggart Cl 2 NG9 183 E1
Biggin St LE11 220 A2
Bigsby Rd DN22 30 A1
Biko Sq 22 NG7 172 C4
Bilberry Wlk NG3 173 F4
Bilbie Wlk NG1 223 D3
Bilborough Coll NG8 171 E4
Bilborough Rd NG8 171 E3
Bilby Gdns 20 NG3 173 F3
Billesdon Dr NG5 160 C2
Billingsley Ave NG16 113 E2
Bilsthorpe Inf Sch NG22 105 F3
Bilsthorpe Rd NG22 92 B1
Bilton Cl NG24 140 B1
Bingham Ave NG17 101 D3
Bingham Ind Pk NG13 177 F3
Bingham Inf Sch NG13 177 F3
Bingham Rd
Cotgrave NG12 187 F2
Langar NG13 190 A2
Mansfield NG18 103 D2
Nottingham NG5 161 E1
Radcliffe on T NG12 176 A2
Bingham Sta NG13 177 F3
Bingley Cl 4 NG8 172 A3
Birch Ave Beeston NG9 184 A2
Carlton NG4 174 B4
Farnsfield NG22 119 F4
Ilkeston DE7 170 A4
Nuthall NG16 159 D3
Rainworth NG21 104 B1
Birch Cl Nuthall NG16 159 D3
Rampton DN22 42 C1
Ravenshead NG15 117 D1
Birch Croft Dr NG19 89 D1
Birch Ct NG22 65 F1
Birch Gr Gainsborough DN21 15 E1
Mansfield NG18 103 D2
Shirebrook NG20 72 B3
Birch Lea Arnold NG5 161 E4
East Leake LE12 205 E1
Birch Pas NG7 222 C3
Birch Rd Hodthorpe S80 45 E3
New Balderton NG24 140 B3
New Ollerton NG22 77 E2
Birch Rise NG14 149 E3
Birch St NG20 73 F3
Birch Tree Cl NG19 89 E2
Birch Tree Cres NG17 114 C2
Birchdale Ave NG15 146 A3
Birchen Holme DE55 113 D2
Birchenhall Ct NG24 139 D2
Birches The NG15 117 D2
Birchfield Dr S80 35 D1
Birchfield Rd NG5 148 A1
Birchlands NG19 88 C1
Birchover Pl DE7 157 F3
Birchover Rd NG8 171 E3
Birchwood Ave
Breaston NG10 193 D4
Long Eaton NG10 193 E3
Birchwood Cl
Ravenshead NG15 117 D1
South Normanton DE55 113 D2
Southwell NG25 121 E1
Sutton in A NG17 100 C3
Birchwood Dr
Ravenshead NG15 117 D1
Sutton in A NG17 100 B4
Birchwood Rd NG8 171 E2
Bird Cl NG18 102 B2
Bird's La NG17 114 C1
Birdcroft La DN10 14 A3
Birding St NG19 88 A1
Birdsall Ave NG8 171 F2
Birkdale S81 36 A3
Birkdale Ave NG22 77 E3
Birkdale Cl Ilkeston DE7 157 E1
West Bridgford NG12 186 A2
Birkdale Dr 5 NG17 114 C3
Birkdale Gr DN22 39 E2
Birkdale Way NG5 160 C4
Birkin Ave Beeston NG9 183 D1
Nottingham NG7 172 C4
Radcliffe on T NG12 176 A2
Ruddington NG11 196 B4
Birkland Ave
Mansfield Woodhouse NG19 88 B2
Market Warsop NG20 74 A2
Nottingham, Mapperley
NG3 162 A2
Nottingham, St Ann's NG1 223 E4
Birkland Dr NG21 76 A1
Birkland St NG18 102 B4
Birklands Ave
New Ollerton NG22 77 E3
Worksop S80 36 B1
Birklands Cl NG20 74 A3
Birklands Prim Sch NG20 74 A2
Birks Cl S80 45 E3
Birks Rd NG19 101 E4
Birley St NG9 182 B3
Birling Cl NG6 159 F4
Birrel St DN21 15 D1
Birrell Rd NG7 173 D4
Bisham Dr NG2 186 A4
Bishop Alexander
Prim Sch NG24 125 D2
Bishop Alexandra Ct
NG24 139 F4
Bishop St Eastwood NG16 143 F1
Loughborough LE11 220 B2
Mansfield NG18 102 A3
Sutton in A NG17 100 C2
Bishop's Dr NG25 136 C4
Bishop's Wlk NG20 74 A3
Bishopdale S81 36 A4
Bishopdale Cl NG10 193 D3
Bishopdale Dr NG16 159 D4
Bishopfield La DN22 19 D3
Bishops Cl NG12 197 F2
Bishops Hill NG21 103 F1
Bishops Rd NG13 177 E3
Bishops Way NG15 146 A4
Bispham Dr NG9 182 C1
Black La LN6 71 F1
Black Scotch La NG18 102 C2
Blackacre NG14 163 F3
Blackburn Cl NG23 98 A1
Blackburn Pl DE7 157 F2
Blackcliff Field Cl S80 45 D3
Blacketts Wlk NG11 195 E4
Blackfriars Cl NG16 159 E2
Blackham Rd LE11 220 A1
Blackhill Dr NG4 174 C4
Blackrod Cl NG9 183 D1
Blacksmith Ct NG12 187 F2
Blacksmith La
Kelham NG23 124 A2
Torworth DN22 19 D1
Blacksmiths Cl LE14 219 E4
Blacksmiths La LN6 83 E1
Blackstone Wlk NG2 173 E1
Blackstope La DN22 40 A4
Blackthorn Cl NG13 178 A2
Blackthorn Way NG17 100 B1
Blackthorne Cl NG24 140 A3
Blackthorne Dr
Lowdham NG14 150 B1
Nottingham NG6 160 A2
Blackwell Rd NG17 99 F2
Bladon Cl NG3 161 F1
Bladon Rd NG11 196 A4
Blair Ct 11 NG2 173 E1
Blair Gr NG10 182 A2
Blaise Cl NG11 195 F4
Blake Cl NG5 162 A4
Blake Cres NG18 102 C4
Blake Ct NG10 193 D3
Blake Rd Stapleford NG9 182 C3
West Bridgford NG2 186 A4
Blake St Ilkeston DE7 157 F1
Mansfield Woodhouse NG19 88 A1
Blakeney Ct NG19 88 C2
Blakeney Dr NG18 102 B2
Blakeney Rd NG12 176 A2
Blakeney Wlk NG5 161 F3
Bland La NG14 150 A3
Blandford Ave NG10 193 D3
Blandford Dr DN22 39 E2
Blandford Gdns NG2 185 E3
Blandford Rd NG9 183 E3
Blankney Cl LN1 57 D2
Blankney St NG5 160 C2
Blantyre Ave NG5 146 C1
Blatherwick Rd NG24 140 B4
Blatherwick's Yd NG5 161 F4
Bleaberry Cl NG2 186 B3
Bleachers Yd NG7 160 C1
Bleak Hill Way NG18 101 F2
Bleasby CE Sch NG14 151 F4
Bleasby Cres NG17 101 D1
Bleasby Rd NG14 151 E4
Bleasby St NG2 173 F2
Bleasby Sta NG14 151 F4
Bleasdale Cl NG4 163 D1
Blencathra Cl NG2 186 B3

Blenheim Ave
Lowdham NG14 150 C1
Nottingham NG3 162 B1
Blenheim Cl
Mansfield NG19 88 B1
Ruddington NG11 196 A4
Blenheim Dr NG9 183 E3
Blenheim Gdns NG13 165 E1
Blenheim Ind Est NG6 159 F4
Blenheim La NG6,NG15 145 F1
Blenheim Pl NG17 99 F2
Blenheim Rise Bawtry DN10 9 F3
Worksop S81 35 F4
Blenhiem Ct NG10 182 A2
Blessed Robert Widmerpool RC Prim Sch NG11 195 F4
Bley Ave LE12 214 B4
Blidworth Cl NG8 159 F1
Blidworth Ind Pk NG21 118 A3
Blidworth La
Blidworth NG21 133 E4
Mansfield NG21 103 E1
Rainworth NG21 117 F4
Blidworth Rd
Farnsfield NG22 119 F3
Kirkby in A NG15 115 F2
Blidworth Waye NG15 131 F4
Blind La NG25 134 B2
Bloomgrove Rd DE7 157 F1
Bloomsbury Dr NG16 159 F2
Bloomsbury Mews NG12 176 C2
Bloomsgrove Ind Est NG7 222 B3
Bloomsgrove St NG7 222 B3
Blue Bell Hill Inf Sch NG3 173 F3
Blue Bell Hill Jun Sch NG3 173 F3
Blue Bell Hill Rd NG3 173 F3
Blue Bell Yd NG22 65 F2
Bluebell Bank NG13 177 E2
Bluebell Cl Hucknall NG15 145 E3
Selston NG16 128 C1
Stanton Hill NG17 100 A3
Bluebell Gr 15 NG17 114 C4
Bluebell Wood Way NG17 100 B1
Bluecoat Cl NG1 223 E3
Bluecoat St NG1 223 E4
Blundell Cl NG3 173 F4
Blyth Cl NG19 87 E1
Blyth Gdns NG3 161 F1
Blyth Gr S81 36 A3
Blyth Rd
Blyth, Bilby S81, DN22 27 F3
Blyth, Nornay S81 18 A4
Elkesley S80 48 C2
Harworth DN11 8 C2
New Ollerton NG22 77 D3
Oldcotes S81 16 C3
Ranskill DN22 19 D2
Walesby NG22 63 D2
Worksop, Kilton S81 36 A3
Worksop, Perlethorpe S80, NG22 48 C2
Blyth St NG3 161 F1
Blythe CE Prim Sch S81 18 A1
Blyton Rd DN21 15 E2
Blyton Wlk NG5 161 D4
Boar La NG24 139 F4
Boat La Aldercar NG16 143 D4
Bleasby NG14 152 B4
Hoveringham NG14 151 F1
Boatmans Cl DE7 157 F1
Bobbers Mill Bridge NG7 172 B4
Bobbers Mill Rd NG7 172 C4
Boden Dr NG16 159 E3
Boden St NG7 222 B3
Bodmin Ave NG15 145 E3
Bodmin Ct NG18 103 D1
Bodmin Dr NG8 160 B1
Body Rd NG9 183 D1
Bohem Rd NG10 182 B2
Bold Cl NG6 160 A4
Bolero Cl NG8 171 F3
Bolham La DN22 29 F1
Bolingey Way NG15 145 E3
Bollard's La LE12 213 D4
Bolsover St Hucknall NG15 146 A4
Mansfield NG18 102 B3
Bolton Ave NG9 183 E2
Bolton Cl NG2 186 A4
Bolton La LE14 211 F4
Bolton Terr NG12 175 F2
Bond Cl LE11 220 B1
Bond St Arnold NG5 161 F4
Nottingham NG2 173 F2
Bonemill La
Clarborough DN22 30 B1
Worksop S81 35 E3
Bonetti Cl NG5 162 B3
Boniface Gdns 4 NG5 147 D1
Bonington Dr NG5 161 F4
Bonington Rd
Mansfield NG19 101 F3
Nottingham NG3 162 A2
Bonner Hill NG14 148 C3
Bonner La NG14 149 D3
Bonner's Rd NG16 158 B2
Bonnington Cl NG6 160 A3
Bonnington Cres NG5 161 E2
Bonnington Jun & Inf Sch NG6 160 A3
Bonny Mead NG12 187 F1
Bonsal Ct NG18 103 D3
Bonsall St NG10 193 F4
Bonser Cl NG4 174 C4
Bonser Cres NG17 99 F1
Bonser Gdns NG17 100 B1
Booth Ave NG19 87 D3
Booth Cl NG3 223 F3
Booth Cres NG19 87 E1
Booth St NG19 88 A2
Boots Yd NG17 99 F2
Borders Ave NG17 114 C4
Borlace Cres NG9 182 C3
Borman Cl NG6 159 F3
Borough St DE74 203 E1
Borrow Bread La NG14 152 A4
Borrowdale Cl NG2 186 B3
Borrowdale Dr NG10 193 D3
Borrowell DE74 203 E2
Boscowan Ct DE7 157 F2
Bosden Cl NG8 171 E3
Bosley Sq NG9 184 A4
Bostock's La NG10 182 A2
Boston St NG1 223 F3
Boswell Cl Kinoulton NG12 200 A1
Mansfield NG18 102 B2
Bosworth Dr NG16 144 A2
Bosworth Prim Sch NG2 173 D1
Bosworth St NG19 101 E4
Bosworth Way NG10 193 F3
Bosworth Wlk 26 NG2 173 D1
Botany Ave
Mansfield NG18 101 F3
Nottingham NG3 173 F4
Botany Cl NG2 185 E1
Botany Dr DE7 157 F3
Bothe Cl NG10 193 E3
Bottesford CE Prim Sch NG13 181 D1
Bottesford Sta NG13 181 E2
Bottle La NG1 223 E2
Bottleacre La LE11 220 A3
Bottom Gn LE14 210 A1
Bottom Row NG24 140 A4
Boughton Cl NG17 100 C3
Boughton Ind Est NG22 78 A3
Boughton Rd S80 35 D3
Bould St NG19 87 F1
Boulevard Ind Pk NG7 184 B4
Boundary Cl NG20 72 C3
Boundary Cres
Beeston NG9 171 F1
Blidworth NG21 118 A3
Boundary Ct NG24 139 F4
Boundary La NG16 143 E2
Boundary Rd Beeston NG9 183 F4
Newark-on-T NG24 139 F4
West Bridgford NG2 185 F2
Boundary Row S80 35 F1
Boundary Wlk NG20 58 C1
Bourne Ave
Kirkby in A NG17 115 D2
Selston NG16 129 D4
Bourne Cl NG9 171 E1
Bourne Dr NG15 117 D1
Bourne Mews NG4 175 D3
Bourne St NG4 175 D3
Bournmoor Ave NG7 184 C1
Bovill St NG7 222 B4
Bovington Ct DN22 29 F1
Bow St NG19 88 C2
Bowbridge Gdns NG13 181 D2
Bowbridge Inf Sch NG24 140 A3
Bowbridge Jun Sch NG24 139 F3
Bowbridge La
Bottesford NG13 180 C2
New Balderton NG24 140 A2
Bowbridge Rd NG24 140 A3
Bowden Dr NG9 184 A3
Bowers Ave 19 NG3 173 E4
Bowes Well Rd DE7 157 F1
Bowland Cl NG3 174 A4
Bowland Rd NG13 177 E2
Bowler Ct 3 LE11 220 B2
Bowling Green Rd DN21 15 D1
Bowling St NG18 102 B3
Bowlwell Ave NG5 160 C4
Bowne St NG17 100 C2
Bowness Ave NG6 160 B1
Bowness Cl NG2 186 B4
Box Cres NG17 114 C3
Boxley Dr NG2 185 E2
Boxwell Ctry Pk NG8 159 F2
Boy La NG21 76 A1
Boyce Gdns NG3 161 F1
Boycroft Ave NG3 173 F4
Boyd Cl NG5 148 A1
Boyer St LE11 220 B2
Boyer's Orch LE14 202 A2
Boynton Dr NG3 161 F1
Bracadale Rd NG5 146 C1
Bracebridge S80 36 A2
Bracebridge Ave S80 36 A2
Bracebridge Ct S80 36 A1
Bracebridge Dr NG8 171 E4
Bracey Rise NG2 185 F2
Bracken Ave NG22 77 F3
Bracken Cl Carlton NG4 162 B1
Gainsborough DN21 15 D2
4 Kirkby in A NG17 114 C3
Long Eaton NG10 182 A1
Market Warsop NG20 74 B2
Nottingham NG8 159 F1
Bracken Ct DN11 8 C2
Bracken Hill NG18 103 D3
Bracken Hill La DN10 4 A3
Bracken Hill Sch NG17 115 E3
Bracken La DN22 40 A3
Bracken Lane Prim Sch DN22 40 A3
Bracken Rd NG10 182 A1
Bracken Way DN11 8 C2
Brackendale Ave NG5 161 F4
Brackendale Dr NG22 64 A1
Brackenfield Ave NG19 88 C2
Brackenfield Dr NG16 158 A4
Brackenfield Rise NG15 117 D2
Brackenfield Specl Sch NG10 182 A1
Brackenhurst Coll NG25 136 B3
Brackenhurst La NG25 136 B3
Brackenwood Cl NG19 89 D1
Brackhills Cl NG19 88 C1
Bracknell Cres NG8 160 B1
Brackner La NG22 106 A2
Bracton Dr NG3 173 F3
Bradbourne Ave NG11 185 D3
Bradbury-Midway Ind Est NG7 184 B4
Bradbury St NG2 174 A2
Bradden Ave NG9 170 C1
Bradder Way NG18 102 A3
Braddock Cl NG7 222 A2
Bradfield Rd NG8 159 F1
Bradforth Ave NG18 103 D4
Bradgate Cl NG10 182 A2
Bradgate Rd 2 NG7 173 D4
Bradley NG11 195 F4
Bradley St NG10 182 B3
Bradley Wlk NG11 195 F4
Bradleys Orch NG14 151 E1
Bradman Gdns NG5 162 A3
Bradmore Ave NG11 196 B4
Bradmore Ct NG18 103 D2
Bradmore La NG12 197 E3
Bradmore Rise NG5 161 E2
Bradshaw St NG10 193 D3
Bradwell Cl NG16 158 B4
Bradwell Dr NG5 161 D4
Braefell Cl NG2 186 B3
Braemar Ave NG16 143 F1
Braemar Dr NG4 163 D1
Braemar Rd Clipstone NG19 89 F2
Nottingham NG6 160 B4
Brailsford Ct NG18 103 D3
Brailsford Rd 1 NG7 172 C1
Brailsford Way NG9 183 E1
Brailwood Cl NG22 106 A3
Brailwood Rd NG22 106 A3
Brake La NG22 77 F4
Brake Rd NG22 63 F1
Brake View NG22 77 F3
Bramber Gr NG11 195 F4
Bramble Cl Beeston NG9 183 E1
Long Eaton NG10 182 A1
New Ollerton NG22 77 E3
Nottingham NG6 160 B2
Shirebrook NG20 72 C3
Bramble Croft NG17 100 B1
Bramble Ct NG4 162 C1
Bramble Dr NG3 174 A4
Bramble Gdns NG8 172 A4
Bramble La NG18 103 D2
Bramble Rd DN22 40 A2
Bramble Way DN11 8 C2
Brambles The NG22 64 A1
Brambleway NG12 188 A1
Brambling Cl NG18 102 C4
Bramblings The S81 35 E4
Bramcote Ave NG9 183 E3
Bramcote CE Sch NG9 183 D4
Bramcote Ct NG18 103 D2
Bramcote Dr Beeston NG9 183 F4
Nottingham NG8 171 E2
Retford DN22 39 E3
Bramcote Dr W NG9 183 E4
Bramcote Hills Comp Sch NG9 171 D1
Bramcote Hills Prim Sch NG9 171 D1
Bramcote L Ctr NG9 171 D1
Bramcote La Beeston NG9 183 E3
Nottingham NG8 171 E2
Bramcote Lorne Sch DN22 51 D3
Bramcote Park Comp Sch NG9 171 D1
Bramcote Rd NG9 183 F4
Bramcote St NG7 222 A3
Bramcote Wlk NG7 222 A3
Bramerton Rd NG8 171 E3
Bramhall Rd NG8 171 E3
Bramley Cl
East Leake LE12 205 F1
Gunthorpe NG14 165 D3
Southwell NG25 136 C4
Bramley Ct
Gainsborough DN21 15 F1
Kimberley NG16 158 C3
Sutton in A NG17 100 C2
Bramley Rd NG8 159 F1
Bramley Wlk NG19 101 E4
Brampton Ave DE75 143 D1
Brampton Ct NG2 186 B4
Brampton Dr NG9 182 C3
Brancaster Cl NG6 160 A2
Brancliffe La S81 34 C4
Brand La NG17 100 B3
Brand St NG2 173 F1
Brandish Cres NG11 184 B1
Brandon Cl NG24 140 C2
Brandreth Ave
Nottingham NG3 173 F4
Sutton in A NG17 100 B2
Brandreth Dr NG16 158 A4
Branklene Cl NG16 158 C4
Branksome Wlk 3 NG2 173 E1
Bransdale S81 36 A4
Bransdale Ave NG19 88 C1
Bransdale Cl NG10 193 D3
Bransdale Rd NG11 184 B1
Branston Ave NG22 119 F3
Branston Cl NG24 125 E3
Branston Gdns NG2 185 E2
Branston Wlk NG5 161 E2
Brantford Ave NG7 184 C1
Brassington Cl NG16 158 A4
Brassington Ct NG19 88 C2
Braunton Cl NG15 145 E3
Brayton Cres NG6 160 B3
Breach Rd DE75 157 D4
Breach The NG16 144 A2
Breadsall Ct DE7 157 F2
Breamer Rd NG23 112 A4
Brechin S81 36 A3
Brechin Cl NG5 148 A1
Brechin Ct NG19 88 A3
Breck Bank NG22 77 E3
Breck Bank Cres NG22 77 E3
Breck Hill Rd NG3 161 F2
Breck La DN10 20 A4
Breckbank NG19 88 C1
Brecks La Elston NG23 154 A1
Stapleford LN6 127 F4
Brecks Rd DN22 39 E2
Breckswood Dr NG11 195 F4
Brecon Cl
6 Long Eaton NG10 193 D4
Nottingham NG8 160 A2
Rainworth NG21 104 B1
Bredon Cl 7 NG10 193 D4
Breedon St NG10 182 B1
Brendon Ct NG9 183 D4
Brendon Dr
Kimberley NG16 158 C4
Nottingham NG8 172 A3
Brendon Gdns NG8 172 A3
Brendon Gr NG13 177 E3
Brendon Rd NG8 172 A3
Brendon Way NG10 182 A1
Brentcliffe Ave NG3 174 A4
Bretby Ct NG18 103 D3
Brett Cl NG15 145 F3
Bretton Rd NG15 117 D2
Brewer's Wharf NG24 124 C1
Brewery La Everton DN10 11 E2
Retford DN22 39 F3
Brewery St NG16 158 C3
Brewsters Cl NG13 177 F2
Brewsters Rd NG3 173 F4
Brewsters Way DN22 29 E1
Briar Ave NG10 182 A2
Briar Cl Beeston NG9 171 F1
Hucknall NG15 145 F3
Keyworth NG12 197 F2
Rainworth NG21 104 A1
Stanton Hill NG17 100 B3
Worksop S80 35 E1
Briar Ct Harworth DN11 8 C2
New Ollerton NG22 77 E3
Nottingham NG2 173 D1
Briar Gate Cotgrave NG12 188 A1
Long Eaton NG10 182 A1
Briar La NG18 103 D2
Briar Lea Retford DN22 39 E2
Worksop S80 35 E1
Briar Rd Eastwood NG16 158 A4
New Ollerton NG22 77 E3
Briarbank Ave NG3 174 A4
Briarbank Wlk NG3 174 A4
Briars The DN10 4 B2
Briarwood Ave NG3 174 A4
Briarwood Cl NG19 89 D1
Briarwood Ct NG3 161 F2
Briber Hill S81 18 A1
Briber Rd S81 18 A1
Brick Kiln La NG18 101 E4
Brick Yard Rd DN22 50 B3
Brickcliffe Rd LE12 205 F1
Brickenell Rd NG14 148 C3
Brickenhole La DN10 13 F3
Brickings Way DN22 32 B3
Brickley Cres LE12 205 F1
Brickyard NG15 146 B3
Brickyard Dr NG15 146 B3
Brickyard La
East Bridgford NG13 165 E1
East Leake LE12 214 A4
Farnsfield NG22 120 A3
Misson DN10 4 B2
Radcliffe on T NG12 176 A2
South Normanton DE55 113 D3
Sutton Bonington LE12 213 F4
Walkeringham DN10 13 E3
Bride Church La DN11 8 A4
Bridegate La LE14 209 F3
Bridge Ave NG9 183 F3
Bridge Cl S80 45 D3
Bridge Ct NG15 146 A3
Bridge End Ave NG16 128 C4
Bridge Farm La NG7 184 C1
Bridge Gr NG2 185 F4
Bridge Green Wlk 6 NG8 159 F1
Bridge Pl Saxilby LN1 57 D2
Worksop S80 35 F2
Bridge Rd
Gainsborough DN21 24 B4
Nottingham NG8 171 E3
Bridge St
Gainsborough DN21 24 B4
Ilkeston DE7 157 F2
Langley Mill NG16 143 E2
Long Eaton NG10 182 B1
Loughborough LE11 220 A2
Mansfield NG18 102 B4
Newark-on-T NG24 139 F4
Bridge St continued
Sandiacre NG10 182 B3
Saxilby LN1 57 D2
Worksop S80 35 F1
Bridgegate DN22 39 F4
Bridgend Cl NG9 182 B3
Bridgeway Ct NG2 173 E1
Bridgeway Ctr NG2 173 E1
Bridgford Rd
Kneeton NG13 166 A4
West Bridgford NG2 185 F4
Bridgford St NG18 102 C3
Bridgnorth Dr NG7 184 C1
Bridgnorth Way NG9 182 C2
Bridle Cl NG17 100 A3
Bridle Rd Beeston NG9 183 D4
Burton Joyce NG14 163 F3
Bridle Ways NG13 165 E1
Bridlesmith Gate NG1 223 E2
Bridleway The NG19 88 C1
Bridlington St NG7 172 C4
Bridport Ave 7 NG8 172 B3
Brielen Rd NG12 176 A2
Brierfield Ave NG11 185 D2
Brierly Gn NG4 175 D4
Brierly Cotts NG17 100 C2
Brierly Rd NG17 100 B2
Brigg Inf Sch DE55 113 D3
Bright Sq NG19 87 E1
Bright St
Gainsborough DN21 24 B4
Ilkeston DE7 157 F2
Nottingham NG7 222 A3
South Normanton DE55 113 D3
Brightmoor St NG1 223 F3
Brimington Ct NG19 88 C2
Brindley Rd NG8 171 E3
Brinkhill Cres NG11 184 C2
Brinkhill Prim Sch NG11 184 C2
Brinkley Hill NG25 137 D3
Brinsley Cl NG8 160 A1
Brinsley Hill NG16 128 B1
Brinsley Prim Sch NG16 143 E4
Brisbane Cl NG19 88 B3
Brisbane Ct NG24 140 B2
Brisbane Dr
Nottingham NG5 160 C4
Stapleford NG9 170 C1
Bristol Rd DE7 157 F1
Britannia Ave NG6 160 C3
Britannia Rd NG10 182 B1
Britannia Terr DN21 24 B4
British Fields NG22 65 E2
British Horological Institute NG23 122 C1
Brittania Ct NG24 139 F4
Britten Gdns NG3 173 F3
Brixham Rd NG15 145 E3
Brixton Rd NG7 222 A3
Brixworth Way DN22 40 A4
Broad Cl NG14 149 E2
Broad Eadow Rd NG6 159 F4
Broad Fen La NG23 156 A4
Broad Gate NG22 66 C4
Broad Gores DN22 30 B2
Broad La Brinsley NG16 143 F4
Hodthorpe S80 45 E3
South Leverton DN22 43 D3
Broad Marsh Ctr NG1 223 E2
Broad Meer NG12 187 F2
Broad Oak Cl NG3 173 F4
Broad Oak Dr
Brinsley NG16 143 F4
Stapleford NG9 182 B3
Broad Pl S80 45 E3
Broad St Long Eaton NG10 193 E4
Loughborough LE11 220 A2
Nottingham NG1 223 F3
Broad Valley Dr NG6 146 C2
Broad Wlk NG6 160 B2
Broadfields NG14 148 C4
Broadgate NG9 184 A4
Broadgate Ave NG9 184 A4
Broadgate La Beeston NG9 184 A4
Kelham NG23 123 F3
Broadhill Rd DE74 203 E1
Broadholme Rd LN1 57 D1
Broadholme St NG7 222 B1
Broadhurst Ave NG6 160 B1
Broadings La DN22 54 A3
Broadlands
Sandiacre NG10 182 A2
South Normanton DE55 113 D2
Broadleigh Cl NG2 185 E2
Broadleigh Ct DN22 39 E2
Broadmead NG14 163 F3
Broadoak Pk NG17 114 C1
Broadstairs Rd NG9 182 C1
Broadstone Cl NG2 185 E3
Broadway Carlton NG3 174 B3
Ilkeston DE7 157 F2
Nottingham NG1 223 F2
Broadway E NG4 174 B3
Broadway The NG18 102 B3
Broadwood Ct NG9 184 A4
Broadwood Rd NG5 161 D4
Brockdale Gdns NG12 197 F2
Brockenhurst Rd NG19 101 E3
Brockhall Rise DE75 143 D1
Brockhole Cl NG2 186 B3
Brockhurst Gdns NG3 173 F3
Brocklehurst Dr NG21 91 E4
Brocklesby Cl DN21 24 C4
Brocklewood Jun & Inf Schs NG8 171 F4
Brockley Rd NG2 186 A4
Brockton Ave NG24 139 D3
Brockwell The DE55 113 D2

Middle St
Barkestone-le-V NG13 ..... 192 B1
Beeston NG9 ..... 184 A3
Hose LE14 ..... 211 F4
Misson DN10 ..... 4 B1
Middle Wood La DN10 ..... 4 B3
Middlebeck Ave NG5 ..... 162 B4
Middlebeck Dr NG5 ..... 162 B4
Middlebridge Rd DN10 ..... 12 C2
Middlebrook Rd NG16 ..... 129 D2
Middledale Rd NG4 ..... 174 B3
Middlefell Way NG11 ..... 184 B1
Middlefield La DN21 ..... 24 C4
Middlefield Rd DN22 ..... 31 F4
Middlefield Sch The DN21 .. 24 C4
Middlegate Field Dr S80 ..... 45 D3
Middleton Bvd NG8 ..... 172 B2
Middleton Cl NG16 ..... 159 E3
Middleton Cres NG9 ..... 171 F1
Middleton Ct
Mansfield NG18 ..... 103 D3
New Ollerton NG22 ..... 77 E3
Middleton Pl LE11 ..... 220 A1
Middleton Prim Sch NG8 .. 172 B2
Middleton Rd
Ilkeston DE7 ..... 170 A3
Mansfield Woodhouse NG19 .. 88 B3
Newark-on-T NG24 ..... 125 E2
Middleton St
Awsworth NG16 ..... 158 B2
Beeston NG9 ..... 183 F4
Cossall DE7 ..... 158 A1
Nottingham NG7 ..... 222 A3
Midfield Rd NG17 ..... 115 D1
Midhurst Cl NG9 ..... 183 D2
Midhurst Way NG7 ..... 184 C1
Midlame Gdns NG6 ..... 159 F4
Midland Ave Carlton NG4 ... 175 D4
Nottingham NG7 ..... 222 A1
Stapleford NG9 ..... 182 B3
Midland Cres NG4 ..... 174 C4
Midland Ct NG7 ..... 172 B3
Midland Gr NG4 ..... 175 D4
Midland Rd Carlton NG4 ..... 174 C4
Eastwood NG16 ..... 143 F1
Sutton in A NG17 ..... 101 D1
Midland St NG10 ..... 193 F4
Midway The NG7 ..... 184 C4
Midworth St NG18 ..... 102 A3
Mikado Rd NG10 ..... 193 E3
Milburn Gr NG13 ..... 177 E2
Mildenhall Cres NG5 ..... 161 E4
Mile End Rd NG4 ..... 174 C3
Miles Yd LE11 ..... 220 A2
Milford Ave NG10 ..... 182 A2
Milford Cl NG6 ..... 160 A4
Milford Cres NG19 ..... 101 E4
Milford Ct NG5 ..... 161 E3
Milford Dr Ilkeston DE7 ..... 157 E2
Nottingham NG3 ..... 174 B4
Milford Prim Sch NG11 ..... 195 F4
Mill Baulk Rd DN10 ..... 14 A3
Mill Cl Huthwaite NG17 ..... 100 A2
North Leverton w H DN22 ..... 32 B1
Sutton on T NG23 ..... 96 C4
Mill Cl The NG8 ..... 160 C2
Mill Cres Arnold NG5 ..... 161 F4
Whitwell S80 ..... 45 D3
Mill Croft NG17 ..... 100 C1
Mill Field Cl
Burton Joyce NG14 ..... 163 F2
Harby NG23 ..... 70 B1
Mill Gate
East Bridgford NG13 ..... 165 E2
Newark-on-T NG24 ..... 139 F4
Mill Gdns S80 ..... 35 E1
Mill Gn NG24 ..... 140 A4
Mill Heyes NG13 ..... 165 E2
Mill Hill DN10 ..... 12 B1
Mill Hill Rd NG13 ..... 177 E2
Mill Holme DE55 ..... 113 D2
Mill La
Annesley Woodhouse NG17 114 C1
Arnold NG5 ..... 161 F4
Caunton NG23 ..... 109 D3
Cossall NG16 ..... 158 B1
Cotgrave NG12 ..... 187 F2
Eagle LN6 ..... 84 C2
East Leake LE12 ..... 214 C4
Edwinstowe NG21 ..... 76 A1
Hickling LE14 ..... 210 B4
Huthwaite NG17 ..... 100 A1
Kegworth DE74 ..... 203 E1
Lambley NG4 ..... 163 D4
Long Clawson LE14 ..... 211 E2
Long Whatton LE12 ..... 212 B2
Loughborough LE11 ..... 220 B3
Morton DN21 ..... 15 E3
Newark-on-T NG24 ..... 139 F4
Normanton on T NG23 ..... 81 E4
North Clifton NG23 ..... 68 C3
North Leverton w H DN22 ..... 42 A4
North Muskham NG23 ..... 110 C1
Orston NG13 ..... 180 A4
Pinxton NG16 ..... 113 E1
Rockley DN22 ..... 51 D1
Sandiacre NG10 ..... 182 B3
Saxilby LN1 ..... 57 D2
Scarrington NG13 ..... 178 C4
Scrooby DN10 ..... 10 A2
South Leverton DN22 ..... 42 B4
Stainsby S44 ..... 85 E4
Upton NG23 ..... 137 F4
Walesby NG22 ..... 63 F1
Walkeringham DN10 ..... 13 F2
Whitwell S80 ..... 45 D3
Willoughby-on-t-W LE12 ..... 217 E4
Mill Lakes Ctry Pk NG6 ..... 146 B2
Mill Meadow View S81 ..... 18 A2
Mill Pk NG25 ..... 121 F1
Mill Rd Eastwood NG16 ..... 144 A2
Elston NG23 ..... 153 F2
Heanor DE75 ..... 157 D4
Stapleford NG9 ..... 182 B4
Mill St Ilkeston DE7 ..... 157 F1
Mansfield NG18 ..... 102 B3
Nottingham NG6 ..... 160 B2
Retford DN22 ..... 39 F3
Sutton in A NG17 ..... 100 C1
Worksop S80 ..... 35 F2
Mill Wlk S80 ..... 45 D3
Mill Yd Beeston NG9 ..... 183 F3
Hucknall NG15 ..... 146 A4
Millash La S80 ..... 45 D2
Millbank DE75 ..... 157 D4
Millbank Cl DE7 ..... 157 E2
Millbaulk La NG22 ..... 93 F4
Millbeck Ave NG8 ..... 171 E2
Millbeck Cl NG2 ..... 186 B3
Milldale Cl NG11 ..... 184 B1
Milldale Ct NG18 ..... 103 D3
Milldale Rd
Farnsfield NG22 ..... 120 A3
Long Eaton NG10 ..... 193 D3
Milldale Wlk NG17 ..... 100 B2
Millennium Way E NG6 ..... 160 A2
Millennium Way W NG6 ..... 160 A2
Miller Hives Cl NG12 ..... 187 F2
Miller's La LE12 ..... 206 B1
Millers Bridge NG12 ..... 187 F1
Millers Cl Retford DN22 ..... 39 F3
Shelford NG12 ..... 164 B1
Millers Ct NG7 ..... 222 A4
Millers Way DN22 ..... 39 E4
Millersdale Ave
Ilkeston DE7 ..... 157 F3
Mansfield NG18 ..... 101 F2
Millfield Ave LN1 ..... 57 D2
Millfield Cl Ilkeston DE7 ..... 157 E2
Retford DN22 ..... 39 F2
Millfield Rd Ilkeston DE7 ..... 170 A4
Kimberley NG16 ..... 158 C4
South Leverton DN22 ..... 42 A3
Millfield View S80 ..... 35 E1
Millicent Gr NG2 ..... 185 F4
Millicent Rd NG2 ..... 185 F4
Millingdon Ave NG16 ..... 159 E2
Millman Way DN22 ..... 29 E1
Mills Dr NG24 ..... 139 E3
Millview Cl 24 NG2 ..... 173 F2
Millview Ct 13 NG2 ..... 173 F2
Millway NG19 ..... 88 B1
Milne Ave DN11 ..... 9 E2
Milne Dr DN11 ..... 9 E2
Milne Gr DN11 ..... 9 E2
Milne Rd DN11 ..... 9 E2
Milner Rd
Long Eaton NG10 ..... 193 E4
Nottingham NG5 ..... 161 E1
Milner St
Newark-on-T NG24 ..... 140 A4
Sutton in A NG17 ..... 101 D3
Milnercroft DN22 ..... 29 E1
Milnercroft Gn DN22 ..... 29 E1
Milnhay Rd Heanor NG16 ..... 143 E1
Langley Mill NG16 ..... 143 E1
Milton Ave DE7 ..... 157 F2
Milton Cl NG17 ..... 101 D2
Milton Cres Beeston NG9 ..... 183 E1
Ravenshead NG15 ..... 117 D1
Milton Ct NG5 ..... 162 A4
Milton Dr
Ravenshead NG15 ..... 117 D1
Worksop S81 ..... 36 A2
Milton Rd
Gainsborough DN21 ..... 15 F1
Ilkeston DE7 ..... 157 F2
West Markham NG22 ..... 65 D3
Milton Rise NG15 ..... 145 E3
Milton St Ilkeston DE7 ..... 157 F2
Kirkby in A NG17 ..... 115 D3
Long Eaton NG10 ..... 193 E4
Mansfield NG18 ..... 102 A4
New Balderton NG24 ..... 140 B3
Nottingham NG1 ..... 223 E3
Milton Wlk S81 ..... 36 A2
Milverton Rd NG5 ..... 161 E4
Mimosa Cl NG11 ..... 184 B1
Minerva St NG6 ..... 160 A4
Minster Cl Hucknall NG15 ..... 146 A4
Kirkby in A NG17 ..... 114 C3
Minster Gdns NG16 ..... 144 A1
Minster Rd DN10 ..... 6 C1
Minster Sch The NG25 ..... 136 B4
Mint Cl NG10 ..... 193 D4
Minver Cres NG8 ..... 160 A1
Mirberry Mews NG7 ..... 222 A1
Mire La DN22 ..... 28 C3
Misk Hollows NG15 ..... 145 F4
Misk View NG16 ..... 144 A1
Mission St NG3 ..... 161 F1
Misson Prim Sch DN10 ..... 4 A2
Misterton Cres NG15 ..... 116 C1
Misterton Ct NG19 ..... 88 A1
Misterton Prim Sch DN10 .... 13 F4
Mitchel Ave NG24 ..... 125 F1
Mitchell Ave NG16 ..... 143 D2
Mitchell Cl
Nottingham NG6 ..... 160 A3
Worksop S81 ..... 35 F4
Mitchell St NG10 ..... 193 F4
Mitchell Terr DE7 ..... 170 A3
Mob La LE12 ..... 217 E4
Model Village S80 ..... 58 C4
Model Village Prim Sch
NG20 ..... 72 C2
Moffat Cl NG3 ..... 173 F4
Moira St LE11 ..... 220 A2
Mollington Sq NG6 ..... 160 A2
Mona Rd NG2 ..... 174 A1
Mona St NG9 ..... 184 A3
Monarch Way LE11 ..... 220 A3
Monckton Rd
Bircotes DN11 ..... 9 E2
Retford DN22 ..... 39 E4
Monk's La NG11 ..... 195 D1
Monks Cl DE7 ..... 170 A4
Monks Mdw LE12 ..... 205 F1
Monks Way S81 ..... 34 C4
Monksway NG11 ..... 185 D2
Monkton Cl DE7 ..... 157 E2
Monkton Dr
Nottingham NG8 ..... 171 F4
Southwell NG25 ..... 121 F1
Monkwood Cl NG23 ..... 98 A1
Monmouth Cl NG8 ..... 171 D2
Monmouth Rd S81 ..... 36 A3
Monroe Wlk 33 NG5 ..... 161 D4
Monsaldale Cl NG10 ..... 193 D3
Monsall Ave DE7 ..... 157 F3
Monsall St NG7 ..... 160 C1
Monsell Dr NG5 ..... 147 F1
Montague Rd NG15 ..... 146 A4
Montague St Beeston NG9 .. 183 F4
Mansfield NG18 ..... 102 C3
Nottingham NG6 ..... 160 B4
Montfort Cres NG5 ..... 161 E2
Montfort St NG7 ..... 222 C3
Montgomery Cl 8 NG9 ..... 183 E1
Montgomery Rd NG24 ..... 140 A3
Montgomery St NG7 ..... 222 C4
Montpelier Rd NG7 ..... 172 C1
Montrose S81 ..... 36 A3
Montrose Ct NG9 ..... 170 C1
Montrose Sq NG19 ..... 88 A3
Montys Mdw S81 ..... 35 E4
Monyash Cl DE7 ..... 157 F2
Moor Bridge NG6 ..... 146 B1
Moor Farm Inn La NG9 ..... 171 D1
Moor La Aslockton NG13 ..... 178 B3
Beeston NG9 ..... 171 D2
Besthorpe NG23 ..... 98 B3
Bingham NG13 ..... 177 F3
Blyth S81 ..... 18 B1
Bunny NG11 ..... 206 B4
Calverton NG14 ..... 149 E3
Elston NG23 ..... 154 A3
Gotham NG11 ..... 205 E4
Dry Doddington NG23 ..... 169 F3
Loughborough LE11 ..... 220 B2
Mansfield NG18 ..... 101 F3
Morton NG25 ..... 137 E2
Normanton on S LE12 ..... 213 E2
North Clifton NG23 ..... 69 D2
Ruddington NG11 ..... 196 B3
South Clifton NG23 ..... 69 E2
Stathern NG13 ..... 202 C3
Syerston NG23 ..... 153 E2
Upper Langwith S44 ..... 72 A4
Moor La Fst Sch NG18 ..... 101 F3
Moor Rd
Bestwood Village NG6 ..... 146 C3
Brinsley NG16 ..... 143 F4
Calverton NG14 ..... 149 D4
Collingham NG23 ..... 98 A1
Nottingham NG8 ..... 159 E1
Moor St Carlton NG4 ..... 175 D4
Mansfield NG18 ..... 102 A3
Moor The NG16 ..... 143 E4
Moor Top Rd DN11 ..... 8 C3
Moorbridge Cotts NG6 ..... 146 B1
Moorbridge Ct NG13 ..... 177 F3
Moorbridge La NG9 ..... 170 B1
Moorbridge Rd NG13 ..... 177 F3
Moorbridge Rd E NG13 ..... 177 F3
Moore Ave DE74 ..... 203 E2
Moore Cl East Leake LE12 ..... 205 F1
West Bridgford NG2 ..... 174 A1
Moore Gate NG9 ..... 184 A3
Moore Rd NG3 ..... 162 A1
Moores Ave NG10 ..... 182 B4
Moorfield Cres NG10 ..... 182 A3
Moorfield Ct NG9 ..... 170 C1
Moorfield La NG20 ..... 58 C2
Moorfield Pl NG20 ..... 74 B3
Moorfields Ave NG16 ..... 143 F2
Moorgate Ave NG19 ..... 86 C4
Moorgate Pk DN22 ..... 39 F4
Moorgate St NG7 ..... 222 C3
Moorgreen NG16 ..... 144 B2
Moorgreen Dr NG8 ..... 159 E1
Moorhaigh La NG19 ..... 87 D2
Moorhouse Rd
Egmanton NG22 ..... 80 B2
Nottingham NG8 ..... 171 F3
Moorings The 19 NG7 ..... 172 C1
Moorland Ave
Stapleford NG9 ..... 182 B3
Walkeringham DN10 ..... 13 F3
Moorland Cl
Sutton in A NG17 ..... 101 D3
Walkeringham DN10 ..... 13 F3
Moorland Way NG18 ..... 103 D3
Moorland Wlk DN10 ..... 13 F3
Moorlands Cl NG10 ..... 182 A1
Moorsholm Dr NG8 ..... 171 E2
Moray Ct NG16 ..... 158 C4
Moray Sq NG19 ..... 101 E3
Morden Cl NG8 ..... 171 E4
Morden Rd NG16 ..... 158 B4
Moreland Ct Carlton NG4 ..... 174 B4
37 Nottingham NG2 ..... 173 F2
Moreland Pl 38 NG2 ..... 173 F2
Moreland St NG2 ..... 173 F2
Moreley Jun Sch NG3 ..... 173 F4
Morello Ave NG4 ..... 174 C4
Moreton Rd NG11 ..... 195 F4
Morgan Mews NG7 ..... 184 C1
Morgans Cl NG24 ..... 126 A1
Morkinshire Cres NG12 ..... 187 F2
Morkinshire La NG12 ..... 187 F2
Morley Ave
Nottingham NG3 ..... 161 F1
Retford DN22 ..... 29 E1
Morley Cl NG18 ..... 103 D3
Morley Ct 5 NG2 ..... 173 F2
Morley Dr DE7 ..... 157 E2
Morley Rd NG3 ..... 162 A1
Morley St Arnold NG5 ..... 161 F3
Gainsborough DN21 ..... 24 B4
Kirkby in A NG17 ..... 115 D2
Loughborough LE11 ..... 220 B3
Stanton Hill NG17 ..... 100 B3
Sutton in A NG17 ..... 100 C2
Morley's Cl NG14 ..... 150 C1
Mornington Cl NG10 ..... 182 B3
Mornington Cres NG16 ..... 159 E2
Mornington Prim Sch
NG16 ..... 159 E2
Morrell Bank NG5 ..... 160 C3
Morris Ave NG9 ..... 183 D1
Morris Cl LE11 ..... 220 B2
Morris Rd NG8 ..... 159 E1
Morris St NG4 ..... 175 D4
Morton Cl Mansfield NG18 .. 103 D3
Morton DN21 ..... 15 D2
Radcliffe on T NG12 ..... 176 B2
Morton Gdns NG12 ..... 176 B2
Morton Gr S81 ..... 35 F4
Morton Hall Gdns DN22 ..... 38 A3
Morton Rd DN21 ..... 15 E2
Morton St NG19 ..... 87 F1
Morton Terr DN21 ..... 15 E1
Morton Trentside
Cty Prim Sch DN21 ..... 15 D2
Morval Rd NG8 ..... 171 F4
Morven Ave
Hucknall NG15 ..... 146 A3
Mansfield Woodhouse NG19 .. 88 A1
Sutton in A NG17 ..... 100 C1
Morven Park Prim Sch
NG17 ..... 115 D3
Morven Rd NG17 ..... 115 D3
Morven St S80 ..... 58 C4
Morven Terr NG20 ..... 74 A2
Mosborough Rd NG17 ..... 100 A1
Moseley Rd NG15 ..... 130 B4
Moses View S81 ..... 34 C4
Mosgrove Cl S81 ..... 35 E4
Mosley St Hucknall NG15 ..... 146 A3
Nottingham NG7 ..... 172 C4
Moss Cl Arnold NG5 ..... 147 E1
East Bridgford NG13 ..... 165 E2
Moss Dr NG9 ..... 183 D4
Moss Rd NG15 ..... 145 F4
Moss Rise NG3 ..... 162 A1
Moss Side NG11 ..... 185 D2
Mosscroft Ave NG11 ..... 184 B1
Mossdale S81 ..... 36 A4
Mossdale Rd
Mansfield NG18 ..... 102 C4
Nottingham NG5 ..... 161 E3
Mosswood Cres NG5 ..... 161 D4
Mottram Rd NG9 ..... 183 E3
Moulton Cres NG24 ..... 140 B2
Mount Ave S81 ..... 35 F3
Mount CE Prim Sch
NG24 ..... 125 D1
Mount Cl DN11 ..... 8 C3
Mount Cres
Market Warsop NG20 ..... 74 B2
South Normanton DE55 ..... 113 D2
Mount Ct NG24 ..... 140 B2
Mount Hooton Rd NG7 ..... 222 C4
Mount La NG24 ..... 140 A4
Mount Milner NG18 ..... 102 B3
Mount Pleasant
Carlton NG4 ..... 174 C4
Ilkeston DE7 ..... 157 F2
Keyworth NG12 ..... 198 A2
Lowdham NG14 ..... 150 B1
2 Mansfield NG18 ..... 102 A4
Nottingham NG6 ..... 160 C1
Radcliffe on T NG12 ..... 175 F2
Retford DN22 ..... 39 F4
Sutton in A NG17 ..... 100 C2
Mount Pleasant Cl DN21 ..... 44 B4
Mount Rd NG24 ..... 140 B2
Mount St
Nottingham, New Basford
NG7 ..... 160 C1
Nottingham, Standard Hill
NG1 ..... 223 D2
Stapleford NG9 ..... 182 C4
Mount The Arnold NG5 ..... 147 E1
Bestwood Village NG6 ..... 146 C2
Clipstone NG19 ..... 89 E2
Nottingham, Broxtowe NG8 .. 159 F1
Nottingham, Portchester
NG3 ..... 162 B1
Stapleford NG9 ..... 182 B3
Mount View Cl NG18 ..... 102 B3
Mountbatten Ct DE7 ..... 157 F2
Mountbatten Gr NG4 ..... 162 C1
Mountbatten Way NG9 ..... 183 E1
Mountfield Ave NG10 ..... 182 A2
Mountfield Dr NG5 ..... 161 D4
Mountsorrel Dr NG2 ..... 186 A3
Mowbray Ct NG3 ..... 223 F3
Mowbray Gdns NG2 ..... 185 F3
Mowbray Rise NG5 ..... 161 F4
Mowbray Str DN21 ..... 15 E1
Mowlands Cl NG17 ..... 101 D1
Moyra Dr NG5 ..... 161 E4
Mozart Cl NG7 ..... 222 A3
Muir Ave NG12 ..... 197 E4
Muirfield S81 ..... 36 A3
Muirfield Cl 8 NG17 ..... 114 C4
Muirfield Rd NG5 ..... 147 D1
Muirfield Way NG19 ..... 88 C3
Mulberry Cl NG2 ..... 185 D3
Mulberry Cres S81 ..... 25 F4
Mulberry Gdns 1 NG6 ..... 160 A4
Mulberry Gr NG15 ..... 146 A2
Mumby Cl NG24 ..... 125 D1
Mundella Rd NG2 ..... 173 E1
Mundy St DE7 ..... 157 F1
Munford Circ NG6 ..... 160 A2
Munks Ave NG15 ..... 145 F4
Murby Cres NG6 ..... 160 A4
Murden Way NG9 ..... 184 A3
Muriel Rd NG9 ..... 183 F4
Muriel St NG6 ..... 160 A4
Murray St NG18 ..... 102 A3
Muschamp Terr NG20 ..... 74 A2
Mushill La LE12 ..... 216 B3
Muskham Ave DE7 ..... 157 F2
Muskham Ct NG19 ..... 88 A1
Muskham La NG23 ..... 110 B1
Muskham Prim Sch
NG23 ..... 110 C1
Muskham St NG2 ..... 173 E1
Musters Cres NG2 ..... 185 F3
Musters Croft NG4 ..... 174 C2
Musters Rd
Bingham NG13 ..... 177 E2
Langar NG13 ..... 190 B1
Newstead NG15 ..... 130 B3
Ruddington NG11 ..... 196 B3
West Bridgford NG2 ..... 185 F3
Musters St NG20 ..... 73 D2
Musters Wlk 13 NG6 ..... 160 A4
Muston Cl NG3 ..... 161 F1
Muston La NG13 ..... 181 E1
Mutton La DN10 ..... 23 D4
Muttonshire Hill DN22 ..... 50 C3
Mynd The NG19 ..... 88 C3
Myrtle Ave
Long Eaton NG10 ..... 193 E3
7 Nottingham NG7 ..... 173 D4
Stapleford NG9 ..... 182 C3
Myrtle Cl NG20 ..... 72 B3
Myrtle Gr NG9 ..... 184 A4
Myrtle Rd NG4 ..... 174 B4
Myrtle St DN22 ..... 39 E3
Myrtus Cl NG11 ..... 184 B1

Nabbs La NG15 ..... 145 F3
Naburn Ct 5 NG8 ..... 172 B4
Nairn Cl Arnold NG5 ..... 148 A1
Farnsfield NG22 ..... 119 F3
Nairn Mews NG4 ..... 174 C4
Nan Sampson Bank DN9 ..... 1 B4
Nansen St NG6 ..... 160 B3
Naomi Cres NG6 ..... 146 B1
Naomi Ct NG6 ..... 146 B1
Narrow La Bawtry DN10 ..... 10 A4
Greasley NG16 ..... 145 D2
Hathern LE12 ..... 213 D1
Wymeswold LE12 ..... 217 D1
Naseby Cl NG5 ..... 160 C2
Naseby Dr NG10 ..... 193 F2
Nash Cl S81 ..... 36 B2
Nathaniel Rd NG10 ..... 193 F3
Nathans La NG12 ..... 187 D4
National CE Jun &
Inf Sch The NG15 ..... 146 A4
National Sch The NG15 ..... 130 C1
National Water Sports Ctr
NG12 ..... 174 C2
Navenby Wlk NG7 ..... 184 C1
Navigation Way LE11 ..... 220 A3
Navigation Yd NG24 ..... 139 F4
Naworth Cl NG6 ..... 160 C3
Naylor Ave Gotham NG11 ..... 195 D1
Loughborough LE11 ..... 220 B1
Neal Ct NG16 ..... 143 D2
Neale St NG10 ..... 193 F4
Near Mdw NG10 ..... 193 F3
Nearsby Dr NG2 ..... 186 A3
Needham Rd NG5 ..... 162 A4
Needham St NG13 ..... 177 F2
Needwood Ave NG9 ..... 170 B1
Neeps Croft NG14 ..... 150 A3
Negus Ct NG4 ..... 163 D3
Neighwood Cl NG9 ..... 182 C1
Nell Gwyn Cres NG5 ..... 147 E1
Nelper Cres DE7 ..... 170 A3
Nelson La NG23 ..... 110 C1
Nelson Rd Arnold NG5 ..... 161 F4
Beeston NG9 ..... 184 A2
New Balderton NG24 ..... 140 A2
Nottingham NG6 ..... 160 B4
Nelson St
Gainsborough DN21 ..... 15 E1
Ilkeston DE7 ..... 157 F2
Long Eaton NG10 ..... 193 E3
Nottingham NG1 ..... 223 F2
Retford DN22 ..... 39 F3
Nene Cl NG15 ..... 145 F2
Nene Wlk S81 ..... 35 F4
Nesbitt St NG17 ..... 100 C1
Nesfield Ct DE7 ..... 157 F1
Nesfield Rd DE7 ..... 157 F1
Neston Dr NG8 ..... 160 B2
Nether Cl Eastwood NG16 ..... 143 F2
Nottingham NG3 ..... 174 A3

Reform St
Annesley Woodhouse NG17 . 129 F4
Sutton in A NG17 100 C1
Regatta Way NG2 186 B4
Regency Ct NG9 184 A4
Regent St Beeston NG9 184 A4
Kimberley NG16 158 C3
Kirkby in A NG17 114 C2
Langley Mill NG16 143 D2
Long Eaton NG10 193 E4
Loughborough LE11 220 A2
Mansfield NG18 102 A4
Nottingham, New Basford NG7 161 D1
Nottingham, Standard Hill NG1 223 D2
Stapleford NG10 182 B3
Sutton in A NG17 100 B1
Regents Cl NG23 112 A4
Regents Park Cl NG2 185 E3
Regina Cl NG12 175 F1
Regina Cres NG15 116 C1
Reid Gdns NG16 159 D4
Reigate Cl NG9 183 F1
Reigate Dr NG9 183 F1
Reigate Rd NG7 160 C1
Reindeer St NG18 102 C3
Rempstone Dr NG6 160 B3
Rempstone Rd
East Leake LE12 214 C4
East Leake, Stanford Hills LE12 214 A3
Hoton LE12 215 E1
Wymeswold LE12 216 A2
Renals Way NG14 148 C4
Rendell Prim Sch LE11 220 A3
Renfrew Ct NG19 101 F3
Renfrew Dr NG8 171 F2
Repton Ct NG19 88 C2
Repton Dr DE7 170 A4
Repton Rd
Nottingham NG6 160 B3
West Bridgford NG2 185 F3
Retford Gate DN22 41 F4
Retford Hospl DN22 39 E4
Retford Rd
Askham DN22 52 C2
Blyth S81 18 A1
Boughton NG22 77 F4
Mattersey DN10 20 B3
North Leverton w H DN22 41 F4
North Wheatley DN22 31 E4
Nottingham NG5 161 D2
Rampton DN22 42 B1
Ranby S81 37 E2
South Leverton DN22 42 A4
Worksop S80 36 B1
Retford Sta DN22 39 F3
Revelstoke Ave NG5 146 B1
Revelstoke Way NG5 146 C1
Revesby Gdns NG8 172 B4
Revesby Rd NG5 161 F3
Revill Cl DE7 157 E1
Revill Cres NG9 182 C4
Revill Ct 13 NG17 114 C4
Reydon Dr NG8 160 B1
Reynolds Dr NG8 171 F3
Rhodes Wlk NG18 101 F3
Rhyl Cres NG4 162 C1
Ribblesdale S81 36 A4
Ribblesdale Ct NG9 183 D2
Ribblesdale Rd
Long Eaton NG10 193 D3
Nottingham NG5 161 E3
Riber Cl
Annesley Woodhouse NG17 115 D1
Long Eaton NG10 193 E3
Richard Bonnington Prim Sch NG5 147 F1
Richard St DN22 40 A3
Richards Cl NG12 189 D2
Richardson Cl NG11 184 B1
Richborough Pl NG8 171 F1
Richey Cl NG5 162 A4
Richmond Ave
Breaston DE72 193 D4
Calverton NG14 149 D4
Eastwood NG16 144 A1
Ilkeston DE7 157 F2
Nottingham NG3 173 F4
Sandiacre NG10 182 A2
Richmond Cl NG24 140 A2
Richmond Dr
Beeston NG9 183 F3
Mansfield Woodhouse NG19 .. 88 B1
Nottingham NG3 161 E1
Radcliffe on T NG12 175 F2
Richmond Gdns NG5 147 F1
Richmond La DN10 9 F3
Richmond Rd
Carlton in L S81 25 F3
Gainsborough DN21 24 C4
Kirkby in A NG17 115 E3
Retford DN22 30 A1
West Bridgford NG2 173 F1
Worksop S80 36 A1
Richmond St NG18 102 C3
Richmond Terr NG12 175 F2
Rick St NG1 223 F3
Ricket La
Blidworth NG21 117 E3
Ravenshead NG15 116 C2
Ricklow Ct 1 NG5 161 D4
Riddell Ave S81 16 C2
Ridding Terr NG3 223 E4
Ridge Cl NG17 100 B2
Ridge Hill NG14 150 B1
Ridge La NG12 176 A3
Ridgeway
Nottingham NG5 161 D4
Shipley DE75 157 D4
Southwell NG25 121 E1
Worksop S81 36 A3
Ridgeway Cl NG22 119 F3
Ridgeway La NG20 74 A2
Ridgeway St NG3 173 F3
Ridgeway Terr NG20 74 A2
Ridgeway The NG22 120 A3
Ridgeway Wlk 17 NG5 161 D4
Ridgewood Dr NG9 183 E2
Ridgewood Gr NG15 117 D1
Ridgmont Walk NG11 195 E4
Ridgway Cl NG2 186 B3
Riding or Ridding La DN10 3 D2
Ridings The
Bulcote NG14 164 A3
East Bridgford NG13 165 E2
Keyworth NG12 198 A2
Mansfield Woodhouse NG19 .. 88 C1
Ridsdale Rd NG5 161 E3
Rifle St NG7 222 A3
Rigg La NG21 132 C4
Rigley Ave 19 DE7 157 F1
Rigley Dr NG5 160 C4
Riley Ave NG17 100 B2
Riley Cl NG17 100 B2
Ring Leas NG12 188 A1
Ringrose Cl NG24 140 B4
Ringstead Cl NG2 185 E3
Ringstead Wlk NG5 161 D4
Ringwood S81 36 A3
Ringwood Ave NG18 102 B2
Ringwood Cres NG8 172 B3
Ringwood Rd NG13 177 E2
Ripon Rd NG3 174 A3
Rise Park Jun & Inf Schs NG5 146 C1
Rise Park Rd NG5 146 C1
Rise The NG5 161 E2
Riseborough Wlk NG6 146 B1
Risegate NG12 187 F2
Riseholme Ave NG8 171 E2
Riseholme Rd DN21 24 C4
Risley Ct DE7 157 F2
Risley Dr NG2 173 D1
Riste's Pl NG2 223 F2
Ritchie Cl NG12 188 A1
Ritson Cl NG3 223 F4
River Cl DN22 29 F1
River La Misson DN10 4 B1
Retford DN22 39 F4
River Rd NG4 174 C2
River View
Market Warsop NG20 74 A3
Nottingham NG2 173 E1
Pye Bridge DE55 128 A3
Retford DN22 39 F2
Riverdale Rd NG9 183 E1
Rivergreen NG11 184 C2
Rivergreen Cl NG9 171 E1
Rivergreen Cres NG9 171 E1
Rivermead
Cotgrave NG12 188 A2
Newark-on-T NG24 139 F3
Riverside Southwell NG25 121 F1
Whatton NG13 179 D2
Riverside Cl
Bottesford NG13 181 D2
Cuckney NG20 60 A2
Riverside Rd
Beeston NG9 184 A2
Newark-on-T NG24 139 E3
Riverside Ret Pk NG11 185 D4
Riverside Way
Mansfield Woodhouse NG19 .. 88 B3
Nottingham NG2 173 D1
Riverside Wlk NG13 181 D2
Riverview Cotts DN10 4 B1
Riverway Gdns NG2 173 E1
Rivington Rd NG9 182 C1
Road No 1 NG4 174 C3
Road No 2 NG4 174 C3
Road No 3 NG4 175 D3
Road No 4 NG4 175 E3
Road No 5 NG4 175 D3
Road No 7 NG4 174 C3
Road No 8 NG4 174 C3
Roadwood La NG23 69 F4
Rob Roy Ave NG7 222 B1
Robbie Burns Rd NG5 161 E4
Robert Ave NG18 101 F3
Robert Dukeson Ave NG24 125 D2
Robert Jones Jun Sch NG21 118 A3
Robert Mellors Prim Sch NG5 161 F4
Robert Miles Jun Sch NG13 177 F2
Robert Shaw Prim Sch NG8 172 B3
Robert's La NG15 145 F4
Roberts Ave NG17 99 F1
Roberts Cl
Dunham on T NG22 54 A1
Kegworth DE74 203 E1
Roberts St Ilkeston DE7 170 A3
Nottingham NG2 173 F2
Roberts Yd NG9 184 A4
Robey Cl Hucknall NG15 131 D1
Mansfield Woodhouse NG19 .. 89 D1
Robey Dr NG16 143 F2
Robin Down Cl NG18 102 B1
Robin Down La NG18 102 B1
Robin Gr NG15 117 D1
Robin Hood Ave
Edwinstowe NG21 91 E4
Market Warsop NG20 74 B1
Robin Hood Cl NG16 143 F1
Robin Hood Dr NG15 145 F3
Robin Hood Ind Est 8 NG3 173 F3
Robin Hood Inf & Jun Sch
Mansfield Woodhouse NG19 .. 88 A2
Nottingham NG5 161 D3
Robin Hood Rd
Annesley Woodhouse NG17 130 A4
Arnold NG5 147 E1
Blidworth NG21 118 A3
Robin Hood St NG3 173 F3
Robin Hood Terr
Nottingham NG3 223 F3
Ravenshead NG15 117 D2
Robin Hood Way NG2 173 E1
Robin's Wood Rd NG8 172 A4
Robina Dr NG16 158 B4
Robinet Rd NG9 183 F3
Robinettes La NG16 158 B1
Robinia Ct NG2 186 A3
Robins Ct NG24 140 A4
Robinson Cl NG24 140 C4
Robinson Dr S80 35 F1
Robinson Gdns NG11 184 B1
Robinson Rd NG3 162 A1
Rochdale Ct NG18 103 D3
Roche Cl NG5 162 B4
Rochester Ave NG4 175 D4
Rochester Cl
Long Eaton NG10 193 D4
Worksop S81 36 A4
Rochester Ct NG6 159 F3
Rochester Rd NG21 118 A4
Rochester Wlk NG7 184 C1
Rochford Ct NG12 186 B2
Rock Ct Mansfield NG18 102 B4
Nottingham NG6 160 B2
Rock Dr NG7 222 C1
Rock Hill NG18 102 B3
Rock St Mansfield NG18 102 B3
Nottingham NG6 160 A4
Rock Valley NG18 102 B4
Rockford Ct NG9 170 C1
Rockford Rd NG5 160 C2
Rockingham Gr NG13 177 E2
Rocklands The NG20 72 C2
Rockley Ave
Eastwood NG16 144 A1
Radcliffe on T NG12 175 F2
Rockley Cl NG15 145 E3
Rockley Way NG20 72 C2
Rockleys View NG14 150 A1
Rockwood Cl NG21 118 A3
Rockwood Wlk NG15 145 F3
Rodel Ct NG3 223 F4
Roden St NG3 173 F3
Roderick Ave NG17 115 D1
Roderick St NG6 160 B2
Rodney Rd NG2 186 A3
Rodney Sch NG22 121 D4
Rodney Way DE7 157 F2
Rodwell Cl NG8 172 B3
Roe Hill NG14 149 E3
Roebuck Cl NG5 161 D4
Roebuck Dr NG18 102 A2
Roebuck Way S80 48 A4
Roecliffe NG2 185 F2
Roehampton Dr NG9 170 B1
Roes La NG14 149 D4
Roewood Cl NG17 114 C4
Roewood La NG22 107 F1
Roger Cl NG17 100 C3
Roker Cl NG8 160 A1
Rolaine Cl NG19 88 B2
Roland Ave
Nottingham NG11 185 D4
Nuthall NG16 159 F2
Rolleston Cl NG15 145 E3
Rolleston Cres NG16 144 C1
Rolleston Dr
Arnold NG5 162 A4
Eastwood NG16 158 A4
Nottingham NG7 222 B1
Rolleston Sta NG25 137 F3
Roman Bank NG19 88 B2
Roman Bank La DN10 18 C3
Roman Dr NG6 160 C2
Romans Ct NG6 160 C1
Romilay Cl NG9 172 A1
Romney Ave NG8 171 E1
Romsey Pl NG19 101 E3
Rona Cl NG19 101 F3
Rona Ct NG6 160 C3
Ronald St NG7 222 B3
Rook's La DN10 6 C1
Rookery Gdns NG5 161 F4
Rookery La NG17 114 A4
Rookery The
Collingham NG23 98 A1
1 Mansfield NG18 102 A4
Rookwood Cl NG9 183 F3
Rookwood Cres NG15 145 E3
Rooley Ave NG17 100 B2
Rooley Dr NG17 100 B2
Roosa Cl NG6 159 F3
Roosevelt Ave NG10 193 E3
Roosevelt Rd NG17 101 D2
Rooth St NG18 102 A3
Rope Wlk LE12 205 E1
Ropery Rd DN21 15 E1
Ropewalk DE74 203 E1
Ropewalk Ind Ctr DE7 158 A1
Ropewalk The
Ilkeston DE7 158 A1
Newark-on-T NG24 140 A4
Nottingham NG1 223 D2
Southwell NG25 121 F1
Ropsley Cres NG2 186 A4
Roscoe Ave NG5 147 F1
Rose Ash La NG5 161 D4
Rose Ave Ilkeston DE7 157 F1
Retford DN22 40 A2
Rose Cl NG3 173 E4
Rose Cottage Dr NG17 99 F1
Rose Cotts NG14 163 F3
Rose Ct NG10 182 A1
Rose Farm Dr NG23 96 C4
Rose Gr Beeston NG9 184 A3
Keyworth NG12 197 F2
Rose Hill NG12 197 F2
Rose La NG19 88 B2
Rose Lea DN22 39 E2
Roseacre NG9 184 A3
Rosebank Dr NG5 148 A1
Roseberry Ave NG2 173 F1
Roseberry Gdns NG15 146 B3
Roseberry St NG17 115 E2
Rosebery Hill NG18 102 B3
Rosebery St NG6 160 C2
Rosecroft Dr NG5 161 E3
Rosedale S81 36 A4
Rosedale Cl NG10 193 D3
Rosedale Dr NG8 171 D2
Rosedale La NG15 116 C2
Rosedale Rd NG3 174 B3
Rosedale Way NG19 88 C1
Rosegarth Wlk NG6 160 B2
Rosegrove Ave NG5 147 F1
Rosehill Cl LN1 57 D2
Rosehill Sch NG3 173 F3
Roseleigh Ave NG3 162 A1
Rosemary Ave NG18 102 A4
Rosemary Cl 1 NG8 159 F1
Rosemary St NG18 102 A4
Rosemont Cl NG17 100 C3
Roseneath Ave NG5 146 C1
Rosetta Rd NG7 160 C1
Rosewall Ct NG5 162 A4
Roseway DN21 15 E1
Rosewood Cl
Newark-on-T NG24 125 D1
South Normanton DE55 113 D4
Rosewood Cres DE75 143 D1
Rosewood Dr NG17 115 E3
Rosewood Gdns
Nottingham NG6 159 F4
West Bridgford NG2 185 E2
Roslyn Ave NG4 162 C1
Ross Cl
Coddington NG24 126 A1
Lowdham NG14 150 C1
Ross La NG4 163 E4
Rossell Dr NG9 182 C3
Rossendale DE7 157 F2
Rossett Cl NG2 186 B3
Rossetti Gdns S81 36 B2
Rossington Rd NG2 173 F3
Rosslyn Dr
Hucknall NG15 146 B4
Nottingham NG8 160 A1
Rosslyn Jun & Inf Sch NG8 160 A1
Rosthwaite Cl NG2 186 B3
Roston Cl NG18 103 D3
Rothbury Ave NG9 170 B1
Rothbury Gr NG13 177 E3
Rotherham Baulk S81 25 E4
Rotherham Rd NG19 86 C4
Rothesay Ave NG7 222 B2
Rothley Ave NG3 173 F3
Rothwell Cl
Gainsborough DN21 24 C4
Nottingham NG11 185 D2
Roughs Wood La NG15 145 E2
Roulstone Cres LE12 205 F2
Roundhill Cl NG17 101 E1
Roundhill Cty Prim Sch NG9 183 F4
Roundwood Jun Sch NG5 161 E4
Roundwood Rd NG5 161 E4
Row The NG13 179 F3
Rowan Ave
Hathern LE12 213 D1
Stapleford NG9 170 C1
Rowan Cl Calverton NG14 148 B4
Kirkby in A NG17 114 C3
Mansfield NG19 88 B1
Rowan Cres S80 35 F1
Rowan Croft NG17 99 F2
Rowan Ct NG16 159 D3
Rowan Dr
Keyworth NG12 198 A1
Kirkby in A NG17 114 C3
Nottingham NG11 185 D2
Ravenshead NG15 117 D1
Selston NG16 128 B4
Shirebrook NG20 72 B3
Rowan Gdns NG6 159 F4
Rowan Way NG24 140 A3
Rowan Wlk NG3 174 A4
Rowe Gdns NG6 160 B3
Rowland Ave NG3 162 A1
Rowland Mews NG3 173 F4
Rowsley Ave NG10 193 D3
Rowston Cl DN21 15 E1
Rowthorne La
Ault Hucknall S44 86 A4
Glapwell S44 86 A4
Roxton Ct NG16 158 C4
Roy Ave NG9 184 A2
Royal Ave NG10 182 B1
Royal Cres S81 35 F3
Royal Mews NG9 183 E2
Royal Oak Ct NG21 76 A1
Royal Oak Dr NG16 129 D4
Royal Way LE11 220 A3
Royce Ave NG15 145 F2
Royds Cres S80 35 D3
Royland Rd LE11 220 A2
Royston Cl NG2 173 D1
Rrith Way NG6 160 A4
Ruby Paddocks NG16 158 C3
Ruddington Ct NG18 103 D1
Ruddington Ctry Pk NG11 196 B3
Ruddington La NG11 185 D3
Ruddington Mus NG11 196 B3
Ruddington Rd NG18 103 D1
Ruddington Village Mus NG11 196 B4
Rudge Cl NG8 171 F3
Ruffles Ave NG5 162 A3
Rufford Ave
Beeston NG9 183 D4
Carlton NG4 162 B1
Mansfield NG18 102 B4
Meden Vale NG20 74 C4
New Ollerton NG22 77 E2
Newark-on-T NG24 139 F4
Rainworth NG21 104 B1
Retford DN22 39 E2
Rufford Cl
Bilsthorpe NG22 106 A2
Hucknall NG15 146 B3
Sutton in A NG17 100 C3
Rufford Ct NG21 104 B1
Rufford Ctry Pk NG22 91 F3
Rufford Dr NG19 88 C2
Rufford Gr NG13 177 E2
Rufford Jun & Inf Sch NG6 160 A4
Rufford La
Edwinstowe NG22 91 F4
Wellow NG22 92 A4
Rufford Rd
Edwinstowe NG21 91 E4
Long Eaton NG10 193 D2
Nottingham NG5 161 E2
Ruddington NG11 196 B4
Rufford Sch The NG21 75 F1
Rufford St S80 47 D4
Rufford Way NG2 186 A3
Rufford Wlk 14 NG6 160 A4
Ruffs Dr NG15 145 F3
Rugby Cl NG5 160 C4
Rugby Rd NG21 118 A4
Rugeley Ave NG10 194 A4
Ruislip Cl NG16 158 C4
Runcie Cl NG12 187 F1
Runnymede Ct NG7 222 C3
Runswick Dr Arnold NG5 161 F4
Nottingham NG8 172 A3
Runton Dr NG6 160 C2
Rupert Cres NG24 139 F4
Rupert Rd NG13 177 E2
Rupert St DE7 158 A1
Rush Leys NG10 193 E3
Rushcliffe Ave
Carlton NG4 174 B4
Radcliffe on T NG12 175 F2
Rushcliffe Ct NG6 160 B3
Rushcliffe Gr LE12 205 F2
Rushcliffe Rd NG15 145 F3
Rushcliffe Rise NG5 161 E3
Rushcliffe Sch NG2 185 F2
Rushes The
Gotham NG11 195 D1
Loughborough LE11 220 A2
Mansfield Woodhouse NG19 .. 88 B3
Rushey Cl S80 36 A1
Rushford Dr NG8 171 E2
Rushley View NG17 100 B1
Rushmere Wlk NG5 161 F3
Rushpool Ave NG19 88 B2
Rushton Gdns NG3 173 F4
Rushworth Ave NG2 185 F4
Rushworth Cl NG3 173 F4
Rushy Cl NG8 171 E3
Ruskin Ave
Beeston NG9 183 E2
Long Eaton NG10 193 D3
Ruskin Cl NG5 161 E4
Ruskin Rd NG19 87 E1
Ruskin St DN21 24 B3
Russell Ave
Harworth DN11 8 C2
New Balderton NG24 140 A2
Nottingham NG8 171 F2
Russell Cres NG8 171 F2
Russell Dr NG8 171 F2
Russell Gdns 5 NG9 183 E1
Russell Pl NG1 223 D3
Russell Rd NG7 172 C4
Russell St
Long Eaton NG10 182 B1
Loughborough LE11 220 B2
Nottingham NG7 222 C3
Sutton in A NG17 100 C2
Russet Ave NG4 174 C4
Russet Gr DN10 10 A4
Russey Cl NG14 150 C1
Russley Rd NG9 183 D4
Ruth Dr NG5 148 A1
Rutherford Ave NG18 102 C2
Ruthwell Gdns NG5 147 D1
Rutland NG17 115 E3

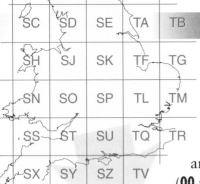

Any feature in this atlas can be given a unique reference to help you find the same feature on other Ordnance Survey maps of the area, or to help someone else locate you if they do not have a Street Atlas. The grid squares in this atlas match the Ordnance Survey National Grid and are at 500 metre intervals. The small figures at the bottom and sides of every other grid line are the National Grid kilometre values (**00** to **99** km) and are repeated across the country every 100 km (see left).

To give a unique National Grid reference you need to locate where in the country you are. The country is divided into 100 km squares with each square given a unique two-letter reference. The atlas in this example falls across the junction of four such squares. Start by working out on which two-letter square the page falls. The Key map and Administrative map are useful for this.

The bold letters and numbers between each grid line (**A** to **F**, **1** to **8**) are for use within a specific Street Atlas only, and when used with the page number, are a convenient way of referencing these grid squares.

Example   The railway bridge over DARLEY GREEN RD in grid square B1 on page 128

Step 1: Identify the two-letter reference, in this case page 128 is in **SP**

Step 2: Identify the 1 km square in which the railway bridge falls. Use the figures in the southwest corner of this square: Eastings **17**, Northings **74**. This gives a unique reference: **SP 17 74**, accurate to 1 km.

Step 3: To give a more precise reference accurate to 100 m you need to estimate how many tenths along and how many tenths up this 1 km square the feature is (to help with this the 1 km square is divided into four 500 m squares). This makes the bridge about **8** tenths along and about **1** tenth up from the southwest corner.

This gives a unique reference: **SP 178 741**, accurate to 100 m.

Eastings (read from left to right along the bottom) come before Northings (read from bottom to top). If you have trouble remembering say to yourself "Along the hall, THEN up the stairs"!

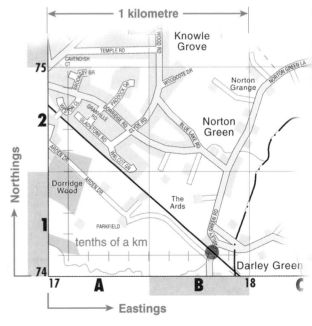

Name and Address	Telephone	Page	Grid Reference

STREET ATLASES
ORDER FORM

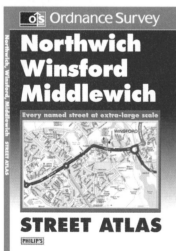

The Street Atlases are available from all good bookshops or by mail order direct from the publisher. Orders can be made in the following ways. **By phone** Ring our special Credit Card Hotline on **01933 443863** during office hours (9am to 5pm) or leave a message on the answering machine, quoting your full credit card number plus expiry date and your full name and address. **By post or fax** Fill out the order form below (you may photocopy it) and post it to: **Philip's Direct, 27 Sanders Road, Wellingborough, Northants NN8 4NL** or fax it to: **01933 443849**. Before placing an order by post, by fax or on the answering machine, please telephone to check availability and prices.

COLOUR LOCAL ATLASES

	PAPERBACK	
	Quantity @ £3.50 each	£ Total
CANNOCK, LICHFIELD, RUGELEY	☐ 0 540 07625 2	➤
DERBY AND BELPER	☐ 0 540 07608 2	➤
NORTHWICH, WINSFORD, MIDDLEWICH	☐ 0 540 07589 2	➤
PEAK DISTRICT TOWNS	☐ 0 540 07609 0	➤
STAFFORD, STONE, UTTOXETER	☐ 0 540 07626 0	➤
WARRINGTON, WIDNES, RUNCORN	☐ 0 540 07588 4	➤

COLOUR REGIONAL ATLASES

	HARDBACK	SPIRAL	POCKET	
	Quantity @ £10.99 each	Quantity @ £8.99 each	Quantity @ £5.99 each	£ Total
BERKSHIRE	☐ 0 540 06170 0	☐ 0 540 06172 7	☐ 0 540 06173 5	➤
	Quantity @ £10.99 each	Quantity @ £8.99 each	Quantity @ £4.99 each	£ Total
MERSEYSIDE	☐ 0 540 06480 7	☐ 0 540 06481 5	☐ 0 540 06482 3	➤
	Quantity @ £12.99 each	Quantity @ £9.99 each	Quantity @ £4.99 each	£ Total
DURHAM	☐ 0 540 06365 7	☐ 0 540 06366 5	☐ 0 540 06367 3	➤
HERTFORDSHIRE	☐ 0 540 06174 3	☐ 0 540 06175 1	☐ 0 540 06176 X	➤
EAST KENT	☐ 0 540 07483 7	☐ 0 540 07276 1	☐ 0 540 07287 7	➤
WEST KENT	☐ 0 540 07366 0	☐ 0 540 07367 9	☐ 0 540 07369 5	➤
EAST SUSSEX	☐ 0 540 07306 7	☐ 0 540 07307 5	☐ 0 540 07312 1	➤
WEST SUSSEX	☐ 0 540 07319 9	☐ 0 540 07323 7	☐ 0 540 07327 X	➤
SOUTH YORKSHIRE	☐ 0 540 06330 4	☐ 0 540 06331 2	☐ 0 540 06332 0	➤
SURREY	☐ 0 540 06435 1	☐ 0 540 06436 X	☐ 0 540 06438 6	➤
	Quantity @ £12.99 each	Quantity @ £9.99 each	Quantity @ £5.50 each	£ Total
GREATER MANCHESTER	☐ 0 540 06485 8	☐ 0 540 06486 6	☐ 0 540 06487 4	➤
TYNE AND WEAR	☐ 0 540 06370 3	☐ 0 540 06371 1	☐ 0 540 06372 X	➤
	Quantity @ £12.99 each	Quantity @ £9.99 each	Quantity @ £5.99 each	£ Total
BIRMINGHAM & WEST MIDLANDS	☐ 0 540 07603 1	☐ 0 540 07604 X	☐ 0 540 07605 8	➤
BUCKINGHAMSHIRE	☐ 0 540 07466 7	☐ 0 540 07467 5	☐ 0 540 07468 3	➤

STREET ATLASES ORDER FORM

COLOUR REGIONAL ATLASES

	HARDBACK Quantity @ £12.99 each	SPIRAL Quantity @ £9.99 each	POCKET Quantity @ £5.99 each	£ Total
CHESHIRE	☐ 0 540 07507 8	☐ 0 540 07508 6	☐ 0 540 07509 4	➤ ☐
DERBYSHIRE	☐ 0 540 07531 0	☐ 0 540 07532 9	☐ 0 540 07533 7	➤ ☐
SOUTH HAMPSHIRE	☐ 0 540 07476 4	☐ 0 540 07477 2	☐ 0 540 07478 0	➤ ☐
NORTH HAMPSHIRE	☐ 0 540 07471 3	☐ 0 540 07472 1	☐ 0 540 07473 X	➤ ☐
OXFORDSHIRE	☐ 0 540 07512 4	☐ 0 540 07513 2	☐ 0 540 07514 0	➤ ☐
WARWICKSHIRE	☐ 0 540 07560 4	☐ 0 540 07561 2	☐ 0 540 07562 0	➤ ☐
WEST YORKSHIRE	☐ 0 540 06329 0	☐ 0 540 06327 4	☐ 0 540 06328 2	➤ ☐
	Quantity @ £14.99 each	Quantity @ £9.99 each	Quantity @ £5.99 each	£ Total
LANCASHIRE	☐ 0 540 06440 8	☐ 0 540 06441 6	☐ 0 540 06443 2	➤ ☐
NOTTINGHAMSHIRE	☐ 0 540 07541 8	☐ 0 540 075426 6	☐ 0 540 07543 4	➤ ☐
STAFFORDSHIRE	☐ 0 540 07549 3	☐ 0 540 07550 7	☐ 0 540 07551 5	➤ ☐

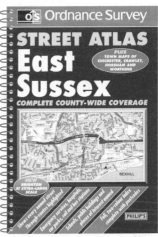

BLACK AND WHITE REGIONAL ATLASES

	HARDBACK Quantity @ £11.99 each	SOFTBACK Quantity @ £8.99 each	POCKET Quantity @ £3.99 each	£ Total
BRISTOL AND AVON	☐ 0 540 06140 9	☐ 0 540 06141 7	☐ 0 540 06142 5	➤ ☐
	Quantity @ £12.99 each	Quantity @ £9.99 each	Quantity @ £4.99 each	£ Total
CARDIFF, SWANSEA & GLAMORGAN	☐ 0 540 06186 7	☐ 0 540 06187 5	☐ 0 540 06207 3	➤ ☐
EDINBURGH & East Central Scotland	—	☐ 0 540 06181 6	☐ 0 540 06182 4	➤ ☐
EAST ESSEX	☐ 0 540 05848 3	☐ 0 540 05866 1	☐ 0 540 05850 5	➤ ☐
WEST ESSEX	☐ 0 540 05849 1	☐ 0 540 05867 X	☐ 0 540 05851 3	➤ ☐
	Quantity @ £12.99 each	Quantity @ £9.99 each	Quantity @ £5.99 each	£ Total
GLASGOW & West Central Scotland	☐ 0 540 06183 2	☐ 0 540 06184 0	☐ 0 540 06185 9	➤ ☐

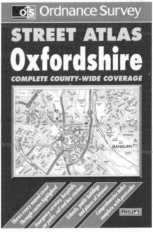

Post to: Philip's Direct, 27 Sanders Road, Wellingborough, Northants NN8 4NL

◆ Free postage and packing

◆ All available titles will normally be dispatched within 5 working days of receipt of order but please allow up to 28 days for delivery

☐ Please tick this box if you do not wish your name to be used by other carefully selected organisations that may wish to send you information about other products and services

Registered Office: Michelin House, 81 Fulham Road, London SW3 6RB

Registered in England number: 3597451

I enclose a cheque / postal order, for a **total** of ☐ made payable to *Octopus Publishing Group Ltd*, or please debit my

☐ Access ☐ American Express ☐ Visa ☐ Diners

account by ☐

Account no

☐☐☐☐ ☐☐☐☐ ☐☐☐☐ ☐☐☐☐

Expiry date ☐☐ ☐☐

Signature...

Name...

Address..

....

....

....POSTCODE

Ordnance Survey

MOTORING ATLAS

Updated annually

Britain

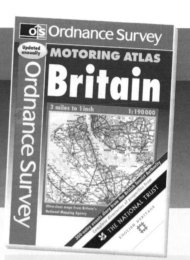

The best-selling *OS Motoring Atlas Britain* uses unrivalled and up-to-date mapping from the Ordnance Survey digital database. The exceptionally clear mapping is at a large scale of 3 miles to 1 inch (Orkney/Shetland Islands at 5 miles to 1 inch).

A special feature of the atlas is its wealth of tourist and leisure information. It contains comprehensive directories, including descriptions and location details, of the properties of the National Trust in England and Wales, the National Trust for Scotland, English Heritage and

Historic Scotland. There is also a useful diary of British Tourist Authority Events listing more than 300 days out around Britain during the year.

Available from all good bookshops or direct from the publisher:
Tel: 01933 443863

The atlas includes:

- ◆ 112 pages of fully updated mapping
- ◆ 45 city and town plans
- ◆ 8 extra-detailed city approach maps
- ◆ route-planning maps
- ◆ restricted motorway junctions
- ◆ local radio information
- ◆ distances chart
- ◆ county boundaries map
- ◆ multi-language legend

Under the Influence of Bright Sunbeams

Centuries of Natural Cuisine in Recipes for Today

Under the Influence of Bright Sunbeams

The Countess
Chiña de Burnay

Illustrated by Dandi Palmer

Photography by Sue Atkinson, Mike Roles Studios.
Food styling for photography in conjunction
with the author.

THORSONS PUBLISHING GROUP
Wellingborough, Northamptonshire
·
Rochester, Vermont

First published 1987

British Library Cataloguing in Publication Data

De Burnay, Chiña
Under the influence of bright sunbeams.
1. Cookery (Natural foods)
I. Title
641.5′637   TX741

ISBN 0-7225-1462-X

Printed in Great Britain by Butler & Tanner Limited, Frome, Somerset

1 3 5 7 9 10 8 6 4 2

Contents

Dedication

To all the cooks of the past, of other cultures and other countries, most of them unknown or long forgotten who made this book possible.

Acknowledgements

I would like to give many thanks to Chris Going for lighting the blue touch paper
before standing back;

To Geoff Marsh and the Museum of London for all their help and encouragement;

To Pamela and Douglas Westland and their many friends for almost eating their way
through the ages and giving me so much encouragement;

To Jackie Brett, Sylvia Merrifield, Gale Watson and Tania de Burnay for their help in
typing the manuscript;

To M. S. de Burnay for all her help in the house while the book was being written;

To Gavin Cook of LBC Radio and all the many people who have sent me recipes and
given me so much help;

To Baroness Valerie von Dahlen for giving me so much help and inspiration during our
many talks on food;

To Paul Kent as 'Consultant Stomach' over a period of years;

To Charmaine Farmer for sharing with me her collection of cookbooks and historical
data;

To my many relations: de Burnays, Pachecos, Pakenhams, Lyalls, and Lerdo de Tejadas
for family food and historical data;

To Fay and Simon Franklin for believing in me and making this book a reality;

To Sue Atkinson for her lovely photographs;

And finally to Malcolm for putting up with me during the birth pains of this book.

Introduction

'Put the fruit into a jar cover with sugar and set by the window
under the influence of bright sunbeams for two days'

— From a Victorian cookery note book.

I love food. I am both greedy and curious. I have always been closely involved with both food and cooking. As a child I was brought up by parents who spent most of their time travelling across Europe. By the time I was twelve I had lived in England, Spain, Portugal and France and had visited several other countries. We always ate the local food and both my parents were great collectors of recipes. My mother, the painter Gill Lyall, came from a family who had for generations not only loved food but had corresponded with great regularity and kept household books dating back for many years.

One of my Grandmother's cousins, Rosemary Hume, carried on the family tradition of food and made it her life's work. She started the Cordon Bleu School of cookery at Winkfield.

My mother, who was a superb cook, spent several years travelling in Europe and the Near East with an uncle who at that time worked for the League of Nations. He not only had a great passion for food, but loved history. During her years with him my mother researched and collected many hundreds of recipes from all over the world.

My father, one of a very large and eccentric Iberian family, had been brought up in a tradition of good food. Whenever a member of the family travelled or visited a different part of the country they always tasted the local specialities and visited the markets. If they came across something which was of special interest, they would make a record of it and in many cases the recipes would be sent to other relations, in time to become part of the 'Comida Burnay' or Burnay food.

My father's family home was situated in the ancient Roman town of Emerita Augusta, Merida of today. Here was the family's base camp, where they had lived for many hundreds of years. There life had changed little over the centuries. Kings came and went, politics and struggles for power brought many new foods to Spain, especially with the discovery and conquest of the New World. This only added to the regional cuisine. Here, in the heart of Estremadura, little really changed. New ideas were tried; if they worked they were absorbed into the local traditions, but the old ways were also preserved. To this day much from the Roman kitchen has survived intact; 'Los Romanos' are fondly mentioned as if they had only been there a few hundred years ago instead of more than a thousand.

It was the food and traditions of my father's family that became the starting point for this book. I began trying to put the vast amount of my family's food related data in some sort of order. This led me to start researching further afield. One period of history led to another.

The first Roman cook book written by Apicius in the fourth century was full of wonderful recipes. Early French, Italian, Catalan and English recipe books, books on agriculture, household account books and records of the spice trade all had something to add to the picture. Many recipe books, often handed down through the ages, contained recipes that often could be traced across Europe through political marriages. When a foreign bride set out for her new home she would take with her, as part of her retinue, cooks who were skilled in the cuisine of her native country, not only to help her to feel more at home but also, I suspect, to try and convert her new countrymen to the customs of her homeland. Every country is quite convinced that their native food is far superior to any other.

Years ago, when I first lived in this country as a student, my aunts used to send me food parcels, full of local cheeses, oil, garlic, saffron, and once a huge sack of rice arrived on my door step to see me through the English winter in case I should starve! I was the most popular student in my year, as I cooked my way through every kind of rice dish I had ever heard of and fed all my friends, in the hope of finishing the rice before the next sack arrived!

This book is a selection of the recipes that I use, some very old some quite new, but all I think good examples of their kind. All I suspect have been cooked and re-invented several times in the last two thousand years, as that is the natural order of both cooks and history.

1.
Soups and Starters

Chick Pea and Lentil Purée

INGREDIENTS

1 lb/450g cooked weight chick peas

4 oz/100g cooked weight red lentils

2 cloves garlic

2 teaspoons coriander seeds

1 tablespoon honey

Sea salt and black pepper to taste

¼ pint/150ml olive oil

PRE-ROMAN EGYPTIAN RECIPE

This is based on the findings in the tombs of Thebes of the remains of purée of chick peas and lentils.

1. Put all the ingredients into a food processor with the exception of the olive oil and process for 2 minutes. Start to add the olive oil gradually until it is all absorbed and you have a smooth paste.

2. Put into a shallow bowl and serve with warm pitta bread or thin wedges of toast.

This dish makes a very good starter, especially if accompanied by a salad of cooked carrots with finely chopped onion, or as part of several hors d'oeuvres.

Before the invasion of Britain by the Romans, we had been visited for some time by those bold Phoenician traders who sailed far from their original home on the Islands of Rhôdes and Crête, and the Libyan and Turkish mainlands. They were ever pressing onwards looking for new markets and new sources of goods. They traded in wine, oil, olives, precious metals, cloth, salt, grains and pulses, anything that would find a ready buyer. They also traded in spices, and bronze goods, jewellery, fine pottery and gems. Once the link with Britain was established, it grew and developed steadily.

Salsa Evissenques

PHOENICIAN PUDDING

This is a very old recipe, almost certainly introduced from the Island of Ibiza, or to use the Catalan word, Evissia, by the Phoenicians who traded and colonized all along the Mediterranean coast and islands. It has been served in its present form in Catalonia for many hundreds of years both in the past as a Lenten dish, and in the last two hundred years as a Christmas dish and eaten only in that season.

1. Put the ground almonds into a large bowl and mix in the saffron, cinnamon and sea salt.

2. Make a well in the centre. Pour in the oil and honey. Work the mixture together until you have a thick paste. Add the eggs.

3. Heat the water or wine in a deep pan.

4. Add the almond paste and blend it well with a wooden spoon. Bring to the boil and simmer very gently for 45-50 minutes.

Serve in individual bowls with grated cheese as a sweet-sour pudding. This makes a warming and unusual starter for 6 or a main dish for 4.

INGREDIENTS

1 lb/450g ground almonds
½ teaspoon ground saffron
1 teaspoon ground cinnamon
½ teaspoon sea salt
4 teaspoons olive oil
5 tablespoons honey
4 eggs
2 pints/1200ml wine or water

Rissoles of Mussels

INGREDIENTS

1 lb/450g shelled mussels
1 oz/25g porridge oats
A little garlic
1 oz/25g pine kernels, chopped
¼ teaspoon freshly ground
black pepper
2 eggs, beaten
2 oz/50g flour
6 fl oz/175ml stock and white
wine mixed

1. Cook the mussels in boiling water until tender.

2. Strain well and chop very finely.

3. Add the oats, garlic, pine kernels, pepper and beaten eggs.

4. Form into small rissoles. Coat with flour and deep fry.

5. Just before serving, heat the stock and pour over the rissoles.

Serve as a side dish with game or with a 'patina'.

Roman Braised Leeks with Black Olives

INGREDIENTS

4 good sized leeks, trimmed,
washed and cut into slices
4 tablespoons olive oil
¼ pint/150ml dry white wine
2 cloves garlic, crushed
10 black olives with the stones
removed
Sea salt to taste
4 oz/100g Ricotta cheese
1 oz/25g chopped nuts
1 teaspoon crushed green
peppercorns (optional)

1. Put the leeks in a shallow oven proof dish.

2. Put the oil, wine, garlic, olives and sea salt into a mortar and pound, or put into a food processor and blend for about 1 minute.

3. Pour the mixture over the leeks.

4. Cover with a layer of Ricotta and sprinkle with chopped nuts and green pepper if using.

5. Cover the dish with foil and put into the oven at 350°F, 180°C, Gas Mark 4 for about an hour or until tender.

Stuffed Calamary or Squid

1. Place your squid on a flat surface or chopping board. Carefully remove the ink sac, intestines and cranial cartilage. Cut off the tentacles but reserve. Repeat with the other three squid.

2. Wash well in cold water.

3. Peel the hard boiled eggs and chop finely. Mix together with oil, herbs, honey and vinegar. Season with salt and black pepper.

4. Chop the tentacles very small. Add to the above mixture and use to stuff the squid.

5. Arrange in a shallow pan and pour the wine over. Cover and cook gently for about 25-30 minutes turning the squid over after about 15 minutes.

6. Sprinkle with fresh herbs and serve.

Several side salads are good with this dish, or it can be used as a starter.

INGREDIENTS

4 calamary or squid
4 eggs, hard boiled
3 tablespoons olive oil
2 teaspoons celery seed
1 tablespoon chopped coriander
1 tablespoon lovage
1 tablespoon honey
1 tablespoon wine vinegar
Sea salt and black pepper
¼ pint/150ml dry white wine

Beetroot Soup à la Roman

INGREDIENTS

1½ lb/675g raw beetroot

2 pints/1200ml stock or half stock half red wine

3 tablespoons olive oil

1 bouquet garni

1 teaspoon coarse ground sea salt

Black pepper to taste

1 oz/25g finely chopped nuts

3 tablespoons chopped dill or chives

This is a beautiful colourful soup that in Roman times was both a soup and a tonic. It was very good for settling the stomach. What more could one want to start a meal with, a guarantee that everything will agree with one!

1. Wash and clean the beetroot. Remove tops, peel and cut into quarters.

2. Place the beetroots, together with the stock, oil, bouquet garni, salt and pepper in a large saucepan. Cook until tender.

3. Remove the beetroot from the pan, reserving the liquid. Pass the beetroot through a sieve or use a food processor so that you have a thick purée.

4. Return the purée to the liquid in the pan, stir well and bring to the boil. Just before serving, sprinkle with chopped nuts and herbs.

If you use ready cooked beetroot, allow it to soak in wine for an hour before using. The quantity of seasoning is very much to personal taste. A larger quantity of salt can be added if wished.

Under the Influence of Bright Sunbeams

From the top: Pumpkin Soup (page 23), Chick Pea and Lentil Purée (page 12) and Chewetts or Medieval Fish Pasties (page 17).

A Roman Meal. Clockwise from the top: Roman Braised Leeks with Black Olives (page 14), Jellied Trout (page 38), French Beans and Chick Peas (page 84) and Tyropatinan (Roman Custard) (page 110).

From the top: Spit Roasted Eggs (page 43), fish covered in pastry (page 197) and Prawns with Chilli (page 41).

Chewetts or Medieval Fish Pasties

These tasty little pasties would have been very popular in Medieval times as they were yet another way of eating fish which added variety on fish days. They look particularly nice if you cut out small fish shapes from the left over pastry and decorate each one. You can use mushrooms instead of fish if you wish, and decorate with small pastry mushrooms.

1. Heat the butter in a shallow pan. Fry the onion gently.

2. Trim off any skin from the fish. Remove any bones and flake the fish. Add to the onions. Add the spices and chopped eggs and stir. Season to taste.

3. Roll out the pastry and cut into circles.

4. Put an equal amount of the filling onto the centre of each circle, fold over to form a purse and pinch the edges together.

5. Glaze with beaten egg.

6. Transfer the pasties to a well oiled baking sheet.

7. Put into the oven at 350°F, 180°C, Gas Mark 4 for 20 minutes.

INGREDIENTS

2 oz/50g butter
1 small onion very finely chopped
½ lb/225g smoked fish — mackerel, trout or eel
½ teaspoon ground mace
½ teaspoon ground ginger
6 eggs hard boiled and chopped
Sea salt and pepper to taste
1½ lb/675g shortcrust pastry
1 egg beaten, to glaze

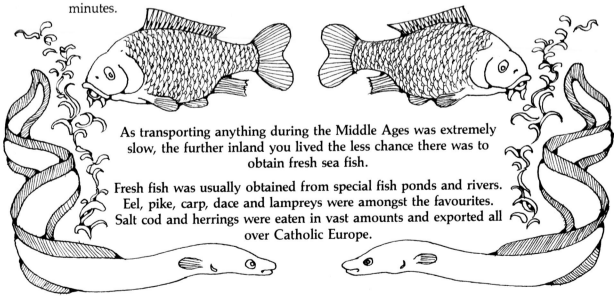

As transporting anything during the Middle Ages was extremely slow, the further inland you lived the less chance there was to obtain fresh sea fish.

Fresh fish was usually obtained from special fish ponds and rivers. Eel, pike, carp, dace and lampreys were amongst the favourites. Salt cod and herrings were eaten in vast amounts and exported all over Catholic Europe.

Bean Butter

Manteiga de Favas
TWELFTH CENTURY

This a very simple country dish that has been made for centuries. To the Romans it was a vegetable 'patina'; in twelfth century Britain it was a Lenten dish, and it can be found to this day in northern Portugal where it retains its original name of Manteiga de Favas *or Bean Butter. Fresh or dried beans were used depending on the season. On the Continent, olive oil takes the place of butter and in the modern version lemon juice is added instead of vinegar. I personally use this version served on very thin fingers of wholemeal toast and sprinkled with black pepper, finely chopped onion and parsley.*

INGREDIENTS

1 lb/450g fresh broad beans cooked and passed through a fine sieve or food processor*

2 cloves garlic, crushed

A little sea salt

1 teaspoon dried thyme

3 tablespoons fresh lemon juice

6 tablespoons olive oil or 2 oz/50g butter

Freshly ground black pepper, finely chopped onion and fresh chopped parsley to garnish

1. Put the beans, crushed garlic, salt, thyme and lemon juice into a food processor and blend until you have a fine purée. Stir in the olive oil or melted butter.

2. Put into a serving dish or spread onto thin fingers of wholemeal toast. Sprinkle with chopped parsley and onion topped with freshly ground black pepper. Serve at once.

This makes a very good starter on its own, or you can serve it with a cheese and watercress pâté and buttered noodles to form part of a main course.

*If you are using a food processor, it is a good idea to remove the skins of the beans first, as they can be rather tough.

Black Death and Famine

Although there were terrible famines and the Black Death decimated the population, wiping out whole villages and towns, in places leaving so few able-bodied people that they were unable to tend the soil to plant the next year's grain, in Britain many people certainly starved through ignorance and prejudice. There were many natural food plants and fruits which were neglected and avoided due to lack of knowledge and understanding.

Fennel

Fennel was known in Anglo-Saxon times and later was laid under bread when baking to give fragrance.

In 1281, Edward I's household was reputed to be using as much as ten pounds a month.

In Tudor England, fennel was supposed to be a protection against enchantment and its seed was often put into keyholes to stop any inquisitive ghost from advancing!

Cold Fennel Soup

FROM THE FORME OF CURY*

1. Put the wine and water into a pan. Add salt and pepper to taste. Bring to the boil.

2. Sprinkle the fennel into the pan and simmer for 4-5 minutes.

3. Remove from the heat and purée in a food processor.

4. Return to a clean pan, stir in the ginger, ground almonds, sugar or honey and sea salt and pepper if required.

5. Simmer very gently for 12-15 minutes, then allow to cool. Pour into individual dishes, sprinkle with chopped fennel and black pepper, and serve.

*The earliest English cookery book known to exist.

INGREDIENTS

(Serves 8)

½ pint/300ml white wine

¾ pint/450ml water

Sea salt and pepper to taste

A good handful of fennel leaves and stalks, chopped very fine

1 teaspoon ground ginger

4 oz/100g ground almonds

3 teaspoons sugar or honey

1 tablespoon fennel finely chopped for garnish

Apple Soup

FOURTEENTH CENTURY

Somewhere in the Victorian era we seem to have forgotten about fruit soups, both hot and cold. You can still find many old recipes being used today throughout Europe for the most mouthwatering and refreshing concoctions of fresh fruit purée.

INGREDIENTS

½ pint/300ml milk
½ teaspoon ground saffron
1 tablespoon honey
2 cloves garlic, crushed
1 oz/25g ground almonds
½ pint/300ml dry white wine
1 lb/450g cooking apples
peeled, cored, sliced and puréed
4 oz/100g curd cheese
Sea salt and freshly ground
black pepper to taste

1. Heat the milk, saffron, honey, garlic and ground almonds together in a pan but do not boil.

2. Combine the wine, apple purée and curd cheese together. Simmer over a low heat stirring constantly.

3. Remove from the heat and stir in the milk and herbs until well mixed. Season to taste and pour into heated bowls. Serve straight away.

You can serve croûtons with the soup, and another variation is to substitute 2 tablespoons chestnut purée for the ground almonds.

This was adapted from a fourteenth century recipe by my mother who was a genius at understanding early recipes.

Arthur Lett-Haynes, the painter, who was a superb cook and a great friend, believed in adding coarsely grated cheese and a little brown sugar to the soup just before serving.

Spinach Dumplings

1540

1. Put 1 oz/25g butter into a pan over a low heat. Add the cooked spinach and the curd cheese.

2. Cook for 3–4 minutes stirring constantly until well combined.

3. Remove from the heat. Add the nutmeg and season to taste.

4. Beat the eggs, flour and 2 oz/50g of the Parmesan cheese. Put into a bowl and add the spinach and curd cheese mixture.

5. When the mixture is cold, form into croquettes or balls and roll lightly in flour.

6. Bring a large pan of salted water to the boil and allow to simmer.

7. Put 4–5 of the croquettes carefully into the water and poach for 5–6 minutes. When the croquettes are cooked, they will float to the surface. Remove the croquettes from the pan carefully and put onto kitchen paper to drain.

8. Repeat this process until all the croquettes are cooked.

9. Lay them in an oven proof dish.

10. Melt the remaining butter and combine with the hazel-nuts. Pour this mixture over the croquettes. Sprinkle with Parmesan cheese and put under the grill for 4–5 minutes. Serve with Parmesan cheese if liked.

This is a delicious starter or main course. A green salad and tomatoes with basil make very good accompanying dishes.

INGREDIENTS

4 oz/100g butter
1½ lb/675g spinach cooked, drained and chopped
12 oz/350g curd cheese
Sea salt and freshly ground black pepper to taste
½ teaspoon nutmeg
2 large eggs, beaten
Approximately 3 tablespoons flour
4 oz/100g Parmesan cheese
Flour for rolling out
2 oz/50g hazel-nuts, finely ground

Pea Soup

1694

INGREDIENTS

3 cloves garlic
½ lb/225g leeks trimmed and thinly sliced
3 oz/75g butter
½ teaspoon ground saffron
¼ teaspoon ground mace
¼ teaspoon ground black pepper
1½ pints/900ml stock
1 vegetable cube
½ lb/225g green peas fresh or frozen
½ lb/225g spinach fresh or frozen and finely chopped
1 head endive or chicory
2 oz/50g savoy cabbage, the heart sliced very fine
1 tablespoons chopped mint
1 oz/25g parsley chopped very fine
1 bunch watercress
½ pint/300ml cream

1. Put the garlic, leeks and butter into a pan and cook for 2–3 minutes. Stir, and add saffron, mace and black pepper. Pour in ¼ pint/150ml stock, stir and cook gently for 5–6 minutes.

2. Add a further ½ pint/300ml of the stock, the cube and all the vegetables and herbs. Bring to the boil and simmer until just soft.

3. Remove the soup from the heat, put into a liquidizer or food processor and purée.

4. Return the vegetable purée to the pan, stir, add the remaining stock and heat gently. Stir in the cream just before serving and sprinkle with grated cheese.

Under the Influence of Bright Sunbeams

Pumpkin Soup

NEW ENGLAND 1750

1. Heat the butter in a large pan and add the saffron and chopped onion. Cook very gently until the onion is soft.

2. Add the pumpkin and potatoes and cook slowly for 5–8 minutes stirring constantly.

3. Pour in water and stir well. Bring to the boil and simmer for 35–40 minutes or until the vegetables are soft.

4. Remove from the heat and pass through a sieve or food processor. Return to the heat and stir in the nutmeg, salt and pepper.

5. Stir in the cream, sprinkle with chopped herbs and serve with croûtons and fresh bread.

INGREDIENTS

4 oz/100g butter
½ teaspoon ground saffron
2 large onions, chopped very fine
1½ lb/675g fresh pumpkin, cut into small cubes
2 large potatoes peeled and very thinly sliced
1½ pints/900ml water
½ teaspoon ground nutmeg
6 fl oz/175ml sour cream
Sea salt and freshly ground black pepper to taste
Fresh herbs to garnish

Fresh Dill Soup

FROM THE 1820s

1. Put the butter into a pan and melt over a low heat. Stir in the flour and make a roux. Cook until golden.

2. Add the water gradually and beat until creamy.

3. Stir in the dill, lemon juice and sugar and cook for 8–10 minutes. Season to taste.

4. Pour a portion of cream into each bowl and then serve.

To vary this soup, serve with a portion of cooked noodles or croûtons.

INGREDIENTS

3 tablespoons butter
1 tablespoon flour
¼ pint/150ml cold water
3 tablespoons freshly chopped dill
Juice of 1 lemon
2 teaspoons sugar
Sea salt and black pepper to taste
¼ pint/150ml sour cream

Pickled Eel

1750

INGREDIENTS

2 lb/900g eel, skinned and cut
off the backbone
3 cloves garlic, crushed
1 teaspoon cayenne pepper
2 sprigs rosemary
3 sprigs thyme
2 sprigs parsley
3 tablespoons brown sugar
1 teaspoon sea salt
1 pint/600ml white wine
vinegar
½ pint/300ml white wine
½ pint/300ml water
1 piece muslin to wrap the
eel in

1. Wash the eel, then rub all over with garlic and cayenne pepper. Leave to stand for 10–20 minutes.

2. Put all the remaining ingredients into a deep pan and bring to the boil.

3. Wrap the eel in a piece of muslin and tie with thread. Lower the parcel into the pan and cook gently for 25–30 minutes.

4. When the eel is cooked, lift out of the liquid and set to one side to cool. Reserve the cooking liquid.

5. Unwrap the eel and put into the cold cooking liquid. Leave overnight before eating.

The original recipe states that this way eel will keep for at least ten days.

Serve with slices of brown bread and butter and a green salad. This dish makes a lovely starter.

Portuguese Soup of Greens

SOPA DE ERVAS

This is a very old Lenten soup from central Portugal. Today it is eaten at anytime of the year, the ingredients varying depending on the season and what is to hand. However, usually they are sorrel, spinach, turnip tops, cabbage or sprouting broccoli. In this instance I have used spinach but it is just as good if made with fresh coriander.

Under the Influence of Bright Sunbeams

1. Heat the oil in a large pan, add garlic, salt, pepper and onion.

2. Simmer slowly for a few minutes until onion is transparent and golden.

3. Add cooked sliced potatoes and stock and simmer for 10 minutes.

4. Mash potatoes slightly and finally add the spinach and cook for a further 10–12 minutes.

Serve with croûtons, or fingers of fried or toasted bread. Sprinkle nutmeg on to the soup just before serving.

INGREDIENTS

2 large tablespoons olive oil
2 cloves garlic, crushed
Sea salt and pepper
1 large onion, finely chopped
½ lb/225g sliced potatoes, either left overs, or specially prepared
¾ lb/340g spinach, finely chopped
1½ pints/900ml chicken or other stock
½ teaspoon ground nutmeg

Elderberry Soup

All the way through history can be found recipes for fruit soups. In Britain they have been out of fashion for a long time but they can still be found in many European countries. This is from an eighteenth century Danish recipe.

1. Put the water and elderberries into a large pan together with the cinnamon and grated lemon zest. Bring to the boil and cook gently for 15–18 minutes.

2. Strain the fruit and press out the juice. Discard the pulp.

3. Mix the arrowroot with the lemon juice and add a little of the soup. Pour into the soup and add the ground nuts and honey. Season to taste.

4. Return to the heat, bring to the boil and cook until the soup has thickened.

Serve with fried croûtons and fresh bread.

INGREDIENTS

3 pints/1½ litres water
1 lb/450g elderberries washed and removed from their stalks
2 sticks cinnamon
Juice and zest of 1 lemon
1 tablespoon arrowroot
4 oz/100g ground nuts
1 tablespoon honey
Sea salt and pepper to taste

Malgre Soup

INGREDIENTS

2 oz/50g butter
1 large onion, chopped fine
2 oz/50g spinach
2 oz/50g parsley
1 oz/25g chervil
3 teaspoons thyme chopped
2 teaspoons sorrel chopped
1 sprig rosemary
1 head of chicory chopped
1 pint/600ml dry cider and 1 pint/600ml water mixed
Juice of 1 lemon
¼ teaspoon ground nutmeg
Seasoning to taste
4 egg yolks beaten
4 eggs to poach

A debased form of Malaga Soup dating from 1700.

1. Melt the butter in a pan over a low heat. Add the onion and cook for 3–4 minutes.

2. Add all the herbs and chicory and cook for 10–12 minutes.

3. Gradually pour in the cider and water. Stir and cook for a further 10–12 minutes. Remove from the heat and set to one side.

4. Stir the lemon juice, nutmeg and seasoning into the egg yolks. Pour in a little of the soup, stirring all the time, gradually adding a little more.

5. Put in a pan and heat very gently until it starts to thicken; return to the main soup pan.

6. Poach 4 eggs and put one into each soup bowl. Pour in the soup. Serve with fresh bread or saffron bread.

Cheese Croquettes

INGREDIENTS

3 oz/75g soft white breadcrumbs
3 oz/75g Gruyère cheese, grated
½ teaspoon coarse ground black pepper
½ teaspoon sea salt
½ teaspoon cayenne pepper
3 egg whites, beaten until stiff
Oil to deep fry
2 tablespoons Parmesan cheese

1. Put the breadcrumbs, Gruyére and seasonings into a bowl.

2. Fold the egg whites into the cheese and breadcrumb mixture.

3. Form into small balls.

4. Heat the oil and fry the cheese balls until they are a light golden colour. Drain on kitchen paper. Sprinkle with Parmesan cheese and serve.

This is an early Victorian recipe. It is quite delicious. You can use Cheddar, but Gruyère is certainly one of the best cheeses for cooking.

Under the Influence of Bright Sunbeams

Chick Pea Croquettes

Pastellinhos de Gräo
NINETEENTH CENTURY

These little croquettes are reputed to have been one of the few savouries that William Beckford was prepared to eat while he was visiting Lisbon in the eighteenth century.

For although he was not received by the Queen of Portugal for some time many of the Portuguese families did welcome him, amongst which was the family of the Marquessa de Tancos whose cook used to make these little croquettes.

1. Put the chick peas and garlic into a food procesor and process until you have a thick light purée.

2. Put into a large bowl with the mashed potato, chopped herbs, spices, nuts, seeds and seasoning. Mix well.

3. Add the beaten egg yolks and seasoning and mix well.

4. Whisk the egg whites until very stiff. Fold into the chick pea mixture.

5. Heat the oil to fry.

6. Take 2 tablespoons and scoop a spoonful of the chick pea mixture into one spoon. Transfer the mixture from one spoon to the other to form the croquette. Drop into the hot fat and cook until golden brown. Continue with the remainder of the mixture. Drain the croquettes on kitchen paper. Garnish with lemon wedges and black olives.

Serve either hot or cold with a mayonnaise dip and vegetable rice. This is a light croquette that just melts in your mouth.

INGREDIENTS

1 lb/450g chick peas, soaked overnight and cooked until tender

2 cloves garlic, crushed

½ lb/225g potato, cooked and mashed

1 oz/25g fresh coriander, chopped very fine

2 oz/50g parsley, chopped

½ teaspoon ground cumin

½ teaspoon dried marjoram

1 oz/25g pine kernels, chopped

1 oz/25g sesame seeds

Sea salt and pepper to taste

2 egg yolks

2 egg whites, beaten until stiff

Oil to deep fry

Lemon wedges and black olives to garnish

Cold Leek and Carrot Soup

INGREDIENTS

3 tablespoons oil

1 onion, very finely chopped

3 good sized leeks, trimmed and sliced

1 lb/450g Granny Smith eating apples chopped, peeled and cored

6 oz/175g potatoes peeled and diced

1 pint/600ml water

½ pint/300ml milk

3 tablespoons sweet sherry

¼ pint/150ml cream

Sea salt and black pepper to taste

2 tablespoons chopped parsley

3 tablespoons chopped chives

NINETEENTH CENTURY

This is another cold summer soup from Scandinavia which is equally good if served hot.

1. Put the oil into a large pan, add the onion and cook very gently until transparent.

2. Add the leeks and apples and continue to cook for a further 10–12 minutes. Add the potato and water, bring to the boil, add the milk and simmer for 20 minutes.

3. Remove from the heat, set to one side and allow to cool.

4. Put into a food processor or blender and purée. Stir in the sherry and cream. Season to taste. Sprinkle with chopped parsley and chives and serve.

Orange and Carrot Soup

INGREDIENTS

2 oz/50g butter

2 medium sized onions, peeled and chopped

1 clove of garlic

1 lb/450g carrots, washed, peeled and cut into slices

2 lemons, juice and zest

2 pints/1200ml water

1 pint/600ml orange juice

Sopa de Naranja
TWENTIETH CENTURY

This is an unusual and colourful soup. I am not sure which of my cousins first sent me the recipe, but I have adapted it to serve four as the original was to feed at least 15!

1. Melt the butter in a large pan, add the onions and garlic. Cook gently until soft.

2. Add the carrots, lemon juice, zest and water, bring to the boil and simmer for 10 minutes. Then add the orange juice and ground nutmeg and continue to cook for 20–30 minutes.

Under the Influence of Bright Sunbeams

3. When the soup is ready, put into a food processor and purée.

4. Return to the pan and heat. Remove from heat, season to taste.

5. Stir in the cream.

6. Pour into a warmed tureen, sprinkle with chopped mint and serve at once.

¼ teaspoon ground nutmeg
½ teaspoon fresh coarse ground black pepper
Sea salt to taste
¼ pint/150ml cream or Greek yogurt
2 teaspoons chopped fresh mint to garnish

Savoury Shortbread

ADAPTED FROM A 1920s RECIPE

These make lovely savoury biscuits to serve with a pâté or terrine or with a hot soup, or just as a snack on their own. Always make more than you need to allow for 'pickers'.

1. Preheat the oven to 200°C, 400°F, Gas Mark 6. Mix the semolina, flour and spices together in a large bowl.

2. Cut the butter into small pieces and work into the flour and semolina until the mixture is of the consistency of fine breadcrumbs.

3. Work the garlic into the cheese, add to the mixture and then add the lemon juice and work again.

4. Put into an 8–10 inch 20–25cm cake tin, pressing the mixture down well. Put into the oven and bake for 12–18 minutes or until the mixture is a golden brown. Remove from the oven, mark into slices and leave to cool in the tin.

INGREDIENTS

2 oz/50g semolina
2 oz/50g wholewheat flour
2 oz/50g plain white flour
½ teaspoon chilli powder
½ teaspoon turmeric
½ teaspoon mustard powder
4 oz/100g butter or 3 oz/75g margarine
1 clove garlic, crushed
4 oz/100g grated cheese
Juice of 1 lemon

Mushroom Fritters

NINETEENTH CENTURY

1 lb/450g mushrooms, stems removed
Sea salt and pepper to taste
6 oz/175g flour
2 egg yolks, beaten
3 tablespoons olive oil
8 fl oz/250ml milk
2 egg whites, beaten very stiff
Oil for frying
Juice of 1 lemon
Fresh parsley for garnish

If people like mushrooms at all, then they tend to be greedy about them. These fritters are an absolutely delicious way of making mushrooms go a long way. 1 lb/450g make a very generous starter. You can halve the amount if you are not a dedicated mushroom eater!

1. Put the mushrooms into a colander or steamer over a pan of boiling water and cook for 10–12 minutes. Remove from the heat and set to one side.

2. Drain the mushrooms onto kitchen paper. Sprinkle with salt and pepper and roll in a little flour.

3. Mix the flour, egg yolks, oil and milk together and beat very well.

4. Fold the stiffly beaten egg whites into the batter.

5. Coat each mushroom in the batter and deep fry until golden.

6. Drain on kitchen paper.

7. Sprinkle with lemon juice and fresh parsley.

This is a delicious and simple starter. You can vary the recipe by adding ½ teaspoon ginger to the flour used to roll the mushrooms in and 1 tablespoon of orange flower water to the milk.

Aubergine Mousse

TWENTIETH CENTURY

First eaten in the Hotel Alentejo in Elvas in 1957.

1. Preheat the oven to 350°F, 180°C, Gas Mark 4. Put the oil into a large pan, add the onion and cook very gently until just transparent.

2. Add the pieces of aubergine and cook for 4–5 minutes.

3. Mix the tabasco sauce, orange flower water and wine together and pour onto the aubergine and onion mixture. Simmer very gently over a low heat for 20–25 minutes stirring from time to time.

4. When the aubergines are cooked, allow to cool for a few minutes before putting into a food processor or liquidizer. Process to a thick purée. Set to one side and allow to cool for 10–15 minutes.

5. Add the eggs and cream. Season with salt and pepper and a little nutmeg.

6. Grease a 1 lb/450g terrine or oven-proof mould. Fill with the aubergine mixture.

7. Put into the oven and bake for 50–60 minutes. Remove from the oven and allow to cool.

8. When cold, turn out of the mould. Cut into thin slices and serve with a sharp sauce or dip such as cucumber and garlic, or a fruit sauce and thin slices of buttered toast.

This is a delicious firm pâté. A good variation is to add 2 oz/50g chopped pistachio nuts to the mixture and a tablespoon of brandy. For those who wish for a variation that will make a dishonest and fat person out of anyone, read on.

Before serving, wrap each mousse in the thinest slices of smoked salmon. Return to the moulds. Press down lightly. When ready to serve, turn out onto individual serving dishes. Garnish with the thinest slices of lemon and a sprig of fresh herbs.

INGREDIENTS

1 tablespoon olive oil
1 medium onion, chopped
1½ lb/675g aubergines, cut into very small slivers
4-6 drops tabasco sauce
2 tablespoons orange flower water
4 fl oz/120ml red wine
2 large eggs, beaten
4 fl oz/120ml cream
Sea salt and black pepper
½ teaspoon ground nutmeg

Mrs Burfield's Coltsfoot Soup

FRANCE 1900s

2 oz/50g spinach or lettuce
leaves
2 oz/50g small coltsfoot leaves
2 tablespoons oil
¼ teaspoon ground nutmeg
Sea salt and pepper to taste
2 tablespoons honey
½ pint/300ml milk
½ pint/300ml cream
2 hardboiled eggs, chopped
Fresh green herbs, chopped

I don't actually know where this recipe originated. It was sent to me by an old lady who had been at school with my grandmother, and having heard from my daughters that I was thinking of collecting family and vegetable recipes, she thought it might be of some interest. They were at school together in France in the early 1900s, and this was one of the country soups served to them, when in season.

1. Wash and dry the spinach and coltsfoot leaves and chop them very fine.

2. Heat 2 tablespoons oil in a pan, add the coltsfoot and spinach and stir quickly. Cook for a minute or so, then add just enough water to cover, sprinkle with nutmeg, salt, pepper and honey and cook till tender, about 8–10 minutes.

3. Put into a liquidizer or blender, or pass through a fine sieve until you have a smooth cream.

4. Mix the milk and cream together.

5. Re-heat if need be. Pour into individual bowls, sprinkle with chopped egg and herbs and serve at once.

This soup freezes very well, and makes an interesting starter.

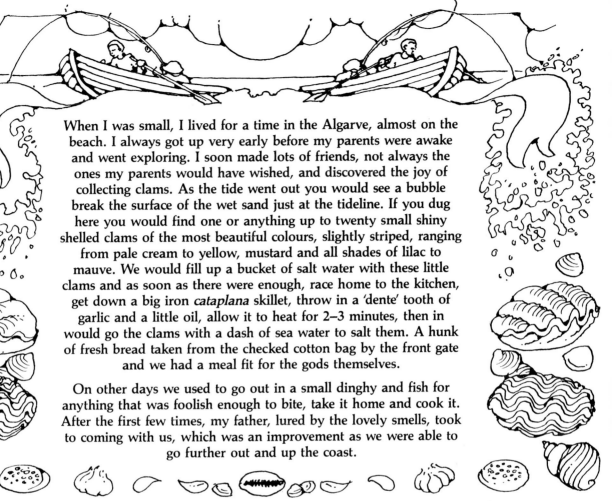

When I was small, I lived for a time in the Algarve, almost on the beach. I always got up very early before my parents were awake and went exploring. I soon made lots of friends, not always the ones my parents would have wished, and discovered the joy of collecting clams. As the tide went out you would see a bubble break the surface of the wet sand just at the tideline. If you dug here you would find one or anything up to twenty small shiny shelled clams of the most beautiful colours, slightly striped, ranging from pale cream to yellow, mustard and all shades of lilac to mauve. We would fill up a bucket of salt water with these little clams and as soon as there were enough, race home to the kitchen, get down a big iron *cataplana* skillet, throw in a 'dente' tooth of garlic and a little oil, allow it to heat for 2–3 minutes, then in would go the clams with a dash of sea water to salt them. A hunk of fresh bread taken from the checked cotton bag by the front gate and we had a meal fit for the gods themselves.

On other days we used to go out in a small dinghy and fish for anything that was foolish enough to bite, take it home and cook it. After the first few times, my father, lured by the lovely smells, took to coming with us, which was an improvement as we were able to go further out and up the coast.

Clams or Mussels with Coriander

1. Heat the oil in a large pan. Drop the garlic in, then the clams.

2. Sprinkle with coriander and brandy. Cover and cook until all the shellfish have opened.

3. Add the remaining ingredients and cook for a further 3–5 minutes. Serve at once with hot fresh rolls to mop up the juices.

INGREDIENTS

3 tablespoons olive oil

2 cloves garlic, crushed

1 tin clams or mussels, fresh, washed and cleaned

1 tablespoon fresh coriander, very finely chopped

2 tablespoons orange juice

2 tablespoons brandy

Sea salt and black pepper to taste

2.
Main Dishes

When Julius Caesar first visited Britain in 55 BC, he later wrote:

Nobody would be foolish enough to go there except to trade. All the Britains paint themselves dark blue with woad which makes them more frightening in battle. The people inland live on meat and milk and dress in skins. They do not grow corn. The trees are of the same varieties that grow in Gaul but there are no pines or beeches.'

During the period Britain was a Roman province, they introduced the vine, the cultivated apple, the fig, the medlar, sweet chestnut, walnut, mulberry, peach and the pear. On the native sloe they grafted the plum. They almost certainly introduced the cultivated cherry. We also have to thank them for introducing coriander, fennel, cumin, pine, borage, penny royal, onions, garlic, leeks, cabbage in many forms, beets, turnips, cucumbers, radishes, celery, peas, lentils, asparagus and the humble nettle.

Within a few generations after the Conquest, all these fruits and foods would have been not only cultivated, but have been available to the population of Roman Britain. The food that would have been eaten in a Romano British household would have differed little from that eaten in Rome, with the exception of some of the Mediterranean fish, and oil which was imported and was certainly very costly.

Wine was imported, for although the Romans taught the Britons the art of viticulture and how to make wine, they preferred imported varieties.

Lentil, Spinach and Almond Flan

For the pastry:

8 oz/225g wholewheat flour
1 teaspoon baking powder
1 teaspoon grated lemon zest
½ teaspoon coarse ground
black pepper
1 teaspoon sea salt
2 oz/50g chopped fresh parsley
(optional)
2 oz/50g butter
6 tablespoons olive oil
1 teaspoon honey
6 tablespoons red wine

For the filling:

3 tablespoons olive oil
1 teaspoon coriander
1 teaspoon cumin
3 large onions very finely
chopped
8 oz/225g split red lentils pre-
cooked in boiling water for
10–15 minutes. Drain and set to
one side.
4 tablespoons lemon juice
1 lb/450g spinach, coarsely
chopped
2 oz/50g fresh chopped parsley
1 teaspoon dried marjoram
1 teaspoon dried basil
1 red pepper chopped into
small pieces
Sea salt and pepper to taste

ROMAN FOURTH CENTURY

Lentils, spinach and nuts, in this case almonds, are the constituents of a typical Roman dish, one of many that helped to lay the foundation of Mediterranean cuisine today.

The Romans would have almost certainly served at least three sauces with this dish, each quite different from the other. This way, one dish would become three. One might be hot, one bland and the other fruity, all helping to give the original dish a different character.

I have changed the pastry recipe slightly as Roman pastry was made with more oil and needs to be eaten hot. This version will keep for some time in the freezer and can be served either hot or cold.

For the pastry:

1. Put the flour, baking powder, lemon zest, pepper and salt into a bowl and mix well, then sprinkle in the parsley.
2. Cut the butter up into tiny pieces and rub into the flour. Add the oil and work in.
3. Mix the honey with the wine, and add to the flour and fat mixture. Work until you have a light easy-to-work dough. If the mixture is too dry, add a little more wine.
4. Put into a cool place for 15–20 minutes.
5. Roll out and line a 9–10 inch 23–25cm flan dish, reserving some of the pastry for decoration.
6. Prick the pastry lightly all over with a fork and put into the oven at 350°F, 180°C, Gas Mark 4 for 5–6 minutes to bake blind.

For the filling:

1. Put the oil into a pan over a low heat. Add the coriander and cumin, stir and then add the onions. Cook very gently until the onions are just crunchy.
2. Mix the lentils and onions together. Add the lemon juice and set to one side.

Under the Influence of Bright Sunbeams

3. Put the spinach into a pan of boiling water for 2–3 minutes. Drain and mix with the lentil and onion mixture.

4. Add the parsley, marjoram, basil and red pepper. Season to taste.

To assemble the flan:

1. When the flan case is cool, fill with the lentil and spinach mixture. Sprinkle with flaked almonds and return to the oven. Cook for 18–25 minutes until the pastry is firm.

2. Decorate with a few strips of green pepper and serve either hot or cold.

Red Mullet

1. Pre-heat the oven to 200°C, 400°F, Gas Mark 6. Clean and wash the fish, making sure that you leave in the livers which give the fish its unique taste.

2. Rub the fish all over with a little oil and crushed garlic. Put a tablespoon of crushed parsley inside each fish and sprinkle with a little salt.

3. Wrap each fish in a piece of well-oiled kitchen foil. Put the fish parcels onto a baking sheet and cook in the oven for 15–20 minutes.

4. Warm a serving dish. When the fish are cooked, remove the foil, reserving the fish juices, and arrange the fish on the serving dish. Keep warm.

5. Put the fish juices and all the remaining ingredients into a pan and bring to the boil. Cook for 2–3 minutes until the anchovies start to soften. Remove from the heat and whisk with a fork until the anchovies have become creamy and the sauce is just thickening. Pour over the fish. Serve at once.

My great grandfather, like the Romans, loved mullet and used to vary the recipe by sprinkling a little grated goat's cheese over the fish and popping it under the grill for 2 minutes.

To assemble:
2 oz/50g flaked almonds
Strips of green pepper to garnish

INGREDIENTS

4 medium sized red mullet

For the Sauce:
3 fillets anchovy
A little oil
1 clove garlic, crushed
3 tablespoons very finely chopped parsley
A little sea salt
1 tablespoon wine vinegar
1 teaspoon honey
¼ pint/150ml red grape juice
¼ teaspoon ground black pepper
¼ teaspoon mustard
2 tablespoons butter

Jellied Trout

INGREDIENTS

4 trout, cleaned and washed. If you can get pink salmon, so much the better.

For the stock:
1 medium onion, very thinly sliced

1 carrot, washed and thinly sliced

1 clove garlic, peeled

1 sprig parsley

1 sprig thyme

2 bayleaves

8 peppercorns

2 cloves

2 or 3 mustard seeds, if available

½ teaspoon salt

¼ pint/150ml dry white wine

¼ pint/150ml red wine

½ pint/300ml water

This is a very early Roman recipe that is quite delicious and very easy to cook. Many of the Medieval fish dishes were coloured with saffron or vegetable juices. Sometimes the jellies would be made into patterns of different coloured jellies and decorated with flowers and herbs.

It is worth searching for a good supply of trout, as at times they can be rather muddy tasting.

1. Put all the ingredients for the stock into a pan and bring to the boil. Set to one side.

2. Put the trout into a shallow pan. Pour on the stock, cover and poach very gently for 10–12 minutes, or until it is possible to lift the fillets off the back bone.

3. Very carefully lift the fish away from the back bone, removing the heads, tails and any skin. Keep the stock and fish bones.

4. Lay the fish in a shallow serving dish. Set to one side.

5. Bring the stock, fish bones and fish heads to the boil and cook until the liquid has been reduced to just over ½ pint/300ml, and strain the stock.

6. Lay a piece of carrot between each fillet.

7. Pour the stock over the fish and put into the refrigerator to set. Serve with a selection of cold salads or vegetable purées.

If you want the dish to look even prettier, you can add other decorations to the pattern before you put it to chill.

Worts and Pastry Roll

TWELFTH CENTURY

1. Wash, peel and slice the turnips, parsnips and onions.

2. Put them into a pan of water, bring to the boil and simmer until just tender. Drain and mash to a rough purée. Set to one side.

3. Melt half the butter in a pan over a low heat with the herbs and spices. Add the mushrooms and cook gently for 4–6 minutes. Remove from the heat and set to one side.

4. Roll the pastry out very thin on a floured board until it forms a rectangle approximately 18×14 inch/ 45×35cm. Moisten the edges with a little water.

5. Starting at one end, place a layer of cooked vegetables and mushroom mixture on the pastry and roll, continuing to fill and roll until you reach within a few inches of the edge.

6. Pinch the ends of the roll together, fold the roll over carefully and place on a well greased baking sheet.

7. Glaze with beaten egg and put into a pre-heated oven at 350°F, 180°C, Gas Mark 4 for 35–40 minutes.

8. Just before the roll is ready to come out of the oven, heat the remaining butter in a pan and stir-fry the shredded cabbage for a few minutes. Put it into a heated serving dish and place the pastry roll on top. Serve at once.

This recipe is a little tricky to start with as the pastry must be rolled out very thin. It is easier if you put the roll in a sheet of greaseproof paper and slide it onto the baking sheet.

Very good side dishes with this are a carrot and chickpea salad, a purée of spinach and a beetroot and cream cheese purée.

INGREDIENTS

6 small young turnips

6 young parsnips

4 medium onions, cut into thin slices

2 oz/50g butter

1 tablespoon finely chopped fresh parsley

2 teaspoons thyme, freshly chopped or 3 teaspoons dried

2 teaspoons chopped mint

1 teaspoon allspice

2 oz/50g mushrooms, sliced

1 lb/450g puff pastry

1 egg to glaze

1 medium spring cabbage, finely shredded

Sea salt and freshly ground black pepper to taste

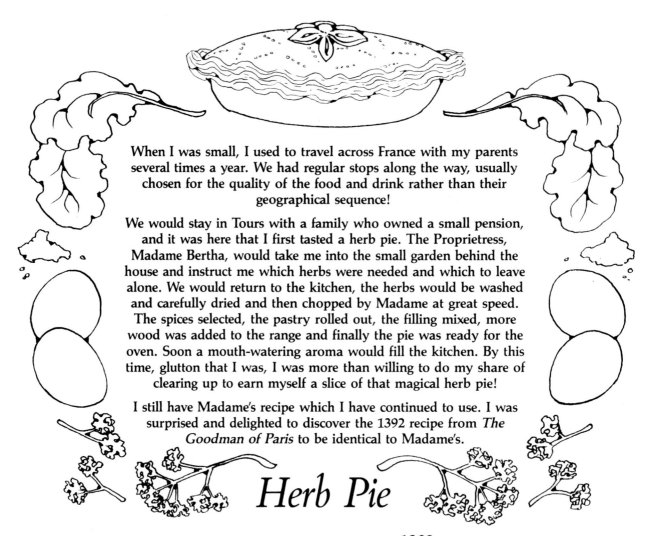

When I was small, I used to travel across France with my parents several times a year. We had regular stops along the way, usually chosen for the quality of the food and drink rather than their geographical sequence!

We would stay in Tours with a family who owned a small pension, and it was here that I first tasted a herb pie. The Proprietress, Madame Bertha, would take me into the small garden behind the house and instruct me which herbs were needed and which to leave alone. We would return to the kitchen, the herbs would be washed and carefully dried and then chopped by Madame at great speed. The spices selected, the pastry rolled out, the filling mixed, more wood was added to the range and finally the pie was ready for the oven. Soon a mouth-watering aroma would fill the kitchen. By this time, glutton that I was, I was more than willing to do my share of clearing up to earn myself a slice of that magical herb pie!

I still have Madame's recipe which I have continued to use. I was surprised and delighted to discover the 1392 recipe from *The Goodman of Paris* to be identical to Madame's.

Herb Pie

1392

INGREDIENTS

1 lb/450g puff pastry

4 oz/100g fresh parsley, very finely chopped

8 oz/225g raw spinach, very finely chopped

2 bunches watercress or Swiss chard, if available, chopped

6 oz/175g curd cheese or Ricotta

Black pepper to taste

1 teaspoon fresh ginger, grated

Pinch of sea salt

1. Roll out the pastry and line a shallow 10 inch flan dish. Put in the oven at 400°F, 200°C, Gas Mark 6 for 10 minutes. When cooked, remove from the oven and set to one side.

2. Mix all the greens together with the cheese, pepper, ginger, salt, chervil and beaten egg yolks in a large bowl.

3. Fold in the whipped egg whites, making sure that all the ingredients are well blended.

4. Pour the mixture into the pastry case, return to the oven and cook for 30 minutes at the same temperature.

Under the Influence of Bright Sunbeams

This pie can be served either hot or cold and makes a delicious meal served with garlic bread and plenty of good wine.

2 tablespoons fresh chervil leaves, if available
4 egg yolks, beaten
4 egg whites, whipped until stiff

Prawns with Chilli

PRE-COLUMBIAN

1. Peel the prawns and reserve the shells.

2. Sprinkle the prawns with lemon juice and a little pepper and set to one side.

3. Put the prawn shells into a pan with ½ pint/300ml water. Bring to the boil and simmer gently until the stock is reduced by half, about 15–20 minutes.

4. Put the garlic, dried chilli and sunflower seeds into a food processor and process to a fine paste. Add the tomatoes, peppers, spice, honey and salt and continue to process until you have a very thick paste.

5. Put the oil into a deep pan. Add the chopped onion and cook very gently until soft. Add the prawns and cook quickly for 2–3 minutes stirring constantly. Add the stock and continue to cook for a further 2–3 minutes.

6. Add the tomato and sunflower seed purée to the onion and prawns. Put into a warmed serving dish and eat.

INGREDIENTS

1½ lb/675g very large uncooked prawns
3 tablespoons lemon juice
½ teaspoon black pepper
½ pint/300ml water
3 cloves garlic, crushed
4 small dried hot chilli peppers
3 oz/75g dried sunflower seeds
1 lb/450g tomatoes, peeled and chopped
3 sweet red pimentos, de-seeded and finely chopped
½ teaspoon ground ginger
2 tablespoons honey
½ teaspoon sea salt
2 tablespoons oil
2 onions, very finely chopped

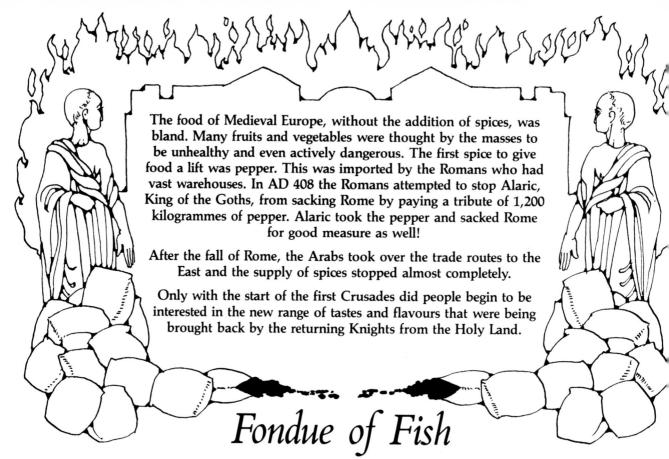

The food of Medieval Europe, without the addition of spices, was bland. Many fruits and vegetables were thought by the masses to be unhealthy and even actively dangerous. The first spice to give food a lift was pepper. This was imported by the Romans who had vast warehouses. In AD 408 the Romans attempted to stop Alaric, King of the Goths, from sacking Rome by paying a tribute of 1,200 kilogrammes of pepper. Alaric took the pepper and sacked Rome for good measure as well!

After the fall of Rome, the Arabs took over the trade routes to the East and the supply of spices stopped almost completely.

Only with the start of the first Crusades did people begin to be interested in the new range of tastes and flavours that were being brought back by the returning Knights from the Holy Land.

Fondue of Fish

VERY EARLY JAPANESE

INGREDIENTS

1 lb/450g cod, boned, skinned and cut into very thin slices

8 small scallops, cut into wafer thin slices

8 oz/225g large prawns or any shellfish, cut into very thin slices

For the Fondue Stock:
½ pint/300ml dry cider
1 pint/600ml vegetable stock
1 bay leaf
3 teaspoons mixed herbs
1 teaspoon ground pepper

1. Bring the stock ingredients to the boil and then stand a heavy saucepan or metal bowl on a trivet over a table heater or spirit burner.

2. Allow each person to help themselves to fish, immerse it in the boiling stock until cooked, and then dip into any one of a variety of sauces.

Serve at least 4 different sauces and a choice of salads and vegetable crudités.

Under the Influence of Bright Sunbeams

Spit Roasted Eggs

FOURTEENTH CENTURY

This is a most spectacular recipe from the Middle Ages and is well worth the effort involved. Serve the spit-roasted eggs with French bread and good wine.

1. Holding each egg over a bowl, make a small hole at each end of the egg with a pin. Blow through one of the holes so as to empty each egg into the bowl, retaining the shells.

2. Mix the chopped herbs and spices with the eggs; beat well. Cook the egg mixture in a pan with the butter until just set.

3. Making sure that the holes at each end of the shells are large enough to take the diameter of the skewers, fill each of the egg shells with the egg mixture.

4. Pass one skewer through two eggs and repeat, or use a smaller skewer for each egg.

5. Put the eggs under a medium hot grill for 4–5 minutes, turning them constantly. You can also cook these over an open fire. DO NOT cook these in a microwave oven, as this does not work!

INGREDIENTS

8 large brown eggs
1 tablespoon chopped mint
1 tablespoon fresh parsley, finely chopped
1 teaspoon dried thyme
1 teaspoon oregano
½ teaspoon ground ginger
½ teaspoon ground saffron
2 oz/50g butter
4 long skewers

Sauce for Roasted Eggs

1. Mix all the ingredients in a pan and heat gently.
2. Put into a heated bowl and serve at once.

INGREDIENTS

4 oz/100g butter
1 teaspoon ground ginger
1 teaspoon honey
Juice of 2 lemons
Pinch of ground saffron
A little sea salt

Eel Pie

St Ethelreda was the Abbess of Ely, which derived its name from the vast quantities of eels that were caught in the surrounding marshes. For many years the local people paid their dues to the Abbey in eels.

INGREDIENTS

4 oz/100g butter
1 teaspoon ground ginger
1 teaspoon honey
Juice of 2 lemons
Pinch of ground saffron
A little sea salt

To prepare the eels:
1 pint/600ml water, or enough to cover the eels
½ pint/300ml cider vinegar
½ teaspoon sea salt
2 lb/900g eels, skinned and cut into inch long pieces

To prepare the Eels:

1. Put the water, vinegar and salt into a pan.

2. Add the eels, and bring to the boil over a low heat. Simmer gently until tender.

3. Drain the fish and reserve the stock to use at a later date.

4. Remove the flesh from the bones, separate and set to one side.

For the pie:

1. Pre-heat the oven to 350°F, 180°C, Gas Mark 4. Divide the pastry in half. Roll out and line a 10 inch/ 25cm flan dish.

2. Put into the oven and bake blind for 10–12 minutes. Remove from the oven and put a layer of spinach in the flan case.

3. Arrange the cooked eels on the spinach. Mix the spices together, stir into the honey and pour over the eels. Top with the remaining spinach.

4. Roll out the pastry lid. Brush the edges with beaten egg or a little water. Put the lid on and decorate with any spare pastry. Brush with beaten egg.

5. Put into the oven and cook for 18–25 minutes or until a deep golden brown. Serve with a vegetable purée.

Under the Influence of Bright Sunbeams

We can thank the Crusaders for sugar. They first tasted it in the East in the twelfth century. As sugar cane does not travel well, it was imported processed in large loaves, some a dirty white and others dark brown.

It was a long time before it was imported in large enough quantities to become popular. Also, like spices, it was very expensive and usually locked up for safety.

The Knights of the Crusades not only encouraged and introduced new dishes to Britain but they founded a very profitable business on the spice trade. From their base in the Meditarranean, they managed to hold the monopoly of certain spices for a very long time. They were not particular who they dealt with and tended to sell to the highest bidder.

The Knights Templars founded their vast and very profitable business by selling spices to German, French and Italian merchants who in turn sold them to English merchants.

By the time spice and sugar reached England, they were very expensive as they had the furthest to travel of almost everywhere in Europe.

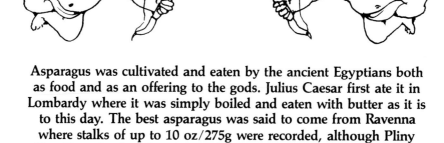

Asparagus was cultivated and eaten by the ancient Egyptians both as food and as an offering to the gods. Julius Caesar first ate it in Lombardy where it was simply boiled and eaten with butter as it is to this day. The best asparagus was said to come from Ravenna where stalks of up to 10 oz/275g were recorded, although Pliny tells of how he found spears so fat that three made a pound (450g). Martial wrote that the best asparagus came from Ravenna. Augustus created the saying 'faster than you can cook asparagus', as he liked it just blanched so as to remain crunchy.

Asparagus-à-la-Pompadour was a dish created by Madame Pompadour which combined asparagus and eggs, which she swore kept up her sexual vigour!

Asparagus Pudding

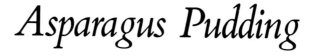

INGREDIENTS

4 oz/100g butter
4 slices white bread
¼ pint/150ml milk
6 tablespoons sour cream
4 egg yolks, beaten
1 bunch fresh asparagus cooked until just tender and cut into small lengths
4 egg whites beaten until stiff

1. Butter an oven proof dish.

2. Soak the slices of bread in the milk.

3. Beat the remainder of the butter until creamy.

4. Squeeze out the soaked bread and add to the butter. Beat.

5. Stir in the sour cream and egg yolks.

6. Combine the mixture with the cooked asparagus.

7. Fold in the whipped egg whites very carefully.

8. Pour the mixture into the buttered dish and cover tightly.

9. Put into a *bain-marie* or a pan half full of boiling water and cook very slowly for about 1 hour. Do not allow the pan to boil dry. Serve at once sprinkled with grated cheese if required.

Under the Influence of Bright Sunbeams

Cucumber, Mushroom and Soya Beans with Lemongrass and Ginger Sauce

This is a lovely spicy tasting dish from the East which I have adapted from Thailand. It is very difficult to date as the same traditions in food have lasted 1000 years and longer.

1. Put the pre-soaked soya beans into a pan with enough water to cover. Bring to the boil and cook very gently for 3–4 hours.

2. When the beans are cooked, drain and set to one side.

3. Wash and trim the spring onions and cut into 1 inch pieces. Chop the green leaves as chives.

4. Heat the oil in a large pan. Add the garlic, onions, cucumber, ginger, lemongrass, mushrooms and a little chopped coriander. Stir well and cook over a low heat for 3–4 minutes.

5. Mix the lemon juice, soya sauce, sherry and orange flower water together. Pour into the pan with the vegetables, stir well, cover and cook for 2–3 minutes.

6. Mix the cornflour with a little of the stock and then add the remaining stock.

7. Add the soyabeans to the vegetables, pour on the stock and cook for 3–5 minutes stirring constantly. Season to taste. Sprinkle with fresh coriander and serve at once.

INGREDIENTS

8 oz/225g pre-soaked soya beans

2 bunches spring onions

3 tablespoons oil

2 cloves garlic finely chopped

1 cucumber peeled and cut lengthways into 2 inch long sticks

1 tablespoon fresh root ginger peeled and finely grated

1 tablespoons chopped lemongrass

4 oz/110g small button mushrooms

3 tablespoons fresh coriander for ganishing

2 tablespoons lemon juice

2 tablespoons dark soya sauce

6 tablespoons dry sherry

2 tablespoons orange flower water

2 tablespoons cornflour

½ pint/300ml stock or water

Sea salt and black pepper to taste

Gratine of Fennel with Eggs and Walnuts

INGREDIENTS

4 heads fennel
2 oz/50g butter
4 eggs, hard boiled and cut into slices
4 oz/100g cheese
2 oz/50g walnuts chopped
3 oz/75g tomato paste
¼ pint/150ml white wine
6 tablespoons Parmesan cheese

FIFTEENTH CENTURY

In Italy and Tudor England, as well as a food fennel was supposed to be a protection against enchantment. Fennel seed was put into keyholes to stop any inquisitive ghost from passing through!

1. Wash and trim the fennel, reserving all the leaves. Cut the heads into small pieces.

2. Put into a pan of water and cook until just crisp. Drain and set to one side.

3. Butter an oven-proof dish and put a layer of fennel, then a layer of cheese, then fennel, then eggs, then fennel, then cheese and finally nuts.

4. Mix the tomato paste and wine together.

5. Pour the tomato and wine mixture onto the fennel. Sprinkle with Parmesan cheese.

6. Put into a preheated oven at 375°F, 190°C, Gas Mark 5 for 15-20 minutes. Garnish with croûtons and chopped fennel leaves and serve.

Orange Marinated Trout

This fifteenth century Italian recipe for trout or perch makes a really interesting and delicious fish course and is very easy to prepare.

1. Wash and very carefully dry the fish. Place in a shallow dish.

2. Rub each fillet with a little garlic and lemon juice. Leave for 10–20 minutes.

3. Mix all the remaining ingredients together. Pour over the fish and leave to marinate for 2–3 hours.

4. Cover with foil and cook in the oven for 25-35 minutes or until just tender at 350°F, 180°C, Gas Mark 4. Garnish with orange slices and chopped parsley and serve at once.

INGREDIENTS

4 trout, filleted

1 clove garlic, very finely chopped

Juice of 1 lemon

1 small onion, very finely chopped

3 tablespoons freshly chopped parsley

½ pint/300ml very dry white wine or vermouth

Juice of 3 oranges

Zest from 3 oranges

¼ teaspoon freshly ground black pepper

4 slices orange for decoration

Sea salt to taste

Vine Leaf Parcels

16 vine leaves, fresh or in packets

For the filling:
5 oz/150g cooked chick peas
2 oz/50g ground almonds
2 cloves garlic, crushed
3oz/75g fresh breadcrumbs
2 tablespoons brandy (optional)
1 oz/25g sultanas
2 oz/50g coarsely chopped nuts
1 egg, beaten
2 oz/50g chopped parsley or for a stronger flavour, fresh chopped coriander
1 teaspoon fresh ginger, grated
3 teaspoons sesame seeds
3 teaspoons poppy seeds
½ teaspoon grated nutmeg
1 teaspoon grated lemon zest
Sea salt and black pepper to taste
Wedges of lemon to garnish

For the sauce:
3 tablespoons olive oil
1 small onion, chopped very fine
2 cloves garlic, crushed
1 tablespoon flour
¼ pint/150ml dry white wine
4 tablespoons tomato purée
½ pint/300ml vegetable stock
Juice of 1 lemon
4 fl oz/120ml cream
3 tablespoons fresh coriander, chopped very fine (If you unable to get coriander, then you can substitute parsley.)

For a main course for 4 people

If you are using fresh vine leaves, put them in a pan of boiling salted water and blanch for 3–4 minutes. Drain and lay them out on a kitchen board.

For the filling:

1. Put the chickpeas into a food processor or mortar and mash to a thick paste.

2. Stir in the ground almonds, garlic and brandy. Allow to stand for 10–15 minutes.

3. Combine all the remaining ingredients with the chick peas and brandy and mix well.

4. Put a spoonful of the mixture onto each vine leaf; roll the leaf up and tuck the ends under to form a neat parcel.

5. Put the parcels into an oven-proof dish.

For the sauce:

1. Put the oil into a pan over a low heat, add the onion and garlic and cook very slowly until soft.

2. Stir in the flour to make a thick paste. Add the wine to the pan and stir, making sure you have no lumps.

3. Stir in the tomato purée and the remaining liquid. Cook very gently for 8–10 minutes.

4. Remove from the heat and stir in the cream and chopped coriander.

To assemble:

Pre-heat the oven to 350°F, 180°C, Gas Mark 4. Pour the sauce over the parcels and put the dish into the oven for 20-25 minutes. Garnish with wedges of lemon and serve with a dish of couscous and a tomato salad, or noodles with a basil and garlic sauce.

Under the Influence of Bright Sunbeams

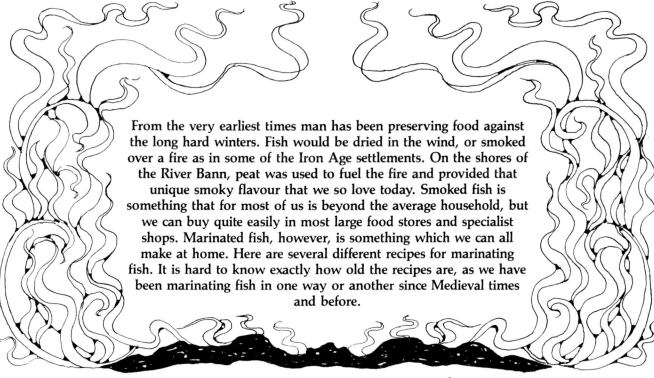

From the very earliest times man has been preserving food against the long hard winters. Fish would be dried in the wind, or smoked over a fire as in some of the Iron Age settlements. On the shores of the River Bann, peat was used to fuel the fire and provided that unique smoky flavour that we so love today. Smoked fish is something that for most of us is beyond the average household, but we can buy quite easily in most large food stores and specialist shops. Marinated fish, however, is something which we can all make at home. Here are several different recipes for marinating fish. It is hard to know exactly how old the recipes are, as we have been marinating fish in one way or another since Medieval times and before.

Marinated Squid

FIFTEENTH CENTURY ITALIAN

To prepare the squid:

1. Cut the squid into pieces and cook very gently with the oil and garlic until just tender. Set to one side and allow to cool.

For the marinade:

1. Mix the ingredients for the marinade together in a jug.

2. Pack the squid into an earthenware casserole and cover with the marinade.

3. Cover and put into a cool place. Leave for 48 hours before eating.

INGREDIENTS

To prepare the squid:

2 lb/900g small squid or cuttlefish, cleaned and cut into small pieces, washed well

2 tablespoons oil

2 cloves garlic

For the marinade:

1 onion, very finely chopped

3 tablespoons olive oil

1 pint/600ml wine vinegar

3 bay leaves

2 good sized sprigs sage

3 cloves garlic, chopped very small

The Arabs gave the word 'escabeche' to the Spanish language. Originally ISKEBÊY, by the time it reached England, it had been mispronounced and misspelt and become CAVEACH. The distinguishing feature of the recipes is that the fish is first fried in oil before being soused or pickled, the main advantage being that it was possible to keep fish in this way for at least a week and often a good deal longer.

Here are two versions, both very good, one dating from 1750 from a recipe book in American and one from an early Catalan recipe.

Caveach Mackerel

To pickle sprats or any other small fish

INGREDIENTS

Stage I
1 lb/450g sprats or other small fish
4 oz/100g flour
1 teaspoon dry mustard
½ teaspoon ground black pepper
Oil for deep frying

Stage II
1 pint/600ml vinegar
½ pint/300ml red grape juice
1 pint/600ml water
2 lemons very thinly sliced
4 bay leaves
3 sprigs rosemary
1 teaspoon cinnamon
½ teaspoon ground mace
½ teaspoon ground nutmeg
4 cloves

Stage I:

1. Clean and wash your fish and cut off the heads. Dry them in a clean cloth or kitchen paper. Mix together the flour, mustard and pepper.

2. Toss the fish in the flour and pepper mixture and set to one side.

3. Heat oil until very hot. Drop the fish in and cook very quickly until just golden.

4. Lift out carefully and drain on kitchen paper.

Stage II:

1. Put all these ingredients into a pan and bring to the boil. Simmer for 10–12 minutes and set to one side.

2. When the fish have drained, pack them in a deep earthenware casserole and pour on the boiled pickle. Make sure the liquid covers the fish. If not, add more vinegar.

3. Leave for at least 2 days before eating.

Under the Influence of Bright Sunbeams

Escabeche of Fish

1. Mix all the marinade ingredients together. Lay the fish in a shallow dish, pour on the marinade and leave for 3–4 hours turning from time to time. Reserve the marinade.

2. Remove the fish from the marinade and dry on kitchen paper. Toss in flour and deep fry in very hot oil until just golden. Drain on kitchen paper.

3. When the fish is cooked, put into a deep casserole. Add ½ pint/300ml olive oil to the reserved marinade and pour over the fish. Leave for at least 12 hours in a cool place before eating.

INGREDIENTS

1-2 lb/450-900g fish (all fish except sprats should be gutted)

For the marinade:
3 cloves garlic, crushed
½ pint/300ml strong wine vinegar
½ teaspoon ground pepper
3 bay leaves
3 tablespoons chopped herbs

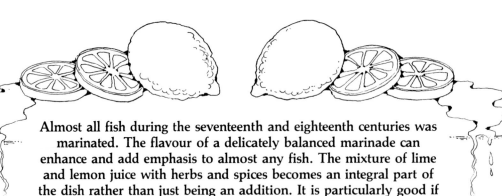

Almost all fish during the seventeenth and eighteenth centuries was marinated. The flavour of a delicately balanced marinade can enhance and add emphasis to almost any fish. The mixture of lime and lemon juice with herbs and spices becomes an integral part of the dish rather than just being an addition. It is particularly good if you are going to grill or barbecue fish, as like meat, you can get tough dry fish no matter how carefully you cook it, and marinating can help ensure a firm tender dish.

Marinade for Fish I

INGREDIENTS

(For 1–2 lb of fish)

6 tablespoons lemon juice
6 tablespoons olive oil
¼ pint/150ml white wine or malt vinegar
2 tablespoons brandy
1 teaspoon sea salt
8–10 black peppercorns, crushed
2 tablespoons brown sugar
2 cloves garlic, chopped
½ teaspoon ground cinnamon

Mix all the above ingredients together in a bowl and leave to stand for 10–15 minutes. Pour over your fish and leave to marinate for 1–2 hours if you are going to grill or bake the fish. To eat without cooking leave to marinate over night.

Marinade for Fish II

This makes a very good marinade for fish that is to be grilled or baked. To marinate the fish to eat without cooking use the above recipe added to 1 pint/600ml of white malt vinegar and leave to marinate over night.

INGREDIENTS

(For 1–2 lb of fish)

3 tablespoons chopped dill
3 tablespoons chopped parsley
3 tablespoons chopped onion
2 cloves garlic, crushed
Juice of 2 lemons
4 tablespoons gin
4 tablespoons white wine
½ teaspoon sea salt
1 teaspoon orange zest
Black pepper to taste

Vegetable Haggis

INGREDIENTS

2 oz/50g coarse oatmeal

8 oz/225g ground almonds

4 oz/100g ground hazel-nuts

2 oz/50g finely chopped mixed
nuts

1 medium onion, minced

2 egg yolks

4 oz/100g finely chopped
parsley

1 oz/25g thyme, sage and
marjoram, chopped together

1 teaspoon ground nutmeg

1 teaspoon ground ginger

½ teaspoon ground green
peppercorns

Sea salt to taste

1 muslin cloth in which to
wrap the 'haggis'

2 pints/1200ml dry cider

8 juniper berries

2 bayleaves

There are all sorts of recipes to be found for 'stuffing' and bag puddings, which contained herbs, nuts and spices. This recipe is based on an early recipe for a 'farce' or stuffing that was rich enough to be a meal on its own.

1. Put all the ingredients, except the juniper berries, bayleaves and cider, together into a large bowl.

2. Mix them together so that you have a firm paste; if need be, add a third egg yolk.

3. Roll into a long sausage, wrap in muslin and tie at each end.

4. Put the cider into a fish kettle or large pan. Add the juniper berries and bayleaves.

5. Bring to the boil and cook the 'haggis' very slowly for 1½ hours. Top the pan up with water if it looks like boiling dry.

6. Allow to cool and unwrap. Cut into slices and serve with a vegetable purée.

Stuffed Sliced Omelette

PIERRE DE LUNE 1656

This is really a mixture between a tortilla and a quiche and it is a direct descendant of the Roman egg 'patina'. It is more versatile, as you can eat it either hot or cold, also in bread as a sandwich or spread with cheese like bread.

1. Pre-heat the oven to 450°F, 230°C, Gas Mark 8. Butter a large flan dish with half the butter.

2. Melt the remaining butter in a pan and cook all of the ingredients together except for the lemon juice and beaten eggs, for 6–8 minutes, stirring constantly. Remove from the heat.

3. Stir in the eggs; pour the mixture into a buttered dish and cook for 10–15 minutes until a good golden colour.

4. Sprinkle with herbs and lemon juice. Cut into slices and serve with fresh bread and a tossed salad. A carrot purée is a very good side dish served with this recipe.

INGREDIENTS

3 oz/75g butter

2 oz/50g fresh sorrel, washed, the stems removed and the leaves chopped

6 eggs, hard boiled and chopped

2 oz/50g fresh parsley, very finely chopped

2 oz/50g fresh spinach, washed and finely chopped

2 artichoke hearts, cooked and mashed to a purée

8 oz/225g very small button mushrooms

2 cloves garlic, crushed

½ teaspoon ground nutmeg

½ teaspoon coarsely ground black pepper

6 eggs, beaten

Juice of 1 lemon

Fricassée of Eggs 1695

INGREDIENTS

To serve 6

1½ oz/40g butter

½ lb/225g mushrooms, very
thinly sliced

2 level tablespoons flour

1 pint/600ml vegetable stock

½ pint/300ml white port wine

¾ teaspoon ground mace

Sea salt and black pepper

1 egg yolk

12 oysters, shelled, retaining
their liquid

1 lb/450g cooked spinach, very
finely chopped

12 eggs, hard boiled, peeled and
cut into quarters

2 tablespoons finely chopped
parsley

1 lemon, cut into thin slices

Take 12 eggs and boil them hard. Cut them into quarters; to which put a Pint of Strong Gravy, and half a pint of White Port Wine; season with a Blade or two of Mace, bruised Pepper and a little salt. Scald a little Spinage to make them look green, with a Pint of Large Oisters to lay around the dish. Put the eggs into a Stew pan, with a few Mushrooms and Oisters, and rowl up a piece of Butter in the Yolk of an Egg and Flower, and shake it up thick for sauce. Garnish with crisp Snippets, Limon and Parsly. A side Dish.'

From *The Family Dictionary* — anonymous

1. Place the butter in a small pan and cook the mushrooms over a low heat until tender.

2. Stir in the flour, then add stock, port and mace, stirring all the time. Blend together well, season to taste and simmer for 8–10 minutes.

3. Add the egg yolk to a little of the sauce in a cup. Add in to the remainder and continue to cook, making sure the mixture does not come to the boil, for a further 2–3 minutes.

4. Heat the oysters gently in their own liquor for 2–3 minutes; no longer or they will become very tough.

5. Heat the chopped spinach and place on a large dish in a ring. Arrange the eggs in the centre, pour over the sauce, place the oysters round the edge, sprinkle with parsley and garnish with lemon slices.

Noodles with Cheese and Fennel Sauce

A CANTABRIAN RECIPE FROM 1720

1. Put the fennel into a pan of well salted boiling water and cook for 8–10 minutes. Drain and set to one side.

2. Heat a pan of water to boiling point. Put in 1 teaspoon oil (to stop the pasta sticking together). Add the pasta and cook until tender.

3. Put the butter into a pan together with the garlic, parsley and ginger and cook for 1–2 minutes.

4. Add the cooked fennel and black pepper; cook for a few minutes. Remove from the heat.

5. Drain the pasta and put into a warmed bowl.

6. Stir the cream into the fennel sauce, pour over the pasta, sprinkle with Parmesan cheese and mix well.

7. Decorate with chopped parsley and serve with lemon wedges.

INGREDIENTS

2 large heads fennel, washed, trimmed and chopped

1 teaspoon oil

8 oz/225g green or white tagliatelli

3 oz/75g unsalted butter

1 clove garlic (optional)

2 tablespoons parsley, chopped very fine

½ teaspoon very finely chopped root ginger

½ teaspoon freshly ground black pepper

3 fl oz/75ml cream

6 tablespoons grated Parmesan cheese

Lemon wedges to serve

Ironpot Stew

This recipe has been adapted from a traditional early eighteenth century American one.

For the stew:

2 tablespoons oil

2 onions, chopped very small

3 cloves garlic (optional)

1 teaspoon dried marjoram

1 teaspoon dried thyme

1 teaspoon fresh or dried rosemary, chopped

8 oz/225g mushrooms, sliced

4 oz/100g leeks, sliced

6 oz/175g swede, peeled and diced

8 oz/225g sweet potatoes, peeled and diced

4 oz/100g celery, cut into thin slices

2 bayleaves

½ pint/300ml sweet cider

1 lb/450g tinned tomatoes

2 tablespoons tomato purée

For the almond and oat topping:

3 oz/75g softened butter

3 oz/75g chopped nuts

3 oz/75g flaked oats

1 oz/25g ground almonds

2 tablespoons sesame seeds

½ teaspoon almond essence

½ teaspoon coarse ground black pepper

¼ teaspoon sea salt

4 poached eggs

For the stew:

1. Heat the oil in a large pan. Add the onions, garlic and herbs and cook for 3–5 minutes over a low heat.

2. Add all the fresh vegetables, stir well, cover and cook for 4–6 minutes. Add bayleaves

3. Mix the cider with the tomatoes, add the tomato purée, stir and pour onto the vegetables. Season to taste, cover and simmer for 35–40 minutes, stirring from time to time.

For the almond and oat topping:

1. Put the butter into a bowl together with all the other ingredients except the eggs for poaching. Rub into the oats and nuts until you have a mixture like coarse breadcrumbs.

2. Sprinkle over the top of the stew. Put it into the oven at 350°F, 180°C, Gas Mark 4 for 25–35 minutes.

3. Just before serving, put 1 freshly poached egg into each person's bowl and ladle the stew on top.

Under the Influence of Bright Sunbeams

Cabbage and Apple Gulbaba

FROM A SIXTEENTH CENTURY RECIPE

This would have been a very good way to use up windfall apples and late cabbages, both available long after most vegetables have finished. Today we are able to go into almost any greengrocer and buy foods that are out of season, but it was not possible to do so until the era of modern methods of preservation and transport.

1. Sprinkle the shredded cabbage with salt, and leave for 2–3 hours.

2. Heat the butter in a large pan and cook the onion very gently for 2–3 minutes.

3. Add the sugar, taking care that it does not burn.

4. Add the cabbage and stir well.

5. Gradually add the stock, stir and then cover and cook for 20–30 minutes.

6. Add the apple slices to the cabbage and cook for a further 10–12 minutes until just tender.

7. Mix the flour in a cup with the lemon juice and a little of the liquid from the cabbage. Add to the cabbage mixture and allow to cook for a further 3–4 minutes, season and serve.

If you want a stronger sweet and sour taste, add a little more lemon juice.

INGREDIENTS

1 lb/450g red cabbage, shredded
very finely
Sea salt
1 oz/25g butter
1 large onion, cut very fine
2 tablespoons brown sugar
½ pint/300ml stock
1 lb/450g cooking apples,
peeled and sliced
1 tablespoon flour
2 tablespoons lemon juice

Marinated Grilled Sole
with Mushrooms

1770

INGREDIENTS

To prepare the fish:

1 large halibut or sole, enough to feed 4, or 4 individual fish, cleaned, fins, tail and gills removed

For the marinade:

Juice of 3 lemons
4 tablespoons wine vinegar
2 bay leaves
4 peppercorns, crushed
½ teaspoon salt
A small sprig fresh coriander (optional)

To assemble:

Black pepper
3 oz/75g melted butter
2 large onions, very finely chopped
½ lb/225g mushrooms, very thinly sliced
6 oz/175g breadcrumbs, toasted
2 hardboiled eggs, chopped
4 slices bread, cut into quarters, either toasted or fried
2 lemons, cut into wedges

To prepare the fish:

1. Wash the fish very well in clean cold water.

2. Make a series of diagonal cuts along the back of each fish.

For the marinade:

3. Mix the ingredients for the marinade together. Lay the fish in a very shallow dish. Pour the marinade over the fish and leave for 2–3 hours turning from time to time.

To assemble:

1. Drain the fish and arrange in a shallow oven-proof dish. Sprinkle with pepper and put under the grill for 20–25 minutes, turning to make sure both sides are cooked.

2. Baste the fish with melted butter.

3. Put the onions into a pan with a little of the butter from the fish. Gradually add the marinade and cook until just tender. Add the mushrooms and cook for a further 5–8 minutes. Remove from the heat and set to one side.

4. Drain the onion and mushrooms. Mix with the toasted breadcrumbs and chopped hardboiled eggs. Pile the mixture onto quarters of toast; arrange round the cooked fish and serve, garnished with parsley and lemon wedges.

A nice variation of this dish is to add a few spoonfuls of Greek cow's yogurt to the mixture before piling onto the toast and a handful of toasted almonds.

Serve with a green salad and lightly steamed French beans with a squeeze of lemon juice.

Under the Influence of Bright Sunbeams

Cheese Fondue

This version of the classic fondue is lovely for almost any occasion.

1. Gently crush the garlic with the flat of a kitchen knife. Rub the inside of a heat proof fondue dish with the crushed garlic.

2. Mix the flour and grated cheese together.

3. Mix the wine, lemon juice and kirsch together, put into a pan and heat very slowly until just boiling. Remove from the heat.

4. Add the cheese and flour and beat for 3–5 minutes until the cheese and flour mixture is completely blended.

5. Add the nutmeg, salt and pepper. Keep warm over a night light or a food warmer. Do not allow to boil. If the mixture becomes very thick, add a little more wine to thin down the sauce.

Dip squares of fresh bread, celery sticks, julienned carrots, pieces of fennel root, small fresh mushrooms etc.

A good variation is to have a small dish of mixed seeds such as sesame, poppy and caraway, and after you have dipped your bread or vegetables in the cheese, dunk it in the seeds.

*You can use only one variety but the mixture produces a subtle flavour.

INGREDIENTS

1 clove garlic
2 tablespoons flour
½ lb/225g Emmental cheese, grated*
½ lb/225g Gruyère cheese, grated*
½ pint/300ml white wine
2 tablespoons lemon juice
3 tablespoons brandy or kirsch
½ teaspoon grated nutmeg
Sea salt and pepper to taste

Polenta with 'Heartwarming' Sauce

SIXTEENTH CENTURY

For the polenta:
2 pints/1200ml water (or for a luxury version 1½ pints/900ml water and ½ pint/300ml wine)
3oz/75g butter
8 oz/225g yellow corn meal
2 tablespoons chopped parsley

For the sauce:
3 tablespoons olive oil
2 cloves garlic, crushed
2 onions, very finely chopped
2 red peppers, seeds removed and flesh chopped into small pieces
3 tablespoons dried marjoram
1 tablespoon sweet red paprika
4 tablespoons tomato purée
1 large tin Italian plum tomatoes
1 glass sweet vermouth
Sea salt and black pepper

To coat the polenta:
1 egg beaten
3 oz/75g cornmeal
Oil to deep fry

For the polenta:

1. Put the water into a large pan with the salt and bring to the boil.

2. Add the butter and sprinkle the cornmeal into the water gradually, stirring all the time so that it does not become lumpy.

3. As the polenta starts to thicken, cover and cook very slowly for 15–20 minutes stirring from time to time to ensure that it does not burn or become lumpy. Sprinkle with chopped parsley.

4. When the polenta is cooked, pour into a shallow dish and allow to cool.

For the sauce:

1. Put the oil into a large deep pan over a medium heat. Add the garlic, onions, peppers, marjoram and paprika, and cook until the vegetables are soft. Add the tomato purée and tinned tomatoes.

2. Cover and simmer for 15–20 minutes, stirring from time to time.

3. Stir in a glass of sweet vermouth. Season to taste and set to one side.

To coat the polenta:

1. Cut the cold polenta into small squares, dip in beaten egg and then dredge in cornmeal.

2. Deep fry in oil and drain on kitchen paper.

3. Arrange the fried polenta in a dish, pour over the hot sauce and decorate with black olives. Serve at once.

Filling for Cannelloni

For the filling:

Mix all the ingredients together.

For the sauce:

1. Heat the butter in a pan. Add the flour and take the pan off the heat. Mix the butter and flour into a thick paste or roux and gradually add the cider. Stir in the lemon juice and zest.

2. Stir in the oil and beat well. Remove from the heat. Stir in the herbs and garlic and leave to stand for a few minutes. Season to taste.

3. Blanch the cannelloni in boiling water for 2–3 minutes, then drain. Fill the cannelloni with the cheese and nut mixture and pour the sauce over. Cover with foil and put into the oven for 35–40 minutes or until the pasta is cooked.

4. Remove from the oven and put under the grill for 3–5 minutes to brown. Serve hot.

INGREDIENTS

For the filling:

4 oz/100g grated Gruyère cheese

2 oz/50g grated Parmesan cheese

2 oz/50g chopped cashew nuts

1 oz/25g sesame seeds

1 bunch watercress

1 teaspoon chopped lavender

½ teaspoon ground nutmeg

½ teaspoon coarse ground black pepper

For the sauce:

1 tablespoon butter

1 tablespoon flour

¼ pint/150ml cider or white wine

Juice of 2 lemons

1 tablespoon grated lemon zest

4 tablespoons olive oil

4 oz/100g chopped green herbs

2 cloves garlic, crushed

Sea salt and black pepper to taste

1 packet dried cannelloni sheets (approximately 3 sheets per person)

Poached eggs have been very popular throughout history. Every country seems to have produced quite a range of different types of egg pans and dishes, those of the very rich often made of precious metals and elaborately decorated. The more humble versions were simply made from terracotta or iron.

These egg dishes could be used for both frying and poaching eggs, depending whether you filled the container with a little water or a few drops of oil and then set it over the hot fire.

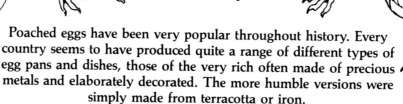

Poached Eggs with Butter and Orange Sauce

SEVENTEENTH CENTURY

INGREDIENTS

8 eggs
1 tablespoon wine vinegar

For the sauce:
2 oz/50g butter
1 medium onion, very finely chopped
3 cloves garlic, very finely chopped
1 teaspoon honey
2 tablespoons chopped parsley
1 fillet anchovy, pounded to a paste (omit for vegetarians)
Juice and zest of 1 orange
1 pint/600ml stock or bouillon
½ pint/300ml very dry white wine*
Sea salt and black pepper to taste

1. To make the sauce, combine in a saucepan, over a low heat, the butter, chopped onion, garlic, honey, parsley and anchovy fillet. Blend together for 2 minutes and gradually add orange juice and zest stirring constantly.

2. Add stock and wine, simmer for 10 minutes or so and season to taste. Remove from the heat and set to one side.

3. To poach the eggs, add 1 tablespoon vinegar to a pan of boiling water. Slide the eggs in one at a time from a ladle or cup. Cook until just firm, about 2½–3 minutes. Remove and drain on kitchen paper.

4. Trim any untidy bits off the eggs with scissors. Heat a shallow serving dish and arrange the poached eggs in the bottom. Cover with the sauce and serve at once.

This is very good served with cheese or saffron bread and lots of butter and also a watercress salad with French dressing.

Under the Influence of Bright Sunbeams

A variation of this recipe is to serve the eggs on a bed of asparagus. A purée of celery hearts and creamed potatoes are also good accompaniments to this dish.

*Portuguese Vine Verde is very good for this recipe and if you are feeling extravagant then dry champagne is delicious.

Mushroom and Basil Couscous

EIGHTEENTH CENTURY

This is based on a very old recipe from Rhodes. Although I suspect that it originally came from Turkey. It makes a delicious accompaniment to any egg dish, in particular poached eggs with orange sauce. The basil and orange flavours combine beautifully. Sliced tomatoes just sprinkled with black pepper and lemon juice are all you need to make a delicious meal.

1. Put the pine nuts, oil, garlic basil, Parmesan and watercress into a food processor with salt and pepper to taste and process to a thick paste. Set to one side.

2. Put the mushrooms into a pan with the vermouth. Cook very gently until just tender, 8–12 minutes. Remove from the heat.

3. Stir the cream or yogurt into the basil and cheese paste. Combine the hot couscous in the sauce. Put in an oven-proof dish, cover with foil and put into the oven for 8–10 minutes at 350°F, 180°C, Gas Mark 4, to heat through. Serve at once.

INGREDIENTS

1 oz/25g pine kernels
2 tablespoons olive oil
3 cloves garlic
1 oz/25g fresh chopped basil
6 tablespoons grated Parmesan cheese
2 oz/50g watercress, chopped
Sea salt and pepper to taste
8 oz/225g tiny button mushrooms
1 glass sweet vermouth
4 fl oz/120ml Greek yogurt or double cream
1 lb/450g couscous, cooked
24 small pearl onions (optional)

Savoury Hazel-Nut Loaf

INGREDIENTS

4 oz/100g grated carrot

¼ pint/150ml milk

½ tablespoon freshly grated root ginger

3 tablespoons orange juice

1 tablespoon turmeric

1 clove garlic, chopped

2 onions, finely chopped

2 tablespoons oil

1 lb/450g courgettes, cut into slices

4 oz/100g chopped hazel-nuts

½ tablespoon dill seeds

½ tablespoon sesame seeds

½ tablespoon cumin seeds

1 oz/50g chopped cashews

2 oz/50g chopped almonds

3 oz/75g rolled oats

Sea salt and black pepper

EIGHTEENTH CENTURY

This tasty crumbly-textured loaf makes a quick and easy main dish that you can eat either hot or cold. I like it served with carrots with lemon and vermouth or homemade tagliatelli and a vegetable purée.

1. Put the grated carrot into a pan with the milk, ginger, orange juice, turmeric and garlic. Cook very gently until the carrot is just tender. Remove from the heat and set to one side.

2. Put the onions into a pan with the oil. Cook very gently for 3–4 minutes. Add the courgettes, nuts and seeds, stir well and cook gently for 10–12 minutes. Remove from the heat.

3. Mix the oats into the onions and courgettes and then the carrots and milk. Make sure that everything is well blended.

4. Season and put into an oven-proof terrine or a well-greased loaf tin. Put into the oven at 350°F, 180°C, Gas Mark 4 for 30–40 minutes. When the loaf is cooked, leave to cool for 10–12 minutes and remove from the tin. Cut into slices and serve.

Under the Influence of Bright Sunbeams

A Gift from Poseidon

BASED ON AN EIGHTEENTH CENTURY RECIPE

For the mousseline:
1. Wash and trim the fish making sure there are no bones or skin. Lift off the fillets and cut the fish into small pieces. Put into a food processor or blender and process to a fine thick purée.
2. Combine the lemon zest, tarragon, paprika, peppercorns and garlic with the egg whites and beat into the fish purée.
3. At this stage it is a good idea either to stand the mixing bowl over some ice or to stand in a pan of very cold water.
4. Gradually start to add the cream a little at a time until all the cream has been combined. Set to one side in a cool place.

For the marinade:
1. Mix together all the marinade ingredients. Pour over the herring fillets and leave to soak for 3–5 hours, turning from time to time. Drain and set to one side.

To assemble:
1. Line a long terrine dish or loaf tin with non-stick baking paper and fill as follows:
   - 1st layer: half the fish purée
   - 2nd layer: prawns
   - 3rd layer: herring fillets
   - 4th layer: salmon
   - 5th layer: mussels and cockles
   - 6th layer: the remainder of the fish purée
   - 7th layer: cover with a layer of well-greased paper and then tin-foil
2. Put into a roasting pan of boiling water in the oven and cook very gently for 35–40 minutes at 340°F, 170°C, Gas Mark 5. Remove from the oven and allow to stand and cool.
3. To demould, lift out of the terrine. Remove the baking paper and decorate with slices of red pepper and anchovy fillets. Serve with mayonnaise and slices of crusty bread, and a good dry white wine.

INGREDIENTS

For the mousseline:

1 lb/450g sole or whiting, skinned and filleted

1 teaspoon grated lemon zest

½ teaspoon dried tarragon

¼ teaspoon sweet paprika

3 black peppercorns, crushed

1 clove garlic, crushed

3 egg whites

½ pint/300ml double cream

A few drops of orange flower water

For the marinade:

Juice of 2 lemons

1 tablespoon white malt vinegar

1 teaspoon brown sugar

1 teaspoon chopped dill

3 tablespoons chopped parsley

2 tablespoons chopped chives

½ tablespoon chopped tarragon

To assemble:

4 oz/100g Herring fillet, skinned and boned

3 oz/75g large prawns, shells removed

4 oz/100g fresh salmon, boned and cut into very small pieces

3 oz/75g small mussels or cockles, shells removed

Red pepper strips to garnish

6 anchovy fillets to garnish

Grilled Cod with Apple and Ginger Sauce

1981

4 good sized cod steaks
1 tablespoon cooking oil
1 large onion, very finely
chopped
½ teaspoon grated fresh ginger
½ teaspoon dry English
mustard
3 medium apples, peeled, cored
and cut into slices
2 tablespoons gin
½ teaspoon sea salt
½ teaspoon ground black
pepper
4 oz/100g Greek cow's yogurt
3 oz/75g grated cheese

This recipe really happened just after I first got my hands on a microwave. I discovered that microwaved apple purée was quick and easy and retained the flavour and colour of true apple like no other method. As we had a lot of apples, apple purée was added to most recipes, just to try.

1. Brush the fish all over with the oil and put under the grill. Cook for 10–12 minutes each side. Put into a warmed serving dish.

2. Put the onion into a pan with a little oil and cook very gently until just soft. Stir in the ginger and mustard.

3. Add the apples to the onion and continue to cook until just starting to break up. Stir in the gin and season to taste. Last of all stir in the yogurt. Continue to cook for 1–2 minutes.

4. Pour the sauce over the fish and sprinkle with grated cheese and black pepper.

5. Return to the grill and cook until all the cheese has melted. Serve at once with vegetables and a green salad.

False Omelette

EIGHTEENTH CENTURY

1. Put the onion, tomatoes and mint into a pan with a little of the oil and cook very slowly for 10–15 minutes. Stir in the flour and paprika and set to one side.

2. Soak the pieces of bread in milk, then squeeze. Add to the beaten eggs, season with salt and pepper and stir in the peas.

3. Heat the oil and pour in the bread and egg mixture. Cook on each side for 3–4 minutes. Set to one side.

4. Cut the omelette into wedges and return to the pan. Spoon the onion and tomato sauce onto the omelette and pour in just enough wine to cover the omelette.

5. Cover and simmer for 12–15 minutes. Serve at once with a salad.

INGREDIENTS

1 onion, finely chopped

2 large tomatoes, finely chopped

2 tablespoons chopped mint

8 tablespoons olive oil to fry in

1 tablespoon flour

2 teaspoons sweet paprika

4 slices bread with the crusts removed

Milk for soaking

4 eggs, beaten

Sea salt and black pepper to taste

¼ pint/150ml white wine

3 oz/75g fresh or frozen green peas

Gruyère Käsekuchen

For the pastry:
2 oz/50g ground hazelnuts
6 oz/175g wholewheat flour
½ teaspoon ground nutmeg
½ teaspoon sea salt
Approximately 2½ oz/65g
butter cut into small pieces
¼ pint/150 milk

For the topping:
8 oz/250g Gruyère cheese
grated
4 oz/100g pre-cooked mashed
potato
3 oz/90ml cream or creamy
yogurt
2 eggs, beaten
Sea salt and pepper to taste
2 medium onions, chopped
very fine

NINETEENTH CENTURY

This is a delicious type of pizza that comes from Switzerland, not far from the northern Italian border. This particular recipe dates from the nineteenth century although variations go back many hundreds of years.

It is difficult to tell how old dishes are as they are handed down in families for many generations by word of mouth and there is no need to write them down. Due to the fact that Switzerland has Italian, French and German neighbours, the cooking reflects a long history of mixed cultures although each area has its own different style of food.

For the pastry:

1. Sieve the hazelnuts, flour, nutmeg and salt into a large bowl. Rub the butter into the flour mixture until it is like coarse crumbs.

2. Make a well in the centre, pour in the milk and mix to make a light dough.

3. Roll out on a floured board to form a large flat pizza-like base about ½ inch/1cm thick. Put onto a well-greased baking sheet and set to one side.

For the topping:

1. Mix all the ingredients together, except the onions.

2. Spread the mixture over the pastry base leaving a margin all round to prevent it falling off the edge. Sprinkle with chopped onion.

3. Put into the oven and cook at 400°F, 200°C, Gas Mark 6 for 20–25 minutes.

Fish with Cider Sauce

NINETEENTH CENTURY

1. Put the fish into a shallow dish and sprinkle with pepper.

2. Mix the garlic, bayleaf, salt and chopped onion into the cider. Pour over the fish and leave to marinate in a cool place for 3–4 hours, turning from time to time.

3. Drain the fish, reserving the liquid, and place under the grill for 10–12 minutes on each side.

4. Strain the onion and bayleaf from the marinade and put onion into a pan with 3 tablespoons oil. Cook gently for 8–10 minutes or until just soft, stirring from time to time.

5. Remove from the heat. Work the ground nuts and flour into the onion. Add the liquid and return to the heat stirring constantly. Sprinkle with paprika, parsley and salt to taste.

6. Arrange the cooked fish steaks in a warmed serving dish, pour over the sauce and serve at once.

Serve with sauté potatoes and a green salad, or with a mixed salad of green beans and mushrooms.

INGREDIENTS

4 thick fish steaks
3 peppercorns, crushed
3 cloves garlic, crushed
1 bayleaf
Sea salt
1 large onion, very finely chopped
½ pint/300ml strong dry cider
3 tablespoons olive oil
1 tablespoon ground almonds or hazelnuts
1 tablespoon flour
1 tablespoon sweet paprika
3 tablespoons fresh parsley, very finely chopped

Celery Meringue Casserole

1830

INGREDIENTS

1 large head celery with leaves,
cleaned and trimmed
1 pint/600ml milk
12 oz/350g fresh breadcrumbs
2 oz/50g butter
¼ teaspoon fresh ground
pepper
¼ pint/150ml sweet white wine
2 anchovy fillets, very finely
chopped (optional)*
2 egg yolks, beaten
4 oz/100g grated cheese — very
mild Cheddar or Emmental
2 egg whites, whipped stiff
¼ teaspoon ground nutmeg

1. Cut the washed and trimmed celery stalks into thin sticks.

2. Chop the green celery leaves very finely.

3. Put the celery into a pan of boiling water, bring to the boil and simmer gently for 45–50 minutes. Drain and chop. Set to one side.

4. Put the milk into a pan. Add the breadcrumbs and stir. Bring to the boil. Set to one side.

5. Melt the butter in a pan and add the chopped celery, wine and the anchovies and cook for 3–6 minutes. Add the pepper.

6. Remove from the heat and stir in the egg yolks.

7. Mix 3 oz/75g of the cheese into the celery. Fold in the beaten egg whites and chopped celery tops.

8. Butter an oven-proof dish and pour in the mixture. Sprinkle with the remaining cheese and ground nutmeg. Bake in a hot oven for 5–6 minutes. Serve straight away.

This is a delicious dish for a cold evening. For a variation, add a layer of steamed spinach sprinkled with 1 oz/75g ground almonds, under the celery.

*If you are omitting the anchovy fillets, then put in ½ teaspoon salt.

Egg Sausage

1830–1840

These little savoury sausages were a favourite of Napoleon III. The recipe is said to have originated in Hungary during the 1830s.

1. Soak the breadcrumbs in half the cream.

2. Mix together with the parsley, rest of the cream and chopped eggs and seasoning. Add the egg yolks to bind, leave to stand for 10–15 minutes.

3. When the mixture has thickened, form into sausage shapes.

4. Melt the butter in a pan and fry the shapes. Drain on kitchen paper.

5. Sprinkle with grated cheese and parsley. Serve at once while still hot.

INGREDIENTS

4 oz/100g soft breadcrumbs
½ pint/300ml double cream
2 oz/50g chopped parsley
8 hard boiled eggs, chopped
Sea salt and pepper to taste
3 egg yolks, beaten
2 oz/50g butter
Grated cheese to garnish

Thunder and Lightning

Thoni e Lampo

This is a version of the old Italian recipe. You can use wholemeal pasta but you will lose the true character of the dish. But if you make your own pasta or can buy freshly made, then do so as it is always tastier than ready-made. Unfortunately so much ready-made wholewheat pasta has the consistency of cork tiles in comparison to really good home-made pasta.

INGREDIENTS

8 oz/225g chickpeas, soaked overnight in water

8 oz/225g fresh pasta shells or macaroni

6 tablespoons olive oil

2 cloves garlic, crushed

Black pepper to taste

2 tablespoons chopped chives and parsley mixed

2 tablespoon lemon juice

½ teaspoon ground nutmeg

2 oz/50g Parmesan cheese

1. Drain the chickpeas and then rinse them in cold water. Put them in a saucepan with enough cold water to cover. Bring to the boil and simmer very gently until tender. Remove from the heat and set to one side.

2. Cook the pasta in a pan of well-salted boiling water. Add 1 teaspoon olive oil to the water which will stop the pasta sticking together. When the pasta is just tender, drain, set to one side and keep warm.

3. Heat the oil in a large pan, add the garlic, pepper and drained chickpeas. Sprinkle with parsley and chives and toss the chickpeas in the seasoned oil. Remove from the heat and sprinkle with lemon juice and ground nutmeg.

4. Mix the chickpeas and pasta together with extra nutmeg and black pepper. Sprinkle with cheese making sure it is well blended. Serve at once with a crisp watercress, tomato and basil salad.

A good variation of this recipe is to omit 2 tablespoons of oil and substitute double cream. This makes a lovely rich coating to the pasta and peas.

Under the Influence of Bright Sunbeams

Vegetable Paella

This is a variation on a paella from Estremadura in Spain which, although traditionally made with meat and shellfish, can be found in a purely vegetable version in the depth of the country.

INGREDIENTS

For the stock:

1. Put all the stock ingredients into a pan and bring to the boil. Cook for 30–35 minutes. Meanwhile put rice in a pan of water and start to cook.

For the paella:

1. While the rice is cooking, heat the oil in a pan, add the onions and gradually all the other ingredients. Cover and cook very slowly for 5–10 minutes.

2. When the rice is cooked, mixed all the vegetables into the rice. Put into a large heat-proof dish and serve.

This is particularly good with a green salad and tomatoes with basil, good red wine and fresh bread.

For the stock:
½ pint/300ml sweet white wine
2 pints/1200ml water
3 cloves garlic, chopped
1 bayleaf
1 teaspoon ground coriander
1 teaspoon ground nutmeg
½ teaspoon coarse ground black pepper
1 teaspoon sea salt
2 teaspoons ground saffron or saffron threads

For the paella:
10 oz/275g rice, uncooked
4 tablespoons olive oil
3 onions, cut into very thin slices
1 green pepper, sliced very thin
1 red pepper, sliced very thin
24 chestnuts, pre-cooked
4 oz/100g tiny button mushrooms
4 oz/100g black olives
8 oz/225g cooked chickpeas
1 tin red pimentos or 4 oz/100g sliced
8 oz/225g fresh or frozen peas, cooked for 2–3 minutes in boiling water

Savoury Carrot and Cheese Savarin

INGREDIENTS

1 oz/25g butter

½ teaspoon ground saffron

1 teaspoon sugar

Zest of 1 lemon

1 lb/450g carrots, washed, peeled and very coarsely grated

¼ pint/150ml vegetable stock

¼ pint/150ml dry white wine

1 tablespoon oil

1 large bunch spring onions, washed, trimmed and very finely chopped including the green stalks or alternatively 1 medium onion, finely chopped

2 oz/50g mushrooms, very finely sliced

3 tablespoons sweet vermouth

4 tablespoons ground almonds or hazelnuts

2 large eggs, beaten

1 oz/25g grated cheese

1 teaspoon sea salt

½ teaspoon black pepper

A little melted butter or oil to grease the mould

For the sauce:

2 tablespoons sweet vermouth

2 oz/50g small whole mushrooms

3 oz/75g Emmental or Gruyère cheese

2 fl oz/60ml creamy Greek yogurt

4 hard boiled eggs

Sea salt and pepper to taste

Toasted almonds and chopped fresh herbs to garnish

TWENTIETH CENTURY — CHINA DE BURNAY

1. Melt the butter in a pan over a low heat. Add the saffron, sugar and lemon zest together with the carrots. Stir thoroughly so that they are well coated with the butter and seasoning. Cook for 3–4 minutes stirring constantly.

2. Pour the stock and wine over the carrots and cook for 18 minutes, stirring from time to time.

3. Heat the oil in a pan and quickly cook the onion and mushrooms. Add the vermouth and cook for 4–5 minutes. Remove from the heat and stir in the ground almonds. Stir in the beaten eggs, cheese, salt and pepper. Mix with the carrots and set to one side.

4. Grease your mould with a little oil or melted butter.

5. Pour the carrot mixture into the mould and cover with foil.

6. Stand the mould in a roasting pan of boiling water in the oven at 400°F, 200°C, Gas Mark 6 for 20–25 minutes.

7. Remove from the oven, leave for 2–3 minutes and then slip a knife blade round the edges of the mould to loosen the contents. Turn out very carefully onto a serving dish. Fill the centre with the sauce.

For the sauce:

1. Put the vermouth into a pan with mushrooms, cover and cook very gently for 3–5 minutes. Stir in the cheese and yogurt. Just allow the cheese to melt.

2. Pour over the sliced hard boiled eggs and season to taste.

3. Fill the centre of the carrot mould with this mixture and garnish with toasted almonds and sprinkle with chopped herbs. Serve at once.

Under the Influence of Bright Sunbeams

Eastern Roast

TWENTIETH CENTURY FROM AMERICA

1. Put the beans, tomato purée, Worcestershire sauce and oil into a food processor or blender. Process until you have a thick smooth purée.

2. Add the yeast, water, ground nuts, wheatgerm and bran. Mix well and set to one side.

3. Heat some oil in a frying pan and add the onion, pepper and ginger. Cook very gently until just tender. Add the green vegetables and heat again. Set to one side.

4. Grease an ovenproof dish. Pour in a quarter of the nut and bran batter, then a layer of onion and greens, then another layer of both and so on until you finish with a layer of batter.

5. Put into a pre-heated oven at 350°F, 180°C, Gas Mark 4 for 1-1¼ hours. Remove from the oven and allow to cool for 5 minutes. Run a knife round the dish and remove the loaf.

Serve with fresh vegetables and a fruit sauce such as apricot.

INGREDIENTS

8 oz/225g pre-cooked soya beans

3 oz/75g tomato purée

1 tablespoon vegetarian Worcestershire sauce

1 tablespoon olive oil

1 packet instant yeast

¼ pint/150ml water

2 oz/50g ground almonds

2 oz/50g ground pine nuts

2 oz/50g wheatgerm

2 oz/50g bran

1 small onion, very finely chopped

1 teaspoon coarse ground black pepper

1 teaspoon ground ginger

4 oz/100g pre-cooked chopped spinach

4 oz/100g pre-cooked chopped kale or calabrese

Stuffed Eggs with Apple Mayonnaise

1870s SCANDINAVIA

This is a lovely delicate tasting mayonnaise that originates in Scandinavia. It is good to serve with salads as part of a main course rather than as a starter.

8 hard boiled eggs
1 tablespoon parsley, chopped very fine
1 tablespoon lemon juice
Sea salt and black pepper

For the sauce:
6 fl oz/175ml apple purée
½ teaspoon creamed horseradish
1 tablespoon gin or vodka (optional)
8 fl oz/250ml mayonnaise
A few green herbs to decorate

1. Cut the hardboiled eggs in half lengthways. Scoop out the yolks and mash with a fork. Add the parsley and lemon juice. Season with a little pepper and salt.

2. Work the yolks to a thick paste. Fill the egg whites with the mixture.

3. Arrange in a shallow dish and serve with the following sauce:

4. Mix the apple purée, horseradish and gin together. Beat for 1–2 minutes, add the mayonnaise. Put into a bowl, cover with film and chill. Before serving, decorate with a few green herbs.

Under the Influence of Bright Sunbeams

On the large plate: Vegetable Spiced Rice (page 100) and on the small plate: Beetroot Salad (page 88).

A Tudor Feast. Clockwise from the top: Portuguese Soup of Greens (page 25), Marzipan Pie (page 116), Vine Leaf Parcels (page 50) and Marinated Squid (page 51).

Pumpkin Pie (page 125).

Asparagus with Kirsch

TWENTIETH CENTURY

It is a really lovely way to eat asparagus and enjoy its subtle taste to the fullest. This dish doesn't really need anything with it, except just crusty bread and a dry white wine. If you do want something to serve with it, steamed carrots with a little lemon juice and pepper are ideal.

1. Put the asparagus into a pan of well-salted boiling water and cook for 15–18 minutes or until just tender. Drain and set to one side.

2. Heat the butter in a pan and brown the potatoes on each side. Remove from the heat.

3. Put a layer of potatoes into an oven-proof dish, then a layer of asparagus, then cheese. Repeat until asparagus, potatoes and cheese are used up, finishing with a layer of cheese. Sprinkle with breadcrumbs, nutmeg and kirsch.

4. Put into the oven at 350°F, 180°C, Gas Mark 4 for 10–15 minutes or until the cheese is just melted.

This is a Swiss recipe that my grandmother used to cook. She got it from a school friend who came from near the Rhône valley.

INGREDIENTS

1½ lb/675g fresh asparagus, washed and tough ends trimmed off

1 oz/25g butter

8 oz/225g cooked potatoes, cut into very thin slices

4 oz/100g very mild cheese, grated

4 tablespoons toasted brown breadcrumbs

½ teaspoon grated nutmeg

2 tablespoons kirsch

3.

Side Dishes

Don't eat vegetables with a spoon. Eat them with a fork. The rule is not to eat anything with a spoon that can be eaten with a fork. Even ices are now often eaten with a fork.

A Manual of Mistakes and Improprieties 1883

French Beans and Chick Peas

Faseoli Virides et Circer
ROMAN

INGREDIENTS

6 tablespoons olive oil
8 tablespoons dry white wine
½ teaspoon coarse ground sea salt
½ teaspoon ground cumin
1 teaspoon honey (optional)
6 oz/175g cooked chick peas
8 oz/225g cooked French or runner beans

1. Place the oil, wine, salt, cumin and honey in a large bowl and mix well together.

2. Add the chick peas and beans.

3. Toss well and serve.

This dish would have formed part of the *hors d'oeuvres* or *Gustum*, but is a very useful dish to serve with roast dishes or grilled fish.

A Medieval Way with Stinging Nettles

INGREDIENTS

3 tablespoons olive oil
2 tablespoons wine vinegar
2 teaspoons honey
1 clove garlic, finely chopped
1 head chicory, very thinly sliced
4 oz/100g young nettle shoots, washed and coarsely chopped
1 medium onion, very finely chopped

'Pick wild nettles when the sun is in the sign of Aires. Take them against illness if you wish.'

1. Mix the oil, vinegar, honey and garlic together in a cup.

2. Put the chicory, nettles and chopped onion into a salad bowl.

3. Pour the dressing over the salad, toss and serve.

Here are just two of the many variations you can serve: use sliced mushrooms and sultanas with your chopped nettles instead of chicory, which is not to everyone's taste, or watercress, grated apple and a little yogurt. Both are very good alternatives to the basic recipe.

Under the Influence of Bright Sunbeams

Cabbage with Raisin and Olive Dressing

ROMAN

1. Bring a pan of water to the boil, add the cabbage and leeks and cook for 3 minutes.

2. Drain and arrange on a dish.

3. Combine all the remaining ingredients in a cup and mix well.

4. Pour over the cabbage and mix. Serve either hot or cold as a side salad.

This is delicious with almost any fish dish.

INGREDIENTS

1 medium cabbage, shredded
2 good-sized leeks, washed, trimmed and cut into thin slices

For the dressing:
1 oz/25g seedless raisins
1 oz/25g pine kernels
3 tablespoons olive oil
3 tablespoons red wine
1 tablespoon sweet wine or sherry
3 tablespoons fresh coriander, chopped
½ teaspoon ground cumin
½ teaspoon fresh ground black pepper
2 teaspoons caraway seed
10 black olives, stoned and cut into small pieces

The earliest known vegetable garden was that created by Ur-Nammu in Mesopotamia 4000 years ago. Among the vegetables that Ur-Nammu grew there were leeks, onions, cucumbers and lettuce.

So highly did he think of his vegetable garden that he built a temple to the god Nanna to save the garden from any harm. Unfortunately, the god was unable to save the garden and Ur-Nammu and the Children of Israel spent two long years in the desert.

But nonetheless traditional recipes for cooking cucumbers and courgettes have been handed down for many hundreds of years.

Stuffed Marrow

TWELFTH OR THIRTEENTH CENTURY

INGREDIENTS

1 medium marrow
4 hard boiled egg yolks
2 oz/50g seedless raisins
1 oz/25g currants
1 oz/25g minced dates
Sea salt and pepper to taste

1. Cut the marrow in half lengthways, scoop out the seeds and wash.

2. Mix together the hard boiled egg yolks, raisins, currants and dates. Season with salt and pepper and beat in the egg yolk to bind.

3. Fill the marrow with the mixture. Put the other half on top and tie with string or wrap in foil.

4. Put into a shallow oven-proof dish or baking tray and cook in the oven for 1–1½ hours at 375°F, 190°C, Gas Mark 5.

Under the Influence of Bright Sunbeams

Apple Flower Fritters

ELIZABETHAN

(You can use rose petals)

This is a lovely old country recipe greatly loved by the Elizabethans. If you have a lot of roses, it is a good way to use up loose petals that are just about to fall.

1. Pound the breadcrumbs and egg yolks together with the mixed spice and galingale if used.

2. Add the apple flowers and beaten eggs and form into small flat cakes.

3. Heat the oil in a large frying pan.

4. Fry the cakes till they are golden brown on both sides. Drain on kitchen paper.

INGREDIENTS

6 oz/175g fresh white breadcrumbs
4 egg yolks, hard boiled
¼ teaspoon mixed spices
¼ teaspoon galingale (optional)
2 handfulls apple flower petals
2 eggs, beaten
Oil to fry

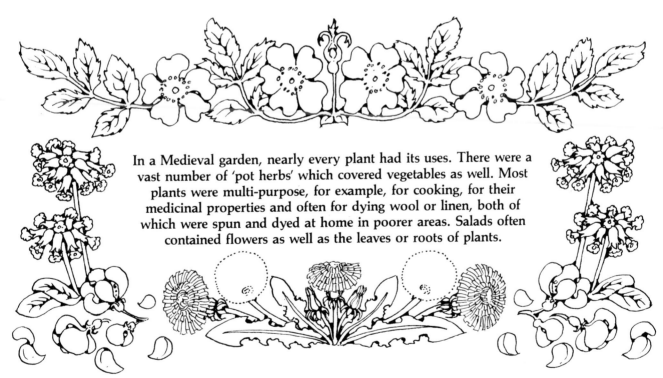

In a Medieval garden, nearly every plant had its uses. There were a vast number of 'pot herbs' which covered vegetables as well. Most plants were multi-purpose, for example, for cooking, for their medicinal properties and often for dying wool or linen, both of which were spun and dyed at home in poorer areas. Salads often contained flowers as well as the leaves or roots of plants.

Beetroot Salad

1 lb/450g cooked beetroot, very
thinly sliced
Sea salt
Juice of 1 lemon
A good pinch chopped tarragon
¼ pint/150ml cream
2 tablespoons olive oil
1 teaspoon honey
Freshly ground black pepper

1. Arrange the slices of beetroot onto a shallow dish or
plate, sprinkle with salt, lemon juice and tarragon and
leave for 2 hours.

2. Mix together in a cup the cream, oil, honey and
pepper, pour over the beetroot and serve.

**For a sharper flavour, add 2 tablespoons wine vinegar
and 1 clove chopped garlic. This salad makes an
excellent side dish for egg salad and rice.**

Chick Pea and Raisin Salad

INGREDIENTS

1 lb/450g pre-cooked chick peas
4 cloves garlic, very finely
chopped
2 large onions, chopped very
small
3 oz/75g chopped parsley
8 almonds, chopped
Juice of 1 lemon
3 oz/75g raisins, soaked in
lemon juice
4 tablespoons olive oil

Cigrons Guisats amb Panses i Pinyons

*This is a typical Catalan dish dating from about 1600. It
is very simple to prepare. You can add black olives and
sliced hard boiled eggs if you want to vary it.*

1. Drain the chick peas and allow to cool.

2. Mix all the remaining ingredients with the chick peas
and serve.

Under the Influence of Bright Sunbeams

Spinach with Raisins

Espinacs amb Panses
SIXTEENTH CENTURY RECIPE
FROM CATALONIA

INGREDIENTS

3 lb/1350g spinach, washed
½ teaspoon sea salt
5 tablespoons olive oil
4 oz/100g raisins
2 oz/50g pine kernels

1. Put the spinach into a large pan with the salt and no water. Cook on a low heat for 10–12 minutes stirring and turning with a wooden spoon several times.

2. When the spinach has rendered down a little, drain it and set to one side.

3. Put the oil into a pan and when it is hot, add the raisins. Turn the heat down, gently stir the raisins and cook for 1–2 minutes until they have swollen.

4. Add the pine kernels and stir until brown, which takes about 1 minute. Then add the spinach, stir and cook for 4–5 minutes.

Serve straight away on hot buttered toast. You can sprinkle the spinach with grated cheese if you wish to vary the recipe.

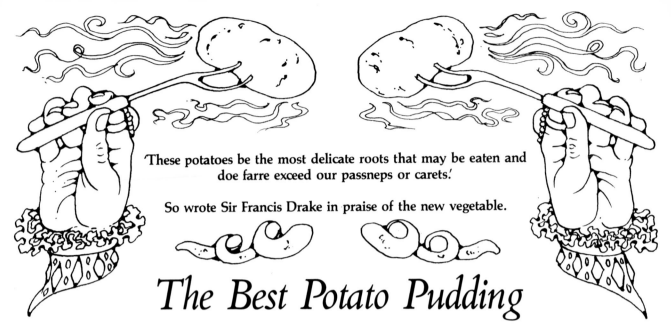

'These potatoes be the most delicate roots that may be eaten and doe farre exceed our passneps or carets.'

So wrote Sir Francis Drake in praise of the new vegetable.

The Best Potato Pudding

5 oz/150g butter
½ teaspoon grated nutmeg
3 oz/75g dark brown sugar
½ teaspoon coarse ground black pepper
Juice of 1 lemon
1 lb/450g potatoes, peeled, washed, cooked and mashed
¾ teaspoon sea salt
6 eggs, beaten
Chopped herbs to garnish

This is a savoury and sweet pudding dating from about 1675. It is very good if served with a variety of sharp salads such as watercress or sorrel.

1. Soften the butter and mix in the nutmeg, sugar, pepper and lemon juice.

2. Stir the butter into the mashed potatoes with a fork.

3. Sprinkle the salt into the beaten eggs and add to the mashed potato. Mix well.

4. Put the egg and potato mixture into an oven-proof dish and bake in a medium oven for 35–40 minutes or until the pudding is brown on top and well risen.

5. Sprinkle with chopped herbs and serve.

Deep Fried Green Beans

1740s AMERICA

The red flowered runner bean, the longest cropping and tastiest of the beans, was first introduced by Charles I's great gardener John Tradescant early in the seventeenth century. This recipe certainly went to the New World with English settlers and only found its way back to Britain via this American recipe of more than a hundred years later.

1. Put the flour and salt into a bowl. Make a well in the centre and pour in the egg and beer mixed together with the seeds.

2. Beat until you have a smooth, thick batter. Allow to stand for at least 2 hours, although this can also be prepared up to 12 hours in advance. Mix well just before using.

3. Trim the beans and remove any strings.

4. Stick the cloves into the onion and put it into a saucepan together with the cinnamon stick, half a lemon, a pinch of salt and the vegetable stock.

5. Bring to the boil. Put the beans in and cook for 5–10 minutes or until just tender.

6. Drain the beans and dry them with a cloth or kitchen paper, or the batter will not stick to them.

7. Heat the cooking oil.

8. Dip each bean into the bowl of batter making sure it is well coated, and deep fry, turning the beans over as soon as they rise to the surface of the oil.

9. When they are golden brown, remove them and drain on kitchen paper. Serve as a side dish with fish.

INGREDIENTS

For the batter:
8 oz/225g flour
1 teaspoon sea salt
1 egg, beaten
1 tablespoon beer
1 tablespoon poppy or dill seeds

10 oz/275g very young string beans
3 cloves
1 small onion
1 stick cinnamon
Half a lemon
1 teaspoon sea salt
1 pint/600ml vegetable stock
Oil to deep fry

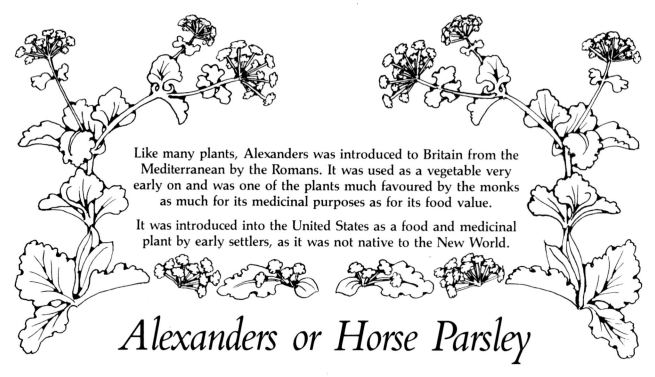

Like many plants, Alexanders was introduced to Britain from the Mediterranean by the Romans. It was used as a vegetable very early on and was one of the plants much favoured by the monks as much for its medicinal purposes as for its food value.

It was introduced into the United States as a food and medicinal plant by early settlers, as it was not native to the New World.

Alexanders or Horse Parsley

INGREDIENTS

3 tablespoons olive oil
5 tablespoons dry white wine
1 tablespoon honey
Zest and juice of 1 orange
1 tablespoon dill seeds
1 tablespoon sesame seeds

Pick young fresh leaves, wash and trim. Cut into small pieces. Put into a salad bowl and serve with the following dressing:

Combine all the ingredients together in a cup, stir well and pour over the Alexanders.

This makes a very interesting salad to serve with grilled fish or any egg dish.

Steamed Leeks with Ginger and Saffron Sauce

EIGHTEENTH CENTURY

This recipe is rather an unusual one in that not many European recipes use saffron and fresh ginger. I suspect that it did originate in the east. It comes from an eighteenth century manuscript book which certainly passed through several hands as the recipes start around 1760 and go on in different handwriting until 1848–50. I find the idea that one recipe book should go on being added to by different generations of cooks delightful.

Often there was what appear to be the same recipes until one starts to look closer and it becomes plain that each cook has added a little something to the recipe over the years, making it often better and occasionally worse!

For the leeks:

1. Put the leeks into a colander or steamer and cook until just tender. Arrange on a serving dish and cover with the following sauce:

For the sauce:

1. Heat the butter in a pan, add the onion and cook very gently for 3–5 minutes.

2. Soak the saffron in 1 tablespoon wine for 10–20 minutes. Add to the onion and cook very gently for 2–3 minutes.

3. Combine all the other ingredients except for the yogurt and heat right through. Stir in the yogurt just before serving. Pour the sauce over the leeks.

For a richer sauce, substitute cream for the yogurt.

You can use this sauce for lots of other dishes containing both eggs and cheese.

INGREDIENTS

For the leeks:

4 large leeks trimmed, washed and cut into 2 inch/5cm lengths

A pan of boiling water

For the sauce:

1 oz/25g butter or oil

1 small onion or shallot, very finely chopped

½ teaspoon ground saffron or 12–15 'threads'

¼ pint/150ml dry white wine

Juice of 1 orange

2 teaspoons fresh chopped ginger

½ teaspoon grated nutmeg

½ teaspoon dried marjoram

Sea salt and pepper to taste

8 fl oz/250ml thick creamy Greek yogurt

Asparagus in Bread and Honey Sauce

INGREDIENTS

½ pint/300ml stock
2 lb/900g asparagus cut into
small pieces
2 cloves garlic
1 tablespoon dry white wine
1 oz/25g soft white
breadcrumbs
2 tablespoons chopped parsley
1 tablespoon honey
8 triangles fried bread

Esparragos Andaluz

When I was about 12 we stayed for a time in a small country house near the Spanish/Portuguese border. Just outside my bedroom window was a steep bank with a few old olive trees and an absolute thicket of wild asparagus. As soon as I discovered how good the young shoots were, I would keep an eye out for the new shoots and try and beat the goats to them! This recipe is my Aunt's, although it is a very old, traditional Andalucian recipe.

1. In a saucepan, heat the stock, add the asparagus and garlic and cook gently over a low heat for 10–12 minutes. Add the wine.

2. In a mortar or food processor, place the breadcrumbs, herbs and honey together with a little liquid from the asparagus and process to make a paste. Add this to the cooked asparagus, stir well and cook for a further 3–4 minutes.

3. Serve in individual dishes with the slices of fried bread.

A Cool Salad

1800

1. Cut one end off the marrows and remove the seeds and pith, leaving a hollow in the centre. Cut a thin slice off the other end so that they will stand upright. Put into a steamer and cook for 20–25 minutes or until just tender. Set to one side and allow to cool.

2. Wash the carrots and cut into thin sticks, put into a pan with a little water; bring to the boil and simmer for 3–5 minutes. Drain and allow to cool.

3. Add the ground nutmeg, mustard and coriander to the mayonnaise.

4. Chop the hard boiled eggs. Divide the mixture into four and fill each marrow with a portion of chopped egg, then a layer of mayonnaise and vegetables.

5. Garnish with chopped herbs and black olives. Chill in the fridge for about an hour. Serve.

INGREDIENTS

4 small young marrows or courgettes
4 oz/100g young carrots
½ teaspoon nutmeg
½ teaspoon dry mustard
½ teaspoon ground coriander
½ pint/300ml mayonnaise
4 eggs, hard boiled
1 good sized onion, finely chopped
4 oz/100g young peas
2 tablespoons fresh garden herbs, finely chopped
12 black olives to garnish

Napoleon's Salad

This recipe was created, so it is said, by Chandelier, chef to Napoleon's sister Pauline. Monsieur Chandelier went to St Helena with Napoleon to cook for him while in exile. This was a salad eaten daily by Napoleon.

1. Drain the beans and allow to cool slightly.

2. Mix together the remaining ingredients.

3. Put the beans into a large serving bowl, pour in the dressing and mix well.

4. Cover and leave to blend well overnight before serving.

This is a lovely salad, easy to make and useful in that it can be prepared the day before. It will keep very well in the refrigerator for several days if covered.

Serve with pasta or egg and cheese dishes. It is also delicious as a side dish for tomato flavoured dishes.

INGREDIENTS

8 oz/225g cooked haricot beans
1 small onion, chopped
6 tablespoons olive oil
2 tablespoons tarragon vinegar
1 teaspoon French mustard
1 tablespoon chopped chives
1 tablespoon chopped chervil
1 tablespoon chopped tarragon
2 tablespoons chopped parsley
2 tablespoons chopped salad burnet
Sea salt and black pepper to taste

Baked Turnip Pudding

*5 or 6 young turnips, washed
and sliced very thinly*

*3 oz/75g Parmesan cheese or
any strong cheese, grated*

1½ pints/900ml creamy milk

*1 oz/25g wholemeal
breadcrumbs*

½ teaspoon cayenne pepper

½ teaspoon grated nutmeg

Sea salt to taste

1 oz/25g butter

*This recipe is based on one of Alexander Dumas' in the
1870s.*

1. Pre-heat oven to 180°C, 350°F, Gas Mark 4. Put a layer of sliced turnips into a pudding basin and then a layer of grated cheese, another layer of turnips and finish with a second layer of cheese.

2. Pour in the milk.

3. Top with breadcrumbs, pepper and ground nutmeg. Season to taste.

4. Cut the butter into small pieces and dot over the top.

5. Put into the oven and bake for 1–1½ hours or until the turnips are just tender.

You can get very good results with pre-cooked turnips if you want to cut down on the cooking time.

Menu suggestion:
Cream soup with croûtons; eggs poached with orange and butter sauce; baked turnip pudding; tomato and basil salad.

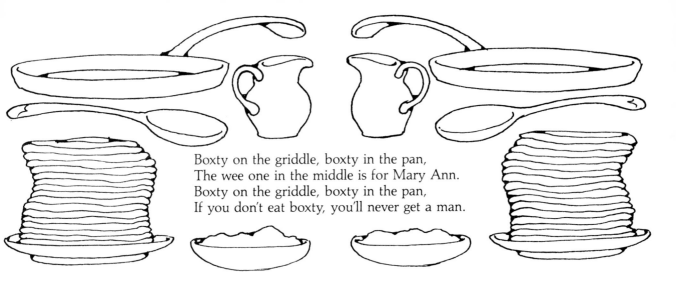

Boxty on the griddle, boxty in the pan,
The wee one in the middle is for Mary Ann.
Boxty on the griddle, boxty in the pan,
If you don't eat boxty, you'll never get a man.

Boxty or Griddle Pancakes

1. Dry the grated potato in a cloth or with kitchen paper.

2. Mix the grated potato, mashed potato, flour and butter together in a large bowl. Season with salt and pepper. Leave to stand for 10–15 minutes.

3. Gradually stir in the milk until the mixture forms a very thick batter.

4. Oil a thick frying pan with a little oil or butter. Drop tablespoons of the batter in and fry on both sides until a deep golden brown. Serve at once with melted butter or grated cheese.

A good variation is to add 2 cloves of crushed garlic and a pinch of nutmeg to the batter.

INGREDIENTS

½ lb/225g potatoes, peeled, washed and grated
½ lb/225g boiled mashed potatoes
½ lb/225g self-raising flour
3 oz/75g butter, melted
Sea salt and pepper
¼-½ pint/150-300ml milk

Chick Pea and Cheese Salad

6 oz/175g dried chick peas, soaked overnight in slightly salted water

1 large onion, very finely chopped

2 cloves garlic, finely chopped

2 tablespoons fresh chopped coriander

2 tablespoons fresh chopped basil

2 tablespoons lemon juice

2 tablespoons wine vinegar

½ teaspoon grated nutmeg

Sea salt and black pepper to taste

8 oz/225g firm goat's cheese, or you can use Greek 'Feta'

Salada Menino Grão de Bico
TWENTIETH CENTURY

In Portugal, chick peas are called Grão de Bico, or Grão for short. As a child, my father used to tell me stories of the famous hero, the bravest of them all, the Menino Grão de Bico, or the 'Chick Pea Kid', and I was always very concerned when we ate chick peas that I would harm him. I was assured that he was only as tall as a chick pea and that he got his strength and wisdom from chick peas much as Popeye does from spinach.

This salad was supposed to be one of his favourite dishes and although I have not found that it does much for wisdom, it is a really lovely salad.

1. Put the chick peas into a pan with enough water to cover. Bring to the boil and cook for about 1 hour until tender. Do not allow to over-cook. Drain and put into cold water to cool.

2. Mix all the other ingredients except for the cheese, together.

3. When the chick peas are cool, put into a bowl and pour on the dressing. Mix well. Allow to stand for 1 hour in a cool place.

4. Cut the cheese into small cubes. Mix into the chick pea salad just before serving. Eat with fresh bread or warm Greek pitta bread.

Under the Influence of Bright Sunbeams

Calabrese with Lemon and Ginger

This southern European recipe shows a marked Moorish influence. This particular version was given to me by Sr Maria del Carmo Madero of Madrid.

1. Heat the oil in a large pan, add the ginger and cook for 2–3 minutes.

2. Add the broccoli and cook for 4–5 minutes stirring all the time. Add the ginger wine and lemon juice and stir. Last of all add the honey and a few spoonsful of water if required.

3. Sprinkle with sesame seeds and serve at once.

INGREDIENTS

6 tablespoons olive oil
1 teaspoon fresh ginger, grated
1 lb/450g calabrese or broccoli, divided into small florets
3 tablespoons ginger wine
3 tablespoons lemon juice
2 tablespoons honey
1 tablespoon sesame seeds

Green Bean and Beetroot Salad with Thyme and Cream Dressing

TWENTIETH CENTURY

1. Put the beans, beetroot and onion into a shallow serving bowl.

2. Mix all the ingredients for the dressing together and pour over the vegetables. Serve.

This is a lovely fresh-tasting salad to serve with a pasta dish or a cheese omelette.

INGREDIENTS

½ lb/225g young green beans, trimmed and pre-cooked
2 oz/50g pre-cooked beetroot
1 oz/25g finely chopped onion
4 fl oz/120ml single cream
1 clove garlic, crushed
2 teaspoons finely chopped thyme
1 teaspoon brown sugar
½ teaspoon Dijon mustard
Juice and zest of 1 lemon

Vegetable Spiced Rice

TWENTIETH CENTURY

INGREDIENTS

3 tablespoons olive oil

2 large onions, chopped

3 cloves garlic, minced

1 teaspoon turmeric

Juice of 2 lemons

2 oz/50g chopped red and green peppers

8 oz/225g raw rice, brown or white

Water or stock: for every cup in volume of rice, you will need 2½ times in liquid

2 oz/50g cooked kidney beans

2 oz/50g cooked carrots, cut into cubes

2 oz/50g cashew nuts

2 oz/50g sultanas

2 oz/50g black olives

2 oz/50g chopped almonds

2 oz/50g sliced mushrooms

1 oz/25g sesame seeds

1 oz/25g chopped celery

½ teaspoon cinnamon

½ teaspoon ground ginger

½ teaspoon crushed sichuan pepper

½ teaspoon star anis, crushed

2 oz/50g mixed fresh herbs, chopped

1. Put the oil into a pan over a low heat and add onions, garlic, turmeric and lemon juice. Cook very gently until the onions are soft. Add the chopped green and red peppers and cook for 2–3 minutes more.

2. Stir in the rice. Add the water or stock and stir well. Bring to the boil, turn to a low heat and simmer until the rice is tender. Stir in all the remaining ingredients and allow to dry out either in the pan or turn out into a large serving dish and put in the oven for 10–12 minutes at 300°F, 150°C, Gas Mark 2. Serve at once.

This recipe is a variation of several recipes combined. It goes very well with many of the main courses.

Gill Lyall's Potato and Carrot Purée

TWENTIETH CENTURY

1. Put the potatoes in a pan of boiling water with a pinch of salt. Bring to the boil and simmer until tender. Remove from the heat and drain.

2. Mash the potatoes while still hot.

3. Put the cooked carrots into a food processor or blender and purée.

4. Combine the orange zest and milk together in a pan and warm.

5. Stir the warmed milk into the mashed potato. Add the carrot purée and softened butter.

6. Season with black pepper and a good pinch of grated nutmeg.

This is a very useful purée. You can vary it by adding chopped basil, or a little brandy to the purée. Another version is, just before serving, stir in a teaspoon of orange flower water and a little grated orange zest.

INGREDIENTS

1½ lb/675g potatoes, peeled and washed
8 oz/225g carrots, peeled, washed and cut into thin slices, then cooked until tender.
Zest of 1 orange
½ pint/300ml milk
2 oz/50g softened butter
Freshly ground black pepper
A good pinch nutmeg

Green Pea and Potato Purée

10 oz/275g peas
Juice of half a lemon
½ tablespoon brown sugar
1 tablespoon finely chopped
fresh mint (optional)
Sea salt and pepper to taste
½ pint/300ml milk
2 lb/900g potatoes, peeled,
washed, cooked and mashed
2 oz/50g softened butter

A recipe by my mother, Gill Lyall, from her Notebooks, 1934–37.

1. Put the peas into a pan with a little water and bring to the boil. Simmer for 4–6 minutes.

2. Drain and put into a food processor or blender with a tablespoonful of cooking liquid and blend to a fine purée.

3. Stir in the lemon juice, sugar, and chopped mint. Season to taste.

4. Heat the milk and gradually stir into the potatoes. Add the pea purée and softened butter.

5. Put into a dish, sprinkle with chopped mint and serve.

This is a very good side dish and makes a pleasant change from ordinary mashed potato. For a richer version, substitute cream for milk or half and half.

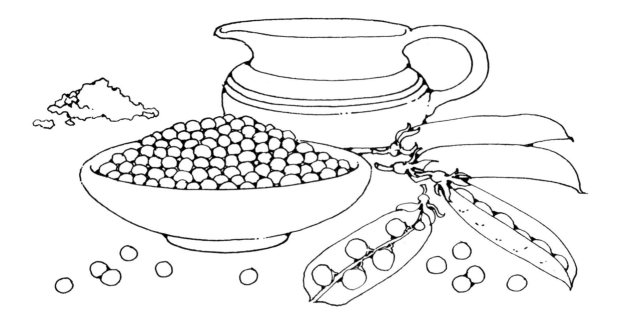

Under the Influence of Bright Sunbeams

Steamed Savoury Custards

TWENTIETH CENTURY

There is a long history of savoury custards. The earliest recipes are Roman although it is certain that something like this was being cooked by the Chinese, judging by the range of kitchen goods that have been found and the many types of steamed dishes that formed part of the oriental cuisine.

This recipe is based on one my father gave me, although I have altered the sauce which he made very hot and which I personally found lost emphasis.

1. Mix the first six ingredients together in a bowl.

2. Grease 4 individual moulds or ramekins and divide mixture between them. Put in a steamer or a colander over a pan of boiling water. Cover and steam for 20–25 minutes.

3. Put all the sauce ingredients into a pan and heat through.

4. Allow the custards to cool for 2–3 minutes and turn out onto individual plates. Pour the sauce over the top and serve.

INGREDIENTS

6 egg yolks
½ pint/300ml cream
Juice of 1 lemon
1 teaspoon orange flower water
1 few drops tabasco sauce
Sea salt and pepper to taste

For the sauce:
1 small onion, minced (optional)
6 tablespoons mango chutney
4 tablespoons white wine
4 tablespoons fresh watercress, chopped very fine

Fennel and Potato Dauphinois

1 large head fennel, washed and trimmed; chop the fennel leaves very finely
2 oz/50g butter
2 cloves garlic, crushed
Juice of ½ lemon
¾ lb/350g potatoes, washed, peeled, dried and cut into very thin slices
Sea salt
Freshly ground black pepper
Grated nutmeg
6 fl oz/175ml double cream

A recipe by Gill Lyall, my mother, from her Notebooks, 1935.

Fennel is one of my favourite vegetables; it is so versatile. Chopped and added to a salad it gives a crunchy aromatic taste; cooked on its own or in this case with potato it is able to share the limelight.

1. Trim the head off the fennel, then slice downwards into long thin slices.

2. Mix the butter and garlic together with a little lemon juice and chopped fennel leaves.

3. Spread half the butter evenly in an oven-proof dish.

4. Put a layer of potato slices into a dish. Season with salt and pepper, and grated nutmeg.

5. Next add a layer of fennel, then another layer of potato and so on finishing with a layer of potato. Season each layer.

6. Pour the cream over the last layer and dab on the remaining butter in small pieces.

7. Put into the oven and cook for 1½ hours at 325°F, 160°C, Gas Mark 3. Raise the heat in the last ten minutes to 350°F, 180°C, Gas Mark 4 to brown the top.

A variation is to put a layer of Mozzarella cheese in with the fennel.

4.

Something Sweet

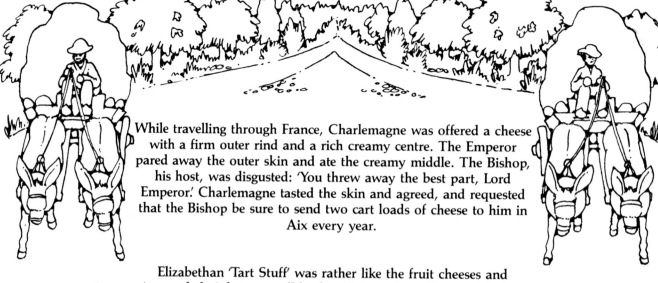

While travelling through France, Charlemagne was offered a cheese with a firm outer rind and a rich creamy centre. The Emperor pared away the outer skin and ate the creamy middle. The Bishop, his host, was disgusted: 'You threw away the best part, Lord Emperor.' Charlemagne tasted the skin and agreed, and requested that the Bishop be sure to send two cart loads of cheese to him in Aix every year.

Elizabethan 'Tart Stuff' was rather like the fruit cheeses and 'marmalades' that can still be found throughout Europe today. It consisted principally of a thick purée of fruit.

'To make all manner of fruit tarts, you must boil your fruit, be it apple, cherry, peach, pear, damson, mulberries or codlins, in fair water, and when they be boiled enough, put them into a bowl, and bruise them and when they be cold, strain them and put in red wine or claret wine, and so season with sugar, cinnamon and ginger.'

Sweet Cheese Tart with a Fruit Purée Topping

THIRTEENTH OR FOURTEENTH CENTURY

In 1265 the Countess of Leicester noted in her account book that she had bought quite a large amount of soft cheese for tarts.

The earliest recipes used curds or curd cheese which was put into a mortar and pounded with egg yolks and honey and a few spices. This was then put into a pastry case and cooked in the oven or just by the fire on a griddle. Later versions started to use nuts and cream and custards, and a crushed biscuit for the base much as we know it today. This recipe is based on one of the very earliest country ones for a 'Sweet Tart'.

INGREDIENTS

For the pastry base:
8 oz/225g plain or wholewheat flour and ½ teaspoon salt mixed together
4 oz/100g butter or margarine, cut into small pieces
2–3 tablespoons cold water

Under the Influence of Bright Sunbeams

For the pastry base:

1. Sieve the flour and salt into a mixing bowl. Add the butter and rub in until the mixture is fine and crumbly.

2. Make a well in the centre and add the water. Blend into the mixture to make a soft dough. If the mixture is too sticky, add a little more flour.

3. Turn out onto a floured board and roll out. Line your flan dish and trim off any excess pastry round the edges. Prick the pastry lightly all over with a fork.

4. Put into a pre-heated oven at 375°F, 190°C, Gas Mark 5 for 15 minutes. Remove from the oven and set to one side.

For the filling:

1. Soak the carrot in the brandy for 10–15 minutes.

2. Drain any watery liquid from the cheese.

3. Mix the cheese with the eggs, honey, carrots and brandy.

4. Blend together the cornflour and cream and combine with the cheese and eggs.

5. Pour into the pre-cooked pastry case and return to the oven at 350°F, 180°C, Gas Mark 4 and cook for 25–30 minutes.

6. When the tart is cooked allow to cool and serve with a fruit purée.

For the fruit purée

1. Cut the fruit into small pieces and put into a pan with the water and honey, (and sugar if used).

2. Cook very slowly until soft and then pass through a sieve.

3. Allow to cool and serve with the tart.

An alternative method is to put your prepared fruit into a microwave dish and cover with cling film. Remember to make a few holes in the film and then microwave on HIGH for 4–10 minutes. The time will vary depending on your microwave voltage.

For the filling:

1 large carrot, peeled and very finely grated

3 tablespoons brandy or any sharp tasting spirit

8 oz/225g cottage cheese

3 eggs, beaten

3 tablespoons honey

½ tablespoon rice or corn flour

4 tablespoons cream

For the fruit purée:

8 oz/225g fruit washed, such as raspberries, stoned plums or damsons

1 tablespoon honey

1 tablespoon brown sugar (optional)

3 tablespoons water

Tyropatinan

'ROMAN CUSTARD'

The concept of a separate pudding or sweet dish to end a meal with is really quite a modern one. Usually a Roman meal would end with fresh fruit or a savoury dish. This Roman custard was almost certainly served as a contrast to a spicy dish to add a 'sweet and sour' taste to the meal, as well as being eaten on its own as just something sweet.

Cooked very slowly, it makes a lovely creamy pudding, half way between custard and creamy scrambled eggs and was probably a great favourite of older Romans who were unlucky enough to have lost a few teeth!

1. Break the eggs into the milk and whisk until well blended.

2. Place in a saucepan over a low heat, stirring constantly until the mixture thickens. Stir in the honey.

3. Remove from the heat, pour into a shallow dish, and allow to cool.

This dish, if sprinkled with pepper, can be used as a side dish with strongly flavoured savoury dishes. Omitting the pepper, it can be served with any fruit.

Honey and Nut Roll

From Badajoz — Torta de Miel y Nueces

1. Make short pastry as follows: Rub the butter into the flour, add the sugar and 1 egg yolk. Carefully add sherry and lemon juice, orange zest and orange flavour water and make into a stiff paste. If need be, add a little more sherry.

2. Roll into a long thin strip, brush with honey and sprinkle with chopped nuts. Roll up and glaze with egg. Sprinkle with sugar.

3. Bake in a moderate oven at 350°F, 180°C, Gas Mark 4 for 25–30 minutes.

This recipe is an old family one and shows the distinct Moorish influence that can be found in so many sweet dishes.

It is interesting to trace the Moorish influence on food in Spain to this day by following the arterial rivers which were the Roman and Moorish 'roads' into the country, and seeing how they have influenced the immediate regions and where the influence stops.

INGREDIENTS

4 oz/100g butter
8 oz/225g flour
1 oz/25g sugar
1 egg yolk
½ glass sweet sherry
Juice of 1 lemon
Zest of 1 orange
½ teaspoon orange flavour water
2 tablespoons honey
2 oz/50g chopped hazelnuts
2 oz/50g chopped walnuts
2 oz/50g chopped almonds
Egg, for glaze

Violet Creams

FOURTEENTH CENTURY

This is a delicious and delicate tasting pudding reflecting fourteenth century tastes perfectly.

1. Mix the rice flour with a little milk in a cup.

2. Heat the honey and milk together in a pan. Stir into the flour with the ground almonds.

3. Bring to the boil and cook until quite thick.

4. Add flavouring and pour into individual bowls. Chill. Cover with whipped cream and crystallized violets. Serve.

INGREDIENTS

4 tablespoons ground rice or rice flour
4 teaspoons ground almonds
2 teaspoons honey
1 pint/600ml milk
1 teaspoon violet flavouring
3 teaspoons rosewater
Crystallized violets or roses for garnish

Moorish Tart

INGREDIENTS

For the pastry:
4 oz/100g plain flour
6 oz/175g ground almonds
2 oz/50g butter, softened
4 egg yolks
2 tablespoons honey
Zest of 1 lemon

For the filling:
1 lb/450g fresh raspberries
2 egg yolks
4 oz/100g fresh thick yogurt
Honey, to taste
Chopped nuts, to decorate

1. Mix the flour and almonds together.

2. Work in the butter and then add the egg yolks one at a time.

3. Add the honey and lemon zest and continue to work until you have a firm dough.

4. Roll out and line a 9 inch flan case. Set to one side.

5. Fill the pastry case with the raspberries.

6. Mix the egg yolks and yogurt together and pour over the fruit.

7. Put into a pre-heated oven at 300°F, 150°C, Gas Mark 2 for 30–40 minutes.

8. Ten minutes before the tart is ready to take out of the oven, sprinkle with honey and chopped nuts and continue to cook.

Soupes Dorye

Bread and Butter Pudding
FOURTEENTH CENTURY

This is a rather nice mixture between a bread and butter pudding and a custard. A good variation is to put a layer of fruit purée or jam under the toast.

INGREDIENTS

3 oz/75g butter
6 slices toasted bread, cut very thin
½ pint/300ml sweet white wine
4 eggs
A few strands of saffron
¼ teaspoon ground ginger
¼ teaspoon ground cloves
¼ teaspoon ground mace
A good pinch sea salt
1 oz/25g sugar

1. Butter the toast and cut off the crusts.

2. Lay them in a shallow oven-proof dish.

3. Sprinkle them with wine.

4. Beat the eggs, add all the spices and salt to the mixture, and pour over the bread.

5. Put into the oven at 325°F, 160°C, Gas Mark 3 for 20–25 minutes or until just set.

6. Sprinkle with sugar and spice and serve.

Under the Influence of Bright Sunbeams

Cream Cheese Tart

Lesefryes or Leschefreys
FOURTEENTH CENTURY

1. Pre-heat the oven to 400°F, 200°C, Gas Mark 6. Line a 10 inch/25cm flan or quiche dish with pastry. Put into the oven and bake blind for 10–12 minutes. Turn the oven down to 375°F, 190°C, Gas Mark 5.

2. Soften the butter in a pan and then beat. Combine with the cheese, salt, eggs and pepper in a bowl and beat until you have a thick cream. Pour into the pastry case and put into the oven. Cook for 20 minutes or until set.

3. Remove from the oven and sprinkle with sugar. Return for a further 10–12 minutes or until the sugar has browned a little. Serve hot or cold.

This pudding dates from a Medieval recipe book that first appeared about 1393. Many of the recipes were almost certainly brought back from the Holy Land by returning Crusaders who seem to have taken to Arab food, even though they spent much of their time fighting the Arabs!

INGREDIENTS

Makes 6–8 slices

12 oz/350g flaky pastry
3 oz/75g butter
8 oz/225g thick cream cheese
½ teaspoon salt
2 eggs
¼ teaspoon black pepper
1 tablespoon sugar

Sambrocade

Elderflower and Cream Cheese Pie

This is a lovely recipe that can be found in various forms throughout Europe. This version comes from a recipe of the fifteenth century.

INGREDIENTS

1 lb/450g flaky pastry
4 oz/100g sugar
1 lb/450g cream cheese
3 egg whites, beaten to peaks
3 handfuls elderflowers, washed

1. Pre-heat the oven to 400°F, 200°C, Gas Mark 6. Roll out the pastry and line a shallow 9 inch/23cm pie dish.

2. Place in the oven and bake blind for 10–12 minutes. Allow to cool. Turn the oven down to 300°F, 150°C, Gas Mark 2.

3. Beat 3 oz/75g of the sugar into the cream cheese and fill the pastry case.

4. Beat the egg whites to peaks, fold in the remainder of the sugar together with the elderflowers. Spread over the top of the cheese filling.

5. Return to the oven and cook for 15–20 minutes, or until the egg white is set and starting to turn a golden brown. Serve at once with cream.

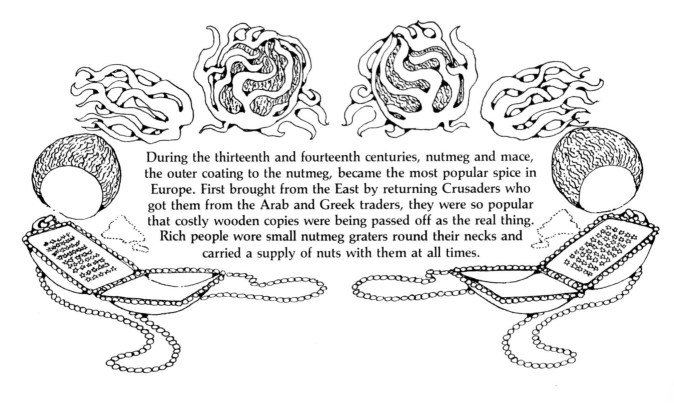

During the thirteenth and fourteenth centuries, nutmeg and mace, the outer coating to the nutmeg, became the most popular spice in Europe. First brought from the East by returning Crusaders who got them from the Arab and Greek traders, they were so popular that costly wooden copies were being passed off as the real thing. Rich people wore small nutmeg graters round their necks and carried a supply of nuts with them at all times.

Rose Hip Tart

ELIZABETHAN

1. Wash the hips and trim off the stalks and calyx.

2. Cut them in half and remove the seeds. Wash well.

3. Put the hips into a saucepan, together with all the other ingredients. Bring to the boil, stir and allow to simmer for 12–15 minutes.

4. Roll out the pastry on a floured board.

5. Line a shallow pie dish with half the pastry and reserve the rest for the lid.

6. When the hips are cool, pour into the pastry case.

7. Dampen the edges of the case with water and cover with the pastry lid. Crimp the edges of the pastry.

8. Put into a pre-heated oven at 375°F, 190°C, Gas Mark 5 for 25–30 minutes. Sprinkle with spices and serve with whipped cream.

INGREDIENTS

8 oz/225g prepared hips
4 tablespoons honey
½ pint/300ml water
½ teaspoon ground ginger
½ teaspoon grated nutmeg
1 lb/450g shortcrust pastry

Gilliflower Syrup

SIXTEENTH CENTURY

Made from sweet scented clove pinks or carnations

1. Put a layer of flower petals into a basin, then a layer of sugar. Repeat until all the petals and sugar are used up.

2. Pour the water into the basin over the flowers and sugar. Cover with foil.

3. Stand in a pan of hot water over a very low heat; allow to infuse for 2–3 hours.

4. Drain and allow to cool before storing in a bottle in a cool place.

You can store the syrup in ice tray compartments and then in the freezer. Defrost when required. Use to flavour creams, custards and drinks.

INGREDIENTS

8 oz/225g gilliflower petals
8 oz/225g sugar
6 tablespoons water

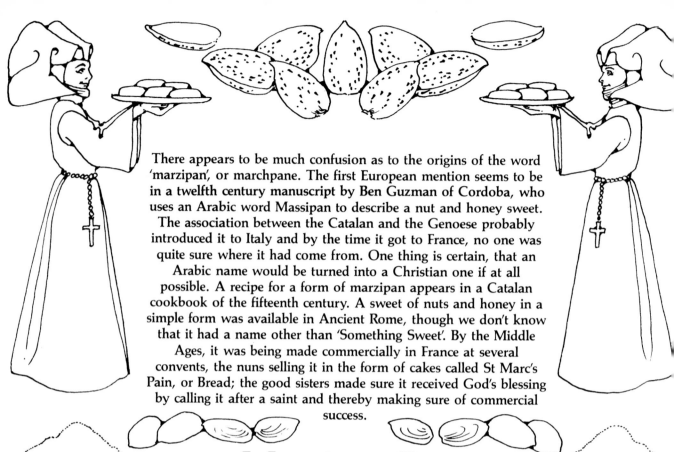

There appears to be much confusion as to the origins of the word 'marzipan', or marchpane. The first European mention seems to be in a twelfth century manuscript by Ben Guzman of Cordoba, who uses an Arabic word Massipan to describe a nut and honey sweet. The association between the Catalan and the Genoese probably introduced it to Italy and by the time it got to France, no one was quite sure where it had come from. One thing is certain, that an Arabic name would be turned into a Christian one if at all possible. A recipe for a form of marzipan appears in a Catalan cookbook of the fifteenth century. A sweet of nuts and honey in a simple form was available in Ancient Rome, though we don't know that it had a name other than 'Something Sweet'. By the Middle Ages, it was being made commercially in France at several convents, the nuns selling it in the form of cakes called St Marc's Pain, or Bread; the good sisters made sure it received God's blessing by calling it after a saint and thereby making sure of commercial success.

Marzipan Pie

INGREDIENTS

For the marzipan base:
1 lb/450g ground almonds
2 egg whites
The grated zest of one lime or lemon
8 oz/225g castor sugar

When this recipe was first written in 1651 both limes and lemons were very expensive as the cost of importing them was very high. This was a very grand pie for special occasions and although it is slightly complicated to make it is well worth the effort involved. For simplicity I have divided the recipe up into 3 parts:

For the marzipan base:

1. Mix the almonds, egg whites, and lime zest together.

2. Mix in the sugar and work for 2–3 minutes.

3. Butter a 10 inch/25cm flan dish and spread the almond paste evenly in it.

4. Put into the oven and cook for 12–15 minutes at 250°F, 130°C, Gas Mark ½.

5. When the marzipan is cooked remove from the oven. Leave in the dish to cool, set to one side.

Under the Influence of Bright Sunbeams

Custard cream topping:

1. Grate the zest from 1 lime and squeeze the juice from both fruit into a double saucepan.

2. Add the sugar and then the cream stirring all the time.

3. Cook very gently, add the egg yolks one at a time, stirring continuously. As soon as the mixture becomes very thick, remove from heat and set to one side.

4. Spread the custard cream over the almond paste. Sprinkle with chopped cherries and nuts.

Meringue topping:

1. Mix the orange flower water and egg whites together and beat until very stiff.

2. Spread the beaten egg whites onto the custard cream and put into the oven to cook for 15–18 minutes or until just golden at 300°F, 150°C, Gas Mark ½.

Custard cream topping:

Zest of 1 lime
Juice of 2 limes
6 oz/175g castor sugar
1½ pints/900ml thick cream
8 egg yolks
4 oz/100g glacé cherries, chopped
1 oz/25g chopped pine kernels

Meringue topping:

4 egg whites
1 tablespoon of orange flower water

Orange and Rosemary Compote

SEVENTEENTH CENTURY

This is a very old country recipe from Southern Portugal, which also appears in almost the same form in England in 1677. The mixture of orange and rosemary produces a unique flavour typical of so many early recipes.

1. Put the rosemary, water, sugar and orange flower water into a saucepan over a low heat.

2. Bring to the boil stirring constantly and simmer for 5–6 minutes. Set to one side.

3. Lay the slices of orange in a shallow serving dish. When the syrup has cooled, pour over the orange slices, decorate with chopped nuts and serve.

INGREDIENTS

6 sprigs rosemary, 4–5 inches long, washed and gently dried
2 fl oz/75ml water
6 oz/75g sugar
A few drops orange flower water
6 large oranges, peeled with the pith removed
Chopped nuts, to decorate

Apricot Pudding

INGREDIENTS

6 large apricots
3 tablespoons castor sugar
4 egg yolks
¼ pint/150ml double cream
2 egg whites
Enough puff pastry to line an
8–10 inch/20–25cm flan dish

The first mention of this recipe that I have found in England is in a cookery book dated 1545 called 'The Proper New Book of Cookery'. It almost certainly originated in Italy as it can be found in an earlier Florentine book. It pops up unchanged almost two hundred years later in a dear little book with the delightful title of 'Adam's Luxury and Eve's Cookery', which is the recipe I give here.

1. Wash the apricots in cold water, drain and cut in half to remove the stones.

2. Arrange the fruit in a steamer or shallow bowl, cover and place over a pan of boiling water. Cook until tender.

3. When the fruit is cooked, break into small pieces and sweeten to taste. Allow to cool.

4. Combine the egg yolks and cream together in a bowl.

5. Add the fruit to the mixture and beat for a few minutes.

6. Whisk the egg whites until stiff and fold into the fruit and cream mixture.

7. Roll the pastry very thinly on a floured board and line the flan case.

8. Pour the mixture into the lined flan case and bake in a hot oven at 375°F, 190°C, Gas Mark 5 for 10–12 minutes, then lower the temperature to 325°F, 160°C, Gas Mark 3 and continue to cook for a further 20 minutes or until the filling is firm.

The First Christmas Pudding

EIGHTEENTH CENTURY

On Christmas Day 1714, King George I was served with the first Christmas Pudding to be made in this country. It was a great success and became a firm favourite with the Royal Family. A Frenchman writing of his visit to London in the 1720's says 'Blessed be he who invented the Christmas Pudding, for it is Manna that hits the palates of all kinds of people.' The recipe below is the one used by George I's chef for that first famous pudding.

1. Mix all the dry ingredients together in a bowl.

2. Add the beaten eggs and milk and stir well.

3. Mix the lemon juice and brandy together and stir into the pudding.

4. Fill two well-greased pudding basins with the mixture, wrap in foil and tie up in cloths. Put the basins into pans filled with hot water making sure that the water comes no further than half way up the basins.

5. Cook for 5–6 hours, making sure that the pans do not boil dry, adding more water from time to time as necessary.

6. To re-heat when required, repeat the procedure and boil for 2–3 hours. Serve with brandy butter and whipped cream.

INGREDIENTS

8 oz/225g cut mixed peel
8 oz/225g stoned prunes
8 oz/225g seedless raisins
8 oz/225g sultanas
8 oz/225g currants
8 oz/225g glacé cherries
8 oz/225g flour
4 oz/100g chopped dates
8 oz/225g Muscovado sugar
2 teaspoons mixed spice
½ grated nutmeg
6 eggs, beaten
¼ pint/150ml milk
Juice of 1 lemon
1 glass brandy

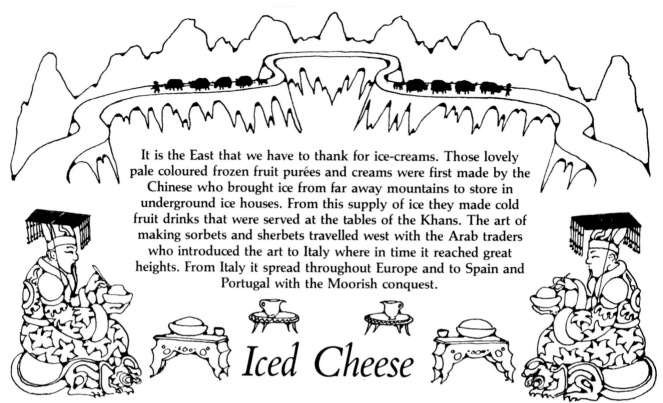

It is the East that we have to thank for ice-creams. Those lovely pale coloured frozen fruit purées and creams were first made by the Chinese who brought ice from far away mountains to store in underground ice houses. From this supply of ice they made cold fruit drinks that were served at the tables of the Khans. The art of making sorbets and sherbets travelled west with the Arab traders who introduced the art to Italy where in time it reached great heights. From Italy it spread throughout Europe and to Spain and Portugal with the Moorish conquest.

Iced Cheese

INGREDIENTS

8 oz/225g cream cheese
4 oz/100g sugar
½ teaspoon cinnamon
10 oz/275g fresh strawberries,
puréed
2 tablespoons cherry brandy
1 teaspoon orange flower water
½ pint/300ml whipped cream
Extra sugar to decorate

This is adapted from a French recipe dated 1717. This was the great age of iced creams and fantastic confections, most of which are too complicated and expensive to make today. This is in many ways one of the less rich and simpler concoctions of the period.

1. Put the cream cheese, sugar, cinnamon and puréed strawberries into a bowl and beat until smooth.

2. Add 2 tablespoons brandy and the orange flower water.

3. Fold in the whipped cream, pour into a dish and put into the freezer for 1½-2 hours.

4. Remove from the freezer, scrape the frozen mixture away from the sides and beat. Return to the freezer for a further 1 hour and repeat the procedure.

5. Press the ice-cream into a mould and freeze for 1 hour. Put the mould into a little warm water for 2–3 minutes and turn the ice-cream out into a serving dish.

6. Garnish with cinnamon and a little sugar. Serve with small biscuits and a fruit sauce.

Under the Influence of Bright Sunbeams

Elderflower Fritters

This recipe for elderflower fritters dates from 1723 and comes from John Notte who was cook to the Duke of Bolton. He was a superb and imaginative cook. He tells us, 'Make sure and gather your bunches of elderflowers just as they start to open, for this is the time of their perfection. They have just then a very fine smell and spirited taste but afterwards they grow dead and faint.'

1. Arrange the elderflowers in a shallow dish or basin.

2. Mix the brandy, sherry, honey and cinnamon together and pour over the flowers. Cover the dish and leave to steep for about 1½ hours, stirring from time to time.

3. Put the flour, egg yolks and wine into a food processor or blender and process to a thinnish batter. Pour into a bowl and leave to stand for an hour.

4. Beat the egg whites until stiff and fold into the batter just before using.

5. Drain the elderflower heads and dip each head in batter.

6. Heat the oil and fry the fritters until they are a golden brown.

7. Drain on kitchen paper. Sprinkle with sugar and cinnamon and serve.

INGREDIENTS

2 pint/1200ml jug full of elderflower heads divided into sections
2 tablespoons brandy
¼ pint/150ml sweet sherry
2 tablespoons honey
2 teaspoons cinnamon

For the batter:
2 oz/50g flour
2 eggs separated
¾ pint/450ml sweet white wine
Oil to fry

Plum Dumplings

1750

INGREDIENTS

1 egg
1½ lb/675g potatoes, peeled,
cooked and mashed
¾ lb/350g flour
½ teaspoon salt
1 oz/25g sugar
½ teaspoon ground cinnamon
16 ripe plums, stoned and cut
in half
3 oz/75g butter
4 oz/100g ground walnuts
Extra sugar to dredge
dumplings

1. Mix the egg, potato, flour and salt together in a large bowl until you have a firm dough.

2. Put the dough onto a floured board. Roll out to ½ inch/1cm thickness and cut into 16 squares, one for each plum.

3. Put a pinch of sugar and cinnamon in the centre of each plum, and put the two halves together.

4. Put a plum onto each section of the dough.

5. Fold the four corners together in the centre and pinch together to form a little parcel.

6. Fill a large pan full of water and bring to the boil.

7. Drop the dumplings into the boiling water one at a time and cook gently for 6–8 minutes. When the dumplings are cooked, lift them from the pan and put onto a sheet of kitchen paper.

8. Heat the butter in a pan and add the ground walnuts. Put the dumplings in the pan and coat all over in the walnut mixture.

9. A variation is to then roll the dumplings in sugar and cinnamon. Serve at once.

There is a great tradition of using fruit for both sweet and savoury dishes throughout eastern Europe, especially in Hungary, where this recipe originated. However several of the early Hungarian kings married foreign princesses, all of whom influenced the national cuisine.

Charles Carter's Carrot Pudding

1730

1. Pre-heat the oven to 350°F, 180°C, Gas Mark 4.

2. Line a flan dish with the pastry.

3. Into a large bowl put grated carrot, breadcrumbs, butter, candied peel and sugar, and mix well together.

4. Add the spices, orange zest, rose water and sherry to the egg yolks and beat well.

5. Combine with the breadcrumb mixture.

6. Finally fold in the whipped cream then the beaten egg whites and pour into the pastry case.

7. Put into the oven for 35–40 minutes or until well risen and golden. Serve with butter sauce or whipped cream.

This unusual pudding is much lighter than one would expect. It is just the thing for cold winter evenings when a hot pudding is very welcome.

INGREDIENTS

½ lb/225g shortcrust pastry
2 oz/50g grated carrot
3 oz/75g white breadcrumbs
4 tablespoons softened butter
2 oz/50g candied peel
2 oz/50g brown sugar
½ teaspoon ground nutmeg
½ teaspoon ground ginger
1 teaspoon ground cinnamon
Zest of 1 orange
1 tablespoon rose water
3 tablespoons sweet sherry
4 egg yolks, beaten
½ pint/300ml cream, whipped
4 egg whites, beaten until stiff

Tansy Pudding

EIGHTEENTH CENTURY

1. Cream the butter and sugar together, beat in the eggs and then add the spices, lemon and brandy. Add the breadcrumbs, rosewater and cream.

2. Grease a deep dish or basin.

3. Mix the chopped spinach and tansy together, sprinkle it into an empty dish, and pour in the pudding mixture.

4. Put in the oven at a cool temperature 150°C/300°F, Gas Mark 2 for about 25–30 minutes or until firm. Allow to cool slightly before turning out on to a dish. Sprinkle with sugar, arrange the orange segments over the tansy and serve.

Brandy Spiced Cherries

1800

1. Combine all the ingredients in a pan and bring to the boil. Simmer very gently for 8–10 minutes. Drain the fruit and set to one side.

2. Combine to cook the liquid to a thick syrup. Add a little extra brandy if wished.

3. Pour over the fruit and allow to cool. Serve with ice-cream or whipped cream.

Pumpkin pies were first taken to America by the early settlers. In the early English recipes, the pumpkin was first cut into small pieces, then fried in a mixture of oil, herbs and spices. Sugar and eggs were added and the pumpkin sandwiched between layers of apples, and a mixture of currants and raisins, to produce a mouthwatering dish.

Deservedly, America recognized a good thing and made pumpkin pie a national dish. In England, unfortunately, prejudice and fashion prevailed and the pie went out of fashion. This is an American version of the Pumpkin Pie sent to England in the eighteenth century.

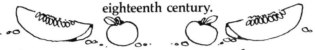

Pilgrim or Pumpkin Pie

1. Heat the butter in a pan over a low heat. Put in the slices of pumpkin and lightly brown all over. Remove from the heat. Reserve the juice. Put the pumpkin into a steamer or a bowl over a pan of boiling water and cook very gently for 18–25 minures until just tender.

2. Put the sliced apple into a pan with currants and any liquid from the pumpkin pan. Cook until just soft; set to one side.

3. Roll out the pastry and line a 9 inch flan dish. Put a layer of apple and currants in the dish.

4. Add the beaten eggs to the pumpkin, stir in the cream and sugar and sprinkle with spices. Mix well and pour into the flan case.

5. Put into the oven at 400°F, 200°C, Gas Mark 6 for 8–10 minutes. Reduce the heat to 350°F, 180°C, Gas Mark 4 and cook for 20–25 minutes. Sprinkle with additional spices and serve.

You can, if you wish, cook the pastry case before you put the filling in. To do this cook at 400°F, 200°C, Gas Mark 6, for 8–10 minutes. Allow to cool for a few minutes then add the filling and cook at 350°F, 180°C, Gas Mark 4, for 16–18 minutes or until just firm.

INGREDIENTS

1 oz/25g butter

1 lb/450g pumpkin, peeled and cut into slices

3 apples, peeled, cored and cut into slices

4 oz/100g currants or sultanas

½ lb/225g rich shortcrust pastry

3 eggs, beaten

¼ pint/150ml cream

4 oz/100g brown sugar

½ teaspoon ground ginger

½ teaspoon ground cinnamon

½ teaspoon grated nutmeg

½ teaspoon allspice

½ teaspoon ground cloves

Additional spices to taste

Chestnut Cake

1760-1770 — FRANCE

INGREDIENTS

For the cake:
6 oz/175g sugar
8 egg whites, beaten until very stiff
4 oz/100g flour
4 oz/100g ground walnuts
1 teaspoon sea salt

For the filling:
3 oz/75g plain chocolate
2 egg yolks
8 oz/225g unsalted butter
6 oz/175g castor sugar
1 teaspoon vanilla essence
1 glass brandy
1 lb/450g tinned chestnut purée

For the cake:

1. Pre-heat oven to 350°F, 180°C, Gas Mark 4. Add the sugar to the beaten egg whites.
2. Mix the flour and walnuts together with a pinch of salt.
3. Fold into the beaten egg whites.
4. Grease a 17×12 inch/42×30cm baking sheet, line with greaseproof paper and sprinkle lightly with flour. Shake off the excess.
5. Pour the case mixture onto the sheet and spread evenly over the sheet.
6. Put into the oven and cook for 15–20 minutes or until firm.
7. Put a sheet of greaseproof paper over the cake when you take it out of the oven. Allow to cool. This prevents the cake from becoming hard on top.
8. When cool, cut lengthwise into three sections.

For the filling:

1. Put the chocolate into a double saucepan or into a bowl over a pan of hot water and melt. Stir in egg yolks and remove from heat.
2. Put the butter, sugar and vanilla essence into a bowl and beat until smooth.
3. Add the brandy.
4. Stir in the melted chocolate and then add the chestnut purée
5. Beat until it is very creamy.
6. Put a layer of chestnut cream between each layer of cake. Decorate with Angelica and whipped cream and serve.

The lady who recorded the recipe comments that it had been sent by a friend who always used wine instead of brandy but that she herself used brandy as she considered that it was better for the digestion!

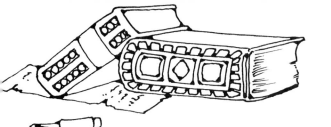
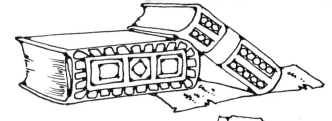
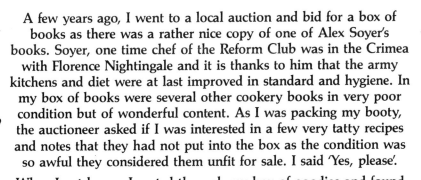

A few years ago, I went to a local auction and bid for a box of books as there was a rather nice copy of one of Alex Soyer's books. Soyer, one time chef of the Reform Club was in the Crimea with Florence Nightingale and it is thanks to him that the army kitchens and diet were at last improved in standard and hygiene. In my box of books were several other cookery books in very poor condition but of wonderful content. As I was packing my booty, the auctioneer asked if I was interested in a few very tatty recipes and notes that they had not put into the box as the condition was so awful they considered them unfit for sale. I said 'Yes, please'.

When I got home, I sorted through my box of goodies and found that though many pages were stained and mouldy, there was much that could be restored. I found I had two handwritten manuscript books, one of which was clearly dated 1780 by a lady in East Anglia, the other starting a little later right up to 1912, in several different hands. Most of the recipes were taken from books of the period and a few earlier ones, but amongst them were a few lovely puddings, this gooseberry cream being one of them.

Norfolk Gooseberry Cream

1780

1. Put the wine, water and gooseberries into a pan over a low heat. Bring to the boil and simmer until just tender.

2. Remove from the heat, add the sugar, honey, rosewater, almonds and butter, and stir until completely dissolved. Set to one side.

3. Beat the cream into the eggs in a bowl. When the gooseberries have cooled a little, combine the cream and eggs with the fruit.

4. Cook very gently over a low heat until the fruit and eggs just start to thicken.

5. Pour into individual dishes and put into the refrigerator to chill. Sprinkle with a few candied rose petals and serve with ratafia biscuits.

INGREDIENTS

¼ pint/300ml sweet white wine

¼ pint/150ml water

2 lb/900g gooseberries, topped, tailed and washed

1 tablespoon brown sugar

1 tablespoon honey

1 tablespoons rosewater

2 tablespoons ground almonds

1 tablespoon butter

½ pint/300ml double cream

4 eggs, beaten

A few candied rose petals for garnish

Orange and Lemon Mousse

INGREDIENTS

Juice and zest of 5 oranges
Juice and zest of 1 lemon
3½ oz/90g castor sugar
6 egg yolks
6 egg whites, whipped until stiff

This is a lovely recipe from Ludlow in Shropshire dating from the eighteenth century.

1. Put the juices, zest and sugar into a pan and heat until all the sugar has been dissolved. Set to one side and allow to cool.

2. Beat the egg yolks until fluffy. Put into a double saucepan or a very thick pan with the fruit juice and sugar syrup. Cook very gently stirring all the time until the mixture has thickened. Remove from the heat and set to one side to cool.

3. Beat the egg whites until very stiff. When the egg and fruit juice mixture is really cool, fold in the egg whites.

4. Pour into a bowl, cover with film and chill. Stir the pudding once or twice in the first ½ hour to make sure the mixture is well blended.

Bilberry and Orange Cake

INGREDIENTS

2 oz/50g butter
4 oz/100g sugar
1 egg yolk
Zest of 1 orange
½ pint/300ml milk
6 oz/175g flour
½ teaspoon ground nutmeg
10 oz/275g bilberries
2 egg whites, beaten until stiff

1. Put the butter and sugar into a bowl and beat until creamy. Add the egg yolk, orange zest and milk. Beat well for 1 minute.

2. Sift the flour and nutmeg in and then add the fruit. Last of all fold in the egg whites.

3. Pour into a 7 inch cake tin and bake for 20–25 minutes at 180°C, 350°F, Gas Mark 4. Serve as a pudding with lots of fresh cream or thick yogurt.

Mixed Red Fruit Salad

GEORGIAN

1. Put the fruit into a large bowl, sprinkle with sugar and brandy and leave for 1–2 hours.

2. Mix the cassis with the jasmine tea and pour over the salad. Leave for 2–4 hours. Just before serving, mix the fruit and juices together.

3. Serve with whipped cream, or for the calorie conscious, plain yogurt.

INGREDIENTS

8 oz/225g dark red cherries, stones removed

8 oz/225g strawberries, hulled and cut into quarters

8 oz/225g dark red grapes, stoned and cut in half

8 oz/225g raspberries or loganberries

3 oz/75g red currants

4 oz/100g castor sugar

3 tablespoons brandy

3 tablespoons cassis or blackcurrant juice

½ pint/300ml jasmine tea medium strength, tealeaves removed and tea allowed to cool

Quince Mould

2 lb/900g quinces
1 lemon jelly
2 tablespoons honey
1 pint/600ml whipped double
cream
Angelica, to decorate

ADAPTED FROM A LYALL FAMILY RECIPE FROM ABOUT 1800.

This is a lovely and unusual pudding. Although it is delicious on its own, my family like it served with a hot custard sauce. It is a great pity that quinces have been out of fashion in England for the last eighty years or so as there are so many good things that can be made from them. When I was a child we had one very old quince tree that produced the most enormous quinces that weighed well over a pound each and it was always a great adventure to climb into the tree and pick the largest before my father did!

1. Cut the quinces into quarters and put into a large pan with enough water to cover.

2. Bring to the boil and simmer until they are a pink mush. Leave overnight.

3. Next day rub the pulp through a sieve.

4. Dissolve the lemon jelly with a tablespoonful of water and combine it with the puréed pulp.

5. Return to the heat and cook gently for 3–4 minutes to ensure that the jelly is well blended.

6. Remove from the heat and allow to cool.

7. Just before the mixture sets, stir in the honey and whipped cream.

8. Pour into a mould or basin, put into the fridge to chill.

9. Turn out onto a serving dish and decorate with angelica.

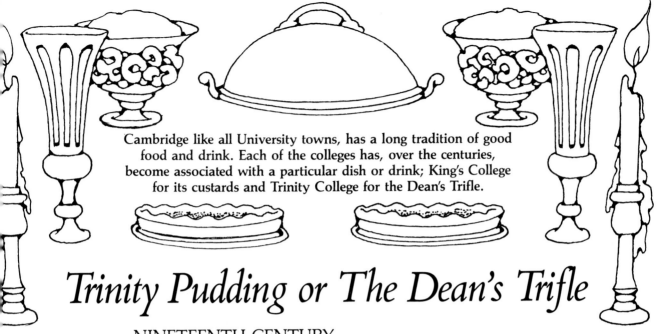

Cambridge like all University towns, has a long tradition of good food and drink. Each of the colleges has, over the centuries, become associated with a particular dish or drink; King's College for its custards and Trinity College for the Dean's Trifle.

Trinity Pudding or The Dean's Trifle

NINETEENTH CENTURY

This pudding comes from Trinity College, Cambridge. One nineteenth century Dean insisted that it should be served at High Table at any college banquet.

1. Spread 8 sponge fingers with raspberry jam and lay them in a deep glass bowl.

2. Spread the remaining 8 with apricot jam and lay them on top of the first layer in the form of sun rays.

3. Crush the ratafias to crumbs and put them over the sponge fingers. Add the halved cherries.

4. Pour the sherry into the bowl and leave for 1 hour.

5. Whip the cream until stiff. Stir in the brandy and sugar. Spoon over the layer of ratafia. Arrange the almonds and crystallized fruit on top and put into the fridge to chill before serving.

INGREDIENTS

Serves 6–8

16 sponge fingers
8 tablespoons raspberry jam
8 tablespoons apricot jam
½ lb/225g ratafia biscuits
4 oz glacé cherries, cut in halves
½ pint/300ml sweet sherry
½ pint/600ml double cream
¼ pint/150ml brandy
3 oz/75g castor sugar
A few toasted almonds
2 oz/50g crystallized angelica, chopped into short lengths
4 oz/100g crystallized pineapple, cut into slices
6 crystallized plums, cut in half

Bread Jelly

INGREDIENTS

4 slices very thinly sliced white bread
¼ pint/150ml port or sherry
½ pint/300ml water
1 stick cinnamon
1 lemon jelly
½ pint/300ml cream, whipped until stiff
A few glacé cherries and angelica to decorate

'Mrs Forrester made some of the bread jelly for which she was so famous. A present of this bread jelly was the highest mark of favour Mrs Forrester could confer.'

Quote from 'Cranford' by Mrs Gaskell

1. Soak the bread in a little sherry and then line a jelly mould or shallow dish with the bread.

2. Bring the water to the boil with the stick of cinnamon.

3. Dissolve the jelly in the boiling water. Pour half the jelly on the bread.

4. When the remaining jelly has nearly set, stir in the whipped cream. Pour onto the layer of jelly and bread. Put into a cool place.

5. When the jelly is completely set, turn out onto a dish and decorate with angelica and glacé cherries. Serve with whipped cream and sweet biscuits.

Printers' Pudding

INGREDIENTS

1 oz/25g butter
4 oz/100g fine breadcrumbs
3 tablespoons honey
Zest of 1 lemon
1½ pints/900ml milk
A pinch sea salt
4 oz/100g brown sugar
4 eggs
2 oz/50g desiccated coconut
1 teaspoon grated nutmeg

MRS HAMMOND'S RECIPE — 1850

1. Butter a large oven-proof dish.

2. Mix the breadcrumbs and honey together and put into the dish.

3. Put the lemon zest into a pan with the milk, salt and sugar. Warm through but do not boil. Set to one side to stand for 20–25 minutes.

4. Beat the eggs. Stir into the milk and pour the mixture onto the breadcrumbs. Sprinkle with desiccated coconut and ground nutmeg. Leave the pudding to stand for 1–2 hours. Then put into the oven at 320°F, 160°C, Gas Mark 3 and cook for 45–50 minutes.

5. Serve with whipped cream and a fruit sauce.

Under the Influence of Bright Sunbeams

Winter Pudding

This Victorian pudding was greatly loved by my grandfather. Born in 1860, he was 84 years older than I, a true Victorian. During the winter months, a good solid pudding that 'stuck to your ribs' was a must — not for the calorie conscious!

INGREDIENTS

3 oz/75g butter
5 oz/150g black treacle
3 oz/75g golden syrup
3 large pears, peeled, cored and cut into halves
2 oz/50g glacé cherries cut in halves
8 oz/225g self raising flour
2 teaspoons ground cinnamon
2 teaspoons ground ginger
4 tablespoons Muscovado sugar
2 eggs, beaten
¼ pint/150ml milk

1. Pre-heat the oven to 350°F, 180°C, Gas Mark 4. Put the butter, treacle and golden syrup into a pan over a very low heat. Bring to the boil, then remove from the heat and set to one side.

2. Line an 8 inch/20cm, deep cake tin with greaseproof paper.

3. Fill the groove in each pear with glacé cherries. Lay the filled pears flat side down in the bottom of the cake tine.

4. Mix the flour, cinnamon and ginger together. Add the sugar and mix well.

5. Pour the syrup and treacle mixture into the flour and beat well. Add the eggs and milk and continue to beat for 2–3 minutes. Pour the pudding mixture into the cake tin.

6. Put into the oven and cook for 40–45 minutes or until the pudding is firm in the centre.

7. Turn the pudding out onto a serving dish and remove the greaseproof paper. Serve with cream or custard.

Peach Upside Down Cake

4 oz/100g unsalted butter
4 oz/100g granulated sugar
2 tablespoons honey
1 teaspoon ground ginger
1 teaspoon ground cinnamon
Juice of 1 lemon

4 large peaches or 8 peach halves. They may be either fresh or tinned. If fresh, just peel and cut into thin slices.

For the cake:
4 oz/100g butter
4 oz/100g castor sugar
4 oz/100g self raising flour
2 oz/50g ground almonds
3 eggs

FROM ESSEX — 1900s

This is a delicious variation of an apple or pear cake. This recipe came to me in a roundabout way. Several years ago, I won a cake at a fête; on the way out of the marquee I dropped the cake. One of the organizers felt so sorry for me that she offered me 'this funny peach topped thing' they had been given. 'This peach topped things' was, of course, the above. I tracked down the donor who was an old lady who had been a baker for many years and this recipe had been given to her by one of her customers, some 60 years before.

1. Put the unsalted butter into a pan over a low heat. When it has melted, add the sugar and continue to cook until you have a pale creamy toffee. Mix in the spices and lemon juice and cook for a further 2 minutes. Remove from the heat and set to one side.

2. Take a shallow 10 inch/25cm cake tin, warm slightly and pour in half the toffee. Arrange the slices of peach so that they overlap and the whole bottom is covered. Pour on the remaining toffee and set to one side.

For the cake:

1. Put all the ingredients for the cake into a large bowl and beat until very creamy. If you are using a food processor, process for 3–5 minutes until it is a pale creamy yellow.

2. Pour the cake mixture onto the toffee and fruit. Put into the oven at 350°F, 180°C, Gas Mark 4 for about 40–45 minutes. The cake should be a deep golden colour and well risen. When the cake starts to shrink slightly away from the edge of the tin, it is ready.

3. Leave to cool for 2–3 minutes. Put a plate over the tin and turn the cake out. Serve either hot or cold with whipped cream.

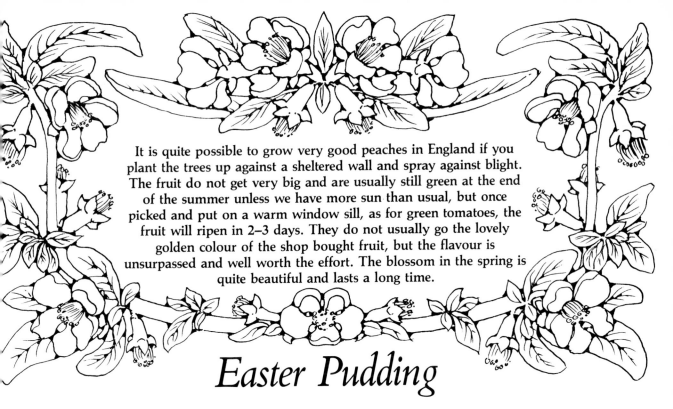

It is quite possible to grow very good peaches in England if you plant the trees up against a sheltered wall and spray against blight. The fruit do not get very big and are usually still green at the end of the summer unless we have more sun than usual, but once picked and put on a warm window sill, as for green tomatoes, the fruit will ripen in 2–3 days. They do not usually go the lovely golden colour of the shop bought fruit, but the flavour is unsurpassed and well worth the effort. The blossom in the spring is quite beautiful and lasts a long time.

Easter Pudding

FROM MALLORCA FROM A RECIPE COLLECTED BY MY MOTHER IN 1926

1. Pre-heat the oven to 350°F, 180°C, Gas Mark 4. Put the sugar, cinnamon, orange and lemon zest into a pan with the milk and bring to the boil. Set to one side to cool.

2. When the milk has cooled, add the beaten eggs and the biscuit crumbs. Pour the mixture into a well greased, oven-proof dish.

3. Put into the oven and cook for 50–60 minutes until golden on top and just risen.

INGREDIENTS

10 oz/275g sugar
1 cinnamon stick
1 tablespoon grated orange zest
2 tablespoons grated lemon zest
1¾ pints/1 litre milk
4 eggs, beaten
4 oz/100g biscuit crumbs

Mrs Larson's Grapefruit Pudding

1950s

INGREDIENTS

3 oz/75g castor sugar
2 egg yolks, beaten
Finely grated zest and juice of 1
grapefruit
1 tablespoon gelatine
¾ pint/450ml double cream
2 egg whites, whipped until stiff
Cinnamon and angelica to
decorate

1. Put the sugar, egg yolks, zest and grapefruit juice into a bowl over a pan of hot water. Heat until the mixture becomes very thick.

2. Sprinkle the gelatine into 3–4 tablespoons very hot water and stir until dissolved.

3. Stir the gelatine into the egg and sugar cream. Leave to stand for 10–12 minutes.

4. Beat the cream until stiff. Add to the mixture. Fold the whipped egg whites into the mixture.

5. Pour into a serving dish, decorate with a layer of ground cinnamon and a few pieces of angelica. Put into a fridge for a few hours before serving.

This is a lovely fresh pudding which I found on the back of an envelope in a second hand cookbook. There was no name except that the envelope was addressed to a Mrs Larson so I have called it Mrs Larson's Grapefruit Pudding.

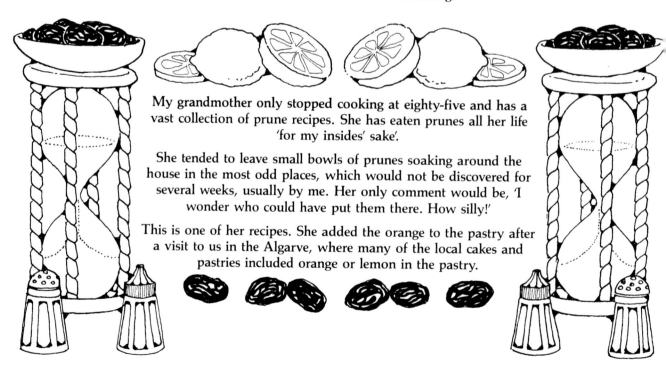

My grandmother only stopped cooking at eighty-five and has a vast collection of prune recipes. She has eaten prunes all her life 'for my insides' sake'.

She tended to leave small bowls of prunes soaking around the house in the most odd places, which would not be discovered for several weeks, usually by me. Her only comment would be, 'I wonder who could have put them there. How silly!'

This is one of her recipes. She added the orange to the pastry after a visit to us in the Algarve, where many of the local cakes and pastries included orange or lemon in the pastry.

Prune Tart with Almond and Orange Pastry

TWENTIETH CENTURY

For the pastry:

1. Put the flour and almonds into a large bowl.

2. Mix the orange flower water, orange zest and lemon juice in a cup, add to the egg and beat.

3. Cut the butter into small pieces and rub into the flour and almonds.

4. Add the egg yolk and lemon juice mixture. If the pastry is too dry, add a little water.

5. Roll out on a floured board. Line an 8 inch/20cm flan dish with the pastry. Put into the oven at 350°F, 180°C, Gas Mark 4 to bake blind for 10–15 minutes. Remove from the oven and set to one side.

For the filling:

1. Put the prunes into a liquidizer or food processor and purée.

2. Beat in the egg yolks, lemon zest and cream.

3. Pour into the pre-cooked pastry case and cook at 350°F, 180°C, Gas Mark 4 for 25–35 minutes or until the filling has just cooked through.

4. Remove from the oven and allow to cool a little. Serve with fresh yogurt or whipped cream.

INGREDIENTS

For the pastry:

4 oz/100g plain or wholemeal flour
4 oz/100g ground almonds
1 tablespoon orange flower water
1 tablespoon grated orange zest
2 tablespoons lemon juice
1 egg yolk
5 oz/150g butter

For the filling:

8 oz/255g pre-cooked stewed prunes, stones removed
3 egg yolks
½ pint/300ml single cream
Zest of 1 lemon

Mrs C's Postcard Sauce

INGREDIENTS

¼ pint/150ml water
½ lb/225g prunes
Zest of ½ lemon
2 tablespoons brown sugar
2 tablespoons brandy or rum

Mrs C was a Village Post Mistress in a small Essex village for 50 years. She was a dedicated reader of other people's post. This recipe came from a postcard which passed through her hands sometime in the 1950s, which she in turn wrote down on a postcard and passed on to my grandmother! We have ever since called it Mrs C's Postcard Sauce.

You can serve this sauce either hot or cold. It is very good with ice cream or meringues, also charlottes or rice pudding.

1. Put the water, prunes and lemon zest into a pan and cook very gently until the prunes are soft.

2. Add the sugar and brandy to the prunes and stir until all the sugar is dissolved.

3. Pass through a sieve.

Raspberry and Cassis Sauce

1. Put the raspberries into a food processor or pass through a fine sieve until you have a smooth purée.

2. Pass the purée through a sieve to remove any seeds.

3. Add the sugar, lemon juice and cinnamon.

4. Put into a pan and bring to the boil over a medium heat, stirring constantly. Cook until all the sugar is dissolved and the purée has formed a heavy syrup. This will take about 10–14 minutes.

5. Remove from the heat, stir in the crème de cassis and allow to chill before serving. You can reheat this sauce if you wish, but it does taste best cold. It is very good served with creamed rice.

INGREDIENTS

8 oz/225g fresh or frozen raspberries

2 oz/50g castor sugar

1 pinch cinnamon

1 teaspoon lemon juice

2 fl oz/60ml crème de cassis (a miniature bottle is a good idea)

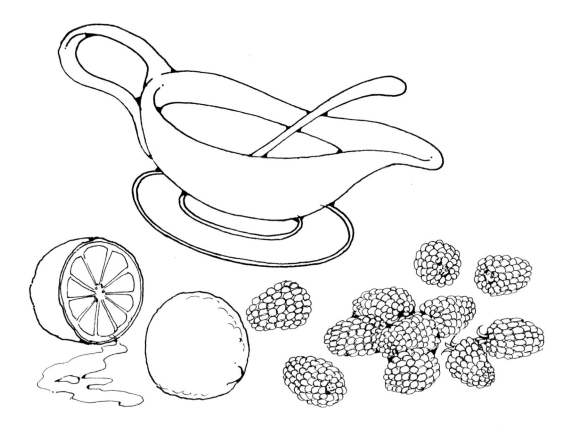

5.

Drinks

Currant Shrub

INGREDIENTS

1 lb/450g redcurrants
½ lb/225g brown sugar
½ teaspoon grated nutmeg
A few blades of mace
Rind of 2 oranges, cut very thin
1 pint/600ml rum
¾ pint/450ml sweet white wine

This is based on a Regency recipe which makes a different and fragrant liqueur.

1. Put the fruit into a pan together with the sugar, nutmeg, mace and orange rinds, and heat gently until the fruit is soft. Pass through a plastic sieve or muslin cloth. Allow to cool.

2. Pour the rum and wine over the fruit, pour into a clean bottle, seal and leave in a cool dark place for 2 days. Filter the liquid and re-bottle. Allow to mature for 3–6 months.

Hipocras

INGREDIENTS

1 bottle (700ml) dry red wine
2 oz/50g fresh ginger root, peeled and sliced
6 sticks cinnamon
½ teaspoon cloves
6 tablespoons honey

This was a favourite drink during the sixteenth and seventeenth centuries.

1. Put all the ingredients into a large pan. Bring to the boil and simmer for 10–15 minutes.

2. Strain and allow to cool. Serve either hot or cold.

Vespetro

SEVENTEENTH CENTURY

INGREDIENTS

8 oz/225g sugar
1 bottle brandy
2 lemons, sliced
1 2 inch piece of angelica root
1 teaspoon orris root
½ teaspoon ground coriander seeds

This is a very old liqueur that was drunk not only as a pleasant drink, but also to cure many ailments; it settles the stomach and is good for rheumatism.

1. Mix all the ingredients together in a large bowl or jar and allow to steep for 10–14 days.

2. Strain and pour into a clean bottle. Cover tightly and store in a cool place.

Under the Influence of Bright Sunbeams

Apricot Ratafia

1. Put the fruit into a large pan with the wine and bring to the boil over a medium heat.

2. Add the sugar and cinnamon sticks. Lower the heat and simmer stirring all the time until the sugar has dissolved.

3. Pour in the brandy and add the orange peel. Remove from the heat and stir. Pour into a large china or plastic container. Cover and put into a cool place to stand for 4 days.

4. Strain off the liquid and filter through a piece of muslin or paper filter. Pour into bottles. Seal tightly and store in a cool place.

Fruit ratafias make delicious flavourings for puddings, sorbets and creams. You can pour them over fresh fruit or drink them as a liqueur, pour them over pancakes or add a few spoonfuls to a sauce.

INGREDIENTS

10–15 ripe apricots
1 lb/450g soft brown sugar
2 bottles (1400ml) white wine
1 pint/600ml brandy
2 sticks cinnamon
Rind of 1 orange

Red Ratafia

1. Wash and dry the fruit.

2. Put the fruit into a cloth and press until all the juice has been removed.

3. Combine the juice with all the other ingredients.

4. Put into a clean glass bottle. Seal and allow to stand.

5. Allow to mature for at least 5 weeks.

6. Strain out the liqueur, re-bottle and used as desired.

INGREDIENTS

1 lb/450g cherries
½ lb/225g redcurrants
½ lb/225g strawberries
1 bottle Vodka, or any liked spirit
5 oz/150g sugar
4 cloves, crushed
4 peppercorns, crushed

Clockwise from the top: Juniper Sauce (page 148), A Variety of Mayonnaise (page 148), Watercress Sauce (page 149) and Raspberry and Cassis Sauce (page 139).

A Georgian Meal. Clockwise from the top: Ironpot Stew (page 60), Asparagus in Bread and Honey Sauce (page 94), Herrings in Marinade (pages 54-5) and The First Christmas Pudding (page 119).

A selection of flavoured oils and vinegars (see pages 161-72).

6.
Sauces

Roman Mayonnaise

6 hard boiled egg yolks
3 tablespoons freshly chopped
green herbs
3 tablespoons freshly chopped
green herbs
1 clove garlic, crushed
1 tablespoon honey
1 oz/25g cream cheese
3 tablespoons cider vinegar
Sea salt and freshly ground
pepper
¼ pint/150ml olive oil

1. Blend the hard boiled egg yolks with all the remaining ingredients except the oil.

2. Whisk in the oil slowly, until you have a thick cream. Put in a serving dish and chill. Serve with poached asparagus or celery hearts.

Almond Milk

For a thick milk to use
as a sauce:
½ pint/300ml water
1 tablespoon honey
½ teaspoon grated nutmeg
4 oz/100g ground almonds
¼ pint/150ml white wine

1398

There are several recipes for almond milk to be found in France, Spain and Italy, but this is one from England dating from 1467 which is certainly derived from a French recipe from 1398 and several Italian versions from the same period.

1. Bring the water to the boil with the honey and nutmeg.

2. Pour over the ground almonds and leave to steep for 1 hour. Stir from time to time.

3. Add the wine, cover with film and put into the refrigerator.

To make the sauce very thick, reduce the amount of water by half. Add salt, pepper and herbs if you want a savoury sauce or extra sweetening if you wish to serve it with stewed fruit or as a sauce for fruit tarts or pudding.

Under the Influence of Bright Sunbeams

Cawdel of Almond Milk

FOURTEENTH CENTURY

This is a simple sauce which has been made since early Medieval times. When you add eggs and milk, you have the basis for a custard. Cawdels were often made with cream beaten into the wine, much as in a later Syllabub.

Place all the ingredients in a pan, bring to the boil and simmer for 20 minutes. Cool and serve as a sauce with fruit tarts or ice-cream.

INGREDIENTS

3 oz/75g blanched almonds
¼ pint/150ml white wine
½ teaspoon ground ginger
3 tablespoons sugar
A few strands of saffron

Walnut Sauce for Fish

FOURTEENTH CENTURY

This sauce almost certainly originated in a Roman kitchen. There is a very similar sauce still eaten today in the north of Italy and it is usually served with pasta. In the Estremadura region of Spain where Roman influence still lingers, the same sauce is eaten with salt fish, the only addition being a few drops of lemon juice.

It is certain that in Britain during the Dark Ages, many recipes were either lost or forgotten and were only re-introduced to Britain in Medieval times from Lombardy and other parts of the Continent, where often traditions in food have remained virtually unchanged.

INGREDIENTS

3 oz/75g very finely chopped walnuts
1 oz/25g fine breadcrumbs
2 cloves garlic, crushed
½ pint/300ml stock
¼ teaspoon black pepper
A few drops of anchovy essence

1. Put all the ingredients into a food processor and purée.

2. Just before serving, put into a pan and heat. Serve with any kind of smoked or salt fish.

Juniper Sauce

FROM A MANUSCRIPT ABOUT 1840

2 oz/50g butter
1 medium sized onion, chopped
very small
1 tablespoon redcurrant jelly
¼ pint/150ml muscatel wine
10 juniper berries, crushed
8 peppercorns, cracked
1 tablespoon wine vinegar
½ pint/300ml stock
1 cinnamon stick
Sea salt to taste

1. Put the butter into a pan and heat gently. Add the onion and cook until soft.

2. Stir in the redcurrant jelly, wine, juniper berries, peppercorns and vinegar.

3. Simmer gently for 2–3 minutes, add the stock and cinnamon stick and cook for 15–20 minutes very slowly. Add salt to taste.

4. When the sauce is cooked, strain and pour over dish or serve separately.

A Variety of Mayonnaise

INGREDIENTS

¼ cucumber, peeled and
chopped
1 pickled sweet gherkin,
chopped
1 tablespoon mango chutney
½ pint/300ml basic
mayonnaise
Sea salt and black pepper to
taste
1 tablespoon chopped green
herbs

From the Fin do Mundo Restaurant, Cascaies
TWENTIETH CENTURY

This is a rather nice variation on a standard mayonnaise.

1. Put the cucumber, gherkin and chutney into a food processor until you have a thick purée.

2. Stir into the mayonnaise. Season to taste.

3. Sprinkle with fresh herbs, chill and serve.

Watercress Sauce

This recipe is adapted from a nineteenth century French one that used cream instead of yogurt. This version is far less cloying.

1. Cut off the ends of the watercress stalks. Put the leaves into a food processor with the garlic. Add the lemon juice and mix well.

2. Add all the remaining ingredients and process. Pour into a sauce boat and serve with cold fish dishes.

INGREDIENTS

2 bunches watercress

2 cloves garlic, crushed

Juice of 1 lemon

8 oz/225g Greek yogurt

1 tablespoon orange flower water

½ teaspoon honey

½ teaspoon cinnamon

½ teaspoon coarse ground black pepper

Sea salt to taste

Tomato, Orange and Basil Sauce for Pasta

NINETEENTH CENTURY RECIPE FROM AMERICA

1. Heat the oil in a pan, add the onion and garlic and cook very gently until just tender. Set to one side.

2. Add the tomatoes, basil and sugar to the onion and simmer for 2–3 minutes. Then add the chopped orange. Cover and cook very gently for 15–20 minutes or until tender. Season to taste.

INGREDIENTS

3 tablespoons olive oil

2 medium onions, chopped very fine

2 cloves garlic, crushed

1 lb/450g tomatoes, skinned and chopped

2 tablespoons dried basil

2 tablespoons brown sugar

2 oranges, peeled and chopped into small pieces

Sea salt and black pepper to taste

Cucumber Sauce

1. Mix all the ingredients together very well in a bowl.

2. Serve as a sauce with shell fish, hard boiled eggs or celery.

1 cucumber, peeled and
chopped into very small pieces
2 cloves garlic, crushed
Juice of 1 lemon
1 teaspoon honey
2 fl oz/75ml yogurt
2 fl oz/75ml thick cream
Sea salt to taste

Harlot's Sauce

Salsa alla Meretrice

'A hot sauce and a harlot have a lot in common' — An Italian country saying that had a hand in naming this sauce.

INGREDIENTS

4 tablespoons olive oil
3 cloves garlic, very finely
chopped
8 anchovy fillets, cut into small
pieces
1 teaspoon lemon juice
2 lb/1 kilo tinned tomatoes
12 black olives, pitted and cut
into slices
12 green stuffed olives, cut into
slices
12 capers
3 teaspoons dried basil
½ teaspoon red cayenne pepper

1. Put the oil into a pan and heat very slowly. Add the garlic and cook very gently until soft.

2. Add the anchovies and lemon juice. Cook until the anchovies have broken up into a creamy consistency.

3. Add the tomatoes, stir well, bring to the boil and simmer for 10–12 minutes.

4. Add the sliced olives, capers, basil and pepper. Stir and continue to cook for 10–15 minutes or until the sauce is really thick.

Serve with tagliatelli or vermicelli, plenty of grated cheese and a green salad, such as endive, or watercress and orange salad.

Under the Influence of Bright Sunbeams

Herb and Vermouth Seasoning and Young Vegetables

1. Just before serving your vegetables, put the lemon juice, vermouth and honey onto a pan and warm. Add the herbs, garlic and pepper.

2. When the vegetables are cooked, drain and put into a warmed serving dish. Pour on the herb and vermouth seasoning and mix well to ensure all the vegetables are well coated with herbs. Serve at once.

INGREDIENTS

1 lb/450g new potatoes or baby carrots or young turnips, boiled until just tender

1 tablespoon lemon or lime juice

3 tablespoons sweet vermouth

1 tablespoon honey

1 tablespoon dill, very finely chopped

1 tablespoon mint, finely chopped

1 tablespoon parsley, finely chopped

1 clove garlic, crushed (optional)

Coarse ground black pepper

Apple and Horseradish Sauce

1. Put the sugar, lemon juice, vinegar and apples into a large pan, bring to the boil and simmer gently for 3–4 minutes.

4. Add the horseradish and cook for a further 2–5 minutes stirring all the time.

3. Allow to cool and then stir in the yogurt and serve, or alternatively store in the fridge until ready to use.

You can omit the yogurt and add a little more apple for a slightly sweeter sauce.

INGREDIENTS

1 tablespoon brown sugar

Juice of 1 lemon

¼ pint/150ml cider vinegar

3 large apples, peeled cored and cut into slices

½ oz/12g grated fresh horseradish

4 oz/120ml creamy yogurt

Tofu and Mint Salad Dressing

INGREDIENTS

8 oz/225g silken tofu
1 clove garlic, crushed
Juice of 1 lemon
Juice of 1 orange
2 tablespoons parsley, finely
chopped
1 tablespoon fresh mint, finely
chopped
1 pinch mustard
¼ teaspoon ground nutmeg
A little sea salt
Black pepper to taste

1. Put all the ingredients into a food processor and blend to a thick cream. Put into a bowl and cover with film.

2. Put into the refrigerator and chill. This dressing will keep for 3–4 days in a cool place.

Curried Mayonnaise

GRANNY PAKENHAM'S NOTEBOOK
1853

'Pound a clove of garlic with 1 teaspoon curry powder and the juice of a lime. Mix into your sauce a little at a time.'

Horseradish Mayonnaise

Add 1 tablespoon creamed horseradish to your basic sauce and 1 teaspoon brandy.

Under the Influence of Bright Sunbeams

Tarragon and Pinenut Mayonnaise

FROM ELVAS IN THE ALENTEJO

To 1 pint/600ml mayonnaise add 1 oz/25g finely
chopped pine kernels, 2 tablespoons finely chopped fresh
tarragon, 1 teaspoon honey, the juice of 1 lemon and a
good pinch of black pepper.

'Smith of the Smiths' Salad Dressing

*This recipe was first written in verse by a nineteenth
century clergyman.*

Put all the ingredients into a food processor or mortar
and purée to a thick cream. Season and serve with fish
or egg dishes.

INGREDIENTS

*1 medium sized potato, pre-
boiled, peeled and chopped*

*1 teaspoon onion, very finely
chopped*

3 hard boiled egg yolks

1 anchovy fillet

1 tablespoon Dijon mustard

1 teaspoon sea salt

2 tablespoons wine vinegar

4 tablespoons olive oil

Sauce Bearnaise

3 tablespoons fresh tarragon,
coarsely chopped

4 tablespoons tarragon vinegar

¼ pint/150ml dry white wine

2 spring onions, very finely
chopped

¾ teaspoon coarse ground
black pepper

4 egg yolks

1 tablespoon cold water

7 oz/200g butter cut into small
pieces

Sea salt to taste

Henry VI of France was one of the country's most popular kings and was a native of Bearn. In the nineteenth century, a restaurant in Paris was named after the King and the chef created this sauce in honour of his memory — as a '"Great Bearnaise", full of the love of life and good things.'

1. Put the tarragon, vinegar, wine, onions and pepper into a pan and bring to the boil. Cook until the liquid has reduced to about 3 tablespoons. Strain and set to one side.

2. Put the egg yolks into a bowl over a pan of boiling water. It is important not to allow the water to touch the bottom of the bowl, only the steam, as the sauce would then cook too fast and not blend.

3. Add 1 tablespoon water to the egg yolks. Whisk the eggs continuously. Add the reduced wine and herb juice and whisk again.

4. Very gradually add the butter, a piece at a time and allow to melt. Continue to whisk. As the butter melts and becomes absorbed, the sauce should thicken to the consistency of fluffy mayonnaise.

5. Season to taste and serve straight away.

You can use this sauce for many dishes. It was originally created to serve with lamb but it is delicious with egg and cheese dishes or over new potatoes, or almost any vegetables.

Lemon and Fennel Basting Sauce

1. Mix all the ingredients together. Leave to stand for at least 2 hours before using.

2. Baste the food frequently with the mixture.

Use with grilled vegetable kebabs or with lentil or chickpea rissoles. Or try basting roast potatoes. Add a little cheese for a really good meal.

INGREDIENTS

2 oz/50g melted butter or
6 tablespoons oil

4 tablespoons fresh fennel,
finely chopped

1 tablespoon brown sugar

1 teaspoon finely grated lemon
zest

4 tablespoons lemon juice

½ teaspoon coarse ground
green peppercorns if available;
alternatively, use black

1 tablespoon Ouzo or Anis

Ginger and Cumin Sauce

Mix all the ingredients together well.

INGREDIENTS

6 tablespoons oil

1 tablespoon very finely grated
fresh ginger

4 tablespoons lemon juice

1 tablespoon ground cinnamon

2 tablespoons cider vinegar

1 teaspoon ground cumin

1 tablespoon brown sugar

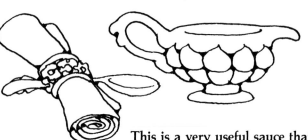

This is a very useful sauce that is almost a pudding in itself. Eat it with yogurt, rice pudding, creamy ice cream or a creamy custard — it is delicious with all of them.

You can use the recipe as a basis for making any number of variations using different fruits and experimenting with flavours.

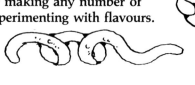

Miss Harper's Lemon Flavoured Brandy

1840

This is a very useful sauce, quite delicious with custards or to flavour a fruit sauce.

INGREDIENTS

Peel of 3 lemons
1 pint/600ml brandy
¼ pint/150ml water
2 tablespoons sugar
3 tablespoons honey

First Day

1. Cut the peel off the lemons very thinly making sure that none of the pith is included.

2. Put the peel into a bottle with the brandy, seal and leave to steep for 24 hours.

Second Day

3. Put the water, sugar and honey into a pan and bring to the boil. Strain to remove any froth. Allow to cool.

4. Add to the brandy and seal.

Under the Influence of Bright Sunbeams

Blackberry or Raspberry Sauce

NINETEENTH CENTURY

For Herrings or Cod

1. Put the berries, apples, honey, ginger and cloves into a pan with the lemon juice.

2. Bring to the boil and simmer very gently for 5–8 minutes until the fruit has just started to soften.

3. Stir in the mustard, port, lemon zest and yogurt and set to one side to cool.

INGREDIENTS

½ lb/225g blackberries or raspberries

½ lb/225g sweet apples, peeled, cored and cut into pieces

1 tablespoon honey

½ teaspoon ground ginger

4 cloves

Juice of 1 lemon

½ teaspoon mustard

3 tablespoons port or sweet sherry

A pinch of lemon zest

3 tablespoons Greek cow's yogurt or 3 tablespoons cream

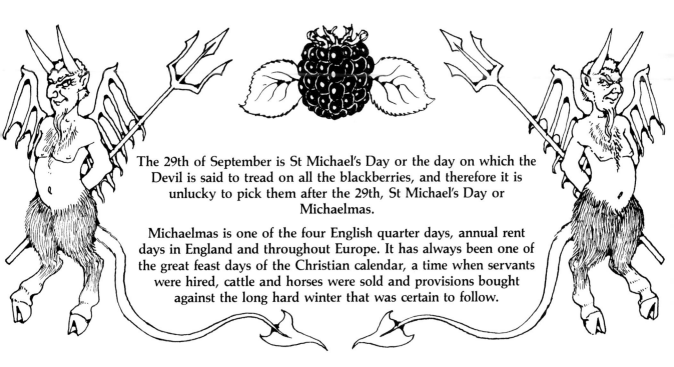

The 29th of September is St Michael's Day or the day on which the Devil is said to tread on all the blackberries, and therefore it is unlucky to pick them after the 29th, St Michael's Day or Michaelmas.

Michaelmas is one of the four English quarter days, annual rent days in England and throughout Europe. It has always been one of the great feast days of the Christian calendar, a time when servants were hired, cattle and horses were sold and provisions bought against the long hard winter that was certain to follow.

Beetroot and Brandy Sauce

TWENTIETH CENTURY

INGREDIENTS

1 oz/25g butter

1 medium onion, chopped very
fine

10 oz/275g cooked beetroot,
diced into small pieces

3 tablespoons white wine
vinegar

1 teaspoon Dijon mustard

3 tablespoons brandy

2 teaspoons brown sugar

2 tablespoons orange flower
water

½ teaspoon ground cloves

½ teaspoon coarse ground
black pepper

Sea salt to taste

6 fl oz/175ml creamy Greek
yogurt or sour cream

3 tablespoons very finely
chopped parsley

This lovely coloured rich sauce is very versatile. You can serve it with vegetables, or with pasta. You can vary the amount of seasoning to your own taste. This was one of my father's favourite recipes; he always used the principle that you doubled all the ingredients you did like and halved the ones you did not. Usually it worked very well!

1. Melt the butter in a pan, add the onion and cook gently for 1–2 minutes.

2. Add the beetroot, stir and cook very gently. Add the wine vinegar, mustard, brandy, sugar, orange flower water and cloves. Stir well, cover and cook for 2–3 minutes.

3. Add the seasoning. Stir in the yogurt and chopped parsley. Heat right through, put into a warmed bowl and serve.

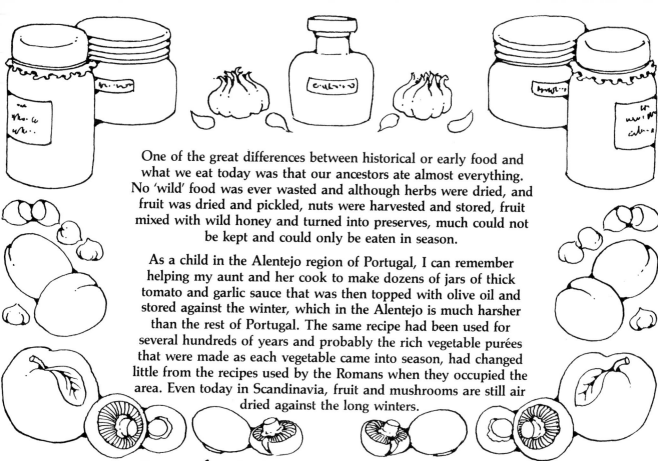

One of the great differences between historical or early food and what we eat today was that our ancestors ate almost everything. No 'wild' food was ever wasted and although herbs were dried, and fruit was dried and pickled, nuts were harvested and stored, fruit mixed with wild honey and turned into preserves, much could not be kept and could only be eaten in season.

As a child in the Alentejo region of Portugal, I can remember helping my aunt and her cook to make dozens of jars of thick tomato and garlic sauce that was then topped with olive oil and stored against the winter, which in the Alentejo is much harsher than the rest of Portugal. The same recipe had been used for several hundreds of years and probably the rich vegetable purées that were made as each vegetable came into season, had changed little from the recipes used by the Romans when they occupied the area. Even today in Scandinavia, fruit and mushrooms are still air dried against the long winters.

Quick Tomato Sauce Purée

1. Put the tomatoes and the tomato paste into a food processor and purée.

2. Heat the oil in a pan and cook the onion gently together with the remaining ingredients.

3. When the onion is tender, add the tomato purée, stir and bring to the boil. Reduce the heat and simmer gently for 45–50 minutes, stirring at frequent intervals.

To make larger amounts just multiply the quantities.

INGREDIENTS

1 large tin tomatoes

1 small tin tomato paste

4 tablespoons oil

1 medium sized onion, finely chopped

½ pint/300ml vegetable stock

2 teaspoons dried oregano

2 teaspoons dried basil

½ teaspoon ground nutmeg

A few drops Holbrook's Worcester sauce

Sea salt and black pepper to taste

7.

Herbs, Oils and Dressings for Salads and Vegetables and Fruit Vinegars

Using and Preserving Herbs

Ideally, fresh herbs are always better than dried ones. Unfortunately not everyone has a herb garden and with the exception of sage, rosemary, thyme and parsley, most herbs disappear at the first sign of frost. If you have access to fresh herbs, the best ways to preserve them are to dry them by the traditional methods, or in the microwave or by freezing them.

To dry herbs, it is best to pick them on a dry day. Wipe them with kitchen paper to remove any dust or dirt and tie into bunches. Put into a loose muslin bag and hang upside down in a cool dry dark airy place for 3–4 weeks by which time they should feel dry and slightly brittle to the touch. Strip the leaves from the stalks and store in airtight jars away from the light. Remember to label as you go along.

To microwave herbs, which in my opinion is now the best method of preserving, as both the colour and the taste are better than the traditional drying method, simply chop the fresh herbs to the fineness you require and microwave them at about setting 9–10 for 2–2½ minutes. Allow to cool completely before storing in jars in the dark.

Freezing is the best method for some delicate herbs. Dill, basil, tarragon and parsley are all herbs that are better frozen. Pick the herbs on a dry day. It's quite a good idea to water them carefully the day before to get rid of any dirt or grit. You can either freeze the herbs in small bunches, or chop them first and put a small spoonful into small envelopes or freezer bags. For soups and casseroles, it is useful to put a small amount of one herb, or mixed herbs, into compartments of ice cube trays and top up with water or wine.

Anise Seed
Pimpinella anisum

Native to Asia Minor and the Mediterranean, it is of the *Umbelliferae* family, growing to a height of 2 feet (60cm). It flowers from June to August, but is rarely seen in gardens in Britain.

It was much praised by the Ancient Greeks to whom bread flavoured with aniseed was a great delicacy. No Roman feast or banquet was complete without cakes and pastries flavoured with anise. Quintus Fabius Cunctator gave his soldiers anis-flavoured sweets called Dragati to celebrate his victories. Pliny recommends it to be taken in the mornings mixed with honey, myrrh and wine.

It should be sown in March or April in light sandy soil in a sheltered spot, as it does not like wind.

Bay Leaves

The Romans used them as a symbol of victory and wore crowns of bay leaves as did the Greeks before them. Julius Caesar was excused by his friends for almost always wearing one, as a means of hiding his baldness!

Bay leaves have a strong aromatic scent, bitter while yet being sweet.

Basil
Ocimum minimum

An annual that can grow up to 20 inches (50cm) tall, it belongs to the *Labiatae* family. It flowers from August to September and is a native of India. It came to Europe via the Egyptians who used it with myrrh and incense as an offering to their gods and it is one of the herbs used in embalming. It then passed to Greece and so to the Romans. It was associated with both love and death, as well as praised for its culinary uses. It was combined with other herbs in bouquets garni and added its delicate taste to many sauces.

It is used in Mediterranean cooking today in many forms. When I was a child in Spain, there were always pots of basil in the kitchen to keep away flies. Basil requires a warm sunny situation. It can be grown in pots and transplanted outside once all danger of frost is over. It is well worth growing to use fresh.

Chervil
Anthriscus cerefolium

An annual plant belonging to the *Umbelliferae* family, it grows to 2 feet (60cm). A native of Western Asia, it reached the Mediterranean long before the birth of Christ. The Romans used it both as a herb and cooked it by itself as a vegetable. It can be grown like parsley, and is a useful plant to have fresh.

Cinnamon and Cassia
Cinnamomum

These were first mentioned in the Ancient Chinese herbals. Cassia was one of the traditional five spice powders used for Chinese cooking.

The Pharaoh Sankhare sent an expedition to the lands of Punt (present day Somalia) in 2500 BC to search for cinnamon, precious metals and spices. A thousand years later, Queen Hatchepsut sent five ships to the land of Punt to bring back ivory, panthers, spices of many kinds and cinnamon.

The Egyptians used both cinnamon and cassia, and other spices in their cosmetics, embalming processes and to flavour food. The Phoenicians introduced it to the Greeks and Arab traders who sold it to everybody.

The Romans learnt the secret of crossing the Indian Ocean using the prevailing south-easterly winter winds and then returning on the north-westerly summer monsoon laden with goods.

Coriander
Coriandrum sativum

It is a biennial plant of the *Umbelliferae* family and reaches just over 2 feet (60cm). It likes a sheltered position and grows well in a warm corner.

One of the oldest spices used by man, coriander seeds have been found in the tombs of the Pharaohs and in the Bronze Age ruins on the island of Thera in the Aegean. It was used in ancient Mycenae.

It was one of the most popular herbs in Roman cooking and finds its way into nearly every dish. Plautus tells us that it was used to flavour boiled greens and porridge, and Varro in his book of agriculture, advises that mixed with caraway seed and vinegar it was good to preserve meat in hot weather. Apicius used it in the greater portion of his recipes. It is also used throughout India and the East, southern Europe and the Mediterranean.

Its flavour is difficult to describe. Elizabeth David, in her *Book of Mediterranean Food* (Penguin, 1970), gets near to it when she says that it has an orange peel scent.

Dill

Anethum graveolens

Like many of our herbs, this belongs to the *Umbelliferae* family. It grows to a height of 4 feet (120cm).

It was greatly valued by the Romans who wore garlands of it at their festivals. It was mixed with the food given to gladiators as a tonic, and used medicinally. Both the seeds and the leaves themselves were used in cooking, to flavour fish and sauces, often combined with caraway seeds and pepper.

Dill is an extremely easy plant to cultivate. Sown in April or May in shallow drills, or singly at the back of a border, it will be ready to harvest 6 or 7 weeks after planting. It can also be grown in pots.

It is a good plant to have fresh for sauces and salads. It will self-seed freely if the seeds are allowed to ripen. It does require watering during the growing season.

Fennel

Foeniculum vulgare

Again, it is a member of the *Umbelliferae* family; it can reach a height of 6 feet (180cm), flowers in July and August and is very like dill in its habits. It grows throughout the Mediterranean and Europe as far as Gaul (France), and was certainly introduced to Britain by the Romans. Apicius wrote that fennel seeds should be in every kitchen. It was used to flavour dishes in combination with other herbs, mixtures of fennel, caraway and coriander seeds were often used to coat fish, also as part of a dressing for salads.

Columnella, in his book of agriculture, tells us how to preserve fennel stalks in brine and vinegar. In Italy, it has long been considered as a vegetable in its own right, the bulbous roots being eaten raw in salads, or cooked and sometimes stuffed.

It is very easy to grow and makes a useful border plant. It likes a dry warm spot with plenty of light. Apart from the usual kind, a modern variety of black fennel with dark bronze red foliage is obtainable from good nurseries, which deserves a place in any herb garden or herbaceous border alongside the normal green plant.

Horseradish
Amoracia Rusticana

Horseradish has been cultivated for at least 2000 years. The strong flavoured pungent root of this plant has long been grated and used as an ingredient for a sauce. It has been used as a medicine as well as a condiment. It has not been used very much in southern Europe, although recipes for sauces can be found throughout Scandinavia.

Juniper
Juniperus Communis

It is a small evergreen shrub with grey-green needles, short and spiky. It flowers in April and May and the small round fruits are green in the first year and a dark bluish-purple in the second.

It is usually sold as dried berries and has a strong pungent and slightly bitter taste. The berries are used in cooking and marinating, as a flavouring for gin and also in sauerkraut. In Sweden the berries are used to make a kind of beer.

Juniper can be grown very easily from cuttings. Juniper oil is extracted from the berries and used in medicine. In England, it grows wild in the south-west and the Lake District. Throughout history it has been used as a protective charm against evil spirits, and was traditionally hung over windows and doors on the Eve of May Day.

Marjoram
Marjoram hortensis or Origanum marjorana

This is a biennial plant, flowering from late June to September. It grows to a height of 2 feet (50cm) and is a member of the mint family closely related to thyme. Its flavour is less sharp than oregano with which it is often confused, and is a different herb altogether. It originated in the Mediterranan, though exactly where is unknown.

It was used by the Ancient Greeks and Romans both as a flavouring for food, and the oil extracted from the plant was much valued in cosmetics and medicines.

It is quite easy to grow in pots or a warm spot in the garden, and worth having to cut fresh for salads and sauces.

Oregano or Wild Marjoram

This is a perennial herb that flowers from late June to September, native to the whole of the Mediterranean and the Middle East. It was much used in cooking by the Romans and is one of the principle herbs for stews and salads. It is still collected wild throughout southern Europe and both its oils and extracts from the plant are used in medicine.

It is easy to grow and well worth the effort in a herb garden, or just as a herbaceous plant. I have in my garden a very pretty golden variety which makes a spectacular plant, as well as being very useful in the kitchen.

Rue
Ruta graveolens

Rue is a perennial semi-shrub, reaching 3 feet (90cm) in height. It belongs to the *Rutaceae* family and flowers from June to September. It has a rather strong, bitter smell and I would recommend using it sparingly. It is native to the Mediterranean region and was introduced to Britain by the Romans, who used it as a flavouring for sauces and salads. It was also used medicinally both dried and fresh.

It is a pretty plant to have in the garden as its blue-grey leaves provide a pleasant background for smaller plants.

Summer Savory/Mountain Savory
Satureja hortensis/Satureja montana

Summer savory is an annual plant which is native to southern Europe, milder in flavour than Winter Savory, and flowers from June to September; it thrives in a warm, dry situation.

Mountain, or Winter Savory, is the wild perennial form, native to the Mediterranean. It is included in nearly every Roman recipe known of to date. It is strongly flavoured and when used on its own, only a small amount is required. When combined with others, it loses some of its potency. It can be added fresh to salads, grilled fish and meat.

It is a pretty plant, with small, pale purple or white flowers, very easy to grow provided it is given a sunny situation. It germinates quickly and does as well in pots as in the open ground.

Thyme
Thymus serpyllum

This is a member of the *Labiatae* or mint family. Wild thyme reaches a height of 8–10 inches, 15–20cm, and grows on dry slopes and roadsides in sunny places. It flowers from May to

Under the Influence of Bright Sunbeams

September. The flowers can be white, pink, deep mauve and there are many varieties. It is a native of the Mediterranean and was used by the Sumerians as early as 3200 BC. Thyme was much loved by both the Greeks and the Romans, who not only used the wild species but cultivated several different varieties. It was used as part of a bouquet garnis for stews and casseroles, and in stuffings for fish. Pliny tells us that it was good when boiled in vinegar to cure headaches and was effective against snake bite. And when burned, it would drive away venomous sea animals! Mixed with honey, it was good for many disorders. It was also associated by the Romans with bravery.

It was almost certainly introduced to Britain by the Romans. Thyme is easily cultivated either by sowing seeds in a sand and soil mixture, or by division of existing plants. There are many different varieties in cultivation, golden thymes, creeping, lemon-scented and trailing. They are evergreen, a constant joy, particularly during the winter months when fresh herbs are very scarce.

Herb Oil

Herb oils go back as far as Ancient Egyptian times and before. They have been used throughout history to preserve the flavour of delicate herbs during the winter. You can use these delicious concoctions for salad dressings and to fry and cook with. They add an extra 'scent' to both the food and the kitchen.

To Make Herb Oils:

It is very important that you make sure that your herbs are completely dry. Either chop your herbs or tie into short bunches. Put a generous portion in a well washed, dry glass jar and fill with any good quality oil. The less flavour the oil has the better as this allows the herbs to flavour the oil to their fullest. Olive oil is not only too strong but works out very expensive. Safflower, soya or sunflower oil are all good.

Cover the jars with cling film and stand on a warm window sill for 3–4 weeks stirring them from time to time. By the third week the herbs will possibly look black and slimy. Don't worry. This shows that they have absorbed a lot of oil which is correct and your herb oil is now ready to strain and bottle, as follows.

1.   First wash and dry a glass bottle with a close fitting lid or cork. Line a small funnel with a coffee filter or a piece of kitchen paper.

2.   Pour the oil in and allow to drip through. Do not press the herbs or you will get a lot of sediment coming through. You may need to strain the oil a second time through a clean filter.

3.   The oil should now be a clear greeny colour. Top up the bottle with fresh oil if there is a large gap, as this will help it keep. Put it into the fridge or a cool place.

It is quite a good idea to make several different flavours in small containers rather than just one. For 1 pint/600ml oil, 2–3 oz/50-75g herbs are sufficient.

Basil Vinegar

KITCHENER'S RECIPE — 1817

This is a very delicate-flavoured vinegar, particularly useful in Britain where basil is quite a short-seasoned herb.

Put 2–3 handfuls of fresh basil leaves into a jar and cover with white wine or vinegar. Allow to steep for 10–12 days. Strain and pour into a bottle. Seal.

This will produce a vinegar which can either be used as it is, or diluted with a mild vinegar, if you wish.

Rose Vinegar for Salad Dressings or Fish

EIGHTEENTH CENTURY

INGREDIENTS

4 oz/100g fresh rose petals (the best are from old roses)
2 pints/1200ml white wine vinegar

Put the petals and wine vinegar in a large china or glass jar. Stand on a warm window sill for 10–12 days, in the sunlight if possible. Strain through a paper filter. Pour into a clean bottle and seal well.

This gives a lovely subtle taste to almost any salad and is also delicious in mayonnaise.

Under the Influence of Bright Sunbeams

Raspberry Vinegar

VICTORIAN — 1847

*This delicious fruit vinegar is one of Eliza Acton's and is
well worth making if you ever have any spare
raspberries. It has a very delicate and distinctive taste
that makes a delightful change from normal vinegars.
Use sparingly.*

'To three quarts of raspberries well crushed, add 1
quart of cider vinegar. Mix them together and put
them in a stone jar; and let them remain in a cool
place for ten days, stirring the mixture every day.
Then strain it and to every pint of juice add one
pound of loaf sugar. Let the whole boil in a stone jar
on a hot hearth, for five minutes. Strain it well, when
cold, bottle and cork it.'

To make a smaller amount, add 1 lb/450g raspberries to
1½ pints/900ml cider vinegar and 4 oz/100g sugar. Put
into a bowl, cover, and keep in a cool place. Stir once a
day as directed above. I found that I could put it into a
large saucepan and bring it to the boil, simmer for 4–6
minutes and then follow the original recipe as to storage.

Hazel-Nut Oil

INGREDIENTS

3 oz/75g hazel-nuts
1 pint/600ml olive or any salad oil

TWENTIETH CENTURY

This recipe came from the painter Cedric Morris who had come across it in France. It is similar to a recipe of Alice B Tolkas, who also found it in France, so I assume that it originates there, where there is a long tradition of flavoured oils, vinegars and nuts in dressings dating from the Romans.

1. Put the hazel-nuts onto a baking sheet in the oven at 225°F, 100°C, Gas Mark ¼ for 10–12 minutes or until they are quite hot.

2. Take them out of the oven and roll them together in a bowl to remove the outer skins.

3. Put them into a food processor and process to a fine powder. Put into a jar and set to one side.

4. Heat the oil until quite hot. Pour onto the processed nuts. Stir and allow to stand overnight. Strain the oil and pour into a bottle and seal. Keep in a cool place.

This makes a delicate, nutty-tasting oil to give an extra lift to almost any salad. It is especially good with pasta and grain salads, chickpeas and pulses, also in mayonnaise. A few fresh chopped nuts added to the dish when you are using it in a dressing give extra flavour.

Under the Influence of Bright Sunbeams

Pistachio-Flavoured Oil for Salads

NINETEENTH CENTURY

1. Shell the pistachio nuts and dip them into a pan of boiling water for 2–3 minutes. Drain and peel off the outer skin, leaving the bright green nut.

2. Chop the nuts and combine with the oil. Seal and leave over night before using. This will last in a cool place the same time as normal oil.

This is quite delicious with anything that needs a vinaigrette, particularly asparagus and artichokes. Try just a few drops poured over cooked or raw vegetables with a squeeze of lemon juice.

INGREDIENTS

3 oz/75g pistachio nuts
1 pint/600ml olive or salad oil

Marinated Black Olives

1880 FROM CATALONIA

1. Drain the olives and retain half the liquid.

2. Combine all the remaining ingredients with the saved liquid from the olives. Put into a container and shake well.

3. Add the olives and leave for 24 hours, then serve.

INGREDIENTS

1 tin or jar (approximately
8 oz/250g) large black olives
4 cloves garlic
6 tablespoons olive oil
3 tablespoons lemon juice
½ teaspoon orange zest
1 teaspoon dried marjoram

8.
Jams, Pickles, Preserves, and Sweets

Candied Cowslips

For whole flowers or petals:
3 tablespoons rosewater
1 oz/25g gum arabic

This recipe comes from a sixteenth century notebook. I have never made it with cowslips as I was always taught not to pick them, but I have made it with yellow garden polyanthus flowers which seemed to me to be a good substitute. They turn out very well although they are conserved rather than candied. I felt that I had to try the recipe as it seemed to be just the kind of thing the woodland folk might make if they took up cooking! Here is the recipe just as it appears in the original.

'Gather the flowers, when the dew is off, and pluck off the green stalks leaving none but the yellow blossoms. Weigh 10 oz (275g) of yellow pips [flowers]. Take 8 oz (225g) of sugar and put the sugar into a pan and candy it with a little spot of water, as you can take off the fire, then shake in the flowers little by little, never ceasing to stir till they be dry enough to put into glasses or gallypots.'

Flowers have been candied and preserved since the early Middle Ages. They were used to decorate puddings and pies, handed round after a meal and sometimes even included in a grand salad! For best results use any of the following: violets, primroses, roses, apple blossom, borage, rosemary, marigold petals, nasturtiums, pinks or carnations, or cowslips.

1. Pour the rosewater over the gum arabic and leave overnight, by which time it should be dissolved.

2. Make sure that the flowers or petals are quite dry. Using a fine paint brush, paint each petal on all surfaces. Make sure that all the surfaces are covered with gum or the petals will not keep properly.

3. Put on a sheet of kitchen paper to dry in a warm place. Store on kitchen paper in an airtight container. Use to decorate cakes and puddings.

Under the Influence of Bright Sunbeams

Peaches were brought to England by the Romans. By the seventeenth century there were 20 different varieties throughout the country.

English grown peaches are far rarer today than they were two hundred years ago when they could be found growing in most orchards of any size. Many houses had their own peach tree along with damsons, greengages, plums and medlars. Brandied peaches make a delicious sweet for a party.

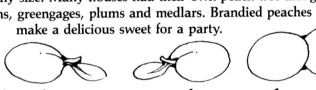

Brandied or Spiced Peaches

1747

1. Bring a pan of water to the boil and dip the peaches in for 2–3 minutes. Drain and peel. Cut in half and remove the stones. Stick a clove into the top of each peach half.

2. Put ½ pint water into a pan with the sugar, spices and honey. Stir and bring to the boil and make sure all the sugar is dissolved.

3. Carefully put the peach halves into the syrup making sure they are covered and simmer very gently for 15–18 minutes.

4. When the peaches are cooked, lift them from the syrup and arrange them in a large glass jar such as a kilner jar.

5. Strain the syrup and stir in the brandy. Pour into the jar of peaches and leave to stand until cook, then seal tightly. Put into a dark cool place for 2–3 days before using.

If you don't have a glass jar, a china pudding basin will do provided that you seal the top with a double layer of cling film. The peaches will mature just as well as in a jar but will not be as decorative!

INGREDIENTS

4 ripe peaches
8 cloves
½ pint/300ml water
10 oz/275g brown sugar
1 cinnamon stick
1 teaspoon ground cinnamon
½ teaspoon ground mace
3 tablespoons honey
6 fl oz/175ml brandy

Jams, Pickles, Preserves, and Sweets

Gooseberry and Orange Flower Preserve

SEVENTEENTH CENTURY

INGREDIENTS

3 lb/1350g gooseberries, topped
and tailed, cut in half and the
pips removed

3 tablespoons orange flower
water

1 lb(450g sugar to each
1 lb/450g prepared fruit

¼ pint/450ml cold water

1 teaspoon cinnamon

1. Put the fruit into a pan with the orange flower water, water and cinnamon. Bring to the boil and cook for 25–30 minutes.

2. Strain the fruit through a sieve.

3. Add the juice to the sugar and cook very gently for 35–45 minutes. Allow to cool, pour into small jars or bowls and cover. Serve as a dessert with cream, yogurt or ice-cream.

Plum and Apple Butter

AMERICAN — 1760s

This is very good both served heated as a sauce with a pudding and with savoury dishes as a relish. This particular version was given to me by an American lady whose family had originally come from East Anglia and had been using it for many years

INGREDIENTS

3 lb/1350g apples, peeled, cored
and cut into slices

1 lb/450g plums, stoned and
cut into pieces

12 oz/350g light brown sugar

1 teaspoon cinnamon

½ teaspoon ground nutmeg

2 tablespoons rosewater

1. Put the fruit into a pan with 3–4 tablespoons water. Cook very slowly until soft. Pass through a sieve.

2. Put the fruit purée into a pan with the sugar, spices and rosewater. Cook very gently until all the sugar has dissolved stirring all the time. Bring to the boil and cook for 6–8 minutes.

3. Pour a little of the purée onto a cold plate to test for setting. Pour into warmed, sterilized jars and seal at once.

Under the Influence of Bright Sunbeams

Pickled Damsons

GEORGIAN

These make a lovely spicy relish to serve with fish.

1. Wash the fruit and trim off any stalks. Prick all over with a fork. Put into a pan in layers with the sugar in between.

2. Mix the spices, wine and vinegar together. Pour onto the fruit. Heat very slowly to boiling point and simmer for 4 minutes. Remove from the heat. Lift the fruit out and put into a shallow dish to cool.

3. Heat the syrup, spices and grated orange peel, and continue to cook for a further 15–20 minutes stirring from time to time. Remove from the heat.

4. Put the fruit into clean sterilized glass jars. Allow the syrup to cool a little and then pour over the fruit. Allow to cool and then cover. Keep in a cool, dark place.

INGREDIENTS

4 lb/1800g damsons or plums
2 lb/900g Muscovado sugar
2 cinnamon sticks
½ teaspoon fresh ginger root, grated
12 cloves
½ pint/300ml white wine
½ pint/300ml white malt vinegar
Grated peel of 1 orange

Pumpkin Preserve or Angel's Hair

CABELLO DE LOS ANGELES

This preserve almost certainly originates from 'Morisco' or Moorish influenced cooking, and this version comes from a family recipe dated 1800.

INGREDIENTS

4 lb/2kg pumpkin or vegetable
spaghetti, peeled and cut into
pieces
2 lb/1kg sugar
3 pints/1800ml water
2 cinnamon sticks
½ teaspoon ground saffron
1 teaspoon ground ginger
Juice of 2 lemons

1. Put the pumpkin into a large pan with enough water to cover. Bring to the boil and simmer gently for 18–20 minutes, or until the flesh is quite tender.

2. Drain and allow to cool.

3. When the pumpkin is cool enough to handle, separate all the 'strings' or fibres.

4. Put the sugar into a large pan with the water, spices and lemon juice and stir until all the sugar is dissolved.

5. Add the pumpkin strings and simmer very gently, stirring from time to time, for 45–60 minutes.

6. Test to see if the preserve is cooked enough by spooning a little onto a saucer of cold water. If it sets it is ready.

7. Remove from the heat and allow to cool for 10–12 minutes.

8. Pour into warmed jars and seal. Store in a cool dark place.

Serve as a jam or preserve with ice-cream or hot as a sauce for puddings.

Under the Influence of Bright Sunbeams

The Best Apple Verbena Jelly

1800

1. Put the fruit into a large pan together with the water, wine, lemon juice, peel and verbena leaves. Bring to the boil and simmer until the fruit is soft. Put the fruit into a cloth or jelly bag and leave to strain overnight into a bowl.

2. Add the sugar to the strained juice. Put into a pan and bring to the boil stirring constantly until all the sugar has dissolved. Boil very fast for 8–10 minutes or until the jelly will set when tested on a cold plate.

3. Allow to cool for 10 minutes or so before pouring into clean, sterilized, warmed jars. Allow to cool before covering. Store away from the light.

A variation of this recipe is to substitute 6–7 rose geranium leaves for the lemon verbena, or to use 2 tablespoons rosewater or rose essence.

INGREDIENTS

5 lb/1.25kg cooking apples, washed and cut into slices (if you are using windfalls, remove any bruised or bad parts)
2½ pints/1500ml water
½ pint/300ml sweet white wine
Juice of 1 lemon
Peel of 1 lemon
10–12 lemon verbena leaves, tied in a piece of muslin or cloth
1 lb/450g preserving sugar to every measured pint/600ml juice

Orgeat Syrup

1800

1. Put the almonds into a food processor with the orange flower water and the orange oil; process to a thick paste.

2. Put the sugar in a large pan with the water; stir until all the sugar is dissolved.

3. Stir in the almond paste; bring to the boil and simmer for 2–3 minutes. Remove from the heat. Allow to cool. Strain and put into sterilized bottles.

Serve diluted with water. Use to flavour sauces and puddings, or to pour over ice-cream.

INGREDIENTS

4 oz/100g almonds, blanched and skinned
½ oz/12g bitter almonds, blanched and skinned
3 tablespoons orange flower water
½ teaspoon sweet orange oil
2 lb/900g sugar
1½ pints/900ml water

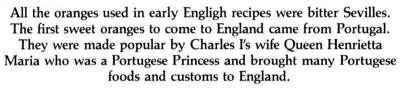

All the oranges used in early Engligh recipes were bitter Sevilles. The first sweet oranges to come to England came from Portugal. They were made popular by Charles I's wife Queen Henrietta Maria who was a Portugese Princess and brought many Portugese foods and customs to England.

In 1669, Samuel Pepys drank a pint of orange juice at a friend's house and was rather uncertain as to whether he liked it or if it might harm him! Oranges were traditionally sold in the London playhouses and it was when she was selling oranges that Charles II first met Nell Gwynn.

Orange Chutney

INGREDIENTS

Makes about 4 lb/2kg

6 sweet oranges, peeled and
pips removed
1 lb/450g stoned dates, chopped
2 oz/50g sultanas
8 oz/225g onions, finely
chopped
1 pint/600ml cider vinegar
1 teaspoon fresh ginger root,
grated
1 teaspoon ground cinnamon
3 tablespoons brown sugar
½ teaspoon sea salt

1. Cut the oranges into small pieces and put into a preserving pan with all the other ingredients.

2. Bring to the boil and simmer very gently for 45–50 minutes or until the chutney is a rich golden brown.

3. Put into warmed jars, cover with film and seal.

Under the Influence of Bright Sunbeams

Orange, Ginger and Date Chutney or Relish

1. Put the chopped onion into a pan with 4 tablespoons water over a low heat. Cover and cook very slowly until soft.

2. Add all the remaining ingredients, cover and simmer very gently for 25–35 minutes, stirring from time to time. Add a little more water or vinegar if it dries out too much.

3. When the mixture is cooked, set to one side to cool. Serve with cheese or any dish that requires a chutney or relish.

INGREDIENTS

1 medium onion, chopped very finely
4 tablespoons water
2 oranges, peeled and cut into small pieces
8 oz/225g stoned dates, chopped
3 tablespoons dark brown or Muscovado sugar
1 tablespoon black treacle
1 tablespoon ground cinnamon
½ tablespoon grated nutmeg
1 teaspoon ground ginger
3 tablespoons wine vinegar
A pinch of sea salt

Ludlow Redcurrant Jelly

1812

1. Put the fruit into a large pan and add the spices and water.

2. Bring to the boil and simmer until the fruit is just soft.

3. Remove from the heat and strain through a muslin cloth or jelly bag.

4. Put the strained juice into a pan with the vinegar and sugar. Bring to the boil and cook for 10–12 minutes or until setting point is reached. Remove from the heat.

5. Allow to cool for a few minutes. Then pour into sterilized jars and cover while still hot.

INGREDIENTS

3½ lb/1½ kilos redcurrants
4 cloves
A blade of mace
3 cinnamon sticks
1 teaspoon cinnamon
2 pints/1200ml water
6 fl oz/175ml malt vinegar
3 lb/1350g granulated sugar

Jams, Pickles, Preserves, and Sweets

Spiced Apricots

VICTORIAN — 1866

This is a really lovely recipe; not only does it taste good but it is so pretty. It was used throughout the Victorian age.

INGREDIENTS

2 lb/900g fresh apricots, washed
8 oz/225g sugar
¼ pint/150ml dry white wine
¼ pint/150ml white wine vinegar
6-8 cloves
1 stick cinnamon
2-3 peppercorns

1. Make sure that the fruit you use is perfect and has no bruises or blemishes.

2. Put the sugar, wine, vinegar, spices and peppercorns into a pan over a low heat.

3. Add the fruit and cook until just tender, 8–10 minutes.

4. Strain the fruit and put into clean jam jars.

5. Bring the cooking liquid to the boil and cook until you have a thick syrup. Allow to cool for a few moments, then pour over the fruit.

6. Add the cloves and cinnamon from the cooking liquid to the fruit in the jars. Seal and store for at least 3 weeks before using.

Samphire or St Peter's Grass

Wash the samphire in clean cold water, cut off any bits of root or dry looking stalk, break into 3–4-inch lengths and put into a colander or steamer over a pan of boiling water. Cook for 8–14 minutes until just tender. It is best to taste a piece to make sure you don't over-cook it. Serve with butter and pepper as a dish on its own, with a fork.

Samphire Sauce

Based on a sixteenth century recipe.

Cook the samphire as above until just tender. Put into a food processor and blend until you have a thick purée. Add a little butter to the purée and re-heat when required. Serve with steamed or poached fish.

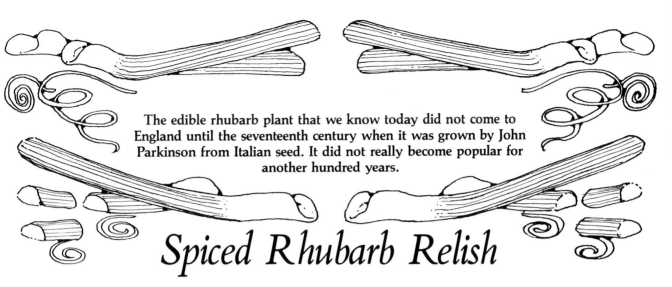

The edible rhubarb plant that we know today did not come to England until the seventeenth century when it was grown by John Parkinson from Italian seed. It did not really become popular for another hundred years.

Spiced Rhubarb Relish

This makes a lovely relish to serve with cheese and egg dishes. This particular version is adapted from a cookery notebook dated 1812.

1. Put the rhubarb into a china or earthenware bowl in layers, sprinkling each layer with sugar. Set to one side.

2. Put the vinegar and spices into a pan and bring to the boil. Simmer for 5–8 minutes, pour over the rhubarb and sugar and leave to stand fro 24 hours.

3. Drain off the liquid. Reboil and pour over the fruit for the second time. Leave for a further 24 hours.

4. Put into a pan and bring to the boil. Remove from the heat, and allow to cool. When quite cold, put into jars and seal. Store in the refrigerator.

INGREDIENTS

2 lb/1kg rhubarb, washed trimmed and cut into 1 inch lengths

8 oz/225g Muscovado sugar

2 pints/1200ml white malt vinegar

1 stick cinnamon

1 teaspoon ground cinnamon

½ teaspoon fresh grated ginger

Rowan and Apple Jelly

1850

INGREDIENTS

2 pints/1200ml water
Peel of 1 lemon
2 cinnamon sticks
3 lb/1350g apples, peeled, cored
and cut into slices
3 lb/1350g rowan berries
2½ lb/1125g soft brown sugar

1. Put the water, peel, cinnamon sticks and apples into a large pan and bring to the boil. Simmer for 15–20 minutes until the fruit is soft.

2. Add the rowan berries and continue to cook for a further 15–20 minutes. Remove from the heat.

3. Strain the fruit and liquid through a jelly bag, squeezing well.

4. Return the strained fruit juice to the pan and heat. Then add the sugar, stirring well to make sure it is all dissolved.

5. Boil the juice and sugar for 10–15 minutes, skimming the froth off the top as it appears. Remove from the heat.

6. Pass through a strainer and pour into sterilized jars. Cover and keep until required.

Under the Influence of Bright Sunbeams

Matilda's Spiced Prunes

TWENTIETH CENTURY

This preserve is really delicious. A nice variation is to remove the stones of 5 or 6 spiced prunes before dishing up the meal, and mash the flesh with 3 oz/75g cream cheese, season with a little salt and lemon juice and serve with oatmeal biscuits.

1. Put the prunes to soak in a strong brew of China tea and leave overnight.

2. Put the fruit into a pan with 1 pint/600ml of the liquid they soaked in. Bring to the boil and simmer for 10–15 minutes.

3. Put the vinegar and wine into a pan with the honey, sugar, spices, lemon juice and crushed cloves. Bring to the boil and simmer for 8–10 minutes. Add the liquid from the prunes and boil for a further 6–8 minutes. Allow to cool.

4. Put prunes into warmed glass jars, cover with liquid and store in a cool dark place.

INGREDIENTS

1 lb/450g dried prunes
2 pints/1200ml cold China tea
½ pint/300ml wine vinegar
½ pint/300ml red wine
3 tablespoons honey
4 oz/100g brown sugar
1 cinnamon stick
1 teaspoon ground nutmeg
1 teaspoon ground ginger
½ teaspoon black pepper
1 tablespoon lemon juice
8 cloves, crushed

Avila Fudge

NINETEENTH CENTURY

This recipe was brought to England by a traveller during the early 1800s.

1. Put the sugar into a pan with the lemon zest and juice over a low heat and stir until all the sugar has dissolved. Add the nuts and essences. Cook for 3–5 minutes.

2. Grease a shallow baking tin with butter or olive oil. Pour in the mixture and leave to set.

3. After about 10–15 minutes, divide the fudge into sections with a sharp knife. Allow to set completely.

4. Wrap in greaseproof paper and store in an air-tight tin.

INGREDIENTS

1 lb/450g brown sugar
Zest and juice of 1 lemon
1 lb/450g flaked almonds
1 teaspoon orange essence
2 teaspoons almond essence

Orange-Flavoured Marron Glacés

GILL LYALL'S RECIPE — 1950

Nearly every year I used to help my mother make Marron Glacés. This is the most delicious tasting sweet. The addition of orange to the chestnuts takes away the over-sweet taste.

2 lb/1 kilo chestnuts
1 lb/450g granulated sugar
1 lb/450g powdered glucose, dissolved in ¾ pint/450ml water
1 tablespoon orange flower water
4 tablespoons orange zest
1 lb/450g additional sugar

To prepare the chestnuts:

1. Cut off the pointed end of each chestnut with a sharp knife.

2. Put the chestnuts into the oven on a baking tray at 400°F, 200°C, Gas Mark 6 for 8–10 minutes.

3. Do not allow the nuts to overcook. As soon as you are able to handle the nuts, cut through the skin with a sharp knife and remove both the outer and inner skin which should now come off easily.

First Day:

1. Put the chestnuts into a pan of water and bring to the boil. Simmer very gently for 18–22 minutes until the chestnuts are tender but still whole. Drain and set to one side.

2. Put the sugar and ¾ pint/450ml glucose water into a pan with the orange flower water and 3 tablespoons of orange zest.

3. Heat the sugar and glucose until all the sugar has dissolved. Bring to the boil.

4. Drop the chestnuts into the boiling sugar and leave on the heat until the syrup comes to the boil again. Remove from the heat and set to one side until the next day.

Second Day:

1. Bring the chestnuts and syrup to the boil over a low heat. Boil for 1–2 minutes. Remove from the heat and set to one side until the next day.

Third Day:

1. Add 1 tablespoon orange zest to the chestnuts and sugar syrup.

2. Put the chestnuts and syrup onto the heat and bring to the boil. Simmer for 2–3 minutes. Remove from the heat.

3. Lift the chestnuts from the syrup with a draining spoon. Arrange over wire racks to drain.

4. Add the remaining sugar to the pan of syrup together with ¼ pint/150ml water.

5. Return to the heat and bring slowly to the boil stirring all the time to make sure all the sugar dissolves. Return the chestnuts to the syrup for 2–3 minutes. Lift them from the syrup a few at a time and arrange on the rack again.

6. Stand the rack in a cool oven (250°F, 120°C, Gas Mark ½) for 25–30 minutes. Dip the chestnuts into the cooling syrup and return to the oven for 1–2 hours. Turn them over and allow to dry for 1 more hour.

7. When the marrons are dry, wrap each one up individually in a small square of grease proof paper and then a square of foil. Store in an airtight box or jar.

These make lovely Christmas presents as they will keep well in an air tight container for many months.

A serving suggestion is to serve them on their own with whipped cream or to put a few into individual dishes, pour 1 tablespoon brandy over each dish and then a little sugar syrup. Leave for 1 hour before serving with whipped cream.

Hereford Snaps

NINETEENTH CENTURY

Traditionally sold at Hereford's May Fair.

INGREDIENTS

8 oz/225g butter
4 oz/100g brown sugar
1 tablespoon golden syrup
2 teaspoons lemon juice
1 teaspoon ground ginger
4 oz/100g flour

1. Put the butter, sugar and syrup into a pan with the lemon juice and ground ginger. Heat gently until all the butter has melted stirring constantly. Remove from the heat and set to one side to cool.

2. Mix the flour into the mixture and beat for 2–3 minutes until it is well blended.

3. Drop teaspoonfuls of the mixture onto a well-greased baking sheet, leaving about 4 inches/10cm between each, as the mixture will spread.

4. Cook in an oven at 375°F, 190°C, Gas Mark 5 for 10–12 minutes or until a golden brown. Remove from the oven and cool for 1–2 minutes. Roll the snaps round a wooden spoon handle and then put onto a rack to finish cooling. Fill with a custard cream or whipped cream. Serve with ice cream.

Almond Halva

INGREDIENTS

4 oz/100g butter
4 oz/100g ground almonds
4 oz/100g ground hazel-nuts
¼ pint/150ml cold water
4 oz/100g castor sugar
¼ teaspoon ground saffron
4 tablespoons rosewater
1 tablespoon vanilla essence

1. Melt the butter in a pan over a low heat. Stir in the ground almonds and hazel-nuts, making sure there are no lumps. Remove from the heat and set to one side.

2. Put the water and sugar in a pan, bring to the boil and cook until all the sugar is dissolved.

3. Stir the syrup into the nuts and beat for 3–4 minutes. Pour onto a lightly-greased plate. Cool, cut into pieces and serve.

Under the Influence of Bright Sunbeams

Toffee has always been one of the most popular English sweets. So great was its popularity during the 1800s that toffee enthusiasts throughout Britain formed local toffee clubs, each trying to out-do the other.

Bonfire Toffee

As a child, one of the English traditions that I loved was bonfire night. The first bonfire night that I remember was in Sussex with my maternal grandparents; my grandfather, who was by then well into his eighties, sitting in a chair with a tartan rug over his knees and a large whisky in one hand and a toffee apple in the other, chanting 'Please to remember the 5th of November, Gunpowder, Treason and Plot'; my grandmother, who was at that time always knitting socks, busily feeding the bonfire. A ball of wool had fallen out of her pocket and was making the whole area like a vast cat's-cradle; and sparklers — we did not have fireworks as they frightened the cats.

Then there was toffee, and potatoes in their jackets, and lovely dark moist gingerbread, and over all the smell of wood smoke and grandmother's Hyacinth perfume and good malt whisky.

INGREDIENTS

14 oz/395g raw cane sugar
1 lb/455g molasses
4 oz/115g butter
1 tablespoon vanilla essence
2 tablespoons vinegar

1. Put the sugar, treacle, butter, and vanilla essence into a large heavy pan and melt very gently, add the vinegar and stir.

2. Bring to the boil and cook for 18-20 minutes stirring continuously.

3. Test by dropping a few drops of the mixture into a cup of cold water. If the toffee hardens at once without clouding the water then it is ready, if not then cook for a further 4–6 minutes.

4. Grease a shallow heat-proof dish and pour in the toffee. Grease both hands and 'pull' the toffee into long strings before it cools. Cut the strings into short lengths before the toffee is quite set.

You can vary the recipe by adding a few drops of peppermint essence.

9.
Pastry

Shortcrust Pastry

Rich Lining

8 oz/225g butter
11 oz/325g plain white flour
2 teaspoons brown sugar
1½ teaspoons sea salt
3 tablespoons very cold water
1 small egg, beaten

This quantity makes enough for 2×8-9 inch/20-23cm pastry shells for tarts and open flans. To make larger amounts just double the quantity. It is not a good idea to make more than twice this amount at once as it is too large an amount to handle quickly.

For a fragrant and tasty variation, substitute 1 tablespoon orange flower water for 1 tablespoon plain water and add the grated zest of 1 orange.

1. Take the butter out of the fridge or larder and leave at room temperature until it is easily worked but not too soft.

2. Cut the butter into walnut-sized pieces.

3. Sift the flour, sugar and salt onto a pastry board. Add the butter and mix together so that the butter becomes coated in flour. Then work by hand pinching the pieces of butter and flour with your fingertips. Work as quickly as you can so that the butter does not get warm.

4. When the butter is worked in, pile the mixture into a mound. Make a well in the centre and pour in the cold water and beaten egg. Stir them into the flour, mix well and work the mixture with the heel of your hand. As soon as the dough ceases to be crumbly, stop.

5. If the dough is too dry and crumbly, add a further ½–1 teaspoon water. If too wet, just dust with a little more flour. Continue to work the dough for a further 2–3 minutes until smooth.

6. Roll the dough into a ball and divide into the number of portions you want. Cut small tarts from one piece of pastry.

7. Pat each piece lightly into shape. Wrap in greaseproof paper and chill in the refrigerator for 1–2 hours. The pastry will keep for 2–3 days in the fridge.

Under the Influence of Bright Sunbeams

Alternatively, when wrapped in foil it will keep in the freezer for 2–3 months. Defrost overnight in the fridge before using.

If you want to use a food processor, do not process much at a time as it is better to divide the ingredients in half and process in two batches.

1. Use the steel blade of your processor.

2. Sift the flour, sugar and salt in the processor bowl.

3. Add the butter cut into walnut-sized pieces.

4. Process just long enough for the mixture to resemble very fine breadcrumbs.

5. With the food processor running, pour the egg and water into the bowl through the feed tube. Process until the pastry dough starts to form a ball on the top of the blade. Stop instantly.

Spiced Hot Water Crust for Raised Pies

INGREDIENTS

6 oz/175g lard
¼ pint/150ml water
1 lb/450g plain flour
½ teaspoon sea salt
1 clove garlic, crushed
½ teaspoon mixed spices
1 egg yolk, beaten
Beaten egg, to glaze
Jellied Stock (see next recipe)

1. Cut the lard into small pieces and put them in a pan with the water and bring to the boil.

2. Put the flour, salt, garlic and spices into a large bowl.

3. Make a well in the centre. When the water and lard come to the boil, remove from the heat and pour into the middle of the flour. Add the egg yolk and mix everything together with a wooden spoon.

4. Let the dough cool just enough so as not to burn your hands. Put ¾ of the dough into the pie tin and work the dough up the sides, making sure that all areas are covered.

5. Fill the case with the filling of your choice.

6. Roll out the remainder of the pastry for the lid and place the lid on the case, making sure that the edges are well sealed.

7. Decorate with strips of pastry cut into leaves and flowers.

8. Glaze with beaten egg and put into the oven at 400°F, 200°C, Gas Mark 6 until the pastry is set, then lower the temperature and cook for 1½–2 hours at 325°F, 160°C, Gas Mark 3. If the top of the pie looks as if it is getting over cooked, then cover with a piece of tin foil.

9. When the pie is cooked, take it out of the oven and remove it from the mould with care. Brush the sides with beaten egg and put into the oven for a further ten minutes.

10. When the pie has cooled for 5 minutes or so, cut a small hole in the centre and pour in the jellied stock (see next recipe). Put into a cool place and leave for 24 hours. Serve with fresh bread and pickles and a green salad.

Jellied Stock

1. Mix the arrowroot and wine together until the arrowroot is dissolved.

2. Put the redcurrant jelly into a small pan and warm over a low heat, gradually add the wine and arrowroot mixture. Add bay leaf and seasonings and continue to cook until the mixture starts to thicken. Remove from heat and set to one side. Warm slightly just before using, discard bay leaf.

INGREDIENTS

2 teaspoons arrowroot
¼ pint/150ml dry white wine
or sherry
4 tablespoons redcurrant jelly
1 bay leaf
A pinch of paprika
¼ teaspoon sea salt
¼ teaspoon black pepper

Nutty Cold Water Crust for Raised Pies

VICTORIAN — 1862

1. Mix the flour, salt, nuts and ginger together in a bowl.

2. Make a hollow in the centre. Put the softened butter in, then the wine and water and work the mixture until you have a firm paste.

3. Line a deep pie tin and work the mixture up the sides reserving enough paste for the lid and any decoration. Fill with your choice of ingredients, put the lid on the pie and decorate with the remaining pastry.

4. Cook in the oven for 1-1½ hours at 340°F, 170°C, Gas Mark 5. You can cook for longer if you wish for a firmer crust.

INGREDIENTS

1 lb/450g wholemeal flour
1 teaspoon sea salt
2 oz/50g ground hazel-nuts
½ teaspoon ground ginger
4 oz/100g butter, softened
6 tablespoons red wine
½ pint/300ml cold water

Easy Puff Pastry

1 teaspoon sea salt
9–10 tablespoons cold water
2 tablespoons butter, just melted
12 oz/350g flour
8 oz/225g very cold butter, cut into small pieces

1. Mix the salt and cold water together and stir into the melted butter.

2. Sift the flour onto a board. Make a small well in the middle.

3. Add the cold butter and coat it in flour.

4. Pour the liquids onto the centre. Mix the flour, butter and liquid together into a loose dough without breaking the butter pieces down.

5. Pat the dough into a rectangular shape, sprinkle with a little flour and roll out to about 16 inches/40cm long and 5 inches/12cm wide. Make sure that your rolling pin is well floured. You will also have to scrape the pastry off the board and dust the board with flour.

6. When you have rolled out the pastry, fold it over like a letter. This will give you three layers. Wrap in greaseproof paper and put into the fridge for 1 hour.

7. Remove the greaseproof paper. Roll the pastry out again and fold as before. This will give you 9 layers.

8. Repeat the process 4 more times putting the pastry into the fridge between each rolling and chill for 1 hour before using.

You can freeze this pastry but you must leave it to defrost overnight before using.

Under the Influence of Bright Sunbeams

To Cover a Fish in Pastry

1. Put a sheet of greaseproof paper or bakewell onto a large board.

2. Roll out your pastry on the paper into the shape of an oval.

3. Allow 2 inches/5cm of extra pastry at each end of the fish.

4. Measure your fish round the widest part with a piece of string or a strip of paper, making sure that the pastry oval is at least 2 inches/5cm wider than the fish. This will allow you to fold the pastry over and seal along the join.

5. Place your fish carefully on the pastry.

6. Fold the pastry over, damping the edges with a little water to seal the join. Make sure the pastry follows the shape of the fish. Reserve any left over pastry.

To make the scales:

7. Roll out the remaining pastry, then using a small pastry cutter or an apple corer, cut out a series of small circles.

8. Brush the fish with a little beaten egg and starting at the tail, press the pastry scales onto the fish in overlapping rows.

9. Cut out the fins and gills. Press them into place. Stick a clove in place for the eye. Brush with beaten egg and put into the oven at 350°F, 180°C, Gas Mark 4 for 25–30 minutes. For a large fish, such as a large trout, allow 11–15 minutes longer.

10. When the fish is cooked, transfer carefully onto a serving dish or board and garnish round the edges with very finely shredded lettuce or green cabbage to form the 'sea', fresh herbs and slices of lemon.

INGREDIENTS

1 amount of Easy Puff Pastry
(see opposite)
Fish of your choice

10.
Breads, Pastries and Cakes

Gingerbread was a favourite sweetmeat from Medieval times onwards. At first, the amount of spices made it very costly. There are records of it being imported from the Netherlands in the thirteenth century in quite large amounts. In 1265 the Countess of Leicester paid over 12 shillings for a box weighing 4 pounds, an enormous sum of money for the day. The cakes themselves were very different from the gingerbread we know today; they were made of very dark, hard paste, often formed into the shapes of heroes and villains of the day. The cakes were glazed with egg white which gave them a high, rich polish, and then gilded with gold leaf. These rich and extravagant figures made beautiful presents and keepsakes. At St Bartholomew's Fair, held at Smithfield from the twelfth century, the gingerbread stall held pride of place and was the last to go after 700 years of trading.

I have adapted the following recipe from a very early cookbook, which was certainly used late into Elizabeth's reign and is well worth trying.

Gingerbread

INGREDIENTS

1¼ lb/550g honey
¼ teaspoon ground saffron
½ teaspoon ground black pepper
2 lb/900g breadcrumbs
3 teaspoons ground cinnamon
2 teaspoons ground ginger

For decoration:
16 bay leaves or box leaves
20 cloves, gilded with gold leaf or gold paint

1. Put the honey into a pan together with the saffron and pepper.

2. Bring to the boil. Remove from the heat and stir in the breadcrumbs and ginger. Beat well until you have a thick paste.

3. Return to the heat and simmer on the lowest heat for about 20–25 minutes stirring constantly.

4. When the paste has dried out, spoon the mixture into a shallow dish, sprinkle with cinnamon and decorate with bay leaves placed in groups of threes to form trefoils.

5. Use the cloves as pins to hold the bay leaves to the gingerbread. Put the remaining 4 cloves in the centre as decoration.

6. Put into a cool place and allow to set for 2–3 days. Cut into small slices.

200   Under the Influence of Bright Sunbeams

Clockwise from the top: Brandied or Spiced Peaches (page 175), Avilla Fudge (page 185), Candied Primroses (page 174) and Almond Halva (page 188).

Numb. 21909.

SUPPLEMENT
TO

The London Gazette

Of FRIDAY the 1st of AUGUST.

Published by Authority.

MONDAY, AUGUST 4, 1856.

An Early Victorian Meal. Clockwise from the top: Peach Upside Down Cake (page 134), Napoleon's Salad (page 95), Mussels with Coriander (page 33) and Savoury Shortbread (page 29).

*From the top: King's Cake (page 208)
and Pilgrim Cakes (page 201).*

Pilgrim Cakes

ST JAMES' CAKES FROM WALES

These little shortbread cakes are a speciality of a small village in Anglesey called Aberffan. They were traditionally moulded in a scallop shell which was the badge of the pilgrims on their way to the Shrine of Santiago de Compostela in Galicia.

1. Mix the flour, sugar and butter together in a bowl and work the mixture until you have a smooth firm dough.

2. If you have a small scallop shell handy, divide the mixture up into small balls and press each one into the shell to form a thin cake or biscuit.

3. Put these biscuits onto a well-greased baking sheet and cook in the oven at 400°F, 200°C, Gas Mark 6 for 8–12 minutes.

4. Remove from the oven and cool on a rack. Top with whipped cream to serve.

INGREDIENTS

6 oz/175g flour
2 oz/50g sugar
4 oz/100g butter, softened

'Knot' or 'Jumble' Cookies

This type of biscuit formed an essential part of any celebration during the seventeenth century. Funerals, christenings and weddings were all occasions to hand round these little treats. They were a traditional 'thank you' present to your hosts after the event. In some parts of Europe, the custom still persists. A small parcel containing two or three biscuits, wrapped in paper and tied with ribbon, is left at the door of your hosts the next day. Everyone expects them and is looking out, to whip them in doors and out of the way of any passing ants, as soon as the donor is out of sight! The prettiest form is 'knots' or 'jumbles' and this recipe dates from about 1660.

1. Pre-heat the oven to 350°F, 180°C, Gas Mark 4. Put the butter, sugar and rose-water into a bowl or food processor and beat until creamy.

2. Add the egg yolks and egg white and beat.

3. Put the caraway and anise seeds into a mortar and bruise. Add to the mixture.

4. Sift in the flour and mace and mix to make a firm dough. Put onto a floured board and knead.

5. Form the dough into long rolls about ½ inch (1.5cm) thick and twist them into knots. Place on a well-greased baking sheet and bake for 15–18 minutes.

6. Remove from the baking sheet and put onto a rack to cool.

If you don't like the taste of the seeds, you can either leave them out or substitute very finely chopped nuts.

Charles I's Portuguese wife, Catherine of Braganza, introduced the habit of taking tea from her native Portugal, where the ladies of the Court were accustomed to meeting for a cup of tisane or tea after the hour of the siesta. Also, I suspect it was a very good opportunity to exchange gossip and plan intrigue.

The idea caught on. Anyone who could afford to, took tea and served a selection of little biscuits and rich cakes. A huge number of recipes of all kinds of rich spicy confections date from this period, as each hostess tried to out-do her neighbour.

Carrot Cake

SEVENTEENTH CENTURY

This is a very old recipe from the Balkans.

1. Pre-heat the oven to 375°F, 190°C, Gas Mark 5. Combine the sugar, butter and egg yolks together in a large bowl.

2. Add the carrot purée, lemon juice and zest to the egg yolks and beat well.

3. Mix the cinnamon, hazel-nuts, baking powder, flour and breadcrumbs together and add to the carrot purée.

4. Fold the egg whites into the carrot and hazel-nut mixture.

5. Grease a 9 inch flancase and pour in the cake mixture.

6. Put into a pre-heated oven and cook for 25–30 minutes or until cooked.

7. Remove cake from the oven. Allow to cool and serve with whipped cream.

INGREDIENTS

6 oz/175g castor sugar

3 tablespoons butter

6 egg yolks

6 oz/175g pre-cooked carrots, puréed

Juice of 1 lemon

Zest of 1 lemon

1 teaspoon ground cinnamon

3 oz/75g ground hazel-nuts

½ teaspoon baking powder

3 oz/75g flour

3 oz/75g wholemeal breadcrumbs

6 egg whites, beaten until stiff

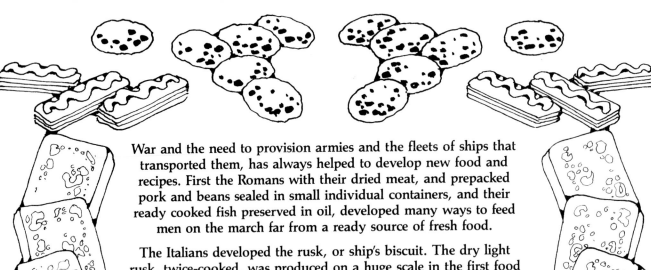

War and the need to provision armies and the fleets of ships that transported them, has always helped to develop new food and recipes. First the Romans with their dried meat, and prepacked pork and beans sealed in small individual containers, and their ready cooked fish preserved in oil, developed many ways to feed men on the march far from a ready source of fresh food.

The Italians developed the rusk, or ship's biscuit. The dry light rusk, twice-cooked, was produced on a huge scale in the first food factories, to feed the Italian fleet.

Biscuits caught on, and rather than just a dry rusk, true biscuits of better quality became part of standard banquet food.

Walnut and Almond Biscuits

Nan-Gerdooi from Persia

This is a very useful recipe as it does not require fat or flour. The biscuits are delicious on their own or served with ice cream or any cream pudding.

INGREDIENTS

5 egg yolks
4 oz/100g sugar
½ teaspoon orange essence
½ teaspoon vanilla essence
2 oz/50g chopped walnuts
3 tablespoons chopped or slivered almonds
4 oz/100g ground almonds or hazel-nuts
Rind of 1 orange, finely grated

This recipe makes about 20 biscuits

1. Put the egg yolks, sugar, orange and vanilla essences into a bowl and beat until creamy.

2. Add the chopped nuts, ground almonds and orange rind.

3. Line a baking sheet with greaseproof paper and spoon the mixture in about 20 rounds onto the baking sheet.

4. Sprinkle the biscuits with chopped nuts and put into the oven at 300°F, 150°C, Gas Mark 2 for 18–20 minutes or until just golden.

Under the Influence of Bright Sunbeams

Guernsey Apple Flavoured Cake

Guernsey Gâche Mêlée

This is a traditional apple cake from about 1750.

1. Put the apple into a bowl. Sprinkle with brandy and a little cinnamon and leave for 8–10 minutes. Add the flour. Mix well together, cover and leave overnight.

2. Next day, cream the butter and sugar together, add the eggs one at a time and then the nutmeg and orange zest. Add to the apple and flour mixture and continue to beat until creamy.

3. Grease an 11×7 inch/27×18cm shallow cake tin, pour in the cake mixture and put into the oven at 300°F, 150°C, Gas Mark 2 for about 1 hour.

4. Remove from the oven, leave in the tin until cool, then turn out onto a wire rack. Decorate with a few pieces of crystallized fruit, if desired.

INGREDIENTS

1 lb/450g cooking apples, cored and cut into small pieces
3 tablespoons brandy
2 teaspoons cinnamon
1 lb/450g wholemeal flour
½ lb/225g butter
1 lb/450g dark brown sugar
3 eggs
1½ teaspoons ground nutmeg
1 teaspoon grated orange zest
A few pieces of crystallized fruit to decorate (optional)

Tipsy Cake

This is a traditional English cake dating from the eighteenth century. This particular version is from near Cambridge in East Anglia and dates from 1770.

INGREDIENTS

5 oz/150g unsalted butter

6 oz/175g castor sugar

2 eggs, beaten

5 oz/150g flour

½ pint/300ml sweet sherry or port

3 tablespoons brandy

½ pint/300ml double cream, whipped until stiff

3 oz/75g toasted almonds

1. Put 5 oz/150g of butter into a bowl with an equal quantity of sugar and beat until creamy. Add the eggs and beat.

2. Sift the flour in gradually and then add 1 tablespoon sherry; continue to beat for 2–3 minutes.

3. Grease an 8 inch cake tin and pour in the cake mixture. Put into a pre-heated oven at 400°F, 200°C, Gas Mark 6 for 35–40 minutes.

4. When cooked, remove from the oven and allow to stand for 5–10 minutes before turning out.

5. When the cake is cold cut into small cubes and put into a glass bowl.

6. Mix the brandy, remaining sugar and sherry together, pour over the cake and leave to stand. Just before serving spoon the whipped cream on top of the cake, sprinkle with toasted almonds and serve.

Under the Influence of Bright Sunbeams

Chelsea Buns

This recipe is especially for my husband who judges a town by its bakers and especially by the quality of its Chelsea Buns.

Richard Hand opened his Chelsea Bun House in the late 1780s. The fame of his delicious hot, spicy buns, bursting with fruit, with hot sugar on top, soon took London by storm.

Mr Hand, as many good cooks were and are, was eccentric; he always dressed in a fez and a dressing gown and was referred to by all as Captain Bun.

1. Sieve the flour, salt and spices together.

2. Mix the yeast with 1 teaspoon sugar and the milk and water mixture and mix until frothy.

3. Mix the fruit with the remaining sugar.

4. Add the yeast mixture, half the flour and mix well. Set to one side to rise.

5. Mix the butter or lard into the remaining half of the flour. Add the egg and fruit and beat well.

6. When the yeast mixture has risen well, mix into the fruit. Beat the two mixtures together and set to one side in a warm place to rise.

7. When the dough has doubled in volume, put onto a well-floured board and knead lightly.

8. Roll out into an oblong strip about ¼ inch thick, sprinkle with sugar and brush with a little melted butter. Roll the strip up as for a Swiss roll. Cut into 10–12 slices. Put onto a well-greased baking sheet and allow to stand for 10–15 minutes.

9. Glaze with melted golden syrup.

10. Put into the oven at 400°F, 200°C, Gas Mark 6 for 15–20 minutes.

INGREDIENTS

14 oz/400g flour
Pinch sea salt
1 teaspoon cinnamon
½ teaspoon ground nutmeg
1½ oz/40g fresh baker's yeast
4 tablespoons warm milk and water
3 oz/75g Demerara sugar
3 oz/75g currants
3 oz/75g sultanas
1½ oz/40g butter or lard
2 small eggs or 1 very large
1 tablespoon melted butter, to glaze
1 tablespoon melted golden syrup

King's Cake

Bolo Rei

A Lusitanian New Year cake; from an eighteenth century recipe that is used all the year round!

INGREDIENTS

¼ oz/6g fresh yeast
10 oz/275g self-raising flour
2 tablespoons milk
¼ teaspoon sea salt
3 oz/75g sugar
3 eggs, beaten
2 oz/50g butter
1½ oz/40g glacé cherries
1½ oz/40g chopped almonds
1½ oz/40g pine kernels
1 oz/25g walnuts
1½ oz/40g raisins
1½ oz/40g chopped dates
Beaten egg, to glaze

1. Dissolve the yeast in a small amount of warm water and place in a warmed bowl.

2. Mix with 3 oz/75g of flour and enough water to make a dough. Cover and put in a warm place to rise for 20 minutes.

3. Warm the milk, add salt, and add to the dough, combining the rest of the flour, sugar and eggs. Beat the mixture, slowly adding the butter.

4. Place on a floured board or slab and knead well.

5. Put into a large bowl and leave in a warm place for 2–3 hours until it has doubled its bulk.

6. Knead again, adding cherries, nuts, raisins and dates. Allow to stand for 10–12 minutes.

7. Grease a large baking sheet or tin. Form the mixture into a rough circle and place a jam jar in the centre to keep it open while it rises.

8. Glaze the top with well-beaten egg yolk and decorate with nuts, sugar and fruit. Place in the centre of a medium oven at 325°F, 160°C, Gas Mark 3 for 25–30 minutes. Remove and place on a wire rack to cool.

This is a traditional cake which is eaten throughout the country on Twelfth Night. It is circular in form to represent the crowns of the three kings. Inside are hidden small trinkets and holy medals, and one dry broad bean to bring luck throughout the year.

Under the Influence of Bright Sunbeams

Potato Loaves

Maria Eliza Rundell
A New System of Domestic Cookery — 1806

This is a very tasty recipe and is delicious served as a tea bread or with hot soup, making it a meal in itself.

1. Boil the potatoes until just soft. Mash them up with the butter and enough of the milk to be able to pass them through a colander.

2. Place in a large mixing bowl. Combine the yeast with a little of the water and allow to stand for 15 minutes in a warm place. Mix the yeast into the potato mixture.

3. Gradually add the flour, salt and milk. Knead the mixture well until you have a light, springy dough. If the dough feels too heavy, add a little more milk or water.

4. Cover the dish and stand in a warm place to rise for 1½-2 hours. Then work the mixture well and form into small loaves or rolls.

5. Place on a greased baking tray and cook in a pre-heated oven at 375°F, 190°C, Gas Mark 5 for 30–35 minutes or until well risen.

6. Allow to cool and serve buttered.

INGREDIENTS

1 lb/450g potatoes
2 oz/50g butter
½ pint/300ml milk
½ oz/12g yeast
3 fl oz/90ml warm water
1½ lb/675g plain bread flour
½ teaspoon rock salt

Anglesey Fruit Cake

1850

This is a lovely variation of the normal rich fruit cake. The thin icing glaze ensures that it retains all its moisture and flavour over a long period of time.

2 teaspoons cinnamon
2 teaspoons mixed spice
1 lb/900g flour
8 oz/225g butter
8 oz/225g dark brown sugar
4 eggs, beaten
4 oz/100g raisins
4 oz/100g currants
4 oz/100g sultanas
10 oz/275g cut mixed peel
3 oz/75g chopped almonds
3 oz/75g chopped walnuts
2 teaspoons almond essence
3 fl oz/90ml brandy
2 teaspoons baking powder
2 teaspoons bicarbonate of soda
mixed with 1 tablespoon lemon
juice and 1 tablespoon water

For the Iced Coating:
6 oz/175g icing sugar
2 tablespoons hot water
1 tablespoon brandy

1. Mix the spices into the flour.

2. Cream the butter and sugar together. Add the beaten eggs.

3. Fold in the flour and spices, and add the fruit and nuts.

4. Mix the almond essence with the brandy, add to the mixture and mix very well.

5. Last of all add the baking powder and bicarbonate of soda and stir carefully so that it is well absorbed.

6. Grease and line an 8 inch cake tin with greaseproof paper. Put into the oven at 325°F, 160°C, Gas Mark 3 for 3–3½ hours.

7. When the cake is cooked, remove from the tin and stand on a rack to cool.

For the iced coating:

1. Mix the icing sugar, water and brandy together. Coat the cake all over with a thin coating of icing not forgetting the bottom.

2. Allow to dry, put into a tin and store in a cool place.

Lavender and Rosemary Scones

SEVENTEENTH CENTURY

1. Sieve the salt, flour and baking powder into a large bowl.

2. Make a well in the centre.

3. Mix the butter, eggs, herbs and milk together. Pour into the well and mix well until you have a soft springy dough. Roll the dough in the chopped nuts.

4. Divide the dough into 15–20 portions and press into shape.

5. Bake on a well-greased baking sheet in the middle of the oven at 400°F, 200°C, Gas Mark 6 for 10–12 minutes.

These scones are very good with butter, or served with soup instead of bread.

INGREDIENTS

Makes 15-20 scones

1 teaspoon sea salt
1 lb/450g flour
2 tablespoons baking powder
2 oz/50g butter or margarine, just melted
2 large eggs, beaten
1 tablespoon very finely chopped rosemary leaves
1 tablespoon very finely chopped lavender leaves
½ pint/300ml milk
4 oz/100g chopped walnuts

Almond Tartlets

1. Pre-heat the oven to 350°F, 180°C, Gas Mark 4. Mix together the sugar, butter, essence and ground nuts until you have a thick cream.

2. Lightly grease 18–20 small tartlet tins.

3. Put 1 teaspoon of mixture into each tin.

4. Put in the oven and cook for 8–10 minutes or until they are a golden brown. Remove from the oven and allow to cool in the tins for 2–3 minutes. Remove from the tins and cool on a wire rack.

5. When the tartlets are cool, fill with a mixture of fruit of your choice and top with whipped cream.

INGREDIENTS

4 oz/100g castor sugar
4 oz/100g butter, softened
1 teaspoon almond essence
4 oz/100g ground almonds or hazel-nuts
Fruit and whipped cream, to garnish.

Granny Pakenham's Apple Purée Cake

INGREDIENTS

8 oz/225g butter
8 oz/225g dark brown sugar
Zest and juice of 1 lemon
¼ pint/150ml thick apple purée
3 eggs
12 oz/350g plain flour
1 teaspoon ground ginger
2 teaspoons powdered cinnamon
2 teaspoons powdered mixed spice
3 oz/75g cut mixed peel
6 oz/175g sultanas
2 oz/50g chopped walnuts
3 oz/75g ground almonds
2 glasses port

1. Cream the butter and sugar together until creamy.

2. Gradually beat in the lemon juice and zest, apple purée, eggs and a little of the flour.

3. Mix the spices into the remaining flour and add mixed peel, sultanas and nuts.

4. Add 1 glass port to the butter and sugar mixture and mix everything together well.

5. Turn the mixture into a well-greased tin (8 inch/20cm round) and bake in the oven at 250°F, 120°C, Gas Mark ½ for 2–3 hours. Cool on a wire rack.

6. When the cake is cool, skewer small holes all over and carefully pour over the second glass of port. Serve with whipped cream or just on its own.

Chocolate and Almond Cake

1880s

The very best of chocolate cakes.

1. Pre-heat the oven to 350°F, 180°C, Gas Mark 4. Mix the rum, almond essence and orange zest together.

2. Break the chocolate into small pieces and put into a bowl with the rum mixture. Put the bowl over a pan of simmering water and melt. Stir until quite smooth. Remove from the heat and set to one side to cool.

3. Put the butter into a bowl with the sugar and beat together until they are very light and fluffy. Beat in the egg yolks one at a time and continue to beat for 2–3 minutes.

4. Add the salt to the egg whites and beat until they are stiff. Add 1 spoonful sugar and continue to beat for 2–3 minutes.

5. Fold half the egg whites into the yolk and sugar mixture, then the other half.

6. Mix ground almonds and flour together and fold in with a spatula.

7. Pour into a well-greased and floured cake tin (8 inch/20cm) and cook in the oven for 30–35 minutes. Cool on a wire rack.

Serve with whipped cream. This is a lovely recipe for a very rich chocolate cake. You can use ground walnuts or hazel-nuts instead of almonds and you can substitute cherry brandy for rum. All are good variations.

INGREDIENTS

3 tablespoons rum or brandy (do not use the essences as they always taste wrong)

2–3 drops almond essence

½ teaspoon orange zest

4 oz/100g bitter chocolate

4 oz/100g unsalted butter, cut into small pieces

4 oz/100g soft brown sugar

3 large eggs, separated

¼ teaspoon sea salt

2 oz/50g flour

3 oz/75g very finely ground almonds

Madeira Cake

FROM GRANNY COMPTON'S COOKERY NOTES 1875–1893

INGREDIENTS

4 oz/100g butter
6 oz/175g sugar
Zest of 1 lemon
4 eggs
6 oz/175g flour
A little sugar
Candied peel, to decorate

1. Cream the butter and sugar together. Add the lemon zest.

2. Separate whites from yolks of eggs and whisk whites until stiff. Beat the egg yolks into the butter cream mixture.

3. Sieve in the flour and fold in the egg whites.

4. Place in a 7 inch/18cm loaf shaped tin and bake in a moderate oven for 30–35 minutes. Then remove from tin and place on a wire rack to cool.

5. Melt a little sugar and glaze the top. Decorate with candied peel.

Grasmere Gingerbread

NINETEENTH CENTURY

INGREDIENTS

4 oz/100g butter
8 oz/225g oatmeal
8 oz/225g dark brown sugar
2 tablespoons black treacle
2 teaspoons ground ginger
½ teaspoon baking powder

One of the main reasons that this recipe has remained so popular is the fact that it is still sold today near what was the cottage of the Wordsworths of Grasmere. Should you be less seriously inclined then you may prefer to think that the 'Wordsmiths of Grasmere' almost certainly would have made it although they may well have called it something else!

1. Melt the butter in a pan.

2. Mix all the other ingredients togehter, put into the melted butter and beat.

3. Press the mixture into a mould or shallow dish and cook in the oven at 350°F, 180°C, Gas Mark 4 for 30–35 minutes or until dry.

Under the Influence of Bright Sunbeams

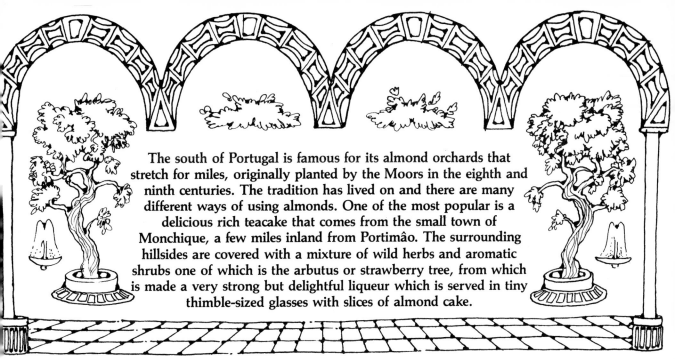

The south of Portugal is famous for its almond orchards that stretch for miles, originally planted by the Moors in the eighth and ninth centuries. The tradition has lived on and there are many different ways of using almonds. One of the most popular is a delicious rich teacake that comes from the small town of Monchique, a few miles inland from Portimâo. The surrounding hillsides are covered with a mixture of wild herbs and aromatic shrubs one of which is the arbutus or strawberry tree, from which is made a very strong but delightful liqueur which is served in tiny thimble-sized glasses with slices of almond cake.

Almond Tea Cake

From Monchique

1. Cream the butter and sugar together until light and creamy. Add the flour and ground almonds and mix well.

2. Add the beaten eggs, lemon zest, saffron and brandy and continue to beat for 3–4 minutes.

3. Grease an 8 inch/20cm cake or bread tin and pour in the cake mixture.

4. Put into a pre-heated oven at 350°F, 180°C, Gas Mark 4 for 35–40 minutes.

INGREDIENTS

8 oz/225g butter
2 oz/50g brown sugar
2 oz/50g flour
5 oz/150g ground almonds
3 eggs, beaten
Zest of 1 lemon
A pinch of powdered saffron
3 fl oz/90ml brandy or arbutus liqueur

Boston Cream Pie

1900 VERSION

This is really a cake! Originally the filling was used in an open pie but later it was incorporated into the cake as a filling.

INGREDIENTS

For the cake:

A pinch sea salt
4 oz/100g plain flour
1½ teaspoons baking powder
4 egg yolks, beaten
3 oz/75g light brown sugar
1 teaspoon vanilla essence
4 egg whites, whipped very stiff

For the filling:

2 tablespoons flour
1 oz/25g castor sugar
A pinch sea salt
A pinch nutmeg
½ pint/300ml cream
2 egg yolks, beaten
1 teaspoon vanilla essence

For the cake:

1. Pre-heat the oven to 375°F, 190°C, Gas Mark 5. Sift the salt, flour and baking powder together.

2. Beat the egg yolks and sugar together in a bowl with the vanilla essence. Stand the bowl over a pan of hot water and continue to beat the egg and sugar mixture until it has nearly doubled in volume and thickened to a pale thick cream.

3. Fold in the beaten egg whites, and last of all the sifted flour.

4. Grease a couple of 7 inch/18cm cake tins and pour half the mixture into each tin.

5. Put into the oven and bake for about 15–20 minutes or until golden and starting to shrink away from the sides of the tins.

6. When cooked, remove from the oven and turn out onto a wire rack to cool.

For the filling:

1. Mix the flour, sugar, salt and nutmeg together in a bowl.

2. Warm the cream in a pan over a low heat. Do not allow to boil. Pour the warmed cream into the flour and sugar stirring all the time so that no lumps form.

3. Add the beaten egg yolks and vanilla essence and stir well.

4. Return to the pan and cook very gently stirring all the time until the mixture has thickened to a creamy purée. Remove from the heat and pour into a bowl. Cover and leave to cool.

Under the Influence of Bright Sunbeams

5. When the mixture has cooled slightly, put into the refrigerator to chill completely.

6. Sandwich the two cakes together with the cream filling and top with the following icing:

For the topping:

1. Melt the chocolate and butter together in a bowl over a pan of hot water. Add the milk and beat until they are well blended. Stir in the vanilla essence and nutmeg and beat for 2–3 minutes. Remove from the heat.

2. Sift in the icing sugar and beat until all the lumps have been removed and the icing is thick and creamy.

3. Leave to cool for a few minutes then spread over the cream filled sandwich. Allow to cool completely before serving.

For the topping:

2½ oz/65g grated plain chocolate
2 oz/50g butter
3 tablespoons milk
2 teaspoons vanilla essence
½ teaspoon grated nutmeg
8 oz/225g icing sugar

Hot Cross Buns

1. Put 2 tablespoons sugar and yeast into a cup with a little warm milk, mix till frothy. Leave to stand for 8–12 minutes.

2. Put the flour into a large bowl. Work the butter in until the mixture is like fine breadcrumbs.

3. Mix the egg, milk, water, sugar and yeast together.

4. Make a well in the centre of the flour, pour in the yeast mixture and knead together until you have a springy dough. Put into a warm place to rise.

5. When the dough has risen, knead again, this time combining the chopped peel, currants, spices and caraway seeds into the dough. Knead well.

6. Divide the dough into about 8 portions; shape each one into a bun and leave to rise for 10–12 minutes. Brush with beaten egg. Put into a pre-heated oven at 400°F, 200°C, Gas Mark 6 for 12–15 minutes or until golden brown. Cool on a wire rack.

INGREDIENTS

2 tablespoons brown sugar
1 oz/25g fresh yeast
½ pint/300ml warm milk
3 lb/1350g flour
8 oz/225g butter or lard
1 beaten egg
1 pint/600ml warm water
8 oz/225g sugar
6 oz/175g candied peel
4 oz/100g currants
1 teaspoon ground nutmeg
1 teaspoon cinnamon
3 teaspoons caraway seeds

Rhubarb and Ginger Tea Cake

1986

This recipe was given to me on holiday by a lady who had heard me bemoaning the lack of interesting rhubarb recipes. Where it originates from I do not know.

INGREDIENTS

2 oz/50g unsalted butter

2 oz/50g dark brown sugar

2 teaspoons ground ginger

1 teaspoon fresh ginger, grated very fine

3 egg yolks, beaten

4 oz/100g black treacle

2 oz/50g candied peel, very finely chopped

2 tablespoons ginger wine or brandy

4 oz/100g wholemeal flour

1 teaspoon bicarbonate of soda

½ lb/225g rhubarb, trimmed and cut into inch lengths

A little icing sugar and a few walnuts.

1. Pre-heat the oven to 325°F, 160°C, Gas Mark 3. Put the butter, sugar and ground and grated ginger into a food processor and blend until very creamy.

2. Blend in the egg yolks, then the treacle, candied peel and ginger wine.

3. Slowly add the flour and bicarbonate of soda. Mix to a thick, moist dough.

4. Grease an 8 inch/20cm loaf tin and put in half the dough, then the rhubarb and top with the remaining dough. Decorate the top with walnuts and put into the oven for 30–35 minutes. Then turn the oven down to 275°F, 140°C, Gas Mark 1 and cook for a further 25–30 minutes or until the cake is firm but not too dry.

5. Remove from the oven and leave for 15–20 minutes. Then pour on a little ginger wine and sprinkle with icing sugar.

Easy Rich Christmas Cake

1860-1870

A family recipe.

1. Wash and dry all the fruit. Sprinkle with brandy and leave to soak overnight.

2. Put the butter, sugar and treacle together in a bowl and cream.

3. Add the remaining dry ingredients to the butter and sugar. Beat in the eggs. Add a little more brandy if the mixture is too dry.

4. Line a large deep cake tin with two thicknesses of greaseproof paper. Allow the paper to stand at least 2 inches higher than the cake tin rim.

5. Spoon the mixture into the tin and put into a pre-heated oven at 325°F, 160°C, Gas Mark 3 for 1½–2 hours, or until a skewer comes away dry.

6. When the cake is cooked, prick the top all over with a fork and pour in 2–3 tablespoons of brandy. Leave to stand.

7. Remove from the tin, wrap in foil and store in a sealed tin. Add a little more brandy every 10 days or so. This cake will keep for up to six months.

INGREDIENTS

8 oz/225g chopped dates
8 oz/225g currants
8 oz/225g stoned raisins
8 oz/225g sultanas
4 oz/100g glacé cherries, chopped
4 tablespoons brandy
8 oz/225g butter
8 oz/225g dark brown sugar
3 tablespoons black treacle
8 oz/225g plain flour
8 oz/225g ground almonds
8 oz/225g chopped walnuts
4 oz/100g candied peel
1 teaspoon ground ginger
2 teaspoons ground cinnamon
½ teaspoon ground cloves
½ teaspoon grated nutmeg
6 eggs, beaten
More brandy, as required

Very Rich Chocolate Cake

Easy to make.

For the cake:
8 oz/225g butter
8 oz/225g dark brown sugar
2 tablespoons very strong black coffee or 1 teaspoon instant coffee powder
2 tablespoons brandy
1 teaspoon rose-water
8 oz/225g self-raising flour
8 oz/225g ground almonds
4 oz/100g cocoa powder
6 eggs, beaten

For the filling:
8 oz/225g icing sugar
8 oz/225g unsalted butter
8 oz/225g plain chocolate
1 teaspoon orange flower water
1 teaspoon rose-water
2 tablespoons Grand Marnier

For the cake:

1. Pre-heat the oven to 350°F, 180°C, Gas Mark 4. Put the butter and sugar together into a food processor or beat by hand until creamy and fluffy.

2. Mix together the coffee, brandy and rose-water. Beat into the butter and sugar.

3. Sift the flour, ground almonds and cocoa together.

4. Add the eggs to the butter and sugar.

5. Gradually add the flour and cocoa. Continue to beat until all the ingredients are well blended.

6. Grease a 10 inch/25cm cake tin and line with greaseproof paper or kitchen parchment.

7. Pour in the mixture, put into the oven and cook for about 55–60 minutes or until the cake has risen slightly in the centre and is firm to the touch.

8. Take the cake out of the oven. Allow to cool for 10–15 minutes. Remove from the tin and put on a wire rack to cool.

For the filling:
The orange flavour water and rosewater give a lovely flavour to the liqueur.

1. Beat the sugar and butter together until light and fluffy.

2. Melt the chocolate and allow to cool. Beat the orange flower water, rose-water and Grand Marnier into the chocolate, making sure the chocolate is quite cool.

3. Beat into the icing sugar and butter. Cover and set to one side until the case has completely cooled.

For the icing:

1. Put the chocolate into a small bowl with the orange juice and melt over a bowl of hot water.

2. Add the icing sugar and beat. Bring to the boil and cook for 3–5 minutes. Stir continuously.

3. Check that the mixture has 'set' by dropping a piece into cold water.

4. When it forms a soft ball, remove from the heat and allow to cool for 1–2 minutes. Stir in the butter and mix well.

To assemble the cake:

1. Slice the cake in half. Sandwich the two portions together with the chocolate filling.

2. Pour the icing over the top. Leave to set for 1–2 hours.

This really rich moist cake will keep very well for a long time if sealed, and will also freeze.

For the icing:
2 oz/50g plain chocolate
2 tablespoons orange juice
3 oz/75g icing sugar
½ oz/12g butter or 1 teaspoon glycerine

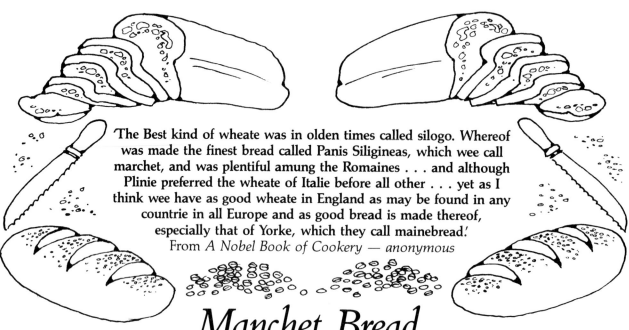

The Best kind of wheate was in olden times called silogo. Whereof was made the finest bread called Panis Siligineas, which wee call marchet, and was plentiful amung the Romaines . . . and although Plinie preferred the wheate of Italie before all other . . . yet as I think wee have as good wheate in England as may be found in any countrie in all Europe and as good bread is made thereof, especially that of Yorke, which they call mainebread.'

From *A Nobel Book of Cookery* — *anonymous*

Manchet Bread

FIFTEENTH CENTURY

From *A Nobel Book of Cookery* — anonymous

INGREDIENTS

1 packet yeast (½ oz/12g)
½ pint/300ml warm water
1 lb/450g wholewheat flour
2 teaspoons sea salt
2 oz/50g softened buter

1. Put the yeast into a small bowl with warm water. Stir to dissolve.

2. Put the flour into a large bowl together with the salt. Make a well in the centre of the flour, pour in the yeast mixture and mix in the buter. Mix well together. Knead for 10–12 minutes, adding more flour if the dough is too wet.

3. Put into a greased bowl and cover with a cloth; put the dough into a warm place and leave to rise for 1½-2 hours, or until it has doubled in size.

4. Knead the dough again for 4–5 minutes, form into round flat loaves and put them onto a greased baking sheet. Cover with a cloth and leave to rise for 40–45 minutes. Just before baking, brush the loaves with beaten egg to give a golden look, and slash across neatly three times, or they can just be pricked with a fork.

5. Put into a pre-heated oven at 375°F, 190°C, Gas Mark 5 for 35–40 minutes.

Kourambiethes

The Greek people are extremely kind and generous. In the little cake shop where I bought these biscuits, in Nauplia, they were only too pleased to give me the recipe when they heard that not only did theirs differ slightly from most of the shortbreads found throughout Greece, but that I was collecting recipes, particularly old ones, and they introduced me to the family and gave me many recipes that had been handed down from mother to daughter for many generations.

INGREDIENTS

8 oz/225g softened butter
8 oz/225g castor sugar
½ teaspoon ground saffron
2 egg yolks
1 tablespoon ouzo
6 oz/150g coarsely ground almonds
3 oz/75g cornflour
9 oz/250g plain white flour
Orange flower water and icing sugar

This recipe can be done by hand or by food processor.

1. Mix the butter and the sugar together with the saffron.

2. When it is very creamy, add the egg yolks, ouzo and ground almonds and continue to beat.

3. Sift the cornflour and the flour together, fold into the mixture and continue to mix until you have a firm dough.

4. Roll out the dough on to a floured board into a long sausage about the thickness of a finger. Cut in to short lengths and bend in to a half moon or a crescent shape.

5. Put the biscuits onto a well-greased baking sheet. Cook in the oven at 350°F, 180°C, Gas Mark 4 for 20–25 minutes or until they are a pale golden brown.

6. When the biscuits are cooked, allow to cool and then dip into a bowl of orange flower water and dredge with icing sugar. Store in an air tight container with plenty of icing sugar. These are particularly good to serve with ice cream or any fruit cream.

Rich Crumpets

1920s

A pinch of sea salt

1 oz/25g dried yeast

2 lb/900g plain strong flour

2 pints/1200ml skimmed milk (you can used dried skimmed milk, 2 oz per 1 pint/600ml water)

2 egg yolks, beaten

½ teaspoon bicarbonate of soda

Butter or oil to grease the skillet

1. Add the salt and yeast to the flour. Mix the milk and egg yolks together. Warm slightly so that the mixture is tepid.

2. Pour into the flour and beat until you have a smooth creamy batter. The more you beat, the more holes you will get in the crumpets.

3. Cover the mixture and put into a warm place for 1–1½ hours. Check the batter from time to time; it should be well-risen and just at the stage of starting to split open at the centre.

4. Dissolve the bicarbonate of soda in a spoonful of water and blend into the crumpet mixture. Beat for 1 minute. Cover and allow to rise for 15–20 minutes.

5. Grease a griddle or iron skillet and heat until very hot. Grease your crumpet rings and place on the hot surface. Put a good couple of spoonfuls of the batter into each ring. The batter should rise and holes start to form. Cook for about 3½ minutes.

6. As soon as the top surface starts to dry, turn the crumpets over and cook for ½–¾ minute. When the crumpets are cooked, remove from the skillet, lift out of the rings and set to one side in a warm place.

7. Repeat the process until you have used up all the batter.

Under the Influence of Bright Sunbeams

Nut and Pear Bread

This is a very old traditional recipe from Switzerland. My mother gave me the recipe which she had learned from a Swiss friend in the 1930s. It is a very good way of using up any windfall pears

1. Put the fruit into a pan with 2 tablespoons water and cook very gently until just soft.

2. Add dried fruit, peel, nuts, spices, kirsch and rose-water and leave to stand overnight, so that the flavours blend together.

For the dough:

1. Mix the flour and yeast together with the salt.

2. Make a well in the centre and pour in the water. Mix together until you have a light springy dough.

3. Form into a ball, put onto a floured board and knead well for 3–4 minutes.

To assemble:

1. Combine the fruit mixture with the dough; knead well until the two have blended completely.

2. Divide the mixture into 4 and shape into loaves.

3. Place the loaves onto a well-greased baking sheet and leave in a warm place to rise for 25–30 minutes. Just before putting in the oven, brush the tops with beaten egg.

4. Put into a pre-heated oven at 400°F, 200°C, Gas Mark 6 for 15–20 minutes, then reduce the heat to 350°F, 180°C, Gas Mark 4 and cook for a further 25–30 minutes or until the bread sounds hollow when tapped. Remove from the oven and stand on a wire rack to cool. Serve with fresh butter and use as a tea bread.

INGREDIENTS

2 lb/900g pears, peeled, cored and cut into slices
2 tablespoons water
4 oz/100g raisins
2 oz/50g mixed peel
4 oz/100g chopped walnuts or hazel-nuts
1 tablespoon ground cinnamon
4 tablespoons kirsch
2 tablespoons rose-water

For the dough:
1½ lb/675g plain strong flour
½ tablespoon dried yeast
½ tablespoon sea salt
1¼ pints/750ml water
Beaten egg, to glaze

Swedish Rye Bread

Limpa

INGREDIENTS

1¼ pints/700ml water
2 tablespoons caraway seeds
3 tablespoons fennel seeds
1 tablespoon butter
4 oz/100g dark brown sugar,
  preferably Muscovado
1 lb/450g wholemeal flour
½ lb/225g white flour
½ lb/225g rye flour
1 sachet instant yeast
2 tablespoons sea salt

1. Heat the water in a pan, add all the seeds, butter and sugar, bring to the boil and simmer for 3–4 minutes. Allow to cool.

2. Mix the flours and yeast together, add the salt, make a well in the centre and pour in the water and seed mixture. Mix well. Knead on a floured board until you have a soft springy dough.

3. Put the dough into a well-greased bowl, cover with a cloth or plastic bag and leave to rise in a warm place for 1–1½ hours.

4. Knead the dough for 4–5 minutes, cover and leave to rise again for 2 hours.

5. Knead the dough for the last time. Divide into three portions. Put the dough into three well-greased loaf tins and leave to rise for about 35–45 minutes in a warm place.

6. Put the risen loaves into a pre-heated oven at 350°F, 180°C, Gas Mark 4 for 1-1¼ hours, until a deep brown. Take the bread out of the oven and put on a wire rack to cool.

Under the Influence of Bright Sunbeams

Iberian Country Bread

1. Mix the flour, yeast and salt together in a large bowl. Add 2 tablespoons oil to the crushed garlic and chopped herbs, mix well together and work into the flour and yeast mixture.

2. Make a well in the centre of the flour, pour in the water and mix thoroughly.

3. Work the mixture into a rough ball. Place on a floured board and knead for 3–6 minutes.

4. Cover the dough with a cloth or a plastic bag and put into a warm place to rise for 1–1½ hours.

5. When the dough has doubled in volume, divide in half. Knead each piece and form into a round loaf.

6. Put the loaves onto a well-oiled baking sheet and brush with the remainder of the oil. Leave in a warm place to rise once again for about 40–45 minutes.

7. Put into a pre-heated oven at 400°F, 200°C, Gas Mark 6 for 35–40 minutes.

8. Remove from the oven and turn out onto a wire rack to cool.

INGREDIENTS

3 lb/1½kg wholemeal flour
2 sachets easy blend instant yeast or 1 oz/25g dried yeast
2 tablespoons sea salt
4 tablespoons oil
2 cloves garlic, crushed
A handful chopped herbs
1 pint/600ml water

Basic Scotch Scone Recipe

1. Mix the dry ingredients together in a bowl.

2. Make a well in the centre and pour in the milk. Work the mixture until you have a soft dough. Roll out on a floured board to about ¾ inch/2cm thick. Cut into rounds and put onto a baking sheet.

3. Bake in the oven at 400°F, 200°C, Gas Mark 6 for 10–12 minutes. Cool on a wire rack.

Variations are:
1. **Fruit Scones** Add 4 oz/100g fruit to the mixture.
2. **Sweet Scones** Add 3 teaspoons mixed spice and 2 tablespoons black treacle to the milk.
3. **Cheese Scones** Add 4 oz/100g grated cheese to the flour.

INGREDIENTS

1 lb/450g flour, either self-raising or wholemeal
2 teaspoons cream of tartar
1 teaspoon bicarbonate of soda
½ teaspoon sea salt
½ teaspoon sugar
Enough milk to make a soft springy dough (about ¼ pint/150ml)

Pitta Bread

3 lb/1½kg flour
1 oz/25g yeast or 2 sachets instand dried yeast
1 tablespoon sea salt
4 tablespoons olive oil
1½ pints/900ml water

1. Mix the flour, yeast and salt together in a large bowl. Make a well in the centre, pour in the oil and water and mix thoroughly.

2. Work the dough into a rough ball, place on a floured board and knead for 3–6 minutes.

3. Cover and leave to rise for 1½–2 hours.

4. When the dough has risen, divide the dough into small portions. Roll each portion into a ball, sprinkle with a little flour and flatten with a rolling pin into a long oval.

5. Lay each piece of dough onto a well-oiled baking sheet, cover and leave to prove (rise) for 20–25 minutes.

6. Pre-heat the oven to 400°F, 200°C, Gas Mark 6. Put the breads into the oven and cook for 8–10 minutes, until well puffed up.

7. Remove from the oven, wrap in a cloth and serve at once.

Under the Influence of Bright Sunbeams

Saffron Bread

This is an unusual and delicious version of Saffron Bread. It is especially good with herb pâté or fish pâté.

1. Pre-heat oven to 375°F, 190°C, Gas Mark 5. Heat 3 tablespoons of wine and water mixture in a pan together with the saffron and garlic. Stir well and simmer for 1 minute. Remove from the heat and set to one side to cool.

2. Mix the yeast with a little liquid and set to one side to work.

3. Mix the flour, salt, pepper and sugar together. Put into a large bowl; make a well in the centre and pour in the liquid, beaten egg, flour and yeast. Work the mixture until you have a light dough. Cover and leave to rise in a warm place until the dough has doubled in volume.

4. When the dough has risen, knead it gently for 3–4 minutes until the volume has been reduced and you have a firm dough. Shape and put into a well-greased 7 inch/18cm round tin. Cover and leave to prove for about 1 hour. Then glaze with beaten egg and put into the oven to cook for about 30–35 minutes.

5. Remove the loaf from the tin and cook for 3–5 minutes more. Turn upside down and bake for 3–5 minutes longer.

INGREDIENTS

7 fl oz/200ml white wine and water, mixed

25–30 strands saffron or ½ teaspoon ground saffron

1 clove garlic, chopped very fine (optional)

1 sachet dried yeast

1 lb/450g strong white bread flour

1 teaspoon sea salt

½ teaspoon black pepper

1 teaspoon brown sugar

1 beaten egg

Egg to glaze

Herb Bread

INGREDIENTS

1 sachet dried yeast
½ pint/300ml warm water
1 teaspoon sugar
1 lb/450g brown or wholemeal flour
2 cloves fresh garlic
4 tablespoons fresh chopped parsley
2 tablespoons fresh chopped coriander
2 teaspoons fresh chopped thyme
2 teaspoons fresh chopped oregano
4 tablespoons fresh chopped dill or fennel
1 oz/25g dill seeds
1 teaspoon sea salt

1. Pre-heat oven to 375°F, 190°C, Gas Mark 5. Dissolve the yeast in the warm water. Leave for 8–10 minutes until frothy.

2. Mix all the other ingredients together in a large bowl.

3. Make a well in the centre of the flour and pour in the yeast liquid.

4. Knead until you have a smooth dough. Cover and put in a warm place to rise for about 1 hour.

5. When the dough has risen, knead it again for 4–5 minutes until it has reduced in volume. Cover and leave to prove for about 1 hour in a warm place. Divide into two small loaves or 1 larger one.

6. Put into a greased loaf tin and cook for 25–30 minutes.

Nutty Bread

Follow method for Herb Bread.

INGREDIENTS

1 sachet dried yeast
½ pint/300ml warm water
1 lb/450g wholemeal flour
1 oz/25g ground hazel-nuts
1 teaspoon sea salt
1 teaspoon sugar
Zest of 1 orange
1 oz/25g sesame seeds
1 oz/25g walnuts
½ oz/12g pine kernels

Under the Influence of Bright Sunbeams

Herb Bread 2

1. Pre-heat oven to 375°F, 190°C, Gas Mark 5. Dissolve the yeast in the warm water. Leave for 8–10 minutes until frothy.

2. Mix all the other ingredients together in a large bowl.

3. Make a well in the centre of the flour and pour in the yeast liquid.

4. Knead until you have a smooth dough. Cover and put in a warm place to rise for about 1 hour.

5. When the dough has risen, knead it again for 4–5 minutes until it has reduced in volume. Cover and leave to prove for about 1 hour in a warm place. Divide into two small loaves or one larger one.

6. Put into a greased loaf tin and cook for 25–30 minutes.

1 sachet dried yeast
½ pint/300ml warm water
1 lb/450g brown flour
2 cloves garlic, chopped very small
4 tablespoons fresh chopped parsley
2 tablespoons fresh chopped coriander
2 tablespoons fresh chopped marjoram
1 teaspoon sea salt
1 teaspoon sugar

Little French Breads

8 fl oz/250ml milk
4 fl oz/120ml white wine
¾ oz/20g yeast
10 oz/275g wheatmeal flour
10 oz/275g unbleached white flour
½ oz/12g sea salt
2 egg whites, beaten until frothy
2 oz/50g pine kernels
1 teaspoon butter
1 egg yolk and a little ground saffron to glaze

Panecitos Franceses

From a family recipe about 1620

1. Warm the milk and wine together.

2. Mix the yeast with a small quantity of the milk until creamy.

3. Mix the flour and salt together and warm for 2 minutes in the oven.

4. Place the warmed flour in a large mixing bowl. Make a shallow hollow in the centre, add the yeast, egg whites, pine kernels and the rest of the milk and wine.

5. Work the mixture well as for ordinary bread dough until you have a light, springy dough.

6. Cover and stand in a warm place to rise for 45–60 minutes.

7. When the dough has risen, knead well and divide into two long or two round loaves as you wish.

8. Place on a well-floured board and leave to prove for about 30 minutes.

9. Melt the butter. Add a few strands of saffron or ¼ teaspoon ground saffron powder. Allow to cool then beat in the egg yolk.

10. When the loaves have proved, place on a greased baking sheet. Decorate the loaves by cutting three lines across the tops with a sharp knife.

11. Glaze with the egg and saffron mixture.

12. Bake in the centre of a pre-heated oven at 400°F, 200°C, Gas Mark 6 for 15–20 minutes. Cover with a sheet of foil and cook for a further 10–15 minutes.

This is a family recipe and has been used constantly since the seventeenth century. The egg whites are said not only to make the bread lighter, but to help it keep better.

Under the Influence of Bright Sunbeams

Wholemeal Bread

This recipe was given to me by a baker in Ludlow, Shropshire and makes the most delicious wholemeal bread I have ever eaten.

1. Put the flour, salt and nutmeg in a large basin and warm in a cool oven for 8–10 minutes.

2. Follow the instructions on the yeast packet and stir into the flour.

3. Mix the treacle with half the water and stir until dissolved. Pour into the flour and mix. Add the remaining water gradually until you have a very soft dough. DO NOT KNEAD.

4. Divide the dough into two, put into well-greased loaf tins and put each tin into a polythene bag. Tie up and put into a warm place for 45–50 minutes.

5. Meanwhile pre-heat the oven to 400°F, 200°C, Gas Mark 6.

6. When the dough has risen, put the tins into the oven and cook for 35–40 minutes.

7. When the bread is cooked, wipe the top over with a little water and put back in the oven for a further 5–6 minutes.

8. Turn the bread out and stand on a wire rack to cool.

INGREDIENTS

2 lb/900g wholemeal flour
4 teaspoons sea salt
½ teaspoon grated nutmeg
2 packets instant dried yeast
2 tablespoons black treacle
1¼ pints/700ml tepid water

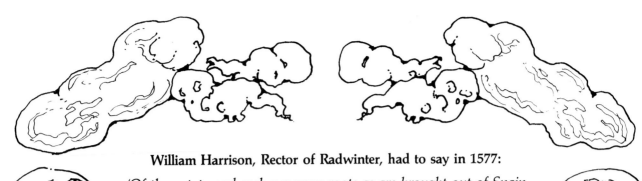

William Harrison, Rector of Radwinter, had to say in 1577:

'Of the potato and such venerous roots as are brought out of Spain and Portugal and the Indies to furnish up our banquets I speak not.'

Irish Apple and Potato Cake

<table>
<tr>
<td>

INGREDIENTS

For the pastry:
1 oz/25g butter
A good pinch sea salt
½ teaspoon ground nutmeg
1 tablespoon brown sugar
1 lb/450g potatoes, peeled, washed and boiled
4 oz/100g flour

For the filling:
1 lb/450g apples, peeled, cored and sliced
1 teaspoon mixed spice
2 tablespoons whisky
1 tablespoon brown sugar
1 egg, beaten, to glaze

</td>
<td>

This is another Irish recipe that uses potatoes for the pastry. The flavour is quite distinctive and you can fill it with anything you fancy, although traditionally it is made with apple.

For the pastry:

1. Mix the water, salt, nutmeg and sugar with the hot mashed potato.

2. Put the mixture onto a well-floured board, add the flour and work until you have a firm dough. Divide in half. Roll out and line a shallow cake tin with half the dough. Reserve the other half for the lid.

For the filling:

1. Lay the slices of apple on the dough in the cake tin, sprinkle with spice, whisky and sugar.

2. Brush the edges of the pastry with a little milk, cover with the pastry lid, trim the edges of the pastry and pinch together to seal.

3. Cut two small slits in the centre of the pastry to allow the steam to escape. Brush with beaten egg to glaze.

4. Put into the oven at 375°F, 190°C, Gas Mark 5 for 35–40 minutes. Serve hot.

</td>
</tr>
</table>

Under the Influence of Bright Sunbeams

Bibliography

The Accomplished Housewife, 1745.

ACTON, ELIZA, *Modern Cookery in All it's Branches*, Longmans, London, 1845.

ADANSON, MME AGLAE, *Arte do Cosinheiro e do Copeiro*, Lisbon, 1845.

Adam's Luxury and Eve's Cookery, Anon., London, 1744.

ALBUQUERQUE, R. M., *Peixes de Purtugal e Ilhas Adjacentes*, Published by Portugaliae acta Biologica, 1954–56.

AMHERST, HON. A. M. T., *A History of Gardening in England*, 3rd edition, 1910.

APICIUS, *The Roman Cookery Book: A Critical Translation of the Art of Cooking*, Flower, B., and Rosenbaum, E.

ASHLEY, SIR WILLIAM, *The Bread of our Forefathers*, Oxford, 1928.

AUSTIN, T. (ed.), *Two Fifteenth Century Cook Books*: Harleian MS 279 and 4016: Early English Text Society, O.S. 91, 1888.

BAILEY, N. *Dictionarium Domesticum*, 1736.

BAILLIE, LADY GRINSELL, *The Household Book, 1692–1733*, Moncrieff, R. (ed.), Edinburgh, 1911.

BARKER, T. C., McKENZIE, J.C. and YUDKIN, J. (eds.), *Our Changing Fare*, 1966.

BEETON, ISABELLA, *Household Management*, Ward Lock, 1912 edition.

BEST, H., *Rural Economy in Yorkshire in 1641*, Surtees Society, 33, 1857.

BICKERDYKE, J., (C. H. COOK): *The Curiosities of Ale and Beer*, 1886.

BLENCOWE, A., *The Receipt Book, A.D. 1694*, 1925.

BONAPARTE, C.L., *Iconografia della Fauna Italica per le Quattro Classi Degli Animali Vertibrati*, Rome, 1834.

A Book of Fruits and Flowers, 1653.

BOORDE, A., *A Compendyous Regyment, or A Dyetary of Helth*, 1542, Furnivall, F. J. (ed.), Early English Text Society, e.s. 10, 1870.

BOSWELL, JAMES, *Journal of A Tour To The Hebrides*, London, 1785.

BRADLEY, R., *The Country Housewife and Lady's Director*, 6th edition, 1736.

BRIDBURY, A. R., *England and the Salt Trade in the Later Middle Ages*, Oxford, 1955.

BRUDEL, FERNAND, *Civilization and Capitalism 15th-18th Century*, Fontana 1979–1982, Vols, I, II, III.

BROTHWELL, D. and P., *Food in Antiquity*, 1969.

BRYENE, DAME ALICE DE, *The Household Book of Dame Alice de Bryene, of Acton Hall, Suffolk, Sept. 1412–Sept. 1413*, trans. Dale, M. K. and Redstone, V. B. (ed.), Ipswich, 1931.

CALERA, A. M., *La Cocina Vasca*, Bilbāo, 1971.

CHEKE, V., *The Story of Cheese-making in Britain*, 1959.

CLAIR, C., *Kitchen and Table*, 1964.

CLARK, LADY, *Lady Clark Of Tillypronie's Cook Book*, 1900, Edinburgh.

CLARK, J. G. D., *Prehistoric Europe: the Economic Basis*, 1952.

The Compleat Cook, 1655.

CROMWELL, E., *The Court and Kitchen of Elizabeth*, 1664.

CUTTING, C. L., *Fish Saving: A History of Fish Processing from Ancient to Modern Times*. Published by Leonard Hill, London, 1955.

DE BURNAY, CONDE A. I., *Livro da Cozinha Regional Portuguesa*, Portalege, 1955.

DE BURNAY, CONDE A. I., *Livro da Cozinha Portugesa*, Badajoz, 1957.

DA CAMPAIO, A. F., *Volupia a Nona Arte a Gastronomia*, Porto, 1940.

DE CASTRO J. DE M. O., *Gabinete de Estudios das Pecas No. 39*, 1967.

DEERR, N., *The History of Sugar*, 2 volumes, 1949.

DEFOE, D., *A Tour through the Whole Island of Great Britain, 1724–5*, 2 volumes, 1927.

DOMÉNECH, I., *La Nueva Cocina Elegante Espanola*, Madrid.

EMMISON, F. G., *Tudor Food and Pastimes*, 1964.

ERNLE, LORD (R. E. PROTHERO), *English Farming Past and Present*, 6th edition, 1961.

EVELYN, J., *Acetaria*, 1699.

FIENNES, C., *Journeys*, Morris, C. (ed.), 1949.

FIGUIER, L., *The Vegetable World*.

FISHER, F. J., 'The Development of the London Food Market, 1540–1640', *Economic History Review*, 5, 1935, pp. 46–54.

FITZHERBERT, SIR ANTHONY, *The Book of Husbandry, 1534*, Skeat, W. W. (ed.), English Dialect Society, D37, 1882.

The Forme of Cury, in *Antiquitates Culinariae*, Warner, R. (ed.), 1791.

FORSTER, E. S. and HEFFNER, E., *Culumella, De Re Rustica*, Loeb Classical Library, 1954.

FRASER, H. M., *History of Beekeeping in Britain*, 1958.

FRAYNE, J. M., *Subsistence Farming in Roman Italy*, Fontwell, 1979.

FUSSELL, G. E., *The English Dairy Farmer, 1500–1900*, 1966.

GERARD, J., *The Herball*, 1597.

GLASSE, MRS HANNAH, *The Art Of Cookery Made Plain And Easy*, 1747.

GLOB, P. V., *The Bog People*, 1969.

The Goodman of Paris, c.1393, (*Ménagier de Paris*), Power, E. (ed.), 1928.

GRAS, N. S. B., *The Evolution of the English Corn Market*, Cambridge, Mass., 1915.

HARRISON, W., *Elizabethan England*, Furnivall, F. J. and Withington, L. (eds.), Scott Library, 1902.

HARTLEY, D., *Food in England*, 1954.

HAZLITT, WILLIAM C., *Old Cookery Books and Ancient Cuisine*, Elliot Stock, 1886.

HELBAEK, H., 'Early Crops in Southern England', *Proceedings of the Prehistoric Society*, 18, 1952, pp.194–233.

HENTZNER, P., *Travels In England*, 1894.

HISTORICUS, *Coco all about it*, London, 1896.

Household Accounts of Brogo de Clare, 1284-1286, Archeologia, 1924.

Household Books of John, Duke of Norfolk, & Thomas, Earl of Surrey, 1481–1490, Collier, J. P. (ed.), Roxburghe Club, 1844.

HUNTER, A., *Cumina Famulatrix Medicinae*, York, 1804.

JONES, P. E., *The Worshipful Company of Poulters of the City of London a Short History*, 2nd edition, 1965.

KERLING, N. J. M., *Commercial Relations of Holland and Zeeland with England from the Late Thirteenth Century to the Close of the Middle Ages*, Leiden, 1954.

KITCHENER, W., *Apicius Redivivus*, 1817.

LABARGE, M. W., *A Baronial Household of the Thirteenth Century*, 1965.

LA VARENNE, F. P. DE, *The French Cook (Le Cuisinier François)*, 3rd edition, 1673.

LEWIS, A. R., *The Northern Seas: Shipping and Commerce in Northern Europe, A.D. 300–1100*, Princeton, 1958.

Liber Cure Cocorum, Sloane MS 1986, Morris, R. (ed.), Berlin, 1862.

M., W., *The Queens Closet Opened*, 1655.

Manners and Household Expenses of England in the Thirteenth and Fifteenth Centuries (Household roll of Eleanor, Countess of Leicester, 1265; and The expenses of Sir John Howard, 1462–1469). Roxburghe Club, 1841.

MARKHAM, G., *The English Hus-wife*, 1615.

MARKHAM, GERVASE, *The English Housewife*, 1649.

MARTIN, M., *A description of the Western Islands of Scotland circa 1695*, and *A Late Voyage to St. Kilda*, McLeod, D. J. (ed.), Stirling, 1934.

MAURIZIO, A., *Histoire de l'Alimentation Végétale*, F. Gidon (trans.), Paris, 1932.

MEAD, W. E., *The English Medieval Feast*, 1931.

MONCKTON, H. A., *A History of English Ale and Beer*, 1966.

MOORE, T. and JACKMAN, G., *The Clematis as a Garden Flower*, The Woking Nursery, 1872.

MORITZ, L. A., *Grain-mills and Flour in Classical Antiquity*, Oxford, 1958.

Myvyrian Archaiology of Wales: Laws of Howell the Good, Owen, A. (trans.), Denbigh, 1870.

NAPIER, MRS A., *A Noble Boke Off Cookry*, Edited from an early MS from the Holkham Collection, 1480. Published 1882.

NELSON, W. (ed.), *A Fifteenth Century School Book*, Oxford, 1956.

NICHOLSON, B. E. and others, *The Oxford Book of Food Plants*, 1969.

Northumberland Household Book. The Regulations and Establishment of the Household of Henry Algernon Percy . . . 1512, New edition, 1905.

NOTT, J., *The Cook's and Confectioner's Dictionary*, 1723.

PIGGOTT, S., *Ancient Europe from the Beginnings of Agriculture to Classical Antiquity*, Edinburgh, 1965.

PLANT, M., *The Domestic Life of Scotland in the Eighteenth Century*, Edinburgh, 1952.

PLATT, SIR HUGH, *Delights for Ladies*, 1605.

A Proper Newe Booke of Cokerye, Frere, C. F. (ed.), Cambridge, 1913.

RABISHA, W., *The Whole Body of Cookery Dissected*, 1673.

RACKHAM, T. (trans.), *Pliny Natural History*, Loeb Classical Library, 1969.

RENNER, H. D., *The Origin of Food Habits*, 1944.

RUNDELL, E., *A New System of Domestic Cookery*, 1806.

RUSSELL, J., *Boke of Burture, in Early English Meals and Manners*, Furnivall, F. J. (ed.), Early English Text Society, O.S. 32, 1868.

——, *English Trade in the Middle Ages*, Oxford, 1931.

SALMON, W., *The Family Dictionary*, 2nd edition, 1696.

——, *The Art and Mystery of Curing, Preserving and Potting all Kinds of Meats, Game and Fish*, 1864.

SHACKLETON-BAILY, D. R., *Cicero, Letters to his Friends*, Penguin Books, 1978.

SHEPPARD, R. and NEWTON, E., *The Story of Bread*, 1957.

SILVA, C. B. DA, *Manual de Confeitaria*, Paris, 1866.

SIMON, A. L., *Bottlescrew Days*, 1926.

A Small Household of the Fifteenth Century, Being the Account Book of Munden's Chantry, Bridport, 1453–60, Wood-legh, K. L. (ed.), Manchester, 1956.

SMITH, M., *The Complete Housekeeper and Professional Cook*, Newcastle, 1772.

SWINFIELD, R. DE., *Roll of the Household Expenses of Richard de Swinfield, Bishop of Hereford, during Part of the Years 1289 and 1290*, Webb, J (ed.), 2 volumes, Camden Society, 59, 62, 1853–54.

THOMPSON, F., *Lark Rise to Candleford*, World Classics, 1954.

THOMSON, G. S., *Life in a Noble Household, 1641–1700*, Bedford Historical Series, 8, 1940.

TUSSER, THOMAS, *Five Hundred Points Of Good Husbandry*, London, 1573. London 1931. J. Tregaskis.

TWEEDIE, ETHEL B., *Through Finland In Carts*, London, 1898.

WALTER OF HENLEY, *Husbandry*, Lamond, E. (trans.), 1890.

WARRENDER, M., *The Humes and Marchmonts of Polworth*, Blackwood, London, 1898.

WINT, HENRY DE, *Finland As It Is*, London, 1901.

WOOLLEY, H., *The Accomplish'd Ladies Delight*, 6th edition, 1686.

WORDE, W. DE, *Boke of Kervynge, in Early English Meals and Manners*, Furnivall, F. J. (ed.), Early English Text Society, O.S. 32, 1868.

WORLIDGE, J., *Vinetum Britannicum*, 1668.

WALTON ISSAK, *The Compleat Angler*, Richard Marriot, London, 1655.

WOODFORDE, JAMES, *Diary of A Country Parson 1758-1802*, Humphrey Milfod, London, 1924.

Index

Index   239

MARGARET M

The Tin Can Band
and Other Poems

illustrated by

Honey de Lacey

J. M. DENT & SONS LTD
London

British Library Cataloguing in Publication Data

Mahy, Margaret,

The tin can band and other poems.
I. Title   II. De Lacey, Honey
821

ISBN 0-460-07042-8

These poems were all originally published
by Dent in *The First, Second* and *Third
Margaret Mahy Story Books*

This edition first published in 1989
Text © Margaret Mahy 1972, 1973, 1975
Illustrations © Honey de Lacey 1989

Contents

Goodness Gracious!

Goodness gracious, fiddle dee dee!
Somebody's grandmother out at sea!

Just where the breakers begin to bound
Somebody's grandmother bobbing around.

Up on the shore the people shout,
"Give us a hand and we'll pull you out!"

"No!" says the granny. "I'm right as rain,
And I'm going to go on till I get to Spain."

The Fairy Child

The very hour that I was born
I rode upon the unicorn.
When boys put tadpoles in their jars
I overflowed my tin with stars.
Because I sing to see the sun
The little children point and run.
Because I set the caged birds free
The people close their doors to me.
Goodbye, goodbye, you world of men –
I shall not visit you again.

8

The Pines

Hear the rumble,
Oh, hear the crash!
The great trees tumble
The strong boughs smash.

Men with saws
Are cutting the pines –
That marched like soldiers
In straight green lines.

Seventy years
Have made them tall.
It takes ten minutes
To make them fall.

And, breaking free
With never a care,
The pine cones leap
Through the clear, bright air.

Sea Song

This is my place, my very own place,
Staring the ocean straight in the face.

Every morning I wake to find
The ocean in front and the hills behind.

Every morning I wake to see
The ocean carefully watching me.

I watch the ocean back again.
It stamps and whinnies and tosses its mane.

Bright and dangerous, bold and free,
Only a fool would trust the sea.

Mighty waters that call and move,
Only a fool could help but love.

Standing here I can know the sea,
But what in the world does it make of me?

Dreaming, dancing, false and true,
I can be bright and dangerous too.

Holding the hills and the sea and the sky,
A little reflection drowned in my eye.

Clowns

Zing! goes the cymbal. Bang! goes the drum.
See how they tipple-topple-tumbling come.
Dazing the country, dazzling the towns,
Here's the procession of the circus clowns.

Hop on the heel and twist on the toe.
See how they wibble-wobble-waddling go.
Bim-bam-balloons in the clear blue air!
Clowns on the march to they-don't-know-where.

Painted-on smiles that are long and loud
Beam at the giggle-gaggle-goggling crowd.
Under the paint do they grin so gay?
Nobody sees so I just can't say.

Look how the clowns all a-cantering come
Riding their donkeys with a hee-haw-hum.
Where have they come from? Where do they go?
They kin-can't say for they din-don't know.

The Tin Can Band

Oh, the tin can band,
Oh, the tin can band!
It's the dinniest band
In the big bright land.
It's a sing-song band, it's a bing-bong band.
It's a miss-a-beat, have-a-treat, skippy-feet band,
As we march along with our pots and pans,
And we bing and bong on our old tin cans.

We're a-singing and a-songing to the binging and the bonging.
We're escaping and a-skipping out
On every hand.

And it sounds like a battle
When our tin cans rattle,
When our tin cans rattle
And our tin cans clang.
Yes, it's sounding like the prattle and the tattle
of a battle
Like a merry monster cannon going
BANG, BANG, BANG!

Though silence falls when the band's gone by,
And the street is bare to the hills and sky,
There's a nitter and a natter,
And a tiny tinny patter,
Like a whisper (only crisper)
Like a tin toy's sigh,
And a flutter like a mutter,
Like a sunny sort of stutter,
Going giggling down the gutter
Where the funny echoes die.

15

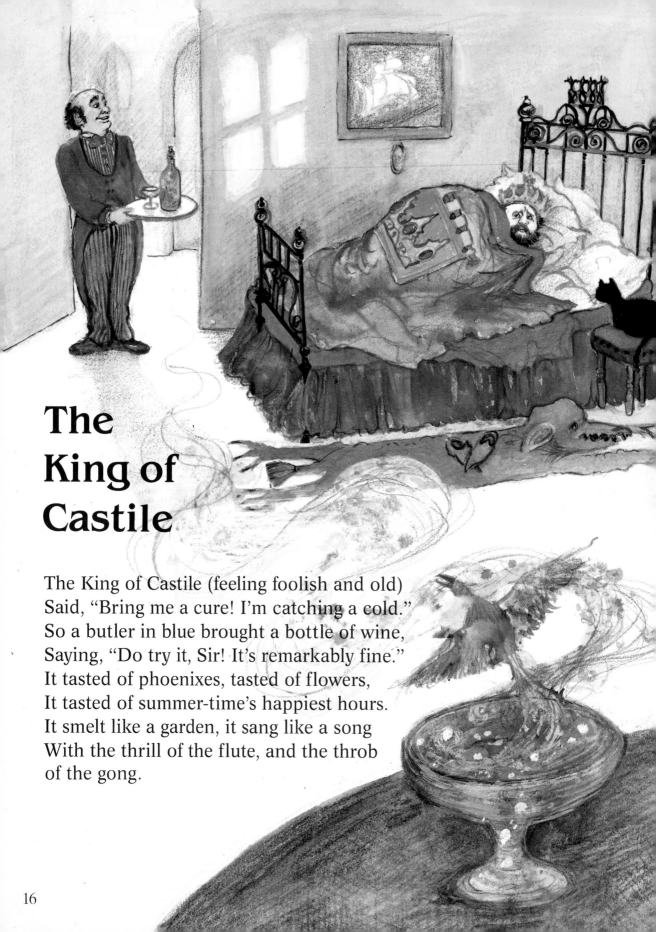

The King of Castile

The King of Castile (feeling foolish and old)
Said, "Bring me a cure! I'm catching a cold."
So a butler in blue brought a bottle of wine,
Saying, "Do try it, Sir! It's remarkably fine."
It tasted of phoenixes, tasted of flowers,
It tasted of summer-time's happiest hours.
It smelt like a garden, it sang like a song
With the thrill of the flute, and the throb
of the gong.

And the King, huddled up in his ivory bed,
Felt it go like a fountain of fire to his head.
In his crown (and pyjamas) he leaped to his feet
And danced, like a dragonfly, into the street.
Away blew his crown, and it looked, as it rolled,
Like a hedgehog whose bristles were covered in gold.
And people who noticed said … "What an odd thing!
It shows that he isn't just any old king.
He's as quick as a cricket, as slick as an eel!
We could do with more kings, like the King of Castile."

Hide and Seek in a Dark House

In and out the window
In and out the door!
Up the path and round again,
Sliding on the floor.

Breathing through the keyhole,
Whispering on the stair,
Hiding by the dust bin,
Crouching by a chair!

Now without a candle,
Turning off the light,
We're a rustling circus,
Entertaining Night.

We're the circus people,
Acrobat and clown,
Pulling shadows round us
Drawing darkness down.

Only Night can see us
Flitting room to room
Wiped away by blackness
Painted out by gloom.

In and out the darkness
Who can really see?
Are the others changing?
Am I really me?

19

When the King Rides By

Oh, what a fuss when the king rides by
And the drum plays *rat-a-plan-plan!*

Oh, what a fuss when the king rides by –
The puss-cat runs and the pigeons fly
And the drum plays *rat-a-plan-plan!*

Oh, what a fuss when the king rides by –
The dogs all bark and the babies cry,
The puss-cat runs and the pigeons fly
And the drum plays *rat-a-plan-plan!*

Oh, what a fuss when the king rides by –
The soldiers stamp and the ladies sigh,
The dogs all bark and the babies cry,
The puss-cat runs and the pigeons fly
And the drum plays *rat-a-plan-plan!*

Oh, what a fuss when the king rides by –
The people throw their hats up high,
The soldiers stamp and the ladies sigh,
The dogs all bark and the babies cry,
The puss-cat runs and the pigeons fly
And the drum plays *rat-a-plan-plan!*

Oh, what a fuss when the king rides by –
Mice in their mouse-holes wonder why
The people throw their hats up high,
The soldiers stamp and the ladies sigh,
The dogs all bark and the babies cry,
The puss-cat runs and the pigeons fly
And the drum plays *rat-a-plan-plan!*

22

Oh, what a fuss when the king rides by –
Rockets dance in the starry sky,
Mice in their mouse-holes wonder why
The people throw their hats up high,
The soldiers stamp and the ladies sigh,
The dogs all bark and the babies cry,
The puss-cat runs and the pigeons fly
And the drum plays *rat-a-plan-plan!*

When I Was But a Little Boy

When I was but a little boy and played
    beneath a tree,
Seven kings and seven queens there came to
    talk with me.
Their hair was blue as lightning beneath their
    crowns of gold,
Their faces all were fair and young – their
    shining eyes were old.

One wore the moon upon her breast, another
    wore the sun,
The others wore the frosty stars that frozen
    courses run.

They talked of wise and wondrous things that
    made my spirits sing.
They made a garland from the winds and
    crowned me as a king.

They took my hand and ran with me and all
    grew hushed and still.
The rivers dwindled as we passed. We strode
    from hill to hill.

The world became a grain of sand washed in a
    mighty sea,
And Time became a withered leaf blown from
    its parent tree.

27

A Witch Poem

The witch my sister from over the sea
Wonderful presents has sent to me.
A whistle to blow and a bell to ring,
Silver ropes for a shining swing,
A golden lion that will play and purr,
Dancing slippers of silver fur,

And, sharp as a needle, bright as a pin,
A mouse that plays on the violin.

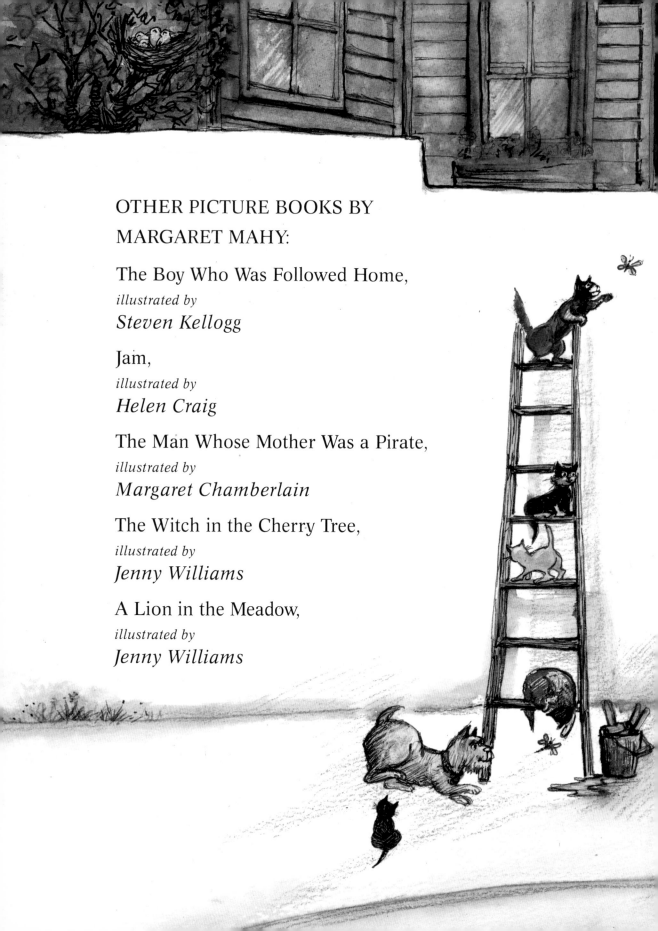

OTHER PICTURE BOOKS BY
MARGARET MAHY:

The Boy Who Was Followed Home,
illustrated by
Steven Kellogg

Jam,
illustrated by
Helen Craig

The Man Whose Mother Was a Pirate,
illustrated by
Margaret Chamberlain

The Witch in the Cherry Tree,
illustrated by
Jenny Williams

A Lion in the Meadow,
illustrated by
Jenny Williams